CONSTITUTIONAL LAW IN SCOTLAND

AUSTRALIA
LBC Information Services
Sydney

CANADA and USA
Carswell
Toronto

NEW ZEALAND
Brooker's
Auckland

SINGAPORE and MALAYSIA
Sweet & Maxwell Asia
Singapore and Kuala Lumpur

GREENS CONCISE SCOTS LAW

CONSTITUTIONAL LAW IN SCOTLAND

By

Christina Ashton, LL.B. (Hons.), M.A. in Ed.
Lecturer in Law, Napier University

and

Valerie Finch, LL.B. (Hons.), M.Sc.
Senior Lecturer in Law, University of Paisley

EDINBURGH
W. GREEN/Sweet & Maxwell
2000

First published 2000

Published in 2000 by W. Green & Son Limited
21 Alva Street
Edinburgh EH2 4PS

Typeset by Dataword Services Ltd, Chilcompton, Somerset

Printed in Great Britain by MPG Books Ltd, Bodmin, Cornwall

No natural forests were destroyed to make this product;
only farmed timber was used and replanted

A CIP catalogue record of this book is available from the British Library

ISBN 0 414 01288 7

PREFACE

For many years, those involved in teaching constitutional law could rest relatively secure in the knowledge that changes in the U.K. constitution would be small, even minimal. This is no longer the case. In the last few years of the twentieth century, there have been many major changes in the U.K. constitution and the pace of change has increased so rapidly that it is difficult to keep abreast of them.

In this book, we have tried to take account of the changes in the law up until September 30, 1999. We were able at proof stage to make some adjustments and alterations to the text to take account of later changes, such as the House of Lords Act 1999, the Freedom of Information Bill and the consultation paper in Scotland and some of the criminal cases involving the implementation of the Human Rights Act 1998 in Scotland. Some of these are discussed within the Introduction, rather than in the text itself.

Thanks go to Karen Taylor at W. Green for her patience and persistence which kept us to the second, if not the first, deadline and to our colleagues at Napier and Paisley Universities for their advice and encouragement, especially Ian Crossland, the law subject librarian at Napier University, for his help with gathering information for the book. Any errors or omission of course are entirely our responsibility. Finally, we are mindful that we have long-suffering partners and families and our thanks go to them for their support and tolerance.

Chris Ashton
Val Finch
October 1999

CONTENTS

TABLE OF CASES

TABLE OF STATUTES

TABLE OF STATUTORY INSTRUMENTS

TABLE OF TREATIES, CONVENTIONS AND EUROPEAN LEGISLATION

TREATIES

CONVENTIONS

DIRECTIVES

Introduction

The devolution of a degree of legislative and administrative power to Scotland by the Scotland Act 1998 has undoubtedly been the most significant constitutional change for nearly 300 years. This is therefore an exciting time to be studying constitutional law and writing this book has been very interesting but has been, at times, rather like walking on shifting sands. The major changes to the law have been laid down by the Scotland Act but the procedures for the day-to-day administration of the government of Scotland are still in the process of development. Constitutional changes of this magnitude will inevitably take some time to come into full operational effect. At the time of writing, two Acts of the Scottish Parliament have been passed and a handful more are in the pipeline. Committees are meeting regularly and are establishing their remits and developing policies and strategies. The exact nature of the relationships between some of the new elements of the Scottish Administration and some of the existing public sector organisations has yet to become clear. In short, we who live and work in Scotland are experiencing a time of great change and a certain amount of upheaval in those institutions with which we are now familiar. We have to become familiar with a new system of government and this book seeks to introduce the reader to some of these changes so that participation in the governance of Scotland will become easier for the ordinary citizen.

Chapter 1 puts the recent changes in the constitution into their historical context. It relates how the two nations of Scotland and England came together, first under the same monarch and then under the same Parliament. The political changes which have occurred in Scotland during the last 50 years are discussed so that the reader can more readily understand why devolution became inevitable.

Chapter 2 seeks to place the British constitution within the context of the constitutions of the world by discussing how a constitution is created and the different types and styles of constitution that may be adopted by a country. The chapter explores the detail of some constitutions so that the British constitution can be better understood. Following on from this discussion, Chapter 3 considers the various sources of the British constitution. The formal sources of legislation and case law are considered along with a more detailed discussion of the royal prerogative and conventions. It is likely that the Scottish Parliament will create its own conventions and it is equally likely that some of these will be based on those used at Westminster. The Procedure Committee of the Scottish Parliament tried to adopt the Westminster convention of holding meetings in private when the activities of members are being discussed. This led to the first judicial review action being brought against the Parliament by *The Scotsman* newspaper in early October 1999[1] and may lead to more careful consideration by the Parliament of the conventions it decides to adopt and create.

In Chapter 4 the three main doctrines of the British constitution are defined. The separation of powers is a relatively straightforward concept but the rule of law requires more reflection. The rule of law drives many of the legal principles of Scots and English law and particularly will be important for the development of Human Rights law after the introduction of the Human Rights Act 1998. The sovereignty of the U.K. Parliament takes on, if not a new meaning, then certainly a new dimension with the introduction of devolution. The sovereignty of the U.K. Parliament is, almost for the first time, stated categorically in an Act of Parliament and, in the years to come, this issue will continue to be one of great importance in Scotland. The relationship between Scotland and England will develop further or may disintegrate depending on how the two Parliaments see the sovereignty issue. The U.K. Parliament has had difficulties in accepting the limitations of its sovereignty by the entry of the United Kingdom to the European Economic Community (now the European Union). This has been reflected in the decisions of judges in cases involving E.C. law and its implementation into the legal systems of the United Kingdom.

Much of the law of the United Kingdom is contained in legislation of various types and such is examined in Chapter 5. The process of making law in the U.K. Parliament and in the Scottish Parliament is discussed and differences highlighted.

Chapter 6 covers the law relating to the procedures for elections in the United Kingdom. Elections to both the Scottish Parliament and the European Parliament took place in 1999 and both elections were significant in constitutional terms because of the introduction of new voting systems, designed to give a degree of proportional representation.

---

[1] The action was later discontinued.

The form of the U.K. Parliament is covered in Chapter 7 where the three institutions required to legitimise an Act of Parliament are studied. Here again major constitutional changes are occurring. The reform of the House of Lords is well advanced although it appears that the process will not be completed for some years. The House of Commons is not immune to change and it has been going through a process of modernisation of its procedures under the current Labour government. Again, this is a long-term process but many changes to the House have already been made.

Chapter 8 introduces the reader to the Scottish Parliament. The Parliament is a complex institution and only a flavour of this complexity and scope can be given. However the text deals with the initial meetings of the Parliament and how the Presiding Officer, First Minister and other ministers are chosen. The procedures of the Parliament are considered, particularly the provisions in the Scotland Act for raising the additional funds for the Parliament. The use or non-use of this power will be closely debated in the years to come. Of importance too are the relationships which will be generated by the Parliament with Westminster, the European Communities and other bodies. If these are neglected, the Parliament will find itself in constant conflict and unable to do its work. One effect should any of these relationships be neglected is the possibility of legal action against the Parliament or Scottish Executive. The Act has set up various procedures to be followed if such legal action becomes necessary and these are discussed in some detail.

Chapter 9 looks at the European constitutional context. European law is becoming increasingly important, with much of the law providing protection for the freedom of the individual being driven by European law. Free movement of persons is becoming a practical reality as well as a notional right under European law and the concept of European citizenship is now developing. The Treaty on European Union 1997 (the Treaty of Amsterdam) represents a new phase in the process of European integration. Following devolution, there will be a higher profile for Scotland in Europe. The Scottish Executive will be involved in the process of policy formation and implementation of E.U. legislation and in links with European institutions. The power to implement European Community law is now one of the shared powers which can be exercised by both the Westminster Parliament and the Scottish Parliament.

The place of local government is considered in Chapter 10. Local authorities were last reorganised in 1996 but it seems likely that the devolution changes will lead to a further reorganisation of this important level of government. The chapter takes a broad overview of local government within Scotland and its place in the new constitutional regime and tries to highlight some of the problems which may occur in its relationship with the Parliament and Scottish Executive.

The executive arm of government is reviewed in Chapter 11 where we discuss how the government is administered. The Prime Minister, the Cabinet and the Scottish Executive are considered together with their relationships with the civil service. The 1980s and 1990s brought about massive changes in the way in which the civil service is organised. The implications of these changes are explored in this chapter as well as Chapter 12 where the discussion centres on the issue of accountability. Here there have been changes to the doctrine of ministerial responsibility as a result of the Scott Inquiry and the Derek Lewis affair. The resolution of the House of Commons on the principle of ministerial accountability has taken the issue out of the realms of convention and made it a parliamentary rule, which will be punishable by the House if it is breached. The differences in approach between the Westminster Parliament and the Scottish Parliament are examined. The 'Lobbygate' affair which hit the Scottish Parliament in early October 1999 has raised the issue of members' interests and conflict of interests; the issue of punishment also arose and the power of the Parliament to punish MSPs who hold ministerial office was questioned. It was unfortunate that this particular affair happened before the Parliament has had an opportunity to adopt its own code of conduct.

Chapters 13 and 14 are devoted to discussion of individual freedoms and human rights. At the same time as the process of devolution to Scotland is developing, there has been a major development in substantive constitutional law. The European Convention on Human Rights and Fundamental Freedoms is, at last, being incorporated into the domestic law of the United Kingdom. This change is being brought into effect by the Humans Rights Act 1998, which will apply throughout the United Kingdom. The Act will make it unlawful for any public authority, including regulators, the police, courts and tribunals, as well as local and central government, to behave in a way which breaches the European Convention on Human Rights. The Government originally announced that the Act will be fully implemented by October 2000 but it is probable that there will be some delay.

The Human Rights Act and the Scotland Act bring to a close an unsatisfactory period in the history of human rights protection in the United Kingdom. Despite the fact that the United Kingdom ratified the European Convention on Human Rights in 1951, there has been a marked reluctance to take the Convention rights into account in proceedings in the domestic courts. At the same time there has been a gradual trend of erosion of fundamental individual freedoms in the United Kingdom. United Kingdom citizens have had to seek redress through the European Court of Human Rights but litigation in this court is a slow process. There is currently a huge backlog of cases waiting to be heard. The Human Rights Act seeks to address this unsatisfactory state of affairs and to bring order and structure to the application of the Convention by courts in the United Kingdom. As a result, courts will be required to look at, and seek to give effect to, the Convention and are more likely to be able to do so effectively. It will no longer be necessary to show that legislation is ambiguous before resort can be had to the Convention in interpreting legislation. Wherever possible, a statute must be interpreted so as to be consistent with the Convention.

The Scotland Act 1998 has implemented this change in Scotland ahead of the rest of the United Kingdom. The sections of the Scotland Act which incorporate the European Convention on Human Rights into Scots law are already in force. Acts of the Scottish Parliament are not within the legislative competence if they are incompatible with the European Convention on Human Rights. Acts which are outwith the legislative competence will be subject to challenge. All acts and decisions of the Scottish Administration must also comply with the Convention. A person who is a victim of a breach of an Article of the European Convention on Human Rights will be able to seek a remedy before the Scottish courts. The jurisprudence of the European Court of Human Rights will thus have greater relevance in Scotland. Actions for judicial review of administrative decisions may become even more common. In fact the impact of these provisions is already apparent. Successful challenges have been made to aspects of criminal procedure on the grounds that they may be in breach of the Convention's right of access to justice. In the milestone case of *Starrs v. Ruxton*,[2] it was held that the involvement of the Lord Advocate in the processes for appointing temporary and permanent sheriffs created a conflict with a person's right to a fair hearing before an independent and impartial tribunal under the European Convention on Human Rights, Art. 6(1). The practice of appointing temporary sheriff for short periods of time had to cease and additional "floating" sheriffs were appointed. The position of temporary judges is also under consideration. The Crown Office is currently appealing a declaration of the High Court of Justiciary, in

---

[2] 2000 S.L.T. 42; 1999 S.C.C.R. 1052.

an appeal against the prosecution for a motoring offence, that in order to be compatible with the appellant's Convention rights, section 172 of the Road Traffic Act 1988 must now "be read" as no longer permitting the Crown to lead self-incriminating evidence by a person who at the time was a suspect.[3] The use of a self-incriminatory statement made under section 172 as evidence in a criminal prosecution would violate the accused's Convention right to silence. Section 172 compels a registered keeper of a motor-vehicle to state who was driving a vehicle at a specified time. The appeal against this decision will be heard by the Judicial Committee of the Privy Council. Other challenges are also being raised and opinions have been expressed that this is the start of an "avalanche" of claims under human rights legislation.

Unlike legislation of the Scottish Parliament, United Kingdom legislation will not be invalid if it is inconsistent with the Convention. It will still be open to Parliament to legislate in a way which is inconsistent with the Convention although any term which attempts to do this will need to be clear and unambiguous as it will be subject to interpretation by the courts on the basis that the intention must have been to legislate in a manner compatible with the Convention.

The incorporation of the European Convention on Human Rights has been welcomed by human rights campaigners. It is a move away from the philosophy that a man is free to do anything except those things prohibited by law towards a culture of assertion of certain fundamental rights. Incorporation of the Convention into domestic law should give speedier access to justice than is afforded at present by the European Court of Human Rights. It will be interesting to observe the developments in this field, particularly since it will be the Scottish courts that are leading the way.

One of the most important rights a citizen can have is to access information, both personal information held by public and private organisations and information regarding issues of government policy and process in which he may have an interest. In Chapter 15 the current position with regard to access to information is discussed together with a consideration of the draft Freedom of Information Bill presented by the Government in the spring of 1999. A statutory right to information will be a major constitutional change that will affect all citizens. In Scotland, the Scottish Executive brought its proposals forward for a Freedom of Information Bill in a consultation paper.

---

[3] *Brown v. Stott,* 2000 G.W.D. 6–237.

Chapter 16 discusses the provision for legal redress for individuals against the state and public authorities. Devolution has led to some new developments in this area. The Scottish Parliament is developing procedures for dealing with complaints of maladministration by office-holders in the Scottish Administration, the Parliamentary Corporation, Scottish public authorities and cross-border public authorities. Challenges to the validity of Scottish legislation may be made in actions in the Scottish courts. In order to avoid the possibility of inconsistency in judicial decisions the Judicial Committee of the Privy Council will act as a final court of appeal for all devolution issues. The Scottish courts will also have to consider compatibility with the European Convention on Human Rights in actions against public authorities and the Scottish Administration.

Certain organisations within the United Kingdom have powers that have a direct impact on the rights and freedoms of individual citizens and Chapter 17 discusses some of these powers. The main emphasis is on the powers of the police as it is these powers which have the most direct and obvious impact on the everyday lives of citizens. Responsibility for the police has been devolved to the Scottish Parliament and a Justice Minister has been appointed. His responsibilities include: civil and criminal justice, criminal policy in relation to drugs, police, fire and emergency planning. In relation to the police forces he will be responsible for developing police policy, providing resources and regulating the police forces. A justice committee supports him in this work.

Chapter 18 deals with the rights and liabilities of the Crown and local authorities in contract and their liabilities in delict. Scottish devolution has lead to some interesting developments. Provision has to be made for the Scottish Administration and the Westminster Administration to make contracts with each other. Property and liabilities may be transferred between the Scottish Administration and Westminster and the two administrations may be co-defenders in litigation. A body called the Parliamentary Corporation has been set up to represent the Scottish Parliament in all legal proceedings, as the Scottish Parliament is an unincorporated body. The relationship between the Scottish Parliament and Administration and Westminster will be founded, at least in the first instance, on relatively informal concordats rather than a complex legal framework.

CHAPTER 1

HISTORICAL DEVELOPMENT OF CONSTITUTIONAL LAW IN SCOTLAND

This chapter will consider the events leading up to the creation of the United Kingdom and the developments which followed thereafter. The drive towards devolution will also be considered here. The chapter is not intended to be a definitive historical text but will introduce the reader to the reasons why devolution became inevitable in the last decade of the twentieth century. 1.01

UNION OF THE CROWNS

Before the Union of the Crowns of Scotland and England in 1603, Scotland was a separate and independent nation state. The union was formed when the Scots King James VI was invited by the English Parliament to become their monarch after the death of Elizabeth of England. The previous four centuries had seen many conflicts between the two countries. In 1503, Henry VII of England sent his daughter Margaret to marry James IV with a view to ending these wars and bringing the two kingdoms closer together. It was through this marriage that James VI came to have the necessary lineage to take the English throne as the great-great-grandson of Henry VII. 1.02

1603–1707

The period between 1603 and 1707 was a turbulent one for the joint kingdom. Those persons born after 1603 owed their allegiance to the same king regardless of whether they were born in Scotland or England. *Calvin's case*[1] decided that these people had dual nationality. Scotland remained an independent state with her own 1.03

---

[1] (1608) 7 Co.Rep 1a.

Parliament and government, except for a short period under Cromwell when the Commonwealth of England, Scotland and Ireland was governed by one legislature and government. The Scottish Privy Council conducted most of the business of government on the king's instructions. The absence of the king from Scotland caused problems, particularly when he tried to assert his authority in religious matters. James VI had converted to the Church of England which was at that time closer to the Roman Catholic Church in its practices than the Presbyterian Kirk in Scotland, with its dour, plain and unadorned way of worship. The religious differences between the two countries caused conflict for most of the seventeenth century.

James' son Charles I tried to impose the Common Prayer Book on the Scottish Kirk; this had already been rejected by the Kirk during his father's reign as "popery".[2] As a result, the book's opponents, the Scots Covenanters, joined with the Parliamentary forces in the Civil War. In 1649, Charles I was beheaded and the Commonwealth led by Oliver Cromwell ruled the two countries until 1660, when the monarchy was restored. Charles II instituted a campaign of persecution against the Presbyterian Scots which resulted in the dissolution of the Scots Parliament and culminated in an uprising against the Crown in 1666. However, the Pentland Uprising, as it was called, led to a more tolerant religious regime.

James VII and II ascended the throne in 1685 but his reign was short-lived. He wanted to reintroduce the Roman Catholic faith as the established church in England and Scotland. Neither Parliament wished this to happen and in 1688 James was ousted from the throne and sent into exile. At this point the English Parliament invited William of Orange and Mary, James' daughter, to take the throne. To ensure that the new monarchs would know from the outset what their powers were and what Parliament's powers were, the Petition of Right was passed by the English Parliament.

In Scotland, however, William and Mary were not welcomed in the same way. The Scots Parliament, known as the Convention of Estates, passed the Claim of Right as their constitutional settlement with the Crown. In it, Parliament claimed the right to depose any king who violated the trust on which his powers were held.[3] William was then invited to take the throne. However, not all Scots were content for this king, a Dutchman, to take power. In the

---

[2] Defined as the Roman Catholic religion and used by Protestants as an offensive term.

[3] Barnett, *Constitutional and Administrative Law* (1995), p. 55.

Highlands, John Graham of Claverhouse, "Bonnie Dundee", raised an army against the Crown but the uprising was quashed at Dunkeld.

Scotland, however, was now divided into followers of William and followers of James (the Jacobites) and this was to cause much grief for the next 50 years. William was pressed to establish a single church in the two kingdoms but he did not do so, preferring to allow the Scots to retain their Presbyterian Church. In 1690, the Church of Scotland was established as the "only government of Christ's church within this kingdom".

The two countries were still separate entities so far as trade was 1.04
concerned; the English excluded the Scots from commercial matters, passing the Navigation Acts which prevented the Scots from trading on equal terms. The English wars in Europe also had the effect of closing off the traditional Scottish markets on the continent. These difficulties led to the disastrous Darien fiasco, where three expeditions were sent to Panama to set up the new settlement of Caledonia. The Scots company, however, was unable to obtain financial backing from England or on the continent, and the Scots were forced to back the expeditions themselves. Most of the would-be settlers died in the attempt from disease and attack by the Spaniards who looked upon the Scots as pirates. There was deep anger in Scotland when it became apparent that English colonies in the West Indies and America had been told to offer no aid to the Scots when they abandoned their settlement and sought medical aid from the English. William was blamed for this and there was a groundswell of opinion that a union of the Parliaments and policies was now necessary to ensure the Scots received equality of treatment with the English. The deep distress of the Scots at the failure of the Darien scheme and England's part in it, is shown in the Act of Union 1707 where article XV ensured that the investors of the Darien company were repaid their investment with interest.

The Scots Parliament meantime continued to flex its muscles against the monarch. In 1703, the Scots Parliament passed an Act to the effect that no future sovereign would have power to make war or peace without its consent.[4] This Act was passed at the height of a war against Louis XIV of France. In 1704, the Act of Security was passed; this stated that if Queen Anne died without an heir, the Scots Parliament would choose a new monarch who would not also be the successor to the English throne unless the two

---

[4] The Act anent Peace and War 1703.

countries had established an acceptable form of government and constitutional, economic and religious liberties were guaranteed to the Scots. This Act challenged the English Act of Succession, passed in 1701, to settle the succession on the Protestant House of Hanover. The English Parliament retaliated by passing the Aliens Act in 1705 which threatened to prohibit trade with Scotland and treat Scots as aliens.

The scene was set for the union of the two Parliaments.

UNION OF THE PARLIAMENTS 1707

1.05 It is probably safe to say that the union of the two Parliaments was inevitable and that Scotland had been made ready for this union for almost a century. James VI was the last king to live in Scotland and his heirs paid only fleeting visits to their northern kingdom. As a result, the Scottish nobility had to go south to the English court to seek favours and patronage. Scottish politics were still controlled by the nobility and their absence in England had a negative impact on Scots politics. They also assumed habits and practices of the English political scene, which were then transferred to the Scottish Parliament. This anglicisation of the Scots nobility was a crucial factor in the eventual political union of the two countries.

The passage of the Union Act in Scotland was assisted by money from the English Parliament. The union was to be an incorporating one, not a federal one, so that Scottish members of Parliament were to be absorbed into the new Parliament of Great Britain, which would always be controlled by an English majority.

> "This was to be a unitary not a federal state; as K. C. Wheare observes (Federal Government: 4th ed. 1963, at page 43) there was no model of federal government in existence which might have been urged against the unitary scheme then proposed and adopted."[5]

However, the money was directed at the Scottish Parliament and its members not at the Scottish people who were unhappy at the prospect of the union. There were many riots and demonstrations in the country and the landowners and burgesses also showed their opposition by publishing addresses against the idea. Indeed, none of the Scottish parliamentary constituencies published an address in favour of the union. In the Scottish Parliament the government

---

[5] Turpin, *British Government and the Constitution* (2nd ed. 1990), pp 222–223.

side refused all requests for a referendum to be held so that the people could voice their opinion.

The union was accomplished by means of a Treaty[6] drawn up between the two Parliaments and then ratified by two separate Acts. The first was passed by the Scottish Parliament whereby it resolved to dissolve itself on May 1, 1707. A separate Act was passed simultaneously to provide for the continuance of the Scottish Presbyterian Church[7] and this was then incorporated into the Treaty. The Act was sent to the English Parliament which ratified the Scots document by passing its own Act of Union and an Act to ensure the retention of the Church of England as the English established church.[8] The two Parliaments disappeared on April 30, 1707 to emerge as a new body, the Parliament of Great Britain. 1.06

The Scots were given 45 seats in the new Commons and 16 peers. The 45 Scots members had been nominated, not elected, by the government party of the Scots Parliament.

Although there were a number of "safeguards" for Scottish institutions stated in the Treaty, as Munro observes: "These were institutions more strongly rooted in the national affection than was the Parliament which was disappearing."[9] The important part of the Treaty so far as the English establishment was concerned was that the English Act of Settlement 1701 was accepted by the Scots and the Crown was to pass to the Hanoverian line on Anne's death. This removed the possibility of the Catholic Stuart line being re-established in Scotland to threaten the Protestant monarchy in England.

Scotland's gains included financial and economic guarantees, the continuance of Scots private law and the Scottish courts, the maintenance of the feudal land system, the privileges of the royal burghs and the maintenance of the Scottish universities. As Bradley and Ewing observe: "Guarantees of a similar kind for English institutions were not required as it was obvious that the English would be politically predominant in the new Parliament of Great Britain."[10]

The union was not popular in England or in Scotland; as soon as 1713 a proposal for the dissolution of the union was introduced

---

6 It is said that the Scots Commissioners who signed the Treaty were unable to do so in the Parliament House because of the rioting mob outside; instead they went to the backroom of a nearby public house and the treaty was signed there.

7 APS XI, 406.

8 6 Anne c.11.

9 *Studies in Constitutional Law* (2nd ed., 1999), p. 25.

10 *Constitutional and Administrative Law* (12th ed. 1997), p. 41.

to the House of Lords and only defeated by four votes.[11] The benefits for Scotland did not appear fully until the late eighteenth century.

1.07 The union of the Parliaments of Scotland and England in 1707 has been described as largely a 'marriage of convenience' whereby "Scotland got access to English markets at home and especially abroad (especially important after the Darien disaster) and England for its turn stabilised its borders and political-military relationship with Scotland."[12] The Union Acts preserved Scotland's distinctive legal system, education and local government and the position of the Church of Scotland, and there is no doubt that these institutions helped to maintain the strong sense of nationhood experienced by many Scots people. Scotland has had a degree of autonomy which made it "not a fully independent state, of course, but far more than a mere province."[13] For many years though, the Scots had little influence in the Westminster Parliament because of the small number of people who could vote and therefore return Members of Parliament. In the late nineteenth century, however, the vote had been given to all men over the age of 21 and pressure grew for better Scottish representation in government. At this time, Scottish affairs were overseen by the Lord Advocate who was responsible for the prosecution and courts system and also the supervision of the police and armed forces. His non-legal functions were transferred to the newly created office of Secretary for Scotland in 1885.[14]

In 1885, a Scottish Office was created to administer matters such as law and order and education and the minister for the Scottish Office, the Secretary for Scotland, was given a seat in the Cabinet in 1892. In 1926, the office became that of a Secretary of State. The functions and powers of the Scottish Office gradually increased over the years so that the Secretary of State for Scotland had responsibility for a wide range of matters including agriculture, fisheries, the arts, education, environmental matters, fire and police services, health services, local authorities, prisons, roads, social work, sport, tourism and planning. Most matters pertaining to the legal system were under the control of the Lord Advocate and the Crown Office. The Secretary of State for Scotland had joint responsibility for some matters with colleagues in Whitehall

---

[11] Munro, *Studies in Constitutional Law*, p. 25.

[12] Brown and McCrone, *A New Parliament and Scotland's Future* (1998).

[13] Paterson, *The Autonomy of Modern Scotland* (1994).

[14] Secretary for Scotland Act 1885.

departments. He was, however, recognised as "the mouthpiece of Scottish opinion in the Cabinet and elsewhere."[15]

There is no doubt that the presence of a Scottish minister in the Cabinet brought benefit to Scotland but given that the internal debates of the Cabinet are not readily available, it is difficult to assess how much benefit was actually obtained. The fact that the Scottish Office was based in Scotland allowed the Scottish people to have access to the executive more easily but the autonomy of the Scottish Office was restrained by the system by which its responsibilities were financed. The Secretary of State for Scotland is still a member of the United Kingdom government; the party he represents may not however have a majority of Scottish seats and thus there may be a democratic deficit. This occurred in 1959–64, 1970–74 and 1979–97 where Conservative governments were elected but each time that party failed to gain a majority of seats in Scotland. Bradley observed: 1.08

> "[A] Conservative Secretary of State's claim to be Scotland's minister becomes rather transparent when his government persist with policies affecting Scottish domestic administration which would be rejected by Scotland's elected representatives."[16]

This complaint was made particularly in the 1980s when the Thatcher government implemented policies such as the community charge or poll tax on a reluctant Scottish population. The question of accountability was also raised since the Secretary of State for Scotland and his ministerial colleagues at the Scottish Office were only called to account in the House of Commons once every three weeks, an inadequate amount of time since it was estimated that the Scottish Office had the same responsibilities as 11 Whitehall departments. There was some improvement in the accountability with the introduction of the Scottish Affairs Select Committee in 1979 and the Scottish Grand Committee in 1994.

The scrutiny of Scottish legislation was another problem area; there were two Scottish standing committees to scrutinise proposed legislation, and the second reading debates and report stages on such Bills could also be heard in the Scottish Grand Committee although the votes on the measure were always taken on the floor of the House.

---

15 Report of the Committee on Scottish Administration (Gilmour Committee) Cmd. 5563 (1937), para. 37.

16 "Devolution of Government in Britain—Some Scottish Aspects" in *Devolution* (Calvert ed., 1975), p. 100.

THE DRIVE FOR CONSTITUTIONAL CHANGE

1.09 It has been observed that the 'marriage of convenience' became less convenient to the Scots during the second half of the twentieth century. Scotland had entered the Union for economic reasons but the discovery of oil and gas deposits around Scotland's coasts fuelled speculation that Scotland might be better off economically outside the Union.[17] In both Scotland and Wales, there had been independence parties active in politics with varying degrees of success. The Scottish National Party and Plaid Cymru did not make any real headway until the late 1960s, although the SNP won a by-election in 1945 at Motherwell with Dr Robert McIntyre. In 1966 Gwynfor Evans won Carmarthen and Winnie Ewing won Hamilton in 1967. The SNP went on to win seats at the 1974 General Election, seven in February and 11 in October, and became the second largest party in Scotland. Plaid Cymru's success was less than the SNP but they still obtained 10.7 per cent of the vote.

The two nationalist parties' success in the 1960s was met with alarm at Westminster and the Labour Government set up a Royal Commission to: "[E]xamine the present functions of the central legislature and government in relation to the several countries, nations and regions of the United Kingdom; and to consider . . . whether any changes are desirable . . . in the present constitutional and economic relationships".[18]

The Commission did not report until late 1973 and was unable to produce a unanimous report; two members wrote a substantial dissenting report.[19] There was agreement that independence for Scotland and Wales should be rejected and that there was no need or desire for a federal structure of government. Eight of the Commissioners then supported a form of legislative devolution for Scotland with a directly elected assembly with power to legislate in those areas covered by the Scottish Office. Six of the eight recommended a similar structure for Wales, but the other two wanted an advisory assembly with no legislative powers. The regions of England should also have some form of assemblies with administrative and scrutinising powers. The authors of the minority report proposed a scheme of intermediate level government with seven directly elected assemblies and governments—five in

[17] Brown and McCrone, *op. cit.*, p. 1.

[18] Royal Commission on the Constitution 1969–73 (Kilbrandon Report) Cmnd. 5460 (1973).

[19] Lord Crowther-Hunt and Professor Alan Peacock: Royal Commission on the Constitution 1969–73, Cmnd. 5460–I (1973), Vol. 2, Memorandum of Dissent.

England and one each in Scotland and Wales. The confusion of the Commissioners led to the report being side-lined; it really did not answer any of the questions the electorate had been asking and its failure to consider fully the implications of independence or federalism was a major flaw in its work.

In the event, it was overtaken by events; that winter of 1973–74 1.10
was riven with strikes and the notorious "three day week" so that within four months of the report's publication, the Conservative Government was fighting a general election. The new minority Labour Government announced plans to consider devolution for Scotland and Wales and in 1976 the Scotland and Wales Bill was introduced. This Bill, however, was poorly drafted and progressed very slowly so that the Government proposed a guillotine motion; the motion was defeated and the Government had to withdraw the Bill. In 1977, the Labour Government entered into a co-operation agreement with the Liberals, the Lib.-Lab. pact, and two Bills were presented to Parliament for consideration. These were eventually passed as the Scotland Act 1978 and the Wales Act 1978. The former introduced an assembly with legislative powers; the latter had only executive powers. In both Bills, the Government had included a provision for referendums to be held to allow the electorate in Scotland and Wales to have their say. However, an amendment was passed that if less than 40 per cent of those entitled to vote voted 'Yes'[20] then the legislation would not come into effect.[21] On March 1, 1979, the referendums were held, but in neither country did the 'Yes' vote exceed the 40 per cent threshold of the Cunningham amendment. In the event, the Scottish result was 32.9 per cent in favour, 30.8 per cent against but 36.3 per cent of the electorate did not vote. In Wales, only 11.9 per cent of the electorate voted in favour. The two statutes were repealed by the incoming Conservative Government.

The Scotland Act 1978 had set up a cumbersome and highly complex scheme of devolution, setting out the topics which could be the subject of legislation by the Scottish Assembly and detailing the sections of U.K. statutes which would fall outside or inside the powers of the Assembly.[22] The Scottish Executive was given powers to introduce legislation to Westminster on subjects that were outside

---

20 Normally all that is required in the U.K. is that a majority of those voting are in favour; here, there had to be 40% of those registered to vote, not 40% of those actually voting on the day.

21 George Cunningham, a Labour backbench M.P. and opponent of devolution proposed the amendment.

22 The Act contained 87 sections and 17 schedules.

the powers of the Assembly. In addition, the way in which the statute was drafted would have made it necessary to amend it on a regular basis to take account of new Westminster legislation. The Act did not give the Assembly any tax raising or varying powers and this omission was a crucial factor in the referendum result.

1.11 The next eighteen years in Scotland were frustrating for many, not least those who wished to see constitutional change. After the disastrous referendum result, there was a feeling of being let down[23] and this was exacerbated when the Conservative Government was returned to power in 1983 and 1987. After the 1987 election in Scotland, the Government had only 10 seats and the Labour Party, with the lion's share of Scottish seats, was helpless to protect Scotland from some of the effects of the Conservatives' policies, particularly the poll tax or community charge, introduced in Scotland a year before it was introduced in England and Wales. The 'democratic deficit' continued to fuel ambitions for devolution.

In 1988 the Campaign for a Scottish Assembly, formed in the aftermath of the 1979 referendum, published *A Claim of Right for Scotland* in which they declared that Scotland had a right to decide her own constitution and called for a convention to be set up to devise a scheme for a Parliament or Assembly.[24] The Claim of Right referred to the democratic deficit where the Scots had voted in large numbers for the constitutional reform proposed by one party but were ignored by the parliamentary majority held by another party which opposed those reforms.[25] The next year, the Scottish Constitutional Convention was set up, drawing support from a wide range of people and organisations. All of the political parties, with the exception of the Conservatives and SNP, were involved as well as the trades unions, religious bodies, local authorities and other organisations. The Conservatives did not join because they were against any constitutional change and the SNP withdrew because it was obvious that the majority of participants would not consider independence as an option.

1.12 The Convention's first report published in 1990 and called *Towards Scotland's Parliament*, was the basis of agreement between

---

[23] For discussion of this and other reasons, see Walker "Constitutional Reform in a Cold Climate: Reflections on the White Paper and Referendum on Scotland's Parliament" in *Devolution and the British Constitution* (Tomkins ed., 1998).

[24] Edwards (ed.), *A Claim of Right for Scotland* (1989).

[25] MacCormick "Sovereignty or Subsidiarity? Some Comments on Scottish Devolution" in *Devolution and the British Constitution* (Tomkins ed., 1998).

the Labour and Liberal Democrat Parties and their respective manifestos in the 1992 General Election reflected this. Again Scotland voted overwhelmingly for Labour policies but the Conservative Party was again returned. However, the Conservatives now realised that the Union was being severely tested and the Government published proposals to extend 'administrative devolution' to the Scottish Office and announced changes in the way Scottish legislation was debated at Westminster.[26] This included increased use of the Scottish Grand Committee, in particular, allowing the second reading debates of Scottish legislation to be heard in the Grand Committee although the ultimate vote would always be in the House.[27] These changes did not stop the bandwagon of constitutional change.

John Smith was elected Labour Party Leader in 1992 and he sought to complete his 'unfinished business' of bringing devolution to Scotland. Smith had been the minister in charge of bringing the Scotland Act 1978 to a successful fruition and he had long campaigned within the Labour Party for devolution to be part of the Party's policy.

After 1992, the Constitutional Convention set to work to develop their ideas on a Scottish Parliament and in 1995 the final report was presented. Called *Scotland's Parliament. Scotland's Right* the report formed the basis of the Labour Government's proposals in 1997. The report recommended a Parliament elected by proportional representation with legislative and tax-varying powers.

In 1997, the Labour Party's manifesto included a commitment to 1.13
hold a referendum on devolution and if this was successful to legislate for a Scottish Parliament within its first year of office. The Referendums (Scotland and Wales) Act 1997 was passed and a referendum was held in Scotland on September 11, and in Wales on September 18. The Scottish referendum was based on proposals set out in a White Paper published in July of that year. *Scotland's Parliament*[28] was a best seller and set out the proposals largely based on the Convention report. The Government sought to ensure that the people of Scotland, and indeed of the United Kingdom, understood that devolution was different from independence. The sovereignty of the U.K. Parliament is stressed in the White Paper:

---

[26] Scottish Office, *Scotland in the Union: A Partnership for Good*, Cm. 2225 (1993).

[27] See discussion in Himsworth, "The Scottish Grand Committee as an Instrument of Government" (1996) 1 Edin.L.R. 79.

[28] Cm. 3658 (1997).

> "The U.K. Parliament is and will remain sovereign in all matters: but as part of the government's resolve to modernise the British constitution, Westminster will be choosing to exercise that sovereignty by devolving legislative responsibilities to a Scottish Parliament without in any way diminishing its own powers."[29]

The referendum asked two questions: the first asked if there should be a Scottish Parliament and the second asked if the Scottish Parliament should have tax-varying powers. This time there was no threshold vote to attain and the referendum result left no doubts as to the wishes of the Scottish electorate. On the first question, 74.3 per cent said 'Yes' and on the second, 63.5 per cent.[30]

The Scotland Bill was published on December 18, 1997 and given the Royal Assent on November 19, 1998.[31] The first election to the Scottish Parliament was held on May 6, 1999 and the first meeting of the Parliament was held on May 12. The Queen officially opened the Parliament on July 1, signalling the transfer of powers from Westminster to the new Parliament and the Scottish Executive.

---

[29] Cm. 3658 (1997), para. 4.2.

[30] For analysis of the results, see Mitchell, Denver, Pattie and Bochel, "The 1997 Devolution Referendum in Scotland" (1998) 51 Parl.Aff. 166.

[31] For discussion of the Bill's passage through Parliament, see Himsworth and Munro, *The Scotland Act 1998* (1999).

CHAPTER 2

WHAT IS A CONSTITUTION?

The study of constitutional law whether of Scotland or the United Kingdom or any other country requires an understanding of what a constitution is. The concept of a constitution is found at all levels of society; for instance a golf club will have a constitution which sets out the rules of the club, saying, *inter alia,* who may become a member, how the club will be organised and how the rules can be changed. The constitution of a state will set out similar rules, such as who will be a citizen of the state, how the government will be elected and how the constitution can be changed. One definition of a constitution is, therefore, that it is a collection of rules and regulations, which govern the organisation of a group of people. It is a code "of norms which aspire to regulate the allocation of powers, functions and duties among the various agencies and officers of government, and [to] define the relationship between these and the public."[1] 2.01

The idea is then that constitutional law is the law concerning nation states and how power is created and regulated within the state. It is: "the whole system of government of a country, the collection of rules which establish and regulate or govern the government."[2]

States are made up of people and constitutional law affects individual citizens as well as governments. One of the twentieth century's most eminent Scots constitutional lawyers, J. B. Mitchell, commented on constitutional law as follows: 2.02

> "State power and individual liberty cannot be separated. Each reacts upon the other. Neither can be regarded in isolation, and the rights and obligations of the state and of the individual should not be regarded as essentially opposed to each other. Rights of the state are . . . nothing but

---

[1] Finer, Bogdanor and Rudden, *Comparing Constitutions* (1995), p. 1.
[2] Wheare, *Modern Constitutions*, (2nd ed. 1966), p. 1.

the communal rights of the individuals who make up that state."[3]

This sentiment was previously uttered by the American, Thomas Paine:

> "A constitution is not the act of a government, but of the people constituting a government, and a government without a constitution is power without right. . . . A constitution is a thing antecedent to a government; and a government is only the creature of a constitution."[4]

Paine's idea was that the constitution precedes the government, and it is the constitution which then gives the government its legitimacy and sets out its powers, duties and functions. This idea can be clearly seen in the constitution of the United States where the original seven articles define the government of the country and set up the checks and balances within which the government will work. The checks and balances include the Supreme Court of the United States and many constitutions with a formal written document will have a constitutional court that has power to declare laws and government actions to be unconstitutional.

Constitutional law can be an instrument of progress and political change where politicians are reluctant to act.[5] Thus in the 1950s and 1960s in the USA, the Supreme Court interpreted the constitution so as to outlaw racial segregation in the southern states. However, the converse can also be true. The U.S. Supreme Court has acted as a brake when the legislature of Texas acted too quickly. In *Texas v. Johnson*[6] the court held that a Texan statute which made it unlawful to burn the U.S. flag as part of a political protest was unconstitutional since it violated the principle of free speech in the First Amendment.

2.03 In practice, the term 'constitution' has two meanings. The first, a narrow meaning, is where it refers to a particular document that sets out the framework of a government and the principal organs to be set up. This document is likely to have a special legal sanctity and may be the supreme law of the land. Examples of states with this type of constitution include the USA, Germany and France. The wider meaning of constitution states that even if a state has a constitution in the narrow sense, the detailed rules necessary for

---

[3] *Constitutional Law,* (1968), p. 3.

[4] *The Rights of Man* (Collins ed., 1984), p. 93 (orig. 1792, Pt. II).

[5] Tushnet, "The Politics of Constitutional Law" in *The Politics of Law* (Kairys ed., 1990).

[6] 109 S.Ct. 2533 (1989).

the running of the government cannot be included. Thus 'constitution' will include the document and the statutes, precedents, rules, customs and practices required to ensure that the constitution can adapt to changing circumstances. Some of these rules will be detailed in ordinary legislation. Others may not be written down at all.

If it is accepted that no one document can contain all of the rules and procedures necessary for a government to operate, it follows that *all* constitutions fall into the second category. All constitutions are comprised of written rules and procedures and unwritten habits and practices. The written elements give stability and continuity; the unwritten elements allow for flexibility.

Constitutional principles are usually given in general or abstract 2.04
terms rather than specific. While this allows some flexibility in their meaning, it is important that the terms are not so general that they can be interpreted too widely. Many written constitutions give power to a constitutional court to interpret the constitution, for instance the Supreme Court of the United States and the German Federal Constitutional Court. In the United Kingdom, none of our laws enjoys any special protection or entrenchment. Technically, any statute can be repealed by passing another statute, and all statutes are passed using the same basic procedure. However, the British courts will have a different attitude to certain statutes because of their perceived status. For instance, the European Communities Act 1972, which allowed the United Kingdom to become a member of the EEC, is seen as one of constitutional importance, whereas the Education (Scotland) Act 1996, which deals with the setting up of the Scottish Qualifications Authority, is not.

The vast majority of countries of the world have a constitution.[7] 2.05
However, a number are suspended, or changed at will, or simply ignored. The constitution is a relatively modern concept and the making of a constitution has usually followed some particular political upheaval, such as, on gaining independence (*e.g.* Kenya, India), after a war (*e.g.* West Germany, Japan), after a revolution (*e.g.* USA, France), after the union of two or more states into one (*e.g.* former Yugoslavia, USSR), and the break-up of a state into a number of smaller ones (*e.g.* Czech Republic and Slovakia). In 1997, South Africa adopted a new constitution to reflect its progress from the apartheid system of government to the democratic, one-man one-vote system known to the western

---

[7] For a list of constitutions, see http://www.findlaw.com/01topics/06onstitutional/03forconst/index.html, July 18, 1999. See also World Constitutions map at http://www.hsrc.ac.za/constitutions/modernconst.html, July 18, 1999.

democracies. In 1982, Canada adopted a Charter of Rights into its constitution after its original constitution had been 'repatriated' from the United Kingdom. The constitution will contain the beliefs and political aspirations of those who framed it.

> "[A] constitution may serve as a binding statement of a people's aspirations for themselves as a nation. A text may silhouette the sort of community its authors/subjects are or would like to become: not only their governmental structures, procedures, and basic rights, but also their goals, ideals, and the moral standards by which they want others, including their own posterity, to judge the community".[8]

The form and content of the constitution will depend on the historical context of its creation. For instance, the constitution of the USA, written in 1787, reflects the desire of its framers to create a system of government where no one body would be in charge but all 13 states would have an equal say. This was a reaction to the British system of government where although the American colonists were heavily taxed they had no representation in the British Parliament to say how those taxes were to be spent. The U.S. model set out that the people are the ultimate source of political legitimacy and authority. It provided for an elected head of state, clear separation of powers and the sanctity of the rule of law by giving the Supreme Court power to decide on the legality of government statutes and actions. Finally, the rights of individuals are protected by the Bill of Rights. In recent times, the rule of law and separation of powers have been closely scrutinised with the various actions against President Clinton. For instance in *Clinton v. Jones*[9] the Supreme Court allowed the federal courts to continue the sexual harassment action by Paula Jones saying that the separation of powers doctrine did not mean that the action had to wait until the President left office.

2.06 If the government is democratic and adheres to the constitution, there will be no problem since the constitution will ensure that the government follows the rules. However, if a government is not democratic, it may ignore the constitution and do as it pleases. The difficulties experienced by Ghana in the early years of its independence illustrate this. Ghana gained her independence from the United Kingdom in 1957. The British government ensured that there was a written constitution, based on a Westminster model

---

[8] Murphy, "Constitutions, Constitutionalism and Democracy" in *Constitutionalism and Democracy* (Greenberg, Katz, Oliviero and Wheatley eds., 1993), p. 10.

[9] 117 S.Ct. 1636, 137 L.Ed. 2d. 945 (1997).

which had been used in other countries. It contained various safeguards for individual and minority interests and it was agreed after an independence conference. In 1960, the head of the government, Dr Nkrumah, ensured the passage of a republican constitution, which omitted any safeguards for minority interests. In 1964, the constitution was again amended, this time to make Ghana a one-party state and thus increase the power of the existing government. In 1969, the government was overthrown and a new constitution was drawn up, once again trying to ensure that abuse of power was impossible and limiting the power of the government. In 1972, there was a military coup and the constitution was suspended.

A constitution may be incomplete or not reflect actual practice. Not all constitutions are the same; a rule included in one may not be included in another. The constitution may also be open to interpretation by the courts, thus changing the meaning intended by the drafters.

The United Kingdom has not seen the major political upheavals 2.07 experienced in other countries, such as France in the eighteenth century and Germany in the twentieth century.[10] There has therefore been little pressure to enact a 'constitution' covering the whole of the government's work. There have been times of unrest which have led to reforms, but no event has been so radical as to require a complete reconstruction of the system of government. Instead reforms were implemented by means of ordinary legislation as and when required. For instance, the crisis between the House of Commons and House of Lords was resolved by passing the Parliament Act 1911 and the abdication of Edward VIII was implemented by His Majesty's Declaration of Abdication Act 1936.

DIFFERENT TYPES OF CONSTITUTION

Constitutions can be categorised in different ways and every 2.08 constitution will fall into more than one category.

Written and Unwritten constitutions

All constitutions are written in the wider sense of the term; 2.09 however, the vast majority of them are written in the narrow sense, that is, there is a specific document to which reference can be made. Indeed only the United Kingdom and Israel have no specific

---

[10] See Wheare, *op. cit.*

written document called "the constitution". Many commentators have thus referred to the British constitution as being unwritten. This is a misnomer; the British constitution is more written than most. Many of our constitutional rules are found in statutes and cases and so technically it would be possible to cut out all of the constitutional statutes and cases and paste them into one very large book and call it the constitution. Jennings reflected:

> "If a constitution means a written document, then obviously Great Britain has no constitution. In countries where such a document exists, the word has that meaning. But the document itself merely sets out rules determining the creation and operation of governmental institutions, and obviously Great Britain has such institutions and such rules. The phrase 'British constitution' is used to describe those rules."[11]

2.10 Writing a constitution is a difficult and complex task. If there are too few articles and clauses, too much detail will be left to the courts to fill in. Too many articles and there may not be enough flexibility to allow change to occur naturally. One of the simplest constitutions is that of the USA. The original constitution consists of just seven articles. Since 1787, only 27 amendments have been added, 10 at one time to form the Bill of Rights in 1791. It has undoubtedly stood the test of time but its terms are very general and this has proved to be a double-edged sword. On the one hand, it has allowed the Supreme Court to interpret the constitution to ensure that it reflects modern life. In 1954, the Fourteenth Amendment came under scrutiny in the segregation case. At section 1 the amendment says:

> "All persons born or naturalised in the U.S. and subject to the jurisdiction thereof, are citizens of the U.S. and of the State wherein they reside. No State shall make or enforce any law which shall abridge the privileges or immunities of citizens of the U.S; nor shall any State deprive any person of life, liberty, or property, without due process of law; nor deny to any person within its jurisdiction the equal protection of the laws."

Some of the southern states operated a segregation policy which meant that black children were bussed miles to all-black schools and white children were treated similarly. The states justified the

---

[11] *The Law and the Constitution* (5th ed. 1959), p. 36. See also Ridley "There is no British Constitution: a dangerous case of the Emperor's clothes" (1988) 41 Parl.Aff. 340.

policy by saying that the children were being educated to the same standards but in a way that encouraged separate development of the races. The Supreme Court had discussed this concept of "separate but equal treatment" in 1896 but at that time the court had held that segregation of the races was not a denial of equal protection of the law.[12] The U.S. Supreme Court finally ruled that such segregation was unconstitutional in 1954. Chief Justice Warren said: "In approaching this problem, we cannot turn the clock back to 1868 when the 14th Amendment was adopted . . . We must consider public education in the light of its full development and its present place in American life".[13]

The other edge of the sword can be seen in a recent decision. The Supreme Court ruled that the viewing of child pornography on the Internet is protected by the First Amendment on freedom of expression, although most citizens would agree that such activity was undesirable.

A further category of written constitution can be identified; it 2.11
can be realistic or part-fictive. A realistic constitution is basically "what you see is what you get". A part-fictive one appears to be fine on the surface but actually omits safeguards and processes in real life. Examples of realistic constitutions include those of France, Germany, Ireland, and the USA. The processes detailed reflect what happens in reality, for instance the U.S. constitution provides that elections for the U.S. President and Vice-President will take place every four years and these occur even if the country is at war.[14] A realistic constitution will also state what will happen if certain circumstances arise. For instance, the French constitution gives power to the President to dissolve the National Assembly and hold fresh elections. The result of these may not be to his liking so can he call for new elections? The constitution prevents him from doing so until a year has elapsed.

There are few part-fictive constitutions left. The best examples were those of the former USSR and the countries of the Eastern Bloc. At first look these constitutions seemed good; they were full of decorative passages that promised much, but the reality was quite different. The 1977 constitution of the USSR gave guidance on how disagreements between the two Houses of the Supreme Soviet would be resolved. However, in reality, both Houses consisted of picked candidates; both Houses met for only a few days each

---

[12] *Plessey v. Ferguson,* 163 U.S. 537 (1896).

[13] *Brown v. Board of Education of Topeka,* 347 U.S. 483 (1954).

[14] Art. II, Section 1; 12th, 20th and 22nd Amendments.

year and sat together, not separately. So disagreements were highly improbable making the 1977 constitutional provision redundant.

A part-fictive constitution may give rights or protection in one place and take them away in another. Article 72 of the USSR constitution stated that every Union Republic had the right to secede (leave) the USSR. Article 3, however, established the principles of "democratic centralism" as a constitutional provision and stated that "lower bodies" such as the Union Republics must "observe the decision of higher ones". In other words, the Union Republics had to follow the decisions of the Union Government.

Rigid and Flexible constitutions

2.12 To be of use to a nation, the constitution has to be amenable to change to meet the different aspirations of a changing society. A flexible constitution is one which can be changed by the same process as any other law. The category is very small; indeed New Zealand and the United Kingdom are the two examples. A rigid constitution is one which can be changed only by means of a special process. Most written constitutions fall into this category. However, the processes used for amending the constitution vary from easy to difficult and thus the degree of rigidity varies. The USSR constitution required a two-thirds majority of each House of the Supreme Soviet; this appears difficult to achieve but the members of the two Houses were handpicked and the Houses sat together, meaning that the constitution could be changed relatively easily. In other countries the constitution may require the consent of other bodies, such as the individual states of the USA, or of the people themselves in a referendum, as in the Republic of Ireland.

When considering the ease, or otherwise, of amending a constitution, it is not sufficient only to consider what the process for amendment is. A number of legal obstacles may be easier to overcome than just one. For instance, the Swiss constitution has a complex amending process and this would appear to make it quite rigid. However, it was changed more often than one of the earlier constitutions of France which required only a joint meeting of the two Houses. On the other hand, the Australian constitution has a similar amending process to the Swiss one but it has been changed only a handful of times. During the period 1900–90, 42 proposals for amendment were made but only eight were successful. It is not therefore just the amending process which has to be taken into account; the political stability of the country also has to be considered. If the constitution suits the party in power, then few changes will be made; if, however, the party in power is unhappy with some aspect of the constitution then changes will be attempted and probably achieved as often as the party sees fit. A democratic government will seek change using the amending process; a non-democratic government will be less likely to use the amending process if it causes them too much difficulty.

The rigidity of a constitution thus depends on three factors: the amending process, the political stability of the country, and the practicality of making the change.

Some constitutions can be amended by the legislature acting 2.13
alone and others require the involvement of the legislature and some other body. The latter constitution is called a supreme constitution. Examples of countries with a supreme constitution are the USA, Australia, Switzerland, Ireland and Denmark. A supreme constitution means that all the organs of the state are subordinate to the constitution. For instance, the U.S. constitution at Article VI, section 2 states the supremacy of the constitution thus:

> "This Constitution and the Laws of the United States which shall be made in pursuance thereof . . . shall be the supreme law of the land; and the Judges in every State shall be bound thereby, anything in the constitution or laws of any state to the contrary notwithstanding."

Amendments cannot be made without the use of the special process stated in the constitution and no one organ has the power to make those amendments. While a supreme constitution has much to commend it, it does make for difficulties if the amending process is too complex. One of the best examples to illustrate this is the U.S. constitution and the operation of the Second Amendment which gives citizens the right to bear arms. This has long been interpreted by the Supreme Court as giving individuals the right to own guns for their own defence and the defence of their property. When the amendment was passed in 1791, the right was understandable, indeed necessary, because most of the USA had no law enforcement agencies and so people had to protect themselves from outlaws. However, today there are many millions of guns in private ownership in the USA, not to mention those held illegally. Many murders are committed each year where guns are used. For instance, during 1998, there were several incidents where teenagers obtained guns from home and used them in their schools to murder their colleagues. During 1999, there were other incidents where gunmen shot people going about their usual business. Many attempts have been made to curtail the ownership of guns by changing the constitutional right to bear arms. However, to change the U.S. constitution, the amendment must be passed by a two-thirds majority in the Congress and accepted by three-quarters of the states, that is 38 out of 50 states. The gun lobby in the USA is exceptionally strong and has been able to ensure that enough states voted against the amendment proposals. There have been other attempts to make it more difficult to obtain a gun; the Brady Act passed in 1993 by the Congress brought in a 14 day waiting time for new purchasers. This was to allow the authorities time to check whether the purchaser had a criminal record and thus should not be granted a licence. Recent case law has mitigated the effects of the Brady Act so that little change has in fact occurred.

Federal and Unitary constitutions

2.14 It is probably easier to identify a constitution as being federal or unitary than flexible or rigid. A federal constitution is one where the powers of government are divided between a government of the whole country and a number of governments of various parts of the country. A unitary constitution is seen where the legislature of the whole country is the supreme law-making body, although there may be other law-making authorities.

The oldest and probably best example of a federal constitution is that of the United States. The USA is a country which comprises 50 individual states. The country has a federal government which comprises the President and his Executive, the Legislature (the Congress comprising the House of Representatives and the Senate) and the Judiciary comprising the Supreme Court and other federal courts. The federal government has specific functions, such as foreign relations, defence, trade, major crime, major projects such as inter-state roads, and so on. The federal legislature makes laws for the whole country and the federal government pays for its programmes by means of taxation of the whole population.

Each of the states also has an executive, legislature and judiciary and has specific functions such as education, health, social welfare programmes, roads and transport, criminal justice and prisons. These are paid for by taxation, but each state has its own rate of local tax which is applicable only in that state. The state government has power to legislate for its own state but no others. Thus there are differences in how each state treats certain matters; for instance some states have the death penalty while others do not. The federal government has power to legislate for the whole country but only in those areas specified in the constitution. There are two forms of legislation in the USA, federal laws and state laws. Both of them are subordinate to the constitution of the United States in that federal laws and state laws may be declared unconstitutional by the Supreme Court. In *Marbury v. Madison*[15] the Supreme Court declared that the power to review legislation was a fundamental power given by the Constitution. Chief Justice Marshall said:

> "The constitution is either a superior, paramount law, unchallengeable by ordinary means, or it is on a level with ordinary legislative acts, and, like other acts, is alterable when the legislature shall be pleased to alter it. If the former part of the alternative is true, then a legislative act contrary to the constitution is not law; if the latter part be true, then written constitutions are absurd attempts, on the part of the people, to limit a power in its own nature unlimitable."[16]

This is commonplace in federal constitutions where the constitution is supreme. Indeed a federal constitution must be supreme, since it must control the two levels of government to ensure that neither has the upper hand. It must also be rigid ensuring that both levels of government are involved in the amending process.

A federal constitution will therefore be supreme and rigid. Each legislature will be limited in power and will be independent of the other. Neither legislature will be subordinate to the other but both will be subordinate to the constitution.

Some constitutions are not truly federal but can be described as 2.15
quasi-federal such as the constitution of Canada. Here, there is an independent government for the whole country but this government has certain, albeit limited, powers of control over the Canadian provinces. The provinces have exclusive jurisdiction over certain subjects specified in the constitution but some bills may be vetoed by the government of Canada. Provincial judges are appointed by the Canadian government, as is the head of each provincial government, the Lieutenant Governor. However, the powers of veto and disallowance are rarely exercised by the Canadian government and so the provinces are in reality independent of the federal government.

The constitution of Australia safeguards the independence of the states, giving the impression of a federal state. The reality is that the government of the Commonwealth of Australia has considerable control over the states because the government controls the purse strings. The state governments are dependent on the Commonwealth government for grants to perform their most important

---

15 (1803) 1 Cranch 103.

16 *Marbury v. Madison* (1803) 1 Cranch 103 at 177.

functions. The constitution is thus written as a federal one but acts like a unitary one with decentralisation or devolution to the states.

2.16 The majority of constitutions are in fact unitary in nature where the legislature with supreme law making power is able to overrule the subordinate lawmakers. Examples here include New Zealand, Ireland and the United Kingdom. The New Zealand constitution is not a supreme one because it is not rigid; the Parliament may change the constitution simply by the ordinary process of law. The constitution of Ireland however is supreme and rigid. The legislature is limited in law making since the constitution does not permit certain laws to be made, for instance to allow divorce. The constitution can only be changed by a special process which includes a referendum.

The constitution of the United Kingdom, although not written in the narrow sense, is both unitary and flexible. Laws are made in the main by Parliament, but certain powers are granted to other bodies to create legislation. For instance, local authorities are permitted to make byelaws. The new Scottish Parliament will have authority to make laws in certain areas but will be prohibited by its creating statute (the Scotland Act 1998) from making laws in areas such as defence, foreign relations and constitutional matters. The U.K. constitution will therefore continue to be a unitary one even though there will be Parliaments or Assemblies established in three of the countries which make up the United Kingdom.

2.17 Occasionally a constitution will be neither federal nor unitary, but will create a confederation. Here the government of the whole country is subordinate to the governments of the individual states. The confederation is a form of association between governments whereby a common organisation is retained by the governments. Before 1789, the thirteen states of America regulated their common affairs through the Articles of Confederation and during the American Civil War the southern states tried to return to this type of constitution when they founded the Confederacy. On the break-up of the USSR there were moves to establish a confederation of independent states but this failed because the smaller republics feared that Russia would again dominate.

A recent text identified states as either federations, unitary states or union states.[17] In this categorisation, the United Kingdom would seem to fall into the last category, as a union of various nation states which came together at different times to create a new state. Keating describes the union state as a pact or contract which does not necessarily treat each partner equally. Such asymmetrical union

---

[17] Keating, *Nations against the State* (1996).

states can work very well; an example would be Spain, where the Basque country, Catalonia and five other regions have been given considerable autonomy in their own affairs.[18] These old 'nations' had been demanding more power to control their own affairs, but other regions of Spain did not appear to be interested in such regional government. The solution adopted was to allow increased autonomy where there was a demand for it.

Presidential and Parliamentary constitutions

The final classification is whether the constitution establishes a presidential executive or a parliamentary one. The distinction between the two is that the president may not sit in the legislature and he will be head of state. In a parliamentary constitution, there will be a prime minister who will invariably sit in the legislature and a separate head of state. The majority of members of the parliamentary executive will not sit in the parliament; they will be civil servants and other officials. Only the heads of government departments will sit in the legislature as members. Other members of the executive as well as the judiciary will probably be precluded from sitting as members of the legislature. Presidential executives are found mainly in countries influenced by the USA such as the Philippines and Liberia. 2.18

CONCLUSION

A constitution can be written or not, rigid or not, federal or unitary, presidential or parliamentary and can be any combination from the four classifications. The classifications are not in themselves important but they serve to explain a country's system of government once the nature of the constitution is established. Most countries operate best if they have a stable democratic constitution since this allows its citizens to predict how the government will act from day to day, but a constitution is not necessary for stable government. The People's Republic of China has a highly stable form of government but the bare minimum of human rights and little in the way of democracy as recognised in western nations. "A constitution has to be read . . . as a living document addressing contemporary situations and problems as and when they arise."[19] 2.19

---

[18] Hazell "Devolution and Constitutional Reform" in *Devolution and the British Constitution* (Tomkins ed., 1998).

[19] O'Neill "A Tale of Two Constitutions" (1997) S.L.T. 205 at 210.

CHAPTER 3

SOURCES OF CONSTITUTIONAL LAW

3.01 The United Kingdom constitution is classified as unitary, flexible, unwritten and parliamentary. The term 'unwritten' is, of course, inaccurate. The U.K., or British, constitution is as much written as any other constitution; the difference is that it is not contained or sourced within one document. It is a constitution created from a number of sources over several hundred years. It is constantly evolving and changing to meet changing circumstances. Further significant changes have recently occurred with the setting up of the Scottish Parliament and Welsh Assembly, the introduction of a Northern Ireland Assembly and changes in the structure of the House of Lords. Further changes will occur when the Human Rights Act 1998 is brought into force and a Freedom of Information Bill is finally passed by the U.K. Parliament. The possibility of the introduction of the Euro as the currency of the United Kingdom will have further implications for the U.K. constitution.

LEGISLATION

3.02 Many Acts of Parliament contain measures which are not constitutional; for instance, the annual Finance Act contains tax alterations and affects individuals and companies. The Sunday Trading Act 1994 allows shops to open on Sundays in England and Wales but again this is not constitutional in nature. On the other hand, there are a substantial number of statutes which have altered the British constitution. Some examples include the following.

Act of Settlement 1701. This Act of the English Parliament was incorporated into the Act of Union 1707. The 1701 Act settled the succession to the throne on the Protestant heirs of Sophia, Electress of Hanover. Queen Anne's children had all died in infancy and the heir according to the constitution was the deposed Catholic king, James VII and II and his heirs. This was unacceptable to the English people because James had tried to impose his religion on the country when he was king. The Parliament enacted the statute with Anne's consent to ensure that the "Auld Pretender" could not succeed on her death. The inclusion of the Act in the Union with Scotland legislation was a crucial element for the English Parliament.[1]

Acts of Union 1707. There were two Acts of Union, one passed by the Scottish Parliament and one by the English Parliament. The two legislatures ceased to exist on April 30, 1707 and the new Parliament of Great Britain came into being on May 1, 1707.[2]

European Communities Act 1972. This Act ratified the treaty obligations signed by the Government for the United Kingdom to become a member of the European Communities on January 1, 1973.[3]

Representation of the People Acts. These Acts are passed from time to time to alter the way in which citizens of the United Kingdom vote in elections.[4]

House of Commons Disqualification Act 1975. This states who may not sit in the House of Commons as a Member of Parliament.[5]

Parliament Acts 1911 and 1949. The 1911 Act curtailed the power of the House of Lords to prevent the passage of a government Bill. The Act stated that the House of Lords could only delay the Bill for two parliamentary sessions; the 1949 Act reduced this to one session.[6]

Scotland Act 1998. This devolves power from the U.K. Parliament to a new Scottish Parliament elected in May 1999.[7]

In addition to statutes, subordinate legislation is used to implement the principles outlined in various statutes. Subordinate, or delegated, legislation is an important method of enacting laws. 3.03

It is important to note the main difference between primary legislation (statutes) and subordinate legislation (statutory instruments). Under the U.K. constitution, once an Act of Parliament

---

1 Further discussed in Chap. 1.
2 See Chap. 1.
3 See Chap. 4.
4 See Chap. 6.
5 See Chap. 7.
6 See Chap. 7.
7 See Chap. 8.

has been through the parliamentary process and received the Royal Assent, it may not be challenged in court as unconstitutional. Any type of subordinate legislation may be challenged in court as being *ultra vires* (literally 'outwith the powers'). If a subordinate instrument is not passed using the correct procedure or it attempts to do something not envisaged in the parent Act, then it may be declared void by the courts.[8] The Acts of the Scottish Parliament will not have the same protection from challenge as those passed by the U.K. Parliament. This is because the Scottish Parliament is a devolved institution whose powers derive from the Scotland Act 1998. The special provisions affecting the Scottish Parliament are discussed in Chapter 8.

COMMON LAW

3.04 There are three main sources for the common law: the royal prerogative, judicial precedent and presumptions of legislative intent.

Royal prerogative

3.05 This has been described as "the inherent legal attributes unique to the Crown". Prerogative powers originate from before Stuart times, that is, before the Union of the Crowns in 1603. The sovereign then held all executive power and was able to do what he or she wished. Parliament met only when the sovereign called it, and that could be infrequently. During the seventeenth century, the power of Parliament gradually increased and the sovereign's powers were transferred to ministers and to Parliament itself.[9] Today, most prerogative powers are actually exercised by government ministers although technically the power is exercised by the Queen on the advice of her ministers.

Prerogative power is a legal source of law and as such is recognised and enforced by the courts. The power is vested in the Crown by the common law and could be described as 'the common law powers of the Crown'. According to the constitutional writer, Blackstone, the power comprises: "those rights and capacities which the King enjoys alone, in contradistinction to others and not

---

[8] For further reading, see Finch and Ashton, *Administrative Law in Scotland* (1997, W. Green), pp. 95–105.

[9] For an account of the history of prerogative powers, see Barnett, *Constitutional and Administrative Law* (2nd ed., 1998); Bradley and Ewing, *Constitutional and Administrative Law* (12th ed., 1997).

to those which he enjoys in common with any of his subjects; for if once any prerogative of the Crown could be held in common with the subject, it would cease to be prerogative any more." This illustrates the crux of the matter: that prerogative powers are separate and distinct from any powers held by individuals either at common law or by statute. The powers of pardon or summoning Parliament are not powers held by an ordinary citizen. However, the Crown, like the ordinary citizen, may enter into contracts and such powers are not part of the prerogative. The exercise of the powers is controlled by convention. So, although the appointment of ministers is made by the Queen, she does not choose them; by convention, she is given their names by the Prime Minister.

In the seventeenth century, the courts and Parliament laid down the limitations of today's prerogative powers. In *Prohibitions del Roy*[10] it was held that the king could not act as a judge, he had to dispense justice through his judges. The king could only make laws through Parliament.[11] During this century there were many disputes between the king and Parliament, culminating of course in the Civil War, the beheading of Charles I and expulsion of Charles II. When the monarchy was restored, there was relative calm until Charles II died and his brother James came to the throne. James VII and II was a Roman Catholic and wanted his religion to be the official religion of the country. Parliament resisted this and James was forced to abdicate in 1688 and his daughter Mary and her husband, William of Orange, were invited to take the throne. The offer of the throne was made by Parliament in the Bill of Rights 1689 which set out the powers of Parliament and declared that certain uses of the prerogative were illegal. In Scotland, the invitation to take the throne was passed by the Scottish Parliament and called the Claim of Right. The Bill of Rights provided that Parliament should meet regularly and that Parliament should approve measures to raise taxation and to maintain the army. The Crown's power to suspend or dispense with a law was declared unlawful and proceedings in Parliament could not be questioned in any court or anywhere outside Parliament. This last provision ensures that anything said in Parliament, whether defamatory or not, cannot be founded on in a court action.

Prerogative powers can be exercised by the sovereign in her 3.06
personal capacity (such as the grant of certain honours including the Order of Merit and the Order of the Thistle) and in her

---

[10] (1607) 12 Co. Rep. 63.

[11] *The Case of Proclamations* (1611) 12 Co. Rep. 74.

capacity as head of state. The most important of these latter powers is the power to order the dissolution of Parliament and the appointment of the Prime Minister. The Queen signs the formal proclamation that Parliament is to be dissolved and a general election held. However, by convention the Prime Minister advises the Queen that he wishes to call an election and the date on which it is to be held. Technically the Queen could refuse his request, but she would be unlikely to do so unless she felt the Prime Minister was acting capriciously or that the country was in danger. The Prime Minister decides the date and may or may not have consulted his Cabinet before doing so. Could the Queen refuse a request from the Prime Minister to dissolve Parliament? However improbable this might seem, it appears that she might if she had "substantial grounds" for believing that another party could form a government and a general election would not be in the national interest at that time.[12]

After the election, the Queen will invite the leader of the party with most seats to form a government. However, the election may have resulted in no party having a clear majority. The current Prime Minister may be able to form a coalition with another party in which case he would remain in office. In February 1974, the Conservative Prime Minister Edward Heath tried to form a coalition with the Liberal Party but failed. He then had to resign as Prime Minister. The Labour Party had 301 seats to the Conservative Party's 297; the Liberals had 14 and other parties 23. The Labour leader, Harold Wilson, was asked to form a government by the Queen. He decided not to form a coalition but made it clear to the House of Commons that his Government would not resign if their legislative proposals were defeated unless the Government had made it clear that the proposal was one of confidence. Wilson called a second election in October 1974 which gave him a small overall majority.

When the Prime Minister retires[13] or loses a party leadership election[14] the government still has the mandate of the people and there is no requirement to hold a general election. Instead the party elects a new leader and that person is asked to form a government. All of the parties now have methods of electing a leader and this simplifies matters for the Queen as to who should be invited to become Prime Minister. Before the mid-1960s, the Conservatives did not have a method of selecting a leader and this

---

[12] De Smith and Brazier, *Constitutional and Administrative Law* (8th ed., 1998).

[13] *e.g.* Churchill in 1955; MacMillan in 1963; Wilson in 1976.

[14] *e.g.* Margaret Thatcher in 1990.

caused them difficulties in 1963 when Harold MacMillan suddenly retired. There were a number of contenders for the post and the Queen had to consult with a number of senior Conservatives before Lord Home was invited to take office.

The term "Royal Prerogative" denotes attributes of the Crown which do not apply to ordinary people. It is difficult to define because of its historical roots and the different meanings given to it by various cases. However, it consists mainly of executive government powers. Dicey said: "every act which the executive government can lawfully do without the authority of the Act of Parliament is done in virtue of the prerogative".[15] 3.07

The powers are essentially 'top-down' in nature where "real power continues to flow from the top of the pyramid to its base."[16]

The prerogative can be abolished or changed by statute, for instance, the Crown Proceedings Act 1947 removed the Crown prerogative that it could not be sued in English civil actions of contract or tort, and confirmed the Scottish position for actions of contract or delict. However, no new prerogative powers can be created. This was established by the decision in *BBC v. Johns*,[17] where Lord Diplock gave the leading judgment:

> "It is 350 years and a civil war too late for the Queen's courts to broaden the prerogative. The limits within which the executive government may impose obligations or restraints on citizens of the U.K. without any statutory authority are now well settled and incapable of extension."

A prerogative power may, however, be applied to new circumstances. In *R. v. Home Secretary, ex parte Northumbria Police Authority*[18] the Home Secretary issued C.S. gas and baton rounds to all police forces in England and Wales. The local police authority objected to this and sought a declaration that the Home Secretary did not have the power to issue such equipment without their consent. The court held that the Home Secretary did have such power, this being derived from the Police Act 1964 and the royal prerogative of keeping the Queen's peace.[19] The Home Secretary 3.08

[15] *Introduction to the Law of the Constitution* (19th ed., 1959), p. 424.

[16] Austin, "Administrative Law's Reaction to the Changing Concepts of Public Service" in *Administrative Law: Facing the Future* (Leyland and Woods eds., 1997), p. 9.

[17] [1965] Ch. 32.

[18] [1989] Q.B. 26. Professor Bradley condemned this decision in "Police Powers and the Prerogative" [1988] P.L. 298.

[19] This prerogative was traced back to 1285.

could "supply equipment reasonably required by police forces to discharge their functions." In *Malone v. Metropolitan Police Commissioner*[20] the limited power to authorise telephone tapping under the prerogative came from extending the power to open articles sent through the post. The power to tap telephones is now given in the Interception of Communications Act 1985, passed after the United Kingdom lost the case before the European Court of Human Rights.[21]

In recent years, the courts have had to decide whether or not the exercise of a prerogative power was reviewable by them. In *Chandler v. DPP*[22] the court decided that they could not review the exercise of a prerogative power. This decision was not however followed in *Council of Civil Service Unions v. Minister for Civil Service*,[23] the GCHQ case. The House of Lords decided that regardless of the source of a minister's powers, whether statute or prerogative, the exercise of the power was reviewable. In this case, the court held that the minister had not exercised her powers properly, there being a legitimate expectation on the part of the unions that they would be consulted before employees' conditions of service were altered. This had not occurred. The minister, however, claimed that the actions were taken on the grounds of national security. The court accepted this and the unions lost the case. However, Lord Roskill listed the prerogative powers which would not be subject to judicial review. He included those relating to the making of treaties, the defence of the realm, the prerogative of mercy, the granting of honours, the dissolution of Parliament and the appointment of ministers. In 1997, the incoming Labour Government reversed the Thatcher Government's decision and restored the right to union membership to those working at GCHQ.[24]

3.09 The 'Roskill list' has, however, been whittled down in recent years by the courts. Matters involving national security and the conclusion of treaties remain matters which may not be reviewed by the courts.[25] In *R. v. Secretary of State for Foreign and Commonwealth Affairs, ex parte Rees-Mogg*[26] the question was whether the government had the power to ratify the Maastricht Treaty without

---

[20] [1979] Ch. 344.
[21] *Malone v. U.K.* (1985) 7 E.H.R.R. 14.
[22] [1964] A.C. 763.
[23] [1985] A.C. 374.
[24] H.C. Official Report, Vol. 294, cols. WA 13–14 (May 19, 1997).
[25] *Blackburn v. Attorney-General* [1971] 1 W.L.R. 1037.
[26] [1994] 1 All E.R. 457.

parliamentary approval. The then Prime Minister, John Major, was doubtful as to whether his government could win a vote in the House of Commons and announced that the treaty would be ratified under prerogative powers. A treaty in the United Kingdom only requires parliamentary approval if a change in the law is required or public money is to be spent. The Queen's Bench Division refused the application for judicial review and the government eventually overcame opposition in the Commons to pass a bill to bring the Treaty into effect. In *Laker Airways v. Department of Trade*[27] the minister had claimed statutory and prerogative powers in the issuing of a designated carrier licence to Laker Airways. The court, however, found that once a right had been conferred by statute, in this case the grant of a licence, it could not be taken away by use of the prerogative. The court also found that the exercise of the prerogative could be examined by them because it was a discretionary power to be exercised for the public good. "The law does not interfere with the proper exercise of the discretion by the executive in those situations; but it can set limits by defining the bounds of the activity; and it can intervene if the discretion is exercised improperly or mistakenly."[28]

In *Ex parte Molyneux*[29] an agreement establishing an intergovernmental conference on the future of Northern Ireland was held to be "akin to a treaty". Taylor J. stated that it was not the function of the court to inquire into the exercise of the prerogative in either entering into or implementing the agreement, but he would look closely at the agreement to ensure it did not contravene any statute, rule of common law or convention and that it did not fetter the discretion of the Secretary of State.

There are further signs that the courts are examining the terms of treaties more closely. For instance in *New Zealand Maori Council v. Attorney-General of New Zealand*[30] the Privy Council looked at the terms of the Treaty of Waitangi between the Crown and the Maori and concluded that the Treaty provisions had not been broken by the Crown.

A number of the other prerogative powers on the list have now 3.10
become reviewable, such as the refusal of grant of a passport in

---

[27] [1977] Q.B. 643.
[28] *ibid. per* Lord Denning at 192.
[29] [1986] 1 W.L.R. 331.
[30] [1994] 1A.C. 466.

R. v. Secretary of State for Foreign Affairs, ex parte Everett[31] in which the granting of a passport was held to be an administrative decision which "affected the rights of individuals and their freedom of travel." Taylor L.J. distinguished such administrative matters that could be subject to review from "matters of high policy" such as making war or mobilising the armed forces, which would not be justiciable. Matters involving the armed forces have now been recognised by the courts as amenable to review. In *R. v. Ministry of Defence, ex parte Smith*[32] it was held that a challenge to the decision to discharge four persons from the armed forces because of their sexual orientation was a justiciable matter. Simon Brown L.J. remarked that the courts would decline to review a matter only in exceptional cases such as those involving security.

The exercise of the prerogative of mercy has less relevance now since the death penalty was abolished in the United Kingdom. However, for many years the courts felt that it was not reviewable by them[33] and this was confirmed in 1985 in the GCHQ case.[34] However, this was overturned by the *Bentley* case in 1993 when the Divisional Court decided that the exercise of the power was subject to judicial review.[35] The court was guided by a New Zealand case in which the view was advanced that: "the prerogative of mercy is a prerogative power in the strictest sense of that term, for it is peculiar to the Crown and its exercise directly affects the rights of persons."[36] The court also decided that the exercise of the prerogative power should be on a case-by-case basis.[37]

The Judicial Committee of the Privy Council has had to consider the death penalty many times in appeals from Commonwealth countries such as Jamaica and Trinidad. In *Reckley v. Minister of Public Safety and Immigration (No. 2)*[38] the appellant's application for stay of execution, on the ground that he had not been able to make representations to the Advisory Committee on the Prerogative of Mercy, was refused. The Judicial Committee decided that

---

31 [1989] 1 All E.R. 655. Note that Directive 68/360 gives E.U. citizens the right to be issued with an identity card or passport valid for travel through and between Member States.

32 [1996] Q.B. 517.

33 *De Freitas v. Benny* [1976] A.C. 239.

34 [1985] A.C. 374.

35 *R. v. Secretary of State for Home Department, ex p. Bentley* [1993] 4 All E.R. 442. In 1998, the Court of Criminal Appeal quashed Bentley's conviction for murder after a reference from the Criminal Cases Review Commission: *R. v. Bentley* [1999] Crim.L.R. 330.

36 *Burt v. Governor General* [1992] 3 N.Z.L.R. 672 at 681.

37 See also *Attorney-General of Trinidad and Tobago v. Phillip* [1995] 1 A.C. 396.

38 [1996] 1 A.C. 527.

the discretion of the minister was a personal discretion which had to be exercised in consultation with the Advisory Committee. The discretion was "an act of mercy which was not the subject of legal rights and thus was not justiciable." In another recent case, the Judicial Committee agreed that death by hanging was not unconstitutional, since that was the only method of execution authorised by the constitution.[39]

Where a miscarriage of justice has occurred, the Home Secretary has both statutory power under the Criminal Justice Act 1988 and prerogative power to make *ex gratia* payments. In a number of cases, the courts held that the decision of the Home Secretary not to use his prerogative power to make an *ex gratia* payment was reviewable on the grounds of *Wednesbury* unreasonableness.[40]

A prerogative power can be abolished or altered by a statutory 3.11
provision.[41] Two cases illustrate the difficulties which may arise when part of the prerogative power is altered by statute. In *Attorney-General v. De Keyser's Royal Hotel Ltd*[42] a hotel was requisitioned for use by the armed forces during the First World War; the requisition was authorised under the Defence of the Realm Acts and Regulations. After the war, the hotel owners sought compensation but the Crown argued that there was a prerogative power to take premises for war purposes and that no compensation was payable for doing so. This power existed even although the Defence of the Realm Act provided for statutory compensation for affected owners. The hotel owners argued that since the Crown had taken the hotel citing statutory authority, the Crown could not now rely on the prerogative. The House of Lords decided that the prerogative had been superseded by the statute and the Crown could not therefore rely on the prerogative. Parliament had given the Crown all necessary powers for the defence of the realm and had included safeguards for individual citizens.

In *Burmah Oil Co. v. Lord Advocate*[43] the company's oil installations in Burma were destroyed in 1942 to prevent them falling into

---

[39] *Boodram v. Baptiste* [1999] 1 W.L.R. 1709.

[40] *R. v. Home Secretary, ex p. Harrison* [1988] 3 All E.R. 86; *R. v. Home Secretary, ex p. Batman* [1985] 7 Admin.L.R. 175; *R. v. Home Secretary, ex p. Atlantic Commercial Ltd* [1997] C.O.D. 381.

[41] *e.g. British Coal Corporation v. R.* [1935] A.C. 500; *De Morgan v. Director General of Social Welfare* [1998] A.C. 275 (New Zealand appeal to Privy Council).

[42] [1920] A.C. 508.

[43] [1965] A.C. 75.

the hands of the advancing Japanese army. The destruction was deliberate; it was not accidental or caused by the fighting. Had the installations been destroyed 'in the heat of battle' no compensation would have been payable by the Crown. However, the circumstances were such that the Crown had taken private property for the benefit of the state and so compensation was payable. Unfortunately for Burmah Oil, the decision was immediately overruled by Parliament passing the War Damages Act 1965 which retrospectively ensured that compensation was not payable for property damaged or destroyed "during, or in contemplation of the outbreak of, a war in which the sovereign is or was engaged."[44]

Where a statute has implemented the power of a prerogative, the prerogative power will go into abeyance. The question of whether such power would be resurrected if the statute were subsequently repealed was considered by the courts in *R. v. Secretary of State for Home Department, ex parte Fire Brigades' Union.*[45] The Criminal Justice Act 1988 provided a scheme for the payment of compensation to victims of crime, but the provisions had not been brought into force by the Home Secretary. In 1993, he published a White Paper[46] in which he proposed a new tariff scheme which offered substantially lower rates of compensation than the scheme in the 1988 Act. This new scheme was to be brought into force using prerogative powers. The Court of Appeal held that the Home Secretary could not bring in a new prerogative scheme while the provisions of the 1988 Act remained on the statute book. He had to either introduce legislation to repeal the 1988 Act scheme thus allowing the prerogative power to be restored, or he could comply with his statutory duty and implement the terms of the 1988 Act. He could not however ignore the duty and act under the prerogative. The statutory scheme took precedence over the prerogative.

The decision of the Court of Appeal was upheld by the House of Lords but their decision did not go quite so far as the lower court. The court held that requiring the Home Secretary to implement the Act would be treading "dangerously close" to the jurisdiction of Parliament but the Home Secretary could not use the prerogative to defeat the purpose of the statute. Following this case, the

---

[44] For discussion of this case and historical development of prerogative, see Payne "The Royal Prerogative" in *The Nature of the Crown* (Sunkin and Payne eds., 1999).

[45] [1995] 2 W.L.R. 1.

[46] Home Office, *Compensating Victims of Violent Crime: Changes to the Criminal Injuries Compensation Scheme,* Cmnd. 2434 (1993).

Government introduced the Criminal Injuries Compensation Act 1995 which repealed the relevant provisions of the 1988 Act and introduced the tariff scheme previously proposed by the Home Secretary in the White Paper.

The continued existence of the prerogative power is surprising in some ways, given the insistence of the current Labour Government to change many other aspects of the constitution. To date, there have been no proposals for reforming the prerogative by making its exercise fully reviewable either by Parliament or the courts. Various suggestions for reform have been made[47]; some of these centre on a written constitution being adopted by the United Kingdom but this would not necessarily be required. The various aspects of the prerogative could be encapsulated in legislation thus ensuring that the authority for government action in these areas was derived from statute. This, as noted above, is not unknown in the U.K. constitution. Lord Brown-Wilkinson observed this in his opinion in the *Fire Brigades' Union* case: "the constitutional history of this country is the history of the prerogative powers of the Crown being made subject to the overriding powers of the democratically elected legislature as the sovereign body."[48] 3.12

Judicial precedent

This important source of Constitutional law is law made by judges during the course of cases heard by them in court.[49] Certain judgments state the law in regard to a particular matter and later cases involving the same issue follow the judgment of the first. In other words, the later cases follow the preceding one, the precedent. Judicial precedent is only a source of law on a legal issue where there is no statute covering the same matter; once a statute is passed, the precedent is overruled and the source of law becomes the statute, as occurred in the *Burmah Oil* case.[50] 3.13

Many of the cases referred to in this chapter are precedents, for instance *Entick v. Carrington*[51]; *M v. Home Office*.[52] Such cases state the law on matters which have not been considered by Parliament.

---

47 *e.g.* Institute of Public Policy Research, *The Constitution of the U.K.* (1991).

48 [1995] 2 All E.R. 244 at 254.

49 For a full account, see White and Willock, *Scottish Legal System* (2nd ed., 1999).

50 [1965] A.C. 75.

51 (1765) 19 St.Tr. 1030.

52 [1994] 1 A.C. 377, but note that the precedent extends to English law only; the position is different in Scotland.

Common law presumptions of legislative intent

3.14 These are presumptions made by the court when interpreting primary or subordinate legislation.[53] Subordinate legislation is also subject to the provisions of the Interpretation Act 1978. The initial presumption of the courts is that "Parliament means what it says"; in other words, the courts use the plain or literal meaning of a word in the context of the whole statute, except where it is clearly intended by the statute that a different meaning should be given. The importance of the context of the words was shown in *Padfield v. Minister of Agriculture, Fisheries and Food*[54] where a phrase, taken in isolation, appeared to confer a power on the minister but, when taken in the context of the Act as a whole, was seen to have imposed a duty on him.

In normal circumstances the words of the statute will be construed without the assistance of any extraneous sources. However, since *Pepper v. Hart*[55] the principle has been established that judges may in certain limited circumstances study Parliamentary debates reported in *Hansard* to aid "the construction of legislation which is ambiguous or obscure or the literal meaning of which leads to an absurdity."[56]

Presumptions of legislative intent are used by the courts to resolve ambiguities, provide answers to problems not foreseen by the legislative draftsman or modify the meaning of the words used to give a meaning which appears to conform with the intention of Parliament. However, all presumptions may be rebutted by clear and precise words in the statute. Among the more important presumptions are the following. Parliament does not intend to exclude access to the courts[57] and does not intend legislation to apply retrospectively.[58] Parliament does not intend to impose a charge of tax unless by clear express statements; this presumption has been particularly considered by the courts, for instance in *Attorney-General v. Wiltshire United Dairies Ltd*[59] and *Daymond v. South West Water Authority*.[60]

---

[53] For a fuller account, see Finch and Ashton, *Administrative Law in Scotland* (1997, W. Green), p. 117.

[54] [1968] A.C. 997; [1968] 1 All E.R. 694.

[55] [1993] A.C. 593; [1993] 1 All E.R. 42; see also *Melluish v. BMI (No. 3) Ltd* [1996] A.C. 454.

[56] *ibid. per* Lord Browne-Wilkinson at 64.

[57] *R. v. Secretary of State for the Home Department, ex p. Fayed* [1998] 1 W.L.R. 763; *Chester v. Bateson* [1920] 1 K.B. 829; *Kerr v. Hood* 1907 S.C. 895.

[58] *Plewa v. Chief Adjudication Officer* [1994] 3 W.L.R. 317.

[59] (1921) 37 T.L.R. 884.

[60] [1976] A.C. 609.

EUROPEAN COMMUNITY LAW

In recent times, E.C. law is perhaps the source which has had the most profound effect on the British constitution. E.C. law has its source in U.K. law in the European Communities Act 1972. This Act will be discussed further in Chapter 4, but it is necessary to note here that it incorporated into U.K. law all of the E.C. law preceding the U.K.'s entry and of course, the law passed since then. 3.15

E.C. law has two sources: primary legislation, that is, the various Treaties, and secondary legislation which is passed under the authority of the Treaties.

Treaties

There are a considerable number of Treaties and each has an effect on the running of the E.C. and thus on the individual member states. Some of the most important are: 3.16

- The Treaty of Paris 1951 setting up the European Coal and Steel Community (ECSC).
- The Treaties of Rome 1957 setting up the European Economic Community (EEC) and European Atomic Energy Community (EURATOM).
- The Treaty of Accession 1972 which allowed the entry of United Kingdom, Ireland and Denmark to the E.C.
- The Treaty on European Union 1993 (the Maastricht Treaty) which created the E.U.
- The Treaty on European Union 1997 (the Amsterdam Treaty).

The three original Treaties (1951 and 1957) set up various institutions which administer the E.C. They are the Council of Ministers, the Commission, the European Parliament and the Court of Justice. A fifth institution of less significance in Constitutional law is the Court of Auditors which, as its name implies, ensures that the accounts of the E.C. are properly monitored. The four main institutions are involved at some stage in the drafting, implementing or interpretation of the secondary legislation. All of the institutions derive their authority and power from the Treaties and all are subject to them.

Secondary legislation

There are three types of secondary legislation in the E.C.[61] 3.17

---

[61] E.C. Treaty, Art. 249.

(1) Regulations

3.18 These are proposed by the Commission and are then sent to the Council of Ministers and the European Parliament. The Council has the final say on whether a regulation will be passed.

Regulations are arguably the biggest "threat" to British parliamentary sovereignty; a regulation passed by the E.C. becomes law in all of the Member States *automatically*. This is called direct applicability. The Member State's legislature does not have to pass the regulation, or indeed discuss it (although draft regulations are always sent to the legislatures for comment). The impact of this type of secondary legislation on British sovereignty will be discussed in Chapter 4.

A regulation is binding in its entirety. It may also have "direct effect" which means that it creates rights for individual citizens. The doctrine of direct effect requires that the regulation (or directive as noted below) is clear, precise and unconditional, and does not leave any discretion in implementation with either the Member State or a Community institution. The doctrine has been revised and refined by the European Court of Justice (ECJ) in a number of cases, some of which are discussed below. Some articles of the Treaties have been held to have direct effect.[62]

(2) Directives

3.19 A directive is also proposed by the Commission and passed by the Parliament and Council of Ministers. It is binding on the Member States as regards the result to be achieved but it requires the Member State to take action to bring them into law. A directive does not therefore have direct applicability. So, in the U.K., the British government has to decide how to implement a directive. Sometimes, an Act of Parliament will be required, or a statutory instrument where domestic legislation already exists but does not go far enough. The directive may even be implemented by changing administrative practices. The difficulties arise where a directive is not implemented by the Member State, or is only partially implemented or incorrectly implemented.

A directive may have direct effect, that is, create rights for individuals who may pursue these rights through the domestic courts. As before, the directive must be clear, precise, and unconditional and leave no room for discretion by the Member State or Community institution.

---

[62] *e.g.* Case 26/62 *Van Gend en Loos* [1963] C.M.L.R. 105.

> "It is settled law, that wherever provisions of a directive appear to be, from the point of view of their content, unconditional and sufficiently precise, they may be relied on against any national provision which is not in accordance with the directive."[63]

The directive may have vertical direct effect; this means that the right conferred by the directive may be enforced against either the government of the Member State or a public body within that state. It may not be enforced horizontally against a private individual or body in the Member State. So, a dental nurse working in a NHS hospital may sue the health authority for non-compliance with a directive, but a dental nurse working in a private dental practice may not sue their employer for the same non-compliance.[64]

Some case examples will help illustrate the doctrine. In 3.20 *Marshall v. South West Hampshire Area Health Authority*,[65] M was told that she was being compulsorily retired at the age of 62. The health authority operated a system whereby female employees retired at 60 and males at 65, but a woman could continue working to age 65 if the authority required her services. M had been asked to stay on when she reached the age of 60 and had intended to work to age 65. She brought an action against the health authority alleging sex discrimination which was contrary to Article 119 of the E.C. Treaty and the Equal Treatment Directive[66] made under Article 119. On a referral to the ECJ, the health authority was found to be a public authority within the terms of the directive (*i.e.* there was vertical direct effect) and was liable for the failure to follow the terms of the directive.

In *Johnson v. Chief Constable of the Royal Ulster Constabulary*[67] a public authority was held to include a police authority. The privatised utilities may also come under this heading.[68]

In *Meyers v. Adjudication Officer*[69] a single parent was denied family credit benefit on the basis that her income exceeded the specified level. However, no allowance was made for child care costs and she argued that this amounted to discrimination against single parents, the majority of whom were women, and who found

---

63 Case C–194/94 *CIA Security International SA v. Signalson SA and Securitel SPRL* (1996) 33 C.M.L.Rev. 1035, para. 42.

64 Case C–91/92 *Faccini Dori v. Recreb Srl* [1995] 1 C.M.L.R. 665.

65 [1986] 2 All E.R. 584.

66 76/207.

67 Case C–222/84 [1987] Q.B. 129.

68 *Griffin v. South West Water* [1995] I.R.L.R. 15.

69 Case C–116/94, *The Times*, July 19, 1995.

it more difficult to organise child care than couples. This was indirect discrimination against women. The ECJ agreed that family credit fell within the scope of the Equal Treatment Directive since it was concerned with access to employment (Art. 3 of directive).

3.21 We have already noted that the ECJ has not recognised the doctrine of horizontal direct effect in directives. However, this might have an adverse effect on citizens suing private companies or bodies for non-compliance with a directive which has not been implemented by the Member State. There would be discrimination between people with a grievance against a public body who could get redress, and those who had a grievance against a private body who could not. The ECJ stated in *Marleasing SA v. La Comercial Internacional de Alimentacion SA*[70] that national courts are required by Article 5 of the E.C. Treaty to do everything possible to reconcile domestic law with a directive's provisions. They should also interpret and apply domestic law so as to be in conformity with E.C. law.

The ECJ had already allowed a private individual to sue the state for non-implementation of a directive. In the joined cases of *Francovich and Bonifaci v. Italy*[71] the two applicants were held to be entitled to compensation from the Italian government for its failure to implement Directive 80/987 which was meant to protect employees on the insolvency of their employer. The ECJ recognised that the directive could not be enforced directly against the private employers, but stated that it could be enforced by way of a "right of reparation" against the Member State.

Where an individual suffers loss caused by a failure or breach of Community law by the Member State, then they may claim compensation for that loss.[72] The breach must be sufficiently serious and there must be a causal link between the breach and the loss suffered.

(3) Decisions

3.22 These are issued by the Commission and are binding on those to whom they are addressed. They can be issued to a Member State, a public body or a private company or individual. They are used particularly in the area of competition law and have direct applicability.

---

[70] [1992] 1 C.M.L.R. 305.

[71] Cases C–6/90 and 9/90 [1991] E.C.R. I–5357.

[72] Case C–48/93 *R. v. Secretary of State for Transport, ex p. Factortame Ltd (No. 4)* [1996] 2 W.L.R. 506.

AUTHORITATIVE WORKS

When no other source of law is available the courts may turn to the works of eminent authors who have collected the law into one place. The authors generally lived in the nineteenth century and the early part of the twentieth century. Of particular importance are the works of Blackstone, Dicey, Anson and Wade in England and T. B. Smith and J. B. Mitchell in Scotland. Their works, however, never have binding force; they are persuasive and will only be consulted when no other authority, such as case law, is available. 3.23

CONVENTIONS

These are non-legal "rules" of the constitution, which exist because they allow the wheels of government to run more smoothly. Dicey described conventions as "constitutional or political ethics, not a body of laws". He said they were "the constitutional morality of the day, not enforced by the courts". Jennings defined them thus: "The short explanation of the constitutional conventions is that they provide the flesh which clothes the dry bones of the law; they make the legal constitution work; they keep it in touch with the growth of ideas."[73] Marshall and Moodie, on the other hand defined them as: "rules of constitutional behaviour which are considered to be binding by and upon those who operate the constitution but which are not enforced by the law courts."[74] 3.24

These definitions give a flavour of what a convention is but do not fully explain its meaning. Barnett offers this definition of a convention which brings together the ideas expressed by other authors:

> "A constitutional convention is a non-legal rule which imposes an obligation on those bound by the convention, breach or violation of which will give rise to legitimate criticism: and that criticism will generally take the form of an accusation of 'unconstitutional' behaviour."[75]

Conventions evolve over a long period of time; they are not necessarily cast in stone, but will change as the habits and practices of Parliament change. They are obeyed because of the political 3.25

---

[73] *The Law of the Constitution* (5th ed., 1959), p. 81.
[74] *Some problems of the Constitution* (5th ed., 1971), p. 23.
[75] *Constitutional and Administrative Law* (2nd ed., 1998), p. 36.

implications if they are not. Munro reflects that "conventions rest entirely on acquiescence" but laws of course do not and have to be obeyed regardless of whether or not they are popular.[76]

The Royal Assent to a Bill is given by the sovereign on the advice of her ministers and the convention is that the sovereign will not refuse the assent. Technically, she may refuse but this would cause a major constitutional crisis since she would then be going against her government and Parliament. Queen Anne was the last sovereign to refuse to give a bill the Royal Assent; this was in 1708 when she refused to sign the Scottish Militia Bill. It is understood however that Anne's refusal was on the advice of her ministers. In 1914, George V was asked by Irish Unionists to refuse his assent to the Irish Home Rule Bill; it appears that the King felt unable to refuse the Royal Assent because he feared that this would set a precedent and he would then be drawn into party politics.

The office of Prime Minister is conventional. No statute states that there must be a Prime Minister, yet it is taken for granted that there will be a Prime Minister at the head of the government. It is now taken as a convention that the Prime Minister will be a member of the House of Commons, not the Lords. In 1962, the Earl of Home (Alec Douglas-Home) disclaimed his peerage and sought a seat in the Commons to continue as Prime Minister. The last peer to act as Prime Minister was Lord Salisbury in 1902.

There is also a convention that all government ministers should be a member of the Commons or a peer in the House of Lords. This is to ensure that government policies can be subjected to scrutiny by members of the two Houses. Where a minister is appointed and does not have a seat in Parliament, he must either fight a by-election to enter the Commons or be granted a peerage. In the summer of 1998, Gus McDonald was appointed as a junior minister in the Scottish Office; he was not an M.P. and so it was announced that he would be made a life peer later in the year. Another example is Linda Chalker who lost her seat at the 1992 general election but after elevation to the House of Lords she was able to continue as Minister for Overseas Development. An exception to the convention was seen with the Lord Advocate and the Solicitor General for Scotland, who did not need to be members of either House. Normally, however, the Lord Advocate was given a life peerage if he was not already a member of the House of Commons. Both officials are now however members of the Scottish Executive and the Law Officer for Scotland in the Westminster Parliament is the Advocate General.

---

[76] *Studies in Constitutional Law* (1999), p. 70.

When a general election is held and the outcome is that the Prime Minister who called the election has lost it, the convention is that he and his government immediately resign. He does not wait until the new Parliament meets. John Major resigned as Prime Minister mid-morning on May 2, 1997 by informing the Queen of his defeat; within the hour, Tony Blair was summoned and asked to form a government. Had the election result been unclear, as happened in February 1974, the Prime Minister may not need to resign until he is certain he cannot form a majority government. Edward Heath waited three days before resigning since he had been seeking the support of the Liberal M.P.s to allow him to carry on.

The breach of a conventional rule does not have legal con- 3.26
sequences, but may have political or constitutional implications. For instance, there is a convention that ministers do not make statements that are contrary to government policy. Should a minister do so, he is expected to resign from the government. In an interview in 1990, Nicholas Ridley, one of Margaret Thatcher's ministers, made inappropriate remarks about the German government's policies on Europe; his remarks were contrary to the Government's published policies and he had no option but to resign.

In 1965, the government of Southern Rhodesia, led by Ian Smith, declared unilateral independence from the United Kingdom. The U.K. Government then dismissed the entire government of the colony although this was of course unenforceable in Rhodesia. The Southern Rhodesia Act 1965 was then passed by the U.K. Parliament giving the U.K. Government power to legislate for the internal affairs of the country. This was contrary to the convention that the U.K. Parliament would not legislate for Rhodesia except when requested to do so by the Rhodesian government. In *Madzimbamuto v. Lardner-Burke*[77] the Judicial Committee of the Privy Council was asked to enforce the convention that there should be no legislation passed by the U.K. Parliament without the agreement of the Rhodesian government. The court held that since the matter was now the subject of legislation (the 1965 Act) the court could not have regard to the convention.

Another case involving the attempted enforcement of a convention was *Attorney-General v. Jonathan Cape Ltd.*[78] This involved the conventional doctrine of collective responsibility which stated that members of the government should not reveal disagreements with Cabinet colleagues. A former Labour minister, Richard Crossman, had kept diaries of his time in office, detailing conversations and

---

77 [1965] 1 A.C. 645.
78 [1976] Q.B. 752.

discussions with Cabinet colleagues, ministers and civil servants. After his death, his family sought to publish the diaries but the Attorney-General intervened by seeking an injunction to prevent publication. He stated that the publication would be a breach of confidence and an injunction should be granted in the public interest. The court held that such a long time had passed since the events described in the book that the public interest plea was not valid.

The issue was further debated by the Canadian courts in *Reference re Amendment of the Constitution of Canada*.[79] The Canadian government sought to 'repatriate' the Canadian constitution by requesting the Queen to present a Bill to the U.K. Parliament to amend the Canadian constitution. This Bill would remove the requirement for the U.K. Parliament to amend the Canadian constitution and would set up a new procedure for amendment and a Charter of Rights. Eight of the 10 provinces however opposed the proposals and stated that there was a convention that such constitutional changes required their consent. The Supreme Court held that there was no legal requirement to obtain the consent of the provinces but there was a convention that such consent should be obtained. The court said:

> "[C]onventions are not judge-made rules. They are not based on judicial precedents but on precedents established by the institutions of government themselves . . . Nor are they in the nature of statutory commands which it is the function and duty of the courts to obey and enforce . . . [W]hile they are not laws, some conventions may be more important than some laws. Their importance depends on that of the value or principle which they are meant to safeguard."

3.27 You could be forgiven for asking why conventions are not written down so that everyone knows what they are and when and how they should be used. However, that would destroy their greatest usefulness, the ability to adapt and change as political "fashions" change. Once something is written down and published, it becomes difficult to change without others asking why the change is necessary. Another reason for not writing down conventions is that they are vaguely drawn in order to be as flexible as possible. If the convention were written down, it would cease to be vague and lose some of its flexibility. Finally, if a convention is observed, is it necessary to write it down? During the hearing of judicial appeals in the House of Lords, it is conventional that non-legally qualified

---

[79] (1982) 125 D.L.R. (3d) 1.

peers will not sit with the Law Lords during the appeal process. In the House of Commons, it is a convention that the Speaker will act impartially; breach of this convention could lead to difficulties for the House in carrying out its business.

During the 1980s, the Australian legislature decided to codify its constitutional conventions. The spur to do so came from events in 1975 when a constitutional crisis had occurred as a result of the dismissal of the Labour Prime Minister by the Governor General (the Queen's representative in Australia) and the subsequent appointment of a 'caretaker' Prime Minister who had agreed to hold a general election. The legislature felt that the conventions had been used to unseat the Labour Prime Minister and his Government in a move which was political rather than constitutional. The legislature was thus suspicious of the use of conventions which seemed too vague. In 1983, a Constitutional Convention adopted a code containing 34 practices which were recognised and declared to be conventions of the Australian constitution. There was no declaration that the code was to be legally enforceable.[80]

Occasionally, a convention will be deliberately disregarded and lead to drastic consequences. In 1909 and 1910, the House of Lords disregarded the convention that the House of Commons, as the elected chamber, should have the final say in the passing of Bills, particularly money or finance Bills. The Parliament Act 1911 was forced through Parliament restating the convention and redefining the relationship between the two Houses. More recently, there have been difficulties between the two Houses where the Labour Government has presented Bills to the Lords after approval by the Commons and the Conservative Party have used their in-built majority in the Lords to amend the Bills against the wishes of the Commons. This has led to Government proposals for reform of the House of Lords, including the removal of voting rights of hereditary peers, who are mostly supporters of the Conservative Party.

CONCLUSION

There are a great variety of sources in which constitutional law in 3.28
the United Kingdom is found. Some of them are legislative, others judicial and some are habits and practices. However, all of them

---

[80] For an account of this experiment, see Sampford, " 'Recognise and Declare': an Australian experiment in codifying constitutional conventions" (1987) 7 O.J.L.S. 369.

are important in helping us to understand what the constitutional law of the United Kingdom is. Of overarching importance is the law of the E.C., which increasingly is affecting the law in the United Kingdom in ways perhaps not envisaged when the United Kingdom joined the E.C. However, the same can also be said for most of the Member States which have found E.C. law to be rather more fundamental in its effect on their domestic laws.

CHAPTER 4

DOCTRINES OF THE CONSTITUTION

"Westminster remains under the British constitution the sun around which the planets revolve."[1] 4.01

The U.K. constitution is made up of legislative documents, legal decisions, habits and practices which taken together create a democratic, sophisticated system of government with many safeguards for the rights and freedoms of the individual citizen. Its 'unwritten' nature allows it to be changed relatively easily to meet changing circumstances. This, of course, can be a double-edged sword; a flexible constitution such as that of the United Kingdom can be changed for the worse as well as the better, and there needs therefore to be a strong system of government that can check any abuses of power. This strong system of government needs to be accountable to the electorate to ensure that what it does is broadly accepted and follows what the majority of the electorate want. If the majority of the electorate do not want what the government is providing, there has to be a method of showing displeasure and this is done through the holding of democratic elections at set intervals. In the United Kingdom, elections are held at intervals not exceeding five years[2] unless Parliament has voted to extend its life for a particular reason, for instance, in time of war. The House of Lords may veto any Bill which otherwise seeks to extend the life of Parliament and in this instance, the Parliament Act 1911 cannot be used to bypass the Lords' consent. This ensures that the government cannot stay in office indefinitely. Most constitutions have a system of checks and balances, and the U.K. system is no different.

This chapter will discuss the three doctrines of the constitution applicable in the United Kingdon: separation of powers, the rule of law and supremacy of Parliament. Of the three, the last is the most important but it is exercised within the confines of the rule of law

---

[1] Bogdanor, "Devolution, The Constitutional Aspects" in *Constitutional Reform in the U.K.* (Cambridge Centre for Public Law, 1998).

[2] Parliament Act 1911.

and acknowledges the different roles of the organs of government through a modified version of the separation of powers.

SEPARATION OF POWERS

4.02 A system of government is normally divided into three branches: the legislature, the executive and the judiciary.[3] In the United Kingdom, these are represented by Parliament, the political government and civil service, and the courts. The doctrine of separation of powers states that the functions carried out by each of the branches should be separate and there should be no overlapping or mixing of these functions. The doctrine was stated by the French jurist, Montesquieu in 1748 as follows:

> "When the legislative and executive powers are united in the same person, or in the same body of magistrates, there can be no liberty . . . Again, there is no liberty, if the judicial power be not separated from the legislative and executive. Were it joined with the legislative, the life and liberty of the subject would be exposed to arbitrary control; for the judge would then be the legislator. Were it joined in the executive however, the judge might behave with violence and oppression. There would be an end to everything, were the same man, or the same body, whether of the nobles or of the people, to exercise the three powers, that of enacting laws, that of executing the public resolutions, and of trying the causes of individuals."[4]

In common with other writers such as Locke, Montesquieu was convinced that there should be a separation of the powers of government to ensure that one branch would not become so powerful that it could override the other two. It was, therefore, a device to control and prevent the abuse of power.

The doctrine expounded by Montesquieu saw its greatest expression in the constitution of the United States of 1789 where it was embraced to great and lasting effect. In the U.S. constitution, the three branches of government are dealt with separately. The legislature is set up in Article I, with Article II providing for the executive in the form of a President. Article III gives judicial power to a Supreme Court and other federal courts. Each article gives the powers, duties and responsibilities of each branch in outline. The independence of the judiciary is emphasised and its powers to

---

[3] First identified by Aristotle in *The Politics* (T. A. Sinclair (trans), 1962).

[4] Montesquieu, *L'Esprit des Lois* (1989).

declare acts of the executive or legislature as unconstitutional were established early.[5] This declaratory power was not specifically stated in the constitution but was held by the Supreme Court to be implicit within its terms. The powers of each branch are not, of course, exercised in isolation from each other. They can influence each other and thus exert a measure of control to ensure that no one branch becomes too powerful. The resignation of President Richard Nixon in 1974 over the Watergate Affair showed that a powerful President elected by popular vote could still be controlled by the combined powers of the Congress and the Supreme Court.[6]

In the United Kingdom, the doctrine has not been developed to give such defined boundaries. Indeed, there is not really a separation of powers between the legislature and the executive; rather it is a division of powers. It is really only in the judiciary that the doctrine can be seen at work. The courts have referred to this idea on a number of occasions. For instance, in *Duport Steels Ltd v. Sirs*[7] Lord Diplock said: "It cannot be too strongly emphasised that the British constitution, though largely unwritten, is firmly based on the separation of powers: Parliament makes the laws, the judiciary interprets them."[8] 4.03

The Master of the Rolls, Sir John Donaldson, picked up this theme in *R. v. H.M. Treasury, ex parte Smedley*[9]: "[I]t is a constitutional convention of the highest importance that the Legislature and the Judicature are separate and independent of one another, subject to certain ultimate rights of Parliament over the Judicature."[10]

However, Lord Templeman explained the doctrine thus: "Parliament makes the law, the executive carry the law into effect and the judiciary enforce the law."[11] Sir Stephen Sedley in the same case remarked: "The proper constitutional relationship of the executive with the courts is that the courts will respect all acts of the executive within its lawful province, and that the executive will respect all decisions of the courts as to what its lawful province is."[12]

The concept of separation of powers states that each branch of government should be separate and have independent status, and

---

[5] *Marbury v. Madison* (1803) 5 U.S. (1 Cranch) 137.
[6] *U.S. v. Nixon*, 418 U.S. 683 (1974).
[7] [1980] 1 W.L.R. 142.
[8] *ibid.* at 157.
[9] [1985] 1 All E.R. 589.
[10] *ibid.* at 593.
[11] *Re M* [1993] 3 W.L.R. 433.
[12] *M v. Home Office* [1992] Q.B. 270 at 314.

no individual should serve in more than one branch. It is obvious that in the United Kingdom the legislature and the executive are closely related and that they have common members. For instance, by convention, all members of the government are also members of either the House of Commons or the House of Lords, so that they may be questioned on their policies and actions. There is a limit of 95 on the number of government ministers who may sit in the House of Commons.[13] Since there are between 110 and 120 ministerial posts, it is obvious that some ministers must of necessity sit in the Lords. The limitation also ensures that the government cannot confine its activities to the House of Commons but must include the Lords in its work.

Civil servants, members of the non-departmental public bodies, members of the armed forces and serving police officers are prevented from sitting in the House of Commons by means of the House of Commons Disqualification Act 1975. This is recognition of the importance of keeping the law-makers separate from those who implement the law.

The Lord Chancellor is a prominent member of all three branches; in the legislature he acts as the Speaker of the House of Lords. In the executive, he is a member of the Cabinet and heads his own government department. He is consulted regarding appointments to the most senior judicial posts[14] although the appointment is made by the Queen acting on the advice of the Prime Minister. Appointments to the High Court of Justice, the crown and county courts are made by the Queen acting on the advice of the Lord Chancellor.[15] Magistrates are appointed by the Lord Chancellor.[16] He is also head of the judiciary in England and Wales, being the President of the Supreme Court as well as a Lord of Appeal in Ordinary in the House of Lords. By convention, however, he does not hear cases in the High Court of Justice and does not normally sit to hear appeals in the House of Lords, particularly where a government department is a party. He is thus able to argue that the doctrine is maintained with regard to the independence of the judiciary. However, a recent decision of the European Commission of Human Rights may affect the position of

---

[13] House of Commons Disqualification Act 1975.

[14] Lord Chief Justice, Master of the Rolls, President of the Family Division, Vice-Chancellor, Lords of Appeal in Ordinary and Lord Justices of Appeal.

[15] Supreme Court Act 1981, s. 10; and see Ganz, "The Supreme Court (Offices) Act 1997: Loss of a Constitutional Safeguard" (1998) 6 *Amicus Curiae* 19.

[16] Magistrates' Court (Procedure) Act 1998.

the Lord Chancellor. In *McGonnell v. United Kingdom*[17] the Commission held that the Royal Court of Jersey was not an independent and impartial tribunal under Article 6 of the European Convention of Human Rights since it was presided over by the Bailiff of Guernsey who is also president of the legislature and head of the island's administration. If a judge has both legislative and executive functions, his impartiality and independence are placed in doubt. The implementation of the Human Rights Act 1998 will make Convention rights, such as Article 6, part of domestic law and thus the position of the Lord Chancellor will have to be reconsidered.

One of the functions of Parliament is to pass legislation, but this 4.04
function is shared with the executive where government departments may pass subordinate legislation. Such delegated legislation is required for a number of reasons, including the lack of parliamentary time to pass primary legislation, the technicality of the subject-matter not being suitable for inclusion in a statute, and the requirement for flexibility to update legislation, for instance to increase the amounts of social security benefits annually. The use of delegated legislation has grown since the end of the Second World War and more than three thousand statutory instruments will be passed each year, compared with around 65 Acts of Parliament. There are problems associated with delegated legislation not the least being the lack of parliamentary scrutiny.[18]

The legislature and the executive are dependent on each other. The executive needs the legislature to pass laws so that it can implement them; similarly the legislature needs the work proposed by the executive so that it has something meaningful to do. The executive controls the legislature by controlling the work and how it is carried out; but the legislature also controls the executive by exerting its power to prevent legislation being passed and ultimately it can bring about the downfall of a government by passing a vote of no confidence in it. This last occurred in 1979 when James Callaghan's Labour Government was forced to call a general election. Members of the government owe their position to the support of their party in Parliament and thus the governing party can exert influence over the government. The system of 'checks and balances' thus shows itself quite clearly in this relationship.

---

[17] *The Times*, Feb. 9, 1999, p. 35.

[18] For further reading, see Finch and Ashton, *Administrative Law in Scotland* (W. Green, 1997), Chap. 5.

Various commentators have argued whether the relationship is necessary or whether it is dangerous. For instance, in 1867, Bagehot argued that it was an "efficient secret" and a "close union" whose "connecting link is the Cabinet".[19] In 1976 Lord Hailsham argued that the executive controlled the legislature by means of the government having a large majority and therefore being able to pass virtually any type of legislation.[20] However, most members of the legislature are mindful, perhaps even jealous, of their position in the constitution and even governments with large majorities may find themselves being criticised and embarrassed by Parliament in debates or select committees reports. Proper scrutiny of the executive by the legislature is crucial for the principle of 'responsible government' whereby members of the government are responsible both individually and collectively to the electorate through Parliament.[21] Further scrutiny of the executive comes from the House of Lords where government measures can be subject to amendment. The government may be forced to use the provisions of the Parliament Acts 1911 and 1949 to progress Bills to royal assent if the House of Lords and House of Commons cannot agree on the Bill's contents.[22]

4.05 The independence of the judiciary is arguably the most important part of the doctrine. Judges in the superior courts cannot be removed easily; the Act of Settlement 1700 gives judges in England and Wales security of tenure of office *quamdiu se bene gesserint* (during good behaviour). The Supreme Court Act 1981, s. 11(3) provides that judges of the superior courts in England and Wales may only be removed by Her Majesty on an address presented to her by both Houses of Parliament. In Scotland, judges in the supreme courts hold office by virtue of the common law and the Claim of Right 1689.[23] Their tenure is *ad vitam aut culpam*[24] (but modified by legislation on retirement ages), and there has been no similar statutory provision to the English one for removal.

However, the Scotland Act 1998 has controversially provided for the removal of any judge by the Scottish Parliament. The procedure originally set out in the Bill required a two-thirds majority

---

[19] Bagehot, *The English Constitution* (1993), 67–68.
[20] (1976) 120 S.J. 693.
[21] Barnett, *Constitutional and Administrative Law* (2nd ed. 1998), p. 143.
[22] See Chap. 5.
[23] See discussion in Bradley, "Constitutional Reform, the Sovereignty of Parliament and Devolution" in *Constitutional Law in the U.K.*, *op. cit.*, p. 37.
[24] "For life or until misconduct".

vote of the entire membership of the Parliament[25] and then a recommendation by the First Minister to the Queen. This method of removal of a judge was seen to offer the judiciary little protection in policing the boundaries of competence of the Parliament and the Scottish Executive.[26] The Act now provides that a judge can only be removed by the Queen on the recommendation of the First Minister and with the approval of the Scottish Parliament.[27] Before the Parliament is asked to approve the recommendation, the First Minister is required to convene a tribunal, headed by a member of the Judicial Committee of the Privy Council (JCPC), which will investigate and report on whether the judge is unfit for office by reason of inability, neglect of duty or misbehaviour.[28] The Act also provides that the judge may be suspended pending the investigation.[29] The procedure to remove a sheriff is similar.[30]

An additional safeguard is that the salaries of judges cannot be reduced because they have displeased either the legislature or the executive. Judges' salaries are a charge on the Consolidated Fund[31] and are not debated in Parliament. The Scotland Act 1998, Sched. 5 provides that the salaries of judges in Scotland are a reserved matter. These safeguards contribute to the judges' independence and their ability to find against the executive in cases brought before them. The judges fulfil an important role in ensuring that the rights of the individual citizen are not infringed by an executive exceeding its powers. The independence of the judiciary is therefore a check on the power of the executive.

The functions of the executive and judiciary do however mingle 4.06
in some respects. For instance, the executive does make decisions which have a judicial element. The reporter in a public inquiry is essentially a civil servant but his role is that of a judge in that he has to weigh the competing arguments and come to a decision. The social security commissioner is another example of a civil servant exercising a judicial function. There is an element of judicial

---

[25] An exceptionally high threshold was proposed here; compare with the U.S. constitution that requires the majority for an impeachment vote to be two-thirds of the senators present, not the whole Senate.

[26] Page, Reid and Ross, *A Guide to the Scotland Act 1998* (1999).

[27] s. 95(6).

[28] s. 95(8).

[29] *Rees v. Crane* [1994] 2 A.C. 173 where the suspension of a judge and the attempted termination of office was held to be unconstitutional.

[30] Sheriff Courts (Scotland) Act 1971, s. 12; *Stewart v. Secretary of State for Scotland* [1998] S.L.T. 385.

[31] Supreme Court Act 1981, s. 12(5).

control over the members of the executive in that abuse or excess of power may be reviewed by the courts. This is a check on the executive by the judiciary and as Barnett points out, an infringement of the doctrine of separation of powers. However, it 'buttresses' the sovereignty of Parliament and the rule of law.[32] Tribunals are administrative authorities but again they fulfil a judicial function and are regarded as part of the machinery of justice. In Scotland, the sheriff has administrative duties as well as extensive judicial functions.

The role of the Law Officers should be mentioned here since there are implications for the doctrine. The Law Officers are the Attorney-General and Solicitor General (for England and Wales), the Advocate General (for Scotland) and the Lord Advocate and Solicitor General for Scotland (for the Scottish Parliament). They are all members of the government and they may be M.P.s or peers at Westminster or MSPs. Before devolution, it was unusual for the Solicitor General for Scotland to be a member of either House. As government ministers they are bound by the principle of collective responsibility and they give legal advice to their respective governments. However, the Attorney-General and the Lord Advocate are also involved in the instigation of criminal prosecutions in their jurisdictions and may bring civil actions in the public interest, or act on behalf of the government in civil actions. In criminal proceedings the Law Officer is required to be independent of the government but there have been a number of occasions when this independence from government influence was doubted. For instance, the Attorney-General was criticised for allowing the prosecution of Clive Ponting[33] and in his actions to prevent the publication of Peter Wright's book *Spycatcher*.[34] Also in 1987, the Attorney-General instructed the Director of Public Prosecutions to investigate possible breaches of the Official Secrets Act with regard to a planned BBC documentary on the Zircon spy satellite being produced by Duncan Campbell. The investigation led to highly controversial warrants of search and seizure being executed at the offices of the BBC in Glasgow and at journalists' homes. Master tapes of the programme were also seized.[35] The Attorney-General denied that he had consulted with any colleagues before taking the action. The Attorney-General and the Lord Advocate have absolute discretion in whether or not they order a

---

32 Barnett, *op. cit.*, p. 153.
33 *R. v. Ponting* [1985] C.L.R. 318.
34 *Att.-Gen. v. Guardian Newspapers Ltd* [1987] 1 W.L.R. 1248.
35 Woodhouse, "The Attorney-General" (1997) 50 *Parliamentary Affairs* 98.

prosecution or action to take place. In *Gouriet v. Union of Post Office Workers*[36] the Attorney General refused to bring a relator action to obtain an injunction against the union to prevent it boycotting mail from South Africa. The court recognised that the Attorney-General's decision was not questionable in a court of law. However, he might have to justify his decision in Parliament under the doctrine of ministerial responsibility.[37]

There are aspects of the powers of the executive in which the judiciary will not interfere. These tend to be areas covered by the prerogative powers such as treaty making,[38] the disposition of the armed forces[39] and matters of national security.[40] In regard to the last power, the courts have declined to ensure that national security is a genuine factor in the case; this is in marked contrast to the finding of the court in *Entick v. Carrington*[41] where a plea of "state necessity" was rejected. In other areas of executive decision-making the courts act as a check on the powers of officials to ensure that the rights of the individual are upheld. This check is seen in the form of judicial review whereby the courts will intervene to prevent an abuse of executive power. They will not, however, intervene where the complaint refers to the merits of a decision or policy; these are political matters which are not for the court to decide. In fact, the courts as an institution do not recognise the political policy of the government of the day: "these are not matters which are in any way relevant to the courts' decisions and are wholly ignored."[42] 4.07

Judges of the superior courts have often been asked to conduct inquiries into disasters and other major events. In Scotland, Lord Cullen has recently been involved in two major inquiries. He conducted the inquiry into the events leading to the shootings at Dunblane Primary School in 1996[43] and in 1989 he chaired the inquiry into the Piper Alpha oil rig disaster of 1988.[44] Other inquiries have included the Profumo Affair (Lord Denning),[45]

---

36 [1978] A.C. 435.

37 See discussion of this and other cases in Walker "The Antmonies of the Law Officers" in *The Nature of the Crown* (Sunkin and Payne eds., 1999).

38 *Blackburn v. Att.-Gen.* [1971] 1 W.L.R. 1037.

39 *Chandler v. DPP* [1964] A.C. 736.

40 *Council of Civil Service Unions v. Minister for the Civil Service* [1985] A.C. 374.

41 (1765) 19 St. Tr. 1030, CCP.

42 *British Airways Board v. Laker Airways* [1984] Q.B. 142, per Sir John Donaldson M.R. at 193.

43 This was conducted under the Tribunals of Inquiry (Evidence) Act 1921; *Report of the Inquiry into the Shootings at Dunblane Primary School on March 13, 1996* (Cullen Report) Cm. 3386 (1996).

44 *Public Inquiry into the Piper Alpha Disaster* (Cullen Report) Cm. 130 (1990).

45 Cmnd. 2125 (1963).

disturbances in Northern Ireland in 1969 (Scarman J.),[46] the collapse of the Vehicle and General Insurance Company (James J.)[47] and the Arms to Iraq Affair (Scott L.J.).[48] Judges are asked to conduct these inquiries because of their training and experience in reviewing evidence and then stating their findings in a clear and logical manner. However, as Lord Woolf points out: "The fact that the judiciary are prepared to take on this task is another aspect of the culture of co-operation between the judiciary and the Government which we tend to take for granted. That they should do this, is often convenient for the government, but the appointments are accepted irrespective of this as a form of public duty."[49]

4.08 The judiciary and the legislature are less intermingled. Members of the judiciary are disqualified from membership of the House of Commons by the House of Commons Disqualification Act 1975, although there are of course judges who sit in the House of Lords to hear appeals from the lower courts. These Lords of Appeal in Ordinary may participate in debates on legislation but they are careful not to intervene in matters which are political in nature. By convention, lay peers do not participate in the work of the Appellate Committee.

A judge of the superior courts in England and Wales may only be removed from office by the Crown on an address from both Houses, an event which has only occurred once since 1707. In 1830 a judge, Jonah Barrington, misappropriated money from litigants. There have been a number of calls by M.P.s for the removal of judges but these are generally more an expression of criticism about a judge's conduct rather than a serious attempt to remove him. For instance, Chief Justice Lane was heavily criticised by M.P.s after the Birmingham Six miscarriage of justice.[50] If an M.P. wishes to criticise a judge he must make a substantive motion before Parliament upon which a vote will be taken. The Speaker ruled in 1973 that this applied to criticisms of the judge's character or motive or any call for his dismissal.[51] This advice was later modified and if the M.P. argues that the judge has made a mistake and does so in "moderate language" a motion may not be required.[52] The last time a motion for removal was put down was in

---

46 Cmnd. 566 (NI)(1972).

47 1971–71 H.C. 133.

48 1995–96 H.C. 115.

49 "Judicial Review—The Tensions between the Executive and the Judiciary" (1998) 114 L.Q.R. 579 at 586.

50 *R. v. McIlkenny* [1991] 93 Cr.App.Rep. 287.

51 H.C. Deb., Vol. 865, col. 1092 (Dec. 4, 1973).

52 H.C. Deb., Vol. 935, col. 1381 (July 19, 1977).

1973 to remove Lord Donaldson, the President of the (now defunct) National Industrial Relations Court. Members of the lower courts and members of tribunals are protected by statute from arbitrary removal by the executive or the legislature.

Judges may not review the validity of an Act of Parliament although this has now been modified by the U.K.'s membership of the E.C. where it is possible, and may indeed be obligatory, for a British court to declare that an Act of Parliament is incompatible with E.C. law. This aspect of the doctrine of parliamentary supremacy is discussed later in this chapter. The inability of the courts to question a statute's validity is at odds with the power of the JCPC when it is acting as the court of final appeal for some former British territories, notably those in the Caribbean.[53] As such it is required to act as a constitutional court, because these states have written constitutions. In *Hinds v. R.*[54] the Judicial Committee held that a Jamaican Act, the Gun Court Act 1974, had infringed the separation of powers implicit in the Jamaican constitution by trying to transfer the sentencing function to a special review board.[55]

The final aspect of the doctrine of the separation of powers to be 4.09 considered here is whether the judiciary exercises the functions of the legislature in making law. In Scotland, the Court of Session and the High Court of Justiciary have certain equitable powers which enable them to declare certain actions to be unlawful or to give a remedy where none is otherwise available. The exercise of the *nobile officium* (equitable power) of the Court of Session is important for the law of trusts where the court can relieve a trust of a condition which makes the trust unworkable.[56] The essence of the equitable power is to allow the law to be implemented in circumstances where a technicality would otherwise have prevented it.

The power may also be used, albeit very sparingly, to insert a provision into a statute or document where this provision was accidentally omitted or was unforeseen. For instance, in *Wan Ping Nam v. German Federal Republic Minister of Justice*[57] a member of a ship's crew was accused of a murder which had been committed while the ship was at sea. When the ship docked at Greenock, the

---

[53] Note, the JCPC will be able to declare Acts of the Scottish Parliament to be *ultra vires*, see Chap. 8.

[54] [1977] A.C. 195.

[55] See discussion in Bradley, "The Sovereignty of Parliament—in perpetuity?" in *The Changing Constitution* (Jowell and Oliver, 3rd ed., 1994).

[56] *Gibson's Trs, Petrs*, 1933 S.C. 19.

[57] 1972 J.C. 43; 1972 S.L.T. 22.

crewman was taken into custody and held pending extradition to Germany where the ship was registered. The relevant extradition statute gave relief to persons so imprisoned by stating that they could apply to the sheriff court for a writ of habeas corpus. This writ, however, is unknown in Scots law and the court therefore invoked the *nobile officium* to give effect to the rights Parliament obviously intended to give.[58]

The High Court of Justiciary has a similar equitable power whereby it can declare acts to be criminal. Again the power is used sparingly although it was used in *Khaliq v. H.M. Advocate*[59] where a shop-keeper was found guilty of selling 'glue-sniffing kits' to children; this offence had not previously been recognised in Scots law but the High Court of Justiciary decided that it was the type of behaviour considered by the common law to be harmful.[60]

However, it must be noted that at anytime a 'law' made by a judge can be overturned by Parliament passing a statute. This was seen after *Burmah Oil Co. v. Lord Advocate*[61] when the War Damages Act 1965 was passed to retrospectively make an unlawful act lawful and thus prevent the payment of full compensation to the company. The decisions of judges in developing areas of law may lead to Parliament legislating to clarify an issue. In *National Provincial Bank v. Ainsworth*[62] Lord Denning interpreted the common law so that wives who had been deserted by their husbands should have rights in the matrimonial home. The government then acted to provide such rights in the Matrimonial Homes Act 1967.

The English courts have also 'created' new criminal offences as in *Shaw v. Director of Public Prosecutions*[63] where publication of a directory of prostitutes' names and contact details was deemed to be a new offence of conspiracy to corrupt public morals. In *R. v. R*[64] the House of Lords concluded that a husband could be guilty of the rape of his wife, thus removing the marital exception to rape.

4.10 The interpretation of both statute and common law is important to ensure that the will of Parliament is taken forward and that common law rights are brought up to date. In *Pepper v. Hart*,[65] a

[58] See also *Roberts, Petr.* (1901) 3 F. 799; *Law Society of Scotland, Petrs*, 1974 S.L.T. (Notes) 6.
[59] 1984 J.C. 2.
[60] See also *Ulhaq v. H.M. Advocate*, 1991 S.L.T. 614.
[61] [1965] A.C. 75.
[62] [1965] A.C.117.
[63] [1962] A.C. 200.
[64] [1992] 1 A.C. 599.
[65] [1992] 3 W.L.R 103.

case involving the interpretation of the Finance Acts, the House of Lords held that it was possible to look to the debates in Parliament to ascertain the will of Parliament. In this case, the provisions of the statute did not accord with a statement made by the minister in committee and the House of Lords agreed to look at the verbatim account of the committee proceedings printed in *Hansard* to find out what the minister had said and clarify the ambiguity. In *Three Rivers District Council v. Bank of England (No. 3)*[66] the use of *Hansard* was allowed to ascertain the purpose or object of the statute as a whole, not just clarify an ambiguous provision in the Act. The use of *Hansard* is however not always justified.[67]

The interpretation and development of the common law is important. "It is now widely recognised that it is proper for the courts in appropriate cases to develop or adapt existing rules of the common law to new conditions."[68] The courts are cautious in their use of this kind of law-making and will not proceed if the matter is one of policy where Parliament is better placed to legislate.[69] However, where the needs of justice require that the common law be developed in a new way, the House of Lords have acted. In *Woolwich Equitable Building Society v. Inland Revenue Commissioners*[70] it was recognised that a citizen is entitled to restitution where he has made a payment of money to a public authority after receiving a demand for tax which was proved to be *ultra vires*.

While judicial interpretation is an important tool to protect against arbitrary executive decisions, it sometimes cannot be used because the statutory provision has been drafted so widely as to allow the action complained of. Dicey argued that once Parliament had legislated, the legislation and its interpretation became the province of the courts and thus the government came under the control of the courts: "Powers, however extraordinary, which are conferred or sanctioned by statute, are never really unlimited, for they are confined by the words of the Act itself, and, what is more, by the interpretation put upon the statute by the judges."[71]

Finally, Parliament retains the power to rule on its own powers and to regulate its proceedings. If a matter before the court relates to a parliamentary privilege the court must decline to rule on it. Thus if a Member of Parliament makes a defamatory statement in

---

[66] [1996] 3 All E.R. 55.

[67] *R. v. Deegan*, *The Times*, Feb. 17, 1998.

[68] *Pettitt v. Pettitt* [1970] A.C. 777, per Lord Reid at 794.

[69] See *Murphy v. Brentwood District Council* [1991] 1 A.C. 398.

[70] [1993] A.C. 70.

[71] *Introduction to the Law of the Constitution* (19th ed. 1959), p. 413.

the House about a citizen, that citizen has no redress through the courts.[72] Parliament also decides on the procedures for passing a statute and the courts will not investigate whether or not a statute, which has the royal assent, was passed properly according to those procedures.[73]

THE RULE OF LAW

4.11 The two doctrines, separation of powers and rule of law, are closely connected. Since the United Kingdom does not have a 'written' constitution, the rule of law and the independence of the judiciary become most important in ensuring that the government does not exceed its powers. The rule of law is thus a limitation on the power of government.

The rule of law is not easy to define but it could be said to mean that the executive and its officials must obey the law and should not act beyond the powers granted to it or without lawful authority. Lawful authority normally means authority derived from a statute, and such authority will in most circumstances be subject to the control of the courts. Aristotle put it thus: "The rule of law is preferable to the rule of any individual." The term, rule of law, has a secondary meaning, however; often Parliament will legislate in such a way that the executive is given very wide discretionary powers so that virtually any exercise of the power is capable of being considered within the law. The rule of law therefore states that such discretionary powers need to be controlled by ensuring that government business is carried on using rules and principles which restrict the use of discretionary power. An example of where the executive abused its powers occurred in *Congreve v. Home Office*[74] where:

> "If he should revoke [a licence] without giving reasons, or for no good reason, the courts can set aside his revocation and restore the licence. It would be a misuse of the power conferred on him by Parliament: and these courts have the authority—and, I would add, the duty—to correct a misuse of power by a minister of his department, no matter how much he may resent it or warn us of the consequences if we do."[75]

---

[72] Bill of Rights 1689, art. IX, which deals with freedom of speech within the confines of Parliament.

[73] *Picken v. BRB* [1974] A.C. 76.

[74] [1976] Q.B. 629.

[75] *per* Lord Denning M.R. at 651.

As with the separation of powers therefore, the rule of law acts to limit the powers of the government. It is therefore important that the government, that is the executive, does not make the law itself but that this is entrusted to another institution, the legislature. It can thus be seen how the two doctrines inter-relate and depend on each other for their validity. Lord Woolf expressed his view thus:

> "Our parliamentary democracy is based on the rule of law. One of the twin principles upon which the rule of law depends is the supremacy of the Parliament in its legislative capacity. The other principle is that the courts are the final arbiters as to the interpretation and application of the law. As both parliament and the courts derive their authority from the rule of law so both are subject to it and cannot act in a manner which involves its repudiation."[76]

The rule of law has a long history in the United Kingdom and 4.12
the courts, particularly in England, have upheld the rule against the King and the executive.[77] The principle was under discussion at an early date in both Scotland and England; Mitchell quotes from George Buchanan, a sixteenth century writer, who wrote of the rule of law: "They [the people] were taught by many experiences that it was better to trust their liberty to laws than to Kings."[78]

The classic case on the rule of law is the English case of *Entick v. Carrington*[79] where the Lord Chief Justice said:

> "No man can set his foot upon my ground without my licence, but is liable to an action, though the damage be nothing . . . If he admits the fact, he is bound to show by way of justification, that some positive law has empowered or excused him."[80] He went on: "And with respect to the argument of State necessity, or a distinction that has been aimed at between State offences and others, the common law does not understand that kind of reasoning, nor do our books take notice of any such distinction."[81]

The principle was thus affirmed that a public official must show legal authority for interfering with a citizen or his property.

---

76 "Droit public—English style" [1995] P.L. 57.
77 *Prohibitions del Roy* (1607) 12 Co.Rep. 63; 77 E.R. 1342.
78 *Constitutional Law* (2nd ed., 1968), p. 53.
79 (1765) 19 St. Tr. 1030, CCP.
80 *ibid.* at 1066.
81 *ibid.* at 1073.

However, there are now many statutes authorising such interference by the state. The broad powers of entry and seizure given to officers of the Inland Revenue under the Taxes Management Act 1970 and other statutes show how the principle in *Entick* can be overcome by the use of general wording and by the executive following the provisions of the statute.[82] Child support inspectors now have the power to effect entry without warrant and to search for evidence.[83] The powers given by statute must, however, be implemented strictly and any discretionary powers may be limited by the purposes of the Act.[84]

Dicey's interpretation of the rule of law

4.13 Dicey argued that the rule of law meant that no one should be punished or should suffer loss except where there was a distinct breach of law which would be established in court. He said that the law was supreme even over discretionary governmental authority or the existence of a prerogative power. These ideas were naïve and took no account of the situation prevailing at the time he wrote his words. People can be punished even though they have committed no offence. For instance, land can be taken from someone by compulsory purchase order to build a road or other public works. A citizen can be compelled to serve on a jury and will be paid little for his contribution to justice although he may have lost considerable wages and time. The use of discretionary power is widespread in government and any abuse of power is subject to review by the courts.

The act of a public authority may be upheld if it was in accordance with the law in the sense that it did not infringe any law.[85] This was seen in *Malone v. Metropolitan Police Commissioner*[86] where the tapping of a suspect's telephone was held to be lawful since it was carried out on the authority of the Home Secretary using the normal procedure. Malone subsequently successfully complained to the European Court of Human Rights that the telephone tapping was a violation of Article 8 of the ECHR, the right to respect for private life and correspondence.[87]

---

82 *R. v. IRC, ex p. Rossminster Ltd* [1980] A.C. 952.
83 Child Support Act 1991, s. 15.
84 *Customs and Excise Commissioners v. Cure and Deeley Ltd* [1962] 1 Q.B. 340.
85 Turpin, *British Government and the Constitution* (3rd ed., 1995), p. 5.
86 [1979] Ch. 344.
87 *Malone v. U.K.* (1984) 7 E.H.R.R. 14; the law was eventually clarified by the Interception of Communications Act 1985.

Those who enforce the law must abide by it; there should be no 'cutting of corners' or 'the end justifies the means'. For instance, in *R. v. Horseferry Road Magistrates' Court, ex parte Bennett*[88] the applicant, a citizen of New Zealand, was wanted in the United Kingdom for a number of offences. He was arrested in South Africa but could not be extradited to the United Kingdom because there was no extradition treaty between the United Kingdom and South Africa. The South African authorities tried to deport Bennett to New Zealand by way of Taiwan but the Taiwanese officials returned him because he had destroyed his passport. The South African authorities again deported him, this time by way of London, where he was arrested. Bennett alleged that he had been returned to the United Kingdom against his will as a result of kidnapping and that this had been done at the request of the English police and that the South African authorities had colluded in his return to the United Kingdom. He argued in judicial review proceedings that this was an abuse of process and the prosecution could not proceed. The House of Lords upheld his appeal saying that a prosecution commenced once the extradition process was set in motion. In this case, the prosecution began when the abduction, instead of extradition proceedings, had occurred. The effect of this case is to uphold the rule of law over the public interest in the prosecution of crime. 4.14

However, the High Court of Justiciary came to a different conclusion in *Bennett, Petitioner*[89] where the same applicant made a petition to the *nobile officium* to have a Scottish warrant for his arrest set aside. The High Court of Justiciary said that the English courts had been too ready to believe that collusion between the English and South African authorities had occurred. The Scottish court said that it would be unreasonable to insist that the police must refrain from arresting a fugitive simply because he was in transit to another country from where he could be extradited. If there was no collusion, the Scottish warrant should be enforced.

The rule of law will of course be undermined if the government indulges in breaches of the law. The Matrix Churchill Affair in 1992 is an example of a government, if not breaching the rule of law, coming very close to doing so. There have also been questions raised over the British government's policies in Northern Ireland in the 1970s and 1980s where there were suspicions that the security forces were operating a 'shoot to kill' policy, and the government

---

88 [1994] A.C. 42.
89 1994 S.C.C.R. 90.

was acceding to this. In such times of civil unrest the rule of law will come under pressure and this can be seen during the troubles in Northern Ireland where the ill-treatment of terrorist suspects was officially, but unlawfully, authorised. A Committee of Privy Counsellors was set up to investigate the interrogation procedures used, but the three were unable to agree and Lord Gardiner produced a minority report which was in fact accepted by the government in preference to the majority report.[90] The issue was raised in the European Court of Human Rights which held that the procedures contravened Article 3 in that they amounted to inhuman and degrading treatment but they did not amount to torture.[91]

4.15 Dicey's idea of the rule of law was formulated in *The Law of the Constitution* in 1885. He defined it as the "absolute supremacy or predominance of regular law as opposed to the influence of arbitrary power". He went on to say that it meant "equality before the law, or the equal subjection of all classes to the ordinary law of the land administered by the ordinary law courts".

His idea was that officials should not be exempt from obedience to the law and should comply with the decisions of the courts. Dicey's ideas have been criticised as lacking foresight and indeed accuracy. Even at the time he was writing, certain people had immunity from suit and prosecution, for instance, the monarch, diplomats, M.P.s and judges. The immunity of the Crown, as opposed to the monarch in her personal capacity, has been changed by the Crown Proceedings Act 1947 and the Crown is now in normal circumstances liable to suit for contract or delict as any ordinary citizen. However, some immunities still exist. Section 10 of the 1947 Act prevents an action for delict where a member of the armed forces has been killed or injured by another and the Secretary of State has certified that the injury was one attributable to service for the purposes of pension entitlement. This section threw up many injustices and it was put into suspense by the Crown Proceedings (Armed Forces) Act 1987 but can be revived by the Secretary of State if he thinks it expedient to do so where there are warlike conditions.[92]

The immunities of the Crown have largely disappeared, including in England and Wales the immunity of a minister from the

---

[90] *Report of the Committee of Privy Councillors appointed to consider authorised procedures for the interrogation of persons suspected of terrorism* (Lord Parker, Chairman) Cmnd. 4901 (1972).

[91] *Ireland v. U.K.* (1978) E.H.R.R. 25.

[92] *Adams v. War Office* [1955] 3 All E.R. 245; *Bell v. Secretary of State for Defence* [1986] 1 Q.B. 322; *Pearce v. Secretary of State for Defence* [1988] A.C. 755.

effects of an injunction. In *M v. Home Office*[93] the Home Secretary was found to be in contempt of court by ignoring an injunction preventing the deportation of a Zairian national who had claimed political asylum. This case, however, has not been followed in Scotland where the Court of Session considered that interdicts against the Crown were prohibited by the Crown Proceedings Act 1947, s. 21.[94]

The rule of law in the United Kingdom today

Turpin maintains that a state can "only claim to uphold the rule of law if it provides effective means for the prevention and redress of illegal action by those who wield public powers . . . There should be courts or other agencies which will check and control the actions of public authorities to ensure their compliance with the law." 4.16

This means *inter alia* that there must be open access to the courts or tribunals so that a citizen may obtain redress of his grievance. In a civilised society, this also means that access to this redress should not depend on your wealth; a state will assist a complainant who has only modest, or less than modest, wealth to bring their action to court. If this does not happen, then only those with financial resources will have access to justice. The National Consumer Council said in evidence to the Home Affairs Select Committee that: "a society that believes in equality before the law must make sure that all sections of society have equal access to legal remedies."[95]

In Scotland, as in the rest of the United Kingdom, those without financial means may receive assistance from the State to bring certain civil actions and also to defend themselves against criminal prosecution. However, the cost of legal aid services are such that the service is means-tested and in reality only those on state benefits are likely to receive assistance. Changes in the criminal legal aid system have led to the requirement for solicitors to be on a central register before legal aid is granted to a client. In addition, a pilot scheme has introduced 'public defenders' to Scots law, whereby accused persons seeking legal aid are required to accept the services of the public defender or pay for their own solicitor. These changes in the legal aid system may make it more difficult for those of modest means to be legally represented in court actions, whether criminal or civil.[96]

---

[93] [1994] 1 A.C. 37.

[94] s. 21. See *McDonald v. Secretary of State for Scotland*, 1994 SLT 692; and see Dickinson, "Still no interdicts against the Crown", 1994 S.L.T. (News) 217.

[95] Fifth Report (1992–93 H.C. 517), App. 15, para. 1.3.

[96] Similar provisions are being introduced in England and Wales.

4.17 It is also important that the government should comply with judgments of the courts and in this regard, it is contrary to the principle of the rule of law that the government should introduce retrospective legislation to mitigate the effects of a decision made against it. In *Burmah Oil Co. Ltd v. Lord Advocate*[97] the House of Lords found that the use of the royal prerogative in the prevailing circumstances had imported an obligation to pay compensation for property destroyed by the British military authorities to prevent the company's installations falling into enemy hands. The company's success in this case meant that others in a similar position would have a claim against the Government; these claims would have amounted to many millions of pounds which the Government was reluctant to pay. The War Damages Act 1965 was quickly passed to prevent such compensation being payable. The Act was retrospective in that actions instituted before the Act was passed were to be dismissed by the courts.

The government has used its legislative powers to pass other statutes which have retrospective effect, perhaps most notoriously, the War Crimes Act 1991. This Act allows charges to be brought for murder, manslaughter or culpable homicide, against a person in the United Kingdom, who was not necessarily a U.K. citizen at the time of the alleged offence, that offence having been committed during the Second World War in Germany or in territory occupied by Germany and where the offence constituted a violation of the laws and customs of war. This Act was only passed after substantial opposition in the House of Lords, and indeed it became the first statute to be passed by a Conservative government using the Parliament Acts 1911 and 1949 to bypass a Conservative dominated House of Lords. It is also notable that retrospective penal legislation of this type may contravene Article 7 of the ECHR.

On many occasions, the government has used its legislative powers to overturn judicial decisions it did not like. In 1995, the Home Secretary proposed legislation to mitigate the effects of the decision in *R v. Home Secretary, ex parte Fire Brigades' Union*[98] so that he could introduce a tariff scheme for criminal injuries compensation. The rule of law is however more than just adhering to the letter of the law. It is also a doctrine of political morality where government is subject to the checks and balances of the laws which protect the individual citizen. It "bears an aura of moral compulsion and is often . . . invoked as a guiding principle by critics of official action of one kind or another."[99]

---

[97] [1965] A.C. 75.
[98] [1995] 2 All E.R. 245.
[99] Jowell, "The Rule of Law Today" in *The Changing Constitution*, *op. cit.*, p. 58.

The rule of law generally requires that laws should be prospective, open, clear and stable.[1] There is a general presumption of law that statutes will not be construed as retrospective unless there is a specific provision in the statute to that effect.[2] In *Secretary of State for Social Services v. Tunnicliffe*,[3] Staughton L.J. defined the presumption thus: 4.18

> "In my judgment the true principle is that Parliament is presumed not to have intended to alter the law applicable to past events and transactions in a manner which is unfair to those concerned in them, unless a contrary intention appears. It is not simply a question of classifying an enactment as retrospective or not retrospective. Rather it may well be a matter of degree—the greater the unfairness, the more it is to be expected that Parliament will make it clear if that is intended."[4]

It is particularly important that criminal laws should not be retrospective for the very simple reason that the citizen must be able to know whether he is committing an offence at the time he carries out a particular action. If subsequent retrospective legislation is passed to make that action unlawful, he will be liable to prosecution although his intention at the time was not to commit an offence but to carry out a lawful activity. The rule of law says this is unfair. Lord Reid remarked that: "it is hardly credible that any government department would promote or that Parliament would pass any retrospective criminal legislation."[5] Nonetheless, the War Crimes Act 1991 appears to do just that, even though it probably contravenes Article 7 of the ECHR which forbids retrospective criminal legislation.

Laws should be open and made known by proper and sufficient publication and publicity. In the United Kingdom it is generally held that 'ignorance of the law is no excuse' and that everyone has access to the law. This of course is somewhat unreasonable; there are so many laws, rules and regulations being created by the executive that it is impossible for the ordinary citizen to know them all. It should also be remembered that many guidelines and rules 4.19

---

1 Raz, "The Rule of Law and its Virtue" (1977) 93 L.Q.R. 195.

2 Dickinson, "Retrospective Legislation and the British Constitution", 1974 S.L.T. 25.

3 [1991] 2 All E.R. 712.

4 *ibid.* at 724; see also *L'Office Cherifien des Phosphates v. Yamashura-Shinnikon Steamship Co. Ltd* [1994] 1 A.C. 486; *Re Barretto* [1994] Q.B. 392.

5 *Waddington v. Miah* [1974] 2 All E.R. 377 at 379.

are not published at all and so the citizen may not be able to find out the laws to which he is subject. The problem of publicity was recognised by the courts in *Fothergill v. Monarch Airlines Ltd*[6] where Lord Diplock said that justice demanded that the rules binding a citizen should be publicly accessible and ascertainable.

Laws should be clear and plain and easily understood by those who have to apply them. In *Merkur Island Shipping Corp. v. Laughton*[7] Lord Diplock remarked: "Absence of clarity is destructive of the rule of law; it is unfair to those who wish to preserve the rule of law; it encourages those who wish to undermine it."[8]

Lord Donaldson, speaking in the same case, but in the Court of Appeal, said:

> "The efficacy and maintenance of the rule of law, which is the foundation of any parliamentary democracy has at least two pre-requisites. First, people must understand that it is in their interests, as well as in that of the community as a whole, that they should live their lives in accordance with the rules and all the rules. Secondly, they must know what those rules are."

The Law Commission reflected that "laws which so many people have to use, often at great personal expense, remain unsimple, unmodern, inaccessible and unreformed."[9]

Further, laws should be stable so that the citizen can plan for the future and to make it easier to know what the law is. For instance, it is not helpful if the tax laws or company laws change too frequently since business people need to be able to plan their affairs for several years in advance.

4.20 The independence of the judiciary has been discussed above, but another point may be made here. The courts must be free to interpret and apply the law as they see fit and various Lords Chancellor have agreed this proposition. Lord Mackay of Clashfern, for instance, in a House of Lords debate in 1994 stated: "I personally believe very strongly and fundamentally in the independence of the Judiciary. I also believe that it is vitally important for the Lord Chancellor to do all he can to preserve the independence of the Judiciary."[10]

This statement has however to be viewed in its context; the debate had been initiated to discuss concerns that the Lord

---

[6] [1981] A.C. 251.
[7] [1983] 2 A.C. 570.
[8] *ibid.* at 612.
[9] 28th Annual Report (Law Com. No. 223, 1994), para. 1.21.
[10] *Hansard*, H.L. Vol. 554, col. 79 (April 27, 1994).

Chancellor had interfered with the way in which the President of the Employment Appeals Tribunal implemented procedures for dealing with notices of appeal to the tribunal. In a series of letters, the Lord Chancellor insisted that a particular rule be applied in full and that if the judge was unable to give an assurance on that, the judge should "consider his position". The judge, Wood J., refused to comply with the Lord Chancellor's request. In the House of Lords debate, the Lord Chancellor denied that he was telling the judge how to do his work but said that he had merely requested an assurance that the rules enacted under the authority of Parliament would be applied. However, the implication in the exchange of letters was clear; the judge should comply with the instructions of the Lord Chancellor, acting in his executive capacity, or resign. Such an implication of course does not accord with Lord Mackay's statement.[11]

Other theories of the rule of law

The rule of law was recognised in the United Nations Universal Declaration of Human Rights in 1948 when it states: "It is essential, if man is not to be compelled to have recourse, as a last resort, to rebellion against tyranny and oppression, that human rights should be protected by the rule of law." Similarly the European Convention on Human Rights recognises the concept in its Preamble. 4.21

In 1959, the International Commission of Jurists compiled the Declaration of Delhi. This declared that the purpose of all law was respect for "the supreme value of the human personality". The Declaration set out minimum standards, which included representative government, basic human freedoms, the right to a fair trial and an independent judiciary. This is a wider description of the rule of law than Dicey's and it probably represents what most people think of as the rule of law.

The concept has been the subject of much philosophical debate over the years. There are three particularly interesting aspects to the debate.

(1) Is the citizen under a duty to obey the law?

Absolute obedience to the law would take away what many regard as a fundamental human right, the right to protest and criticise. However, if society is to be peaceful, then the majority of 4.22

[11] For discussion of this, see Allen and Thompson, *Cases and Materials in Constitutional and Administrative Law* (4th ed., 1996), pp. 197–206.

citizens must obey the law, whether they like the law or not. Indeed the law obtains its authority from the obedience of the people. Laws must be passed which are recognised to be for the good of the majority; if they are not perceived as such then a sizeable minority, and perhaps the majority, will not obey them, and law and order may break down. In 1990, there was general concern, and some violent demonstrations, against the introduction of the community charge (the poll tax) and many people refused to pay it. The government was forced to reconsider the tax and it was abolished in the Local Government Finance Act 1992.

(2) Is there a right to disobey the law?

4.23 Sometimes citizens will feel that the lawmakers are not dealing fairly with them and will protest, perhaps resorting to illegal acts as part of that protest. Examples of such protests include the Suffragette movement of the early twentieth century which led eventually to the franchise being extended to women as well as men. In India, Mahatma Gandhi led a peaceful civil disobedience campaign which led to independence for that country in 1947. The Civil Rights Movement in the United States of America was led by Martin Luther King and resulted in the reform of racial segregation laws.

Looking back at these, most people would maintain that their outcomes led to major advances in society, although some of the methods employed might still be disapproved of. Each protest was met with opposition from government sources; these often cited the breakdown of law and order as their reason for trying to end the protests, sometimes using force. The response by government to civil disobedience is difficult to judge. Should the government be tolerant even where the lawbreaking ends in violence? Or should the rule of law be upheld, no matter the cost to civil liberties? Dworkin has argued that the state should be careful how it handles civil disobedience and should not be quick to prosecute those involved.[12] Such prosecutions could have two opposite effects. On the one hand, it will uphold the law of the land, but on the other it will highlight whether the law is defective and whether it has popular support. In *R. v. Ponting*[13] the jury refused to convict Ponting even though the judge had indicated that there was clear evidence of criminal action by him. More recently, the prosecution of protesters against tolls on the Skye road bridge has highlighted their grievances and led to some concessions by the government.

---

[12] *A Matter of Principle* (1986).

[13] [1985] Crim. L.R. 318.

(3) Is there a duty to disobey the law?

If the state violates the law, does the citizen have a duty to disobey it? An example here is the situation prevailing in Germany from 1933 to 1945. Hitler's government passed many laws that were found to be morally repugnant to other nations. However, the laws were passed according to the constitution (at least in the early days) and the rule of law thus required that the laws be obeyed. In moral terms, the laws could not be justified. Many of the people who upheld these laws were tried after the war at Nuremberg for crimes against humanity. The International War Crimes Tribunal found many of the people guilty for obeying the laws of their own state but disobeying the laws of morality. 4.24

In the United Kingdom during the First World War, some men refused to obey the conscription laws and join the armed forces. As conscientious objectors, they were treated very harshly. Some were imprisoned for long periods; others were dressed in uniform, sent to the front line then shot as traitors when they refused to fight. Their objections to fighting were often moral rather than political; many were Quakers or members of other religious groups and their religious beliefs did not allow them to fight. They felt they had a duty to disobey the law.

SUPREMACY OF PARLIAMENT

Introduction

Although the doctrines of separation of powers and rule of law are important in their own right, there is no doubt that the doctrine of the supremacy of Parliament is crucial to our understanding of constitutional law and the respective places of government and Parliament within the law. 4.25

The doctrine is also called "sovereignty of Parliament". This idea of sovereignty can be confusing since it can also be construed as having something to do with the sovereign or monarch. Supremacy, or sovereignty, in its U.K. sense refers to the supreme legal and political authority of Parliament to make laws for the United Kingdom. Political supremacy could be said to lie with the people since the people elect those who sit in Parliament and make laws. "Sovereignty, as a political concept, ultimately resides with the people; if the people accept the new legal order they will thereby give it validity and legitimacy."[14] This idea could be seen in the

---

[14] Allen and Thompson, *op. cit.*, p. 60.

United States during their struggle for independence. The Declaration of Independence in 1776 and the Constitution of 1787 were illegal according to the law which had existed, that is British law, but the people of the United States validated them because they accepted the new order by agreeing to abide by the constitution.

Legal supremacy in the United Kingdom, however, rests with the "Queen in Parliament", that is the House of Commons, House of Lords and the Queen acting together to pass laws and it is expressed at the beginning of all statutes by the form of words known as the 'enacting formula'. The normal form of words is: "Be it enacted by the Queen's most Excellent Majesty, by and with the advice and consent of the Lords Spiritual and Temporal, and Commons, in this present parliament assembled, and by the authority of the same, as follows".

Mitchell defined the doctrine as "the absence of any legal restraint upon the legislative power of the United Kingdom Parliament."[15] This view is also known as legal positivism and it contends that law is the command of a legal sovereign, whether a person or a body, these commands being backed by sanctions. The concept distinguishes between law and morality, saying that even a law which is morally repugnant must be upheld by the courts if it has been legally passed by the sovereign.[16]

The doctrine is an old one, predating the 1707 Union of the Parliaments of Scotland and England and seems to have its roots in the Bill of Rights in 1689. In that document, the grant of the Crown to Mary and William of Orange was made conditional on terms set by the English Parliament and thus the powers of the sovereign were dependent on Parliament, rather than vice versa. "What was asserted and accepted in 1689 was the principle of parliamentary sovereignty whereby Parliament secured legal supremacy amongst the institutions of the state. Thus not only was the monarchy subordinated to Parliament but, also, the last vestiges of the claim of the courts that Parliament could not legislate in derogation of the principles of the common law were removed."[17]

4.26 The doctrine of parliamentary sovereignty, of course, has been modified by the effect of the U.K.'s membership of the E.C. and this will be considered later in this chapter. In Scotland, the courts have questioned the validity of the doctrine in Scots law, although

---

[15] Mitchell, *op. cit.*, p. 64.
[16] Le Sueur and Sunkin, *Public Law* (1997).
[17] Judge, *The Parliamentary State* (1993), p. 20.

it has never been tested beyond the Scots courts.[18] The challenges have mainly centred on the status of the Act of Union 1707 and whether it was a founding document of the U.K. Parliament.[19]

An Act of Parliament has to be passed by the House of Lords, the House of Commons and receive the royal assent. Although an Act may be passed without the consent of the House of Lords, the power to do so derives from two statutes, the Parliament Acts 1911 and 1949. The House of Commons and the House of Lords acting alone may not pass statutes; the three elements of the Queen in Parliament are required for a statute to claim its legitimacy. A resolution of one of the Houses does not have the force of law unless a statute or subordinate legislation is enacted to bring it into law.[20] A proclamation by the Crown similarly does not have the force of law.[21]

The Traditional Doctrine

The traditional doctrine is one of the common law and has three main elements: (1) Parliament is the supreme lawmaker in the U.K.; (2) an Act of Parliament is the highest source of law in the U.K.; and (3) no Parliament can bind its successors. The basis of the power of supremacy is not found in any statute, since "no statute can confer this power upon Parliament, for this would be to assume and act on the very power to be conferred."[22] 4.27

(1) Parliament can make or unmake any law it pleases

This aspect of the doctrine states that Parliament is the supreme lawmaker and that there is no matter which cannot be legislated for.[23] However, the proposition is limited by the realities of what Parliament can and cannot do. It is, for instance, possible for Parliament to legislate to ban smoking on the streets of Paris; the reality is that such a law would be neither practicable nor possible.[24] 4.28

---

[18] See *MacCormick v. L.A.*, 1953 S.C. 396; *Stewart v. Henry*, 1989 S.L.T. (Sh.Ct.) 34; *Fraser v. McCorquodale*, 1989 S.L.T. (Sh.Ct.) 39; *Pringle, Petr.*, 1991 S.L.T. 330.

[19] Bradley and Ewing, *Constitutional and Administrative Law* (12th ed., 1997), p. 79.

[20] *Stockdale v. Hansard* (1839) 9 Ad. & E. 1; 3 St. Tr. (NS) 723: *Bowles v. Bank of England* [1913] 1 Ch. 57.

[21] *Case of Proclamations* (1611) 12 Co. Rep. 74; see also *Hoffman-La Roche & Co. v. Secretary of State for Trade* [1975] A.C. 295.

[22] Salmond, *Jurisprudence* (12th ed., 1996), p. 111.

[23] *R. v. Jordan* [1967] Crim. L.R. 483.

[24] Jennings, *The Laws of the Constitution* (5th ed. 1959) at 170.

Such a law would be absurd and could not be enforced. Parliament is thus restricted by its territorial jurisdiction, in that it can only make effective laws for those areas it controls. "If a minister was to have power to make an order under a statute making acts done by foreigners abroad triable in English criminal courts that power had to be conferred on him by words in the statute so clear and specific as to be incapable of any other meaning."[25] However, Parliament can pass laws so that a person abroad committing a particular offence under U.K. law may be tried in this country. So in recent years, legislation has been passed making it illegal for a British citizen to engage in procuring children for sexual purposes in another country. The War Crimes Act 1991 is a further example of this type of legislation. The Hijacking Act 1971 gave effect to the Convention for the Suppression of Unlawful Seizure of Aircraft.[26] The Act allows the U.K. courts to hear cases on hijacks wherever they occur and whatever the nationality of the hijacker.

Parliament may extend the boundaries of the state by legislation. So in 1964 the Continental Shelf Act was passed to give the United Kingdom sovereignty over the continental shelf out to 200 miles from the coast or to a half way mark where the coastal waters of another state intervened. In 1972, the Island of Rockall Act was passed to extend British sovereignty to that small rocky outcrop in the Atlantic Ocean and thus ensure control over any mineral wealth on the surrounding seabed.

Parliament may legislate to extend its own life; for instance the Parliament Act 1911 reduced the length of a Parliament from seven to five years. During both World Wars, Parliament extended its life so as to prevent the holding of a general election during the war. Parliament has altered the succession to the throne by the Act of Settlement 1700 and again by His Majesty's Declaration of Abdication Act 1936. The composition of the House of Lords has been altered by the Life Peerages Act 1958, which allowed the creation of non-hereditary peerages and the Peerage Act 1963 which allows an hereditary peer to renounce his title. Further changes to its composition will occur when the House of Lords Act 1999 comes into force. The composition of the House of Commons has been altered on many occasions by extending the franchise to both men and women.[27] Parliament may alter local democracy by abolishing authorities such as the Greater London Council and five

---

[25] *Wiggins v. Air India* [1980] 2 All E.R. 593.
[26] Now contained in the Aviation Security Act 1982.
[27] Representation of the People (Equal Franchise) Act 1928.

other large metropolitan authorities and by reorganising them.[28] In 1996, local authorities in Scotland were reorganised by the Local Government etc. (Scotland) Act 1994. These are all examples of the powers of Parliament to reorganise both itself and other public bodies.

Does Parliament then have the right to make and unmake any law it pleases? In recent years commentators have suggested that this is no longer the case. Leaving aside the question of E.C. law obligations, there are "limits on the supremacy of Parliament which it is the court's inalienable responsibility to identify and uphold."[29] The limits relate to matters involving democratic principles such as free elections and free speech and it is suggested that these are matters which should be left to the judiciary to police rather than to legislation.[30] Thus Parliament should not legislate to restrict democratic principles but where legislation is necessary should ensure that the principles are extended or enhanced. The enactment of a Bill of Rights may provide the security required for fundamental rights since it would be protected to a certain extent from legislative interference but would still be subject to judicial interpretation. "The very purpose of a Bill of Rights is to withdraw certain subjects from the vicissitudes of political controversy, to place them beyond the reach of majorities and officials and to establish them as legal principles to be applied by the courts."[31] The incorporation of the ECHR into U.K. law will extend the rights available to citizens and, incidentally, will curtail the power of Parliament to legislate in any way it pleases.

(2) No other body may question the validity of an Act of Parliament

This has been interpreted as meaning that the courts may not 4.29
question an Act's validity and the courts have indeed shown considerable reluctance to interfere in how a statute has been passed.[32] In *Edinburgh and Dalkeith Railway Co. v. Wauchope*[33] a private Act of Parliament was challenged on the grounds that it had been passed without the respondent having had notice of its

---

[28] Local Government Act 1985.

[29] Woolf, "Droit Public—English style" [1995] P.L. 57 at 69.

[30] Marshall "Parliamentary Sovereignty: The new horizons" [1997] P.L. 1.

[31] *West Virginia State Board of Education v. Barnette* (1943) judgment of the U.S. Supreme Court quoted in Loveland, "Incorporating the ECHR into U.K. law" (1999) 52 *Parliamentary Affairs* 113 at 119.

[32] *Ex p. Canon Selwyn* (1972) 36 J.P. 5.

[33] (1842) 8 Cl. & F. 710.

provisions as was required by Standing Orders. However, this argument was rejected by the court, with Lord Campbell stating:

> "[A]ll that a court of justice can look to is the parliamentary roll; they see that an Act has passed both Houses of Parliament, and that it has received the royal assent, and no court of justice can inquire into the manner in which it was introduced into Parliament, what was done previously to its being introduced, or what passed in Parliament during the various stages of its progress through both Houses of Parliament."

The matter was again raised in *Pickin v. British Railways Board*[34] where the courts refused to challenge the Act on the basis that it was prima facie valid. The House of Lords held that the appellant was not entitled to examine proceedings in Parliament to show that fraud had occurred and that any question as to the validity of the statute would require to be investigated by "the High Court of Parliament", in other words by the internal procedures of the two Houses. Further confirmation came in *Manuel v. Attorney-General*[35] when Sir Robert Megarry V.C. said: "Once an instrument is recognised as being an Act of Parliament no English court can refuse to obey it or question its validity."[36]

The courts will, however, now look at the proceedings in Parliament where they are considering the interpretation of a statute and there is some ambiguity in the terms of the statute and the intention of its proposers. The courts will then look at the official record of proceedings in the House, *Hansard*, to determine the words used and their meaning. However, only the words of the proposer of the Bill, whether minister or private member, may be considered.[37]

The Human Rights Act 1998 will be brought into force in October 2000. The Act provides that all courts and tribunals in the United Kingdom will be required to interpret Westminster legislation in a way which is compatible with Convention rights in so far as it is possible to do so. If a provision is found to be incompatible with Convention rights, the court may make a declaration of incompatibility but will not be able to strike down provisions in the U.K. statute. Instead, the Human Rights Act provides a fast track procedure to allow Westminster to amend legislation which has been declared incompatible. The courts will be able to quash

---

34 [1974] A.C. 765.
35 [1983] Ch. 77.
36 *ibid.* at 86.
37 *Pepper v. Hart* [1992] 3 W.L.R. 1032.

incompatible subordinate legislation unless the parent Act makes it clear that the provisions will contravene Convention rights. Thus an Act may not be declared to be incompatible and thus unenforceable; Parliament still requires to amend the legislation if it so desires. This contrasts with the position of an Act of the Scottish Parliament: an Act of the Scottish Parliament is unenforceable if it contravenes Convention rights.

(3) No Parliament can bind its successors

This element of the doctrine has itself a number of aspects flowing from the supposition that the ultimate lawmaker cannot bind itself or its successors, or it will then be subject to some higher law and thus not be the ultimate lawmaker. Dicey declared it thus: "The logical reason why Parliament has failed in its endeavours to enact unchangeable enactments is that a sovereign power cannot, while retaining its sovereign character, restrict its powers by any particular enactments."[38] 4.30

(a) Doctrine of implied repeal

This doctrine states that a later Act of Parliament will repeal an earlier contradictory statute by implication. This is an extension of the 'Parliament can make or unmake any law it pleases' aspect in that if a later statute were to be read subject to an earlier one, then the later Parliament is in effect bound by its predecessor. The courts recognised the principle of implied repeal in *Ellen Street Estates Ltd v. Minister of Health*[39] where the wording of the Acquisition of Land (Assessment of Compensation) Act 1919, s. 7 said that the provisions of any Act authorising compulsory acquisition "shall . . . have effect subject to this Act, and so far as inconsistent with this Act those provisions shall cease to have or shall not have effect." It was argued that this Act applied to a later Act, the Housing Act 1925. The Court of Appeal, however, rejected this argument and held that the 1919 Act had been overridden by the provisions of the later Act since the terms of the 1919 Act could not control future Parliaments.[40] "The legislature cannot, according to our constitution, bind itself as to the form of subsequent legislation, and it is impossible for Parliament to enact that in a subsequent statute dealing with the same subject-matter there can be no implied repeal."[41] 4.31

---

[38] *op. cit.*, p. 68.
[39] [1934] 1 K.B. 590.
[40] See also *Vauxhall Estates Ltd v. Liverpool Corp.* [1932] 1 K.B. 733.
[41] *ibid.* Maugham L.J. at 597.

(b) Independence statutes

4.32 There must be some limitations to the exercise of this element of the doctrine. For instance, from the 1940s to 1960s, Parliament granted many previous colonies their independence by passing a statute for that purpose.[42] It would be ludicrous to suppose that Parliament could now repeal any of those independence statutes. Parliament had itself acknowledged the reality of this situation. The Statute of Westminster 1931 enacted that Parliament would not legislate for a dominion unless the dominion so requested and then consented to such legislation.[43] The dominions at that time were Canada, Australia, New Zealand, Irish Free State, Newfoundland and South Africa and they were all autonomous states, although not independent. The request and consent referred to in section 4 had to be included in the preamble to any such statute.

Parliament's power to legislate for Canada was challenged in *Manuel v. Attorney-General*[44] where Manuel argued that the consent required by the 1931 Act had not been properly given and so the Canada Act was invalid. The preamble of the Canada Act stated that the Act had been requested by the Canadian Parliament who had consented to the passing of the Act by the Westminster Parliament. The Court of Appeal held that prima facie the Act was valid and could not be questioned.

The ability of Parliament to legislate for a self-governing colony was seen during the Southern Rhodesian crisis where the white minority population sought to make a unilateral declaration of independence. Parliament passed the Southern Rhodesia Act 1965 to return power to legislate to Parliament itself. Of course, the government in Rhodesia ignored the Act, but the British courts recognised Parliament's power to pass such a statute in *Madzimbamuto v. Lardner-Burke*[45] where Lord Reid remarked that it "does not mean that it is beyond the power of Parliament to do such things. If Parliament chose to do any of them, the courts could not hold the Act of Parliament invalid."[46]

The courts have nonetheless recognised the reality of the doctrine with respect to independence statutes. Lord Denning declared it in *Blackburn v. Attorney-General*[47]:

---

[42] *e.g.* Nigeria Independence Act 1960, Zimbabwe Independence Act 1979.
[43] s. 4.
[44] [1982] 3 All E.R. 786; see also *British Coal Corporation v. R.* [1935] A.C. 500.
[45] [1969] 1 A.C. 645.
[46] *ibid.* at 723.
[47] [1971] 1 W.L.R. 1037.

> "We have all been brought up to believe that, in legal theory, one Parliament cannot bind another and that no Act is irreversible. But legal theory does not always march alongside political reality. Take the Statute of Westminster 1931, which takes away the power of Parliament to legislate for the Dominions. Can anyone imagine that Parliament could or would reverse that statute? . . . Freedom once given cannot be taken away. Legal theory must give way to practical politics."[48]

This part of the doctrine of parliamentary supremacy is interesting for another aspect. The Parliaments of the Dominions depended for their validity on the various statutes passed by the Westminster Parliament. The same kind of relationship was created by the Scotland Act 1998 when the Scottish Parliament came into being in 1999. The Act states which powers have been devolved to the Scottish Parliament and which powers have been reserved to the U.K. Parliament. The question will arise therefore as to whether this will be a fettering of the U.K. Parliament.

(c) Statutes with 'special status'

Do any statutes have a special status and can they be considered to be irreversible, or as constitutional law would term it, are they entrenched in the constitution? 4.33

In the past, the Union Acts have apparently attempted to prevent their repeal by their wording. The Act of Union with Ireland 1800 established the United Kingdom of Great Britain and its wording implied that the union was intended to be permanent. Article 5 of the Union Act provided that the United Church of England and Ireland should be the established church; this was "deemed and taken to be an essential and fundamental part of the Union." However, that provision was inconsistent with the position of religion in Ireland where the majority of the population was of the Roman Catholic faith. As a result the article was repealed in 1869 by the Irish Church Act which disestablished the Irish Church.[49]

However, after a century of conflict, the Government of Ireland Act 1920 was passed to establish two Parliaments for Ireland, one for the south in Dublin and one for the six counties in the north, where the population was largely Protestant. However, only one

---

[48] [1971] 1 W.L.R. 1037 at 1040.

[49] See *ex p. Canon Selwyn* (1872) 36 J.P. 54.

Parliament, in the north, was actually established. The Irish Free State was established in 1922 thus finally breaking the terms of the 1800 Union Act. The 1920 Act however, while giving the Stormont Parliament a large degree of autonomy, reserved the right of the U.K. Parliament to legislate for Northern Ireland.[50] Independence was granted to the southern part of the island by the Ireland Act 1949. This Act also made provision for the future governance and status of Northern Ireland at section 1(2), by saying that Northern Ireland "remains part of His Majesty's dominions and of the United Kingdom and it is hereby affirmed that in no event will Northern Ireland or any part thereof cease to be part of His Majesty's Dominions and of the United Kingdom without consent of the Parliament of Northern Ireland."

During the period from 1920 to the start of the civil unrest in the late 1960s, the British Parliament consistently refused to interfere with events in Northern Ireland. Indeed in 1964, the Home Secretary told the House of Commons that religious discrimination in Northern Ireland could not be raised at Westminster since it was a matter solely for the Northern Ireland Parliament.[51] Westminster was finally forced to take back the power to legislate fully for the province in the early years of the 'Troubles' when the Northern Ireland Parliament was abolished.

The Northern Ireland Constitution (Amendment) Act 1973, however, tried to reassure the Unionists by stating that Northern Ireland would remain part of the United Kingdom unless a majority of the people voting in a referendum determined otherwise. The commitment has been repeated verbally several times and in the Anglo-Irish Agreement of 1985,[52] the Joint Declarations of the governments of the Republic of Ireland and the United Kingdom in 1994 and again in the Northern Ireland Act 1998. This Act, however, not only requires the consent of a majority of the people in Northern Ireland voting in a referendum, it also requires an agreement between the government of the United Kingdom and of the Republic of Ireland.

4.34 Unlike the Irish union, the union between Scotland and England still subsists and in Scotland at least is the subject of a belief that the Act of Union 1707 has a special status not found in other statutes. The Treaty of Union abolished the two existing parliaments and set up a new Parliament of Great Britain and appears to

---

[50] s. 75.
[51] H.C. Debs, Vol. 698, col. 1151.
[52] Cmnd. 9657 (1985).

state that this Parliament could freely legislate in most areas of law, but acknowledged there would be some areas which were declared to be fundamental and unalterable. The question of special status is a difficult one. The Treaty was ratified by an Act of each Parliament, first in Scotland, then in England; the English Parliament recognised and agreed the terms of the Treaty and the contents of the Scottish Act. It could therefore be said that it agreed that certain parts of the Treaty were accepted as being unalterable. However, one of the unalterable provisions was repealed by the Universities (Scotland) Act 1853, which abolished the requirement that University professors should be Presbyterians. The provisions of the Treaty and the Act to protect the Protestant religion and the Church of Scotland as the established church in Scotland, were also eroded by the Church Patronage (Scotland) Act 1711 and the Scottish Episcopalians Act 1711. The organisation of the Church of Scotland was altered by the Church of Scotland Act 1921.

Article XIX of the Treaty retained the Court of Session and the High Court of Justiciary as the supreme courts of Scotland: "subject nevertheless to such regulations for the better administration of justice as shall be made by the Parliament of Great Britain." The courts in Scotland have reserved their judgment on the hypothetical case of Parliament trying to pass legislation which would seek to abolish the Scottish supreme courts. Lord President Cooper said in *MacCormick v. Lord Advocate*[53]:

> "The principle of unlimited sovereignty of Parliament is a distinctively English principle which has no counterpart in Scottish constitutional law . . . Considering that the Union legislation extinguished the Parliaments of Scotland and England and replaced them by a new Parliament, I have difficulty in seeing why it should have been supposed that the new Parliament of Great Britain must inherit all the peculiar characteristics of the English Parliament but none of the Scottish Parliament, as if all that happened in 1707 was that Scottish representatives were admitted to the Parliament of England. That is not what was done. Further, the Treaty and associated legislation, by which the Parliament of Great Britain was brought into being as the successor of the separate Parliaments of Scotland and England, contain some clauses which expressly reserve to the Parliament of Great Britain powers of subsequent modification, and other clauses which

---

[53] 1953 S.C. 396.

either contain no such power or emphatically exclude subsequent alteration by declarations that the provision shall be fundamental and unalterable in all time coming, or declarations of a like effect. I have not found in the Union legislation any provision that the Parliament of Great Britain should be 'absolutely sovereign' in the sense that Parliament should be free to alter the Treaty at will."

4.35 In *Gibson v. Lord Advocate*[54] the provisions of article XVIII came under scrutiny. Article XVIII had acknowledged that laws regarding trade and customs and excise duties should be uniform throughout Great Britain but that laws concerning 'private right' should not be altered "except for evident utility of the subjects within Scotland". Gibson argued that membership of the EEC would harm 'private rights' by granting other EEC nationals access to the Scottish fishing grounds. The court held, however, that fishing rights in territorial waters were part of public law and were not protected by article XVIII.

In *Sillars v. Smith*,[55] Jim Sillars and a colleague were prosecuted for an offence under the Criminal Justice (Scotland) Act 1980 but they appealed arguing that the Scotland Act 1978 had been passed to create a legislative Assembly for Scotland with power to legislate for criminal law. Sillars argued that the U.K. Parliament had no power to repeal the Scotland Act and thus no power to pass the Criminal Justice (Scotland) Act 1980. Unsurprisingly the court rejected the arguments and the traditional view of supremacy of Parliament was upheld.

The Scottish courts have therefore shown a reluctance to be drawn into the debate regarding the status of the Union Treaty; they have tended to treat it as a political problem rather than a justiciable one.[56] However, Lord Hope was unconvinced that all matters regarding the Treaty would be non-justiciable. In *Pringle, Petitioner*[57] Article IV of the Treaty came under scrutiny as a result of the introduction of the community charge[58] in Scotland one year ahead of its introduction to England and Wales. The petitioner argued that the statute contravened article IV which stated that all subjects should be treated similarly in respect of taxation and he asked for relief from the assessment to tax made upon him.

---

54 1975 S.L.T. 134.
55 1982 S.L.T. 539.
56 1975 S.L.T. 134.
57 1991 S.L.T. 330.
58 Abolition of Domestic Rates Etc. (Scotland) Act 1987.

The government argued that the matter was non-justiciable. The court however found against the petitioner on the basis that his remedy was not one they could grant.

The imposition of toll charges on the Skye bridge also raised questions in the Scottish courts on the validity of the toll as regards article XVIII of the Treaty. In *Robbie the Pict v. Hingston (No. 2)*[59] R was charged with criminal offences of refusing to pay the toll. He maintained that the toll was a tax or excise within the meaning of article XVIII and had been imposed in Scotland in a different way from similar provisions in England where alternative routes existed, bypassing toll bridges. On appeal to the High Court of Justiciary, the court held that the toll was not an excise with the meaning of the article. Whether it was a tax depended on the circumstances of its imposition. However, Lord Coulsfield, giving the court's Opinion, said that article XVIII might prohibit a different application of identical legislation.[59a]

The comment of De Smith is interesting:

> "The position of the Established Church in Scotland and the Scottish system of judicature, entrenched as fundamental and unalterable in the Acts of Union, remains largely intact. Although the immunity of the surviving fundamental principles of the Union from legislative encroachment by the U.K. Parliament without Scottish consent is probably to be regarded now as a matter of convention rather than of strict law, one cannot be certain that Scottish courts would take this view."[60]

The establishment of a new Scottish Parliament will undoubtedly have an effect on sovereignty. The Scotland Act 1998 provides for the retention of sovereignty by the U.K. Parliament and section 28(7) states that the U.K. Parliament retains the power to make legislation for Scotland. However, there must be doubts as to whether the U.K. Parliament will be able to exercise this power, particularly given the position of the Stormont Parliament from 1920 to 1972 when the U.K. Parliament refused to interfere with the government of Northern Ireland. Arguably the Scottish Parliament is in a stronger position than Stormont, because it has been established after a referendum and it can claim to represent the Scottish nation. Bogdanor argues: 4.36

---

[59] 1998 S.L.T. 1201.

[59a] The status of the Treaty was considered by the House of Lords in *Re Lord Gray's Motion, The Times,* Nov. 12, 1999.

[60] De Smith and Brazier, *Constitutional and Administrative Law* (7th ed., 1994), p. 79.

> "A Scottish Parliament will create a new locus of political power in Scotland, making it extraordinarily difficult for Westminster to continue to exercise its supremacy. In practice, therefore, sovereignty is being transferred and Westminster will not be able to recover it, except under pathological circumstances . . . Power devolved will become power transferred."[61]

It should also be remembered that the concept of sovereignty in Scotland is quite different from that expressed in the English common law. In Scotland, sovereignty lay with the people and this view has held true over the years, being reiterated quite recently. The Claim of Right for Scotland[62] taken up as the declaration inaugurating the Scottish Constitutional Convention in 1989 states: "We . . . do hereby acknowledge the sovereign right of the Scottish people to determine the form of government suited to their needs". The signatories to the declaration included all of the 50 Scottish Labour M.P.s, bar one, and it could therefore be assumed that they at least agreed the spirit of the definition of sovereignty thus declared.

(d) International law

4.37 Finally, we consider the position of international law. British courts do not recognise international law as limiting the supremacy of Parliament. International law and domestic law are two separate systems and international law has no status within the United Kingdom unless and until it is incorporated into U.K. law by means of legislation. This is called a dualist approach and is contrasted with the monist approach whereby international law is automatically incorporated into domestic law, with no requirements for domestic legislation to be passed. Such international law then takes precedence over the domestic legislation. The monist approach is used in countries such as France and Italy. The dualist approach of U.K. law was acknowledged in *Attorney-General for Canada v. Attorney-General for Ontario*[63] where Lord Atkin remarked: "If the government of the day decide to incur the obligations of a Treaty which involve the alteration of the law they have to run the risk of

---

[61] *op. cit.*, p. 12. Bogdanor's "pathological circumstances" referred to the civil unrest in Northern Ireland at the start of the 1970s when the Stormont Parliament was abolished. He argues that only in such circumstances could Westminster take back the power granted to the Scottish Parliament.

[62] *A Claim of Right for Scotland* (O. Edwards ed., 1989).

[63] [1937] A.C. 326.

obtaining the assent of Parliament to the necessary statute or statutes."

Ratification by the government may not be sufficient; many treaties have been ratified by the British government but not enacted by statute. The European Convention on Human Rights is a good example of this. For many years, persons claiming a breach of the Convention in the British courts had no case because the Convention is not part of U.K. law. The British government ratified the Convention and British citizens are free to take a complaint to the European Court of Human Rights and if the court finds in their favour, the British government is bound to abide by it and change the law to give effect to the decision. However, the Human Rights Act 1998 will incorporate the Convention into U.K. law when it is brought into operation, in October 2000. If a treaty is to be ratified by the government but does not require to be brought into U.K. law, the text of it is laid before Parliament before the ratification takes place. This ensures that the legislature is aware of what the executive is doing.[64]

The courts will not interfere in the ratification process since it is seen as a prerogative of the Crown and not justiciable. In *Blackburn v. Attorney-General*[65] the court did not recognise the contents of the EEC Treaty which was about to be ratified by the Crown, that is the British government. Lord Denning remarked famously: "Even if a Treaty is signed, it is elementary that these courts take no notice of treaties as such. We take no notice of treaties until they are embodied in laws enacted by Parliament, and then only to the extent that Parliament tells us."[66]

The rights of individuals under international law are not pro- 4.38
tected in the United Kingdom unless they are incorporated in a legislative act. In *Civilian War Claimants Association v. R.*[67] the German government had agreed in the Treaty of Versailles to pay sums in compensation to British victims of war damage. The claimants did not receive any sums and sued the Crown for the payments. The House of Lords said that the negotiation of the Treaty was a prerogative of the Crown and the Crown was not acting as an agent or trustee for any claimant, unless it declared itself expressly to be doing so. The claim failed when the claimants were unable to show that the Crown had acted as trustee or agent for its nationals.

---

64 H.C., Vol. 171, ser. 5, col. 2001 (April 1, 1921).

65 [1971] 1 W.L.R. 1037.

66 See also *R. v. Secretary of State for Foreign and Commonwealth Office, ex p. Rees-Mogg* [1994] A.C. 14.

67 [1932] A.C. 14.

Where domestic law conflicts with international law, the courts will always implement the domestic law. In *Mortensen v. Peters*[68] the Scandinavian captain of a fishing vessel was caught fishing in the Moray Firth and charged with and convicted of fishing illegally contrary to byelaws made under the Herring Fishery (Scotland) Act 1889. At the time of the offence, the boat was outside the three-mile limit, in international waters. However, the byelaw prohibited fishing in the whole of the Moray Firth, most of which was in international waters. On appeal, the High Court of Justiciary upheld the conviction; the terms of the legislation were unambiguous and affected everyone including foreigners. "For us an Act of Parliament duly passed by Lords and Commons and assented to by the King is supreme, and we are bound to give effect to its terms." This decision has been upheld in other cases, including *Croft v. Dunphy P.C.*[69] where Lord MacMillan said: "Legislation of Parliament, even in contravention of generally acknowledged principles of international law, is binding upon, and must be enforced by, the courts of this country."[70]

Although the courts try to interpret domestic law as not being in conflict with international law[71] if there is a conflict the court will uphold the domestic law even if this results in the United Kingdom breaching a Treaty obligation. In *Cheney v. Conn*[72] the plaintiff objected to part of the money paid by him in income tax being used to purchase nuclear weapons. He argued that the Finance Act 1964, under which the tax assessment was made, was contrary to the Geneva Convention to which the United Kingdom was a signatory. The court declared: "What the statute itself enacts cannot be unlawful, because what the statute says and provides is itself the law, and the highest form of law that is known to this country. It is the law which prevails over every other form of law, and it is not for the court to say that a parliamentary enactment, the highest law in this country, is illegal."

PARLIAMENTARY SUPREMACY AND E.C. LAW

4.39 The principles of the traditional view of the doctrine have to be read in conjunction with the principles set out below.

---

[68] (1906) 8 F. (J.) 93.
[69] [1933] A.C. 156.
[70] *ibid.* at 164.
[71] *R. v. Secretary of State for the Home Department, ex p. Brind* [1991] 1 A.C. 696.
[72] [1968] 1 All E.R. 779.

The United Kingdom became a member of the European Economic Community on January 1, 1973, having ratified the Accession Treaty in 1972 and having implemented it by means of the European Communities Act 1972.[73] Parliament had to recognise the special status of the E.C. Treaties in the Act and in particular recognise the common requirements and objectives of E.C. law. However, it must be noted from the outset that the acceptance of E.C. law is under the 1972 Act, which is a statute with no special status or provisions seeking to entrench E.C. law. During the debates on the Act, the Government acknowledged that a future Parliament might wish to repeal the Act and that the wording of the Act did not affect Parliament's ultimate sovereignty. The Government refused to allow a statement on this point to be included in the statute.[74]

The E.C. is a supranational body with its own institutions exercising executive, legislative and fiscal powers accorded to them by the treaties. The ECJ acts like a constitutional court in interpreting, applying and enforcing Community law. That law may become part of the law of member states automatically, as in the case of Regulations, and may create rights which are directly enforceable by individuals in the national courts. The Community is thus a unique international organisation. The Parliament at Westminster has no role in the making of Community legislation except in so far as it is required to enact legislation to incorporate some Community law into the U.K. law. Even laws that appear to be essentially U.K. laws may be influenced by E.C. laws, for instance, the Criminal Justice Act 1993 contains provisions to give effect to the Insider Dealing Directive and the Data Protection Act 1998 was passed to give effect to a Council Directive.

The tensions between the doctrine of supremacy of Parliament and membership of the EEC were highlighted before the treaty was even signed by the British government. In *Blackburn v. Attorney-General*[75] Blackburn sought a declaration that signing the EEC Treaty would amount to a surrender of part of Parliament's sovereignty and this was unlawful because no Parliament could bind a successor. Lord Denning's remarks on this are stated above.[75a] In 1994, a further challenge was made to the government's power to enter into treaties in *R. v. Secretary of State for the Foreign and Commonwealth Affairs, ex parte Rees-Mogg*.[76] Here the

---

[73] U.K. also joined the ECSC and Euratom at the same time.

[74] Bradley, *op. cit.*

[75] [1971] 1 W.L.R. 1037.

[75a] See para. 4.37.

[76] [1994] 2 W.L.R. 115; [1994] 1 All E.R. 457.

applicant sought a declaration that the Government could not ratify the Treaty on European Union 1992 without the consent of Parliament. The Court of Appeal followed earlier cases and the application was refused, as was leave to appeal to the House of Lords.

4.40 The European Communities Act 1972, s. 2(1) incorporates all existing E.C. law into U.K. law and states:

> "(1) All such rights, powers, liabilities, obligations and restrictions from time to time created or arising by or under the Treaties, and all such remedies and procedures from time to time provided for by or under the Treaties, as in accordance with the Treaties are without further enactment to be given legal effect or used in the United Kingdom shall be recognised and available in law, and be enforced, allowed and followed accordingly; and the expression 'enforceable Community right' and similar expressions shall be read as referring to one to which this subsection applies."

Future E.C. law is given effect by virtue of section 2(4):

> "(4) The provision that may be made under subsection (2) above includes, subject to Schedule 2 of this Act, any such provision (of any such extent) as might be made by Act of Parliament, and any enactment passed or to be passed, other than one contained in this Part of this Act, shall be construed and have effect subject to the foregoing provisions of this section."

The Act gives power to the government to amend existing legislation or create new legislation by means of regulations introduced by the appropriate minister.[77] This has the beneficial effect of allowing changes to be made quickly. However, some matters may require to be enacted by a statute rather than subordinate legislation; for instance, where an E.C. Directive had to be implemented with retrospective effect, this could only be achieved by passing a statute.[78] The section is subject to the provisions of Schedule 2 of the Act, which sets out areas where secondary legislation may not be made by the section 2(2) procedure, such as a provision with retrospective effect, or a provision to impose or increase taxation. Such regulations require to be made by a statutory instrument which is subject to annulment by either House.

---

[77] s. 2(2).

[78] Case 150/85 *Drake v. Chief Adjudication Officer* [1987] E.C.R. 1995.

Section 3(1) of the Act states that questions of the interpretation of E.C. law are to be determined "in accordance with the principles laid down by any relevant decision of the European Court". Thus the primacy of the ECJ is recognised.

Section 2(1) clearly provides that E.C. law in existence on January 1, 1973 is to be given effect; this therefore provides that if a rule of E.C. law conflicts with a domestic law made before January 1, 1973, the E.C. law will prevail.[79] There is no difficulty with this; the principle in fact accords with the traditional doctrine of implied repeal that a later Act (here the E.C. Act) will prevail over a conflicting earlier Act. The problem occurs when a provision of E.C. law is inconsistent with a post-1972 Act.

The ECJ has always made it clear that it views E.C. law as 4.41 supreme over domestic law. This has a number of implications. First, Community law must always prevail over domestic law. Secondly, all Member States must apply Community law to the same effect and extent. Thirdly, only the ECJ may interpret E.C. law and domestic courts must follow previous judgments of the ECJ or refer the matter to the Court for decision. Finally, Member States are required to amend their domestic laws where these are found to be incompatible with E.C. law. Failure to do so will now result in a fine being imposed on the Member State by the Court on the application of the Commission.

In *Costa v. E.N.E.L.*[80] the Court remarked that Member States had limited their sovereign rights and created a body of law which bound their nationals and themselves: "The transfer by the states from their domestic legal system to the Community legal system of the rights and obligations arising under the Treaty carried with it a permanent limitation of their sovereign rights, against which a subsequent unilateral act incompatible with the concept of the Community cannot prevail."[81]

In *Walt Wilhelm v. Bundeskartellamt*[82] the Court said: "The Treaty has established its own system of law, integrated into the legal systems of the member states, and which must be applied by their courts. It would be contrary to the nature of such a system to allow member states to introduce or to retain measures capable of prejudicing the practical effectiveness of the Treaty."

The ECJ also decided that E.C. law prevails over even the constitutional provisions of Member States. In *Internationale*

---

[79] *R. v. Henn* [1981] 2 All E.R. 166; *R. v. Goldstein* [1982] 1 W.L.R. 804.

[80] Case 6/64 [1964] E.C.R. 585.

[81] *ibid.* at 586; see also Case 26/62 *Van Gend en Loos v. Nederlandse Administratie der Belastigen* [1963] E.C.R. 1.

[82] [1969] E.C.R. 1.

Handelsgesellschaft[83] the ECJ held that even the German constitution had to conform to E.C. law. The *Simmenthal* case[84] ruled that where there was a conflict between domestic law and a directly applicable E.C. law, the domestic law was rendered inapplicable. The ECJ declared:

> "A national court which is called upon . . . to apply provisions of Community law is under a duty to give full effect to those provisions, if necessary refusing of its own motion to apply any conflicting provisions of national legislation, even if adopted subsequently, and it is not necessary for the court to request or await the prior setting aside of such provisions by legislation or other constitutional means."

Note that the ECJ did not state that the conflicting national law was void, only that it could not be applied.

4.42 With this background, it was inevitable that the British courts would have difficulty in reconciling the doctrine of supremacy of Parliament with the idea of supremacy of E.C. law.

Where a statute is passed after January 1, 1973 (or comes into effect after this date) and conflicts with E.C. law, the British courts have tried to interpret the statute so as to conform with the E.C. law. In a 1980 case involving Article 119 of the E.C. Treaty[85] the position of conflicting U.K. law was summarised by Lord Denning:

> "In construing our statute, we are entitled to look to the Treaty as an aid in its construction: and even more, not only as an aid, but as an overriding force. If on close investigation it should appear that our legislation is deficient—or is inconsistent with Community law . . . then it is our bounden duty to give priority to Community law. Such is the result of s. 2(1) and (4) of the European Communities Act 1972."[86]

In *Garland v. British Rail Engineering Ltd*[87] Lord Diplock referred to the general presumption that Parliament does not intend to legislate contrary to an international treaty obligation and said that: "the words of a statute passed after the Treaty has been

---

[83] Case 11/70 *Internationale Handelsgesellschaft GmbH v. Einfuhr-und Vorratstelle fur Getriede und Futtermittel* [1972] C.M.L.R. 255.

[84] Case 106/77 *Amministrazione delle Finanze dello Stato v. Simmenthal SpA* [1978] E.C.R. 629.

[85] Now renumbered Art. 141 by the Treaty of Amsterdam 1997.

[86] *Macarthys Ltd v. Smith* [1981] Q.B. 180; [1980] 2 C.M.L.R. 20; see also *H. P. Bulmer v. J. Bollinger SA* [1974] Ch. 410.

[87] [1983] 2 A.C. 751.

signed and dealing with the subject-matter of the international obligation of the U.K., are to be construed, if they are reasonably capable of bearing such a meaning, as intended to carry out the obligation, and not to be inconsistent with it."[88]

Thus the U.K. courts have interpreted the words in U.K. enactments as widely as possible to achieve consistency. This was seen in *Pickstone v. Freemans plc*[89] where the House of Lords interpreted the Equal Pay Amendment Regulations so that they did not conflict with Article 119; this was done by supplying words by implication into the Regulations.[90] Where a U.K. statute cannot be construed as in conformity with E.C. law, then E.C. law must be applied in preference to the U.K. statute.

This was the ruling of the House of Lords based on section 2(4) 4.43 of the 1972 Act in *R. v. Secretary of State for Transport, ex parte Factortame*[91] which concerned a conflict between E.C. law and the Merchant Shipping Act 1988 and associated regulations governing the registration of fishing vessels. The common fishing policy of the E.C. required that fishing vessels from all Member States should have equal access to the fishing grounds of other Member States. In 1983, the Council adopted conservation measures to prevent over-fishing; these included setting quotas on the amount of fish to be caught, with these being distributed among the Member States. The quotas were based on the number of ships registered in a Member State. The Merchant Shipping Act 1894 prohibited non-nationals from owning British boats but allowed corporate ownership by British companies. Directors of 96 Spanish boats registered under the 1894 Act and these were counted as part of the U.K. quota. The government imposed additional requirements for registration in 1986 and then in 1988 passed the Merchant Shipping Act, requiring that those registering should be able to show a "genuine and substantial connection with the U.K." as well as other qualifying conditions. Factortame did not comply with these requirements and challenged the Act as being incompatible with E.C. law, on the grounds of discretion as to nationality and the rights of companies to establishment in other Member States.

The case went to the ECJ for a preliminary ruling and on its return to the House of Lords, Lord Bridge declared:

---

[88] [1983] 2 A.C. 751 at 771.

[89] [1988] 2 All E.R. 803.

[90] See also *Duke v. G.E.C. Reliance Ltd* [1988] 1 All E.R. 626; *Litster v. Forth Dry Dock Co. Ltd* [1989] 1 All E.R. 1134.

[91] Case C–213/89 [1990] 2 A.C. 85.

"Whatever the limitation of its sovereignty Parliament accepted when it enacted the European Communities Act 1972 was entirely voluntary. Under . . . the Act of 1972 it has always been clear that it was the duty of an U.K. court, when delivering final judgment, to override any rule of national law found to be in conflict with any directly enforceable rule of Community law."

When the divisional court decided to refer the case to the ECJ, Factortame requested that an injunction be granted to protect their Community rights by preventing the government from imposing regulations under the 1988 Act. Both the Court of Appeal and the House of Lords stated that such an injunction was not available against the Crown.[92] The 1988 Act would have to be presumed to be valid until the contrary was shown. In a preliminary ruling, the ECJ held that the provisions of the 1988 Act should be suspended until the full case was heard. They based this on the principle that E.C. law must be given full effect throughout the Community and that interim relief should be available to ensure full effectiveness. The House of Lords accepted the ruling and granted the injunction. Thus provisions of Community law may confer jurisdiction on U.K. courts to grant injunctions against the Crown. However, the circumstances in which such interim relief may be granted against primary legislation will require to be "most compelling" according to the Court of Appeal in *R. v. H.M. Treasury, ex parte British Telecommunications plc*.[93]

In a related action, the European Commission brought an action in the ECJ against the United Kingdom seeking a declaration that the United Kingdom had failed in its obligations under the E.C. Treaty by imposing nationality requirements in the 1988 Merchant Shipping Act.[94] The ECJ made an interim order that the United Kingdom suspend the application of the nationality requirements. The House of Lords granted an injunction against the Secretary of State requiring him to suspend the nationality requirements, although this had already been done by an Order in Council.[95] The *Factortame* case has continued to proceed through the courts, with a finding by the ECJ in 1996 that the applicants were entitled to reparation for the loss they sustained.[96]

---

[92] Note that this position was reversed for English cases by *Re M* [1993] 3 W.L.R. 433.

[93] *The Times*, Dec. 2, 1993.

[94] Case 246/89R *Commission v. U.K.* (*Re Nationality of Fishermen*) [1989] E.C.R. 3125.

[95] Merchant Shipping Act 1988 (Amendment) Order 1989 (S.I. 1989 No. 2006).

[96] *R. v. Secretary of State for Transport, ex p. Factortame (No. 4)* [1996] 2 W.L.R. 506.

The principle of the supremacy of E.C. law was further reinforced in *R v. Secretary of State for Employment, ex parte Equal Opportunities Commission*[97] where the provisions of the Employment Protection (Consolidation) Act 1978 were held to be incompatible with Article 119 and with Council Directives.[98] In this case, there was no reference to the ECJ; the British courts decided for the first time without prompting from the ECJ that British statutory provisions were unenforceable. Potential conflict with the concept of sovereignty was avoided by the House of Lords declaring the incompatibility of the legislation, rather than declaring the U.K. provisions to be void. 4.44

These cases have had a marked impact on the traditional doctrine of the supremacy of Parliament. This is expressed by Bradley thus: 4.45

> "Dicey asserted that 'no person or body is recognised by the law of England as having a right to override or set aside the legislation of Parliament' (Law of the Constitution, page 40). In fact, U.K. law now recognises that Community organs have the right to make decisions and issue regulations, which may have the effect of overriding legislation by Parliament."[99]

The doctrine of supremacy of Parliament has at its heart the principle that no Parliament can bind its successors. Yet there can be no doubt that the Parliament of 1972 attempted to do just that and apparently succeeded. The wording of section 2(4) includes the phrase "any enactment passed *or to be passed*".[1] These words bind future Parliaments and subordinate all future legislation to E.C. law. The judgments in the *Factortame* cases are evidence that the European Communities Act 1972 may be entrenched in U.K. law.[2] It should be remembered that the 1972 Act does not use any wording attempting to entrench its provisions; it is a statute like any other, and, like any other, may be amended or repealed. Its 'entrenchment' lies in its political importance, not in its legal form.

However, an interesting question still arises: what would happen if Parliament deliberately legislated contrary to E.C. law, using words which were express and unambiguous? The United Kingdom would of course then be in default of its treaty obligations and 4.46

---

[97] [1995] 1 A.C. 1.

[98] See also *Marshall v. Southampton Health Authority (No. 2)* [1993] 4 All E.R. 586.

[99] *op. cit.*, p. 91.

[1] Emphasis added.

[2] Wade and Forsyth, *Administrative Law* (7th ed., 1994), p. 31.

there would be political repercussions, but would the courts then apply the U.K. statute or the E.C. law? The basis of all of the cases above is that Parliament gave authority by means of the European Communities Act 1972 for the implementation of E.C. law in the United Kingdom and authorised the U.K. courts to refer questions of E.C. law to the ECJ for interpretation of that law. If Parliament then chooses to override the 1972 Act by the specific and express enactment of a statute which is contrary to E.C. law, it could be argued that the U.K. courts would have no alternative but to implement the later statute.[3] Lord Bingham in *Factortame (No. 2)*[4] thought this would be unlikely: "any rule of domestic law which prevented the court from giving effect to directly enforceable rights established in Community law would be bad."

The courts' generally pragmatic approach is shown in this quotation by Hoffman J., in *Stoke on Trent Council v. B. & Q. plc*,[5] when he said:

> "The (E.C.) Treaty is the supreme law of this country, taking precedence over Acts of Parliament. Our entry into the European Economic Community meant that (subject to our undoubted but probably theoretical right to withdraw from the Community altogether) Parliament surrendered its sovereign rights to legislation contrary to the provisions of the Treaty on matters of social and economic policy which it regulated. The entry into the Community was in itself a high act of social and economic policy, by which the partial surrender of sovereignty was seen as more than compensated by the advantages of membership."[6]

Bradley also accepted this pragmatic viewpoint: "so long as the U.K. wishes to remain in the E.C., the supremacy of the law made by Parliament must if necessary give way to the greater supremacy of Community law."[7]

E.C. SECONDARY LEGISLATION AND THE SUPREMACY OF PARLIAMENT DOCTRINE

4.47 The principle of direct effect of Community legislation states that if a Community Treaty provision, or a Regulation, or a Directive, is

---

[3] See dicta of Lord Denning in *Macarthys Ltd v. Smith* [1979] 3 All E.R. 325.
[4] [1991] 1 A.C. 603.
[5] [1991] Ch. 48.
[6] *ibid.* at 56.
[7] *op. cit.*, p. 97.

held to have direct effect, then individuals may claim that rights or obligations have been created directly by that Community legislation without the need for implementation by legislation of a Member State. The individual may then rely on such Community legislation in the courts of their own state in the same way as a statute made by the legislature.[8]

Not all Treaty provisions are directly enforceable and it has been left to the ECJ to define these. However, some examples are: Article 48 on freedom of movement of workers,[9] Article 52 conferring the right of freedom of establishment,[10] and Article 119 conferring the right of equal pay for equal work for men and women.[11]

An E.C. Regulation has special status within the legal systems of the Member States. Article 189 E.C. states that: "A regulation shall have general application. It shall be binding in its entirety, and directly applicable in all member states." The concept of direct applicability is different from direct effect. Direct applicability means that the Regulation automatically becomes law in the Member State with no legislation from the Member State's legislature required to implement it. A Regulation will always be directly applicable; it does not necessarily have direct effect. For a Regulation to have direct effect, it must be clear and precise, unconditional and leave no room for discretion in its implementation.

An E.C. Directive is binding as to its effect, but it is left to the Member State to decide how it is to be implemented. To have direct effect, the Directive must fulfil the conditions above and in addition, the period for implementation of the Directive must not have expired.[12] In the U.K., Directives are implemented either by Act of Parliament or by subordinate legislation. The ECJ has indicated that a Directive may have vertical direct effect, but not horizontal.[13] This can create anomalies; for instance an employee working for a public body can claim rights contained in a Directive, but a person working in the same kind of job in the private sector may not. It is left to the national legislatures to correct such anomalies and injustices by implementing legislation to bring the private and public sectors into line.

---

[8] Case 26/62 *Van Gend en Loos*, above.

[9] Now Art. 39, TEU; Case 41/74 *Van Duyn v. Home Office* [1975] Ch. 358.

[10] Now Art. 43, TEU; the *Factortame* cases.

[11] Now Art. 144, TEU; Case 149/77 *Defrenne v. Sabena (No. 2)* [1978] E.C.R. 1365.

[12] Case 148/78 *Pubbico Ministerio v. Ratti* [1979] E.C.R. 1629.

[13] Case C–188/89 *Foster v. British Gas* [1990] E.C.R. I-3313; Case 152/84 *Marshall v. Southampton and South West Hampshire Area Health Authority* [1986] E.C.R. 723; Case 103/88 *Fratelli Constanzo v. Comune di Milano* [1992] 1 C.M.L.R. 1045 (state includes local authorities).

4.48 As well as the doctrine of direct effect of a Directive, the ECJ has developed the principle of indirect effect, although the development has been less consistent than for direct effect. Indirect effect involves the duty of a Member State under Article 10[14] to take "appropriate measures" to ensure that obligations arising from the Treaty are given effect, facilitate the achievement of the Community's tasks and refrain from taking measures which would prevent the attainment of the Treaty's objectives. If a Member State fails in any of its duties under Article 10, then the Member State may be liable in compensation for any loss incurred by an individual as the direct result of that failure. In *Von Colson v. Land Nordrhein-Westfalen*[15] the ECJ ruled that Article 10 imposed a duty on the governments of Member States and on all national authorities, including the courts. The national courts have the duty of interpreting their national law "in the light of the wording and the purpose of the directive." This decision meant that where a provision was not directly effective it could still be applied by means of interpretation, that is indirectly. The *Marleasing* case[16] extended this principle, in effect allowing Directives to have horizontal direct effect by requiring national law to be interpreted to achieve the result envisaged by the Directive, even as against private parties, and even though no national provisions had been passed to give effect to the Directive.

CONCLUSION

4.49 The doctrine of supremacy of Parliament appears to have taken a substantial knock with the entry of the U.K. to the E.C. "Section 2 is an attempt by one Parliament to fetter the continuing supremacy of Parliament by providing that, while future parliaments may legislate in breach of Community law, the courts must (to the extent of any inconsistency) deny it any effect."[17]

Wade, commenting on the *Factortame* case, said that: "the Parliament of 1972 had succeeded in binding the Parliament of 1988 and restricting its sovereignty, something that was supposed to be constitutionally impossible."[18]

---

14 Formerly Art. 5.

15 Case 14/83 [1984] E.C.R. 1891.

16 Case 106/89 *Marleasing SA v. La Comercial Internacional de Alimentacion SA* [1992] 1 C.M.L.R. 305.

17 Bradley and Ewing, *op. cit.*, p. 15.

18 "Sovereignty—Revolution or Evolution?" (1996) 112 L.Q.R. 568.

However, on closer examination, it can be seen that the U.K.'s continued membership is dependent on Parliament not passing another statute to take the United Kingdom out of the E.C. As such then the doctrine is intact although it depends for its validity not on its legality, but on the political views of the government of the day. "The common law doctrine of the legal sovereignty of Parliament remains potentially in force, albeit in temporary suspension, while, in virtue of the 1972 Act and Treaty of Accession, the British and European courts are required to review Acts of Parliament for compatibility with Community law."[19] The effects of devolution and the development of the E.U., taken together, will squeeze Parliament which "will have to get used to sharing power with these rival institutions, and will have to adapt to survive . . . taken together this decentralised, more pluralist, more legally controlled system will amount to a new constitutional order."[20]

---

[19] MacCormick, "Sovereignty or Subsidiarity? Some Comments on Scottish Devolution" in *Devolution and the British Constitution* (A. Tomkins ed., 1998), p. 7.

[20] Hazell, "Reinventing the Constitution: Can the state survive?", CIPFA/*Times* Lecture, Nov. 1998.

CHAPTER 5

LEGISLATION

SCRUTINISING LEGISLATION IN THE U.K. PARLIAMENT[1]

5.01 There are three types of Bill passed in Parliament. Private Bills affect particular bodies such as a local authority or public corporation. The procedure for passing these Bills is slightly different from that for a Public Bill. There is often little or no discussion of the contents of the Bill within Parliament. A hybrid Bill is one which, on the whole, has general application but also contains particular provisions applying specifically to particular persons or bodies. For instance, the building of the Channel tunnel required an act which involved a private company being given compulsory purchase powers to buy the land required to build the northern end of the tunnel. The final, and most important type, is the Public Bill. These take up the greater part of the legislative programme of Parliament. There are two types of Public Bill, the Government Bill and the Private Member's Bill.

The proposal for a Private Member's Bill may come from the M.P., or from a pressure group or indeed from the government. M.P.s who are lucky in the ballot for a Private Members' Bills will find themselves inundated with ideas for a Bill. Increasingly the government is suggesting to M.P.s that they might present Bills on matters which the government would like to see promoted but is unable to devote time to or with which they do not wish to be too closely associated because of the controversial nature of the Bill. Such a Bill will receive preferential treatment compared to Bills put forward without the blessing of the government. For instance, the Hunting with Dogs Bill put forward in the 1997–98 session did not have the blessing of the government and ran out of time, although the vast majority of M.P.s voted in its favour at second reading.

---

[1] For a detailed account, see M. Zander, *The Law-making Process* (5th ed., 1999).

The methods of initiating a Private Member's Bill are by the ballot, the 10-minute rule procedure or Standing Order 39. At the start of each session of Parliament a ballot of backbench M.P.s is held. The first 20 names drawn out are allowed time to present a Bill. The debates take place on six Friday mornings and if the Bill fails to achieve a vote in its favour, then it will fall. The chances of Bills completing the process are very small; to have a chance, the Bill has to be one of the top six in the ballot, it has to be non-controversial and have cross-party support. Only six or so of these Bills will be passed in a session. Some major laws have been passed by Private Members' Bills from the ballot. They include the Abolition of the Death Penalty Act 1965, the Abortion Act 1967, the Sexual Offences Act 1967, the Theatres Act 1968, the Divorce Reform Act 1969, the Disabled Persons (Services, Consultation and Representation) Act 1986 and the Age of Legal Capacity (Scotland) Act 1991.

The 10-minute rule Bill[2] is introduced on a Tuesday or Wednesday afternoon before ministerial question time. It is a popular way of introducing a Bill to Parliament because of its timing but a Bill introduced in this way is highly unlikely to become law. The proposer of the Bill speaks for 10 minutes, then anyone opposed to it speaks for 10 minutes and a vote is then called. Even if it passes this stage, it is unlikely to become law because no government time will be given to it. Each year, only one or two Bills will be passed using this procedure, for instance the Bail (Amendment) Act 1993, which gave the prosecution the right of appeal against a grant of bail. The Standing Order procedure 39 allows a Bill to be introduced to Parliament during the course of the day; no particular time is set aside and again the chances of it becoming law are slim, only one or two each year.

A government Bill is prepared by parliamentary draftsmen in 5.02
consultation with the department proposing the Bill. It will have been considered by a Cabinet committee and the Cabinet and will have their approval. Very often too it will have been the subject of extensive consultation with pressure and interest groups before it reached the draft stage. The current Labour Government now publishes draft Bills for discussion before the Bill proper is introduced to Parliament.

A Bill may be introduced in either House but certain Bills will always be introduced first to the House of Commons; these are

---

[2] Brought under Standing Order 13.

money Bills, controversial Bills and Bills of constitutional significance.[3]

A recent innovation regarding Bills is the introduction of explanatory notes which are published with the Bill. The notes explain in plain English the background to the Bill, summarise the provisions, give worked examples where appropriate and explain difficult concepts.[4]

Stages of a Bill

5.03 A Bill must be passed by each House and receive the Royal Assent before it becomes law. In each House, the same procedure is carried out.

First reading

5.04 A Bill is taken as read for the first time if certain formalities are complied with.[5] At the start of business the Speaker calls upon the minister in charge of the Bill who stands up and nods; the clerk reads out the short title of the Bill and the minister names a date for the second reading. This allows the Bill to be printed.

Second reading

5.05 This is a general debate held about two weeks after the first reading. The debate is on the principles of the Bill and no amendments are allowed at this stage. At the end of the debate the motion is put and voted on. A Bill can be lost at this stage although it is uncommon. In 1986, the Shops Bill was lost at second reading stage despite the Government's large majority. The second reading of a Bill may be referred to a second reading committee. This may occur for a non-controversial measure, often one which has already been passed by the House of Lords. The minister will propose that the Bill be referred to a second reading committee and this will be set up unless 20 M.P.s object. However, any vote on the Bill must be taken on the floor of the House.

---

[3] For discussion of what constitutes a constitutional Bill, see J. Seaton and B. Winetrobe, "The Passage of Constitutional Bills in Parliament" (1998) 4(2) J.L.S. 33.

[4] C. Jenkins, "Helping the Reader of Bills and Acts" (1999) Vol. 149 (No. 6980) N.L.J. 798.

[5] Standing Order 58.

Committee stage

The Bill is considered clause by clause and amendments are proposed and debated. Amendments are voted on as they occur. The government usually opposes amendments but may support some. There are two types of committee, the standing committee and the committee of the whole House. A standing committee has between 16 and 50 M.P.s chosen to reflect the political make-up of the House. It is not a permanent committee as the name suggests; it is set up to consider the Bill and when that business is concluded, the committee is disbanded. It acts as "amending and improving machinery on behalf of the government."[6] A standing committee is quite different from a select committee and this is reflected in the form of the committee where the members of a standing committee sit in government and opposition benches facing each other (as in the Chamber) but in select committee members sit at a horseshoe-shaped table with witnesses in front of them. Appointment to the standing committees is made by a committee of selection and the chairman is appointed by the Speaker. In 1986, the House approved Standing Order 91, which allows a special standing committee to be set up. During the first 28 days of a Bill being sent to this committee, it may take written and oral evidence from witnesses to assist in its deliberations. Thereafter the committee reverts to the ordinary standing committee procedure. 5.06

The Grand Committees (for Scotland, Wales and Northern Ireland) and the Regional Affairs Committee are all standing committees, not select committees. The Scottish Grand Committee can consider Scottish Bills in relation to their principle, this being the equivalent of a second reading. Since 1994, the Scottish Grand Committee has also been able to debate various issues of its own choice, take oral questions for the Scottish Office ministers and hear ministerial statements from ministers who sit in both the Commons and the Lords. It is also able to sit in places other than Westminster and it has regularly sat in various locations in Scotland. It is not yet clear what effect devolution will have on the work of the Scottish Grand Committee. The Welsh Grand Committee has similar functions. The Northern Ireland Grand Committee may hear matters relating to Northern Ireland but it meets rarely. A standing committee on regional affairs is included in the Standing Orders but has not met since 1978. The Leader of the House of Commons announced in January 1999 that it may be revived in an adapted form.[7]

---

[6] P. Madgwick and D. Woodhouse, *The Law and Politics of Constitution of the UK* (1995), p. 172.

[7] Statement by Margaret Beckett, *Hansard*, H.C. Vol. 323, col. 238 (Jan. 14, 1999).

A Committee of the Whole House comprises all M.P.s who consider the Bill clause by clause on the floor of the House. It is chaired by the Chairman of the Ways and Means Committee, not by the Speaker. Another difference between the Committee of the Whole House and a sitting of the House itself is that members may speak more than once during the Committee's discussions. The Committee will be set up for Bills of constitutional importance such as the Scotland Bill in 1998. Other Bills included in this procedure would be those which the government wants passed very quickly, for instance, during a state of emergency. The annual Finance Bill is taken partly before the whole House and partly in standing committee,[8] and this procedure is available for other Bills, *e.g.* clauses relating to the age of consent for homosexual acts were considered by a Committee of the Whole House during the 1993–94 session, since they were considered to be matters of individual conscience.

There are two European standing committees to consider E.C. draft proposals for legislation and other documents on matters relating to the E.C. legislation. The first committee deals with documents relating to agriculture, fisheries, food, forestry, the environment and transport, while the second committee deals with any other matter. Each committee has 13 members appointed for a session. The E.C. documents are first considered by the Select Committee on European Legislation, which then recommends that the documents be considered further by one of the standing committees.

Report stage

5.07 If the Bill has been before a Committee of the Whole House, this stage is a formality. Otherwise the stage informs M.P.s who were not on the standing committee of any amendments. The new clauses will be debated and the government may make further amendments if it had agreed to do so in committee. There is no vote and the third reading usually follows immediately.

Third reading

5.08 This is similar to the second reading except for amendments made in committee. The Bill is debated in principle and a vote taken. It is unusual for a Bill to be lost here.

After both Houses have agreed the Bill, it is sent for Royal Assent and comes into effect either immediately, or on a date

---

[8] Standing Order 61.

specified in the Act, or on a date to be decided by the minister. The Act will state which of these dates is to be followed. It is not unusual for an Act to be brought into effect in stages. For instance, the Consumer Credit Act 1974 was not fully implemented for more than 10 years.

If a Bill is rejected by the other House or is amended by them, a different procedure comes into play. A Bill from the House of Lords rejected by the Commons will fall. A Bill from the Commons rejected or amended by the Lords returns to the Commons where the amendment is considered. If the Commons rejects the Lords amendment, it goes back to the Lords for them to reconsider. If the Lords still do not like the Bill as passed by the Commons, then there are discussions among the party managers to try to come to a consensus. If this fails, the Bill is withdrawn. If the government reintroduces the Bill in the next session of Parliament and the same happens again, the Parliament Acts 1911 and 1949 are brought into play and the Bill may be passed without the consent of the House of Lords.

Curtailing debate on legislative proposals

There is always considerable pressure on parliamentary time and 5.09
there is still a need for most Bills to be passed within one parliamentary session. Opposition parties will, not unnaturally, attempt to hold up government business whenever possible. For these reasons, a government will have to use one of two methods of controlling the amount of time spent on debating a Bill. The closure motion can be put by any member, although it is usually put by a government whip, during a debate in the House or in standing committee and the Speaker (or committee chairman) will then decide whether or not to accept the motion. If at least 100 M.P.s vote in favour of closure, the debate is concluded. Although not often used, the closure motion is a useful device for moving a Bill along more quickly.

The allocation of time motion, or guillotine, is a more common method of controlling the time spent on debate. The motion will set a strict timetable for discussion of a Bill at its various Commons stages. The motion must first be passed by the House after a debate of at least three hours. Thereafter there will be specific time-limits set for the discussion of each stage of the Bill. This is done by the Business Committee of the House, which divides the Bill up into portions and allocates a specified period of time for discussion to each portion. If the time-limit is reached before all of that portion of the Bill has been discussed, discussion comes to an end and the members move on to the next portion. Those measures which are guillotined tend to be important ones which the government wants passed quickly or where there has been considerable debate already in the committee and the Bill is in danger of running out of time. Thus the Dangerous Dogs Act 1991 was guillotined for its second reading, committee stage, report and third reading and again when the House of Lord's amendments were being discussed. The Referendums (Scotland and Wales) Act 1997 was guillotined as was the Finance Act 1997, both after second reading.

The use of the guillotine motion restricts the scrutiny of legislation and should therefore only be used sparingly. However, there has been increased use of the motion in recent years, particularly by the Conservatives during the period 1988 to 1992, when no less than 19 Bills were guillotined.

LEGISLATION OF THE SCOTTISH PARLIAMENT

5.10 In Scotland there is now a plethora of legislation to be consulted. There is the law of the E.C., legislation from the U.K. Parliament and legislation of the Scottish Parliament, together with all of the associated subordinate legislation. "Ignorance of the law is no excuse" goes the legal maxim, but it will be increasingly difficult for the Scottish people to know what the law is and who is responsible for passing it.

Legislative competence of the Scottish Parliament

5.11 There are two models of devolving the law-making power from a central authority to a subordinate authority.[9] The retaining model occurs where the central authority devolves all of its powers with the exception of specific powers for itself. An example of the retaining model was the Government of Ireland Act 1920 which established the Northern Ireland Parliament. The Act set out the powers reserved (retained) to the U.K. Parliament in section 4 with the implication being that any powers not listed as reserved were devolved. The reservations included the Crown, the armed forces and the making of war and peace. To ensure that the reserved powers were not usurped, the Act also states: "Any law made in contravention of the limitations imposed by this section shall, so far as it contravenes those limitations, be void." The Northern Ireland

---

[9] See McFadden, "The Scottish Parliament: Provisions for Dispute Resolution", 1998 J.R. 221.

Constitution Act 1973 was set out in similar terms, reserving specific matters but devolving everything else.

In the second model, called the transferring model, the central authority devolves power to the subordinate authority to make laws in particular specified areas. Anything not so specified is reserved to the central authority. The Scotland Act 1978 created a transferring model; the Act contained long lists of statutes, some of them devolved some of them not. It was a complicated and complex piece of legislation that would have required constant updating and thus would have caused uncertainty as regards the powers actually devolved.

The Scotland Act 1998 is based on a retaining model, along the lines of the two Northern Ireland Acts mentioned above. Thus the Scottish Parliament is limited in the types of laws it may enact.

"The Parliament may make laws, to be known as the Acts of the Scottish Parliament."[10] This power in section 28 is read subject to section 29, which lays down the limitations of the Scottish Parliament, in other words, section 29 sets out the Parliament's legislative competence. Section 28 sets out some of the procedures for passing legislation. Thus a proposed act is called a Bill, and a Bill becomes an Act of the Scottish Parliament when it is passed by Parliament and has received the Royal Assent.[11] The validity of an Act of the Scottish Parliament is not affected by any invalidity in the proceedings and Acts of the Scottish Parliament are to be judicially noticed, *i.e.* the Act does not require evidence of its existence and contents to be led in court proceedings.[12] The power of the U.K. Parliament to make laws is confirmed by section 28(7).[13]

Section 28 has to be read with section 29, which sets out the 5.12
limits on the power to make laws conferred on the Scottish Parliament. Section 29 however has also to be read with Schedule 4, section 30 and Schedule 5 so that the full significance of the Parliament's competence can be understood. Section 29(1) states: "An Act of the Scottish Parliament is not law so far as any provision of the Act is outside the legislative competence of the Parliament." This confirms that Acts of the Scottish Parliament are not of the same status as Acts of the U.K. Parliament. Acts of the Scottish Parliament may be struck down as being *ultra vires*,

---

[10] s. 28(1).

[11] s. 28(2).

[12] There is an equivalent rule for U.K. statutes in the Interpretation Act 1978, s. 3.

[13] See para. 4.36.

whereas an Act of the U.K. Parliament may not be so declared. The section then proceeds to detail the areas in which any attempt to legislate by the Scottish Parliament would be invalid.

(a) The Scottish Parliament cannot legislate for another country or territory, nor confer or remove functions exercisable otherwise than in Scotland. This subsection will therefore prevent the Scottish Parliament from legislating for another part of the United Kingdom.
(b) The Scottish Parliament may not legislate on a matter which is a reserved matter, as detailed in Schedule 5. Reserved matters are discussed fully below.
(c) The Scottish Parliament may not legislate in breach of the restrictions in Schedule 4. The Scottish Parliament has the power generally to amend or repeal Acts of the U.K. Parliament, which relate to devolved matters. Certain limitations are placed on the exercise of this general power by stating in Schedule 4 that certain enactments may not be modified. The Acts of Union 1706 and 1707 are protected as well as the European Communities Act 1972, Human Rights Act 1998 and Scotland Act 1998 itself, although there are a small number of excepted sections. The prohibition against amending the Scotland Act is of course necessary to ensure that devolution in this form continues, otherwise the Scottish Parliament and U.K. Parliament might have been continually at odds with the Scottish Parliament taking more powers to itself than the U.K. Parliament had envisaged.
(d) Legislation of the Scottish Parliament must not be incompatible with Convention rights or E.C. law. Convention rights are defined in the Act by reference to section 1 of the Human Rights Act 1998 and include most of the rights stated in the ECHR. Community law is also mentioned here as it is important that the United Kingdom as a member of the E.C. complies with Community law and the United Kingdom would be liable if the Scottish Parliament passed laws which were incompatible with Community law. The Scottish Parliament is also responsible for implementing Community obligations in areas that have been devolved.
(e) The Scottish Parliament may not legislate to remove the Lord Advocate from his position as head of the systems of criminal prosecution and investigation of deaths in Scotland. Thus the traditional independence of the Lord Advocate as prosecutor in Scotland is maintained.

The Act recognises that it may be difficult sometimes to distinguish between reserved and devolved matters and gives rules for interpretation at section 29(3) and (4). The primary test is that of purpose; if the purpose of a provision is a devolved one, the provision is not outwith the legislative competence merely because it incidentally affects a reserved matter. In the parliamentary debates, the minister gave an example of the thinking behind this section. If an Act of the Scottish Parliament had a provision relating to pollution caused by water seeping from a coal-mine, or dust coming from an open-cast mine, the devolved matter of pollution control would be trespassing on the reserved matter of coal-mining. Section 29(3) allows the courts to look at the purpose of the legislation in pollution control and allow the provision to stand even though it affects a reserved matter. 5.13

Section 29(4) deals with a special category of overlap between reserved and devolved matters. It refers to Scots private law and Scots criminal law. Where legislation affects either of these two areas and the legislation would not otherwise have related to a reserved matter, it will be treated as a reserved matter unless its purpose is to make the law apply consistently to reserved matters. The effect of this subsection is to act as a 'catch-all' for any legislation which would normally relate to a devolved matter but because it changes the private law or criminal law must be regarded as relating to a reserved matter until it is proved that it is necessary to bring the Scots law into line with U.K. law.

As we all know, the law does not remain static and the Scotland Act recognises that there may have to be changes in the contents of Schedules 4 and 5 to take account of changing circumstances. Section 30(1) states that Schedule 5 shall have effect and then goes on at subsestion (2) to allow for modifications of the boundaries between devolved and reserved matters. The modification or adjustment may be made by an Order in Council which has to be approved by the U.K. Parliament and the Scottish Parliament. Amendments to the Scotland Act other than Schedules 4 and 5 are authorised by section 114(1).

Section 30(3) states that the functions exercisable (or not exercisable), in or as regards Scotland, may be specified in an Order in Council. This subsection was apparently inserted by the Government to regulate the devolution arrangements for sea fisheries. It aims to enable the government to clarify which existing functions may be transferred to Scottish Ministers under section 53 so that Scottish Ministers and U.K. Ministers will not attempt to exercise the same functions.[14]

---

[14] For a detailed discussion of s. 30(3) see Himsworth and Munro, *The Scotland Act 1998* (1999), p. 43.

Reserved matters

5.14 It was expected that a number of matters would be reserved to the U.K. Parliament. The Scottish Constitutional Convention suggested defence, foreign affairs, immigration and nationality, social security policy, and central economic and fiscal responsibilities. The Government's White Paper added a few more including the constitution of the United Kingdom, common markets for goods and services, employment legislation, regulation of certain professions, transport safety, broadcasting, abortion and equality legislation.

The reserved matters are detailed in Schedule 5 of the Act. The Schedule is in three parts: Part I contains general reservations; Part II contains reservations grouped by subject matter; and Part III contains explanatory and interpretative provisions. The Schedule has to be read as a whole since a subject may be reserved under one paragraph but part of it excepted in another.

5.15 Part I contains general reservations under the headings of the constitution, political parties, foreign affairs, public service, defence and treason. Paragraph 1 states that certain aspects of the constitution are reserved matters, including succession to the Crown, the Union of the Kingdoms of Scotland and England, the Parliament of the United Kingdom, and the continued existence of the supreme courts of Scotland, the Court of Session and the High Court of Justiciary. Additional specific matters are reserved in paragraph 2(2), (3) and (4) and these include honours and dignities, the management of the Crown Estate and the functions of the security service, secret intelligence service and GCHQ. There are exceptions to the general reservation at paragraph 2(1) and these include the royal prerogative and other executive functions, functions exercisable by a person acting on behalf of the Crown or any office of the Scottish Administration.

Paragraph 7 relates to foreign affairs and reserved matters involving international relations, E.C. and international organisations, regulation of international trade and international development assistance and co-operation. The paragraph does not prevent Scottish ministers or representatives of the Scottish Parliament from consulting with international organisations and other countries but does not allow the Scottish Ministers or others to purport to speak for the United Kingdom or reach agreements that commit the United Kingdom. Paragraph 7(2)(b) allows Scottish Ministers to assist Ministers of the Crown with international relations and this will be appropriate particularly in E.U. negotiations where a devolved matter is under discussion. Paragraph 7(2)(a) also specifically requires that the Scottish Parliament and Scottish Executive need to observe and implement international obligations, convention rights and Community obligations.

The civil service is a reserved matter[15] but matters relating to the staff of the sheriff courts, the procurators fiscal and officers of the High Court of Justiciary and the Court of Session are not reserved, thus allowing these staff to be transferred to the Scottish Administration. However the staff of the Scottish Ministers and the Lord Advocate are members of the Home Civil Service[16] and their terms and conditions of service, etc., will not be matters upon which the Scottish Parliament may legislate.

As one might expect, the defence of the realm and most matters relating to the armed forces are reserved matters.[17] The Parliament may legislate on civil defence functions and may also confer enforcement powers on the armed forces with respect to sea fishing.

Part II of the Schedule is highly detailed in places and very 5.16
general in others. Entitled "Specific Reservations", it is set out first in 'Heads', such as "Head B—Home Affairs", then in sections, such as "Section B1. Misuse of Drugs". Under each section specific matters will be detailed as being reserved, followed by any exceptions to the reservations, or any interpretation of the reservation.

The various Heads are as follows, with short notes on their contents.

Head A—Financial and Economic Matters. This Head includes general fiscal, economic and monetary policy, the issue of money, taxes and excise duties, government borrowing and lending, the exchange rate and the Bank of England. Local taxes to fund local authority expenditure is excepted. The currency, banking and financial services, financial markets and money laundering are also reserved matters.

Head B—Home Affairs. These matters tend to be matters which are within the remit of the Home Office and include the possession, production, supply, import and export, and trafficking in drugs; the Data Protection Act 1998; all aspects of elections for the U.K. Parliament, European Parliament and Scottish Parliament; the franchise for local elections (the Scottish Parliament may legislate for local elections); firearms; classification of films, cinemas and videos; immigration and nationality; scientific procedures on live

---

[15] para. 8.
[16] s. 51.
[17] para. 9.

animals; national security, interception of communications, official secrets and terrorism; betting, gaming and lotteries; emergency powers and extradition. Some of these matters were in fact previously exercised by the Secretary of State for Scotland under an executive arrangement and it is anticipated that they will be transferred to Scottish Ministers using an order under section 63.

Head C—Trade and Industry. The general headings for these reserved powers are business associations; insolvency (although there are exceptions here to take account of the differences in insolvency law and practice in England and in Scotland); competition; intellectual property; import and export control; sea fishing outside the Scottish zone, except in relation to Scottish registered fishing boats; consumer protection; product standards, safety and liability; weights and measures; telecommunications and wireless telegraphy; postal services; and research councils.

Head D—Energy. In general, the provision and supply of energy is a reserved matter whether the type of energy is electricity, oil and gas, coal or nuclear energy. There are some exceptions such as pollution control in respect of electricity, the manufacture of gas and the conveyance, shipping and supply of gas otherwise than through pipes and certain environmental matters with regard to coal.

Head E—Transport. The main methods of transport are mentioned here—road, rail, marine and air—and specific reservations and exceptions are made. For instance, in the section on rail transport, the provision and regulation of railways is reserved but grants to provide railway services are excepted.

Head F—Social Security. This reservation is couched in general terms to include the social security system and how it is delivered rather than specifying individual statutes or types of benefits. Illustrations are given and include national insurance, social fund, administration and funding of housing benefit, council tax benefit and so on. The power to require people such as employers to keep records and supply information is also reserved. The exceptions to the social security benefit scheme refer to the promotion of social welfare by local authorities. The Head also includes sections relating to child support, occupational and personal pensions and war pensions.

Head G—Regulation of Professions. Various professions are specified here so that their regulation is a reserved matter. These are architects, auditors and health professionals, such as pharmacists, vets, doctors, dentists, nursing personnel and osteopaths.

Head H—Employment. The reserved matters here relate to employment and industrial relations (except provisions regarding agricultural workers); health and safety, although some matters involving public safety are excepted, *e.g.* food safety; job search and support, except for careers services and certain duties regarding Scottish Enterprise and Highlands and Islands Enterprise.

Head J—Health and Medicines. Under this head are a number of matters involving moral or ethical aspects such as xenotransplantation, embryology, surrogacy, genetics and abortion. One of the most contentious issues in the parliamentary debates was the inclusion of abortion as a reserved matter since it comes within the health and criminal areas, both of which are devolved. The Government's arguments were that these ethical issues should remain within the powers of Westminster so that all parts of the British mainland were treated the same. Also under this Head are issues relating to medicines and poisons.

Head K—Media and Culture. Again some of the reserved matters here caused controversy, particularly those which reserve broadcasting to Westminster. However, it is likely that section 63 orders will be used to ensure that Scottish ministers are consulted before members (with Scottish interests) of the broadcasting regulatory bodies are appointed and before the National Governor for Scotland of the BBC is appointed.

Head L—Miscellaneous. The independence of the judiciary in Scotland is further protected by reserving the power to determine their salaries. Scottish Ministers are responsible for the payment of those salaries from the Scottish Consolidated Fund. Equal opportunities issues are also reserved although there are two exceptions here. The Scottish Parliament may legislate to encourage the observance of equal opportunities but this may not involve the use of prohibition or regulation. The Scottish Parliament may also impose duties on office-holders of the Scottish Administration or Scottish public authorities to ensure that they carry out their functions giving due regard to meeting equal opportunities requirements. Similar duties may be imposed on cross-border public authorities with respect to their Scottish functions. Also included under this Head is a reservation regarding the designation of timescale, time zones, the subject-matter of the Summer Time Act

1972 and issues relating to the calendar and the date of Easter. Excepted from the reservation are computations of legal periods of time so that the Scottish Parliament may legislate to change, for instance, the periods of prescription used for the enforcement of obligations. The term dates used for legal documents and Scottish bank and public holidays are also excepted.

5.17 The list of reserved matters is quite long although this was to be expected. The list will also change over time as new U.K. legislation is passed which adds new reserved matters or existing statutes mentioned in the Schedule are amended or repealed. There is however, no provision in the Act to allow for official reprints to be published to update it as it is amended. It may therefore become difficult to ascertain what the reserved powers are.

Apart from the matters stated in section 29 and Schedules 4 and 5, the Scottish Parliament may legislate on any other matter since it is by implication a devolved matter. The Parliament also has the power to amend or repeal existing Acts of the Scottish Parliament, which relate to devolved matters.

Scrutiny of proposed legislation

5.18 Before a Bill is presented to the Scottish Parliament for scrutiny and enactment, it must go through a pre-legislative scrutiny phase, which is designed to ensure that the Parliament does not legislate outwith its competence.

A Bill may be presented by a member of the Scottish Executive, by a committee of the Parliament or by an individual member. The processes for the pre-legislative scrutiny are slightly different for each type of Bill and these will be discussed separately below. However, it should be recalled that the Law Officers have the power to refer a Bill (or a provision in a Bill) to the Judicial Committee of the Privy Council (JCPC) if they believe that the bill is outwith the legislative competence of the Parliament. This power is exercised in the four-week period after the Bill has gone through its legislative stages and before it receives the Royal Assent. A similar power is accorded to any Secretary of State under section 35 where they believe the Bill is incompatible with Convention rights or E.C. law or the interests of defence or national security, or if they believe that the Bill modifies a law which relates to a reserved matter and there is reasonable ground to believe the modification will have an adverse effect on the law.

Before a Bill is presented to Parliament, the member of the Scottish Executive presenting it must make a statement that the provisions of the Bill are, in their view, within the legislative competence of the Parliament.[18] The Presiding Officer must also consider the Bill before it is submitted to Parliament and state whether in his view it is within legislative competence.[19]

(1) Executive Bills

The general stages of any Bill are set out in section 36. The Parliament's Standing Orders must include these general stages but may also make a provision for an accelerated procedure where a Bill has to be passed quickly in an emergency. Standing Orders may also provide a different procedure for Bills that restate the law, repeal spent legislation and Private Bills. If a Bill has been referred to the JCPC under section 33(1) on the *vires* of the Bill, and the JCPC has upheld the reference, the Standing Orders must include a phase to allow for a reconsideration of the Bill. 5.19

The Consultative Steering Group (CSG) proposed Standing Orders for the Parliament, suggesting a model for the passage of Bills and these were incorporated into a transitional statutory instrument.[20] One of the CSG's proposals was that Bills should be subjected to extensive consultation before they are presented to Parliament and this should continue throughout their passage. This will help to ensure that any ambiguities or anomalies are resolved early in the process and will also meet the Parliament's stated objective of encouraging maximum public involvement in the work of the Parliament. The CSG was keen to ensure that the consultation by the Scottish Executive was not just cursory but was appropriate in the circumstances and recommended that a memorandum should accompany the Bill, stating what consultation had taken place, an explanation of the Bill's purpose, an estimate of the costs, benefits and financial implications, and its impact on other issues such as equal opportunities, sustainable development and so on.

The Standing Orders give a three-stage process, but in reality, there are five, one pre-legislative phase and a post-legislative phase before Royal Assent.

(a) Introduction of the Bill and consideration by the relevant committee. The Bill is introduced by being lodged with the Parliamentary Clerk who is then responsible for giving notice of the Bill in the Parliament's Business Bulletin.[21]

---

[18] s. 31(1).

[19] s. 31(2).

[20] The Scotland Act (Transitory and Transitional Provisions) (Standing Orders and Parliamentary Publications) Order 1999 (S.I. 1999 No. 1095).

[21] Standing Orders, Rule 9.2.

No bill can be introduced, unless it is a Budget Bill, which will authorise sums to be paid out of the Scottish Consolidated Fund. The Presiding Officer is required to make a statement that the Bill is, or is not, in his view within legislative competence. The Executive memorandum is also included. The Bill is then authorised to be printed and published with its accompanying documents.

(b) The Bill then enters Stage 1 of the legislative process. It is sent to the relevant committee where the principles of the Bill are considered. The committee prepares a report for the Parliament plenary. The report may include comments on the Executive memorandum accompanying the Bill and the committee may recommend further evidence be obtained if it considers that the memorandum is deficient. There is then a debate and vote in Parliament plenary on the principles of the Bill.

(c) If approved, the Bill passes to Stage 2, where it is referred to one or more committees for detailed consideration. Standing Order 9.5.3 states that there must be a period of at least two weeks between Stage 1 and Stage 2. Any MSP may propose amendments at this stage for consideration by the committees. The Bill is considered in detail and amended as appropriate. The committee stage may be held in Parliament plenary if necessary.

(d) After a lapse of two weeks,[22] the Bill then moves to Stage 3 where the amended Bill is sent back to the Parliament plenary. If the amendments confer powers to make subordinate legislation, the Bill must be referred to the Subordinate Legislation Committee to consider and report on these amendments. There will be a debate and vote in the Parliament and amendments may be made although these are likely to be tightly controlled and would not include reopening issues which had previously been discussed at any earlier stage.

A fifth and final stage is the submission for Royal Assent by the presiding officer under section 32. The Bill must wait for four weeks before being given the Royal Assent to give the Law Officers time to consider its implications and whether they need to make a reference to the JCPC under section 33. It also allows the Secretary of State to consider whether an order under section 35 needs to be

---

[22] Standing Orders, Rule 9.5.3.

made. The four-week period may be curtailed if the Law Officers or Secretary of State indicate that they do not intend to refer the Bill.

Table 5.1

Procedure for passing an Executive Bill

Pre-legislative scrutiny	Draft Bill or proposals. ↓ Committee scrutiny. ↓ Introduction of Bill with Executive Memorandum Statement by member of Scottish Executive and presiding officer as to legislative competence. ↓
Stage 1	Committee considers and reports on general principles. ↓ Parliament plenary debates and votes on general principles. ↓
Stage 2	Committee considers details. Amendments proposed. ↓
Stage 3	Parliament plenary considers details and amendments. Debate and vote on Bill. ↓ Parliament votes in favour of the Bill. ↓
Post-legislative scrutiny	Four week period begins. ↓

Legal challenges by Secretary of State or Law Officers.		
Yes ↓	↑	↓ No
Reconsideration of Bill as amended by challenge →	Debate in Parliament plenary and vote	ROYAL ASSENT

(2) Committee Bills

This is a new development in U.K. parliamentary affairs and 5.20 indicates the view of the government that the MSPs should be involved in the work of government. The committee system of the Scottish Parliament is therefore in many ways likely to prove more powerful than its counterpart in Westminster.

The Presiding Officer, Sir David Steel, gave his view on the importance of the committees to the work of the Parliament. "I hope that we can develop a climate in the Parliament where members will make their reputations in the committees. These will be the real driving force of this Parliament."[23]

The CSG recommended that committees should be given the right to initiate legislation. The committee would conduct inquiries into whether legislation was required and report on this to the Parliament plenary with a recommendation for legislation. The Scottish Executive has five 'sitting days' to decide whether or not to bring forward legislation. If it declines to bring legislation forward, the Parliament plenary may decide to adopt the committee's report thus giving authority for the drafting of the necessary legislation. The Bill would then be introduced to the Parliament with a general debate (Stage 1) and if approved would then proceed to committee (Stage 2) and final debate in Parliament (Stage 3). At Stage 1 there is no requirement for a committee to consider the general principles of the Bill.[24]

(3) Members' Bills

5.21 As at Westminster, there are opportunities for MSPs to propose legislation. The CSG's proposals give two methods for an MSP Bill. The first involves the MSP submitting a written proposal to the relevant committee which may then decide to hold an inquiry into whether such legislation is required. If it decides to do so, the procedure will then follow the same route as committee Bills. The second method requires the MSP to obtain sufficient support form other MSPs to present a proposal to the Parliament plenary. The MSP first lodges the Bill with the Parliamentary Clerk and then within a month has to obtain the support of 11 other members who co-sign the Bill. The Presiding Officer has to rule on the legislative competence issue but thereafter the Bill will follow the same route as an Executive Bill.

(4) Budget Bills

5.22 A Budget Bill is an Executive Bill and will authorise payments to be made from the Scottish Consolidated Fund. It can only be introduced by a member of the Scottish Executive and does not require a financial memorandum, explanatory notes or policy memorandum. Stage 1 of the Bill does not include consideration of

---

[23] "Scottish Parliament User's Guide", *The Scotsman*, Sept. 1, 1999, p. 10.

[24] Standing Orders, Rule 9.15.

the general principles by a committee and Stage 2 is taken by the Finance Committee. The timescales detailed in Rule 9.5.3 do not apply to Budget Bills although Stage 3 may not begin earlier than 20 days after the introduction of the Bill and it must be completed before the expiry of 30 days from introduction.

A Budget Bill may not be amended except on the motion of a member of the Scottish Executive. If a Budget Bill falls or is rejected at any stage by the Parliament, another Budget Bill in the same terms may be introduced at any time.

(5) Private Bills

This is defined as a Bill introduced by an individual, a body 5.23 corporate or an unincorporated association for the purpose of obtaining powers to benefits in excess or in conflict with the general law. It can only be introduced on March 27 or November 27 each year (or the next sitting day following if either of these dates in not a sitting date).

At Stage 1 of a Private Bill, the committee may require the promoter to provide additional documents, advertise the Bill, require the Bill and papers to made available for public inspection and invite objections. The committee must prepare a report on the need for the provision in the Bill and detail any objections to it.

(6) Emergency Bills

The first measure to be considered by the Scottish Parliament 5.24 was an Emergency Bill, the Mental Health (Public Safety and Appeals) (Scotland) Act 1999. The procedure is an accelerated one but the Scottish Parliament must first agree to a motion proposed by a member of the Scottish Executive or a junior Scottish Minister that the Bill be treated as an Emergency Bill. Stage 1 dispenses with the need for a committee scrutiny and Stage 2 will be taken by a Committee of the Whole House. The usual time-limits of Rule 9.5.3 do not apply to an Emergency Bill. Rule 9.21.5 specifies that all of the stages of an Emergency Bill are to be taken on the day the Parliament decides to treat the Bill as an emergency one. However the Parliament may on the motion of the parliamentary bureau decide to take the matter over a longer period, and this is what occurred with the Mental Health Bill.

Subordinate legislation

The Act gives power to H.M. in Council, Ministers of the Crown 5.25 and Scottish Ministers to make subordinate legislation. If a section confers a power to make subordinate legislation but does not specify who is to exercise the power, then it is to be exercised by H.M. by Order in Council or by a Minister of the Crown by order.[25] This power is referred to in section 112(2) as an open power and its use gives more flexibility to the way in which the power is to be exercised. An important measure would be enacted by Order in Council, while a less important measure would be enacted as a ministerial order. Schedule 7 of the Act states the procedure to be used when enacting subordinate legislation under specific sections of the Act. For instance, subordinate legislation made under section 30 (legislative competence of the Parliament) has to be passed using Type A procedure which requires an Order in Council to be laid before each House of Parliament and the Scottish Parliament and approved by resolution of each House and the Scottish Parliament.

United Kingdom ministers are given the power under section 113(5) to modify Acts of Parliament although the power to modify the Scotland Act itself is not granted (s. 113(6)) unless the Scotland Act specifically grants them that power. Examples of the power of modification being granted can be seen at section 89 (cross-border public authorities) and section 107 (legislation to remedy *ultra vires* acts). Schedules 4 and 5 of the Act are not included in section 113(5), but the power to modify them is given at section 30(2).

Of course, the power to make subordinate legislation relating to devolved matters is granted to the Scottish Parliament and Scottish Ministers. Section 118 refers to the powers of U.K. ministers given in pre-commencement statutes which are to be exercised by the Scottish ministers. The procedures for scrutiny required by the pre-commencement statute are to be used by the Scottish Parliament in the same way. Thus if a pre-commencement statute requires that the subordinate legislation be approved by the affirmative procedure, *i.e.* a vote in favour, then this procedure must be used in the Scottish Parliament to enact subordinate legislation after devolution.

The CSG recommended that subordinate legislation proposals should be scrutinised by a delegated legislation committee which would consider the technical aspects of the subordinate legislation and whether it is *intra vires*. In addition, the subordinate legislation would be scrutinised by the relevant subject committee. If the subordinate legislation requires an affirmative resolution, the CSG recommended that the committee report to the Parliament plenary with its recommendations. If the negative resolution procedure is

---

[25] s. 112(1).

required, the committee would have 40 days to consider the subordinate legislation and if it wished to oppose it, might then report this to the Parliament plenary.

Section 63 of the Act allows the transfer of functions from a U.K. minister by Order in Council to the Scottish Ministers in so far as the functions relate to Scotland. This means that Scottish Ministers may have the power to make subordinate legislation in areas that are not devolved matters. The transfer can only be made with the approval of both Houses of Parliament and the Scottish Parliament.[26]

The procedure for the laying of subordinate legislation in the Scottish Parliament is given in Chapter 10 of the Standing Orders. 5.26
An instrument is laid before the Parliament by lodging it in the Clerk's office. The Clerk then refers the instrument to the subject (called the 'lead') committee and the Subordinate Legislation Committee. The Subordinate Legislation Committee may determine whether the attention of the Parliament should be drawn to the instrument on various grounds:

(a) The instrument imposes a charge on the Scottish Consolidated Fund or contains provisions requiring payments to be made to the Fund in consideration of any licence or consent or services to be rendered.
(b) The instrument seeks to exclude challenge in the courts.
(c) It purports to have retrospective effect although the parent statute does not confer such express authority.
(d) There appears to have been unjustifiable delay in its publication or laying.
(e) There is doubt as to its *vires*.
(f) It raises a devolution issue.
(g) It has been made by an unusual or unexpected use of the powers in the statute.
(h) For any special reason, its form or meaning could be clearer.
(i) Its drafting appears to be defective.
(j) Any other ground which does not impinge on its substance or the policy behind it.

The Subordinate Legislation Committee has to report to the Scottish Parliament and lead committee no later than 20 days after the instrument has been laid.

---

[26] Sched. 7, para. 2.

Rule 10.4 gives the procedure for a motion for annulment. Any MSP may, no later than 40 days after the instrument has been laid, propose a motion to the lead committee that nothing further is done under the instrument. A debate may be held on this motion in the committee. The MSP proposing the motion, the Scottish Executive member or junior Scottish Minister may attend the committee but not vote (unless they are a member of the committee). The lead committee must send its recommendations to the Parliament within 40 days of the instrument being laid.

Where an instrument may be made without the approval of the Parliament, any member may (within 40 days of the instrument being laid) by motion propose that the committee recommend that the instrument not be made. There are similar provisions for debate and recommendations to the Parliament as in Rule 10.4.

If an instrument requires the affirmative approval of the Scottish Parliament the lead committee will decide whether to recommend its approval.[27] The provisions regarding debate and recommendations to the Parliament are similar to Rule 10.4.

---

[27] Standing Orders, r.10.6.

CHAPTER 6

ELECTORAL PROCESS

INTRODUCTION

To many people the right to vote in elections is regarded as the most important, or possibly the only way, in which they can participate in the government of their country. The opportunities for the citizen living in Scotland to use this power have been increased by entry into the European Community and by the establishment of a Scottish Parliament. We now have four levels of government in which democratically elected members represent the people of Scotland: 6.01

(1) the United Kingdom Parliament at Westminster,
(2) the European Parliament,
(3) the Scottish Parliament,
(4) local councils.

The right of citizens to participate in democratic elections is the primary indicator that a government is truly accountable to the members of the society it represents. The fact that universal adult suffrage is a relatively modern phenomenon means that voting in elections is seen as a great privilege, particularly amongst women who had a much longer struggle than men to secure the right to vote. Unlike in certain other countries,[1] there is no legal duty to vote in the United Kingdom, although there is a duty to register as a voter in a constituency.

Principles of a democratic election process

In a modern democratic state every adult member of society should have an equal right to participate in the electoral process. It is therefore of fundamental importance that the electoral system is conducted in a way which will ensure fairness and integrity, in particular: 6.02

[1] *e.g.* Australia, Belgium, Greece and Italy.

(a) There should be a full franchise with only limited restrictions; *i.e.* every adult should have the right to vote.
(b) The voting system should be designed so as to result in both a government which is representative of the electorate and a government which will be able to govern effectively.
(c) The value of each vote cast should be equal to every other vote.
(d) The conduct of the elections should be regulated to ensure legality and fairness.

Development of the franchise in the United Kingdom

6.03 At the beginning of the nineteenth century only a small minority of the population had the right to vote. The qualification to vote depended on the ownership of property. Men who did not own property and all women were excluded from the franchise. The Representation of the People Act 1832 increased by 50 per cent the number of people entitled to vote but this still left over 85 per cent of the population disenfranchised. The Representation of the People Act 1867 doubled the number of people entitled to vote by extending the franchise to skilled and unskilled male labourers. This reform did not meet with universal approval because of a widespread belief that ordinary working men were not qualified to make judgments on such intellectual matters as the choice of suitable people to govern the country.

Votes for women

6.04 It was not until 1928 that women were granted the same rights to vote as men. The campaigns for equal rights for women in politics, education and certain professions had been running for nearly three-quarters of a century by this time, having begun in the mid-nineteenth century. The numerous separate campaigns were united as one large campaign under the National Union of Women's Suffrage Societies in 1897. The campaign became increasingly militant under the leadership of Emmeline and Christabel Pankhurst and began to win significant public support in 1909 when sympathies were aroused by the violent force-feeding of imprisoned suffragettes. Bills intended to give women rights to vote were introduced into Parliament in 1910, 1911, and 1913, but they had only half-hearted support from members of Parliament and none of them became law.

It was the changes in society, in particular the increasing tendency for women to work during the First World War, which finally led to the extension of the franchise to women. The suffragettes continued to campaign during the war years at a time when women were regarded as being of more value to society, as they were increasingly needed to replace men in jobs in offices and factories. Women began to have expectations of achieving equal status in society.

The Representation of the People Act 1918 introduced universal adult male suffrage and the right to vote in Parliamentary elections for all women over the age of 30 who were either local government electors or who were married to local government electors. The Parliament (Qualification of Women) Act 1918 provided that a woman would not be disqualified by sex or marriage from being elected to or sitting or voting as a member of the House of Commons. In 1948 the Representation of the People Act established a universal adult franchise (for people over the age of 21) on the principle; "one person, one vote".

ORGANISATION OF THE FRANCHISE

Earlier Representation Acts were consolidated into the Representation of the People Act 1983. Section 1 gives every person over 6.05 the age of 18, who is resident in a parliamentary constituency on the previous qualifying date and who is not subject to a legal incapacity, the right to vote. The franchise is not restricted to British citizens but includes citizens of the republic of Ireland and citizens of commonwealth countries, provided that residence requirements are satisfied.[2] Commonwealth citizens include British Overseas citizens, British Dependent Territories citizens and citizens of various commonwealth countries.[3] The qualifying date is currently October 10.[4] A temporary absence on the qualifying date does not necessarily prevent a person being recorded as resident at their main address.[5]

Persons who qualify as resident but who are unable to attend within the constituency on polling day may apply for a postal vote. One category of persons entitled to a postal vote is those unable or likely to be unable to go in person to the polling station because of

---

[2] Representation of the People Act 1983, s. 1(1)(b)(ii).

[3] British Nationality Act 1981, ss. 37 and 50.

[4] See also *Daly v. Watson*, 1960 SC 216; 1960 S.L.T. 271; *Dumfries Electoral Registration Officer v. Brydon*, 1964 SC 242; 1964 S.L.T. 266; *Keay v. MacLeod*, 1953 S.C. 252; 1953 S.L.T. 144.

[5] *Marr v. Robertson*, 1964 S.C. 448.

the general nature of their occupation, service or employment.[6] In the case of *MacCorquodale v. Bovack*,[7] it was confirmed that students who are normally resident in university accommodation but who have to vacate their accommodation during vacations are entitled to register as absent voters in the university constituency. In the case of *Dumble v. Electoral Registration Officer for Borders*,[8] it was held that Parliament envisaged the possibility of a person having a qualifying address in more than one constituency. Where a person had two careers, each of which was a major interest in their life and each of which required an address in a separate constituency, it was allowable that the name of that person should appear in the register of electors for each constituency.[9] Students therefore may be registered in the constituency where their university or college is located and in the constituency where their permanent home is located. Naturally they are only entitled to vote in one of the constituencies in which they are registered.[10] Absent voting is permitted for people who are unable to attend at a polling station. Sailors on ships and offshore oil workers, for example, are granted postal votes. Absent voting rights are also permitted on the grounds of physical incapacity where this is attested by a registered nurse. Applications relating to absent voting must be received by the registration officer before the prescribed deadline in order to be effective at a particular election.[11]

Each year the electoral registration officer in each constituency draws up a Register of Electors. The maintenance of the register is the responsibility of the local council. After canvassing all households in the constituency a draft register is published. At this stage amendments may be made. There is right of appeal against decisions in relation to the register to a sheriff, and then to an Electoral Registration Appeal Court, which comprises three Court of Session judges.[12] Once the register has been finalised it remains unchanged for the ensuing year and only a person whose name

---

[6] Representation of the People Act 1983, s. 19(1)(b)(i).

[7] 1984 S.L.T. 328.

[8] 1980 S.L.T. (Sh.Ct.) 60.

[9] See also *Scott v. Phillips*, 1974 S.L.T. 32; *Fox v. Stirk* [1970] 3 All E.R. 7; *Ferris v. Wallace*, 1936 S.C. 561; 1936 S.L.T 292.

[10] See also *Strathclyde Electoral Registration Officer v. Boylan*, 1980 S.C. 266 (Prisoner on remand).

[11] Representation of the People (Scotland) Amendment Regulations 1997 (S.I. 1997 No. 979 (S.88)) (amending the Representation of the People (Scotland) Regulations 1986 (S.I. 1986 No. 1111)).

[12] Representation of the People Act 1983, ss. 10 and 57.

appears on the register may vote.[13] There is, however, provision for the electoral registration officer to make corrections where there has been an error in drawing up the register such as the wrongful omission of a name.[14]

Legal incapacity

There are certain categories of people who are not entitled to vote because they suffer from a legal incapacity. They include minors (those under the age of 18), mental patients who are compulsorily detained, aliens, peers other than Irish peers and convicted persons in detention.[15] Anyone who is found guilty of certain election offences is not entitled to vote for five years.[16] 6.05a

Constituencies

Constituencies are geographical areas containing generally similar numbers of electors. Each constituency is represented in Parliament by the person who has secured a majority of votes cast in either a general election or, if the seat becomes vacant, in a by-election. 6.06

The Parliamentary Constituencies Act 1986[17] provides that the number of constituencies in Great Britain shall not be greater or less than 613 and the number of constituencies in Scotland shall not be less than 71. Constituencies are based partly on an electoral quota of voters. The number of people comprising the eligible voting population in the country is divided by the number of constituencies.[18] This quota is calculated separately for Scotland. There are currently 72 constituencies in Scotland for elections to the Westminster Parliament and 73 constituencies for elections to the Scottish Parliament. The extra constituency is created because Orkney and Shetland are divided into two separate Scottish Parliamentary constituencies, although they remain united for Westminster elections. The number of electors per constituency in Scotland is smaller than in many constituencies in England and

---

[13] Representation of the People Act 1983, s. 1(3).

[14] *ibid.* s. 11(2). Prior to this the only recourse for an error in the register was to appeal to the *nobile officium* of the Court of Session. See *Ferguson, Petr.*, 1965 S.C. 16.

[15] Representation of the People Act 1983, s. 3, as amended by the Representation of the People Act 1985, Sched. 4.

[16] Representation of the People Act 1983, s. 60.

[17] Parliamentary Constituencies Act 1986, Sched. 2.

[18] R. W. Blackburn, *The Electoral System in Britain* (1995, Macmillan), pp. 114–115.

Wales thus each vote has a higher value. The average number of voters per constituency in 1992 was 69,279 in England and 54,369 in Scotland. The Western Isles constituency had only 23,015 electors.[19] The Scotland Act has removed the requirement for there to be at least 71 Westminster constituencies in Scotland and established that in future the same electoral quota will be used as for England.[20] This will lead to a reduction in the number of Scottish constituencies at the next Boundary Commission review. The review is due between 2002 and 2006. Orkney and Shetland will still however be treated separately. They cannot be joined with any other constituency except each other for Westminster elections and they will remain as separate constituencies for Scottish Parliament elections.

Review of Constituencies

6.07 The constituency boundaries are reviewed regularly by the Boundary Commissions which report every eight to 12 years.[21] Regular review is required partly because of overall changes in the population and partly because of changes in residential patterns. There has been a recent trend of depopulation of city centres as people have moved to housing developments on the outer edges of the cities. There are four separate Boundary Commissions, one each for England, Scotland, Wales and Northern Ireland.[22] The Boundary Commission for Scotland reports to the Secretary of State. The latest review of constituencies was completed in 1994[23] and increased the number of constituencies in the United Kingdom from 651 to 659. Although one aim of the Boundary Commissions is to ensure that each vote cast has approximately the same value, equality in the number of voters is not the sole criterion by which constituency boundaries are set. They also consider factors such as special geographical considerations (*e.g.* for remote or island communities). The Speaker of the House of Commons heads each Boundary Commission. A senior judge acts as deputy and there are two other members from outwith the Houses of Parliament.

Boundary Commission reports are not always accepted without challenge. Changes in constituency boundaries may cause a political

---

[19] Office of Population Censuses and Surveys, Electoral Statistics 1992, 1992, HMSO, Series EL No. 19, p. 2.

[20] Scotland Act 1998, s. 86.

[21] Boundary Commissions Act 1992.

[22] Parliamentary Constituencies Act 1986, s. 2.

[23] Boundary Commission Reports for England, Scotland and Wales, H.C. 433–1 (1994), S.I. 1995 Nos 1036, 1037 and 1626.

party to lose a safe seat or may change a marginal constituency into a safe seat for one party. In 1969 a challenge was made on the ground that the Labour Government had not implemented all of the Boundary Commission recommendations.[24] They were reluctant to implement the report because of the potential political disadvantage. They nevertheless failed to win a majority of votes in the general election and the changes were introduced by the incoming Conservative Government. Boundary Commissions do not have unfettered powers but there are only limited grounds on which a court may review the exercise of a power, jurisdiction or authority such as that exercised by the Boundary Commissions. The most widely recognised statement of the possible grounds of challenge is that of Lord Diplock in the case of *Council for Civil Service Unions v. Minister for Civil Service*.[25] Lord Diplock stated that the grounds are: (i) illegality, (ii) irrationality, and (iii) procedural impropriety.

In *R. v. Boundary Commission for England, ex parte Foot*,[26] 6.08
Michael Foot M.P. sought an order of prohibition and injunctions to prevent the Boundary Commission putting its report to the Home Secretary. He alleged that the Commission had misinterpreted the rules. It was held that the Parliamentary Constituencies Act gave a wide discretion to the Boundary Commissions and the argument was rejected. As long as the Boundary Commissioners make recommendations which any reasonable body of men in their position could properly make, exercising the best of their skill and judgment in the light of the instructions given to them by Parliament the courts cannot intervene. In other words, only if their decision showed evidence of the type of irrationality classified as Wednesbury unreasonableness could the decision be challenged.[27] The term "Wednesbury unreasonableness" applies to a decision which is so outrageous in its defiance of logic or of accepted moral standards that no sensible person who had applied their mind to the question to be decided could have arrived at it.[28] The 1994 Boundary Commission review in Scotland was challenged in relation to the constituency boundaries of Ayr; Carrick, Cumnock and Doon Valley; and Port Glasgow and Kilmacolm.[29] It was argued that the Commission had fettered its discretion to make

---

[24] *R. v. Home Secretary, ex p. McWhirter* (1969) 119 N.L.J. 926; *The Times*, Oct. 21, 1969.

[25] [1984] 3 W.L.R. 1174.

[26] [1983] Q.B. 600.

[27] *Associated Picture Houses v. Wednesbury Corporation* [1948] 1 K.B. 233.

[28] For further discussion of the grounds for challenge, see V. Finch and C. Ashton, *Administrative Law in Scotland* (1997, W. Green), pp. 250–362.

[29] *Re Philip Roy Gallie M.P.*, O.H., Dec. 16, 1994.

suitable judgments in relation to each constituency by adopting a policy of adhering to the local government boundaries for the Regional, District and Islands councils, which were about to be replaced by single tier local authorities. It was also argued that the decisions of the Commission were unreasonable. Neither argument was successful. The Court of Session held that the Boundary Commission had operated within the statutory guidelines and that the decision was not so unreasonable that no reasonable authority would have arrived at it. The reluctance of the courts to intervene in a situation which could result in the substitution of the discretion of the court for that of an administrative body appointed by Parliament is understandable.

Criticisms of boundary commissions

6.09 The main criticism of the role of the Boundary Commissions stems from the fact that the reviews which take place are not based on a simple and objective quota system whereby the countries of the United Kingdom are divided into geographical constituencies solely on the basis of population size. The Commissions try to respect local government boundaries and to take into account any special geographical considerations. The process of review is also very slow. The population statistics on which a review is based are no longer valid when the Commissions report several years later. A third criticism is that the four Boundary Commissions operate autonomously and there is a body of opinion to the effect that a single authority, independent from Parliament, should act as Boundary Commission throughout the United Kingdom.[30]

Regions

6.10 In addition to the division into 72 or 73 constituencies, Scotland is divided into eight regions. The regions operate as constituencies for the European Parliament[31] and each return seven regional members to the Scottish Parliament.[32] The regions are:

Central Scotland, containing the parliamentary constituencies of: Airdrie and Shotts, Coatbridge and Chryston, Cumbernauld and Kilsyth, East Kilbride, Falkirk East, Falkirk West, Hamilton North

---

[30] H. Barnett, *Constitutional and Administrative Law* (2nd ed., Cavendish Publishing, 1998), pp. 491–492.

[31] European Parliamentary Constituencies (Scotland) Order 1996 (S.I. 1996 No. 1926).

[32] Scotland Act 1998, Sched. 1, para. 2.

and Bellshill, Hamilton South, Kilmarnock and Loudon, Motherwell and Wishaw.

Glasgow, containing the parliamentary constituencies of: Glasgow Anniesland, Glasgow Ballieston, Glasgow Cathcart, Glasgow Govan, Glasgow Kelvin, Glasgow Maryhill, Glasgow Pollok, Glasgow Rutherglen, Glasgow Shettleston, Glasgow Springburn.

Highlands and Islands, containing the parliamentary constituencies of: Argyll and Bute, Caithness, Sutherland and Easter Ross, Inverness East, Nairn, and Lochaber, Moray, Orkney and Shetland, Ross, Skye and Inverness West, Western Isles.

Lothians, containing the parliamentary constituencies of: Edinburgh Central, Edinburgh East and Musselburgh, Edinburgh North and Leith, Edinburgh Pentlands, Edinburgh South, Edinburgh West, Linlithgow, Livingston, Midlothian.

Mid Scotland and Fife, containing the parliamentary constituencies of: Central Fife, Dunfermline East, Dunfermline West, Kirkcaldy, North East Fife, North Tayside, Ochil, Perth, Stirling.

North East Scotland, containing the parliamentary constituencies of: Aberdeen Central, Aberdeen North, Aberdeen South, Angus, Banff and Buchan, Dundee East, Dundee West, Gordon, West Aberdeenshire and Kincardine.

South of Scotland, containing the parliamentary constituencies of: Ayr, Carrick, Cumnock and Doon Valley, Clydesdale, Cunninghame South, Dumfries, East Lothian, Galloway and Upper Nithsdale, Roxburgh and Berwickshire, Tweeddale, Ettrick and Lauderdale.

West of Scotland, containing the parliamentary constituencies of: Clydebank and Milngavie, Cunninghame North, Dumbarton, Eastwood, Greenock and Inverclyde, Paisley North, Paisley South, Strathkelvin and Bearsden, West Renfrewshire.

These regions are very large both in terms of population size and geographical area. They have been used as single member constituencies for the European Parliament but for the European Parliament elections from 1999 onwards a form of proportional representation, with the whole of Scotland being treated as one region, will be used in place of single member constituencies.[33]

Review of regions

6.11 The regions will be subject to review by the Boundary Commission in the same way as constituencies.[34] They may recommend changes to boundaries and changes to the number of members to be returned. Whenever there is a general review of constituencies, corresponding changes to the regions will be necessary. There are specific rules governing review of the regions.[35] The regions should all comprise the same numbers of electors so far as is reasonably practicable, having regard to special geographical considerations. No constituency can be split between regions. The number of regions is fixed at eight, but the number of members returned by each region may be varied. The same proportion of regional to constituency seats as currently pertains will be maintained.[36] There are currently 56 regional seats and 73 constituency seats therefore a proportion of approximately seven regional seats to nine constituency seats will be maintained at each review. Assuming that the number of regional seats is divisible by eight, each region will be allocated one-eighth of the number of regional seats. If the number is not divisible by eight a more complicated system of allocation will operate.[37] First as many seats as possible will be divided equally between all the regions. The left over seats, "residual seats", will then be distributed by the Boundary Commission. A maximum of one residual seat may be granted to a region. The Commission is required to take into account whether a region is comparatively over-represented or under-represented by the allocation of constituency and regional seats after the first allocation. This is to be calculated by ascertaining the total number of electors in each region and dividing this figure by the number of constituency and regional seats already allocated to the region. The residual seats are to go to under-represented regions, *i.e.* those with the highest number of electors for each seat. The Boundary Commission is required to follow similar procedures to the review of constituencies for the review of regions. Proposed changes must be advertised and wherever local authorities or a significant

---

[33] European Parliamentary Elections Act 1978, amended by the European Parliamentary Elections Act 1999.

[34] Scotland Act 1998, Sched. 1 paras 4–5.

[35] *ibid.* Sched. 1 para. 7.

[36] *ibid.*

[37] *ibid.* para. 7(2)(4).

number of individuals object to the proposed changes local inquiries must be held. Any report proposing changes to regions will have to be laid before the Scottish Parliament.[38]

Wards

Wards are the equivalent to constituencies for local authority elections. A local council area is divided into smaller wards, each of which elects a single councillor on a "first past the post" system, to represent the ward. Wards are also subject to periodic review by the Boundary Commission.[39] The Commission, when carrying out a review, may make proposals to the Secretary of State for effecting changes which appear to them desirable in the interests of effective and convenient local government.[40] They ways in which they may make changes are specified by statute.[41] 6.12

The Commission must first decide on the appropriate number of councillors required for effective and convenient local government. Then it is the duty of the Commission so far as is reasonably practicable to secure, as nearly as may be, electoral equality.[42] The requirement for parity of electors may yield to special geographical considerations.[43]

To summarise, each citizen of Scotland is represented by the following democratically elected members of government:

(1) A group of members of the European Parliament representing Scotland as a region.
(2) A member of the Westminster Parliament representing the constituency in which they are registered as an elector.
(3) A member of the Scottish Parliament representing that same constituency (Except in the case of Orkney and Shetland where the single constituency for the purposes of general elections is divided into two separate constituencies for elections to the Scottish Parliament).
(4) A group of members of the Scottish Parliament representing the electoral region.

---

38 Scotland Act 1998, Sched. 1, para. 3(5).

39 *Aberdeen City Council v. Local Government Boundary Commission for Scotland*, 1998 S.L.T. 613.

40 Local Government (Scotland) Act 1973, s. 16(2) and Sched. 5, as amended by the Local Government (Scotland) Act 1994.

41 *ibid.* s. 13.

42 *London Borough of Enfield v. Local Government Boundary Commission for England* [1979] 3 All E.R. 747 at 751.

43 *Re Shetland Islands Council*, O.H., Jan. 14, 1999.

(5) A member of the local council representing the ward in which he resides or works.

THE ELECTORAL PROCESS

6.13 The turnout for elections is often disappointingly low, especially for local government elections. The turnout for the first elections to the Scottish Parliament was only approximately 56 per cent of those entitled to vote. This has been attributed to several factors including, general political apathy, a failure to understand the voting system and a lack of accessibility caused by the restricted voting hours and the small number of polling stations. The fact that there are now four types of election must also be a factor which contributes to voter apathy.

Voting systems

6.14 Until 1999 the voting system which has been used for elections to all levels of government in the United Kingdom has been the majority system. A majority system is one whereby the person who obtains a majority of votes in a constituency is elected and the party with the most seats forms the government. Some of the political parties in the United Kingdom, notably the Liberal Democrats who have often been under-represented in Parliament in relation to the votes cast for their candidates, have campaigned for many years for a move towards a system of proportional representation. A system of proportional representation is one which aims to achieve proportionality between the votes cast for a political party and the seats which they gain. Until this year governments of the United Kingdom have clung tenaciously to the majority system of territorial representation on a first past the post basis. In this respect the United Kingdom has been lagging behind the rest of the world in terms of electoral systems. The majority of countries in Europe now use some sort of system of proportional representation. List systems are the most common. France uses a system which involves two ballots. When no candidate wins an absolute majority of the votes cast in the first ballot, a second ballot is held to determine which of the candidates who gained more than 12.5 per cent of the registered electorate in the first ballot are to be elected. Austria uses two systems; compulsory preferential voting for election to the House of Representatives and proportional representation for election to the Senate.

Simple majority system

The origins of the simple majority system lie in tradition. It is the easiest and probably the most economical method to administer. The simple majority voting system is not based on any form of constitutional law but has developed out of past political practice. It is known as the "first past the post" or "relative majority" system. It is based on single member constituencies. The candidate for whom the greatest number of votes is cast relative to each of the other candidates is elected as the member for the constituency. Where there are only two candidates he or she will have obtained the majority of the votes cast but where there are more than two candidates the elected candidate will frequently have obtained fewer votes than the total votes cast for the unsuccessful candidates. 6.15

The benefit of the simple majority system is that it will usually result in one political party gaining a majority of seats in the House of Commons and therefore being in a strong position to form a government and to carry out the policies proposed in the party manifesto. The democratic disadvantage of the simple majority system is that the party which wins the election may have obtained a majority of the Parliamentary seats without having obtained an overall majority of the votes cast. In the 1992 general election the Conservative Party secured 52 per cent of the seats despite having achieved only 42 per cent of the votes cast and in 1997 the Labour party gained 63 per cent of the seats having secured only 44 per cent of the votes cast. Minority parties fare particularly badly in a simple majority system. Their share of the vote may be substantial but because they fail to win many constituencies they are under-represented in Parliament.

The Electoral Reform Society calculates that the results of the general election of 1997 would have been much different if there had been a system of proportional representation in operation. The Labour Party would still have secured the most seats (44 per cent), the Conservative Party would have secured 30 per cent of the seats, the Liberal Democrats would have secured 17 per cent and other parties 10 per cent. This would have more than doubled the number of seats held by the Liberal Democrats and the other parties.

Membership of the European Community gave rise to increased pressure for change. The procedures for elections to the European Parliament were the subject of particular criticism. There was strong feeling that a vote in England, Scotland or Wales did not have the same value as a vote in other parts of the European Community, including Northern Ireland where a system giving 6.16

proportional representation was in use. The pressure to introduce a system of proportional representation even included litigation which attempted (but failed) to challenge the validity of the simple majority system of the European Parliament elections. The challenge was based on the ground that the rights of voters in Scotland under the Treaty of Rome were violated by the simple majority system operated under authority of the European Parliamentary Elections Act 1978.[44]

Several alternative systems exist, some of which offer proportional representation and others, which do not achieve proportional representation, but which would be an improvement on the simple majority system. Those which offer proportional representation are the additional member system and the single transferable vote. The alternative vote and the supplementary vote are enhanced majority systems.

Supplementary vote

6.17 The supplementary vote system was recommended by the working party on electoral systems set up by the Labour Party, chaired by Lord Plant, which reported in 1993.[45] It is based on single member constituencies. Voters express their preference by voting for two candidates. If no candidate secures 50 per cent of the vote, the second preferences cast for all candidates other than the top two are redistributed between the two leading candidates until a clear winner emerges. This system is effective where the number of candidates is small but it can become very complex where more than three candidates are standing in a constituency. If a system is too complex the process of calculating the result becomes expensive and slow. There is also a risk that the electorate will fail to understand the system and, in trying to vote tactically will fail to elect the candidate whom they prefer.

Alternative vote

6.18 This system also retains individual constituencies. The voter indicates their preferences in numerical order. A candidate who secures 50 per cent of the first preference vote is elected. If no candidate achieves 50 per cent the votes of the candidate who achieves the lowest number of first preference votes are redistributed according to their supporters' second preference

---

[44] *Prince v. Secretary of State for Scotland*, 1985 S.C. 8; 1985 S.L.T. 74.
[45] *Report of the Working Party on Electoral Systems*, Labour Party, 1993.

votes. This process is repeated until one candidate achieves an overall majority of the votes that have been cast relative to all the other candidates. This system ensures that the candidate with the most support in the constituency is elected. It does not solve the problem of under-representation for minority parties. Indeed it may lead to fewer candidates from the smaller parties being elected. Although the system represents a small improvement in comparison with a simple majority system the level of improvement is probably not sufficient to justify the additional costs of administering the elections.

Single transferable vote

Election on the basis of a single transferable vote would require a rearrangement of the current single member constituencies into larger regional units, each of which would return several members of Parliament. It would therefore retain the principle of territorial representation but with several members of Parliament rather than a single member. The method of calculation of transferable votes varies from country to country but it generally involves allocation on the basis of a quota for the first preference votes cast or the redistribution of the votes cast for the losing candidates. A single transferable vote system is used for local elections and elections to the European Parliament in Northern Ireland.[46] The single transferable vote is the most complex electoral system from the point of view of administration of elections but it is relatively easy for the voter to understand. The voter expresses their preferences in numerical order. A quota is decided which represents an appropriate share of the votes cast, *e.g.* in a six-member constituency the quota would be one seventh of the votes cast. If a candidate achieves this quota and obtains more votes than their rivals they are elected. Second and third preference votes are redistributed until the required number of candidates achieve the quota. If necessary the candidate with the lowest number is eliminated and their share of the vote reallocated until the quota is reached for all of the required elected members. A disadvantage of this system is that relatively slow and costly counting procedures are required. 6.19

Party list system

This system requires that a list of candidates be nominated by each political party. The votes for each party are calculated on a national basis and each party is awarded a number of seats in 6.20

---

[46] European Parliamentary Elections Act 1978, Sched. 1, para. 2(2)(b).

direct proportion to the votes cast. This system produces the fairest representation on a party by party basis but it is not without drawbacks. The major criticisms are twofold. First, it places too much power in the hands of the leaders of the political parties responsible for drawing up the party lists. Secondly, it deprives the citizen of a constituency member who is accountable to the local electorate for the standard of representation that they provide for those who have elected them. A party list system was used for the 1999 European Parliamentary elections but on a regional rather than a national basis. This will not provide the same degree of proportionality on a national basis but it has the advantage that it provides an element of local representation albeit for a large geographical area. The whole of Scotland is one region for the purposes of the European Parliamentary elections.

Additional member system

6.21 The additional member system is designed to maintain the advantages of single member constituencies whilst achieving overall proportionality between the votes cast for each party and the seats which they gain. People like to feel that they have an individual member of Parliament whom they can approach with their problems and who will take a special interest in local affairs. This is the system that is used in elections to the Scottish Parliament and the Welsh Assembly.

VOTING SYSTEM FOR ELECTIONS TO THE SCOTTISH PARLIAMENT

6.22 The Scottish Parliament has 129 members. There are 73 constituency members and 56 regional members—seven for each of the eight regions. At a Scottish Parliament election each voter has two votes. The first vote is used to elect a constituency member. These are elected in the same way as candidates under a simple majority system. Candidates may stand in a constituency on behalf of a party or as independent candidates. The candidate with the largest number of votes will gain the seat. The second vote is for a political party, or for a candidate standing as an individual, within a larger electoral area called a Scottish Parliament region. There are eight Scottish Parliament regions. Each region covers a group of constituencies and has seven additional seats in the Parliament. The members chosen to fill these seats are known as regional members. The total number of seats held by a political party depends on the number of constituencies it has won, plus the number of additional seats it wins in the regions.

The allocation of the regional seats is based on a comparison between the number of votes each party has received in the second ballot and the number of constituency seats it has won. A party may win some constituencies but not enough to reflect properly its share of votes in the regional ballot. That party may then gain one or more of the additional seats, according to the number of votes cast for it in the regional ballot. It may be the case that a party with significant support within a region fails to win any constituency seats. The additional member system allows such a party to be represented in the Parliament on the strength of the regional ballot. The Conservative Party benefited in this way in the 1999 Scottish parliamentary elections.

A party which already has enough constituencies to reflect its share of votes in the regional ballot will not be allocated any additional members. An independent candidate can stand as an individual in the regional ballot. They can gain one of the additional seats in their own right, if they win enough regional votes. In practice parties, or candidates standing as individuals, will generally need to win at least 6–7 per cent of the votes cast in a Scottish parliamentary region in order to have a chance of gaining an additional seat.

Example[47]

	Party 1	Party 2	Party 3	Party 4
Votes on regional ballot	61,974	63,362	61,189	37,206
Constituencies won	2	4	1	0
Additional seats allocated	2	0	3	2
Total seats in the Parliament	4	4	4	2

The number of votes cast for each party in the regional ballot is divided by the number of constituency seats gained plus one. The addition of one allows parties which have not won any constituencies to be included in the rest of the calculation.

[47] "The Scottish Parliament", Factsheet 1, Scottish Office (1999).

After that the party with the highest resulting figure gains the first additional seat. In the above example the total votes for Party 1 would be divided by three, the votes for Party 2 would be divided by five, the votes for Party 3 would be divided by two and the votes for Party 4 divided by one. The calculation is then repeated with the newly allocated seat being included in the parties total. Thus the votes for Party 4 would be divided by two in the second round and the next seat would go to Party 3. By the end of the process the ratio of votes to seats for each party has been made much more even. However, this is only in proportion to the regional votes cast not to the total regional and constituency votes cast.

Each political party puts forward a list of candidates for the regional ballot. These candidates are specified on the regional ballot paper. Only those whose names appear on the ballot paper can take up additional seats in that region. Candidates whose names appear on a party list for a region may also stand for election in a constituency, provided that they stand as a representative of the same political party. The names on the list are shown in a fixed order. The maximum number of names per party is 12. The first person named on the list will take the first additional seat which the party wins, the second person will take the second seat allocated to that party and so on. Any person who has already won a constituency seat will be passed over in favour of the next person on the party's list. A candidate standing as an independent may take one of the additional seats, depending on how many votes they receive. It is possible for an independent to receive a higher share of the vote than merits a single seat. In such a case the next seat goes to the party which achieved the next highest number of votes. It is not necessary for either parties or individuals to stand both for a constituency and in the regional list. Smaller parties may choose to stand only in the regional ballot, if they decide that they stand a stronger chance of winning seats in that part of the election. This allows parties or individuals to have a chance of becoming a Member of Parliament without having to expend funds on a large scale. If a regional seat becomes vacant between general elections it may be filled by the next person on the relevant party list without requiring a by-election.

The additional member system has the advantage of remaining close to the system that is already in use, while departing from it sufficiently to improve proportionality. The disadvantages are that it is more expensive to administer and that it is difficult to explain to the electorate.

ELECTIONS TO THE WESTMINSTER PARLIAMENT

General elections

The maximum term of years for any Parliament is five years and so general elections have to be held every five years.[48] The Prime Minister controls the timing of general elections. There is no constitutional regulation specifying an exact term for a Parliament or a fixed time of year for a general election. Although the dissolution of Parliament and the power to order the issue of writs for the election of a new Parliament is a prerogative power of the Crown, it is a power exercised in practice at the behest of the Prime Minister. This gives the Prime Minister the power to decide to hold a general election at a time which will be politically advantageous to their party. As long as the election is held within the five year period they can decide to hold an election at any time of the year and may even choose to hold it a year or more in advance of the end of the maximum term. In 1974 the Parliament lasted less than one year. In theory the Crown could refuse to dissolve Parliament if it were considered that a second general election within a short time would be contrary to the public interest. The Prime Minster is not bound by any constitutional rules with regard to the amount of notice which has to be given prior to dissolving Parliament. In 1974, Edward Heath gave only one day's notice before Parliament was dissolved.[49] 6.23

By-elections

By-elections take place following the death or retirement of a Member of Parliament. It may also be necessary to hold one when a Member of Parliament becomes disqualified from holding office as, for example, when a member is convicted of a criminal offence in the course of gaining election. Any Member of Parliament may put down a motion to the House, which if it is successful, will result in the Speaker making a warrant for the issue of a writ to commence the election procedure. Normally the Chief Whip of the party to which the former member belonged will move the motion for the writ. 6.24

---

[48] Septennial Act 1715, as amended by the Parliament Act 1911, s. 7.
[49] O. Gay and B. Winetrobe, "Putting out the Writs" [1997] P.L. 385.

Eligibility of candidates

6.25 There is no statutory definition of the qualifications for membership of the House of Commons. However, the House of Commons Disqualification Act 1975 disqualifies certain persons from membership of the House of Commons.

The following classes of persons are disqualified form membership of the House of Commons[50]: holders of judicial office; civil servants; members of the armed forces; members of police forces; members of non-commonwealth legislatures; members of the boards of nationalised industries, commissions, tribunals and other bodies whose members are appointed by the Crown.[51]

In addition to these specific disqualifications there are several other restrictions on eligibility:

(a) Persons under the age of 21. The Family Law Reform Act 1969 reduced the age of majority from 21 years to 18 years for many purposes, including the right to vote in elections, but the qualifying age for membership of the House of Commons remains at 21 years.

(b) Peers. Members of the House of Lords, or persons succeeding to a peerage, are not eligible for membership of the House of Commons. A person who succeeds to a peerage may disclaim their peerage and restore their eligibility to be a member of the House of Commons.[52] If a person who is a serving member of the House of Commons succeeds to a peerage they either have to disclaim the peerage within one month or resign from the House of Commons.

(c) Persons suffering from mental illness. If an elected Member of Parliament is authorised to be detained on grounds of mental illness, the Speaker of the House is notified and, if the illness is confirmed, the Member's seat is declared vacant.[53]

(d) Members of the clergy. A person may not stand for election to the House of Commons if they have been ordained to the office of priest or deacon or who is a minister of the Church of Scotland.[54] A clergyman or woman may relinquish their office and thus become eligible to stand for election.[55]

---

[50] House of Commons Disqualification Act 1975, s. 1 and Sched. 1.
[51] *ibid.* Sched. 1, Pt. II.
[52] Peerage Act 1963.
[53] Mental Health Act 1983, s. 141.
[54] House of Commons Disqualification Act 1975, s. 10(2).
[55] Clerical Disabilities Act 1870.

(e) Bankrupts. A person who is declared bankrupt may not be elected to the House of Commons. If an existing Member is declared bankrupt they are barred from sitting or voting in Parliament until the bankruptcy is discharged by the court or the adjudication annulled.[56]

(f) Persons convicted of certain crimes. Those sentenced to more than one year in prison are disqualified during their sentence or while unlawfully at liberty.[57] Persons convicted of treason are disqualified from election to Parliament. If a Member of the House of Commons is convicted of treason they may not sit or vote until a pardon has been received or the sentence of the court has expired.[58]

(g) Persons found guilty of corrupt practices during elections. If a person is found guilty of corrupt practices during an election they may be disqualified from taking up their seat in the House. If the corrupt practice was only discovered after the election, the Member may be disqualified from sitting in Parliament. In December 1997 charges of election fraud were made against Mohammed Sawar, the Member of Parliament who had been elected to represent the Govan constituency. He was suspended from the House but was reinstated on his acquittal in 1999. A disqualification for corrupt practices lasts for a period of five years for any constituency and for an additional five years in relation to the constituency in which the offence took place.

Choice of candidates

On the whole the citizens of the United Kingdom do not select 6.26
their government directly. Candidates for election are selected by political parties to represent constituencies (for the Westminster and Scottish Parliaments) and regions (for the Scottish and European Parliaments). The process of selecting these candidates is determined by the procedural rules of each party. Occasionally individuals who are not aligned to a political party put themselves forward for election but they are rarely elected. Their chances of success have been increased in relation to the Scottish Parliament however. It appears that the electorate may be more willing to use one of their votes to support an individual when they have a second

---

[56] Insolvency Act 1986, s. 427.
[57] Representation of the People Act 1981, s. 1.
[58] Forfeiture Act 1870, ss. 2 and 7.

vote which they can use to express their preference for a political party.

ELECTIONS TO THE EUROPEAN PARLIAMENT

6.27 The system of elections based on individual constituencies returning a single member on the basis of territorial representation and "first past the post" has been replaced by a system of proportional representation similar to that used for the Scottish Parliament with effect from the June 1999 European Parliamentary election. Scotland will be a single region of the United Kingdom returning eight members from party lists. Individual candidates may also be listed.[59]

In *Prince v. Secretary of State for Scotland*,[60] voters in the elections to the European Assembly sought declarator of their right to a system of proportional representation against the Secretary of State and interdict against the returning officer from conducting the election. The basis of the claim was that the existing system was *ultra vires* and contrary to section 2 of the European Communities Act. The interim interdict was refused because it had not been established that the election system was *ultra vires*.

ELECTIONS TO THE SCOTTISH PARLIAMENT

6.28 The first election was held on May 6, 1999. Elections to the Scottish Parliament normally take place every four years. If circumstances arise which cause an extraordinary general election to be held before the four year term has expired it does not affect the normal quadrennial cycle. Therefore if an extraordinary general election is held after three years, the new Parliament will only last for one year. If, however, an extraordinary general election is held within six months before an ordinary general election would be due the extraordinary general election replaces the ordinary general election. Therefore if there was an extraordinary general election after three years and seven months, the duration of the newly elected parliament would be four years, Despite the fact that some members of the Scottish Parliament are elected as constituency representatives and others are regionally elected members, all of the members have equal status once they have been elected.

---

[59] European Parliamentary Elections Act 1978, s. 3, as substituted by the European Parliamentary Elections Act 1999.

[60] 1985 S.L.T. 74.

Eligibility of candidates

The rules relating to disqualification for election to the Scottish Parliament are broadly similar to the rules for the Westminster Parliament.[61] Most of the disqualifying categories apply to the Scottish Parliament as well as to the Westminster Parliament.[62] The following groups are disqualified: those holding judicial office; civil servants; members of the armed forces; members of police forces; and members of a legislature outwith the commonwealth. 6.29

The major differences in eligibility are that: (i) citizens of the E.U. resident in Scotland can be members of the Scottish Parliament[63]; (ii) there is no disqualification for peers; and (iii) clergymen and women are not disqualified.[64]

Those disqualified because they hold judicial office include judges in the Court of Session and sheriffs. The Lords of Appeal in Ordinary are expressly excluded from membership of the Scottish Parliament.[65]

The Scotland Act makes provision for further disqualifications for the holders of certain public appointments to be made by Order in Council. This list may differ from the equivalent list of disqualifications for the Westminster Parliament.[66] Certain posts will be incompatible with membership of the Scottish Parliament but not with membership of the Westminster Parliament and vice versa. It is also possible to have disqualifications that relate only to office holders in a particular region or constituency. The Scottish Parliament may resolve to disregard a disqualification in an individual case.[67] This can only be done if the following conditions are met: (i) the ground for disqualification no longer exits; (ii) Parliament considers that it is proper for the disqualification to be disregarded; (iii) the disqualification has not been determined by the courts (iv) the disqualification is not the subject of current legal proceedings.

The practical consequence of this provision is that a member of Parliament who holds a disqualifying office may continue as a member provided that he resigns the other office. The general disqualifications which apply both to the House of Commons and to the Scottish Parliament cannot be disregarded by the Scottish Parliament. The following persons are disqualified: persons under

---

[61] Scotland Act 1998, s. 15.

[62] House of Commons Disqualification Act 1975, s. 1 and Sched. 1.

[63] Scotland Act 1998, s. 16(2).

[64] *ibid.* s. 16 (1).

[65] *ibid.* s. 15(1)(c).

[66] House of Commons Disqualification Act 1975, Sched. 1.

[67] Scotland Act 1998, s. 16(3)–(5).

21 years of age, persons suffering from severe mental illness, bankrupts, persons convicted of certain crimes and persons convicted of election offences.

In the case of mental illness the Presiding Officer has to arrange for the member to undergo a medical examination. Disqualification will take effect if a member has been detained on the ground of mental illness and six months have elapsed without their recovering sufficiently to be released.[68] Members who are declared bankrupt are suspended when the court order is made. Their seat is declared vacant after six months unless the order has been recalled.[69]

If a disqualified person is returned as a member their election is void and the seat is then vacant. If a member becomes disqualified during office they cease to be a member and the seat becomes vacant. In the case of bankruptcy and insanity, where there is a six month delay before the disqualification takes effect the member is suspended from office in the interim period and cannot participate in any parliamentary proceedings. The Parliament may withdraw their rights and privileges.[70]

Proceedings for disqualification

Disqualification claims during election proceedings

6.30 A claim that a candidate is disqualified is dealt with by an election petition under the Representation of the People Act.[71] A petition must be lodged within 21 days after the election. Petitions are considered by an election court which consists of two nominated judges of the Court of Session. Depending on the grounds of challenge the respondent to the petition will be either the returning officer or the member whose eligibility is being contested.[72] In order to discourage frivolous applications there is a requirement that the applicant must provide caution of up to £5,000 for the expenses of the proceedings.

Disqualification claims at times other than an election period

6.31 A person who wishes to claim that a member is disqualified may apply to the Court of Session for a declarator to that effect.[73] The defender in such an action will be the member in person. The

---

[68] Mental Health Act 1983, s. 141, as amended by Scotland Act 1998, Sched. 8, para. 19.

[69] Insolvency Act 1986, s. 427.

[70] Scotland Act 1998, s. 17(4).

[71] 1983 Act, s. 121.

[72] *Stair Memorial Encyclopaedia*, (Butterworths, 1996), Vol. 15, paras 1436–1492.

[73] Scotland Act 1998, s. 18.

Court of Session may not make such a declarator if the Parliament has already resolved that the disqualification should be disregarded.[74] Parliament may not resolve to disregard a disqualification which has been declared by the Court of Session.[75] There is no appeal to the House of Lords from a Court of Session declarator that a member is disqualified. The decision is final. In the same way as for proceedings before an election court the applicant must provide security of up to £5,000 for the expenses of the action.

Vacancies

Constituency seats falling vacant

If a constituency member resigns, dies or becomes disqualified, the seat will be filled by means of a by-election in that constituency.[76] The Presiding Officer will determine the date of the by-election subject to a requirement that it must be held within three months of the vacancy occurring or coming to their notice.[77] A by-election will not be held if the last day on which it could be held is within three months of the scheduled date for the next general election. Generally this will mean that if a seat falls vacant within six months of the next general election it will remain vacant until the election. As general elections are normally scheduled in May this means that seats falling vacant after the first Thursday in the December prior to a general election year will be left vacant until the general election. Existing members are prohibited from standing as candidates in by-elections.[78] This means that a member who has been elected from a party list as a regional member cannot stand for election as a constituency member during the life of a Parliament. It is also not permissible to stand as a candidate for more than one by-election at a time. 6.32

Regional seats falling vacant

Where a member who has been elected as a regional member resigns, dies or becomes disqualified the seat is filled directly or is left vacant depending on the way in which the member was elected.[79] 6.33

---

[74] Scotland Act 1998, s. 18(3)(b).
[75] *ibid.* s. 16(5).
[76] *ibid.* s. 9.
[77] The exact date will be fixed according to Standing Orders.
[78] Scotland Act 1998, s. 9(6).
[79] *ibid.* s. 10.

If the member was returned from a party list, the seat is filled by one of the unsuccessful candidates on that party's list at the previous general election. The regional returning officer must ascertain which of the unsuccessful candidates from the list are willing to serve as regional members. The seat then goes to the available candidate whose name was the highest on the party list. This procedure avoids time being wasted by offering seats to unsuccessful candidates who are no longer willing or available to sit as members. The returning officer notifies the Presiding Officer of the name of the candidate at which time that candidate becomes a member of Parliament. If there are no available candidates left on the list the seat will remain vacant until the next election. It is therefore strategically important for each party to include sufficient names on their party list both to fill the places won at the election and to provide sufficient numbers to fill any seats becoming vacant during the life of the parliament.

If the member who has left was returned as an individual candidate from a regional list, then the seat remains vacant until the next general election.[80]

VOTING IN A REFERENDUM

6.34 Elections used to provide the only opportunity for members of the general public to assert their political power, but referendums have been used on occasion to ascertain the level of support for particularly important changes in the constitution of the United Kingdom. Every referendum requires statutory authority. Referendums have been held on: whether or not Ireland should remain part of the United Kingdom,[81] whether or not the United Kingdom should remain part of the European Community,[82] and devolution of government and legislative powers to Scotland and Wales.[83] The statute which gives the authority for the holding of a referendum will also specify the rules and regulations under which it will be held. The Scotland Act 1978 proposed the creation of a Scottish Assembly, with law-making powers in certain areas of devolved responsibility; it was, however, subject to the requirement that it would only come into force if, in the referendum of the Scottish electorate, it gained a majority of those voting and a majority of at

---

[80] Scotland Act 1998, s. 10(2).

[81] Northern Ireland (Border Poll) Act 1972.

[82] Referendum Act 1975.

[83] Scotland Act 1978; Wales Act 1978; *Scotland's Parliament*, Cmnd. 3658 (1997).

least 40 per cent of those registered to vote.[84] The result of the referendum showed that the Scotland Act was supported by a majority of those who voted but, as this voting majority was only equivalent to 32.8 per cent of those entitled to vote, the Act was repealed without coming into force.[85] Further referendums were held in 1997[86] with the referendum in Scotland producing a large majority in Scotland for the establishment of a Scottish Parliament and a comfortable majority for the proposition that it would have tax-raising powers. Although there have been calls for referendums on other political issues it is unlikely that the use of referendums will become widespread as they are seen as a challenge to the idea of representative democracy.

REGULATION OF THE CONDUCT OF ELECTIONS

As well as ensuring that an electoral system is in operation which is 6.35
fair, effective and accessible it is essential that the electoral process should be regulated so that it is as free as possible from corruption and coercion. "A wide and equal suffrage loses its value if political bosses are able to gerrymander constituencies so as to suit their own interests; there is no point in having an elaborate system of proportional representation if the electors are all driven in one direction by a preponderance of bribes and threats."[87] The rules on the conduct of elections are intended to secure fairness in the electoral process at individual constituency level.

The returning officer for each constituency is responsible for ensuring the proper conduct of elections. This role is normally filled by an official of the local council.[88] The purpose of the regulation of the conduct of elections is to ensure that there is fairness and a reasonable degree of parity between the candidates regardless of their financial resources. The regulations control the amount of expenditure and the manner in which it can lawfully be spent, proscribing certain unlawful practices and providing procedures for challenge in the event of irregularities during a campaign. Where there has been a failure to follow prescribed

---

[84] Scotland Act 1978, s. 85.

[85] Scotland Act 1978 (Repeal) Order 1979 (S.I. 1979 No. 928).

[86] *Scotland's Parliament*, Cmnd. 3658 (1997).

[87] R. Mackenzie, "Free Elections" in *Law and the Electoral Process* (H. Rawlings ed., Sweet & Maxwell, London, 1988), p. 19.

[88] Representation of the People Act 1983, s. 25.

procedures the court may grant relief for failure to follow procedures in certain circumstances. The case of *Curran v. Lord Advocate* concerned a failure on the part of an election agent to have the return and declaration signed in the presence of a justice of the peace as required by sections 81 and 82 of the Representation of the People Act 1983. An election agent, who had acted for Mohammed Sarwar in the 1997 general election petitioned for relief from the failure to comply with the terms of the Act. Evidence was accepted that the failure resulted from inadvertence on her part caused mainly by allegations against the candidate and the stressful and unpleasant media attention. It was held that relief could be granted where the failure to follow prescribed procedures was attributable to: (i) inadvertence, (ii) absence of bad faith, and (iii) that it was just and equitable in the circumstances that relief be granted.[89]

The focus of the regulation for elections to the Westminster Parliament is still the local campaign within the constituency or region.[90] This is seen by many commentators as anomalous since the bulk of the campaign expenditure is now devoted to mass media campaigns by political parties at national level.[91]

Each candidate must be nominated by 10 registered electors from the constituency in which he intends to stand. The sum of £500 must be deposited. The purpose of this requirement is to deter frivolous candidates. The deposit is refunded after the election provided that the candidate has secured five per cent of the votes cast.[92] Once a candidate has been nominated they must then nominate an election agent. The candidate may however nominate themself. A declaration that they are not disqualified from membership of the House of Commons is also required at this stage.

In the case of elections to the Scottish Parliament, the Secretary of State for Scotland has the power to make detailed rules governing the conduct of elections.[93] These will cover such matters as registration of electors, the appointment of returning officers, limitations on election expenditure by individual candidates and by

---

[89] 1999 S.L.T. 332, See also *Clark v. Sutherland* (1897) 24 R 821; (1897) 4 S.L.T. 363; *Munro v. Mackintosh*, 1920 S.C. 218; 1920 1 S.L.T. 93; *Pole and Scanlon, Petrs*, 1921 S.C. 98; 1921 1 S.L.T. 38; *Smith v. Mackenzie*, 1919 S.C. 546; 1919 2 S.L.T. 29.

[90] Representation of the People Act 1983, Sched. 1, as amended by the Representation of the People Act 1985.

[91] See M. Deans, *Scots Public Law* (1995).

[92] Representation of the People Act 1985, s. 13.

[93] Scotland Act 1998, s. 12.

parties and challenges to election results. The Secretary of State can apply with or without modification, the rules found in existing legislation regulating local, parliamentary or European elections although some matters, such as the management of the counting of the regional list votes need specific consideration.

Corrupt practices

Corrupt practices include bribery, treating and undue influence. 6.36
Undue influence may be caused by threats or attempts to intimidate electors. Although a completely secret ballot is preferable in order to give the voter confidence in the election process some concessions are made in order to ensure that investigations may be carried out if there is a suspicion that corrupt practices have taken place. It is possible to trace the identity of each voter from the serial number on the ballot paper. This number is recorded opposite the voter's name on the electoral register by the polling clerk at the time of voting.[94] Allegations of election fraud were made in 1997 against the candidate elected in the Glasgow Govan constituency. The allegations, which were not upheld, included a charge that personation of voters had taken place. There were also allegations of financial irregularities. Breaches of the restrictions on expenditure are the most common subject of allegations of corrupt practices.

Expenditure

Expenditure by or on behalf of candidates for election is strictly 6.37
limited. The purpose of this restriction is to promote fairness by preventing the wealthy candidate gaining an unfair advantage by spending large amounts of money on the campaign in the constituency. A maximum limit is placed on expenditure on behalf of each candidate.[95] The Secretary of State is permitted to set and to raise the permitted amounts of expenditure, in line with inflation, by way of statutory instrument. Every candidate must appoint an election agent and all expenditure to promote the election of a candidate must be authorised by the candidate or their agent. A breach of this requirement is classed as a corrupt practice under electoral law.[96] Accounts must be kept of all expenditure on public meetings, advertisements and circulars, or other means by which the candidate

---

[94] Representation of the People Act 1983, s. 66.

[95] *ibid.* ss. 76 and 76A, as amended by the Representation of the People Act 1985.

[96] *ibid.* s. 75.

or their opinions are made known to the electors. A return of these accounts must be submitted to the returning officer within 21 days of the election result.

Where expenditure limits have been exceeded the result of the election may be challenged by petition to an election petition court comprising two judges of the Court of Session. In 1965 such a challenge was made to the election of Sir Alexander Douglas-Home who was at that time the Prime Minister and leader of the Conservative Party.[97] The defeated Communist Party candidate petitioned to have the election declared void on the ground that national party political broadcasts made by Douglas-Home were not authorised in writing by the candidate's election agent nor were they included in the statutory return of expenses. It was held that the broadcasts were not made with a view to promoting the election of the individual candidate in his constituency but rather to inform the public about the Party's national policies and therefore there had been no infringement of the statute by the respondent and the petition was refused.

An alternative way to challenge excessive expenditure is to seek an interdict to prevent or to halt expenditure which contravenes the statutory restrictions. An interdict was granted to prevent unauthorised expenditure in relation to local government elections in Lothian region in 1983.[98] Members of one political party petitioned the Court of Session to interdict the local authority, which was run by another political party, from distributing a publication known as the Lothian Clarion. They alleged that an article in the publication was calculated to promote the election of the majority party's candidates and to disparage candidates of the petitioners' party. An interim interdict was granted on the ground that the article complained of was calculated to promote the election of the majority party's candidates.[99]

More recently two local election candidates sought interdict preventing a trade union from carrying on an advertising campaign against the national government and its policies with a view to discouraging electors from voting for the political party for which the petitioners were standing. The interdict was refused on the ground that the statutory provisions were not contravened by an advertisement in the form of a generalised attack on one or more

---

97 *Grieve v. Douglas-Home*, 1965 S.C. 315; 1965 S.L.T. 186.

98 *Meek v. Lothian Regional Council*, 1983 S.L.T. 494.

99 See also *R. v. Tronoh Mines Ltd* [1952] 1 All E.R. 697; *DPP v. Luft* [1977] A.C. 962.

of the policies of a political party at the time of a general election or of local government elections throughout Scotland.[1]

The matter of restriction of election expenses has been considered by the European Court of Human Rights. Mrs Bowman, who had been prosecuted under section 75 for incurring expenditure with a view to promoting or procuring the election of a candidate in the 1992 general election whilst she was not authorised so to do, applied to the European Court of Human Rights. She claimed that there had been a breach of Article 10 of the European Convention on Human Rights which protects freedom of expression. She had in fact been acquitted because of a delay in bringing the prosecution. Mrs Bowman was executive director of the Society for the Protection of the Unborn Child. She distributed 25,000 leaflets in Halifax shortly before the 1992 general election outlining the views on abortion of the three main candidates. She alleged that section 75 of the Representation of the People Act 1983 amounted to a restriction on her freedom to express her views. The European Court of Human Rights recognised that the intention behind section 75 was not to restrict freedom of expression but rather to regulate expenditure so as to promote equality between candidates. This aim was considered to be legitimate. However, the means of achieving this legitimate aim need to be balanced against the fundamental democratic principle of freedom of expression and in particular, freedom of political debate during the period of an election campaign. The court ruled (by a majority of 14 to six) that Mrs Bowman had no other effective means of communicating information to the electorate on an issue which could affect the public perception of the candidates. Section 75, which limited the expenses that Mrs Bowman could legitimately incur to a maximum of £5, effectively operated as a total ban on her freedom of expression during the election period. This was made more unfair by the lack of any financial controls on the expenditure by political parties at a national level. There were also no restrictions upon the freedom of the press to support or oppose the election of any particular candidate. The restriction was held to be disproportionate to the purpose intended and was therefore a violation of Article 10. The court awarded the applicant a specified sum for legal costs and expenses.[2] 6.38

This case highlights the major anomaly in the regulation of election expenses. The restrictions on expenditure at constituency

---

[1] *Walker v. Unison*, 1995 S.L.T. 1226.

[2] Case 141/1996/762/959, *Bowman v. U.K.*, *The Times*, Feb. 23, 1998.

level were adequate to meet their purpose in times when election campaigns consisted of distribution of leaflets, hustings in local halls and doorstep canvassing. Nowadays the most influential elements of an election campaign are the national party campaigns in particular the party political broadcasts on television. There are however no restrictions on expenditure at a national level. This makes it very difficult for any minor party to mount a successful campaign when they have limited resources and the established political parties have substantial funds.

Broadcasting

6.39 Broadcasting is controlled by sections 92 and 93 of the 1983 Act. Expenditure on national party election broadcasts is met out of the central funds of each party. Party election broadcasts may only be made by the British Broadcasting Corporation and under the authority of the Independent Broadcasting Authority. Political advertising is not permitted on television or radio. Following the case of *Grieve v. Douglas-Home*[3] the law was amended to allow broadcasting authorities to incur expenditure in disseminating material relating to elections provided that the material does not take the form of advertisements.[4] No broadcast may be made without the consent of any candidate who appears in the programme.[5] If a candidate participates in a broadcast for the purpose of promoting their own election, every other candidate in the constituency must consent to the broadcast. Participation in a broadcast is taken to mean active participation. In *Marshall v. BBC*,[6] an objection was raised because a candidate who had refused to take part in a broadcast was filmed while canvassing in the streets. It was held that the broadcast did not breach any regulation. No offence had been committed because to "take part" in a broadcast about a constituency means to take an active part in the programme.

Independent broadcasting authorities are under a duty to maintain accuracy and impartiality.[7] Although direct television advertising by political parties is prohibited, each party is allowed a number of party political broadcasts.[8] The amount of time allocated to each

[3] 1965 S.C. 315; 1965 S.L.T. 186.
[4] Representation of the People Act 1983, s. 75(1)(c)(i).
[5] *Marshall v. BBC* [1979] 3 All E.R. 80.
[6] [1979] 3 All E.R. 80.
[7] Broadcasting Act 1990, s. 6.
[8] Registration of Political Parties Act 1998, ss. 13–15 disallow any political broadcast from a party which is not registered.

party is determined according to the proportion of the overall vote which the party secured at the previous election. This allocation applies during election campaigns and during other political campaigns such as political broadcasting prior to referenda. In 1979 a successful challenge was brought against the allocation of party political broadcast time prior to the Scottish devolution referendum. Allocation of time had been made to four political parties, three of which were campaigning in favour of the referendum proposals. The opponents of the referendum proposals argued successfully that they were being treated unfairly.[9] During the 1987 general election campaign the Scottish National Party challenged their allocation of party political broadcast time. The SNP claimed that they were being treated less favourably in Scotland when compared to other parties who campaigned throughout the United Kingdom.[10]

Registration of political parties

Problems have arisen when candidates have been nominated for 6.40
election as representatives of groups with titles which are designed to cause confusion on the part of the voters because of the similarity with the name of an established political party.
The case of *R. v. Acting Returning Officer For the Devon and East Plymouth Constituency, ex parte Sanders*[11] was a challenge by Sanders, who was the Liberal Democrat candidate for the Devon and East Plymouth constituency to the acceptance of the nomination of another candidate. This other candidate was nominated as the "Literal Democrat" candidate. Sanders applied for leave to move for judicial review of the returning officer's decision to accept the nomination papers as valid. The action failed for technical reasons, but it was held that it was arguable that the returning officer should not have accepted the nomination. This problem has now been resolved by the requirement for political parties to register their names and their pictorial symbols, which appear on ballot papers.[12] This decreases the risk that voters will be confused by parties with similar names. The register of political parties is used for the following elections, namely, Parliament, the European Parliament, the Scottish Parliament, the National Assembly for Wales, the Northern Ireland Assembly and local authorities.

---

[9] *Wilson v. IBA*, 1979 S.L.T. 279.

[10] *Wilson v. IBA (No 2)*, 1988 S.L.T 276; see also *Scottish National Party v. Scottish Television*, O.H., Apr. 15, 1997.

[11] [1994] C.O.D. 497; *The Times*, May 30, 1994.

[12] Registration of Political Parties Act 1998.

Irregularities in election procedures

6.41 Where there has been an irregularity in the conduct of the election procedures the election of a candidate may be declared void and the election has to be repeated.

An example of procedural irregularity arose in the case of *Miller v. Dobson*.[13] At a local government election two ballot papers were rejected at the count because polling officials at the polling stations had inadvertently omitted to stamp them with the official mark when issuing them to voters. After several recounts the candidate declared duly elected had a majority of one. The candidate who had narrowly lost petitioned the court for a declaration that the other candidate was not duly elected, by virtue of the Representation of the People Act 1983, s. 48(1), as the breach of the officials' duty had affected the result. The petitioner also sought a declaration under section 145(1) that she had been duly elected, or alternatively that the election was invalid and that a further election should be held. It was held that the election had to be declared invalid as the omission by the polling officials had affected the result. The court could not determine that another person had been duly elected and so a further election would have to be held.[14]

---

[13] *Miller v. Dobson*, 1995 S.L.T. (Sh.Ct.) 114.

[14] See also *Fitzpatrick v. Hodge*, 1995 S.L.T. (Sh.Ct.) 118; *Morgan v. Simpson* [1975] 1 Q.B. 151.

CHAPTER 7

THE UNITED KINGDOM PARLIAMENT

The "Sovereign in Parliament" is the supreme lawmaker in the United Kingdom. There are three elements to the proposition—the House of Commons, the House of Lords and the sovereign. In common with many of the legislatures of the world, the U.K. Parliament is bicameral, meaning that it has two chambers, both of which are involved in the law-making process. This chapter will discuss the place of each of the three elements in the constitution and consider the changes to them which are being brought about by the Labour Government's extensive programme of constitutional reform. These changes were referred to by the Lord Chancellor in a speech to the Constitution Unit when he said that the reforms are designed to produce a "maturer democracy with different centres of power." He answered critics of the programme by saying that there was a long tradition of constitutional reform and the Government's programme was consistent with this.[1] He further argued that change was part of our constitutional tradition and that the government must act to resolve long-standing dissatisfaction with many areas of constitutional practice. Many of these are concerned with changes seen to be required in Parliament itself. 7.01

THE SOVEREIGN

The head of state for the United Kingdom is the sovereign, who performs many ceremonial as well as constitutional functions. The present Queen performs the annual State Opening of Parliament at which she reads out a speech prepared for her by the Prime Minister. This speech gives an indication of the government Bills to be presented to Parliament during the forthcoming parliamentary session. 7.02

---

[1] Lord Irvine of Lairg, "Government's Programme of Constitutional Reform," Lecture to Constitution Unit, Dec. 8, 1998, http://www.open.gov.uk/lcd/speeches/lc-const.htm (Dec. 13, 1998).

Many of the powers of the sovereign are now exercised through a government minister but the Queen does have some personal prerogative powers, three of which are of considerable constitutional importance. These are the appointment of the Prime Minister, the dismissal of ministers and the dissolution of Parliament. These are all governed by convention. The appointment of a Prime Minister is usually clear-cut; after a general election the Queen will invite the leader of the party with the largest number of M.P.s to form a government. This occurred in May 1997 when the Conservative Prime Minister, John Major, tendered his resignation to the Queen on the morning after the general election and she then invited the Labour Party leader, Tony Blair, to form a government. If the Prime Minister resigns following some other event, such as losing a leadership election (such as Margaret Thatcher in 1990) or by reason of ill health (such as Harold MacMillan in 1963) the Queen will invite the new leader to form a government. In 1990, Margaret Thatcher did not resign until the Conservative Party had had a leadership election so that the transfer was achieved without delay. All of the political parties now have procedures for choosing and replacing their leaders. However, in 1963, the Conservative Party did not have a selection process and the Queen had to consult with senior members of the Party to ascertain who could form a government and command the confidence of the House of Commons. In the event, she had to exercise her discretion and chose the fourteenth Earl of Home, Sir Alec Douglas-Home, who subsequently renounced his title, fought a by-election and took his seat in the House of Commons.

The Queen may also have to exercise her discretion if the general election produces a "hung Parliament". This occurred in February 1974 when the Conservative Government failed to win a majority of seats. The Prime Minister, Edward Heath, tried to enter into a coalition with the Liberal Party to give him an overall majority but failed to do so. The Labour Party had the largest number of seats but not an overall majority; nonetheless the Queen invited Harold Wilson to form a government when Heath resigned four days after the election.[2]

The second personal power of the Queen is that of dismissing ministers. This is by convention exercised on the advice of the Prime Minister and it is unlikely that the Queen would dismiss a minister against the advice of the Prime Minister. However, what

---

[2] See discussion of this in Brazier, "The Constitution in the New Politics" (1978) P.L. 117.

would happen if the Prime Minister and government had lost the confidence of Parliament but refused to resign? Would the Queen then be justified in exercising her powers of dismissal? This would of course cause a constitutional crisis of some proportion and would require very careful handling. There is a precedent that occurred in 1975 in Australia when the Queen's representative, the Governor-General, dismissed the Prime Minister of Australia and the Labour Government to try to resolve a political and constitutional impasse. The Liberals controlled the Upper House of the Australian Parliament and had refused to pass the Government's Appropriation Bills to authorise the raising of money. The Liberal leader assured the Governor-General that, if he were Prime Minister, he could get the Appropriation Bills through the House and that he would then dissolve Parliament and call a general election. On this basis, the Governor-General appointed him as Prime Minister. The subsequent general election was won by a coalition of the Liberal and Country parties.

The final power is the dissolution of Parliament but again this is exercised by the Queen on the advice of and at the request of the Prime Minister. Such a request will be made by the Prime Minister either when they feel they have a good chance of winning a General Election, or after the government has been defeated in the Commons on a vote of confidence. No monarch has refused the Prime Minister's request for dissolution since the Representation of the People Act 1832.

HOUSE OF LORDS

Until late 1999, the House of Lords consisted of unelected 7.03
members, who were members either because they held a hereditary peerage or were appointed by the Crown. There were three main categories of members making a total membership of just under 1300. The membership on January 4, 1999 was 759 hereditary peers, 26 spiritual peers (such as the Archbishop of Canterbury and Bishop of London)[3] and 510 life peers including 26 Law Lords, both serving and retired.[4] Life peers are created under the Life Peerages Act 1958; these are conferred on the recipient for the duration of their life and do not pass to their heir on their death.

---

[3] The Lords Spiritual sit only so long as they are bishops; once they retire their seat is given to their successor in office.

[4] See White Paper, *Modernising Parliament: Reform of the House of Lords*, Cm. 4183 (1999).

The objective of the Act was to increase the number of Labour peers in the upper House. The House of Lords had a 'built in' Conservative majority because most hereditary peers were Conservative. In 1998, 43 per cent of peers were Conservative, 14 per cent Labour, six per cent Liberal Democrat, 28 per cent Cross benchers (*i.e.* had no party affiliation) and nine per cent others. Relatively few hereditary peers have been created since 1963; Margaret Thatcher created three in 1983 and 1984 but two of the peers did not have heirs and their titles lapsed when they died.[5]

Life peers tend to be working peers who attend the debates in the House and participate in its work. Hereditary peers, on the other hand, did not attend in large numbers except when there was a vote which is of importance to them, for example during debates in 1998 and 1999 on measures to ban hunting with hounds, or to reduce the age of consent for homosexuals, or when the Conservative Party called on them to attend and vote to defeat a proposal put forward by the other parties.

Peers who sit in the Lords were disqualified from voting in elections to the Commons but may vote in local elections, elections to the European Parliament and elections to the Scottish Parliament or Welsh Assembly. According to the Peerages Act 1963, if a peer or peeress does not sit in the House of Lords, they may vote in general elections for the United Kingdom Parliament. The Act also clarified the position of Scots peers, allowing them to sit in the Lords. Prior to this, only the 16 representative peers from Scotland provided for by the Act of Union 1707 could sit. The House of Lords Act 1999, s. 3(1)(b) allows peers who do not sit in the Lords to vote in elections for the House of Commons.

In recent years a Political Honours Scrutiny Committee has been set up to examine the nominations for life peerages and other honours made by the political parties. This was created to prevent the parties nominating people who had, for instance, given them large donations but who did not otherwise merit such an honour.[6]

7.04 The Labour Party has campaigned for a long time to have the House of Lords reformed. In the 1967–68 parliamentary session, the two Houses considered proposals for reform and in 1969, the Labour Government brought forward a Bill to modernise Parliament but this was later dropped by the Government. The new Labour Government announced that these reforms would take

---

[5] Viscounts Whitelaw and Tonypandy in 1983, Earl of Stockton (Harold MacMillan) in 1984.

[6] For description of role and function of Committee see Neill Report on Funding of Political Parties, Cm. 4057 (1998).

place during the lifetime of the current Parliament. The first reform proposed was to remove the right of hereditary peers to sit and vote in the Lords.[7] In early 1999, the Government published a White Paper entitled *Modernising Parliament: The Reform of the House of Lords*[8] in which various reforms were proposed with the intention of bringing the composition of the Lords more into line with the proportion of votes cast for each party at the last general election.

The first stage was to create a transitional House of Lords. This contains the existing life peers and a small number of hereditary peers who are sitting temporarily. The second stage which would bring about the reformed House has not yet been finalised. The Government set up a Royal Commission on the Reform of the House of Lords, under the chairmanship of Lord Wakefield, to look at the long-term reform. Its remit was wide-ranging and the timescale tight; it was required to submit a report before December 31, 1999. The terms of reference were:

> "Having regard to the need to maintain the position of the House of Commons as the pre-eminent chamber of Parliament and taking particular account of the present nature of the constitutional settlement, including the newly devolved institutions, the impact of the Human Rights Act and developing relations with the European Union:
>
> - To consider and make recommendations on the role and functions of a second chamber; and
> - To make recommendations on the method or combination of methods of composition required to constitute a second chamber fit for that role and those functions."[9]

The Royal Commission issued a consultation paper in March 1999, requesting written evidence from interested people and also stating its intention to hold open meetings in various locations throughout the United Kingdom The paper identified a number of issues that need to be addressed, including the role and functions of the House of Lords and its powers, procedures and composition. The paper recognised that there was a need to preserve the pre-eminence of the House of Commons and to take into account the effects of devolution, the United Kingdom's position in Europe

---

[7] Members of the Royal family who have the right to sit and vote in the Lords will also be affected by the reforms—White Paper, Cm. 4183 (1999), para. 5.16.

[8] White Paper, Cm. 4183 (1999).

[9] *ibid.*, para. 10.

and the integration of the European Convention on Human Rights into U.K. law.[10]

When a Bill for reform is eventually presented to Parliament, a joint committee of both Houses will be set up to look at the parliamentary aspects of reform.

The Government in its White Paper gave assurances that the transitional House of Lords would not be flooded by Labour appointments. "The government will ensure that no one political party commands a majority in the Lords. The government presently plans to seek only broad parity with the Conservatives."[11] Specifically the Prime Minister has agreed to establish an independent Appointments Commission to recommend non-political appointments to the transitional House and agreed not to veto these recommendations or those appointments suggested by other party leaders and agreed by the commission.

The commission will be an advisory non-departmental public body, consisting of representatives from the three main political parties and independent people, who will comprise the majority and from whose ranks the chairman will be chosen. The commission will operate an "open and transparent system of nominations" and will ask the public and organisations to make nominations. The awards of peerages will continue to be made by the Queen with names being submitted by the Prime Minister in accordance with normal convention for the exercise of the prerogative. The Prime Minister will decide how many nominations are needed and the commission will forward that number to the Prime Minister. These will be passed to the Queen along with the Prime Minister's own nominations and those from other party leaders. The Prime Minister will not be able to influence names except where matters of national security are concerned.

The Royal Commission reported in January 2000[11a] making 132 recommendations and setting out its views on the selection of members to the second chamber. In particular, it recommended that the House of Lords should comprise around 550 members, with some elected from a regional list, some nominated by an independent Appointments Commission and the remainder drawn from existing life peers who wish to continue to sit.

---

[10] For discussion of the Royal Commission, see Winetrobe and Gay, *The House of Lords Bill: Options for Stage Two,* House of Commons Library Research Paper 99/6 (1999).

[11] White Paper, Cm. 4183 (1999), para. 9.

[11a] Royal Commission on the Reform of the House of Lords, *A House for the Future,* Cm. 4534 (2000).

Powers and functions of the House of Lords

The House of Lords is one element of the supreme lawmaker and as such its members have the power to introduce legislation. However, this is not commonly done by individual peers but is done by ministers where the Bill is being introduced first in the Lords rather than in the Commons. This often occurs for legislation which is not contentious. A Bill that purports to raise or spend revenue must always start in the Commons because the Commons is the elected chamber and is subject to the will of the people. 7.05

The Parliament Acts 1911 and 1949 had a marked effect on the powers of the House of Lords. In 1906 a Liberal Government was elected on a mandate to bring about social reform. The Lords was, as it has always been, dominated by the Conservative Party and conflict between the two Houses was inevitable. In 1909 the Lords voted against the Finance Bill. This Bill had proposed increases in taxes on income and property to finance old-age pensions and unemployment insurance. The tax increases, particularly on property, would have affected members of the Lords badly. The Government called a general election which they won although with a reduced majority. The Finance Bill was then enacted. The Government decided that the powers of the Lords should be curtailed so that a similar situation could not arise. However, it was obvious that the Lords would not willingly vote to curtail their powers so the Prime Minister, Asquith, asked the newly crowned King George V to create around 400 new Liberal peers so that there would be a Liberal majority in the Lords. The King agreed provided there was direct electoral support for the proposals. Another general election was called and the Liberals were returned with their mandate. The Lords then realised that they could not win and did not oppose the Parliament Bill.

The 1911 Act has had three main consequences. First, the House of Lords no longer has the power of veto over public Bills, except one which tries to extend the life of Parliament beyond five years. The power of veto remains for private Bills and subordinate legislation. Secondly, the House of Lords was given a delaying power on public Bills. This power enables the Lords to delay the passage of a Bill for two years, but if the House of Commons passed the same Bill for three consecutive parliamentary sessions then it would become law without the consent of the Lords. A certificate is signed by the Speaker of the House of Commons detailing the process. This procedure is not used often; indeed since 1911, only four Bills have been passed without the Lords' consent.[12] The lack of use of the procedure does not mean, however, that the Lords and Commons rarely disagree. On the contrary, there are often times when the Lords amend government Bills substantially but the resulting disagreements are resolved either by compromise by the Lords or the government accepts the amendments. Thirdly, money Bills certified as such by the Speaker of the House of Commons may be presented for the Royal Assent if not passed by the Lords within one month of being sent there by the Commons. A money Bill is a public Bill dealing only with central government taxation, supply, appropriation and government loans.

The Parliament Act 1949 was proposed by the Labour Government elected in the post-War landslide of 1945. The Government had a huge nationalisation programme and decided to extend it into other areas, in particular the shipbuilding industry. The Lords had indicated that they would not oppose nationalisation measures which were included the Government's manifesto but they were unhappy that this nationalisation was being proposed. The convention that the Lords would not oppose legislation which had been proposed in the Government's manifesto is called the Salisbury convention, after the Leader of the Opposition in the Lords in 1945 to 1951. It means that the Lords should not frustrate the declared will of the people but rather should wherever possible amend and improve any such Bill.[13] A Party leaders' conference was held in 1948 to discuss the future of the Lords and this agreed that no party should be assured of permanent majority and hereditary alone should not be a qualification to sit and vote. However, the leaders could not agree on changes to powers of Lords so the Government then decided to curtail the delaying power of the Lords further by reducing the two year period to one year.

7.06 The position now is that a Bill passed by the House of Commons but rejected by the House of Lords in two successive sessions may be presented for Royal Assent provided one year has elapsed between its Commons second reading in the first session and its third reading in the same House in the following session. Such a Bill is accepted as law only because it is authorised by the Parliament Acts. The enacting formula for the new Act includes the wording that it has been passed "in accordance with the Parliament Acts 1911 and 1949 and by the authority of the same".

---

[12] Government of Ireland Act 1914, Welsh Church Act 1914, Parliament Act 1949, War Crimes Act 1991.

[13] See discussion in Brazier, "Defending the hereditaries: the Salisbury convention," (1998) P.L. Autumn 371.

The House of Lords has a number of functions, including: "considering and amending legislation, questioning the Government through debates and questions to Ministers, debating matters of public interest and carrying out specialist investigations through select committees of the House."[14]

"Check and balance"

The Lords is regarded by many as the "Protector of the Constitution". If the government has a very large majority in the Commons[15] it can pass any legislation it pleases since there will be no Opposition in the Commons to stop it. The Lords, however, have traditionally taken a more 'conservative' view and thus might try to stop legislation which was very radical, such as legislation to abolish the monarchy. The Lords also have the power to prevent the government introducing legislation to extend the life of Parliament.[16] If this were not so, then a government could pass a Bill which could mean it staying in office indefinitely. 7.07

Revision of legislation

This is one of the most important roles of the Lords, particularly where a Bill has been 'guillotined' in the Commons. This occurs when a government curtails debate on a Bill to ensure it is not talked out by the Opposition. There is no guillotine or closure motion in the Lords and so there can be a full debate on the implications of the Bill. The Lords may make amendments to the Bill to clarify it or change its meaning entirely. During the summer of 1998, the Lords amended the Government's Higher Education Bill twice to try to mitigate the effects of the £1,000 tuition charge being levied in Scotland on English and Welsh students taking a four year honours degree. This seriously embarrassed the Government and negotiations took place between the party managers of the two Houses to resolve the problem. The Government's provisions were eventually passed but only after the Lords had extracted a promise that the matter would be reviewed in 1999. 7.08

The Lords have the same powers as the Commons in respect of subordinate legislation and may in effect veto instruments that require to be passed by either the affirmative or negative resolution procedure. This power is used sparingly but in 1968 the Conservative majority in the Lords voted to reject an affirmative resolution,

---

14 White paper, Cm. 4183 (1999) para. 6.

15 Such as the current Labour Government and the Thatcher Governments of 1983–87 and 1987–92.

16 Parliament Act 1911, s. 7.

the Southern Rhodesia (United Nations Sanctions) Order.[17] The result was that the relationship between the two Houses deteriorated and the inter-party discussions on the reform of the Lords were suspended. In the event the Lords approved the order soon afterwards.

Debates

7.09 The working peers include many former ministers, former M.P.s, business people, professionals and so on, people who have achieved much and are therefore able to make a worthwhile contribution to debates. There is no guillotine, no closure motion and no votes of confidence, which if lost would endanger the government. The debates can therefore be more open and wide ranging and less political.

Select committees

7.10 The Lords has a number of select committees whereby it obtains information from civil servants, academics, business people, pressure groups and so on. They are also involved in joint committees with the Commons, the most important ones being the Joint Committee on Subordinate Legislation and European Communities Legislation.

Final court of appeal

7.11 The House of Lords is the final court of appeal in all civil cases in the United Kingdom and the final court of appeal for criminal cases in England and Wales. Only the legally qualified peers who are judges sit on appeals; by convention, no non-legally qualified peer may do so.

This final word on the House of Lords sums up what it does and how its work is now seen:

> "The most distinctive and important role of the present House of Lords is the specialist expertise and independent perspective it can bring to the scrutiny of legislation. But the House of Lords and the work it carries out suffer from its lack of legitimacy, because the presence of the hereditary peers creates a permanent, inbuilt majority for a single party. For its functions to be properly performed, the House of Lords needs a degree of legitimacy which it does not now enjoy. This limits

---

[17] S.I. 1968 No. 299.

the extent to which it can make a proper contribution as a second parliamentary chamber. The anachronistic and unrepresentative nature of its own composition is at the root of this deficiency."[18]

HOUSE OF COMMONS

The third arm of the legislature is the House of Commons and at least every five years its composition changes after a general election when individual citizens across the United Kingdom elect Members of Parliament to sit in the House. The right to vote, called the franchise, is controlled by various Representation of the People Acts passed to regulate who may vote and when. The most recent consolidating Act was in 1983 and provides that the right to vote is given to every British citizen who is at least 18 years old, is resident in the United Kingdom, is not subject to a disqualification and whose name appears on the electoral register of the constituency in which they reside. 7.12

Generally those entitled to vote are residents of the United Kingdom who are either British citizens, or citizens of British dependent territories, or British overseas citizens, or Commonwealth citizens, or citizens of the Irish Republic. A citizen of the E.U. may vote in European Parliament elections and local elections but not in general elections or elections to the Scottish Parliament.

If a person's name is not included on the electoral register for the constituency in which they live, then they do not have the right to vote. If their name is included on the register but they are subject to a disqualification, such as age, then again they do not have the right to vote. At every election there are stories in the press of young children's names being included on the register erroneously. If a person's name is included on two registers, for instance a student being included on the register for their home constituency and also on the register for their university address, they may still only vote once. Casting a vote while subject to a disqualification may be an electoral offence.

Those who are disqualified from voting include aliens (people who are not citizens as described above), minors (young people under 18 years), hereditary peers and peeresses (they have seats in the House of Lords and so do not have the right to vote for members of the other House),[19] prisoners, some patients in mental 7.13

[18] White Paper, Cm. 4183 (1999), para. 6.

[19] Note that the House of Lords Act 1999 confers the franchise on those hereditary peers who lose the right to sit and vote in the Lords.

hospitals[20] and overseas voters who are British citizens residing abroad for more than 20 years.

A person may be elected to sit in the Commons but be unable to take that seat because of some disqualification. These are detailed in the House of Commons (Disqualification) Act 1975. Note that there are no qualifications to be a Member of Parliament, only disqualifications. Those who may not sit in the Commons include those under the age of 21 years,[21] aliens, peers, and members of the established churches of England, Wales, Scotland and Northern Ireland and the Roman Catholic Church.[22] If a member becomes mentally ill, the Speaker of the House of Commons must be informed and after six months the seat may be declared vacant if the member is still certified ill. A bankrupt may not be elected to the Commons and if a member becomes bankrupt they will have to resign their seat unless the bankruptcy is cleared within six months.[23] A person who has been sentenced to imprisonment for a term of more than one year or an indefinite sentence (as for murder) is also disqualified. No such person may now be nominated as a candidate. This provision was introduced after Bobby Sands, an IRA prisoner in the Maze Prison, was elected to Parliament in 1981. He was unable to take his seat because he died while on hunger strike.

The holders of certain public offices are also disqualified. These include judges, police officers, members of the armed forces, civil servants and members of certain boards and tribunals. These people are disqualified because they are deemed to be members of the executive arm of government and thus, according to the doctrine of separation of powers, should not also be members of the legislature. Persons who are convicted of corrupt or illegal electoral practices are also disqualified for certain periods of time.[24]

If a member inherits a peerage, they will be expelled from the House of Commons unless they renounce the title. Tony Benn

---

[20] Those who are insane are regarded as not having the capacity to understand why they are voting and are thus denied a vote. However, many patients in a mental hospital will be able to understand the process and thus be able to vote by post.

[21] The Family Law Reform Act 1969 reduced the age of majority to 18 but expressly preserved the age for candidature for Parliament as 21.

[22] The clergy of other religions are not disqualified, *e.g.* Baptist or Methodist ministers, clergy of the Jewish and Muslim faiths.

[23] Jeffrey Archer, now Lord Archer, was declared bankrupt and had to resign his seat.

[24] Representation of the People Act 1983.

inherited the title of Lord Stansgate in 1961 while he was an M.P. He did not wish to sit in the Lords but his Commons seat was declared vacant. He fought a by-election and won. He was again expelled. In 1963, the Peerage Act was passed allowing him to renounce his title and regain his seat in the Commons. This Act also allowed Sir Alec Douglas-Home to renounce his title to become Prime Minister. In 1996, Lord James Douglas-Hamilton renounced a title to which he might have been heir (the issue was in doubt at the time) so that he could stay in the Commons as a member of the government and, incidentally, ensure the survival of the Major Government which would have been left without a majority.

Finally, there is a limitation on the number of ministers who may sit in the House of Commons. The limit, currently 95, was set to ensure that there was no excessive use of patronage by the Prime Minister. Any ministers appointed over the limit are required to sit in the House of Lords. 7.14

The parliamentary session

As mentioned above, the life of a Parliament will last for up to five years but may be curtailed if the Prime Minister decides to call an earlier general election. Most Parliaments do not last the full five years because the Prime Minister uses their power to call the election at the time of greatest advantage to the government party. Thus Margaret Thatcher called a general election in June 1983 after being in power for four years one month and in May 1987 after three years 11 months. However John Major's Government elected in April 1992 lasted almost the full five years until April 1997. 7.15

The Parliament is divided into sessions which in most years last from November to the following October. During a general election year, Parliament will run from the State Opening after the general election to the October in the next calendar year. Thus the parliamentary session 1997–98 lasted from May 1997 to October 1998. The parliamentary session is ended when the Queen prorogues Parliament, that is formally concludes the session. Prorogation is an important event because it means that all business in Parliament is suspended until the new session and any Bill that has not received the Royal Assent by then will fall. However, a new procedure has been introduced whereby a Bill progressing through the House of Commons at the end of the session may be carried over into the next if a suspension motion is agreed. This procedure was previously available for private Bills but has now been extended to public Bills, although it may not be used for contentious Bills over which the two Houses are in disagreement.[25] The prorogation proclamation now also calls the members to attend on a particular day for the opening of the new session.

The House normally sits from Monday to Thursday from 2.30 p.m. to around 10 p.m. although it now also sits on Wednesday mornings. On Fridays, the House sits from 9.30 a.m. until the early afternoon. However, the House does not sit every Friday, thus allowing M.P.s to return early to their constituencies to attend to business there.

Functions of M.P.s

7.16 The current electoral system for the United Kingdom means that an M.P. is elected to represent a constituency. However, most M.P.s are elected because they represent a particular political party. The question of conflict of interest may sometimes arise; is the M.P.'s principal loyalty to their party or their constituents? For most the answer will be the party. Indeed, many people now believe that an M.P. is not elected for their special qualities or opinions but because of the party they represents. This means that the M.P. is bound to uphold the policies of the party before those of their constituency or even their own conscience.

Arguably the most important power of the members of the House of Commons is to vote together to pass a vote of no confidence in the government, as occurred in 1979. In 1907 the Leader of the Opposition, Mr Balfour, expressed the Commons collective power thus: "We can put an end to a government; we can bring a government into being; we can destroy the career of a Minister; and we can pass a vote of censure which carries with it an immediate resignation."[26]

The particular functions of M.P.s include acting as a check on the activities and power of the government. In this regard the government's own back-bench M.P.s will have more power than those of the Opposition since the government is more likely to listen to the concerns of their own supporters. An M.P. will act for their constituents in any grievances they may have against central or local government. The M.P. may ask questions of ministers, or lobby on behalf of the constituent or refer the matter to the Parliamentary Ombudsman. The M.P. may represent pressure

---

[25] See Select Committee on Modernisation of the House of Commons, *Third Report: Carry-Over of Public Bills,* H.C. 543 (1997–98).

[26] Parl.Deb. Vol. 176, col. 928 (June 24, 1907).

groups and many M.P.s do have links with such groups as trade unions, the CBI, charities and so on. These links, particularly where the M.P. receives payment, have to be disclosed in the Register of Members' Interests. Members of Parliament are expected to represent and support their party and to work in committees of the House of Commons to further the party's aims.

Functions of the House of Commons

The House of Commons does not govern the country; this is 7.17
done by the Executive, that is the central government departments, local authorities and other bodies which are charged by legislation to perform these functions.

The House of Commons is a body which has four main functions: to scrutinise proposed legislation brought to it by government ministers, individual members and other private bodies; to question the actions of government ministers and departments; to debate various issues and ensure that different opinions are heard; and to check the financial probity of the government. The scrutiny of legislation is discussed in Chapter 5.

The House of Commons' business is led by the government, as evidenced by Standing Order 14(1) which states: "Save as provided in this order, government business shall have precedent at every sitting." In many ways the House is subordinate to the government because of the way in which the government controls the work of Parliament. The power of the government to control Parliament's business was seen in the early days of the current Labour Government when it was announced that the Prime Minister would answer parliamentary questions once each week on a Wednesday afternoon for 30 minutes, rather than twice a week for 15 minutes on Tuesday and Thursday afternoons. The House was powerless to prevent this happening.

Questions

Ministerial question time is an important constitutional process; 7.18
it allows members to obtain information from ministers and to scrutinise the work of government in the full glare of publicity.

At the beginning of business on Monday to Thursday each week ministers are required to answer questions that have been laid down in advance by back-bench M.P.s.[27] Questions are asked from 2.35 p.m. to 3.30 p.m. The ministers take it in turn to answer

---

[27] Standing Order 17.

questions; usually they will appear every three or four weeks and will answer questions for up to an hour. The Prime Minister is the exception, answering questions for 30 minutes every Wednesday. Tony Blair changed the format of Prime Minister's question time when he came to office; previously it was held on Tuesdays and Thursdays for 15 minutes.

Ministers may only be questioned on matters for which they have responsibility. This has caused much confusion in recent years. During the late 1980s, the Thatcher Government introduced reforms of the civil service, implementing the "Next Steps Initiative" which set up agencies to carry out functions which were previously carried out by central government departments. These were under the leadership of agency chief executives who had day-to-day control of the agency's functions. The government decided that any parliamentary questions which involved the work of an agency would be passed for answer to the agency chief executive and would no longer be answered on the floor of the House by the minister. This outraged many Opposition M.P.s but the practice persisted and is still in place. Thus a question on a matter which is within the remit of an agency will be sent to the chief executive who will reply directly to the M.P.; the minister will not be involved and the M.P. will not be able to ask supplementary questions on the floor of the House. The answers are now published in *Hansard* at the end of the day's debate.

The Scott Inquiry into the Arms for Iraq affair in 1992 highlighted that ministers were answering some questions in a dubious manner. Answers are usually prepared for ministers by their civil servants and they are now instructed to be as open and truthful as possible. In particular an answer should not be given which is literally true but likely to give rise to misleading inferences.

A minister should try to answer questions where possible, but there are instances when they may decline to do so:

- The question does not relate to the minister's departmental responsibilities.
- They are statements not questions.
- The matter is currently *sub judice*.
- The matter was asked in the previous three months.
- The cost of finding the answer would be too high.
- The answer might damage national security.
- The matter involves confidential exchanges between governments.
- The question relates to commercial or contractual confidentiality.

There are two main ways in which a member of the U.K. Parliament can ask questions of a minister: either by putting a question for oral answer or by putting a question for a written answer. In addition, there is a special process for urgent questions, known as the private notice question.

(a) Questions for oral answer

With the exception of Fridays, a period of approximately one hour is set aside daily for ministers to answer questions in the House. The questions are put down for answer two weeks in advance of the minister's question time and appear on the daily Order of Business. The process of asking the question is simple; the Speaker asks the member to ask the question and the member does so by referring to the number of the question on the order paper. There is no need to read out the question since it is already printed in the paper. The minister will give the answer prepared by the department. The member then has the opportunity of asking a supplementary question which should broadly relate to the original question. This supplementary question, however, is often used by Opposition members to try to catch out the minister. The Speaker may then call on other members to ask supplementary questions on the same subject. When the Speaker has decided that sufficient time has been given to that matter, they will call the next member to ask their question. At the end of the time allotted for that question time, any remaining questions not answered orally will be given a written answer and printed in *Hansard* at a later date. 7.19

Ministers answer questions approximately every three to four weeks, except for the Prime Minister who now answers questions every Wednesday afternoon for 30 minutes. Ministers in charge of minor departments, such as the Attorney-General, will answer questions for 15 to 20 minutes every four weeks.

There are always many more questions tabled than can be answered in the given time and to ensure that each member has an equal chance to ask a question, a ballot is held, called the 'five o'clock shuffle'. This occurs on the tenth sitting day before the relevant question time at 5 p.m. A number of questions are 'drawn out' and printed in order on the Order of Business. Up to 40 questions are drawn out for the large departments which have a question time lasting one hour, 30 questions for the departments which have 40 minutes, and 20 for Prime Minister's question time and smaller departments.

There are rules regarding the content of questions. The question should seek information or press for action and it should not be a statement of the opinion of the questioner or seek a statement of opinion. It must relate to a matter for which the minister is responsible as minister and the answer must not be readily available elsewhere. The question must not seek an opinion on a matter of law, nor relate to a matter that is *sub judice*. The question must not have been asked and answered within the previous three months and must not relate to the security services or matters of commercial confidence.

During Prime Minister's question time, a number of questions asked will be an inquiry about the Prime Minister's official engagements for that day. The Prime Minister does not have departmental responsibility but is in overall charge of the government and its activities; thus questions can range over all of the activities of government. The 'official engagements' question hides the real purpose of the member's question: to ask a supplementary question on any topic and hope to surprise the Prime Minister. The question can therefore be on any topical matter.

The Leader of the Opposition is allowed up to four supplementaries and the leader of the next largest party is allowed up to two. These 'questions' often sound more like statements denigrating government policies but since the Prime Minister always has the last word, they can frequently miss their mark. Prime Minister's question time is the most closely observed period in Parliament, when the House is full and television and radio broadcast the proceedings.

(b) Questions for written answer

7.20 There is no limit to the number of questions a member may table for written answer. The procedure is an excellent way of obtaining detailed information from a department. Normally an answer will be given within seven days of tabling the question.

There are of course many more questions for written answer than oral questions, around 40,000 tabled in a year compared to 2,500. A question tabled for oral answer however does not have any cost limit attached to it. If a question for written answer is likely to cost more than £500 (the cost limit) the minister can refuse to answer. The annual cost of answering questions, both written and oral is around £4.5 million.

(c) Private notice questions

7.21 These are used when a question needs to be asked and answered urgently. The matter must be urgent and of public importance, so that advance notice is impossible. The procedure involves the member applying to the Speaker before noon on the day the answer is required. The department and the minister are informed immediately. If the Speaker allows the private notice question, the question will be put immediately after the end of that day's question time. Only about four private notice questions are raised each month. In 1989, however, the budget was delivered as the reply to a private notice question because it was anticipated that a member would try to delay the budget by raising other business.

Debates

Members of Parliament participate in debates on the second 7.22
readings of Bills, motions to approve some aspect of government policy, motions set down by the Opposition parties to challenge government policies, the budget proposals and many other matters. There are 20 Opposition days on which the Opposition parties may debate issues of their own choosing.

Each day there is an 'adjournment' debate, taking place at the end of the day for 30 minutes. The topic is chosen by a back-bench M.P. who has competed successfully in a ballot to bring the matter to the attention of a minister and the House. The M.P. cannot call on the government to initiate legislation; rather they will use the time to put forward their case for action by the minister. The topic is often a matter involving one of their constituents and the debate is an excellent way of publicising the problem, although it is rare for many M.P.s to be in the chamber to hear the debate.

The government may also initiate an adjournment debate and will do so where an issue is controversial but still needs to be aired. This type of debate is useful because the motion cannot be amended and no vote is taken at the end of it.

There is also provision in the House's Standing Orders to hold an emergency debate at the request of an M.P. and with the agreement of the Speaker that it is a "specific and important matter that should have urgent consideration."[28] However, it is difficult to persuade the Speaker that such a situation exists and thus emergency motions of this type are rarely granted.

A further type of motion is available to back-bench M.P.s to put their views forward to the government. These are called Early Day Motions (EDMs) and are technically a request for a debate to be held at some time in the future. However, their purpose now is to test the opinion of the House on a particular matter rather than have a debate. The motion is tabled and printed on the daily order paper of the House. Any M.P. may add their name to the motion

---

[28] Standing Order 20.

and the new list of supporters is then circulated the following day and each day a new name is added. The EDM is useful for party managers to gauge opinions of back-bench M.P.s. An EDM may eventually lead to a debate; in 1979 an EDM put down by the Leader of the Opposition, Margaret Thatcher, and five senior Conservatives led to a debate censuring the Labour Government under James Callaghan, and thus to the Government's resignation and a general election.

There has been a dramatic rise in the number of EDMs each year from 97 in 1950–51 to 2595 in 1992–93. The EDM can thus be viewed as a barometer of parliamentary opinion.

Select committees

7.23 The current structure of select committees was adopted in 1979[29] and it is credited to Lord St John of Fawsley who described them as "a necessary preliminary to the more effective scrutiny of government".

There are more than 30 select committees which are generally set up for the whole Parliament. They fall into three categories: around 12 domestic committees such as Accommodation and Works, Finance and Services, Standards and Privileges, Procedure, and Modernisation of the House of Commons; around seven scrutiny committees such as Deregulation, E.C. Legislation, Public Accounts, and Public Administration; and 16 departmental select committees which 'shadow' a government department and investigate the workings of the department and its associated public bodies and agencies. Other committees are concerned with the internal workings of the House.

Departmental select committees are set up under Standing Order 130, which allows them to hear witnesses, send for papers, appoint specialist advisers and report to the House their opinion and observations on the matters they have investigated. They are required to "examine the expenditure, administration and policy of the principal government departments." In practice, select committees do not scrutinise the expenditure of departments; this is left to the Committee of Public Accounts. The committee itself will decide the matters they wish to investigate and who they wish to call to give evidence. The size of the departmental select committees varies from 11 up to 17 members.[30] Each committee has a

---

[29] For detailed discussion, see Drewry (ed.) *The New Select Committees* (1979).

[30] For Education and Employment, and Environment, Transport and Regional Affairs.

permanent staff of three or four civil servants to assist in the operation of the committee and preparation of reports.

The departmental select committees can investigate any matter they wish connected with the government department or any of the department's executive agencies and associated public bodies. The committees of course are highly dependent on the co-operation of the government to allow ministers and officials to appear before the committees to give evidence and to release documents to the committees. There is no formal requirement that the government does co-operate but successive governments have generally done so. However, there have been a number of high profile investigations during which governments were less than helpful. Three select committees held separate investigations into the Westland Helicopter affair in 1985 but they were hampered by the Government's refusal to allow senior civil servants to give evidence on the leaking of a letter written by the Solicitor-General.[31] Instead the head of the civil service appeared and gave answers to specified questions. In 1988, the Select Committee on Agriculture invited Edwina Currie to give evidence to the committee on her remarks, which had led to her resignation from her post as junior minister at the Department of Health, that "most eggs produced" in the United Kingdom were infected with salmonella. Mrs Currie at first refused to do so, but after the chairman insisted that it was for the committee to decide who should give evidence, she agreed to do so.

Prime Ministers and former Prime Ministers do not normally appear before select committees and indeed there appears to be a convention that they do not do so. In 1994, Margaret Thatcher refused to give evidence to the Foreign Affairs Select Committee on the Pergau Dam affair, citing the convention as her reason. Other ministers may be called to give evidence but may refuse to answer questions. Leon Brittan refused to answer certain questions put to him by the Defence Select Committee in 1986 regarding the Westland Helicopters affair.

Select committees may ask government departments for documents but are unable to order such production. In 1978, the now defunct Select Committee on Nationalised Industries asked the Secretary of State for Industry for papers relating to the future prospects of British Steel. The request was denied, but the committee then sought and obtained the documents from the Chairman of British Steel, who, being a private person, was unable to refuse since he would then have been in contempt of Parliament.

---

[31] See Report of Defence Select Committee, H.C. 518, 519 (1985–86).

During various committee inquiries into the Arms for Iraq affair, it was found that some witnesses either did not tell the truth or were 'economical with the truth'. Now witnesses before select committees are required to take a formal oath. If it is subsequently discovered that they have lied, they may be reported to the Crown Prosecution Service for prosecution. If the witness is an M.P., the committee will ask the House of Commons to vote to remove the M.P.'s immunity from prosecution.

The effectiveness of select committees has long been debated. On the one hand, there is no doubt that they have increased the amount of government information available and have provided some routine departmental accountability. Some of the reports are exceptional documents containing detailed research and recommendations. On the other hand, there are serious limitations. The restrictions on evidence from government ministers and officials mean that their reports are incomplete while the lack of staff and resources means that their reports are not as well presented and researched as they might be. In addition, there is always a government majority on the committee and this may preclude effective discussion and criticism. Lastly, it is unfortunate that the reports receive little publicity and are rarely debated in the House.

Financial proceedings

7.24 A government cannot function if it is unable to raise and spend revenue. This principle was seen at work in the conflict between the House of Commons and House of Lords in 1909–11 which led to the passage of the Parliament Act 1911, curtailing, *inter alia*, the power of the House of Lords to delay financial Bills of the government.

Taxation without the consent of Parliament is unlawful[32] and only the government can initiate legislation to raise or spend money. "It is a principle of the highest importance that no public charge can be incurred except on the initiative of the Crown."[33] This means that Parliament may not increase expenditure submitted to it by the government or vote for expenditure to be incurred on items of its own choice. It also means that private members' Bills may not purport to raise or spend taxation. Although many forms of taxation are provided for in permanent legislation, others require to be passed every year in the Finance Bill. These include rates of income and corporation taxes. The Finance Bill incorporates the budget which is read out by the Chancellor of the

---

[32] Bill of Rights 1689, art. 4.

[33] Erskine May, *Parliamentary Practice* (21st ed. 1989), p. 691.

Exchequer around mid-March each year. Debates on the Finance Bill follow very quickly after the budget speech and although M.P.s have an opportunity to question the details of the budget proposals, it is unusual for any major amendments to be made.

All revenue is credited to the Consolidated Fund, the government's main account at the Bank of England. The authority to withdraw money must be given in a statute and this is called the Consolidated Fund Act. About one-third of the expenditure authorised in the Consolidated Fund Act is expenditure of a permanent nature and is not subject to debate in the House. The type of expenditure (called in parliamentary terms 'supply') authorised are the salaries of judges, the Speaker and the Leader of the Opposition, the Parliamentary Ombudsman, the Comptroller and Auditor-General, payments to meet the country's obligations to the European Community and the Queen's Civil List. These payments are not subject to political scrutiny because they are deemed to be for services which should remain outside political influence and interference.

Most public expenditure is of an annual nature, where the amounts must be approved by Parliament. The cost of the armed forces must be approved by Parliament every year. These types of expenditure are known as Supply Services and the government has to lay its estimates of what they will cost before Parliament in the form of resolutions. When these are passed, they are included in the Consolidated Fund Bill or in an Appropriation Bill. The main Appropriation Bill is passed in July each year and authorises the allocation of money to the purposes contained in the estimates. Money must be appropriated for specific purposes in the year in which the authority to spend was given, so if money is not spent in the current financial year, it cannot be taken forward for spending in the next year.

Taxation is called 'ways and means'. The Chancellor of the 7.25
Exchequer will present proposals in the annual budget statement, setting out tax proposals and the government's expenditure plans for the following three years. At the end of the speech, ways and means resolutions are tabled, forming the basis of the debates on the budget. The Finance Bill is then introduced.

Income tax rates are annual taxes and require to be reviewed in each Finance Act. The authority to collect taxes expires on April 5 each year but the Finance Bill does not receive the Royal Assent until July. In *Bowles v. Bank of England*[34] it was held that a resolution of the House of Commons could not authorise the

[34] [1913] 1 Ch. 57.

Crown to levy a tax. According to the Bill of Rights, the levying of a tax required the authority of statute. Thus to ensure that the government can continue to collect taxes during the period April to July, the Provisional Collection of Taxes Act 1913 (now 1968) was passed.[35] The Finance Act must now be passed by August 5 each year to ensure that the government can still collect taxes.

The courts have been vigilant in ensuring that any taxation levied by the government has parliamentary authority. In *Congreve v. Home Office*[36] the Home Office were prevented from revoking the television license of C who had purchased a new licence before the expiry of his old one to avoid a price increase. The threat of revocation of the licence if C did not pay the difference between the new price and the old was held to be an attempt to levy money without the authority of Parliament and was unlawful. In *Woolwich Building Society v. Inland Revenue Commissioners (No. 2)*[37] the Inland Revenue made a demand for tax from the building society and this was held to be unlawful. The building society then sued for the return of the money but there was no statutory right available to authorise its repayment. The House of Lords subsequently held that the repayment was due at common law. Lord Goff stated, *obiter dicta,* that the principle of repayment might extend to "cases in which the tax or other levy has been wrongly exacted by a public authority not because the demand was *ultra vires* but . . . for example, because the authority has misconstrued a relevant statute or regulation."[38]

The basic rules for spending and taxing are:

- Legislative approval is required for taxation and expenditure proposals.
- Only the Crown (*i.e.* a minister) may move such proposals.
- Proposals must originate in the Commons.
- Estimates and related supply must be voted in the same session.
- Spending and taxing proposals in a Bill must be approved separately—they are usually voted on after the second reading of the Bill.

7.26 The timetable for expenditure proposals has been modified recently. The Chancellor of the Exchequer announced in 1998 that

---

[35] See also *Attorney-General v. Wiltshire United Dairies Ltd* (1921) 37 T.L.R. 884.
[36] [1976] Q.B. 629.
[37] [1992] 3 All E.R. 737.
[38] *ibid.* at 764 d-e.

the departmental estimates would be for three years rather than the previous one. The Treasury receives all of the departmental "bids" for funding and allocates the available funds according to government policy. Negotiations for funds go on for several months. Eventually the proposals are set before the House for debate, usually around March of each year. Three days are set aside for the debates, which must be concluded before August 5. Once the estimates are approved, an annual Appropriation Bill is enacted; this usually occurs in late July.

Where a department has underestimated the amount of money it requires for a particular year, it will present a supplementary estimate for approval. This is then authorised in the main Appropriation Bill (if presented before July) or in the Consolidated Fund Bill. The supplementary estimates are submitted by departments in June, November and February and take account of sums the departments have underestimated in their normal estimates. A supplementary estimate may be required to take account of additional spending caused by a change in government policy or unforeseen circumstances, such as a large increase in unemployment leading to more people claiming benefits.

The control of income and expenditure falls to the Treasury. As such it is a very powerful department and the Chancellor thus occupies one of the most important offices of State. Individual departments put forward their spending proposals to the Treasury which must approve them before they are included in the government's spending proposals. As well as this supervisory role, the Treasury will advise departments on the financial implications of any legislation and the departments are required to consult the Treasury when such legislation is proposed. Each department has an accounting officer, a senior civil servant appointed by the Treasury to ensure that the department's financial affairs are properly conducted. The accounting officer signs the department's accounts and will appear on behalf of the minister at hearings before the Committee of Public Accounts. The accounting officer is also concerned with policy and is responsible for advising ministers on 'all matters of financial propriety and regularity'. During the Pergau Dam affair it emerged that the accounting officer for the Foreign Office had warned the Foreign Secretary that the proposed offer of £234 million to build the Pergau Dam in Malaysia was uneconomic and wasteful. He was overruled and the money was paid out of the Overseas Development Administration budget. The grant was linked to an agreement with Malaysia that the Malay government would buy weapons worth £1.3 billion from British companies. Under international law, such a link between aid and arms sales was illegal and indeed the grant was contrary to section 1 of the Overseas Development and Co-operation Act 1980.[39] The Government subsequently changed its procedures so that if a minister overrules the accounting officer a report may be sent to the Chairman of the Committee of Public Accounts. In any event, the Comptroller and Auditor-General should also be informed.

7.27 As we have seen, the debates on the financial processes are unlikely to produce much change in the government's proposals and indeed are not long enough to properly scrutinise the details of the spending plans. Parliament has therefore developed other methods of scrutinising the financial affairs of individual departments. These involve the Committee of Public Accounts (PAC) the most powerful and oldest select committee of the House of Commons.[40] The power of this committee is not just rooted in the fact that its members are senior M.P.s and it is chaired by a senior Opposition M.P. Its real power comes from the detailed reports and accounts it receives from the Comptroller and Auditor-General (C&AG) who is head of the National Audit Office (NAO). Other select committees have only four clerks to assist them in collecting information; the PAC has the resources of the NAO at its disposal and its reports are accordingly highly authoritative and detailed.

The PAC is not confined to hearing only that evidence the government determines it shall hear. Instead it receives reports from the NAO which has the right under the National Audit Act 1983 to obtain any information reasonably required for its investigations. The PAC's weaknesses are that its inquiries are held after the expenditure has been incurred and that it discusses the administration of the expenditure, not the policy that required the expenditure to be made. The recommendations of the PAC are normally accepted by the government since these are based on the detailed analysis of the departmental annual accounts prepared by the NAO.

The C&AG is an officer of the House of Commons[41] and is independent of party politics and the political influence of the government. The C&AG is head of the NAO, which again is independent of government and civil service. The NAO recruits and trains its own staff. The NAO's functions are to examine the accounts of central government departments and associated bodies

---

[39] See *R. v. Secretary of State for Foreign and Commonwealth Affairs, ex p. World Development Movement* [1995] 1 All E.R. 611.

[40] First set up by Gladstone in 1861.

[41] National Audit Act 1983.

and to carry out value for money (VFM) audits.[42] Departmental accounts are audited each year to ensure their accuracy and probity. VFM audits are carried out from time to time on areas of a department's work to ensure that there is no extravagance or waste. The NAO has carried out many investigations into various privatisations of public assets to ensure that the taxpayers received a good return on the sale. It should be noted, however, that neither the C&AG nor the NAO are able to comment on the merits of any government policy.[43]

The NAO is itself subject to audit and this is carried out by the Public Accounts Commission which was set up under section 2 of the 1983 Act. The commission comprises a total of nine M.P.s, including two *ex officio* members, the Leader of the House of Commons and the Chairman of the Committee of Public Accounts. No ministers may sit on the commission. The commission appoints an accounting officer for the NAO, appoints auditors and examines the estimates with the advice of the Treasury or the PAC.

Self-regulation of the House

The House of Commons has long had the right to regulate the 7.28
activities of its own members, including punishing members who have breached parliamentary privilege or been found to be in contempt of the House. Punishment ranges from admonition, to suspension, to expulsion. In July 1999, Ernie Ross, M.P. for Dundee West, was suspended from the House for the premature release of a report of the Foreign Affairs Select Committee to the Foreign Office officials; the report criticised the Foreign Office for its handling of the Arms to Sierra Leone affair. The matter had been referred to the Committee of Privileges.

While such matters as the Ross episode are important, there have been more problems associated with the external interests of M.P.s and the effect these have on their activities in Parliament. The Conservative Government of the early 1990s was plagued by accusations of 'sleaze' with a number of members of the Government being accused of acting inappropriately or even of accepting money or services in return for lobbying ministers on behalf of businesses.

There were allegations that Neil Hamilton and Tim Smith accepted payments form the owner of Harrods, Mohamed Al-

[42] 1983 Act, s. 6.

[43] For a good account of public finance see McEldowney, *Public Law* (2nd ed. 1997).

Fayed, and further allegations by the *Sunday Times* that two other M.P.s (Graham Riddick and David Tredinnick) had stated that they would accept money in return for asking questions in Parliament. These allegations came at the same time as ministers, David Mellor and Tim Yeo, had been forced to resign because of inappropriate behaviour in their private lives. In addition, there was disquiet that a number of former ministers had obtained well paid directorships in private companies soon after leaving office. The companies had had direct dealings with the departments in which these ministers had held office. The appointments of apparent supporters of the Conservative Government to remunerated posts in quangos also caused concern. The overall impression to the country was that M.P.s had access to a lucrative 'gravy train'.

John Major appointed the Committee on Standards in Public Life in October 1994, under the chairmanship of Lord Nolan and with the remit to "examine current concerns about standards of conduct of all holders of public office, including arrangements relating to financial and commercial activities." The first report dealt with matters relating to M.P.s, ministers and civil servants, quangos and N.H.S. bodies and set out the "Seven Principles of Public Life"—selflessness, integrity, objectivity, accountability, openness, honesty and leadership. As regards the conduct of M.P.s, the report made 11 recommendations falling into six areas—paid outside employment, parliamentary consultancies, disclosure of interests, conflicts of interest, code of conduct and enforcement of obligations. Most of the recommendations only required changes in the procedures and practices of the House of Commons; the only recommendation requiring legislation was on the clarification of the law on the bribery of M.P.s. This recommendation was necessary after a case in 1992 when a Conservative M.P., Harry Greenway, was accused of accepting bribes from an engineering company based in his constituency. Although the prosecution was not proceeded with, the court decided in a preliminary ruling that parliamentary privilege was not a bar to prosecution.[44]

7.29 The House responded to the Nolan recommendations in various ways. A Select Committee on Standards in Public Life was set up in June 1995 to consider the Nolan recommendations and in its first report it proposed a draft resolution for the House to the effect that a Code of Conduct be drawn up as soon as possible.[45] In

---

[44] For discussion of the ruling see Bradley, "Parliamentary Privilege and the common law of Corruption: *R. v. Greenway and Others*" (1998) P.L. Autumn 356.

[45] Select Committee on Standards in Public Life, First Report, H.C. 637 (1994–95).

July 1995, the House passed resolutions to set up a new Select Committee on Standards and Privileges to replace the existing Privileges Committee and Select Committee on Members' Interests, to appoint a Parliamentary Commissioner for Standards and set out additional requirements for members to declare an interest and regarding consultancies. The new select committee and the office of Parliamentary Commissioner for Standards were set up in late 1995.

The Code of Conduct was devised by the Committee on Standards and Privileges in 1996.[46] The Code itself is short, only three pages, but it is accompanied by a 21 page guide which gives detailed guidance on the rules in the Code. The Code's purpose was to "assist members in the discharge of their obligations to the House, their constituents and the public at large."[47] It reiterates Nolan's Seven Principles and adds some principles of its own, including, that M.P.s should avoid conflicts of interest, maintain the integrity of Parliament, register their interests, act openly with ministers, other members and public officials, and not misuse confidential information.

The new Standards and Privileges Committee had a busy time in its first two years, publishing 25 reports, of which 21 concerned complaints against 41 members. Fourteen complaints were upheld, although only one suspension resulted and in five others no action was possible because the individuals were no longer M.P.s.[48]

If an M.P. receives money from a source outside Parliament, they are expected to declare a pecuniary interest should they be involved in any debate or committee during which there is discussion affecting the business interests of the person or company which gave them the money. The House of Commons passed a resolution in 1974 that required disclosure of any pecuniary interests or benefit, direct or indirect.[49] A second resolution authorised the setting up of the Register of Members' Interests. The responsibility for compiling and maintaining the register now lies with the Parliamentary Commissioner for Standards. Members are required to register matters such as directorships, travel and

---

[46] Select Committee on Standards and Privileges, Third Report, *The Code of Conduct and the Guide to the Rules relating to the Conduct of MPs*, H.C. 604 (1995–96).

[47] House of Commons, *The Code of Conduct together with the Guide to the Rules Relating to the Conduct of Members*, H.C. 688 (1995–96), para. I.

[48] For discussion of this, see Rush, "The Law Relating to Members' Conduct," in *The Law and Parliament,* (Oliver and Drewry eds., 1998).

[49] H.C. Deb. Vol. 874, cols. 537–538 (May 22, 1974).

accommodation paid for by persons other than the M.P., contracts involving the provision of parliamentary services by M.P.s, sponsorship of an M.P. by a trade union, blind trusts for Opposition front-bench spokesmen to pay for research and costs associated with their front-bench duties, and so on.

CHAPTER 8

THE SCOTTISH PARLIAMENT

The current Government was elected on a manifesto which promised devolution to Scotland and Wales and new initiatives leading to power sharing in Northern Ireland. It is noticeable that the three structures are all quite different. The Scottish Parliament will be a body with legislative, executive and tax-raising powers, while the Welsh Assembly has been given only executive powers. The power sharing arrangements suggested for Northern Ireland are unique to that part of the United Kingdom. For England there are proposals for an Assembly for Greater London, but little other decentralisation of power. Scottish electors and Northern Irish electors voted in large numbers for their respective forms of devolution; Welsh electors barely registered their vote. English electors have yet to be given the opportunity to decide whether or not they wish some form of devolution and this "asymmetrical devolution" throughout the United Kingdom may cause difficulties in the future.[1] However, it has to be said that as yet English voters have shown no desire for devolution and so have not been catered for. 8.01

The drive towards a devolved Parliament is dealt with in Chapter 1; in this chapter we consider what form that devolution has taken and how it will work.

SCOTLAND ACT 1998

The scheme of devolution stated in the Scotland Act 1998 sets out new constitutional arrangements for Scotland. Throughout the discussions in the Scottish Constitutional Convention, the White Paper and the Act's parliamentary debates, the idea was mooted that the Scottish Parliament should not be made in the image of the Westminster Parliament. Rather the opportunity should be 8.02

[1] See Brown "Asymmetrical devolution: the Scottish case" (1998) 69 Political Quarterly 215.

taken to create a new and innovative Parliament using the most up-to-date information technologies and adapting the best practice of other Parliaments and Assemblies to obtain a Parliament reflecting the needs and aspirations of the Scottish people. "Scotland has a unique and enviable opportunity: a blank sheet of paper to devise a new Parliament fit for the 21st century."[2]

The Scottish Parliament is set up differently from the Westminster Parliament in a number of ways. The system of election is different and makes one party government in Scotland less likely. The balance of parties within the Parliament will be different, thus making majority government unlikely but allowing a more collaborative and consultative form of government. The elections in May 1999 confirmed the expectation that there would not be a majority government. The Labour Party won 56 seats, nine short of a majority, and were forced to negotiate with the Liberal Democrats to form a coalition Government. The appointment of ministers is made with the agreement of the Parliament, a major departure from Westminster politics. It was hoped that committees would be more collegial in their deliberations and less partisan but this will depend very much on the style of the committee chairmen and the individual members of the committees. Where there are a number of members who are, or have been, M.P.s, it is possible that their experience of Westminster politics will affect their behaviour. It was intended that committees should meet outside Edinburgh on occasions, but the number of committees set up and the estimated costs of taking members round the country would seem to have curtailed that hope. The CSG in its last report and other organisations have expressed the hope that there will be public participation in the work of the Parliament, with the formation of civic forums, handling of public petitions and a partner libraries scheme whereby parliamentary papers are made available in local libraries.

The coalition Government created by the Labour and Liberal Democrat Parties is headed by the "Partnership Executive" whose operation is based on a written agreement, *Partnership for Scotland: An agreement for the first Scottish Parliament*.[3] The agreement set out how the two Parties intend to conduct themselves to ensure that the government of Scotland is carried out. The agreement stated that the doctrine of collective responsibility was to apply to ministers and each party was required to make its own business

---

[2] Mitchell, *Standing Orders for the Scottish Parliament* (1998), p. 2.
[3] http://www.scotland.gov.uk, May 1999.

management arrangements to ensure "effective Party support for the Executive".[4]

The doctrine of collective responsibility has since been defined and clarified by the Scottish Ministerial Code published in August 1999.[5] The doctrine applies to members of the Scottish Executive and is specifically extended to include deputy ministers appointed under section 49.[6] The Code states: 8.03

"2.1 The Executive operates on the basis of collective responsibility. The internal process through which a decision has been made should not be disclosed. Decisions reached by the Executive are binding on all its members . . .

2.3 Collective responsibility requires that Ministers should be able to express their views frankly in the expectation that they can argue freely in private while maintaining a united front when decisions have been reached. This in turn requires that the privacy of opinions expressed and advice offered within the Executive should be maintained. It is therefore essential that, subject to guidelines on the disclosure of information set out in the Code of Practice on Access to Scottish Executive Information, Ministers take the necessary steps to ensure that they and their staff preserve the privacy of Executive business and protect the security of Executive documents.

2.4 Collective responsibility as defined above also applies to any junior Scottish Ministers who are appointed by the First Minister under the terms of Section 49 of the Scotland Act even though they are not members of the Executive."

The Code is further clarified by another document published concurrently, *The Scottish Executive: A Guide to Collective Decision Making*.[7] Published by the Executive Secretariat, this Guide explains the arrangements for collective decision-making and the way in which the First Minister and Deputy First Minister work together. It contains specific guidance for members of staff of the Scottish Administration and particularly those who work with Scottish ministers. It outlines the procedures for sending minutes to ministers and others and prints in table form who should receive

---

[4] May 13, 1999, para. 2.4.

[5] http://www.scotland.gov.uk/library2/doc03/smic-00.htm, Aug. 24, 1999.

[6] *Partnership for Scotland: An agreement for the first Scottish Parliament*, para. 2.4.

[7] http://www.scotland.gov.uk/library2/doc03/sedc-00.htm, Aug. 24, 1999.

copies of minutes. The conduct of meetings of ministers, officials and others is covered, as are meetings of the Scottish Cabinet.

Form of the Parliament

8.04 The Scotland Act sets out the framework for devolution but leaves many of the decisions on the procedures and practices to the Scottish Parliament itself. In the White Paper, the Government said that it expected that "the Scottish Parliament will adopt modern methods of working; that it will be accessible, open and responsive to the needs of the public; that participation by organisations and individuals in decision making will be encouraged; and that views and advice from specialists will be sought as appropriate."[8]

The Act commences with the simple but highly significant statement: "There shall be a Scottish Parliament".[9] The Parliament thus established is unicameral (as opposed to the bicameral U.K. Parliament) and is created by force of an Act of the U.K. Parliament. Thus the Scottish Parliament is a creature of statute and is not a sovereign body in its own right; its powers, duties and functions derive from the statute. It is a subordinate body, subject to the control of the Scotland Act and thus to the U.K. Parliament. It is important to remember that the constitutional change that has occurred in the United Kingdom has not created a federal structure but remains unitary.[10] Neither is the sovereignty of the U.K. Parliament denied or altered by the Scotland Act; indeed the Act states clearly at section 28(7): "This section does not affect the power of the Parliament of the United Kingdom to make laws for Scotland." The form of words of section 28(7) is interesting; it contrasts with the form used in the Government of Ireland Act 1920, s. 75: "Notwithstanding . . . anything contained in this Act, the supreme authority of the Parliament of the U.K. shall remain unaffected and undiminished over all persons, matters and things in (Northern) Ireland and every part thereof." The words in the Scotland Act expressing supremacy are mild in comparison to this declaration. Brazier suggests that the wording was deliberate "so as not to offend Scottish susceptibilities too easily."[11]

---

[8] *Scotland's Parliament*, Cm. 3658 (1997), para. 9.9.

[9] 1998 Act, s. 1(1).

[10] For discussion of the possibility of a U.K. federal structure, see Olowofoyeku, "Decentralising the U.K.: The Federal Argument" (1999) Vol. 3 E.L.R. 57.

[11] Brazier, "The Scotland Bill as Constitutional Legislation" (1998) Vol. 19(1) Stat. L.R. 12 at 27.

The section means that power to legislate for Scotland is not granted to the Scottish Parliament exclusively; even in those areas devolved to the Parliament, the U.K. Parliament retains the right to legislate for Scotland if it so wishes. MacCormick reflects:

> "If Parliament does not choose to invade or to recall (the Scottish Parliament's powers) perhaps on the ground of political wisdom and received convention, it will nevertheless remain a real power of choice. Westminster will be in the position of continually choosing not to revoke a delegation of its powers, and that is different from having given up or lost the power of choice."[12]

In the parliamentary debates on the Bill, Lord Hope of Craighead observed that section 28(7) "simply states the obvious."[13] The doctrine of supremacy of Parliament, he continued, would not allow Parliament to "abandon its own sovereignty." Critics of the section expressed the view that the section was unnecessary and even provocative and offensive since it could be construed as an invitation to Westminster to "meddle in the future in the law-making of Scotland on those matters which this Bill devolves to Scotland."[14] The Government responded to these concerns by saying that the section was needed to emphasise that the Act was setting up a system of devolution, not a federal system. They also emphasised that they did not foresee the section being used in any areas of law that had been devolved to the Scottish Parliament without the consent of the Parliament. The Government suggested that the U.K. Parliament might legislate for the whole of the United Kingdom where international obligations had to be incorporated into domestic law; they said it might be simpler and quicker for one legislature to enact such laws. The Government considered that a convention would be developed to prevent Westminster legislating without the Scottish Parliament's consent, rather like the situation that existed between Westminster and the Northern Ireland Parliament from 1920 to 1972.

Since the Scottish Parliament is a subordinate body, created by a 8.05
U.K. statute, the laws it enacts are also subordinate. This means that, like the subordinate legislation made by the U.K. Parliament, the Acts of the Scottish Parliament are subject to the scrutiny of

---

[12] MacCormick, "Sovereignty or Subsidiarity? Some Comments on Scottish Devolution" in *Devolution and the British Constitution* (Tomkins ed., 1998), p. 9.

[13] *Hansard*, H.L. Vol. 592, col. 796.

[14] Lord Steel of Aikwood, *Hansard*, H.L. Vol. 593, col. 1947.

the courts and can be declared invalid. This is discussed later in this chapter. Scottish legislation will be valid so long as it does not trespass upon the reserved matters detailed in the Act. There is however the possibility that the U.K. Parliament may legislate to remove some of the Scottish Parliament's powers or even to abolish it outright. In legal terms this is perfectly possible, although in political terms it is highly unlikely to occur without the consent of the Scottish electorate.

The Act does not set out a constitution for Scotland but it is a curious mix of constitutional sections and those of a more mundane nature. For instance, none of the sections of the Act are entrenched and no special procedures are required to change it. There are no lofty statements or principles setting out the relationship between the new Parliament and the Scottish people. However there are statements such as section 28(7) regarding the sovereignty of the U.K. Parliament while details of the aspects of "the constitution" which are reserved matters are given in Schedule 5, paragraph 1. The appointment and removal of judges is tucked away at section 95 although the constitutional implications of this section should normally have indicated a more prominent place. The more mundane matters tackled by the Act include the remuneration of MSPs and members of the Scottish Executive[15] and exemption from jury service.[16]

The parliamentary drafters of the Scotland Bill had to decide whether some matters should be allowed to develop as conventions or whether detailed rules should be enacted. Again there is a mixture of the two. The appointment of Ministers of the Crown is ruled by the prerogative and convention, but the appointment of Scottish Ministers is specified in the Act since they are creatures of statute. The Act specifies the circumstances when a First Minister is to be nominated but leaves the actual procedure to be set by the Parliament in Standing Orders. The nomination for First Minister will usually be the leader of the party able to command a majority in Parliament but this is not specified in the Act and will therefore probably evolve into a convention. However improbable, the Parliament could nominate someone who had been elected as an independent MSP. The First Minister nominates the Scottish Ministers with the agreement of the Scottish Parliament and the approval of the Queen, but the number of Scottish Ministers and junior ministers is a matter for the First Minister alone. Presumably if the Scottish Parliament thought that there were too many or

---

[15] s. 81.
[16] s. 85.

too few they could withhold their agreement. Again it is thought that these matters will become the subjects of convention.

Elections to the Scottish Parliament

The process for electing the Scottish Parliament is contained in sections 1 to 18 of the Act and Schedule 1. The system adopted is mixed; it retains the first past the post electoral system for 73 constituencies with the additional member system of proportional representation to elect a further 56 members on a regional basis. The existing U.K. Parliament constituencies are retained with the exception of Orkney and Shetland constituency which is split in two, to give each island group its own constituency. There are eight regions, based on the boundaries set for the European Parliament elections and each region returns seven members. The Boundary Commission for Scotland will review the number of constituencies and indeed the number of Scottish constituencies at Westminster may be altered. Section 86 of the Act first removes the requirement that there must be at least 71 Scottish constituencies and then goes on to state that the electoral quota to be used in calculating the number of seats at the next boundary review will be the quota for England. It is thought that this will have the effect of reducing the number of Scottish constituencies to around 56, and so the number of constituency seats at the Scottish Parliament will automatically also be reduced. This will also trigger a reduction in the number of regional seats. The electoral quota for the following boundary review will revert to the Scottish quota. 8.06

The next review of electoral boundaries will occur between 2002 and 2006 and it is at this time that it is expected that the number of Scottish constituencies will fall. There is precedent for reducing representation at Westminster where a devolved system of government has been introduced. When the Northern Ireland Parliament was set up, the number of Westminster constituencies was reduced, rising again in the 1970s when the Parliament was abolished and direct rule reimposed. However the reduction in the number of Scottish M.P.s will not occur until after the next general election which must be held before May 2002. As Himsworth and Munro point out, the reduction in the number of Scottish M.P.s does not resolve the 'West Lothian question' but does go some way to alleviate it.[17] The 'West Lothian question' refers to the situation whereby Scottish M.P.s may debate and vote on measures which are applicable to English constituencies only, but English M.P.s may not

[17] Minsworth and Munro, *The Scotland Act 1998* (1999), p. 107.

debate and vote on similar measures affecting Scotland, since these have been devolved to the Scottish Parliament. It appears therefore that Scottish M.P.s would have an unfair influence over what happens in England but both Scots and English M.P.s would have no influence over what happens in Scotland. The West Lothian question is not answered by the Act and there remains the possibility of English M.P.s reacting badly to this anomalous situation. Indeed, questions were asked in June 1999 when former Scottish Office minister Helen Liddell was moved to the DETR as Transport Minister; an M.P. for an English constituency asked why an M.P. for a Scottish constituency was Minister for Transport in England. The Government's proposals for an elected mayor in London[18] and regional development agencies throughout England[19] may not be sufficient to allay fears that Scotland, Wales and Northern Ireland have been given unfair advantage at the expense of England.

8.07 Elections to the Scottish Parliament will be held every four years[20] although there is provision for extraordinary general elections to be held outwith the four-year normal term.[21] The extraordinary general election will be held if Parliament resolves, with a two-thirds majority, to dissolve itself or if there is no nomination for First Minister within the first 28 days after a general election or vacancy occurring.[22] The holding of an extraordinary general election will not normally disturb the four year cycle of elections unless the extraordinary general election has been held within six months of an ordinary general election. In this circumstance, the extraordinary general election replaces the ordinary one.

The date of the ordinary general election is set as the first Thursday in May[23] but there is provision for this date to be moved forward or back one month from the normal date. The Presiding Officer of the Parliament will propose whether the date should be moved thus removing the possibility of any political advantage in the date of the general election.

The Scottish Parliament is required to meet within seven days of the result of the poll being announced.[24]

8.08 The method of election chosen for the Scottish Parliament is a combination of first past the post and additional member system. Thus electors receive two ballot papers on polling day and may

---

[18] Greater London Authority Act 1999.
[19] Regional Development Agencies Act 1998.
[20] s. 2(2).
[21] s. 3.
[22] s. 46 deals with the appointment of the First Minister.
[23] s. 2(1).
[24] s. 2(3).

vote twice.[25] The first is the traditional ballot paper on which the names and parties of the candidates are printed and the elector places a cross in the box against the name of the candidate they wish to support. The number of votes for each candidate is counted and the one with the greatest number is elected to represent that constituency.

In the second ballot, the elector is able to vote for a specific party or individual candidate from a regional list. This second paper contains the names of the various parties and any person who wishes to stand as an individual 'independent' candidate. The elector again has only one vote. Each party will have nominated a list of its candidates for that region and this list is also printed on the ballot paper. A candidate for a constituency election may also be named as a candidate on the party's regional list. The actual voting process is straightforward and indeed it appeared that electors in the first election had few problems in voting, given that the number of spoilt papers did not increase appreciably.

The counting of the regional seats is the complicated part of the 8.09
process. The actual count for the regional seats cannot commence until all of the results for the constituencies in that region have been declared. If a candidate is elected for a constituency and their name was also on a party's regional list, their name will be deleted from the list. Then the constituency returning officers notify the regional returning officer of the total votes cast in the second ballot for each political party and any independent candidate. These are totaled for the region. The total for each party is then divided by the number of constituency seats won by the party, plus one. An example may help: if Party X has a total of 100,000 votes in the region and has won three constituency seats, the calculation will be 100,000 divided by four (*i.e.* 3 + 1) = 25,000. This process is carried out for each party and individual candidate. The first seat will be allocated to the party or person with the highest figure. If Party X with 25,000 is highest, it will gain one seat. That one seat changes the party's divisor to five (4 seats + 1) and the figure now will be 20,000. The next seat will again be allocated to the party or person with the highest figure, and so the process continues until all seven regional seats have been allocated.[26]

The results for the region should broadly reflect the proportion of votes cast for each party or person. In the May 1999 election,

---

[25] There is no compulsion on electors to vote in both the constituency and the regional election; they can choose to abstain in one or other.

[26] For a detailed examination of how this process works, see McFadden and Lazarowicz, *The Scottish Parliament: An Introduction* (1999), p. 26.

the Labour Party won 53 constituency seats but only three regional seats. The Conservatives won no constituency seats but 18 from the regional list. The SNP won seven constituencies and 28 from the regional list while the Liberal Democrats won 12 constituency seats and five regional seats. Labour won 73 per cent of the constituency seats with 39 per cent of the constituency vote, thus illustrating that the first past the post system does not give proportional results. The additional member system helps to adjust this result by allocating additional seats from the regional vote to other parties, so that Labour's final allocation of seats worked out at 43 per cent. The SNP was the main beneficiary of the new system but it also helped the Conservatives and smaller parties such as the Green Party and the Scottish Socialist Party, both of whom won one regional seat.[27]

8.10 Sections 9 and 10 detail how vacancies are to be filled. A vacancy occurring in a constituency seat will trigger a by-election, normally to be held within three months[28] unless the date for an ordinary general election falls within that three months. The precise date is fixed by the Presiding Officer, thus again removing the possibility of political advantage to any of the political parties. Section 9(6) forbids existing MSPs to stand in the by-election; so a member elected on the party list may not try to win a constituency seat at a by-election unless they resign their seat. Regional vacancies are dealt with in section 10. Here there is no by-election. Instead, where the MSP was returned as an individual candidate the seat will remain vacant until the next general election.[29] If the MSP was returned from a party's regional list, the next unelected person on that party's list will be offered the seat.[30] The regional returning officer then notifies the person's name to the Presiding Officer and the person takes the vacant seat. If however, there is no unelected person on the party's list who is willing to serve, the seat remains vacant until the next general election.

A member may resign their seat by giving notice in writing to the Presiding Officer[31] and the vacancy will be treated as discussed above. This simple procedure contrasts with the position in the House of Commons where an M.P. may not simply resign; they must seek a disqualifying office under the House of Commons

---

[27] See analysis of the results in Curtis and Vidler, *Scottish Parliament Election Results* (1999).

[28] s. 9(3).

[29] s. 10(2).

[30] s. 10(3).

[31] s. 14.

Disqualification Act 1975, such as the Stewardship of the Chiltern Hundreds. By accepting the office, the M.P. becomes disqualified and their seat is declared vacant.

Disqualification from membership of the Scottish Parliament under section 15 will occur if the person is disqualified under the House of Commons Disqualification Act 1975, s. 1(1)(a) to (e), or is otherwise disqualified by some other statute, or is a Lord of Appeal in Ordinary or the holder of an office specified in an Order in Council made under this section. The persons disqualified under the 1975 Act include judges, civil servants, members of the armed forces, police officers and members of foreign legislatures. Also disqualified are aliens (but citizens of the E.U. who are resident in the United Kingdom are excepted from the disqualification by s. 16(2)), those who are mentally ill, undischarged bankrupts and persons convicted of corrupt or illegal electoral practices. Section 16 details various exceptions to section 15. These include peers and peeresses who may stand for election to the Scottish Parliament, and priests and ministers of any religious denomination. If a person is disqualified from being an MSP but is so elected, the return is held to be void and the seat is declared vacant.[32] Questions of disqualification may be referred to the Court of Session for resolution under section 18. This section has no time-limit so anyone wishing to challenge the election of a candidate may do so at any time. This contrasts with the position under the Representation of the People Act 1983 whereby an election petition must be presented by a registered elector within 21 days of the declaration of the result of the poll. 8.11

Officers of Parliament

The Parliament is required to elect a Presiding Officer and two deputies at its first meeting after the general election.[33] The Presiding Officer and the deputies hold office until the next such election which would normally occur at the first meeting of a newly elected Parliament. Thus the tenure of these officials does not cease when Parliament is dissolved. Schedule 3 provides that the Parliament's Standing Orders will provide that the Presiding Officer and deputies will not all represent the same political party. The Presiding Officer has a number of statutory functions such as being responsible for declaring the date of the next general election, being a member of the Scottish Parliamentary Corporate 8.12

[32] s. 17(1).
[33] s. 19.

Body and submitting Bills for Royal Assent. The Government's White Paper, *Scotland's Parliament*,[34] declared that the Presiding Officer would "ensure the efficient conduct and administration of Scottish parliamentary business" as well as chairing the meetings.

Section 20 provides for the appointment of a Clerk of the Parliament by the Scottish Parliamentary Corporate Body. It also provides for the Clerk's functions to be exercised by an assistant clerk. Both the Clerk and the assistants are members of the staff of Parliament and their terms and conditions of employment are determined by the Corporate Body.[35]

The Scottish Parliamentary Corporate Body, also referred to as the Parliamentary Corporation, is set up under section 21 and Schedule 2. The members of the parliamentary corporation are the Presiding Officer and four MSPs and their main function is to ensure that Parliament has the property, staff and services it requires. The Scottish Parliament is not a body corporate, unlike the National Assembly of Wales, which is such a body.[36] Accordingly there is a need for a legal body to be created to hold property, enter into contracts and bring or defend legal actions. Similar arrangements were made for the House of Commons under the House of Commons (Administration) Act 1978 which set up the House of Commons Commission as a body corporate. Separate corporate officers for the two Houses were established by the Parliamentary Corporate Bodies Act 1992.[37]

The parliamentary corporation is able to hold property and may accept the transfer of property from a minister of the Crown or department. According to Schedule 3, paragraph 4, the corporation can enter into contracts, charge for goods or services, make investments and accept gifts. The corporation is important since it ensures that all members are provided with facilities and these are not dependent on the Scottish Executive.

Members of the Scottish Parliament

8.13 Although there is a difference in how the constituency and regional members are elected, thereafter there is no difference in their status and they all have the same rights, responsibilities and privileges.

---

[34] *Scotland's Parliament*, Cm. 3658 (1997), para. 9.5.

[35] Sched. 2, para. 3.

[36] Government of Wales Act 1998, s. 1.

[37] See *Harmon (CFEM) Facades (U.K.) v. Corporate Officer of the House of Commons* (1997).

All members must take the oath of allegiance, usually at the first meeting of the Parliament after the general election.[38] The form of oath is prescribed by the Promissory Oaths Act 1868 and must be taken within two months of being elected. The member may not participate in the proceedings of Parliament or receive a salary or allowances until the oath has been taken. The oath has also to be taken each time the member is returned regardless of whether or not they have previously taken the oath.

The Parliament is required to decide on the level of remuneration of members of the Parliament and of the Scottish Executive.[39] This remuneration includes salary, pension provision and allowances such as secretarial support and travel. The White Paper stated that the Government would ask the independent Senior Salaries Review Body to set the initial salaries and thereafter that any changes should be related to changes in the salaries of M.P.s.[40]

When the Parliament was proposed there were a number of Scottish M.P.s who expressed their intention to stand for the Scottish Parliament. This raised the issue that an M.P. could also become an MSP and be able to draw two salaries. Section 82 seeks to address this by requiring the Scottish Parliament to ensure that the salary from the Scottish Parliament is reduced by an appropriate amount. Most of those M.P.s who were returned as MSPs in 1999 have indicated that they will either resign their Westminster seats over the coming year or will not seek re-election at the next U.K. general election. The section applies to MSPs who are also returned as MEPs.

Members of the Scottish Parliament are protected against action 8.14
in defamation regarding remarks made by the MSP in the Parliament.[41] Such statements are held to be absolutely privileged.[42] The privilege is necessary to ensure that MSPs enjoy freedom of debate within Parliament. The publications authorised by Parliament are also protected by section 41(1)(b) and by the provisions of the Defamation Act 1996, s. 15 where privilege is granted to a report of proceedings which is fair and accurate and made without malice.[43]

The Scottish Parliament is subject to the general law on contempt of court and is required to adopt Standing Orders which will include a *sub judice* rule to restrict discussion of cases before

---

[38] s. 84.

[39] s. 81(1).

[40] *Scotland's Parliament*, Cm. 3658 (1997), para. 9.3.

[41] s. 41.

[42] Members of the U.K. Parliament enjoy such privilege by virtue of the Bill of Rights 1689.

[43] *Beach v. Freeson* [1972] 1 Q.B. 14; *Cook v. Alexander* [1974] Q.B. 279.

the courts.[44] However a limited form of immunity is granted by section 42 whereby proceedings in relation to a Bill or subordinate legislation will not be covered by the strict liability rule of the Contempt of Court Act 1981.

Finally, the Parliament is subject to the provisions of the Prevention of Corruption Acts 1889 to 1916.[45]

Members' interests

8.15 During the Major Government years (1990–97) there was increased disquiet in Parliament and the country as a whole over 'sleaze'. In 1994, John Major attempted to resolve this issue by establishing the Committee on Standards in Public Life (originally called the Nolan Committee after its first chairman, now called the Neill Committee). The committee was asked to look at how standards in the House of Commons could be enforced. The committee's first report made recommendations that were largely accepted and implemented and since then the committee has investigated other areas of public life.[46] However, none of the recommendations made with respect to the U.K. Parliament has been incorporated into statute and the House still operates a system of self-regulation.[47]

The members of the Scottish Parliament are required by section 39 to enter any relevant interests in the Register of Members' Interests which is open to public inspection and indeed is available on the Parliament's web site. The Parliament is required to provide by statute for the conduct of MSPs in respect of their financial interests and in this regard, a transitional order was made by the Secretary of State for Scotland under the 1998 Act.[48] The 1998 Act also requires the Parliament to regulate the lobbying of MSPs and the Parliament's staff.

Proceedings of Parliament

8.16 Section 22 of the Act states that the procedures to be used in the Parliament will be regulated by Standing Orders, and goes on to state that Schedule 3 will provide for certain matters to be dealt with in those orders. Some of these matters must be included in the

---

[44] Sched. 3, para. 1.
[45] s. 43.
[46] First Report of the Committee on Standards in Public Life, Cm. 2850 (1995).
[47] For fuller discussion, see Chap. 12.
[48] Scotland Act (Transitory and Transitional Provisions) (Members' Interests) Order 1999 (S.I. 1999 No. 1350).

Standing Orders but others are discretionary. While the Scotland Bill was being debated in the U.K. Parliament, the Secretary of State for Scotland set up a consultative steering group (CSG) to consider how the Parliament would operate and what its procedures should be. The CSG included members from the four main political parties under the chairmanship of Minister of State, Henry McLeish. The CSG produced its final report in January 1999.[49]

The Secretary of State for Scotland promulgated an order for Standing Orders, based on the CSG recommendations, to be used during the first few months of the Parliament.[50] These will cease to operate once the Parliament makes and brings into force its own Standing Orders. The CSG recommended that the Standing Orders should be accompanied by guidance on the operation of the Parliament so that the lay person would be able to understand them.

The mandatory requirements for the Standing Orders include provision for preserving order in the proceedings of Parliament, proceedings to be held in public, reporting and publishing the proceedings of Parliament, and ensuring that committees and sub-committees are politically balanced with regard to their membership. Discretionary requirements include provision for excluding a member from proceedings, withdrawing a member's privileges and excluding a member of the public from Parliament.

Powers and privileges of Parliament

Parliament is given power to call for witnesses and documents,[51] 8.17
and anyone who is properly summoned to attend or produce documents[52] but fails to do so, is guilty of an offence which is punishable by a fine of up to Level 5 on the Standard Scale[53] or up to three months' imprisonment.[54] It is important that the Parliament is able to fully investigate issues within its competence and thus the power to compel witnesses to attend is crucial to its work. The Scottish Parliament does not however have the same powers of punishment as the U.K. Parliament, which is itself able to punish individuals for contempt of Parliament. Failure to adhere to a summons from the Scottish Parliament is punished by the Scottish courts.

---

49 CSG, *Shaping Scotland's Parliament* (1999).

50 Scotland Act (Transitory and Transitional Provisions) (Standing Orders and Parliamentary Publications) Order 1999 (S.I. 1999 No. 1095).

51 s. 23.

52 s. 24.

53 Currently £5,000.

54 s. 25.

A witness summoned to give evidence to the Parliament must be given notice in writing. If a person is required to produce documents, the notice must specify which documents are required and when they are required. The Standing Orders may provide that the Presiding Officer administers an oath to witnesses[55] and provide that refusal to take the oath is an offence.

Sections 23 to 26 do not however confer a specific right of scrutiny of the Executive by the Parliament although section 91 requires that arrangements be set up to investigate complaints of maladministration against a member of the Scottish Executive or an office-holder in the Scottish Administration. The Parliamentary Ombudsman was appointed as Ombudsman for the Scottish Parliament in July 1999.

Scottish Administration

8.18 The Scottish Administration is composed of four elements: the Scottish Executive, junior ministers, non-ministerial office-holders and civil servants. These are detailed in Part II of the Act which sets out their respective functions.

Scottish Executive

8.19 This comprises the First Minister, ministers appointed by the First Minister and the Scottish Law Officers, the Lord Advocate and the Solicitor General for Scotland.[56] The Act states that the members of the Scottish Executive are to be known collectively as the Scottish Ministers[57] and it is this body to whom statutory functions are given and transferred from Ministers of the Crown. The Act provides that a person may not hold concurrent office as a minister of the U.K. government and a member of the Scottish Executive.[58] This provision was inserted by the Government at a late stage of the Bill because it was accepted that it would be inappropriate for someone to hold office in both governments. However this argument was not accepted for the Government of Wales Act.

The Scottish Ministers are collectively responsible for the actions of each individual and the actions of individual ministers are binding on all.[59] Any functions conferred on Scottish Ministers may

---

[55] s. 26(1).
[56] s. 44(1).
[57] s. 44(2).
[58] s. 44(3).
[59] s. 52(4).

be exercised by any other minister[60] except where the functions are conferred on the First Minister alone or retained functions of the Lord Advocate. Their actions in these circumstances are not attributable to the Scottish Executive as a whole.[61] If one minister is censured by the Parliament and a vote of no confidence in the Scottish Executive is then passed the whole Executive must resign. There is no provision for forcing the resignation of one minister alone.

The First Minister is appointed by the sovereign[62] from a nomination made by the Parliament,[63] and holds office at their Majesty's pleasure. Accordingly, in theory he may also be dismissed by the sovereign. In any event he will cease to hold office as soon as another First Minister is appointed.[64] The First Minister must be an MSP and he may resign at any time and is required to do so if Parliament passes a vote of no confidence in the Scottish Executive. The First Minister is nominated after a general election or if the office becomes vacant following resignation or some other event, such as death or incapacity, or if the First Minister is no longer an MSP. The nomination of the Parliament is notified to the sovereign by the Presiding Officer and it must be made within 28 days of the event which has made the nomination necessary. It appears that after a general election a victorious First Minister must still be nominated by the Parliament, unlike a victorious Prime Minister who simply continues in office. After the first election in May 1999, three candidates stood for the nomination as First Minister. The CSG had recommended that a ballot or series of eliminating ballots should be held until one candidate emerged with majority support. This ballot occurred and Donald Dewar emerged as the person nominated for First Minister.[65]

The inclusion of the two Scottish Law Officers as members of 8.20
the Scottish Executive has raised concerns regarding their independence, both during the passage of the Bill and more recently. They

---

[60] s. 53(2).

[61] s. 52(5).

[62] s. 45.

[63] s. 46.

[64] s. 42(3).

[65] The procedure for appointing the Scottish First Minister is in contrast to the procedure for the First Minister in the Northern Ireland Act 1998 at s. 16 which requires the First Minister and Deputy First Minister to be elected from the Assembly on a cross-community vote, *i.e.* they must secure a majority of members voting, as well as a majority of Nationalists voting and a majority of the Unionists voting. None of the ministers holds office at H.M.'s pleasure and thus none is dismissible.

are appointed or removed under section 48 by the sovereign on the recommendation of the First Minister after the First Minister has obtained the agreement of the Parliament. They may resign at any time and are required to do so if the Parliament passes a vote of no confidence in the Scottish Executive. The Scottish Parliament, however, has no power to remove the Lord Advocate from the position as the head of the systems of criminal prosecution and investigation of deaths in Scotland.[66] If the Parliament resolves that the Scottish Executive should resign, then the Lord Advocate will continue in office for all retained functions until a new Lord Advocate is appointed, thus ensuring continuity.[67] The independence of the Lord Advocate in the criminal justice matters is preserved by section 48(5) and certain 'retained functions' of the Lord Advocate may not be carried out by other ministers of the Scottish Executive.[68] The Scottish Law Officers may be members of the Scottish Parliament and so participate in its business, but if either or both of them are not MSPs, they may still participate in the proceedings of Parliament but not vote.[69] The Law Officers thus may not necessarily be MSPs; they may continue to be appointed from members of the Scottish legal profession. Traditionally, the appointments have been made from the ranks of the Scottish Bar but during the Bill's parliamentary proceedings, the Lord Advocate admitted that there was no reason to restrict appointments to members of the Bar.[70] If the Law Officers are questioned on a matter regarding a criminal prosecution, they may decline to answer or produce documents if this would prejudice the criminal proceedings.

The Law Officer functions of the Lord Advocate in relation to reserved matters are transferred to a new Law Officer, the Advocate General for Scotland who will advise the U.K. government on constitutional, reserved and devolved matters.[71] The Advocate General for Scotland is appointed by the Prime Minister and may or may not be a member of either House.[72] During the parliamentary debates on the Bill the Government conceded that the Advocate General for Scotland should be a person with 'appropriate standing and qualification in Scots law' but need not

---

66 s. 29(2)(e).
67 s. 48(3).
68 s. 52(5).
69 s. 27.
70 593 H.L. Official Report (5th series) col. 2032, Oct. 28, 1998.
71 s. 87.
72 The first Advocate General for Scotland is Dr Lynda Clark, Q.C., MP.

be a solicitor or advocate, thus raising the possibility that the position could be held by an academic.

The First Minister appoints ministers with the agreement of Parliament and the approval of the sovereign.[73] Such ministers hold office at the pleasure of the sovereign and thus may be removed from office by the sovereign on the recommendation of the First Minister; they may resign at any time and must do so if there is a vote of no confidence in the Scottish Executive. It is worth noting that a nomination by the First Minister to appoint a minister requires the agreement of Parliament, but no such agreement is required by the First Minister to dismiss a minister. Deputy Scottish Ministers may also be appointed in a similar way by the First Minister.[74] Note that the First Minister must seek the agreement of the Parliament for all nominations for ministers whereas the U.K. Prime Minister does not seek such approval or agreement. The First Minister's nominations for ministers may be agreed by the Parliament but it is for the First Minister alone to decide which nominee will hold which ministerial portfolio. There is no limit to the number of ministers who may be appointed; Donald Dewar appointed nine ministers and a similar number of junior ministers, thus creating a surprisingly large Scottish Executive. 8.21

Section 51 enables the First Minister to appoint persons to be members of the staff of the Scottish Administration and provides that such staff will be members of the Home Civil Service. Salaries and expenses of the staff are to be met out of the Scottish Consolidated Fund. The terms and conditions of service of staff are determined by the Civil Service Management Code. Non-ministerial office-holders who are deemed to be part of the Scottish Administration are the Registrar of Births, Deaths and Marriages for Scotland, the Keeper of the Registers and the Keeper of the Records of Scotland, and any other office specified in an Order in Council made under section 128(8)(b).[75] These office-holders and their staff remain as members of the Home Civil Service. It was thought important by the U.K. government and Parliament that the staff of the Scottish Administration should remain part of the U.K. civil service to preserve the Union[76] but it is equally important for these civil servants to retain the ability to seek promotion within a unified service. Responsibility for the

---

[73] s. 47.

[74] s. 49.

[75] *e.g.* the Accountant in Bankruptcy.

[76] McFadden and Lazarowicz, *op. cit.*, p. 60.

management of the civil service remains with U.K. Minister for the Civil Service[77] although day-to-day management is delegated to Scottish Ministers in the same way as happens in U.K. government departments. The Scottish Parliament has no power to legislate for the civil service, this being a reserved matter.[78]

Functions of the Scottish Ministers

8.22 Functions which are conferred by statute on Scottish Ministers are exercisable on behalf of the sovereign[79] and may be exercised by any member of the Scottish Executive. However there are certain functions conferred on the First Minister alone and some retained functions of the Lord Advocate which may not be exercised by anyone else. Initially the powers conferred on the Scottish Ministers come from sections 53 and 54 but eventually their powers will come from Acts of the Scottish Parliament. Section 52(6) defines the "retained functions" of the Lord Advocate and is one of a series of measures designed to protect the independence of the Scottish Law Officers and in particular the place of the Lord Advocate as head of the criminal prosecution service and system of investigation of deaths.[80]

Section 53 specifies the functions to be exercisable by the Scottish Ministers instead of Ministers of the Crown. These functions may have been conferred on Ministers of the Crown by the Royal Prerogative or statute and they were transferred to the Scottish Ministers on "devolution day", that is July 1, 1999. The functions are exercisable so far as they relate to matters of devolved competence. The test as to whether a function is a devolved function is given in section 54; it is defined by reference to what is outside devolved competence and this is any matter which would be outside the legislative competence of the Scottish Parliament.[81]

Normally, where a statute confers a function on the Secretary of State that function may be exercised by any Secretary of State unless the Act also names the Secretary of State.[82] Thus any Scottish Minister may exercise any devolved function with the exception of those conferred on the First Minister or the Lord Advocate as

---

[77] s. 51(4); note that the Minister for the Civil Service is normally the Prime Minister.
[78] Sched. 5, Pt 1, para. 8.
[79] s. 51(2).
[80] s. 29(2)(e).
[81] s. 54(2).
[82] *Agee v. Lord Advocate*, 1977 S.L.T. (Notes) 54.

mentioned above, and any pre-commencement enactment referring to a Minister of the Crown is to be read as if it referred to a Scottish Minister.[83]

In many pieces of U.K. legislation, there is a statutory obligation on a minister to exercise a function after consultation with, or with the agreement of, another minister such as a Treasury minister. Where a function has been devolved, it becomes exercisable by a Scottish Minister and it would have been difficult, particularly in political terms, to leave the requirement for agreement or consultation with an U.K. minister in respect of a devolved power. Thus section 55(1) removes any requirements or such agreement or consultation to be required, but section 55(2) retains a requirement for such agreement to be sought from the Treasury when designating or modifying enterprise zones.

Inevitably there will be instances when U.K. ministers need to 8.23
exercise their powers within Scotland and section 56 deals with the sharing of such powers. They include matters such as grants and loans for the construction of railways and harbours, the enforcement of United Nations Security Council resolutions, contributions towards mineral exploration, assistance for arrangements for employment and training, and road safety information and training. These shared powers could cause difficulty for the two sets of ministers and their departments and in the anticipation of this, the U.K. Government announced that the Scottish Administration and U.K. departments would develop 'concordats' or agreements to co-ordinate their shared functions. These concordats are not legally binding but will have political force. Himsworth and Munro[84] reflect that breach of a concordat might give rise to judicial review on the grounds of breach of legitimate expectation.

Section 57 allows a Minister of the Crown to exercise functions to implement obligations under Community law even if that function has been transferred to a Scottish Minister under section 53. The power to use section 2(2) of the European Communities Act 1972 to make legislation to implement E.C. law is available to Scottish Ministers as well as to U.K. ministers. Scottish Ministers, however, are specifically prevented from making legislation that is incompatible with Convention rights or Community law.[85] Thus by section 29, the Scottish Parliament is prohibited from enacting legislation which is contrary to Convention rights or E.C. law and the Scottish Ministers are similarly prevented by section 57.

---

[83] s. 117.

[84] Himsworth and Munro, *The Scotland Act 1998* (1999), p. 73.

[85] s. 57(2).

8.24 If the Secretary of State has reasonable grounds to believe that proposed action by a Scottish Minister will be incompatible with any international obligations, the Secretary of State may by order direct that the action should not be taken.[86] Conversely if the Secretary of State believes that action should be taken by a Scottish Minister to implement an international obligation the Secretary of State can order that the action be taken.[87] The word "action" in both subsections is defined in section 58(3) as including the introduction of a Bill into the Parliament or making subordinate legislation. Further if subordinate legislation made by a member of the Scottish Executive contains provisions which are incompatible with international obligations, to the interests of defence or national security, or appear to be modifying the law relating to reserved matters to the detriment of the operation of the law, then the Secretary of State may by order revoke the legislation.[88] Section 58 deals with the activities of the Scottish Executive in similar ways to section 35 which provides for ways to prevent the Scottish Parliament legislating in matters which have not been devolved.

The Secretary of State referred to in section 58 is any Secretary of State, not just the Secretary of State for Scotland. So if a Scottish Minister wished to change the speed limit on motorways in Scotland, the Secretary of State for the Department of the Environment, Transport and the Regions would be able to prevent that from happening since speed limits are a reserved matter specified in Schedule 5, Part II, section E1. If the Secretary of State exercises their powers under section 58 they must state their reasons for making the order. This will of course assist if the decision is challenged by way of judicial review.

However, the Act allows the U.K. government to transfer powers in reserved matters from Ministers of the Crown to the Scottish Executive.[89] This has been called 'executive devolution'.[90] The transfer of such powers does not however include the transfer of legislative competence in these matters to the Scottish Parliament. The powers will be exercisable by Scottish Ministers instead of U.K. ministers, or indeed they may be exercisable jointly. In addition a function may be exercisable by a U.K. minister but this will only occur after consultation with or with the consent of

---

[86] s. 58(1).
[87] s. 58(2).
[88] s. 58(4).
[89] s. 63.
[90] Page, Reid and Ross, *A Guide to the Scotland Act 1998* (1999).

Scottish Ministers. The White Paper[91] clearly envisaged that the government would confer additional powers on the Scottish Ministers and this is done by using the order-making power of section 63. During the Act's passage through Parliament, a draft Order in Council was published listing the functions that might be devolved under section 63.[92] These included measures regarding betting, gaming and lotteries; firearms licensing; extradition; appointments to tribunals; roads and transport; funding for Gaelic broadcasting and the running of public sector pensions. Many of these functions were performed by the Secretary of State for Scotland before devolution. Such executive devolution orders are subject to the affirmative resolution procedure in both the Scottish Parliament and at Westminster.[93]

The Act also gives authority to transfer a function from a Scottish Minister to the U.K. government and this is done by an Order in Council made with the agreement of both Parliaments.[94] This provision was added at the Commons report stage to allow the U.K. government to recover devolved functions where it has become necessary to do so. The function may have been added to the list of reserved matters under Schedule 5 or the government may wish to vary the executive devolution settlement of section 63. In either event, the transfer has to be agreed by both Parliaments.

Financial provisions of the Act

The Scottish voters in the referendum of March 1979 rejected 8.25
the 1978 Scotland Act partly because of the lack of any tax-raising powers for the proposed Scottish Assembly. The Government's 1997 White Paper[95] advocated arrangements whereby the Scottish Parliament would receive a block grant from the U.K. government together with powers to vary the basic rate of U.K. standard rate income tax by 3p in the pound. These arrangements would allow the Parliament to determine its own spending priorities while the U.K. government would retain control over public spending and public borrowing at U.K. level. Part III of the Act sets out, in a fairly skeletal form, the way in which the finances of the new Parliament will be dealt with.

A Scottish Consolidated Fund is established in section 64(1). The block grant from the U.K. Treasury is paid into the Scottish

[91] *Scotland's Parliament*, Cm. 3658 (1997), para. 2.7.
[92] Transfer of Functions (Scottish Ministers) Order 1999 (S.I. 1999 No. 1104).
[93] Sched. 7.
[94] s. 108.
[95] *Scotland's Parliament*, Cm. 3658 (1997).

Consolidated Fund by the Secretary of State and it is from this fund that payments are made to the Scottish Parliament and the Scottish Administration. Any sums received by these bodies will be paid into the fund.

The amount of the block grant is calculated in virtually the same way as the amounts previously allocated to the Scottish Office. The amount of grant is negotiated in the annual spending round and agreed by the Cabinet and then a formula is used to adjust the amount by which the departments with responsibility for equivalent services in England have had their spending increased or reduced for that year. This formula is called the Barnett Formula, after the former Chief Secretary to the Treasury, Joel Barnett, and was introduced in 1978 to adjust the spending plans for the three territorial departments, Scotland, Wales and Northern Ireland. Barnett defined the formula in his evidence to the Treasury Select Committee in 1997: "Put simply, the Barnett Formula set percentages for changes in comparable expenditure in Great Britain. That is to say, it would be 85 per cent for England, 15 per cent for Scotland and five per cent for Wales."[96] The proportions are population based and Scotland received 11.76 per cent of the total Great Britain expenditure, while Wales received 5.88 per cent. In 1995, these proportions were revised to take account of the 1991 Census of Population data; Scotland now receives 10.66 per cent and Wales 6.02 per cent. In addition, the proportions are applied to any increases (or reductions) in the budget for a particular service, not on the total budget itself. So if the Cabinet decide that there should be an increase in expenditure in education across Great Britain of £1 billion, Scotland will receive an additional sum of £106.6 million, while Wales will get £60.2 million.

The Barnett Formula will continue to be used to calculate how much money the Scottish Parliament and Administration will receive. There will be additional sums for additional devolved responsibilities: agriculture, forestry, council tax benefit and nationalised industries. The formula will be updated annually to take account of changes in population estimates and so based on this, the amount of increased expenditure will reduce for Scotland since the proportion of population in Scotland compared to England is now 10.45 per cent compared to the Barnett Formula of 10.66 per cent.

---

[96] Second Report of the Treasury Select Committee, *The Barnett Formula* (1997–98 H.C. 341), Q.1.

The formula is not statutory and is not included in the Scotland Act. The White Paper envisaged that any substantial revision of the formula "would need to be preceded by an in depth study of relative spending requirements and would be the subject of full consultation between the Scottish Executive and the U.K. Government."[97] However, the lack of a statutory requirement to consult with the Scottish Parliament, or even the U.K. Parliament, gives considerable power to the U.K. Treasury with whom the discretion to change the method of calculating the formula will remain. The ability of the U.K. government to control the finances of the Scottish Parliament may lead to a weakness in the devolution system. Hopkins points out that in Europe, the Italian system of regional government is weak because of a lack of financial autonomy whereas the German, Belgian and Spanish regions do have financial autonomy and are strong institutions. "When policy differences arise between the centre and the devolved entities it will take a very restrained U.K. government not to use its financial leverage to its advantage."[98] The amount of the block grant has to be negotiated each year by the Secretary of State with the Treasury and the Barnett Formula is then used to 'top up' the block grant when English departments negotiate increased expenditure. The Scotland Act 1998 says that the Secretary of State: "shall from time to time make payments . . . out of money provided by Parliament of such amounts as he may determine."[99]

This gives the Secretary of State considerable power over the Scottish Executive and Parliament and illustrates the dependence of the Parliament on the goodwill of the Secretary of State and the U.K. Parliament. In addition, the Scottish Parliament depends on the Secretary of State fighting hard in Cabinet to obtain the maximum resources for the Scottish Parliament. These raise some interesting questions. First, will the Secretary of State fight hard if the Scottish Parliament and Executive are controlled by a party not his own? Secondly, how will the negotiations proceed if, as is rumoured may happen, the office of Secretary of State for Scotland is no longer a Cabinet post? The annual budget settlements will undoubtedly cause much of the inevitable friction that will occur between Edinburgh and London in the next few years.[1]

---

[97] *Scotland's Parliament*, Cm. 3658 (1997), para. 7.7.

[98] Hopkins, "Devolution from a Comparative Perspective" (1998) Vol. 4(3) E.P.L. 323 at 327.

[99] s. 64(2).

[1] For discussion of the Barnett Formula, see Twigger, *The Barnett Formula* (1998).

8.26 The operation of the Scottish Consolidated Fund is strictly controlled and the same kind of measures for payments out of the fund exist here as in the U.K. Consolidated Fund. So money may only be paid out of the fund if it has been authorised by any enactment, whether of the United Kingdom or Scottish Parliament, or is authorised by the Scotland Act, or it is paid out in accordance with rules made by an Act of the Scottish Parliament to meet expenditure of the Scottish Administration.[2] The amounts paid out of the fund can only be used for the purpose for which they were appropriated.[3] Scottish Ministers do not have a general power to borrow but are given borrowing powers under section 66 to meet temporary shortfalls of cash or to provide a working balance in the fund. An upper limit of £500 million is specified in section 67 for such borrowings although this may be increased by the Secretary of State with the Treasury's consent. The Scottish Parliament does not have power to confer borrowing powers on the Scottish Executive and the Scottish Executive may only borrow by using section 66 or by powers granted by a U.K. statute. The members of the Scottish Executive have limited power to make loans to statutory bodies[4] but these must not be at preferential rates of interest. The interest must be the same or higher than the lowest rates determined by the Treasury for similar loans made from the National Loans Fund.

The Act requires the Parliament to legislate in a financial framework for the operation of the Scottish Parliament and Scottish Administration. This legislation will have to be one of the earliest Bills considered and passed by the Scottish Parliament since the transitional arrangements run out at the end of the financial year 1999–2000. In a Consultation Paper published in August 1999, the Scottish Executive stated its intention to introduce a Public Finance and Accountability Bill in September 1999.[5] The Paper is based on the recommendations of the Financial Issues Advisory Group (FIAG) which was set up in early 1998 to consider the financial management of the Scottish Parliament and the procedures which would be required. The FIAG Report proposed a different process of parliamentary approval for the allocation of resources to spending programmes by giving the

---

[2] s. 65(1).

[3] s. 65(3).

[4] s. 68.

[5] Scottish Executive, *Consultation Paper on a Financial Framework for the Scottish Parliament* (1999) http://www.scotland.gov.uk/library2/doc02/fdcon-00.htm, Aug. 5, 1999.

Parliament more financial control than the House of Commons has. There would be three stages of scrutiny as given in Table 1.

Table 1

Stage		Timescale
1.	Consideration of spending strategy and broad priorities by Parliament.	Before summer recess
2.	Examination of draft budget in detail at the level below the main programme. Finance Committee will collate alternative proposals.	Late autumn
3.	Formal consideration by Parliament of firm budget proposals. Parliament able to reject or approve the package but NOT amend it.	November/December

The FIAG recommended that the Scottish Parliament should seek the views of the public on the initial spending proposals and the Scottish Executive has indicated that it will have public consultations on the firm budget proposals.

The Scottish Executive's annual budget proposals will be approved by primary legislation and only a member of the Executive is able to introduce such Bills or propose amendments to them. The Scottish Executive proposed in its consultation paper that changes to the funding proposals should not require primary legislation because of the four-week delay inherent in passing any Act of the Scottish Parliament. The Public Finance and Accountability (Scotland) Act 2000 confers on Scottish Ministers the power to approve budgets or budget revisions by Budget Orders which would require approval by Parliament.

The Act also sets up a system of audit and financial control. An Auditor General for Scotland is appointed by Her Majesty on the nomination of the Scottish Parliament.[6] The Auditor General is given reasonable security of tenure by requiring the Scottish Parliament to vote with a two-thirds majority for his removal and by specifying the independence of his office from direction or control by either the Parliament or Scottish Executive.[7] The specific functions of the Auditor General are to be determined by the Parliament but section 70 requires these to include the examination of parliamentary accounts, issue of credits for the payments out of the fund, carrying out examinations into the way in which the Scottish ministers and Lord Advocate have used their

---

[6] s. 69(1).
[7] s. 69(4).

resources to ensure economy, efficiency and effectiveness, the preparation of accounts, appointment of staff of the Scottish Administration to act as accounting officers, and the publication of accounts and reports. The FIAG recommended that there should be an audit body, Audit Scotland, comprising the audit staff of the Accounts Commission and the National Audit Office in Scotland to carry out audit work for the Auditor General for Scotland and the Accounts Commission.

8.27 One of the most contentious aspects of the devolution proposals was the tax-varying power. During the elections for the Scottish Parliament, three of the main parties promised not to use the power either for the time being or not at all, while the fourth main party, the SNP, promised to spend more on education by raising income tax by one pence using the Acts' powers. Many political commentators have surmised that this promise led to a poorer than expected showing by the SNP in the poll.

The tax-varying power is set out in Part IV of the Act and it is based on the proposals made by the Scottish Constitutional Convention in their final report.[8] The Convention was adamant that such powers of taxation were essential if the Parliament was to function effectively. The 1997 referendum included a second question in which the electorate was asked to approve such powers being given to the Parliament. There was considerable support for the idea. Note that the provisions in the Act for the tax-varying powers are comprehensive compared to those pertaining to the block grant; this was necessary since the power to levy taxes is a power reserved to the U.K. Parliament.[9]

The power is given in section 73 to vary the basic rate of income tax by a maximum of three pence in the pound and this variation can be an increase or decrease in the rate. This would raise around £450 million each year (or cost £450 million in lost revenue to the Scottish Parliament if the rate is reduced). The tax will not be levied on income from savings or dividends[10] and the rate of variation may be specified as a whole or half number.

The variation is made by the Scottish Parliament passing a resolution to that effect[11] and this resolution may be moved only by a member of the Scottish Executive.[12] The first year in which such a resolution can have effect is the tax year of assessment 2000–01.

---

[8] *Scotland's Parliament. Scotland's Right* (1995).

[9] Sched. 5, Pt II, s. A.1.

[10] s. 73(3).

[11] s. 73(1)(a).

[12] s. 74(5).

Where a resolution is passed to vary the rate of income tax, the resolution must relate to a year of assessment which begins after the resolution is passed, but not more than 12 months afterwards.[13] If however, the U.K. Parliament has not determined the U.K. rate until after the commencement of the tax year then the Scottish Parliament is given one month from the time the U.K. rate is set to pass its own resolution for that tax year.

The resolution will apply to Scottish taxpayers only and they are 8.28
defined in section 75 as people resident within the United Kingdom for tax purposes and Scotland is "the part of the United Kingdom with which (they have) the closest connection during that year."[14] The 'Scottish taxpayer' refers to individuals and includes sole traders and partners in firms but the tax will not apply to non-natural persons such as companies. The concept of residence is well settled in tax law but difficulties may arise in establishing the meaning of "closest connection". Section 75(2) tries to clarify this by setting out three tests or conditions and saying that if one or more of these applies to a person then that person has "closest connection" with Scotland under the Act.

The tests are that the person has their principal U.K. home in Scotland, the person has spent the same or more days in Scotland than elsewhere in the United Kingdom, and the person represents a Scottish constituency as a member of the U.K. Parliament, the Scottish Parliament or the European Parliament. The principal U.K. home test has three elements, each of which must be met. First, the person must spend part of the year in Scotland. Secondly, the person's principal home must be in Scotland and the person must reside there for part of the year. Thirdly, the amount of time spent in the Scottish residence must equal or exceed the amount of time spent elsewhere. The section refers to "place of residence" and defines "place" as including a vessel or other means of transport.[15] Page *et al.* reflect that a person could qualify as a Scottish taxpayer if they spend six months of the year sailing on the west coast of Scotland or even living in a camper van in the north west Highlands.[16]

The 'number of days' test requires a person to have spent at least as many days in Scotland as elsewhere in the United Kingdom and a day is spent in Scotland if the person is in Scotland at the end of

---

[13] s. 74(2)(a).
[14] s. 75(1)(b).
[15] s. 75(6).
[16] Page, Reid and Ross, *A Guide to the Scotland Act 1998* (1999), p. 147.

the day.[17] A day spent elsewhere in the United Kingdom requires the person to be elsewhere than in Scotland at the end of the day. Thus if a businessman from Glasgow travels by the early morning plane to London and returns the same evening, the day will count as being spent in Scotland if he arrives home before midnight. If however he catches the early morning plane but returns by the overnight sleeper train, the day will not count as a day spent in Scotland.

If the tax-varying power is used to increase tax, the Act requires that the Inland Revenue will pay the amount of the tax received into the Scottish Consolidated Fund.[18] The Inland Revenue must inform the Scottish Ministers as soon as possible after the tax-varying resolution has been passed what the amounts will be and when they will be paid in. Where the tax-varying resolution is for a tax reduction, the administrative arrangements are given in section 78. This will entail a reduction in the resources available to Scottish Ministers and payments will be taken from the Scottish Consolidated Fund to make up the shortfall in income tax receipts. The sums will be transferred to the Consolidated Fund for the United Kingdom.

DEVOLUTION AND THE COURTS

8.29 The Scottish Parliament is a devolved body whose powers come from the Scotland Act 1998. Thus the legislation passed by the Scottish Parliament is subject to review by the courts. The normal powers of judicial review are available, *e.g.* to decide whether or not the decision or action complained of is irrational. In addition, however, a number of other actions are available. The legislative powers of the Parliament are limited by the 1998 Act so an Act of the Scottish Parliament may be challenged on the grounds that it is outwith the competence of Parliament. Section 29(1) of the Act states: "An Act of the Scottish Parliament is not law so far as any provision is outside the legislative competence of the Parliament." A provision will be outside the competence if it tries to legislate in the following areas:

(1) A reserved matter as specified in Schedule 5 as reserved to the U.K. Parliament (s. 29(2)(b)).

---

[17] s. 75(4)(a).
[18] s. 77(1).

(2) A harmonisation matter whereby the Scottish legislation makes incidental modifications of Scots private law or Scots criminal law as it applies to reserved matters (s. 29(4)(b)).
(3) A protected enactment under Schedule 4 (s. 29(2)(c)).
(4) The Scottish legislation is not compatible with Convention rights as specified by the Human Rights Act 1998 (s. 29(2)(d)).
(5) The Scottish legislation is not compatible with E.C. law (s. 29(2)(d)).
(6) The legislation purports to remove the Lord Advocate from being the head of the systems of criminal prosecutions and investigation of deaths in Scotland (s. 29(2)(e)).
(7) Extra-territorial matters where the law purports to make law for a country or territory outside Scotland (s. 29(2)(a)).

Full discussion of protected statutes and reserved matters is made in Chapter 5.

The action of a Scottish Minister may also be open to challenge 8.30
on the ground of being outside devolved executive competence. These actions are referred to as "devolution issues" and they may arise in ordinary cases before the courts or in judicial proceedings instituted by the Law Officers. "Devolution issues" are defined in Schedule 6 of the 1998 Act. There are six questions:

(1) Whether an Act of the Scottish Parliament, or a provision within it, is within the legislative competence of the Parliament.
(2) Whether a function is a function of a Scottish Minister or the First Minister or the Lord Advocate.
(3) Whether the exercise of a function by a member of the Scottish Executive would be within devolved competence.
(4) Whether the exercise of a function by a member of the Scottish Executive is or would be incompatible with E.C. law or Convention rights.
(5) Whether a failure to act by a member of the Scottish Executive is incompatible with E.C. law or Convention rights.
(6) Any other question as to whether a function is within devolved competence and any other question arising by virtue of the Act about reserved matters.

Although there are provisions in the Act to refer a Bill to the Judicial Committee of the Privy Council (JCPC) before it is passed,[19] it is still possible to challenge the legitimacy of an Act of the Scottish Parliament at a later date. However, the validity of an Act of the Scottish Parliament cannot be challenged on the ground that the proceedings leading to its enactment were invalid.[20] Thus an Act of the Scottish Parliament is similar to an Act of the U.K. Parliament in that the parliamentary procedures may not be challenged.[21] During the passage of the Scotland Act through Parliament, the Government indicated that they wanted to differentiate between an Act of the Scottish Parliament and subordinate legislation. "It is intended to make the position of an Act of the Scottish Parliament similar to that of an Act of the U.K. Parliament . . . [and] in a different position from subordinate legislation which can be challenged on the basis that the procedure prescribed for making the subordinate legislation has not been complied with."[22]

The courts are required to interpret Acts of the Scottish Parliament and subordinate legislation in such a way as to facilitate its effect, by reading it "as narrowly as is required for it to be within competence, if such a reading is possible."[23] During the Lords stages of the Scotland Act, the Lord Advocate explained that the section was to enable the courts to give effect to legislation wherever possible.[24] He gave an example of how the interpretation could be made. If the Scottish Parliament passed an Act to allow Scottish Ministers to hold a referendum on any matter, this might be *ultra vires* since it could be interpreted as allowing a referendum on reserved matters. The legislation could be given effect if it was construed as referring to referendums on devolved matters, so that a referendum on education in Scotland would be *intra vires* but a referendum on the monarchy as a reserved matter would not.

8.31 A devolution issue could conceivably come to light in any case, civil or criminal, in Scotland, England, Wales or Northern Ireland. The Act provides at Schedule 6, paragraph 2 for the court or tribunal to hold that the issue is frivolous or vexatious and not a devolution issue. The issue may be raised by any party to the

---

[19] s. 33.
[20] s. 28(5).
[21] *Pickin v. British Railways Board* [1974] A.C. 765.
[22] *Hansard,* H.L. Vol. 593, col. 1946 (Oct. 28, 1998).
[23] s. 101(2).
[24] *Hansard,* H.L. Vol. 593, cols. 1952–1956 (Oct. 28, 1998).

proceedings but in criminal cases there are time-limits for raising the issue.[25]

In Scotland, proceedings for the determination of a devolution issue may be instituted by the Lord Advocate or the Advocate General for Scotland[26] and the Lord Advocate may defend any such proceedings raised by the Advocate General. However, paragraph 4 does not prevent others from raising or defending devolution issues. Where a devolution issue arises, the Lord Advocate and the Advocate General must be given notice[27] and either, or both of them, may then participate in the case as far as it relates to the devolution issue.

When a devolution issue is raised in a tribunal from which there is no appeal, the tribunal must refer the devolution issue to the Inner House of the Court of Session; any other tribunal may choose to do so (para. 8). Any civil court (except the House of Lords or the Court of Session sitting with three or more judges) may refer the devolution issue to the Inner House (para. 7). Any criminal court (except the High Court of Justiciary sitting with two or more judges) may refer the issue to the High Court of Justiciary (para. 9). These provisions are designed to ensure that where necessary a lower court may refer a devolution issue to a superior court and they will be dealt with by the superior court, not just passed upwards to another court. The superior courts may themselves refer a devolution issue to a higher court. This applies to the Court of Session convened as a court with at least three judges and the High Court of Justiciary convened with at least two judges. The court to which the reference will made, in both civil and criminal cases, is the JCPC.

Once a decision on a reference has been given, the right of appeal against that decision will come into operation. Where a reference has been made under paragraphs 7 or 8 to the Inner House of the Court of Session, appeal is to the JCPC. Where the reference has been made under paragraph 9 or the devolution issue has arisen in the ordinary course of proceedings before the High Court of Justiciary as an appeal court, then any appeal requires leave to appeal from the High Court or the JCPC, and is made to the JCPC (para. 13(a)). Where there is a reference to the

---

25 Cases on indictment — issue must be raised within seven days of the indictment being served. Summary cases — notice of devolution issue must be given before the accused is asked to plead. Rules of Court, Ch. 40 http://www.scotcourts.gov.uk/justiciary/ch40.htm, June 14, 1999.

26 Sched. 6, para. 4(1).

27 para. 5.

Inner House in a case from which there is no appeal to the House of Lords (*e.g.* the Lands Valuation Appeal Court), then appeal may be made to the JCPC with leave of the Inner House or the JCPC (para. 13(b)). The routes for reference and appeal are set out in Table 2.

Table 2

Court in which devolution issue is raised	Court for Reference	Appeal
Any tribunal (except those where there is no appeal).	Inner House of the Court of Session (para. 8).	JCPC (para. 12).
Civil court, *i.e.* sheriff court, Outer House of the Court of Session.	Inner House (para. 7).	JCPC (para. 12).
Criminal court, *i.e.* district court, sheriff court, High Court of Justiciary as trial court.	High Court of Justiciary as an appeal court (para. 9).	JCPC but only with leave to appeal (para. 13(a)).
Court of Session with at least three judges, but not if devolution issue was raised under paras 7 or 8.	JCPC (para. 10).	JCPC but only with leave to appeal and if no right of appeal to House of Lords (para. 13(b)).
High Court of Justiciary with at least two judges, but not if devolution issue was raised under para. 9.	JCPC (para. 11).	JCPC but only with leave to appeal (para. 13(a)).

8.32 Part III of Schedule 6 sets out the various routes for references from courts in England and Wales and these are set out in Table 3. The proceedings may be instituted by the Attorney General and the Lord Advocate may defend any such proceedings.[28] The court or tribunal before which a devolution issue arises must order that the Attorney General and the Lord Advocate are informed of the matter[29] and either, or both, may then be party to the proceedings.[30] A tribunal from which there is no appeal must refer a devolution issue to the Court of Appeal; other tribunals may choose to do so.[31]

---

[28] para. 15.
[29] para. 16.
[30] para. 17.
[31] para. 20.

Where a devolution issue arises in proceedings before a court in Northern Ireland, Part IV of Schedule 6 applies. The provisions are similar to those outlined above. The Attorney General for Northern Ireland may institute the proceedings and both he and the Lord Advocate must be informed if a devolution issue is raised in an action. All lower courts may refer the matter to the Court of Appeal in Northern Ireland, from which the appeal will lie with leave to the JCPC.

Table 3

Court or Tribunal in which devolution issue is raised	Court for Reference	Appeal
Magistrates' court—civil proceedings (para. 18).	High Court of Justice.	JCPC but only with leave.
Any civil court (except the Magistrates' court, Court of Appeal, House of Lords, or High Court under reference from para. 18).	Court of Appeal.	JCPC but only with leave.
Any criminal court (except Court of Appeal and House of Lords (para. 21) — summary proceedings — proceedings on indictment.	 — High Court of Justice — Court of Appeal.	JCPC but only with leave.
Court of Appeal where issue arises in proceedings before it not under reference (para. 22).	JCPC.	

On occasion (admittedly rare) the devolution issue may be first raised in proceedings before the House of Lords. In these circumstances, the House may refer the issue to the JCPC or deal with the matter itself.[32] The House of Lords therefore has discretion in how it deals with the matter, but is bound to follow any previous relevant decisions of the JCPC since section 103 provides that any decision of the JCPC is binding on all other courts. In any event it is unlikely that the House of Lords would depart from the decisions of the JCPC given that the two courts (for issues under the Scotland Act) have common members.

[32] para. 32.

Where the devolution issue concerns the proposed exercise of a function by a member of the Scottish Executive, then the person making the reference must notify a member of the Scottish Executive that the issue has been raised.[33] The devolution issue may not have arisen in judicial proceedings but any of the Law Officers may refer the issue of the proposed exercise. O'Neill suggests that this is tantamount to asking the JCPC to rule on a hypothetical matter.[34] Thereafter no member of the Scottish Executive may exercise the function until the matter is disposed of. If a member of the Scottish Executive does exercise the function, the Advocate General, or any other person, may bring proceedings against the Scottish Executive.

8.33 To all intents and purposes, the JCPC is now the constitutional "court" for the United Kingdom with regard to matters involving devolution.[35] The establishment of a separate constitutional court was proposed during the parliamentary debates but this idea was rejected by the Government. The JCPC, for the Act's purposes, has a reduced membership in that those from Commonwealth countries will not sit in cases involving the Act. The membership is limited to serving or retired Law Lords and those who hold or have held the posts of Lord Chancellor, judge of the High Court of Justice or Court of Appeal, judge of the Court of Session or judge of the High Court or Court of Appeal in Northern Ireland.[36] The inclusion of the Lord Chancellor was controversial since it was felt that there might be doubt as to the court's independence from the government's influence.

The Act does not require that the membership of the JCPC, when sitting to consider a devolution issue, should include a judge from the country concerned. However, it is likely that a convention will develop whereby a Scottish judge will sit on cases involving the Scotland Act; this would be in line with the practice of the House of Lords where a Scottish Law Lord is usually assigned to the bench considering a case from Scotland.[37]

---

[33] para. 35.

[34] O'Neill, "The Scotland Act and the Government of Judges", 1999 S.L.T. (News) 61.

[35] The JCPC is technically not a court since it does not pass judgments; instead it offers advice to the sovereign which is then enacted by the government in an Order in Council.

[36] s. 103(2).

[37] Rules of Procedure for the determination of devolution cases have been published: Judicial Committee (Devolution Issues) Rules Order 1999 (S.I. 1999 No. 665).

Normally, when a legal provision or action is found to be *ultra vires* the provision or action is treated as null and void. However actions in court to challenge the validity of a provision or action made under the Scotland Act will take time to be heard and decided and before the case is raised the provision or action may have been acted upon. This would mean that anyone who had relied on the provision or action would be in difficulty since any decision of invalidity would be retrospective. The Act accordingly allows the court to limit the effect of such a decision. Section 102 allows the court to remove or limit any retrospective effect of the decision or to suspend the effect of the decision pending its being corrected.[38] The court is required to have regard to the effect the making of the order would have on persons who are not parties to the proceedings. Before an order is made the court must order intimation to the Lord Advocate, and, if the matter relates to a devolution issue, to the appropriate Law Officer.[39] The Law Officer may then participate in the proceedings relating to the order.

Powers to remedy defects in legislation

The Act gives power to various bodies to correct defects in legislation. The powers are intended to allow amendment to be carried out as quickly as possible using a 'fast track procedure'. The various powers are discussed below by reference to their respective sections in the Act. 8.34

(1) Section 33

This section allows for the pre-legislative judicial review of proposed legislation. The Lord Advocate, Advocate General for Scotland or the Attorney-General may refer to the JCPC a question of whether a legislative Bill, or one of its provisions, is within the legislative competence. The Law Officer has a period of four weeks after the passing of the Bill to make the reference and the Bill may not be presented for Royal Assent until the matter has been resolved.[40] The delay in presenting the Bill for Royal Assent was deemed necessary by the Government in the White Paper to ensure that the U.K. government had time to consider whether the Bill was within the competence of the Scottish Parliament. There 8.35

38 s. 102(2).

39 s. 102(4): the appropriate Law Officers are the Advocate General for Scotland for cases in Scotland, the Attorney-General for cases in England and Wales, and the Attorney-General for Northern Ireland for N.I. cases.

40 s. 32.

are provisions to allow a Bill to proceed quickly to Royal Assent if all of the Law Officers have decided that they will not refer the Bill.[41] If the JCPC decides that the Bill is outwith the competence, the Scottish Parliament may reconsider the Bill and amend it.

(2) Section 35

8.36 The Secretary of State for Scotland may intervene to prevent a Bill being passed by the Scottish Parliament by making an order prohibiting the Presiding Officer from submitting the Bill for Royal Assent. There are two grounds for making such an order:

(a) The Bill contains provisions which "the Secretary of State has reasonable grounds to believe would be incompatible with any international obligations or the interests of defence or national security."
(b) The Bill contains provisions to modify the law as it applies to reserved matters and which the Secretary of State "has reasonable grounds to believe would have an adverse effect on the operation of the law."

This power could be used by any Secretary of State but is more likely to be used by the Secretary of State for Scotland, although with the current doubt as to the future status of the office, it may be that it will be left to other U.K. ministers. The section is politically controversial, since it may be perceived as allowing the Secretary of State for Scotland to override the wishes of the Scottish Parliament and act rather like a Governor General of a British colony. However, given that Bills will take some time to pass through their parliamentary stages, there is likely to be ample time for the U.K. government to persuade the Scottish Parliament to reconsider those aspects of the Bill which cause difficulty.

The Secretary of State must give reasons for making an order under section 35 and the order may be made at any time during the four weeks after the Bill has been passed or, if a reference has been made to the JCPC under section 33, then the four weeks beginning when the reference was decided or disposed of.

(3) Section 58(1)

8.37 This section is similar to section 35 but affects action proposed to be taken by a member of the Scottish Executive which the

---

[41] s. 33(3).

Secretary of State believes would be incompatible with an international obligation. The Secretary of State may by order direct that the action is not to be taken.

(4) Section 58(2)

The Secretary of State may order that action be taken by a member of the Scottish Executive to implement an international obligation.[42] However the Secretary of State does not have the power to order the Scottish Parliament to enact it. 8.38

(5) Section 58(4) and (5)

This relates to subordinate legislation that has been made or may be revoked by a minister of the Scottish Executive. It applies if the Secretary of State has reasonable grounds to believe that the subordinate legislation is incompatible with an international obligation or the interests of defence or national security, or it makes modifications to the law applying to reserved matters which will have an adverse effect on the operation of such law. The Secretary of State may revoke the legislation but must give his reasons for doing so. During the Parliamentary debates on the Scotland Act, there was concern that this power could be used by the Secretary of State as a 'general over-ride' but this was denied by the then Secretary of State for Scotland, Donald Dewar, who pointed out that the order had to be laid before the U.K. Parliament which would ensure that no arbitrary order would be passed.[43] 8.39

(6) Section 107

In this section, subordinate legislation may be made as considered necessary or expedient in consequence of an Act of the Scottish Parliament or a provision of an Act of the Scottish Parliament which is not, or may not be, within the legislative competence of the Scottish Parliament, or the exercise of a function by a member of the Scottish Executive where that exercise is not, or may not be, a proper exercise of the function. The power here has been referred to as an 'open power' exercisable either by Her Majesty by Order in Council or by a Minister of the Crown.[44] The provision allows an Act of the Scottish Parliament to be 8.40

---

[42] See McFadden, "The Scottish Parliament: Provisions for Dispute Resolution", 1998 J.R. 221.

[43] 306 H.C. Official Report col. 243 (Feb. 16, 1998).

[44] s. 112(1).

remedied by the U.K. government where it is not possible to refer the matter back to the Scottish Parliament. The power could be used after a decision by a court that a provision in an Act of the Scottish Parliament was *ultra vires* and would allow the Act to be amended. It may also be used before court proceedings are commenced. During the parliamentary debates on the Scotland Act the Government indicated that if there was no court decision involved, they would not act without the consent of the Scottish Ministers. If this were not forthcoming, the matter would have to be decided by the courts.[45]

RELATIONS WITH OTHER BODIES

The U.K. government and Parliament

8.41 The setting up of the Scottish Parliament does not mean that the U.K. government and U.K. Parliament no longer have any interest or influence in what happens in Scotland. On the contrary, the reserved powers to the U.K. Parliament are of immense importance to those living in Scotland and thus the U.K. Parliament will continue to be of interest.

Scotland will still return M.P.s to the U.K. Parliament and for the time being there will be no reduction in the number of such M.P.s. As noted above,[46] however, this will change after the next boundary commission review. Members of Parliament for Scottish constituencies can therefore be expected to play a full role in the governance of the United Kingdom as a whole even though their influence over everyday matters such as education and health in Scotland will be curtailed.

The discussion of Scottish issues in the U.K. Parliament is likely to become subject to convention. When the Northern Ireland Parliament was created in 1922, the Speaker of the U.K. House of Commons ruled that matters delegated to the government of Northern Ireland had to be raised with them in Northern Ireland and questions on reserved matters addressed to the appropriate U.K. minister. The Speaker of the Northern Ireland House ruled that matters which were reserved were not proper subjects for discussion in that House. The basis for each ruling was the doctrine

[45] 594 H.L. Official Report (5th series) col. 599 (Nov. 9, 1998).
[46] See para. 8.06.

of ministerial responsibility in the House of Commons and the lack of power to legislate in the Northern Ireland House.[47]

The making of legislation for Scotland in areas which have been devolved is also expected to become the subject of a convention. Generally, the U.K. Parliament will not seek to legislate for Scotland in devolved areas, but on occasions it may be necessary and expedient to do so. For instance, if the United Kingdom is required to enact legislation to implement an E.C. obligation, it may do so for the United Kingdom as a whole.[48] The Government minister in the Lords, Lord Sewel, said that it was expected that, as had happened in Northern Ireland, "a convention (will) be established that Westminster would not normally legislate with regard to devolved matters in Scotland without the consent of the Scottish Parliament."[49] The example of the former Northern Ireland Parliament is a useful predictor of what might occur in the new devolved bodies. The U.K. Parliament did legislate for Northern Ireland but "invariably" this occurred only with the consent of the Northern Ireland government although such consent was not always willingly given. The U.K. Parliament also ensured that the Northern Ireland government introduced legislation to the Parliament even though that government was not willing to do so.[50]

At present the Standing Orders of the House of Commons do 8.42 not preclude an M.P. from introducing a private member's Bill to the House of Commons on a matter that has been devolved to the Scottish Parliament. For example, an M.P. could introduce a private member's Bill to require all NHS bodies to abolish private hospital facilities. This is a devolved matter, but suppose that it has the support of a majority of M.P.s and it passes through its various stages and becomes law. The government has not supported the Bill and the Scottish Parliament has not consented to the Bill's enactment. There is a clear possibility that a constitutional crisis will occur. Even if a Scottish M.P., rather than an English M.P., introduced the Bill, it will only have slightly more political legitimacy and it will be seen as interfering with the intentions of the Scotland Act. However there may be times when the intervention of an M.P. will be welcomed, for instance if the Scottish Executive fail to act. For example, during the summer of 1999, a mental patient from the State Hospital at Carstairs was released although

---

47 Hadfield, "The Nature of Devolution in Scotland and Northern Ireland" (1999) Vol. 3 E.L.R. 3.

48 s. 28(7).

49 H.L. Debs col. 791 (July 21, 1998).

50 Calvert, *Constitutional Law in Northern Ireland* (1968).

his doctors considered that he was still a danger to the public. The man was able to exploit a 'loophole' in mental health legislation that stated that he could only be held while he was receiving 'treatment'; he was able to argue that he had an untreatable personality disorder and so should be released. The Scottish Executive was heavily criticised for their apparent inability to prevent his release and the possibility that more patients would be able to seek release using the same argument. Although the Scottish Executive acted to close this 'loophole', had they not done so, it would have been open to an M.P., whether from Scotland or elsewhere, to introduce a private member's Bill to change the law, even though this is a devolved matter. In all probability the Bill would have had the support of the majority of the Scottish electorate. Although the Scottish Parliament and Executive would have been unhappy at the Bill it would be unable to prevent its passage. Would a constitutional crisis arise in these circumstances, or would they more likely cause a crisis of confidence in the Scottish Executive?

8.43 The House of Commons Select Committee on Procedure has been considering the procedural consequences of devolution. In a report published in May 1999, the committee expressed the view that in the long-term it may be necessary to establish a 'constitutional affairs committee' to consider the relationships between the constituent parts of the United Kingdom.[51] In respect of private member's Bills the committee noted the Government's statement that any such Bill would be opposed by the Government. The committee supported the Government's view that the House should not legislate on devolved matters without the consent of the legislature concerned.

The committee also considered the setting up of liaison committees and joint hearing between the House of Commons and the devolved legislatures. The committee pointed out two areas of difficulty. The first concerned the exchange of documents where the difficulty highlighted involved their status as a proceeding in Parliament and the official publication of such documents. The second area was the holding of joint meetings. The committee felt that these should be informal in nature, with M.P.s being warned that parliamentary privileges would not necessarily be available to them. If however a select committee ordered a witness to attend or produce documents, then the meeting would have to be formal.

---

[51] Select Committee on Procedure, Fourth Report, *Procedural Consequences of Devolution* (1998–99).

This would raise questions of what legal restraints, if any, could be imposed on the meeting. Arguments over the legal powers of a committee of the Scottish Parliament could lead to legal action; the question of how such would affect the joint proceedings has not been clarified. The committee thus recommended that no formal joint meetings should be held without the express authority of the House.

The Secretary of State for Scotland is a member of the U.K. government and his role as a conduit between the two government administrations will be important. His role in negotiating the size of the block grant has already been discussed[52] and he will also represent Scottish interests in reserved matters. However, the Scottish Ministers will want to discuss matters directly with their counterparts in Whitehall and liaison arrangements have been set up between the two governments and two Parliaments. 8.44

These arrangements are formal but non-statutory understandings between the various departments. They were called "concordats" by the Secretary of State for Scotland when he issued draft guidance on these in February 1998. There is no statutory provision to cover these concordats and they were not finalised until October 1999. The Memorandum of Understanding and supplementary agreements between the United Kingdom Government, Scottish Ministers and the Cabinet of the National Assembly for Wales[53] provides for a Joint Ministerial Committee to be set up and sets out four concordats covering E.U. matters, financial assistance to industry, international relations touching on the responsibility of the devolved administrations, and statistical work across the United Kingdom. In addition, there will be bilateral concordats between U.K. departments and their counterparts in the devolved administrations; these have not yet been published. The memorandum is not a binding agreement and does not create legal obligations. "It is intended to be binding in honour only."[54] The memorandum does not create any additional right for the Scottish Executive to be consulted by the U.K. government.

The Joint Ministerial Committee will consist of U.K. government ministers, Scottish Ministers and members of the Cabinet of the National Assembly for Wales and a plenary session will take place at least once a year attended by the Prime Minister, the Deputy Prime Minister, the First Minister and another Scottish

---

[52] See para. 8.26.
[53] http://194.247.69.28/library2/memorandum/default.htm
[54] *ibid.* para. 2.

Minister, the Welsh First Secretary and another Assistant Secretary, together with the Secretaries of State for Scotland and Wales. The Joint Ministerial Committee will consider non-devolved matters which impinge on devolved responsibilities, keep arrangements for liaison between the U.K. government and the devolved administrations under review, and consider disputes between the administrations. A committee of officials will shadow the Joint Ministerial Committee and prepare papers for their meetings.

Relationships with the E.C./E.U.

8.45 The relationship between the Scottish Parliament and Executive and European Union institutions will be dependent on the U.K. government allowing such a relationship to develop. The negotiation of E.C. obligations is a reserved power[55] and so the involvement of Scottish Ministers in E.U. matters will be by invitation. However there is no doubt that the implementation of E.C. obligations will be smoother if the Scottish Ministers are involved in negotiations. Indeed since the Scottish Executive will be responsible for implementing Community obligations on devolved matters, it is commonsense that their involvement in negotiations is early and continuing.

The Act provides that the Scottish Parliament's legislation must not be incompatible with E.C. law or Convention rights[56]; any such law that is incompatible is outwith the legislative competence of Parliament and is not law. There is a similar provision with regard to the making of subordinate legislation by a member of the Scottish Executive.[57] The U.K. Parliament, of course, has retained the right to legislate for Scotland, even in devolved matters, and this power may be used to ensure the Scottish Parliament and Executive comply with E.C. obligations or to enact U.K. legislation to implement an E.C. obligation. This legislation would normally be passed with the agreement of the Scottish Executive.

The Scottish Parliament and Scottish Executive do not have a statutory right to be involved in the E.C. law-making process. Instead the government proposed consultative, non-statutory means such as the involvement of the Scottish Executive in discussion within the U.K. government about formulating the U.K. government's policies and allowing a Scottish Minister to speak for the United Kingdom in negotiations with the E.C. The U.K. lead

---

[55] Sched. 5, Pt I, para. 7.
[56] s. 29.
[57] s. 57(2).

minister would retain overall responsibility for the negotiations. The Scottish Parliament may scrutinise E.U. legislative proposals and forward their comments to the U.K. government and Parliament. The Scottish Executive and Scottish Parliament will be able to participate in informal discussion in Europe and they will have the right to nominate Scotland's representation on the Committee of the Regions and the Economic and Social Committee. All in all, however, the impression is given that the Scottish Parliament and Scottish Executive will be the 'poor relations' when it comes to involvement in European matters. U.K. departments will always lead the negotiations whereas in the past, the Scottish Office was often lead department for matters involving fishing and offshore mineral exploration.

The CSG recommended that a European Committee be set up and this has occurred. It is a mandatory committee required by Rule 6.1.5 of the Standing Orders and is appointed for the whole session of Parliament. Its remit is "to consider and report on proposals for, and implementation of European legislation, and any E.C./E.U. issue."[58] It has a membership of 13 and is thus one of the larger committees. The CSG suggested that the committee's main role should be to "sift incoming EU-related documents on behalf of the Parliament and to determine where further investigation or debate is necessary."

Relationships with local authorities

Although the Act does not specifically mention local authorities, 8.46
the relationship they will have with the Scottish Parliament is particularly important. Both institutions are democratically elected and accountable and both have tax raising powers.[59] The 1998 Act devolves power over local authorities to the Scottish Parliament and many of the functions carried out by local authorities are the subjects of ministerial portfolios, such as education, housing, transport and environment. A special relationship will therefore have to develop whereby the Scottish Parliament ensures that national policies are given legislative effect and local authorities are allowed to carry these out on a local basis. With this in mind the Scottish Constitutional Convention in its last report stated that there should be a "culture of co-operation and stability at the heart of the relationship between the Parliament and local authorities."[60] The

---

[58] http://www.scottish.parliament.uk/whats_happening/whisp90–00/wh08–11.htm, July 28, 1999.

[59] McFadden and Lazarowicz, *The Scotish Parliament: An Introduction* (1999), p. 78.

[60] *Scotland's Parliament. Scotland's Right* (1995).

White Paper indicated that the Government did not envisage the Scottish Parliament 'calling in' functions to be centrally administered where these "would be more appropriately and efficiently delivered by other bodies within Scotland."[61] The White Paper endorsed the principle of subsidiarity whereby decisions are taken as close as possible to the citizens of Scotland. The Constitution Unit had previously proposed that the principle could be fulfilled by drawing up a concordat between Scottish local and central government to commit Scottish government to extensive consultation with local authorities on all matters of concern.[62]

The Scotland Act reserves to the U.K. Parliament the franchise at local government elections but excepts from the reserved powers the power to alter the system of local taxation. Thus the local government elections held on May 6, 1999, at the same time as the Scottish Parliament elections, were conducted under the first past the post system and future elections will be held using whatever method of election the U.K. Parliament decides is appropriate. The system of local taxation, currently the Council Tax and business rate, may be changed by the Scottish Parliament to almost any type of tax it pleases.

8.47 Local government areas were completely reorganised in 1996 as a result of the Local Government etc. (Scotland) Act 1994[63] and it is therefore unlikely that any further reorganisation will occur for some years to come. However the form of local councils largely stayed the same with the traditional councillor/official format being retained. The Labour Government recognised that there was apprehension in local authorities as to how the Scottish Parliament would see them and indeed, treat them. The Scottish Parliament has control over what functions are exercised by local authorities and could take over certain functions. Rumours have abounded that the education service would be taken in by the Scottish Parliament with local boards being set up to look after the day-to-day affairs of groups of schools. The place of the social work function has been in doubt with the various functions of social work departments being divided up among various ministers in the Scottish Executive. Some local authorities are following the trend and 'breaking up' their social work departments into smaller units which are then allocated to other departments.

---

[61] *Scotland's Parliament*, Cm. 3658 (1997), Chap. 6.

[62] Constitution Unit, *Scotland's Parliament: The Fundamentals for a new Scotland Act* (1996).

[63] With the exception of the three Islands Councils which remained as unitary authorities but with additional powers.

The Labour Government tried to allay some of these fears by setting up the Commission on Local Government and the Scottish Parliament (the McIntosh Commission) in 1997. The commission's remit was:

> "To consider how to build the most effective relations between local government and the Scottish Parliament and Scottish Executive, and
> To consider how councils can best make themselves responsive and democratically accountable to the community they serve."

The commission issued two consultation papers during its existence and published its findings in June 1999 in *Moving Forward: Local Government and the Scottish Parliament*. The report is wide-ranging and makes a number of recommendations regarding the relationship between local authorities and the Scottish Parliament. The commission's recommendations regarding the operation of local authorities are dealt with in Chapter 10.

The commission reiterates the general principles on which their report and recommendations were based. These are worth repeating here: "Local authorities and the Scottish Parliament have in common the democratic mandate; and share a common responsibility to the people of Scotland. In view of this their relations with each other should be conducted on a basis of mutual respect and parity of esteem."[64]

The principle of subsidiarity is mentioned very early in the report and the commission in its principles notes that where the reverse of subsidiarity is implemented, *i.e.* centralisation, this must be justified as being of benefit to the public. The commission refers to the European Charter of Local Self-Government to which the United Kingdom became a signatory in June 1997.

The commission recommends that the Parliament and all 32 local authorities should agree a 'covenant' in which the basis of their relationship would be set out. A draft covenant is set out in Appendix B of the report. It proposes a Joint Conference with equal numbers drawn from the Scottish Parliament and local authorities. The proposal has been supported in principle by the Scottish Executive but the minister felt that the operation of the covenant needed more consultation. A proposal to set up a similar joint body for ministers and councillors has been agreed by the Scottish Executive and a first meeting was arranged for September

---

[64] McIntosh Report (1999), p. 4.

1999. The 'leadership forum' will probably take on the agreement concluded between COSLA and the Scottish Office in 1997.

The final important recommendation made by the commission is that local authorities should be given a statutory power of general competence. Currently local authorities may only do what statutory provisions empower them to do. In other countries, such as France and the USA, local authorities may do anything "for the benefit of their communities which is not specifically reserved or prohibited or already provided for through other legislation."[65] The commission argued that a power of general competence would give specific statutory form to the principle of subsidiarity and would help "to facilitate the process of community planning by increasing the freedom of councils to take part in joint action in partnership with other agencies to address particular issues."[66] The Scottish Executive's response was that ministers would "consult carefully on the case for a power of general competence". The Minister for the Communities also stated in August 1999 that she would be publishing a consultation paper with proposals for developing the McIntosh recommendations.[67]

Relationships with other bodies

8.48 The White Paper listed around one hundred non-departmental public bodies (NDPBs) or quangos, which would become the responsibility of the Scottish Parliament. These bodies deliver a wide range of public services. They are invariably unelected bodies, being appointed by ministers. The range of the work is extensive; there are judicial bodies such as the children's panels and various tribunals; advisory bodies such as the Health Appointments Advisory Committee and the Secretary of State's Advisory Group on Scotland's Travelling People; regulatory bodies such as the Scottish Environmental Protection Agency; bodies with executive functions and large budgets, such as Scottish Homes, Scottish Enterprise and the water authorities. The lack of direct accountability to a democratically elected body has long been seen as a problem with regard to these bodies. The Scottish Parliament and Scottish Executive will now have responsibility for the quangos and will be able to set them up, wind them down, alter them and merge

---

[65] McIntosh Report (1999), para. 48.

[66] *ibid.* para. 51.

[67] Bulletin of Scottish Local Government Information Unit, No. 114, July/Aug. 1999.

them. The power of appointment is given to the Scottish Executive, as is the power to fund them and direct their activities.

The Scottish Office Guide to the Scotland Bill published in June 1998 lists the Scottish public bodies and includes NDPBs, certain nationalised industries, tribunals, public corporations and health bodies.[68]

There are certain bodies which are categorised as 'cross-border public authorities' concerned with devolved matters in Scotland and reserved matters in Scotland and elsewhere. Examples of these include the Meat and Livestock Commission, the British Council, the Scottish Law Commission, the United Kingdom Transplants Support Service Authority and the Central Council for Education and Training in Social Work.

The Scotland Act deals with the issue of cross-border public authorities at sections 88 to 90. The Act provides that a Minister of the Crown must consult with the Scottish Ministers before he appoints or removes a cross-border public authority or any of its members, or where the exercise of one of his functions may affect Scotland in a matter which is not entirely a reserved matter.[69] If a cross-border body is required to lay a report before the U.K. Parliament, it must now also do so with the Scottish Parliament.[70] Section 89 allows for alteration of the functions of the cross-border bodies to take account of the devolution settlement. This is done by an Order in Council subject to the affirmative resolution of both Houses of Parliament and the Scottish Parliament, and subject also to consultation with the cross-border body concerned.

It is possible for the Scottish Parliament to legislate to remove functions from a cross-border body in respect of functions falling within the legislative competence of the Parliament.[71] The transfer of property in such a case would be made by Order in Council and the Scottish Parliament could therefore set up its own Scotland based public authority.

There are bodies which operate on a United Kingdom or Great Britain basis within the reserved areas. Such bodies will continue to be accountable to the U.K. Parliament and government but some of them will be of great interest and importance in Scotland, and the White Paper thus proposed that the Scottish Parliament should

---

[68] http://www.scottish-devolution.org.uk/scotland%20bill/billcon.htm, Oct. 1, 1998.
[69] s. 88(2).
[70] s. 88(3).
[71] s. 90.

be able to invite the bodies to present reports and give oral evidence to the Parliament's committees. The Government has also proposed that the Scottish Executive should be consulted before the national governor is appointed to the Board of Governors of the BBC.

CHAPTER 9

EUROPEAN CONSTITUTIONAL CONTEXT

INTRODUCTION

9.01 The European Community is a unique constitutional entity. It has its own institutions and law-making powers. It can create rights and duties within the legal systems of Member States. It represents far more than a forum for inter-governmental co-operation. When duties are imposed on Member States, these may imply rights for individuals which may be enforced in the domestic courts or in the European Court of Justice.

In constitutional terms the European Union is an organisation with superior status to individual states. When new States are admitted to membership they become bound by the entire law of the Union which pertains at the time of their accession. This body of law is known as the *acquis communitaire*, which means "Community patrimony". This contrasts with the principle of international law which provides that normally, when a state becomes a signatory to a treaty it is not bound by any acts done under the treaty before it became a signatory.[1] In order to become a member of the European Union a state has to ensure that its national law conforms with the provisions of the E.C. Treaty.

MEMBERSHIP OF THE EUROPEAN UNION

9.02 The United Kingdom became a member of the European Communities in 1973 by signing the Treaty of Rome. At the time the Community consisted of six countries: Belgium, France, the Federal Republic of Germany, Italy, Luxembourg and the Netherlands. Eire and Denmark joined at the same time as the United Kingdom. In 1979 Greece became a member. Spain and Portugal joined in 1986 and Austria, Finland and Sweden in 1995. There are

[1] See J. Steiner, *Textbook on EEC Law* (5th ed., Blackstone, 1996).

actually three communities: the European Atomic Energy Community, The European Coal and Steel Community and the European Community (formerly known as the European Economic Community). The Communities became known collectively as the European Union under the Treaty of Union signed at Maastricht in 1992. Membership of the European Community required the United Kingdom to accept a new legal order. In order to implement the changes in U.K. law which were necessary to make Community law part of U.K. law, the European Communities Act 1972 was enacted. The Treaty of European Union was adopted into the United Kingdom by the European Communities (Amendment) Act 1993. Expansion of the European Union has been accompanied by measures towards closer economic and political union of the Member States. The Treaty on European Union 1997 (the Treaty of Amsterdam) reflects this trend, representing "a new stage in the process of European integration undertaken with the establishment of the European Communities."[2]

OBJECTIVES OF THE EUROPEAN UNION

9.03 The objectives of the European Union are set out in Article 2 of the 1997 Treaty[3] as follows:

> "To promote economic and social progress and a high level of employment and to achieve balanced and sustainable development, in particular through the creation of an area without internal frontiers, through the strengthening of economic and social cohesion and through the establishment of economic and monetary union, ultimately including a single currency;
> To assert its identity on the international scene, in particular through the implementation of a common foreign and security policy including the progressive framing of a common defence policy, which might lead to a common defence;
> To strengthen the protection of rights and interests of the nationals of its Member States through the introduction of a citizenship of the Union;
> To maintain and develop the Union as an area of freedom, security and justice, in which the free movement or persons is assured in conjunction with appropriate measures with respect

---

[2] E.U. Treaty, Preamble.
[3] *ibid.* Art. 2.

to external border controls, asylum, immigration and the prevention of and combating of crime;
To maintain in full the acquis communitaire and build on it with a view to considering to what extent the policies and forms of co-operation introduced by this Treaty may need to be revised with the aim of ensuring the effectiveness of the mechanisms and the institutions of the Community."

Principles of the E.U.

The objectives are intended to be considered in the light of the following principles[4]: 9.04

1. The Union is founded on the principles of liberty, democracy, respect for human rights and fundamental freedoms, and the rule of law, principles which are common to the Member States.
2. The Union shall respect fundamental rights, as guaranteed by the European Convention for the Protection of Human Rights and Fundamental Freedoms signed in Rome on November 4, 1950 and as they result from the constitutional traditions common to the Member States, as general principles of Community law.
3. The Union shall respect the national identities of its Member States.
4. The Union shall provide itself with the means necessary to attain its objectives and carry through its policies.

DIVISION OF FUNCTIONS BETWEEN THE EUROPEAN UNION AND THE MEMBER STATES

There has to be a realistic balance between the powers which the Union needs to fulfil its objectives and the need for Member States to conserve their autonomy. The allocation of functions and the powers required to fulfil those functions is determined mainly by the provisions of the major treaties. The principle of subsidiarity has become a major concept in the allocation of powers and functions. 9.05

---

[4] E.U. Treaty, Art. 6.

Subsidiarity

9.06 The principle of subsidiarity is central to European Community law, however the exact meaning of the term is far from clear.[5] It has been interpreted as meaning that the Community should only act: (a) where the objective cannot be achieved by regulation at the national level; (b) where the objective can be better, or more effectively, achieved by action at Community level; or (c) where the matter in question can be more effectively regulated at Community level.[6]

Other decisions should be taken at national level. The EC Treaty provides:

> "The Community shall act within the limits of the powers conferred upon it by this Treaty and of the objectives assigned to it therein.
>
> In areas which do not fall within its exclusive competence, the Community shall take action, in accordance with the principle of subsidiarity, only if and so far as the objectives of the proposed action cannot be sufficiently achieved by the Member States and can therefore, by reason of scale or the effects of the proposed action, be better achieved by the Community.
>
> Any action by the Community shall not go beyond what is necessary to achieve the objectives of this Treaty."[7]

The basic principle of subsidiarity is therefore that action should be taken at the level which is most appropriate for the achievement of its purpose. It is a dynamic concept which will develop and become clearer as the Court of Justice adjudicates on its scope and application on a case by case basis. The principle of subsidiarity is sometimes confused with the concept of proportionality. Subsidiarity is a principle which determines the appropriate level at which an action should be taken whereas the principle of proportionality is concerned with the nature and scale of the action taken. The principle of proportionality requires that administrative measures must not be more drastic than is necessary for attaining the desired result.[8]

---

[5] See D. O'Keefe and P.M. Twomey (eds), *Legal Issues of the Maastricht Treaty* (London, Chancery, 1994).

[6] J. Steiner, "Subsidiarity under the Maastricht Treaty" in *Legal Issues of the Maastricht Treaty*, *op. cit*.

[7] Art. 5, as revised by E.U. Treaty.

[8] See V. Finch and C. Ashton, *Administrative Law in Scotland* (1997, W. Green), pp. 297–299.

It is not entirely clear from the E.C. Treaty which are the areas in which the Community has exclusive competence and which are the areas where power is shared between the Community and the Member States. Where there is a concurrent power the Member State can take any action provided that the Community has not exercised its power in relation to the relevant matter. Once the Community has taken action the power of the Member State is pre-empted and the power to act rests thereafter with the Community.[9] In a situation where the Community has exclusive competence to act but has not done so and urgent action is required, it has been held that a Member State may take action as "trustee of the common interest".[10] The concept of subsidiarity was debated by the European Council at the Edinburgh Summit meeting in December 1992. As a consequence of the discussion on that occasion guidelines were agreed which now have a legal basis under the protocol to the Treaty of Amsterdam.

EUROPEAN INSTITUTIONS

The number of European Community institutions continues to increase but the backbone of the European framework comprises the four major institutions established by treaty: (i) the Council of Ministers; (ii) the Commission; (iii) the European Parliament; and (iv) the European Court of Justice. 9.07

Council of Ministers

The Council of Ministers consists of the appropriate government minister from each Member State. Its membership therefore varies depending on the subject-matter under discussion. If, for example, an issue relating to transport is under discussion, the Council will consist of the Minister of Transport from each Member State. Ministers who represent the United Kingdom in decision-making in the Council of Ministers and European Council are then accountable to the Westminster Parliament for their actions under the principles of ministerial responsibility. 9.08

The Council of Ministers is the principal decision-making body of the Community, having both legislative and executive powers. In

---

[9] See D. O'Keefe and P.M. Twomey (eds), *Legal Issues of the Maastricht Treaty*, *op. cit*.

[10] Case 804/79 *Commission v. United Kingdom* [1981] E.C.R. 1045.

practice it operates as several councils, each dealing with a specific field of activity such as agriculture or commerce. They meet to approve Community law or policy. Article 202 sets out the powers of the Council:

> "To ensure that the objectives set out in this Treaty are attained, the Council shall, in accordance with the provisions of this Treaty:
>
> (a) ensure co-ordination of the general economic policies of the Member States;
>
> (b) have power to take decisions;
>
> (c) confer on the Commission powers for implementation of rules which the Council lays down. The Council may impose certain requirements in respect of the exercise of these powers. The Council may also reserve the right, in specific cases, to exercise directly implementing powers itself. The procedures referred to above must be consonant with principles and rules to be laid down in advance by the Council, acting unanimously on a proposal from the Commission and after obtaining the opinion of the European Parliament."

The European Council, which meets twice a year, is made up of the heads of government of each Member State. In order to communicate and negotiate between meetings of the Council or heads of government each Member State has an office with a permanent representative in Brussels. The permanent representatives are senior diplomats. They delegate tasks to working groups dealing with specific subjects. They meet together as the Committee of Permanent Representatives.

The Council of Ministers has a major role in the instigation of Community legislation. This role is regarded as an essential device to maintain the status of the individual Member States. Ministers can ensure that their government's interests are protected and that they are not dominated by larger states. The secrecy and "behind the scenes" nature of the activities of the Council leads to criticisms that the Community is not sufficiently open and democratic.

There are three ways by which the Council can reach a decision: (1) unanimously, (2) by qualified majority vote, or (3) by a simple majority vote.

Where a new policy is to be instigated or where the policy framework is to be changed, a unanimous vote is normally required. Unanimity is also necessary when the Council decides to amend a Commission proposal against the wishes of the Commission. Unless otherwise provided in the Treaty the Council acts on a majority vote.[11] Qualified majority voting is required for matters such as those relating to incentives in employment and social matters, equal opportunities, social exclusion, foreign and security policy, public health and anti-fraud measures. Where a qualified majority is required the voting power of each Member State is weighted in favour of the larger states. In the past difficulties have arisen where a single state has blocked proposals because of a conflict with national interests. Article 11 provides that where a Member State raises an objection to a proposal because of important national interests, the Council shall refer the matter to the European Council for unanimous decision.

Commission

The Commission was originally called the High Authority. It has 9.09
been described as "the guardian of the Treaties". It is centrally concerned with all aspects of Community decision-making at all levels. The Commission consists of 20 members who are appointed following consultations between the governments of the Member States.[12] The number of commissioners may be changed by the Council if there is a unanimous decision. The commissioners are appointed for a fixed term of five years, which may be renewed. They cannot be dismissed during their term of office by their governments.[13] A government may however block the reappointment of a commissioner.[14] They may also be compulsorily retired by the European Court of Justice for incompetence or serious misconduct.[15] The European Parliament has the power to pass a motion of censure to remove all of the commissioners at once.[16] The commissioners must be nationals of a Member State and no more than two may be nationals of the same Member State.[17] The

[11] E.C. Treaty, Art. 205.

[12] *ibid.* Art. 213.

[13] *ibid.* Art 214. They may however be subject to political pressure which could force them to resign. In 1999 all of the commissioners tendered their resignations following a scandal involving corruption.

[14] This happened in 1989 when the renewal of the appointment of Lord Cockfield was blocked by the U.K. Prime Minister because he was too "pro-European".

[15] E.C. Treaty, Art. 216.

[16] *ibid.* Art. 201.

[17] *ibid.* Art. 213.

five largest Member States (France, Germany, Italy, Spain and the United Kingdom, each have two commissioners, the other Member States each have one. Once appointed they are deemed to serve the Community, not to be representatives of the government of their own country. Article 213(2) provides:

> "The Members of the Commission shall, in the general interests of the Community, be completely independent in the performance of their duties.
>
> In the performance of these duties they shall neither seek nor take instructions from any government or from any other body. They shall refrain from any action incompatible with their duties. Each Member State undertakes to respect this principle and not to seek to influence Members of the Commission in the performance of their tasks."

The Commission is headed by a President. He is appointed from the Commission for a renewable period of two years. The Commission may appoint one or two vice-presidents.[18] The President provides political guidance to the Commission. Decisions in the Commission are reached by majority voting.[19] Each commissioner has responsibility for a specific area of Community policy. The role of the Commission is to initiate and implement Community policy. The Commission does not legislate except in relation to certain delegated matters. It makes proposals for legislation to the Council of Ministers.

Article 211 of the EC Treaty sets out the basic powers of the Commission:

> "In order to ensure the proper functioning and development of the common market, the Commission shall:
>
> (a) ensure that the provisions of this Treaty and the measures taken by the institutions pursuant thereto are applied;
>
> (b) formulate recommendations or deliver opinions on matters dealt with in this Treaty, if it expressly so provides or if the Commission considers it necessary;
>
> (c) have its own power of decision and participate in the shaping of measures taken by the Council and by the Assembly (Parliament) in the manner provided for in this Treaty;

---

[18] E.C. Treaty, Art. 217.

[19] *ibid.* Art. 219.

(d) exercise the powers conferred on it by the Council for the implementation of the rules laid down by the latter."

The Commission therefore has powers to initiate measures and powers of supervision and enforcement in addition to its administrative functions.

Instigating Community action

The Commission may be requested by the Council[20] or the European Parliament[21] to draft proposals for legislation. The Commission does not have complete freedom of action. Where it is under an obligation to submit legislative proposals within a time-limit specified by the Treaty, failure to act within the time-limit may lead to a challenge by the European Court of Justice.[22] 9.10

Ensuring compliance with community obligations

Where a Member State has failed to fulfil its Treaty obligations, the Commission has the power to deal with the breach of duty. Article 226 provides: 9.11

> "If the Commission considers that a member State has failed to fulfil an obligation under this Treaty, it shall deliver a reasoned opinion on the matter after giving the State concerned the opportunity to submit its observations.
>
> If the State concerned does not comply with the opinion within the period laid down by the Commission, the latter may bring the matter before the Court of Justice."

These powers are exercised regularly. There may be as many as 50 references to the European Court of Justice in any one year. The sanction used to enforce compliance is the imposition of financial penalties. The Commission specifies a lump sum to be paid by the defaulting State in the event that the Court rules against the State.[23]

Acting as executive of the community

The Commission provides a permanent administration for the Community, centred in Brussels. It has an administrative staff of approximately 15,000 people. Once a policy decision has been 9.12

---

[20] E.C. Treaty, Art. 208.
[21] *ibid.* Art. 192.
[22] *ibid.* Arts 232, 233.
[23] *ibid.* Art. 228.

taken by the Council, the detailed implementation of that policy is the responsibility of the Commission.

European Parliament

9.13 The European Parliament was originally called the Assembly. Its members were, until 1976, delegates appointed by the Member States. They were both members of their national Parliaments and of the European Parliament. In 1976 the Council decided that the members of the European Parliament would be elected by direct universal suffrage in the Member States.[24] Elections to the European Parliament were first held in the United Kingdom in 1979. Members of the European Parliament are elected for a term of five years. Seats in the European Parliament are allocated according to the size of the population of each Member State, within a total number of 700 seats. The allocation is not directly proportionate to the number of electors in each country and the smaller countries have a smaller proportion of constituents to members. Luxembourg, for example, has six seats and the United Kingdom has 87 seats although on a direct calculation of the populations Luxembourg should have only one seat. Members of the European Parliament may also be members of their own national parliaments. This facilitates close links between the European and national parliaments but it does give rise to a risk of conflicts of interest.[25]

The Members of the European Parliament are grouped according to political affiliation rather than nationality. The major political parties are the European Democrats, Socialists, Communists, European People's Party and Liberals.

The E.C. Treaty provides that: "The Assembly, which shall consist of the peoples of the States brought together in the Community, shall exercise the advisory and supervisory powers, which are conferred upon it by this Treaty."[26]

The European Parliament has to meet at least once a year and may also meet at the request of a majority of its members or at the request of the Commission or the Council.[27] In practice it meets 12

---

[24] The Council Decision and Act of September 1976 on Direct Elections [1976] O.J. L278.

[25] House of Lords Report, *Relations Between the United Kingdom Parliament and the European Parliament After Direct Elections*, H.L. (1977–78).

[26] Art. 189.

[27] E.C. Treaty, Art. 196.

to 15 times each year and each session lasts for several days. Plenary sessions are held in Strasbourg and committee meetings are held in Brussels. Standing committees normally consider proposals before they go before a full parliamentary session. The secretariat of the European Parliament is in Luxembourg.

Until 1986 the role of the European parliament was to act as an advisory body, except that it had the function of approving the Community budget on an annual basis. With the exception of the power to approve the budget, its decisions had no legal effect. Budget proposals originate from the Commission who submit them to the Council. A draft budget is drawn up by the Council and submitted to Parliament. Parliament has power to accept, amend or reject the budget. In so far as the budget relates to compulsory expenditure (expenditure directly required by Treaty provisions) Parliament may suggest amendments to the Council but the Council may accept or reject the suggestions. Any budget proposals for non-compulsory expenditure may be amended by Parliament. Parliament may reject the entire budget but only if "there are important reasons so to do".[28] Such a decision requires a special majority of two-thirds of the votes cast, which figure must also be an overall majority of the eligible votes.

The European Parliament may instigate policy changes. This is achieved by means of an initiative report to the European Commission. Parliament, however, has no power to require the Commission to adopt a proposal. Parliament has the right to ask questions of both the Council and the Commission. Replies are published in the Official Journal of the European Communities. It also has the power to dismiss all of the commissioners on a vote of censure. This vote requires a special majority. If the vote is carried the Commission resigns as a body. Paradoxically there is no power to prevent a new set of commissioners following exactly the same policy as that for which the original Commission was censured.

Legislative procedures

Traditional procedure

Under the traditional procedure, the role of the Parliament is 9.14
only advisory. The Commission takes a view on the opinion of Parliament and the Council of Ministers then takes the final decision. Since 1992 the Parliament has had a more significant role in the passing of Community legislation. The Council of Ministers

---

[28] E.C. Treaty, Art. 272.

is obliged to seek the advice of the Parliament, usually in the form of the relevant standing committee, in relation to specific matters. Failure to consider the view of Parliament would be a serious violation of the procedural requirements of Community law and would render any decision liable to be declared void by the European Court of Justice. This does not mean that the Council is bound to accept the advice of the Parliament and to follow its recommendations. Provided that it has followed the appropriate procedures for consultation it may then disregard the advice which has been given.

Co-operation procedure

9.15 Where there is a consultation requirement for certain matters relating to monetary union the co-operation procedure is followed.[29] This is a complex procedure, which formerly had a wider application, but which has since been superseded in many instances by the conciliation procedure and co-decision powers. Instead of taking a final decision after receiving the Parliament's advisory opinion, the Council adopts a common position by a qualified majority and the proposals are then sent to Parliament for a second time. Under the system of qualified majority voting in the Council, Member States are given different numbers of votes according to the size of their population. Parliament then has three months to reach a decision. If it takes no decision or approves the proposal the Council may adopt it. If the majority in the Parliament reject the Council's common position the proposal is not lost but may then only be accepted by a unanimous vote in the Council. A particular piece of legislation can be defeated by a majority in the Parliament together with one Member State.

Co-decision and conciliation procedure

9.16 Parliament now has powers of co-decision in relation to a wide range of policy areas including: the internal market; consumer affairs; culture; education; racial discrimination; freedom of movement; social security for migrant workers; right of establishment for foreign nationals; rules governing professions; implementation of transport policy; social fund; vocational training; public health, research; environment; development co-operation; equal opportunities and equal treatment; openness; measures to counter fraud;

---

[29] E.C. Treaty, Arts 6, 7. Introduced by the Single European Act 1986, given effect in the U.K. by the European Community (Amendment) Act 1986.

statistics; creation of an advisory body on data protection; incentive measures for employment; customs co-operation and measures to combat social inclusion.[30] Under this procedure, the Council also prepares a common position for presentation to the Parliament. If Parliament rejects this, the proposals will proceed no further.

Conciliation Committee

If Parliament rejects or amends a proposal a Conciliation Committee is convened. This consists of equal numbers of representatives of the Council of Ministers and the European Parliament.[31] The Conciliation Committee attempts to reconcile the views of the Council and the Parliament within a time-limit of six weeks.[32] If the conciliation is unsuccessful the proposal will not be adopted. 9.17

European Court of Justice

The European Court of Justice is the highest adjudicatory authority on the interpretation and application of Community law. Judges are appointed from each Member State for a period of six years.[33] The Court interprets Community law in areas of Community competence and interprets the treaty provisions, which define the powers of the European institutions. When carrying out this function it is operating as a constitutional court. 9.18

The Court is presided over by a President, who holds office for a period of three years. The judges are assisted by eight Advocates General.[34] They examine each case and present the legal arguments before the Court.

The Court's function is to consider issues of Community law but these issues are often considered in the light of the national law of the Member State. This approach improves the effectiveness of the Court's decisions. It also has the advantage that harmonisation of the laws of the Member States is facilitated.

---

30 E.U. Treaty 1992; E.C. Treaty, Arts 251, 252.

31 E.C. Treaty, Art. 251(3).

32 *ibid.* 251(5). The period may be extended by two weeks under E.C. Treaty, Art. 251(7).

33 E.C. Treaty, Art. 223.

34 *ibid.* Art. 222.

Referrals to the European Court of Justice from the Commission

9.19 A failure by a State to implement Community law may be referred by the Commission to the ECJ.[35] An early example was the case of *Commission v. United Kingdom*.[36] The Council issued a Regulation, which came into force on January 1, 1976, requiring Member States to legislate for compulsory use of tachographs in certain categories of commercial vehicles. The United Kingdom prepared a draft statutory instrument for a voluntary, rather than a compulsory scheme. The Commission repeated the requirement for a compulsory scheme but the U.K. Government indicated that it would not comply with the regulation. In October 1977 the Commission initiated action against the United Kingdom. In January 1978 the U.K. Government again declined to comply and the Commission gave a reasoned opinion requiring compliance and a two-month period from February in which to comply. In June 1978 the matter went to the European Court of Justice and in February 1979 the Court ruled that the United Kingdom was in breach of the Treaty.

Actions by States against other States

9.20 There is also a procedure by which one Member State may bring another State before the Court. The State which is aggrieved must first refer the matter to the Commission.[37] The Commission then considers oral and written submissions from the State in question and gives a reasoned opinion. The Member State then has a discretion whether or not to bring the matter before the Court. If the Commission fails to deliver its reasoned opinion within three months from the date of referral, the Member State may proceed with an action before the Court without further delay.

Actions by States against the Council and Commission

9.21 Member States and institutions of the Community can challenge the Council and the Commission on the ground that they have failed to act as required under the Treaty. Such action was threatened by the Assembly (Parliament) against the Council in 1969 because the Council had failed to develop procedures for direct elections to the assembly.

---

[35] E.C. Treaty, Art. 226.

[36] *Commission v. U.K.* [1979] 2 C.M.L.R. 45.

[37] Case C–265/95 *Commission of the European Communities, supported by Kingdom of Spain and United Kingdom v. French Republic, The Times*, Dec. 11, 1997.

Preliminary rulings

The Court may give preliminary rulings on certain matters.[38] Article 234 provides that: 9.22

> "The Court of Justice shall have jurisdiction to give preliminary rulings concerning:
> (a) the interpretation of this Treaty;
> (b) the validity and interpretation of the institutions of the Community and of the European Central Bank;
> (c) the interpretation of the statutes of bodies established by an act of the Council, where those statutes so provide.
>
> Where such a question is raised before any court or tribunal of a Member State that court or tribunal may, if it considers that a decision on the question is necessary to enable it to give judgment, request the Court of Justice to give a ruling thereon.
>
> Where any such question is raised in a case pending before a court or tribunal of a Member State against whose decision there is no judicial remedy under national law, that court or tribunal shall bring the matter before the Court of Justice."

Preliminary rulings play a very important part in the harmonisation of the laws of the Member States. The courts and tribunals of individual jurisdictions follow their own rules of statutory interpretation, which if applied to Community law, can give widely differing interpretations. The ability to refer matters for a preliminary ruling promotes greater consistency of interpretation.

Remedies

The Court has been criticised because it has lacked power to enforce its rulings effectively. If it finds that a Member State has failed to fulfil its obligations it issues a ruling requiring the Member State to take the measures which are required to comply with the ruling of the Court. If a State refused to comply with the ruling there was no sanction which the Court can impose. In the 1980s France refused to comply with rulings regarding the free movement of British lamb. Ultimately compliance depended upon political pressure from the other Member States. The Court can now impose a penalty payment on any Member State, which fails 9.23

[38] E.C. Treaty, Art. 234.

to respect the judgment of the Court.[39] The level of fines is related to the size of the economy of the State.

Interpretation of Treaty provisions

9.24 The ECJ has jurisdiction to make rulings on the interpretation of Treaty provisions in relation to certain matters including free movement of persons, immigration and asylum. It also has jurisdiction to rule on the validity or interpretation of acts of the institutions of the Community. It may not rule on matters relating to internal security or law and order.[40] Member States have made a declaration that they will accept preliminary rulings from the Court in relation to Justice and Home Affairs.

European Court of First Instance

9.25 The Court of First Instance was introduced by the Single European Act 1986. It sat for the first time in 1989. It consists of 12 members. Cases are usually heard by three to five judges sitting in Chambers. Its jurisdiction is limited with regard to subject-matter. The matters which it can consider include disputes between the Community and its servants, cases involving E.C. competition law and applications for judicial review and damages in respect of certain matters under the European Coal and Steel Community. There is a right of appeal from this court on matters of law to the Court of Justice.

EUROPEAN COMMUNITY LAW

9.26 The Primary sources of European Community law are the Treaties. Secondary legislation is law made by the Community institutions. This takes the form of Regulations, Directives and Decisions. They are defined by the E.C. Treaty as follows:

> "A regulation shall have general application. It shall be binding in its entirety and directly applicable in all Member States;

---

[39] E.C. Treaty, Art. 228.
[40] *ibid.* Art. 68.

> A directive shall be binding, as to the result to be achieved, upon each Member State to which it is addressed, but shall leave to the national authorities the choice of form or methods;
>
> A decision shall be binding in its entirety on those to whom it is addressed;
>
> Recommendations and opinions shall have no binding force."[41]

Regulations may be passed which are designed to have direct effect in Member States. This means that no change in national law is required to bring them into force in each State.

Directives could be described as instructions to the government of Member States to implement a change in national law to bring it into line with European policies. Each Member State may choose how to bring the Directive into effect.

THE EUROPEAN UNION AND THE EUROPEAN CONVENTION ON HUMAN RIGHTS

The Convention for the Protection of Human Rights and Funda- 9.27
mental Freedoms was drafted and prepared in 1950 by the Council of Europe. It established rights and freedoms protected by the Commission and Court of Human Rights in Strasbourg. Article 303 of the E.C. Treaty concerns links between the European Community and the Council of Europe but the European Community itself is not bound by the Convention. The original Treaties did not refer explicitly to human rights although Article 119 of the Treaty of Rome requires equal treatment for men and women in employment. Article 6 of the Treaty on European Union 1997 states that:

> "The Union shall respect fundamental rights, as guaranteed by the European Convention for the Protection of Human Rights and Fundamental Freedoms . . . and as they result from the constitutional traditions common to Member States, as general principles of Community Law."

The development of the jurisprudence of the European Court of Justice on rights and freedoms has been aided by the principle that Community law takes precedence over national law where there is

---

[41] Art. 249.

a conflict. In *Stander v. City of Ulm*[42] the European Court of Justice stated that it had a duty to protect the rights of individuals as provided for by the constitution of the Member State, and that such provisions formed part of the general provisions of Community law. *In Internationale Handelsgesellschaft GmbH v. EVST*,[43] the ECJ expressed its opinion that respect for fundamental rights forms an integral part of the general principles of law protected by the Court of Justice. The protection of such rights must be ensured within the framework of the structures and objectives of the Community.

Although it is clear from the case law that respect for internationally protected human rights is an important principle of Community law, the relationship between the European Community and the European Convention on Human Rights remains indistinct. It is clear, however, that the principle of respect for human rights is binding on Member States when acting within the scope of Community law, when the national government is implementing a Community law.[44]

EUROPEAN COMMUNITY LAW AND NATIONAL LAW

9.28 The European Community Treaties were incorporated into U.K. law by the European Communities Act 1972. In other words all Community law became directly applicable. It applies as part of U.K. law without any further action by the government of the United Kingdom. Community law also became capable of forming the basis of rights and obligations enforceable by individuals before the courts of the jurisdictions comprising the United Kingdom. It could therefore be described as having direct effect. The two terms direct application and direct effect cause some confusion and may be used interchangeably. Directly applicable laws are those which apply without any further law-making procedures being required and directly effective measures give enforceable rights to individuals within the State. Often measures will be directly applicable and will have direct effect. Other measures will be binding on and be enforceable by Member States alone.

---

[42] Case 29/69 *Stander v. City of Ulm* [1969] E.C.R. 419.

[43] Case 11/70 *Internationale Handelsgesellschaft GmbH v. Einfuhr -und Vorratsstelle für Getreide und Futtermittel* [1970] E.C.R. 1125.

[44] Case C–5/1998 *Wauchaul v. Bundescourt für Ernahrung und Fortwistschalt* [1991] E.C.R. I–2925.

Where a provision has direct effect domestic courts must apply it. Where there is a conflict between Community law and national law, it is Community law which prevails.

The relationship between the new Scottish Parliament and the European Community was an important element of the pre-devolution White Paper.[45] The Government set out a guiding principle that there should be the closest possible working relationships and involvement of the Scottish Executive in E.U. matters. The Scottish Executive would be involved in the process of policy formation and negotiation, in the scrutiny and implementation of E.U. legislation and in links with European institutions. Specifically in relation to implementation of Community obligations, it was stated that the Scottish Executive would itself be held liable for any failures for which it was responsible. The power to implement European Community law is one of the shared powers which can now be exercised by both the Westminster Parliament and the Scottish Parliament.[46]

The Scotland Act 1998 ordains that an Act of the Scottish Parliament is not law so far as any provision of the Act is outside the legislative competence of the Parliament.[47] The Act also provides that a provision is outside that competence if it is incompatible with Community law.[48] This paragraph reconfirms the principle that where there is inconsistency between Community law and national law it is Community law which prevails. Any provision which is incompatible with Community law is *ultra vires*. The Act also expressly prohibits any member of the Scottish Executive from doing anything incompatible with Community law.[49]

Vertical and horizontal direct effect

Direct effect may have two consequences. If a measure has vertical direct effect, rights arising from it may be enforced by a citizen against the government of the state or an emanation of the government of the state. In other words the central government administration, Scottish Administration, local authorities and other public bodies are deemed to be "emanations of the state". Examples of other public bodies include health authorities and 9.29

---

[45] *Scotland's Parliament*, Cm. 3658 (1997).
[46] Scotland Act 1998, s. 57(1).
[47] *ibid.* s. 29.
[48] *ibid.* s. 29(2)(d).
[49] *ibid.* s. 57(2).

police authorities. If a measure also has horizontal direct effect, it will give rise to rights which may be enforced by one citizen, or non-public body against another citizen or organisation.

Treaty Articles

9.30 Some Treaty Articles have been held to have direct effect. The question of direct effect of Treaty Articles was first raised in *Van Gend en Loos v. Nederlandse Administratie der Belastingen*.[50] The Dutch administrative tribunal asked the Court of Justice whether Article 12 of the EEC Treaty (now Art. 25) has an internal effect and whether the nationals of Member States may, on the basis of that Article, enforce rights which a judge should protect. Article 25 provides; "*Customs duties on imports and exports and charges having equivalent effect shall be prohibited between Member States. The prohibition shall also apply to customs duties of a fiscal nature.*" The Dutch firm of Van Gend en Loos protested that customs duties of eight per cent were imposed on imports of glue from Germany. The ECJ held that if a Treaty provision is to confer individual enforceable rights, it must indicate that it applies not just to Member States but also to individuals within the State. The provision must be clear and precise. The provision must also be unconditional and unqualified and not subject to any further measures on the part of Member States. The provision must be one which does not leave any substantial latitude or discretion to Member States. It was held that the Article did have direct effect.

Regulations

9.31 As Regulations are of general application and are binding in their entirety and directly applicable in all Member States, they take effect in each State immediately without the need for further implementation. It is therefore often taken for granted that they will have direct effect, but direct effects are not always automatic. There may be cases where a provision in a Regulation is conditional, or insufficiently precise, or requires further implementation before it can take full effect. Since a Regulation is of general application, where the criteria for direct effect are satisfied it has both vertical and horizontal direct effect.

---

[50] Case 26/62 *Van Gend en Loos v. Nederlandse Administratie der Belastingen* [1963] C.M.L.R. 105.

Directives

Directives are not directly applicable. Further action is required by each Member State in order to modify the laws of the State so as to meet the objectives of the Directive. The government has a discretion as to the method by which this will be achieved. Because of this it was originally thought that Directives would not have direct effect. 9.32

The Member States, however, do not always implement Directives with alacrity and do not always legislate in a way that achieves the full purposes of Directives and so the European Court has developed a doctrine that a Directive may have direct effect, without national legislation. One consequence of this is that an action may be raised against the government or an emanation of the State which is failing to implement the Directive.[51] Direct effect is only possible where the European provisions, whether in a Treaty or a Directive, are clear and precise and render it certain exactly what rights and obligations should exist without leaving discretion to the Member States in implementing the measures. These conditions were met in the case of *Marshall v. Southampton and South West Hampshire Health Authority (Teaching) (No. 2)*.[52] M had established, in a claim for wrongful dismissal, that her compulsory retirement at the age of 60 constituted sex discrimination contrary to an E.C. Directive. She was awarded the meagre statutory maximum damages under national employment law and no interest. When she won her first victory in 1986, the maximum compensation available was £6,250. The tribunal did not think this was adequate and awarded her £19,405, which included an interest amount of £7,710 from the date of her dismissal to the date of award. This award was appealed by the employers and they won; M then appealed and lost; appealed again, this time to House of Lords on the ground that the statutory upper limit for compensation and the exclusion of interest payments were contrary to E.C. law. The House of Lords referred the matter to the ECJ. The Court held that the United Kingdom had not properly implemented the Equal Treatment Directive by capping the amount payable to M and refusing to pay interest. The Directive required an effective remedy and that the limit to compensation and the

---

[51] *Van Duyn v. Home Office* [1975] Ch. 358, ECJ; *Marshall v. Southampton and South West Hampshire Health Authority* [1986] Q.B. 401, ECJ; *Marshall v. Southampton and South West Hampshire Health Authority (No. 2)* [1993] 3 W.L.R. 1054, ECJ.

[52] [1993] 3 W.L.R. 1054, ECJ.

rule that no interest would be paid were obstacles to adequate compensation they were contrary to E.C. law. The Health Authority, as an emanation of the State was liable for this breach. The Government then had to pass the Sex Discrimination and Equal Pay (Remedies) Regulations 1993[53] which abolished the limit on compensation payable. In the case of *R v. Secretary of State for the Health Department, ex parte Richardson*,[54] R, aged 64, contended that, as a result of regulation 6(1) of the National Health Service (Charges for Drugs and Appliances) Regulations 1989, he had suffered discrimination contrary to Directive 79/7. The regulations provided for differences in the charges for men and women between the ages of 60 and 65 years. The Secretary of State argued that prescription charges did not fall within the scope of the Directive and the Queen's Bench Divisional Court sought a preliminary ruling from the ECJ. It was held that as prescription charges were part of a statutory scheme to provide protection against the risk of sickness, regulation 6(1) fell within the scope of Directive 79/7. Discrimination was permitted where it was necessarily and objectively linked to the difference in retirement age set by a Member State for the purpose of granting retirement pensions. The discrimination underlying regulation 6(1) was not a necessary consequence of different ages for retirement. The ECJ also ruled that the direct effect of the Directive could be relied upon to support claims for damages for periods prior to the date of the judgment.[55]

9.33 Directives which are directly effective are enforceable only against the national government and not against other individuals or bodies. They are described as having vertical but not horizontal effect. A failure to comply with a Directive cannot give rise to an action against private individuals so the *Marshall* case was only competent as it was a case against a public authority as an employer and not a private employer. Where a person suffers harm because a Directive has not been incorporated into national law they will not have an action against another citizen or organisation but an alternative form of redress may be an action for damages against the government itself. A Directive normally contains a time-limit within which it must be implemented by each Member State. If a Member State fails to implement a Directive within the time-limit indicated it may render itself liable to pay compensation

---

[53] S.I. 1993 No. 2798.

[54] C–137/94, ECJ; *The Times*, Oct. 27, 1995.

[55] See also *Thomas v. Chief Adjudication Officer* [1993] E.C.R. I–1247.

to any individual who suffers damage as a direct consequence of this failure to implement in time. This liability will only arise if it was the intention of the Directive to confer rights on individuals and that the content of those rights is identifiable from the Directive itself. In the case of *Francovich v. Italy*,[56] the ECJ ruled that a Member State might be liable in damages in respect of the loss and damage suffered by a private individual which was directly caused by the State's failure to implement a Directive which conferred directly enforceable rights. The case concerned the failure by the Italian government to give effect to a Directive requiring state guarantees for wages owed to employees by bankrupt employers. The employers were a private firm, and so the claims of the employees could not be enforced directly. It was immaterial whether or not the Directive had direct effect since the liability was for failure to translate the Directive into national law. Some of the remarks made in the judgment of the ECJ in this case support a wider principle that a Member State is liable to indemnify any individual injured under these conditions by any breach by the State of E.C. law and not merely where the breach consists of non-implementation of a Directive.

Liability for failure to implement a Directive may be strict. The case of *Wagner Miret v. Fondo de Garantia Salarial*[57] arose because Spain had taken no action to implement a particular Directive since it considered that the national law of Spain was adequate for this purpose. This view was held to be incorrect but there was no discussion in the judgment as to whether the argument put forward by Spain was a reasonable one. It appears therefore that liability is strict and does not depend on a deliberate or culpable failure to implement the Directive in question. This was confirmed in two linked cases, *Brasserie du Pêcheur*,[58] wherein it was held that reparation for loss or damage cannot be made conditional upon fault (intentional or negligent) on the part of the organ of state responsible for the breach. A serious breach of Community law may be sufficient alone to give a right to compensation. In *Brasserie du Pêcheur* the ECJ held that individuals who have suffered damage have a right to reparation where three conditions are met: (1) the rule of law infringed must have been intended to confer rights on individuals; (2) the breach must be sufficiently serious; and (3) there must be a direct causal link between the breach of

---

[56] Case 6/90; [1992] I.R.L.R. 85; [1991] E.C.R. I–5357.
[57] Case C–334/92; [1993] E.C.R. I—6911.
[58] C46/93 *Brasserie du Pêcheur SA v. Germany* [1996] 1 C.M.L.R. 889.

the obligation resting on the State and the damage sustained by the injured parties.

9.34 Breach of a directly effective Treaty provision by a Member State or its failure to correctly transpose a Directive into national law gives rise to liability where a manifest and serious breach is present. A breach of Community law is sufficiently serious if a Community institution or a Member State, in the exercise of its rule-making powers, manifestly and gravely disregards the limits on those powers.[59] It has subsequently been held that failure to take any measures to transpose a Directive in order to achieve the result it prescribes within the period laid down for that purpose constitutes *per se* a serious breach of Community law. Such a breach will give rise to a right of reparation for individuals if the result prescribed by the Directive entails the grant to individuals of rights.[60]

In *R. v. Ministry of Agriculture, Fisheries and Food, ex parte Hedley Lomas*,[61] it was stated that if, at the time when it committed the infringement, the Member State in question was not called upon to make any legislative choices and had only considerably reduced, or even no, discretion, the mere infringement of Community law may be sufficient to establish the existence of a sufficiently serious breach. The case related to a refusal by the Ministry to issue licences for the export of live sheep to Spain. The refusal to grant the licences was on the ground that their treatment in Spanish slaughterhouses was contrary to Directive 74/577 on stunning of animals before slaughter. The Directive had been implemented in Spanish law but the Ministry considered that it was not being complied with in some Spanish slaughterhouses. It was held that the United Kingdom Government had little discretion at the time when it committed the infringement. It was obliged to comply with the Directive. Failure to do so constituted a sufficiently serious breach to give rise to liability to an individual who suffered a loss. It was observed that the United Kingdom was not even in a position to produce any proof of non-compliance with the Directive by the slaughterhouse to which the animals for which the export licence was sought were destined.

---

59 *Brasserie Du Pêcheur III*, above ; C392/93 *R. v. H.M. Treasury, ex p. British Telecommunications* [1996] 2 C.M.L.R. 217.

60 C178/94 *Dillenkofer v. Germany* [1996] All E.R. (E.C.) 917; [1996] 3 C.M.L.R. 469.

61 C–5/94 *R. v. Ministry of Agriculture, Fisheries and Food, ex p. Hedley Lomas (Ireland) Ltd* [1996] 2 C.M.L.R. 391.

Member States may claim that the period allowed for the implementation of a Directive is too short but it has been established that a Member State may not rely on provisions and practices within its own legal system to justify a failure to observe a time-limit for implementation.[62] If the period allowed for implementation is too short, the only step available to a Member State is to take appropriate initiatives within the Community in order to have the competent Community institution grant the necessary extension of the period.[63]

In *Brasserie du Pêcheur*,[64] it was held that reparation for loss or damage caused to individuals as a result of breaches of Community law must be commensurate with the loss or damage sustained. In the absence of relevant Community provisions, it is for the domestic legal system of each Member State to set the criteria for determining the extent of reparation. The criteria must be no less favourable than those applying to similar claims based on domestic law and must not be such as in practice to make it impossible or excessively difficult to obtain reparation. The injured party must show reasonable diligence in limiting the extent of the loss or damage. A State may not exclude liability for loss of profit in the case of a breach of Community law. It was also held that, in circumstances where an award of exemplary damages may be awarded in a similar action under domestic law they must also be awarded in an action based on Community law.

CONFLICT BETWEEN UNITED KINGDOM LEGISLATION AND EUROPEAN COMMUNITY LAW

Although the United Kingdom has joined the E.C. and has 9.35
accepted that European laws may have direct effect within the United Kingdom, U.K. governments have been reluctant to relinquish the doctrine of supremacy of Parliament. An Act of the Westminster Parliament will not be declared invalid by a U.K. court on the ground that it is incompatible with E.C. law. The courts will declare that an Act of Parliament is incompatible with E.C. law.[65] They will not declare that an Act of the Westminster Parliament is *ultra vires*. The language used is advisory. It is then

---

62 *Commission v. Belgium* [1988] E.C.R. 3271, para. 7.

63 *Commission v. Italy* [1976] E.C.R. 277, para. 12.

64 [1996] 1 C.M.L.R. 889.

65 See *R. v. Transport Secretary, ex p. Factortame (No. 2)* [1991] 1 A.C. 603; *R. v. Employment Secretary, ex p. Equal Opportunities Commission* [1995] 1 A.C. 1.

up to Parliament to correct the incompatibility to which the courts have drawn attention. In theory Parliament could ignore the declaration and leave the law unchanged. Parliament decides what measures are necessary to correct the incompatibility and the extent to which the law will be amended. In practice Parliament has always acted to correct incompatible provisions but the fact that it cannot be compelled to do so preserves the principle that Parliament can make or unmake any law and no court may set aside an Act of Parliament.

CHAPTER 10

LOCAL GOVERNMENT IN SCOTLAND

From 1999, there will be four tiers of government in Scotland affecting Scottish voters: the European Community, U.K. Parliament, Scottish Parliament and local authorities. Local government now comes under the control of the Scottish Parliament and there may be tensions between the two bodies as time goes on. 10.01

The Scottish Parliament is restricted in its powers to those that have been granted by the Scotland Act 1998. Undoubtedly, the Scottish Parliament will want more powers or to extend its power-base. Since such new powers will be difficult to obtain from Westminster, the Scottish Parliament may be tempted to increase its power-base at the expense of local government. There is historical precedent for this with the Northern Ireland Parliament set up by the Government of Ireland Act 1920. That Parliament affected the working of the local authorities in Northern Ireland to their detriment and it is arguable that they have never recovered. Local government areas were reorganised in Scotland in 1996 and in this chapter we will consider why this reorganisation occurred and how local government now works.

THE REORGANISATION OF 1996

A major reorganisation of local authorities in Scotland occurred in the 1970s. From more than 400 councils of varying sizes, the new structure reduced the number to 53 district, nine regional and three islands councils. The system enacted in the Local Government (Scotland) Act 1973 was a two-tier structure, with the regional councils providing major services such as education, social work and roads, and the districts providing services of a more local or community based type such as housing and environmental services. The islands councils (Shetland, Orkney and Western Isles) were unitary in nature although they shared some services with Highland Region such as police, fire and planning. The system had 10.02

been suggested by the Wheatley Commission in 1969[1] after extensive research and consultation. The Wheatley Commission recommendations sought to rationalise the then fragmented local government system by providing economies of scale by introducing large regions with strategic functions, by improving the co-ordination of service delivery and ensuring better accountability by reducing the need for joint boards. By contrast, the reorganisation carried out by the Local Government etc. (Scotland) Act 1994 was not the result of a Royal Commission and the research and consultation was limited. In England an independent commission took evidence and then made suggestions as to the best solution in particular areas.

The reorganisation in Scotland was heralded by two consultation papers and a White Paper, all written by officials at the Scottish Office. The first paper was published in 1991, and was called *The Structure of Local Government in Scotland: The Case for Change*.[2] In it, the Government made out its case for changing the structure, giving three main reasons: the impact of previous legislative changes had meant that local authorities were no longer providers of services but "enablers"[3]; the existing regional councils were too remote from the people; and the people did not know whether a service was provided by the district or regional council and this caused confusion and delay.

It is debatable whether any of the given reasons in the paper was sufficient to justify the upheaval of a reorganisation in terms of time, effort and expense. However, there were unwritten, and probably overriding, reasons behind the Government's thinking. Local government cost too much and in Scotland, at least, local councils had too much power and influence. The economic argument seemed to be of paramount importance:

> "The key moment in the reform process was the collapse of the poll tax. At that time, the Secretary of State [for Scotland], in common with his colleagues in England and Wales explicitly linked the search for economy with the desirability of structural change."[4]

---

[1] *Report of the Royal Commission on Local Government in Scotland*, Cmnd. 4150 (1969).

[2] Scottish Office, *The Structure of Local Government in Scotland: The Case for Change* (1991).

[3] *ibid.* para. 12.

[4] Alexander, "Wheatley To . . . What?" in *The Constitutional and Political Impact of Re-organisation* (Black ed., 1995), p. 27.

The second consultation paper, issued in 1992, was eventually translated into legislation almost without alteration to its substance. Called "The Structure of Local Government in Scotland: Shaping the New Councils"[5] the paper suggested four different structures, ranging from 15 councils to 24, to 35, and up to 51. It included maps of how the boundaries might be drawn. The two extremes of 15 and 51 councils were quickly rejected and most of the discussion centred on the two middle groups of 24 and 35. The 1992 paper presented reorganisation as a *fait accompli*, moving the debate on from whether reorganisation was necessary to how it could be achieved. The arguments then centred on the boundaries of the proposed new councils and an acceptance of the "need for change" occurred almost by default. People were more interested in where their town or village would be after reorganisation than whether there should be a reorganisation at all.

In the event, 32 council areas were selected, 29 new ones and the three existing islands councils which were left unaltered. All of the councils were to be single tier or unitary, providing almost the entire range of local authority services previously handled by the regional and district councils.

THE NEW LOCAL AUTHORITIES

The new councils are unitary, providing a wide range of services 10.03
such as education, social work, local roads, housing, planning and leisure and recreation. They range in population size from 623,000 in the City of Glasgow to 48,000 in Clackmannan. Ten of the new councils have a population of fewer than 100,000 while eight have more than 200,000. They vary in geographical size also, from Clackmannan which is about 300 square miles to Highland which is about 160,000 square miles, the size of Wales. Few of the councils created in 1975 survived intact.

Although the 1994 Act reorganised the structure and form of the local authorities, the powers and responsibilities of local authorities remain as in the Local Government (Scotland) Act 1973, as amended. Many of the particular functions of councils are set out in separate statutes, for instance the Social Work (Scotland) Act 1968 and the Education (Scotland) Act 1980.

---

5 Scottish Office, *The Structure of Local Government in Scotland: Shaping the New Councils* (1992).

The changes were not however merely cosmetic. Strategically and structurally the changes were more significant. "The creation of smaller units was achieved through a loss of functions such as trunk roads, water and sewerage, the reporters' administration, and the need for extended use of joint arrangements for service provision."[6]

The Local Government etc. (Scotland) Act 1994 removed responsibility for water and sewerage services from the councils and transferred them to three newly created quangos whose boards were selected by the Secretary of State. This was seen as a precursor to water privatisation in Scotland; something the Conservative Government had been unable to do because of the political implications north of the border where Conservative supporters were also against such a move. The Government justified the move by saying that the 32 small councils could not provide the funding required to bring the services up to E.C. standards; this could only be done efficiently and effectively by water authorities created for the purpose. The boards for these authorities do not consist of members nominated by the local authorities but are appointed by the minister who ensures that the best possible people for the job are selected.

10.04 The second major strategic change for local authorities was that the Government suggested in its consultative paper that some councils would join together to provide services in a more efficient and economical manner. The Local Government etc. (Scotland) Act 1994 gives power to the Secretary of State (now the Scottish Executive) to create joint boards for the provision of a service where he considers a function should be carried out jointly.[7] The minister has exercised these powers in respect of police and fire services. The Act also envisages joint boards for structure planning[8] and traffic control.[9]

The Act allows councils to set up joint committees for services; here each council retains the responsibility for the particular service but the function is carried out jointly. A third type of joint arrangement was recognised in the 1992 consultation document, contracting. Here one or more councils will contract with another to provide a service; for instance, it may be cheaper for a council to contract out the rubbish collection of a rural community to a

---

[6] Midwinter and McGarvey, "Local Government Reforms in Scotland: Managing the Transition" (1997) Vol. 23(3) *Local Government Studies* 73 at 75.

[7] s. 20.

[8] s. 33.

[9] s. 49.

council which is geographically better placed to provide the service. Alternatively, two or more councils may set up a consortium to provide a service, for instance, school catering.

Joint committees and contracting do not in the main have the same accountability problems seen in joint boards. The councils have, however, resisted setting up these joint arrangements; there appears to be a preference in Scotland for a local authority to provide the full range of services itself—a quirk of political culture between Scotland and England.[10] The widespread use of joint arrangements in England became necessary after the abolition of the metropolitan county councils in 1986. Statutory joint boards were set up for police, fire and passenger transport services and these operated on a county-wide basis. There remains the possibility that Scottish councils will be forced to set up joint boards if the minister wishes to use his powers.

However, the use of joint arrangements in a unitary system does appear to be a regressive step. It seems to create another tier of government which is not as democratic since the joint board or committee has no direct link with the electorate. "Joint action for anything other than a very limited range of services should be seen as an additional (indirectly elected) tier of government which actually undermines, in a fundamental sense, the 'unitary authority' principle."[11]

Other problems exist: smaller partner councils may feel 'swamped' by a larger partner; the chief officer of the joint board or committee will invariably be employed as an official of one partner and thus a conflict of interest may arise; the lead partner will have the advantages of extra expenditure in ancillary work and property and will be perceived to have additional power through agenda-setting. Research in England found that joint boards and committees encountered problems with the way in which charges for the service were calculated, since smaller partners often felt they were being overcharged.[12]

In 1993, the *Re-organisation* White Paper was published express- 10.05
ing support for the idea of joint arrangements and maintaining that accountability would not suffer as a result:

---

[10] Black, "Constitutional and Political Issues in the Re-organisation of Scottish Local Government" in *The Constitutional and Political Impact of Re-organisation, op. cit.*, p. 8.

[11] Leach, Davies, Game and Skelcher, *After Abolition: The Operation of the Post 1986 Metropolitan Government System in England* (1992), p. 5.

[12] Travers, "More and More Go Hand in Hand", *Local Government Chronicle*, June 9, 1995.

> "This need not however mean that an individual authority would relinquish control or responsibility for the provision of a service . . . There is nothing new in local authorities combining to provide services: various arrangements already exist in the current system ranging from joint boards for police and fire to the use by smaller authorities of specialist facilities which are provided only by the larger authorities."[13]

The Government did not mention the number of existing arrangements which would have indicated the use of these in Scotland. Before the reorganisation there were three statutory police joint boards and three fire joint boards, one joint water board and only one voluntary joint committee.[14] In 1997, these had increased to 23 joint boards, of which six were police and six were fire, and only four joint committees. These have been referred to as 'secondary local government' where the number of 'primary' local government units fell from 65 before reorganisation to 32 while the number of 'secondary' units rose from seven to 32, including five new quangos which took over some of the responsibilities of the regional councils.[15] The three water authorities have been discussed above. The other two quangos are the Scottish Children's Reporters Administration and the Scottish Environmental Protection Agency (SEPA). The latter took functions from both local councils and the river purification boards which were wound up. SEPA has no local accountability for its performance and, in common with other agencies, is responsible to the minister by means of an annual report and thus has little accountability to Parliament.

10.06 In addition to these changes the 1994 Act gave the Secretary of State for Scotland (now the Scottish Executive) over one hundred new powers to make orders, directions and so on. His existing powers such as capping of local authority expenditure remain and the Act strengthened his powers with regard to capital controls. Taken with the other changes—the requirement for joint arrangements and the creation of new quangos—these powers represent a further move away from local to centralised decision-making. The Act also required councils to prepare decentralisation schemes. At present, the schemes appear to decentralise services rather than

---

13 Secretary of State for Scotland, *Shaping the Future—The New Councils*, Cm. 2267 (1993), p. 8.

14 Kerley and Orr, "Joint Arrangements in Scotland" (1993) Vol. 19(3) *Local Government Studies* 309.

15 Alexander, "Wheatley To . . . What?" in *The Constitutional and Political Impact of Re-organisation, op. cit.*

power or influence, which was the spirit, if not the intention, of the White Paper. The net effect of the centralisation of powers upwards to the Scottish Executive and other government bodies and the decentralisation of services down to local communities must be regarded as a further emasculation of local authorities.

The reorganisation restructured the boundaries and brought most of the services from regions and districts together into one authority. As discussed above, it failed to touch the way in which councils operate. Management structures are still broadly the same as before, with a chief executive and a number of chief officers heading a number of departments which provide either a service such as education or housing, or administrative support such as finance or personnel. On the elected members' side, the committee structures follow broadly the same pattern as before with a full council meeting to which the service and administrative committees report. The 1994 Act did not require any changes to be made. However, it specifically removed the statutory requirement for councils to appoint a director of social work and a director of education, raising fears that these important positions would be abolished or merged with other functions. In the event, most councils have retained the two positions.

There have been some amalgamations of functions with around one-third of the councils combining services such as housing and social work in one department. Throughout Scotland the number of chief officers who comprise the management team of a council has been reduced, although it is likely that the second management tier has increased in number.

Recent research on how the reorganisation affected the housing function found that the structures adopted were varied and confirmed that the decentralisation of the service was mainly physical rather than political and managerial. "There is only limited local discretion over policy, procedures and financial arrangements, reinforcing the picture of decentralisation arrangements emphasising local service delivery with the centre retaining a high degree of control."[16]

The 1993 White Paper had seen advantages for housing being on the same tier as social work, education, roads and transport since this would lead to "improved co-ordination" of the services.[17] The research does not address this issue but since the majority

---

[16] Taylor and Douglas, *Local Authority Structures for Housing after Reorganisation* (1998).

[17] Secretary of State for Scotland, *Shaping the Future—The New Councils*, *op. cit.*, p. 10.

of councils have a dedicated housing committee it is unlikely, certainly at member level, that there will be as much co-ordination as the White Paper expected. At officer level, it is likely that they will try to protect their own service particularly given the financial strictures imposed by central government since the councils were formed.

10.07 The Minister for Communities has overall responsibility for most local authority functions, but there are other aspects of local government work, which are controlled by other ministers, such as the Minister for Children and Education, the Minister for Enterprise and Lifelong Learning, the Minister for Health and Community Care, the Minister for Rural Affairs and the Minister for Transport and Environment. The Scottish Parliament has set up a Local Government Committee but other committees will also be concerned with how local authorities carry out their functions, *e.g.* education, culture and sport; health and community care; rural affairs; and social inclusion, housing and voluntary sector.

The local authorities also have to work with an array of government agencies and quangos. For instance, in housing, the councils have to consult with Scottish Homes and various housing associations regarding the provision of housing within their council area. Housing is still an important function of local authorities despite the diminution of council housing stock to only 34 per cent of homes in Scotland in 1994 compared to 56 per cent in 1979. The government encouraged the sale of council houses to sitting tenants and a number of councils are now considering the large scale voluntary transfer of their housing stock to the private sector, either to a housing association or a local housing company. So far in Scotland, only one such transfer has occurred[18] but more than 40 have occurred in England. The transfer of stock has to be problematic for a council in fulfilling its statutory functions, particularly with respect to homeless persons. The 1993 White Paper[19] thought that councils should be "more strategic and enabling in character" declaring that councils had the responsibility for assessing housing need but did not need to fulfil those duties by being a landlord.

Throughout the United Kingdom, local councils may only do those things which are provided in the legislation setting them up. In Scotland, the Local Government (Scotland) Act 1973 is still the basic legislation setting out the powers and duties of councils. This

---

[18] Berwickshire District Council transferred its entire stock to a local housing company in 1995, a few months before it ceased to exist under reorganisation.

[19] Secretary of State for Scotland, *Shaping the Future—The New Councils, op. cit.*

doctrine of *ultra vires* is different from the position of local government bodies across Europe where local government have a power of general competence, defined as the right to intervene and take initiatives on any matter which affects the local community in so far as the law does not explicitly provide otherwise.[20] The Wheatley Commission in 1969 recommended that this power of general competence be given to the councils.[21] The 1973 Act kept the *ultra vires* doctrine but gave limited power to a local authority to spend money which the authority thought was in the interests of the inhabitants of their area. This limited power was, however, curtailed by section 164 of the 1994 Act so that the new councils are now only able to incur expenditure which is in the interests of their area and will bring "direct benefit" to it. There are further restrictions on this, including an obligation to ensure that the direct benefit is commensurate with the expenditure. The minister may set a limit on the expenditure that can be incurred under this section.

The minister has considerable powers: for instance, he is responsible for the funding of many bodies in Scotland, particularly local councils; his permission may be required before certain expenditure is incurred; and he has considerable powers of patronage affecting many areas of Scottish public life. This includes the appointment of members to the many advisory, consultative and executive bodies now funded by the Scottish Executive, although these powers of appointment are now exercised under the advice of a panel of independent advisers[22] set up as a result of the recommendations of the Commissioner for Public Appointments.[23] 10.08

The 1973 Act section 211 gives the minister default powers to establish a local inquiry into a council's performance of a statutory duty. If he finds there has been a failure, he may make an order giving directions on how the default is to be rectified. These default powers are used rarely since direct intervention by central government in local affairs is not seen as appropriate except in the most extreme circumstances. Such an occasion occurred in 1995 when the Secretary of State ordered an inquiry into the allegations of

---

[20] See Hughes, Clarke, Allen and Hall *The Constitutional Status of Local Government in other Countries,* (1999).

[21] In England, the Maud Committee Report on the Management of Local Government had made a similar recommendation in 1967.

[22] At Sept. 30, 1998, the panel comprised 29 members drawn from various walks of life.

[23] The Commissioner for Public Appointments issued a Code of Practice and Guidance in 1996.

impropriety in the recruitment practices of Monklands District Council. If the default is not rectified, the Lord Advocate may apply to the Court of Session for an order of specific performance. This occurred in 1986 when the Government prevented a local authority from transferring funds from the rate fund to the housing revenue account in an attempt to hold down council house rents.[24] Later in 1990, a council was prevented from trying to circumvent the "right to buy" legislation by inserting unlawful conditions into its offers to sell council houses.[25]

The minister has default powers in other legislative provisions. The Education (Scotland) Act 1980, s. 70 deals with the failure of a local authority to discharge its duties under the Act, whereupon the minister may declare the authority is in default and require a remedy by a specific date.

Many actions taken by a local authority under statutory authority require the express approval of the minister, such as orders for the compulsory purchase of land. He has appellate powers in respect of planning applications turned down by the local authority and in this respect he has a considerable influence on the decisions of local planning authorities since these will be taken with his policies in mind.[26] He has the power to "call in" planning decisions, and has used this power particularly in respect of planning applications for large out-of-town retail parks.

10.09 The relationship between the Scottish Executive and local authorities is supervisory in nature. Indeed, the Scottish Office declared that "local authorities are independent and the management of their day-to-day business is for them to conduct as they think fit."[27] Essentially this is accurate but the statement is simplistic and somewhat fictional, given that the Scottish Executive controls local authorities by means of policy advice and financial controls. The department issues circulars as required advising councils on how the government wishes legislation to be enacted in their area. It will thus be a brave council that ignores such advice. Such circulars do not normally have legal effect since they are not subordinate legislation, but a statute may authorise the issue of directions and these may be embodied in a circular.[28] Circulars are also used to set out the criteria to be used by the minister in

---

[24] *L.A. v Stirling District Council*, 1986 S.L.T. 179.

[25] *L.A. v City of Glasgow District Council*, 1990 S.L.T. 721.

[26] Himsworth, *Local Government in Scotland* (1995).

[27] Scottish Office Website http://www.scotland.gov.uk/library/documents3/fs12–07.htm

[28] See Finch and Ashton, *Administrative Law in Scotland* (1997).

exercising a discretion and as such may give rise to legitimate expectation by persons relying on the criteria.

The Scottish Executive has to rely on local authorities to carry out a range of central government functions and thus the relationships between the two sets of officials become even more important. The central local relationship in Scotland is an individual one, since the minister generally exercises his powers with each individual local authority, not collectively. However, there are occasions when he consults with the local authorities on a collective basis, and this will usually be done under the auspices of the Convention of Scottish Local Authorities (COSLA). For instance, the Local Government Finance Act 1992, Sched. 12, requires the minister to consult associations of local authorities "as appear to him to be concerned". COSLA was set up after the 1975 reorganisation and has played an important part in the development of central local government relations since then. Local government in Scotland, and thus COSLA, has been dominated by Labour controlled authorities over the last two decades and so COSLA's influence has waxed and waned according to the party in power at Westminster.

THE RELATIONSHIP BETWEEN THE SCOTTISH PARLIAMENT AND LOCAL AUTHORITIES

The Scottish Parliament has taken over the areas which comprised 10.10
the responsibilities of the Secretary of State for Scotland and the Scottish Office. The White Paper which preceded the referendum of September 1997 referred to the principle of subsidiarity that decisions should be made as close as possible to the citizen.[29] The government thus recognised that the new Parliament would have a marked effect on the position of local authorities. A consultation paper was issued suggesting the setting up of an independent commission to look at the tripartite relationship which would exist between the Parliament, the Scottish Executive and local government. The commission's remit was also "to consider how councils can best make themselves responsive and democratically accountable to the communities they serve."

The 1998 Act does not amend the various local government statutes which remain intact but become subject to alteration by the Parliament as new policies are developed in that forum. The White Paper set out the broad relationship:

---

[29] *Scotland's Parliament*, Cm. 3658 (1997).

> "The Scottish Parliament will have the power to set the framework within which local government operates and to legislate to make changes to the powers, boundaries and functions of local authorities. The Scottish Parliament will be responsible for supporting local authority current expenditure and for controlling and allocating capital allocations to the Scottish councils. It will also be responsible for the system of local taxation."[30]

The Act does not restore any of the powers removed from local authorities in the 1996 reorganisation. Indeed, the Act does not contain any provision recognising the principle of subsidiarity as stated in the White Paper. This is in contradiction to the proposals for the Parliament put forward by the Scottish Constitutional Convention in 1995 when it suggested that the Scottish Parliament should be required "to secure and maintain a strong and effective system of local government."[31] The statute establishing the Welsh Assembly, the Government of Wales Act 1998, at section 110 requires the Assembly to "sustain and promote local government in Wales."

What does this omission mean for local government in Scotland? It could be concluded that the government wanted the Parliament to have a free hand in its dealings with local authorities. However, there was a hint of the Government's thinking in the White Paper at paragraph 4: "The best guarantee that local government will enjoy its proper place under the Scottish Parliament is a system of local government able to demonstrate that it is fully responsive to the electorate which it serves."

This suggests that local authorities will have to become more democratic and accountable to their electorate by taking steps to increase the participation of the population in the democratic process. The remit of the Commission on Local Government and the Scottish Parliament reflected this. The commission was charged to present its final report to the Scottish Parliament or the Scottish Executive but could make an interim report to the Secretary of State for Scotland giving its ideas on ways in which voter participation might be increased. The implications for local authorities were that their relationship with the Parliament would depend upon them increasing democratic accountability.

---

[30] Scotland's Parliament, Cm. 3658 (1997), para. 6.5.

[31] Scottish Constitutional Convention, *Scotland's Parliament. Scotland's Right* (1995), p. 17.

The Labour Government had recognised that the issue of the relationship between the Parliament and local authorities could become a major problem unless it was addressed at an early stage. Consequently, the commission, now known as the McIntosh Commission, was set up with the remit, first, to consider how to build the most effective relations between local government and the Scottish Parliament and Scottish Executive, and secondly, to consider how councils could best make themselves responsive and democratically accountable to the communities they serve. 10.11

The commission published its first consultation paper in the spring of 1998 setting out its initial views and asking for responses to various matters. At paragraph 9 of the document, the commission reflected: "[The creation of a new Parliament] is an opportunity to look at existing systems and see if they are working, or if they need an overhaul".

The paper suggested the drawing up of a concordat between the Scottish Parliament and the Scottish local authorities, in which the Parliament would set out how it intended to exercise its powers of scrutiny, monitoring and consultation. In its submission to the commission, COSLA stated that: "Parliament's role should be to set the framework in which it expects councils to meet. Once that is done it should accept local government's right to do things differently and to find local solutions which best meet local needs."[32]

The submission went on to state that local government has three roles: the provision of services (*e.g.* education, social work), the regulation of services (*e.g.* development control) and community planning (*e.g.* establishing the needs of the community and bringing local service providers together to meet these needs). The Secretary of State for Scotland indicated that he wished local government to take on a community planning role[33] and indicated his willingness to look at more radical reforms such as Cabinet government, directly elected civic heads and new voting systems, in a bid to modernise local government.

Most of the commission's consultation paper was concerned with questioning the system of local government itself. It asked for comments on the electoral system, arrangements for voting, recruitment of candidates for election, decentralisation, the role of community councils and the role of councillors and chief officers.

---

[32] Response of COSLA to First Consultation Paper of Commission on Local Government and the Scottish Parliament: http://www.lg.scot.commission.gov.uk/root-comm/submissions

[33] *The Scotsman*, Oct. 8, 1998.

The commission took a 'root and branch' approach to its remit by inquiring into all aspects of the system of local government. This is in fact the proper consultation which should have taken place before the 1993 White Paper and the 1996 reorganisation.

10.12 In its final report *Moving Forward: Local Government and the Scottish Parliament*,[34] the commission suggested a draft covenant between the Scottish Parliament and Scottish local authorities and a draft agreement between the Scottish Executive and the authorities. The draft covenant declares a commitment "to work together in an atmosphere of mutual trust and respect, recognising the value and legitimacy of the role that both have to play in the governance of Scotland." It goes on to suggest a joint conference which would meet annually with all council leaders attending and on a more regular basis with around 15 members from the Parliament and 15 from local authorities. The draft agreement between the Scottish Executive and local authorities starts with a similar commitment and then proposes more formal ties with COSLA.

The commission recommended that the internal organisation of local councils should be reviewed. The work of councillors and the work and role of committees were discussed with the recommendation that they should also be reviewed. During the summer of 1999, ministers have indicated that councils must reform their internal procedures and structures and stated that 'the status quo was not an option.' Neil McIntosh, the former chairman of the commission, has been given the task of advising councils on how to achieve the changes wanted by the Scottish Executive. It is obvious that the reorganisation of 1996 is to be followed by further reorganisation, this time to the committee structures and council departments which were left largely unaltered in 1996.

---

[34] Commission on Local Government and the Scottish Parliament (1999).

CHAPTER 11

GOVERNMENT AND THE ADMINISTRATION

The executive organ of government is the largest of the three organs identified in the doctrine of separation of powers. It consists of the Prime Minister, the Cabinet, the other government ministers and civil servants who implement the policy passed by the legislature. Civil servants are of course involved at two levels in the policy process. They are responsible for formulating policy according to the instructions of their ministers and they are also involved in implementing the policy. This division between policy and operation has been used to make major changes in the structure of the civil service and these will be discussed below. 11.01

The Scottish Executive and Scottish Administration have been newly formed but already similarities and differences between Edinburgh and Whitehall can be seen. The implications of devolution on the civil servants who undertake the work of government in Scotland will be discussed later in this chapter.

THE U.K. GOVERNMENT

Prime Minister

The Prime Minister is chosen as a result of either a successful general election, in which his party is returned as the largest party, or on the resignation of a former Prime Minister, such as occurred in 1990 when Margaret Thatcher was forced to resign by her parliamentary party. In either event, the party leader must be invited by the sovereign to form a government. The sovereign invokes the prerogative to choose a Prime Minister although by convention the choice is effectively limited to the leader of the largest party or the new leader of the party already in government. Thus it could be argued that the choice of Prime Minister always rests with the political parties. The sovereign's discretion to choose a Prime Minister is limited to the situation where a general election does not produce a majority for one party and there is no possibility of the parties entering into a coalition government; in these circumstances 11.02

the sovereign would have to decide which party leader was more likely to command sufficient support in the House of Commons to form a government.

By convention, the Prime Minister must be a member of the House of Commons. There are two reasons for this requirement. First, as leader of a political party he must be able to stand for election in a general election and obtain popular support for his party's manifesto. Secondly, the Prime Minister has to be accountable to the electorate and this can only happen on a day-to-day basis if he is subject to the scrutiny process of the House of Commons. The last peer to be selected as Prime Minister by the Queen was Lord Home in 1963 but he immediately renounced his title under the Peerage Act 1963, stood as a candidate in a by-election and was elected as an M.P.

The Prime Minister has extensive powers.

(1) Powers relating to the Cabinet

11.03 The Prime Minister appoints his Cabinet and all of the other ministerial posts. He has the power to "hire and fire" and the provisions of employment law with regard to unfair dismissal do not apply. However his power is not unlimited; he has to try to reconcile the various "wings" of the party and there may be people who have helped him attain his position and therefore need to be rewarded. Thatcher's first government contained ministers who were to the left of the Conservative Party, since she needed to retain the support of the whole party. Later, as more right wing M.P.s were elected, she was able to dispense with most of these "wets" as they were called. Similarly, Tony Blair has had to involve people who were traditionally on the left wing of his party to ensure party unity.

In addition, the Prime Minister is able to appoint people who are his friends since he will need friends in the Cabinet to balance those who have ambition for higher office. An example here is David Mellor, who was appointed by John Major in 1992 but who quickly had to resign because of his inappropriate activities. Tony Blair appointed Peter Mandelson to a Cabinet post in 1997 as Minister without Portfolio and then in 1998 promoted him to Secretary of State for Trade and Industry. He had to resign a few months later because certain loans he had received had not been declared in the Register of Members' Interests. He returned to the Cabinet in late 1999 as secretary of State for Northern Ireland.

The Cabinet is normally composed of 20 to 22 senior M.P.s and peers. There are no set rules for deciding which ministers should be in the Cabinet, but it is inconceivable that the Cabinet would not include the holders of the great offices of state, such as the Chancellor of the Exchequer, the Home Secretary, the Foreign Secretary and the Defence Secretary. The Lord Chancellor is invariably a member of the Cabinet and he will be joined by the Leader of the House of Lords (who is also Lord Privy Seal).

The Prime Minister has the right to require a minister to resign or he may dismiss him. It has become the custom each summer for the Cabinet to be subject to a "re-shuffle" when the Prime Minister moves ministers to other jobs or dismisses them to the back benches. Again it is for the Prime Minister to decide whether to rearrange his Cabinet in this way and he may do so at any time. In 1962, Harold Macmillan dismissed seven of his 20 Cabinet ministers in an effort to revitalise his flagging government.

(2) Dissolution of Parliament

The Prime Minister decides when he will call a general election, 11.04
unless he is unlucky enough to have lost a motion of no confidence in his government when he will be obliged to call an election, such as James Callaghan in 1979.

The Prime Minister will decide the date of an election after consulting close colleagues. He does not have to consult the Cabinet. Thatcher did apparently consult others regarding the timing of the elections in 1983 and 1987 but on both occasions her ministers accepted that it was her decision to make.

John Major took a risk when he threatened to call an election in November 1994 if his backbench M.P.s voted against a government Bill to increase U.K. budgetary contributions to the E.C. He won the vote but probably alienated more members of his party and thus contributed to their defeat in 1997.

Once he has decided to call a general election, the Prime Minister must ask the sovereign to dissolve Parliament.

(3) Cabinet meetings

The size and composition of the Cabinet is decided by the Prime 11.05
Minister alone, as are the sizes and composition of Cabinet committees which discuss proposed legislation and other matters. The Prime Minister decides when the Cabinet will meet, what will be discussed and what will be written in the minutes. It is not usual for a vote to be taken in Cabinet; rather the Prime Minister "senses the mood of the meeting" and sums up for the minutes. Thatcher's control over her Cabinet is legendary but this did not mean that there was no dissent. In 1986, Michael Heseltine resigned as Defence Secretary after Thatcher refused to allow

discussion on the impending sale of Westland Helicopters to an American company instead of the European consortium Heseltine favoured. The Prime Minister also refused to allow ministers to discuss the matter outside Cabinet, invoking the doctrine of collective responsibility.

(4) Patronage

11.06 As well as the power to hire and fire ministers, the Prime Minister has other powers of patronage and influence over the appointment of people to senior positions. The Prime Minister's consent is required for the appointment of the most senior civil servants and his nomination is also required for the appointment of senior judges, bishops of the Church of England, the Parliamentary Ombudsman and many others. He makes recommendations to the sovereign for the conferment of new life peerages, honours and dignities and appointments to the Privy Council.

Cabinet

11.07 The choice of members of the Cabinet is left to the Prime Minister, as discussed above. How the Cabinet works will depend on the style of the Prime Minister. It is however the central core of the government and its support is necessary if the Prime Minister is to survive in office. This was seen most clearly in November 1990 when Margaret Thatcher won the first ballot in the Conservative Party leadership election but found that the majority of her Cabinet were unwilling to support her in the second ballot. She was thus forced to resign.

The style of government will depend on the relationship between the Cabinet and the Prime Minister. If the Cabinet is freely involved in the decision-making process it is said that there is Cabinet government. However, if the Cabinet is subordinate to the Prime Minister and a small coterie of ministers, the government is styled prime ministerial. In Cabinet government, the Prime Minister is said to be *primus inter pares*, or first among equals. The prime ministerial government however is more presidential in style where the Prime Minister is likened to a chief executive and the Cabinet ministers are heads of departments. The Thatcher government was said to be prime ministerial while the Wilson government of the 1960s was considered to be an example of Cabinet government.

The Cabinet meets usually once a week to discuss forthcoming business in Parliament and current and future issues needing the government's attention. However it would be impossible for the Cabinet to discuss all of these issues in detail and thus the practice has evolved over the years of discussing the detail of policies in committees and bringing the policy statement to the Cabinet for approval.

Until 1992, the existence of the Cabinet committees was an open secret; everyone knew they existed but the government would not admit their existence or their membership or remit. The arguments for secrecy were that decisions taken by Cabinet were subject to collective responsibility and to scrutiny by the House of Commons. It was not therefore appropriate that the committees were identified since their decisions could not be scrutinised. Further, the existence of the committees and publication of their membership would lead to lobbying by M.P.s and other groups and would therefore interfere with their deliberations. John Major decided that his government would operate in a more open manner and he published the names and remit of 27 Cabinet committees and their membership in 1992. He further streamlined the structure in 1995 by reducing the number of committees to 19 to try to produce greater efficiency.

In September 1999, there were 30 ministerial committees and sub-committees and a Joint Consultative Committee with the Liberal Democratic Party, this last having been formed by the Labour and Liberal Democratic Parties shortly after the general election in 1997 to pursue issues of common interest, particularly matters involving constitutional changes. The committees are arranged into four groups, Economic and Domestic, Constitution, Overseas and Defence, and European.[1] They cover many varied matters including public services and public expenditure, utility regulation, drug misuse, food safety, constitutional reform policy, Northern Ireland and European issues.

Cabinet committees are comprised of Cabinet ministers, non-Cabinet ministers and officials and will be chaired by the Prime Minister or a senior member of the government. They are set up to "relieve pressure on Cabinet itself by settling business in a smaller forum or at a lower level or at least by clarifying issues and defining points of disagreement . . . They act by implied devolution of authority from the Cabinet and their decisions therefore have the same formal status as decisions by the full Cabinet."

The Cabinet Office

The Cabinet Office was created in 1917 originally to co-ordinate 11.08
the work of the War Cabinet. It is headed by the Secretary to the Cabinet, who is the most senior civil servant. The Cabinet Office is

---

[1] See http://www.cabinet-office.gov.uk/cabsec/index/cbcom/index.htm, Sept. 9, 1999.

responsible for recording Cabinet meetings and circulating the minutes and other papers. The Cabinet Office is not the Prime Minister's department; it is a co-ordinating department which serves the Cabinet and government as a whole. The aim of the Cabinet Office as published in its Public Service Agreement is "to help the Prime Minister and Ministers collectively to reach well informed and timely decisions on policy and its presentation, and to drive forward its implementation, together with their agenda for modernising government, for improving the quality, coherence and responsiveness of public services, and for promoting a strong and well-managed Civil Service."[2]

Currently the Minister for the Cabinet Office holds the position of the Chancellor of the Duchy of Lancaster and he has day-to-day responsibility for the civil service.

The department was extensively reorganised in 1998 and now includes a wide range of secretariats and units. These include the Social Exclusion Unit, Women's Unit, the U.K. Anti-Drugs Co-ordination Unit, Better Regulation Unit, Civil Service Corporate Management and Government Information and Communication Service. The department's predecessor, the Office of Public Service, included the Freedom of Information Unit, but responsibility for this was transferred to the Home Office in July 1998 so that the Home Office could "co-ordinate the detailed preparation and implementation of the (Freedom of Information) Bill alongside related legislation on data protection and human rights."

The Cabinet Secretariat is under the direct supervision of the Prime Minister through the Secretary to the Cabinet. It services a number of Cabinet committees and includes a number of specialist secretariats, such as the Constitution Secretariat, the European Secretariat and the Joint Intelligence Organisation. The Central Secretariat is responsible for providing advice to the Cabinet Secretary and his private office as well as ministers and departments on matters such as ministerial responsibility and accountability, the machinery of government, standards and ethics issues in relation to ministers, civil servants and specialist advisers and public appointments.

The Prime Minister is also served by the 10 Downing Street office which provides policy advice and ensures that the government's policies and decisions are communicated effectively to Parliament, the media and the public. The office is not part of the Cabinet Office.

---

[2] Cabinet Office Memorandum to the Public Administration Select Committee (1998), http://www.cabinet-office.gov.uk/1998/memo/index.htm, Sept. 9, 1999.

Civil service

The civil service has undergone a major transformation during the last decade and this has led to some problems, particularly with regard to the distinction between the making of policy and its operation or implementation. 11.09

The civil service is part of the executive arm of government. Its traditional role is to advise ministers on policy matters and, once the policy has been decided, to implement that policy. Each government department is headed by a senior civil servant, the permanent secretary whose job it is to oversee all the workings of the department and advise the minister of progress on policy formulation and implementation. However, it was recognised in the 1960s that this dual function of the permanent secretary was an impossible one; the two tasks are quite different and should be separated. This idea was the basis of changes which were to take place, slowly at first, and then gathering pace under the Conservative Government in the late 1980s.

The definition of a civil servant is to be found in the Fulton Committee Report: "a civil servant is a servant of the Crown, other than holders of political or judicial offices, who is employed in a civil capacity and whose remuneration is paid wholly and directly out of monies voted by Parliament."[3] This definition helps to clarify who is not a civil servant or Crown servant. Thus, politicians and members of the judiciary are not civil servants; members of the armed forces are not civil servants since they are employed in a military rather than a civil capacity. Officials of local authorities are not civil servants since they are paid partly from monies raised through local taxation. Similarly police officers' salaries are partly funded from local taxation. Staff in the National Health Service are not civil servants although their salaries are funded from central government funds; most of them are employed by NHS trusts and do not have the status of Crown servants.

A civil servant is generally a permanent employee who should remain politically neutral and may expect that their advice to a minister will remain anonymous. These are the three constitutional principles upon which the British civil service is founded: permanence, neutrality and anonymity.

The concept of permanence is no longer one upon which any 11.10
civil servant may rely. A civil servant holds office "at the pleasure of the Crown" and generally will have the same rights of employment protection as any other employee although some of them

---

[3] Report of the Committee on the Civil Service, Cmnd. 3638 (1968).

may be revoked under the royal prerogative. In 1985, the right of civil servants employed at GCHQ to belong to a trade union was revoked by the government using prerogative powers.[4] A civil servant may also be dismissed with no action at common law for wrongful dismissal.[5] However, in reality, the position of most civil servants is as secure as any other employment and their terms and conditions of employment are regulated under the prerogative.

The main idea of permanency rests in the fact that while a government may change every five years or so, the civil service does not. The civil servant is expected to serve whichever government has been elected and this means that an incoming government will have the benefit of the expertise of civil servants who have been in their post for some time and who know the background to the problems which may arise for a minister.

11.11 However, if a civil servant serves a government of one political hue, how can he then serve a new government of a different hue? This is the second constitutional principle of the civil servants, that they should be able to serve any government and that they owe their loyalty to the government of the day. The political neutrality of the civil servant is crucially important, otherwise incoming governments would need to replace senior civil servants when they came to office and the expertise and knowledge of the civil servant would be lost. To preserve their political neutrality, senior civil servants are prevented from participating in political activities. They may not participate in national elections or European Parliament elections and they may not express their views on matters of national political controversy. They are also prevented from standing for election as local councillors or hold office in a political party or take part in political activity such as canvassing. Civil servants in the more junior grades may be able to participate in local politics but only if they have the permission of their head of department.

Civil servants will still have their own political opinions and they may find themselves in a dilemma if those opinions and the government policy conflict. The Ponting case is an example of this. In 1984, the Defence Select Committee was examining the conduct of the Falklands War in 1982 and an M.P., Tam Dalyell, had asked a number of questions in the House relating to the sinking of the Argentine ship *General Belgrano*. Clive Ponting was responsible for preparing answers to the parliamentary questions being asked but his answers were altered by his superior before the minister gave

---

[4] *Council of Civil Service Unions v. Minister for the Civil Service* [1985] A.C. 374.
[5] *Riordan v. War Office* [1959] 1 W.L.R. 1046.

them out. Ponting felt that the answers given were misleading and he then anonymously sent papers to Dalyell giving the true circumstances of the sinking. Dalyell passed the papers to the Chairman of the Select Committee who passed them to the minister and Ponting was found out. He was charged under the Official Secrets Act 1911, s. 2 with communicating information to an unauthorised person. Ponting argued that Dalyell was a "person to whom it was, in the interests of the state, his duty to communicate" the information. The judge directed the jury that the 'interests of the state' meant 'the policy of the state as laid down by the government' and Ponting's duty was the official duty imposed on him by his position.[6] Ponting was acquitted, the jury having decided that his action was justified.

A civil servant who feels that his personal opinions are in conflict with some action he has been asked to take must consider carefully before declining to take the action (or refrain from doing something). The Civil Service Code advises the civil servant to consult a senior officer and if the conflict remains unresolved he may then take the matter up with the Permanent Head of the Department. An appeal from the decision of senior officials lies to the Civil Service Commissioners. Ultimately if the civil servant is unable to resolve the conflict he will either have to carry out the instructions he has been given or resign. The Civil Service Code states at paragraph 5 that the civil servant "must not knowingly mislead Parliament or the public." However he must at no time disclose the information to the public or to an unauthorised person.

Civil servants now see their loyalties as lying with the government of the day, not directly with Parliament, and this was clearly indicated by those civil servants who gave evidence to the Scott Inquiry.[7] For instance, one civil servant admitted: "It was simply a matter of us not telling the truth, of knowingly not telling the truth to the public and Parliament. The policy was bent and we concealed that policy."[8]

The third principle is that of anonymity. This is tied up with the 11.12
idea of ministerial responsibility, in that the minister is responsible for the actions of his department and accountable to Parliament for any shortcomings. The minister takes credit and blame, and civil servants are shielded from public inquiry and opprobrium. The

---

[6] *R. v. Ponting* [1985] Crim.L.R. 318.

[7] Report of the Inquiry into the Export of Defence Equipment and Dual-Use Goods to Iraq and Related Prosecutions (Scott Inquiry) (1995–96 H.C. 115).

[8] Mark Higson quoted in Fenwick and Philipson, *Source Book on Public Law* (1996), p. 599.

anonymity afforded civil servants thus will enhance their political impartiality.[9] However, in recent years senior civil servants have become less anonymous. This has occurred for a number of reasons. First, the changes in the civil service from large departments to smaller ones with associated executive agencies has led to the identification of agency chief executives, who are able to speak for their agencies in press briefings and select committee hearings. The strengthening of the select committee system is another reason as is the televising of their hearings. In addition, ministers have been less willing to take responsibility for the wrongdoings of their civil servants and more willing to identify civil servants. This was seen in the Westland Affair where the Head of Information at the Department of Trade and Industry leaked part of a letter written by the Solicitor General in which he disputed the accuracy of information given by Michael Heseltine. The letter was released after the civil servant had consulted with members of the Prime Minister's staff. The furore caused by the leak led to the resignation of Leon Brittan, the Secretary of State for Trade and Industry, who accepted responsibility for the actions of his staff. However the Head of Information's identity and that of four other civil servants was released by the Prime Minister in Parliament, breaching the principle of anonymity. The five civil servants were subsequently forbidden to give evidence to the Defence Select Committee when it decided to investigate the affair although the Head of the Home Civil Service appeared to give evidence on the matter.

As a result of the difficulties experienced by civil servants in the Westland Affair and the Scott Inquiry, the Nolan Committee recommended that the constitutional framework within which civil servants work should be clarified.[10] A new Civil Service Code was issued under the royal prerogative and came into force in 1996. The Civil Service Management Code says:

> "[T]he constitutional and practical role of the civil servant is, with integrity, honesty, impartiality and objectivity, to assist the duly constituted government, of whatever political complexion, in formulating policies of government, carrying out decisions of the government and in administering public services for which the government is responsible."[11]

---

[9] The idea of ministerial responsibility is discussed in Chap. 12.

[10] *Standards in Public Life* (Nolan Report), Cm. 2850–I (1995).

[11] The Management Code was issued by the Civil Service Order in Council 1995 (as amended in 1995 and 1996).

Civil servants are appointed on merit and recruitment is based on fair and open competition.[12] This is overseen by the Civil Service Commissioners, who also operate the appeals system referred to above. Overall responsibility lies with the Minister for the Civil Service, who is usually the Prime Minister, although he may delegate this to another minister. The minister decides the terms and conditions of employment of civil servants.

Government departments and executive agencies

Cabinet ministers in the government and certain other ministers are responsible for particular government departments; these may be very small, such as the Lord Chancellor's Department, or very large, such as the Department of Environment, Transport and the Regions (DETR). Each Secretary of State will be assisted by three or four junior ministers who will take on a particular policy responsibility within the department. Most of the departments are responsible for a particular function, *e.g.* Ministry of Defence and the Treasury. Others have many functions, such as the DETR and Department of Trade and Industry. Currently there are also three territorial departments, the Scotland Office, the Wales Office and the Northern Ireland Office, although there are indications that following devolution, these departments will be amalgamated into one 'Department for Devolution' or 'Department of the Isles'. At the time of writing it is unlikely that such an amalgamation will take place until the Northern Ireland peace process is more stable and a devolved government established in that unhappy area. 11.13

The senior civil servant of a department is the permanent secretary and he is responsible for the day-to-day management of the department and for advising the minister on policy. He is also the department's principal accounting officer and has the responsibility of ensuring that proper accounting records are kept and expenditure complies with the authorisation given by Parliament. The day-to-day control of expenditure is handled by an accounting officer, appointed by the Treasury and personally responsible for "the propriety and regularity of the public finances for which he or she is answerable."[13] These officers have the duty of advising their ministers against taking any action which would breach the requirements of the rules on propriety and regularity. If their advice is ignored, the accounting officer should seek written instructions

[12] Civil Service Order in Council 1995, art. 2.

[13] Public Service Committee, Second report on Ministerial Accountability and Responsibility (1995–96 HC 313–I), para. 77.

from the minister before carrying out the minister's decision.[14] The advice of the accounting officer and the fact that the minister overruled it is then reported to the Public Accounts Committee of the House of Commons.

Civil servants in departments will propose policy to their ministers and once that policy has been agreed by the politicians, the civil servant will then be required to carry out that policy. As mentioned above, formulating policy and implementing it are two distinct activities and if a senior civil servant is involved in formulating policy, he will not necessarily have the time or skills to ensure it is put into operation properly. This distinction was recognised in the Fulton Committee Report in 1968 but not properly put into effect until the 'Next Steps' reforms of the late 1980s.

11.14 The process was started in 1979 when Margaret Thatcher set up the Rayner Unit, a small unit of civil servants under Derek Rayner. Thatcher's intention was to reduce the size of the public sector by 'deprivileging' civil servants and introducing privatisation to enable reductions in the public sector borrowing requirement. The Rayner Unit started by requiring all departments to question all of their activities, propose solutions and begin to implement them within 12 months. The Department of Environment introduced the Management Information System for Ministers (MINIS) a relatively simple scheme which ascertained departmental economic targets, how they were set and how they were being achieved. This kind of information had not previously been available to ministers and it led to the department being reorganised and substantial staff savings being made.

The next stage was the introduction of the Financial Management Initiative (FMI) whereby managers at all levels were given greater responsibility and control by ensuring they had clearly defined objectives and responsibilities and the training to ensure they could exercise those responsibilities. Performance related pay was introduced in 1985 and new running costs were imposed on departments in 1988, with individual managers being set cash limits.

The biggest cultural change occurred in 1988 with the publication of the Ibbs Report.[15] This proposed a split between service delivery (or operation) and the making of policy. The idea was that departments would divide themselves, with a small policy formulation core sponsoring government policies and services, and a large

---

[14] *R. v. Secretary of State for Foreign and Commonwealth Affairs, ex p. W.D.M.* [1995] 1 All E.R. 611.

[15] Jenkins, Caines and Jackson, *Improving Management in Government—The Next Steps: Report to the Minister* (1988).

number of agencies concentrating on the delivery of a particular service. The agencies would employ their own staff and would be managed by an agency chief executive.[16] Since 1988, most of the civil service has moved into the agency status. The Department of Social Security, for instance, moved 97 per cent of its staff into five agencies.

The real impetus of the changes in the departmental structures was the Conservative Government's search for efficiency and economy. Once the Rayner Unit asked departments to look at their activities, it was only a matter of time before the question became "do you need to carry this out at all? Can it be provided more cheaply in the private sector?" The Treasury required all departments to consider options for each activity: abolition, privatisation, contracting out, agency status and status quo. The Treasury's preferred option was abolition and any department opting for the status quo had to be prepared to give specific arguments in its favour. The options are reconsidered every four or five years, although this may take place earlier if it appears that privatisation has become a strong option.

Executive agencies are controlled by a chief executive who is 11.15
responsible for providing the specific service within a given budget. The agency chief executive is a civil servant and is subject to the same restrictions as other civil servants in respect of answering the questions of select committees and individual M.P.s in the House. A civil servant appearing before a select committee represents his minister and thus his answers must reflect the policy of the minister. He may not give his own views. However an agency chief executive appearing before a select committee is able to answer questions on operational matters on their own account but must answer questions on policy according the minister's views. If an M.P. asks a question of a minister and the question relates to a matter which is within the responsibility of an agency, the minister will refer the question to the agency chief executive. The reply from the agency chief executive is not given by the minister in the House; instead, it is published in *Hansard*. This procedure has the effect of removing a minister from the line of fire, and thus from taking responsibility for any shortcomings of an executive agency.

At present civil servants who are transferred to an executive agency will remain as civil servants but their conditions of service will not necessarily remain the same. The civil service used to have an image of being a uniform service, where staff could move from

---

[16] For a fuller discussion, see V. Finch and C. Ashton, *Administrative Law in Scotland* (1997), Chap. 4.

one department to another on being promoted. Pay grades were universal; a higher executive officer in the Ministry of Defence would be on the same scale as a higher executive officer in the Scottish Office. Conditions of service were also uniform.

Now agency chief executives can implement pay scales and conditions of service, as they think appropriate. This means that civil servants wishing to transfer back into the mainstream service to perhaps become involved in policy making may have difficulty in doing so without losing seniority or pay.

THE GOVERNMENT IN SCOTLAND

11.16 Until July 1, 1999, the government of Scotland was handled by the Secretary of State for Scotland and the civil servants of the Scottish Office. Devolution has seen most of the powers and responsibilities of the Secretary of State for Scotland pass to the First Minister and the Scottish Executive. The Scottish Office is now called the Scotland Office, to distinguish the new U.K. body from its predecessor.

The Secretary of State for Scotland is still a member of the Cabinet and will answer questions in the House of Commons on non-devolved matters relating to Scotland. There is still a Scottish question time every four weeks but it will now have a shorter time allocated for it. The Secretary of State for Scotland is responsible for ensuring that there is dialogue between the Scottish Executive and the U.K. government so that matters of mutual interest are discussed. Under the Scotland Act 1998 the Secretary of State for Scotland has specific responsibilities, for instance in relation to a bill which may be incompatible with Community obligations or Convention rights, and he may make an order to prohibit the Presiding Officer from submitting the bill for Royal Assent.[17]

Scottish Administration

11.17 The Scottish Administration comprises the First Minister, the Scottish Executive, the other junior ministers, other office holders specified in the Act and the members of staff of the Scottish Administration, *i.e.* the civil servants.

The First Minister, the ministers appointed by him and the two Law Officers collectively are known as the Scottish Ministers and make up the Scottish Executive.[18]

---

[17] 1998 Act, s. 35.
[18] *ibid.* s. 44(1).

First Minister

The First Minister is appointed by the sovereign following a nomination by the Scottish Parliament and the recommendation of the Presiding Officer.[19] The First Minister then may appoint ministers to the Scottish Cabinet; again these are appointed with the approval of the sovereign and the agreement of the Parliament.[20] There is no limit on the number of ministers who may be appointed and the First Minister, Donald Dewar, appointed nine ministers and 10 junior ministers. 11.18

The First Minister has other statutory functions:

(1) appointment and dismissal of junior Scottish ministers[21];
(2) recommendation of the appointment and dismissal of the Law Officers[22];
(3) nominating the Lord President of the Court of Session and the Lord Justice Clerk[23];
(4) recommending the appointment of other Court of Session judges, sheriffs principal and sheriffs[24];
(5) recommending the removal of Court of Session judges and the Chairman of the Scottish Land Court.[25]

The Scottish Cabinet

The First Minister chose nine ministers to form the first Scottish Cabinet along with the Lord Advocate. The ministers have a variety of portfolios: Finance, Justice, Children and Education, Enterprise and Lifelong Learning, Health and Community Care, Parliament, Rural Affairs, Communities, and Transport and Environment. Only two ministers do not have a deputy minister to assist them (Finance, and Transport and Environment) and of the other seven, three have two deputies. The Scottish Executive has adopted the title of Deputy minister rather than junior minister. 11.19

Law Officers

The Law Officers, the Lord Advocate and the Solicitor General for Scotland, are appointed directly by the sovereign on the recommendation of the First Minister and with the agreement of 11.20

---

19 1998 Act, ss. 45(1), 46(4).
20 *ibid.* s. 47.
21 *ibid.* s. 49.
22 *ibid.* s. 49.
23 *ibid.* s. 95(2).
24 *ibid.* s. 95(4).
25 *ibid.* s. 95(6).

the Scottish Parliament.[26] Other ministers are appointed by the First Minister with the sovereign's approval. The difference in appointment is important; it helps to ensure the independence of the Law Officers, particularly the Lord Advocate, from being dismissed by the First Minister because the Lord Advocate has not been able to support the First Minister politically. The Parliament must agree to a recommendation by the First Minister that the sovereign be asked to remove the Lord Advocate from office.

The Law Officers need not be MSPs and if they are not, they may participate in proceedings in which they have an input although they may not vote.[27]

The Act seeks to preserve the independence of the Lord Advocate by means of his appointment and removal, and by ensuring that he may not be removed by the Parliament from his position as head of the system of criminal prosecution and investigation of deaths.[28] The Lord Advocate is also required to act independently when taking decisions on matters relating to criminal prosecutions or investigation of deaths.[29] If the Parliament passes a vote of no confidence in the Scottish Executive the Lord Advocate must resign along with the other members[30] but he will remain in office until a successor takes office to ensure that the 'retained functions' of the Lord Advocate may still be carried out. The 'retained functions' are those which are exercisable only by the Lord Advocate.[31]

The Scottish Cabinet and other ministers are subject to the doctrine of collective responsibility.[32] In August 1999, the Scottish Executive published the Scottish Ministerial Code which sets out a Code of Conduct and guidance on procedures.[33]

---

26 1998 Act, s. 48(1).
27 *ibid.* s. 27(1).
28 *ibid.* s. 29(2)(e).
29 *ibid.* s. 48(5).
30 *ibid.* s. 48(2).
31 *ibid.* s. 48(3).
32 See Chap. 12.
33 http://www.scotland.gov.uk/library2/doc03/smic-00.htm.

CHAPTER 12

GOVERNMENT AND ACCOUNTABILITY

> "In every free state, for every public act, someone must be responsible; and the question is, who shall it be? The British Constitution answers: 'the Minister and the Minister exclusively'."[1] 12.01

This is the traditional view of the accountability of ministers and it is a simple and relatively straightforward view. However, it is a view of its time. When Gladstone was making his proposition, the government and civil service were small and the minister was able to control what was happening in his department. He would know his civil servants personally and be aware of their individual duties. So if something went wrong, the minister took responsibility because it was his responsibility to have known about it and to have taken steps to prevent the occurrence. In the late twentieth century however, government is very different. There are many more civil servants, departments are much larger and handle many more functions. It would be impossible for any minister to know precisely what is happening in his department and control it. In addition, the introduction of executive agencies to take over many functions of departments has meant that much of the work of a department is now carried out at arm's length from the minister. The doctrine of ministerial responsibility therefore has had to change to take account of these changing circumstances and it is no longer a simple straightforward proposition; it is now a highly complex and highly political issue.

This chapter will try to define ministerial responsibility as it affects the U.K. government and the Scottish Executive. Ministerial responsibility is a constitutional convention and it is central to the relationship between the executive and the legislature. The idea is that government should be conducted in as open a way as

---

[1] Gladstone (1879) quoted in Public Service Committee Second Report, Ministerial Accountability and Responsibility (1995–96, H.C. 313–I).

possible, while taking account of the requirements of the national interest. The concept is explained thus: "Ministers are responsible for the general conduct of government, including the exercise of many powers legally vested in the Monarch; and ultimately, through Parliament and parties, to the electorate."[2]

There are two aspects to the doctrine of ministerial responsibility: collective responsibility and individual responsibility.

COLLECTIVE RESPONSIBILITY

12.02 The convention of collective responsibility is the mechanism by which a government shows a united front to Parliament and to the country at large. It is rigidly adhered to by government for a number of reasons. First, the government must be seen as strong and united so that other governments will know that it is able to carry out its policies and to reassure the stock market and money markets that the business of government will carry on smoothly. Secondly, if a minister is under pressure in Parliament over his policies, the rest of the government will rally round to support him since his policy is their policy. The doctrine protects and defends ministers who are unpopular, or even incompetent. Finally, the doctrine reinforces the belief that the executive is one body and that all government departments are part of that body. During the annual financial discussions between departments, it could be harmful if one department is seen to be benefiting at the expense of another thus communications between departments are secret as are the final expenditure discussions made by the Cabinet.

There are two main rules underlying the convention. First, once a decision has been reached by the Cabinet, all members of the government, whether in the Cabinet or not, are bound by that decision and are required to support it publicly. Decisions made in a Cabinet committee, particularly when it is chaired by the Prime Minister, will also be binding on all members of the government. If a minister dissents from the decision, such as occurred with Michael Heseltine in 1986 and Geoffrey Howe in 1990, then the minister must either agree to the policy, accept and support it, or resign. In 1986, Michael Heseltine was unable to accept the Prime Minister's decision that no statements on the take-over of Westland Helicopters should be made without her authority and he was unhappy at her refusal to discuss this decision in Cabinet. He

[2] Marshall and Moodie, *Some Problems of the Constitution* (5th ed. 1971).

resigned. In 1990, Geoffrey Howe, who was Deputy Prime Minister, was unable to accept the Prime Minister and the Cabinet's position regarding the United Kingdom's relationship with the E.C. He resigned and made a damning resignation speech in the House of Commons, thus setting in train the events that were to lead to a leadership challenge and the eventual downfall of Margaret Thatcher.

The second rule requires all Cabinet discussions to remain secret. Ministers may openly discuss the issues in Cabinet and their discussions will remain completely confidential. This aspect of the doctrine of course depends on all ministers agreeing to be bound by the collective decision. The Code of Conduct and Guidance of Procedures for Ministers[3] sets out the government's views on collective responsibility. "Collective responsibility requires that Ministers should be able to express their views frankly in the expectation that they can argue freely in private while maintaining a united front when decisions have been reached. This is turn requires that the privacy of opinions expressed in Cabinet and Ministerial committees should be maintained."[4]

The Cabinet records are protected by confidentiality. Cabinet papers of the previous government may not be seen by an incoming government without the consent of the previous Prime Minister. Thus during the inquiry into the conduct of the Falklands War, the consents of five Prime Ministers were required before Cabinet papers could be released. The rule is justified on the basis that the incoming government should not be able to make political capital out of any Cabinet discussions held by their predecessor. There are three exceptions to this rule: papers which are already in the public domain, such as letters from former ministers to constituents, M.P.s or others; papers dealing with matters already known to foreign governments as a result of intergovernmental negotiations; and the written legal opinions of the Law Officers. These last documents should not, however, be disclosed outside the government without the authority of the Law Officers.[5]

The status of ministerial memoirs has arisen in recent years. The 12.03
celebrated case is *Attorney-General v. Jonathan Cape Ltd*[6] which involved the publication of the diaries of the late Richard Crossman, a Labour Cabinet Minister in the 1960s. The Attorney-General sought an injunction to prevent the publication on the

---

[3] http://www.cabinet-office.gov.uk/central/1997/mcode/index.htm
[4] *ibid.* para. 17.
[5] *ibid.* para. 24.
[6] [1976] Q.B. 752.

ground that publication was not in the public interest because the diaries revealed the details of Cabinet decisions, differences of opinion between ministers and the disclosure of advice given by civil servants. The court had to consider the doctrine of collective responsibility and the confidentiality of discussions within the Cabinet. Both the doctrine and the issue of confidentiality as being in the public interest were upheld by the court but with the proviso that at some time the issue of confidentiality would lapse. The court considered that a lapse of 10 years was sufficiently long that much of the material contained in the diaries would have been made public or would have lost their sensitivity.

After the Crossman diary case, a committee of privy councillors was set up to consider when such memoirs might be published and in what circumstances. The Radcliffe Committee Report[7] stated that a minister should be free to use his experience to give an account of his own work but this should be subject to four restrictions: national security; relations with other nations; confidential relationships between ministers or ministers and civil servants; and opinions or attitudes of ministers together with advice given by ministers or civil servants. The report went on to recommend that the Cabinet Secretary should be consulted on the contents of the memoirs and if the contents related to the first three restricted categories, his decision on whether to publish the information would be final. With regard to the fourth restriction, there should be no publication within 15 years except with the approval of the Cabinet Secretary. Now, any minister writing his memoirs is required to submit the manuscript to the Cabinet Secretary for approval.[8]

On occasion, the convention of collective responsibility comes under severe pressure. In 1975 for instance, the government had agreed to hold a referendum on whether the United Kingdom should remain a member of the EEC. The government was advising electors to vote 'Yes' but the Cabinet was clearly split on the issue. The Prime Minister announced a waiver of the convention, saying: "ministers who do not agree with the government's recommendation in favour of continuing membership of the E.C. are, in the unique circumstances of the referendum, now free to advocate a different view during the referendum campaign."[9]

The statement, however, limited the ministers' freedom to disagree by saying that the waiver did not apply to parliamentary

---

7 Report of the Committee of Privy Councillors, Cmnd. 6386 (1976).
8 Code of Conduct, para. 18.
9 H.C., Vol. 889, col. 351 (Apr. 7, 1975).

proceedings and official business, and ministers were asked not to appear on the same platform and give dissenting views. In 1977, a similar situation arose for the Labour Government on the issue of direct elections to the European Parliament. Once again the Cabinet was divided and the Prime Minister had to suspend the convention: "I think the doctrine (of collective responsibility) should apply except in cases where I announce that it does not."[10]

The convention of collective responsibility helps to bind the government together but there are occasions where a minister disagrees with the collective decision but does not resign. He may then give an unattributed briefing to a journalist setting out his point of view. This can be very damaging to a government since it gives an impression of dissent and the government will then have to spend time denying that dissent exists. If there is considerable 'leaking' in a government, its authority will be undermined, as happened in the later stages of the Major Government of 1992–1997.

INDIVIDUAL RESPONSIBILITY

There are two aspects to this, one of which has little or no bearing 12.04
on the constitutional question of ministerial responsibility. A minister is constitutionally responsible for the conduct of his department and a minister is also responsible, but not in a constitutional sense, for his own personal conduct. The second aspect has been in the news many times over the years. In 1963, John Profumo, the Secretary for War, resigned after he lied to the House regarding a sexual relationship he was having with a prostitute, Christine Keeler, who in her turn was involved with an attaché at the Soviet Embassy. The scandal led to a judicial inquiry into the security implications. In 1983, the Secretary of State for Trade and Industry, Cecil Parkinson, was forced to resign after revelations about his affair with his secretary. In 1992, David Mellor, Secretary of State for Heritage, had to resign after his sexual dalliance with an actress and revelations that he and his family had enjoyed the hospitality of the wife of an officer of the Palestinian Liberation Organisation. In 1998, Peter Mandelson resigned after allegations of impropriety over a loan to purchase a house and the lender, Geoffrey Robinson, was also forced to resign from his position as Paymaster General. In the main, resignations

---

[10] Prime Minister James Callaghan, H.C., Vol. 993, col. 552 (June 16, 1977).

of this type occur when an M.P. is found to be leading a 'double life', often pretending to have a happy marriage while conducting affairs with others. There are no formal qualifications for office as a minister and there are no formal means by which suitability for office is ascertained, although it seems likely that the Security Services will run a security check on likely candidates for ministerial office. In constitutional terms, however, the personal conduct of a minister is not of importance except in the sense that a person who has an illicit affair while married is untrustworthy in one respect and that may raise doubts about their character to hold office.

The most important issue is the level of accountability and responsibility of a minister for the shortcomings of his department. This has long been a political 'hot potato' and there have been major changes in the way ministerial responsibility is seen.

The current Ministerial Code states:

> "(ii) Ministers have a duty to Parliament to account, and be held to account, for the policies, decisions and actions of their Departments and Next Steps Agencies;
> (iii) It is of paramount importance that Ministers give accurate and truthful information to Parliament, correcting any inadvertent error at the earliest opportunity. Ministers who knowingly mislead Parliament will be expected to offer their resignation to the Prime Minister;
> (iv) Ministers should be as open as possible with Parliament and the public, refusing to provide information only when disclosure would not be in the public interest, which should be decided in accordance with the relevant statute and the Government's Code of Practice and Access to Government Information (Second edition, January 1997)."

This is rather different from the concept of ministerial responsibility previously adhered to and it is worth considering why these changes have occurred.

12.05 The classic exposition of the doctrine was seen in the Crichel Down Affair in the early 1950s. Farm land, including land called Crichel Down, was compulsorily acquired in 1937 by the Air Ministry and was used by them as a bombing range until the end of the Second World War, when it was transferred to the Ministry of Agriculture to be administered by the Commissioners for Crown Lands. In 1950, the commissioners decided to lease the land as a single farm. Part of the land had been owned by the Martin family and they tried in 1950 and 1952 to buy it back. When they were unsuccessful they asked their M.P. to intervene on their behalf.

The Ministry requested a report from the commissioners but their official was told to treat the whole matter as highly confidential and not to approach the previous owners or inspect the land. The report was full of inaccuracies but was accepted by the Ministry which decided to continue with the lease to a tenant farmer. The Martins then asked to lease the land but the Ministry ignored their letters. An inquiry was set up and this found that there had been inaccuracies in the report and the matter had been dealt with by officials in a highhanded and deceitful manner. In 1954, the Minister for Agriculture, Sir Thomas Dugdale, accepted responsibility and resigned.[11] Although a good example of the doctrine at work, it was not really an example of an 'innocent' minister taking responsibility; apparently Sir Thomas had been involved personally in the decisions. The civil servants were not accorded anonymity as the doctrine implies; they were all named in the inquiry report.

The Public Service Committee investigated the doctrine in 1996 and quoted extensively from a memorandum of the Permanent Secretary to the Treasury in 1954, at the time of the Crichel Down Affair. His interpretation of the doctrine was as follows:

> "It follows that a civil servant, having no power conferred on him by Parliament, has no direct responsibility to Parliament and cannot be called to account by Parliament. His acts, indeed, are not his own. All that he does is done on behalf of the Minister, with the Minister's authority express or implied: the civil servant's responsibility is solely to the Minister for what he may do as the Minister's servant."[12]

He maintained that no civil servant should be named either to praise them or to blame them. The minister will take responsibility for the errors of his department, although he is not liable for conduct of which he had disapproved or even expressly forbidden. The Home Secretary also gave his interpretation of how the doctrine should work. He said that a minister must protect a civil servant who has carried out his explicit order or has acted in accordance with the minister's policy. The minister will accept responsibility for an error where there is no important issue of policy involved. If, however, the civil servant has acted contrary to the minister's orders and without his knowledge, the minister need

---

[11] Report of the Inquiry into the disposal of Land at Crichel Down, Cmnd. 9176 (1954); see also Griffith "Crichel Down: The Most Famous Farm in British Constitutional History" (1987) 1 *Contemporary Record* 35.

[12] Second Report, Ministerial Accountability and Responsibility, above, para. 8.

not defend the civil servant, although he will remain "constitutionally responsible to Parliament for the fact that something has gone wrong."[13]

12.06 From 1954 to the 1980s, there were a number of very serious incidents in which defects in departmental administration were found but the ministers concerned did not resign. These included the collapse of the Vehicle and General Insurance Company in 1971. An inquiry blamed an official at the Department of Trade and Industry and the minister stayed in office. A breach of security at Buckingham Palace in 1982 led to an intruder entering the Queen's bedroom, but the Home Secretary did not resign. In 1984, the Secretary of State for Northern Ireland refused to resign after the violent escape of terrorist prisoners from the Maze Prison. An inquiry was held into the circumstances surrounding the escape and this found that the prison governor should be held accountable for the failure in the prison's security arrangements.[14] The Secretary of State had previously stated that if the inquiry found that there had been a failure in his policy then he would accept responsibility and resign. However, he maintained that the inquiry had found that there was a failure in the implementation of the policy, and that was not his responsibility. His distinction between policy and implementation of policy is one that has been taken up by ministers in subsequent similar affairs, but it is one which was most eloquently questioned and derided by the late Enoch Powell:

> "The responsibility for the administration of a Department remains irrevocably with the Minister in charge. It is impossible for him to say to the House or to the country, 'The policy was excellent and that was mine, but the execution was defective or disastrous and that was nothing to do with me' . . . If the responsibility for administering so central to a department can be abjured by a Minister, a great deal of our proceedings in the House is a beating of the air because we are talking to people who, in the last resort, disclaim the responsibility for the administration."[15]

The Government, and successive governments, did not accept Mr Powell's views.

12.07 A few resignations have occurred since 1982. The failures of the Foreign and Commonwealth Office in events leading to the

---

13 H.C. Vol. 21, cols. 1286–1287 (July 20, 1954).

14 Hennessy Report (1983–84 H.C. 203).

15 H.C., Vol. 53, col. 1061 (Feb. 9, 1984).

Falklands War led to the resignation of the Foreign Secretary, Lord Carrington, and two junior ministers. It is clear that Lord Carrington's resignation was made in response to the failures of his department but there were other underlying reasons that are detailed in his memoirs. He resigned partly for political reasons and partly to provide a scapegoat to take pressure off the Prime Minister and the Government.[16]

In 1986, at the height of the Westland Helicopter Affair, a letter was leaked to the press by an official at the Department of Trade and Industry; this letter was embarrassing to Michael Heseltine who had resigned over the issue. In the furore which followed this breach of convention, the Secretary of State, Leon Brittan, was forced to resign, again partly to save further embarrassment to the Government and take pressure away from the Prime Minister, whose office, it appeared, had given permission for the letter to be released to the press.

The 1990s have seen two major incidents in which the doctrine 12.08 has come under severe pressure and after which the doctrine was changed to the one now propounded in the Ministerial Code. The two incidents are the Derek Lewis Affair and the Matrix Churchill prosecution.

The Derek Lewis Affair involved the Director General of the Prison Service, Derek Lewis, in a confrontation with the Home Secretary, Michael Howard, regarding the meaning of the policy/operation distinction. In 1994, the Prison Service became an executive agency and its framework agreement stated that day-to-day operational matters were to be entrusted to the Director General and a board of 10 directors. The Home Secretary was said to be "accountable to Parliament for the prison service"; he was not, however, to be involved in the day-to-day management but would be "consulted . . . on the handling of operational matters which could give rise to grave public or Parliamentary concern." The Home Secretary and the Director General were to meet fortnightly and the Home Secretary was to be informed of anything which might give rise to grave public or parliamentary concern. In late 1994, there was an attempted breakout from Whitemoor Prison of a number of prisoners who had been convicted of terrorist offences. In January 1995, the alleged serial murderer Fred West hanged himself in prison, while supposedly under close supervision to prevent suicide. A few days later, three convicts escaped from Parkhurst Prison on the Isle of Wight and were at

[16] Lord Carrington, *Reflect on Things Past* (1988), p. 371.

large for several days before being recaptured. This sequence of events led to an inquiry and in October 1995 the Learmont Report was published. It was highly critical of the prison service. However, the report also referred to the high degree of political interference endured by the agency and recommended that there should be a change in the relationship between the Home Office and the agency, to give the agency greater operational independence. The Home Secretary, Michael Howard, interpreted the report as identifying that all of the problems were related to the way in which the policies had been carried out, and he asked Lewis to resign. Lewis declined to do so and was dismissed. He later successfully negotiated a substantial compensation package after threatening legal action for wrongful dismissal. He has since maintained that there was persistent political interference with the way in which the agency operated to the extent that he indicated that he could not carry out his job properly. When the Learmont Report was debated in Parliament, Howard was able to resist Opposition demands for his resignation by calling on the support of the Prime Minister and his Party and by claiming that operational matters were the sole concern of the agency chief executive.[17] In May 1997, the veracity of Howard's version of the affair was put in doubt when his former junior minister, Ann Widdecombe, made a parliamentary statement to the effect that there had been substantial interference by the Home Secretary.[18]

12.09 The second incident was the Matrix Churchill prosecution or the Arms to Iraq Affair, which was the subject of a wide-ranging inquiry by Sir Richard Scott. The case involved a company, Matrix Churchill, which supplied machine tools to Iraq. One of the consignments was stopped by the Customs and Excise and the directors of the company were charged with trying to export goods in breach of the export regulations. These regulations required that export licences were required for the sale of goods to Iran or to Iraq, since these countries had been at war with each other from 1980 to 1988. At the end of the war, the regulations were revised to allow a more liberal policy in respect of Iraq, but this information was not reported to Parliament. In 1989, the Government Minister, William Waldegrave, answered questions on the Government's policy saying that the policy had not changed. At the trial in 1992, the defence argued that the Government knew about the exports and had authorised them. Four Government ministers signed

---

[17] H.C. Vol. 264, cols. 502–520 (Nov. 18, 1995).

[18] See also Tomkins, *The Constitution after Scott* (1998), p. 45.

public interest immunity certificates to prevent disclosure of documents relating to meetings and communications between the Department of Trade and Industry and the Foreign Office. One of the Ministers, Michael Heseltine, did not want to sign the certificate since he felt that the interests of justice required disclosure of the documents but he was persuaded to sign a modified version of the certificate after seeking advice from the Attorney-General. The effect of the certificates was to prevent crucial evidence being laid before the court which would have tended to prove the innocence of the accused. The trial collapsed when a former Minister, Alan Clark, admitted in evidence that the Government had known about the exports. The Scott Inquiry was set up by the Prime Minister the day after the trial was halted.

The inquiry took much longer than expected, and the report was not published until February 1996. Scott found a number of matters of concern regarding the involvement of ministers before the prosecution was brought and in the manner of the prosecution. As regards the behaviour of ministers in 1989 and later in answering parliamentary questions, Scott found that the Government had deliberately failed "to inform Parliament of the current state of government policy on non-lethal arms sales to Iraq."[19] However, he found that Waldegrave had not noticed the changed wording in documents indicating a change in policy and thus there was no intention on his part to be misleading. Scott endorsed the recommendations made in the First Nolan Report that the Questions of Procedure for Ministers (the predecessor of the Ministerial Code) should state that "ministers must not knowingly mislead Parliament and the public . . . They must be as open as possible with Parliament and the public, withholding information only when disclosure would not be in the public interest." Scott went further: "the withholding of information by an accountable minister should never be based on reasons of convenience or for the avoidance of political embarrassment, but should always require special and carefully considered justification."[20]

In evidence to the Scott Inquiry, the Cabinet Secretary, Sir Robin Butler, defined the meaning of ministerial responsibility, as he believed it to be:

---

[19] Report of the Inquiry into the Export of Defence Equipment and Dual-use Goods to Iraq and Related Prosecutions (Scott Inquiry) (1995–96, H.C. 115), para. D4.25.

[20] *ibid.* para. K8.5.

"I am using 'accountability' to mean that the Minister must always answer questions and give an account to Parliament for the action of his department, whether he is 'responsible' in the sense of attracting personal criticism himself, or not. So I am using 'accountability' to leave out, as it were, the blame element of it. The blame element is an open question. There are cases where he is accountable in which he may be personally blameworthy, and there will be occasions when he is not personally blameworthy."[21]

This definition was later taken up by the government in its response to the Treasury and Civil Service Select Committee's Report on the Civil Service.[22] The arguments were:

"(a) [A] minister is accountable for everything that happens in his or her department in the sense that Parliament can call the minister to account for it;
(b) a minister is responsible for the policies of his or her department, for the framework through which policies are delivered and for the resources which are allocated; and
(c) a minister is not responsible for everything in his or her department in the sense of having personal knowledge and control of every action taken and being personally blameworthy when delegated tasks are carried out incompetently or when mistakes or errors of judgment are made at operational level."[23]

This approach appeared to have been accepted by Scott in his conclusions and in evidence to the Public Service Committee. However, he maintained that this approach would mean that the minister would be under an obligation to provide information to Parliament: "if ministers are to be excused blame and personal criticism on the basis of the absence of personal knowledge or involvement, the corollary ought to be an acceptance of the obligation to be forthcoming with information about the incident in question."[24]

12.10 The Public Service Committee examined the concept of ministerial responsibility after the Scott Inquiry Report was published.[25]

---

[21] Evidence given to the Inquiry on Feb. 9, 1994, transcript pp. 23–24, cited in Scott "Ministerial Accountability" [1996] P.L. 410.

[22] *The Civil Service: Taking Forward Continuity and Change*, Cm. 2748 (1995).

[23] Code of Conduct, para. 50.

[24] Scott Inquiry Report, above, para. K8.16.

[25] Second Report, Ministerial Accountability and Responsibility, above.

The Committee's conclusions expressed doubt about the usefulness of the accountability/responsibility distinction and put forward its own ideas, 'the obligation to give an account' (*i.e.* to give information to Parliament) and 'the liability to be held to account' (*i.e.* the requirement on ministers to respond to concerns and criticism raised in Parliament about the actions and failures of their department).[26] The Government's response in late 1996 to the conclusions was that ministers "must fully discharge their obligations to account to Parliament for their own and their department's policies, decisions and actions . . . and must respond to criticism made in Parliament. It is for Parliament to determine whether it is satisfied with the account it receives and what sanctions, if any, should follow."[27] Although the wording of the response appears to accept that ministers should respond when a failure occurs and should inform Parliament and the public what action has been taken to prevent a recurrence, the rhetoric of the Major Government did not follow the reality. In early 1997, the Minister for Agriculture denied any responsibility for his department's failures in respect of the BSE crisis and the Minister for the Armed Forces denied any knowledge of the Ministry of Defence's awareness of the alleged connection between the use of pesticides and the Gulf War Syndrome.

The Public Service Committee proposed that the House of Commons should pass a resolution setting out a minister's duty to give full and accurate information to the House. Shortly before Parliament was prorogued for the general election in 1997, a resolution was proposed and passed, and this resolution forms the basis of the current Ministerial Code.

The Ministerial Code[28] emphasises that ministers must give truthful and accurate information and correct any errors at the earliest opportunity. If a minister 'knowingly' misleads Parliament he is expected to resign. The next paragraph requires ministers to be as open as possible and provide information except where it is not in the public interest to do so, but here there is no requirement for a minister to resign if he is not as forthcoming as he should be. Tomkins argues that the House of Commons resolution means that the unwritten constitutional convention known as ministerial responsibility is now a clear parliamentary rule.[29] He says that

---

[26] Second Report, Ministerial Accountability and Responsibility, above, para. 32.

[27] Government Response to the Report of the Public Service Committee on Ministerial Accountability and Responsibility (1996–97 H.C. 67), p. vi.

[28] Code of Conduct and Guide of Procedures for Ministers, above.

[29] *The Constitution after Scott*, *op. cit.*, p. 62.

although the words 'accountability' and 'knowingly mislead' are used in preference to 'responsibility', nonetheless ministers are required to give an accurate and truthful account to Parliament and the tendency of ministers to be 'economical with the truth' is no longer to be tolerated.

In conclusion, when will a minister be required to resign? If a minister makes a "grievous and foreseeable error in a very high policy" then a resignation is likely, but there must be no one else to take the blame and the Prime Minister must be content to lose the minister. There must be media pressure and the minister must have a "sense of constitutional propriety".[30] Certainly this view of the requirements for ministerial responsibility is cynical but it is borne out by the activities of the Major Government of 1992–97. It has yet to be seen whether the Blair Government will react in the same way when scandal hits the government and ministerial resignations are called for.

MINISTERIAL RESPONSIBILITY AND CIVIL SERVANTS

12.11 The Civil Service Code was revised in May 1999 to take account of devolution and it forms part of the terms and conditions of employment of every civil servant. They should not "deceive or knowingly mislead Ministers, Parliament or the public" and should "conduct themselves with integrity, impartiality and honesty."[31]

The Civil Service Code is closely allied to the Ministerial Code and the latter code requires that civil servants must give truthful and accurate information. "Ministers should require civil servants who give evidence before Parliamentary Committees on their behalf and under their directions to be as helpful as possible in providing accurate, truthful and full information in accordance with the duties and responsibilities of civil servants as set out in the Civil Service Code."

The Ministerial Code, however, perpetuates one of the difficulties perceived by select committees in recent years, that civil servants are only able to give answers which reflect the minister's policies and are not able to answer on their own account. According to the government, the purpose of a civil servant appearing is to "contribute to the central process of ministerial accountability,

---

[30] Woodhouse "Ministerial Responsibility in the 1990s: When do ministers resign?" (1993) 46 Parl.Aff. 277 at 292.

[31] Civil Service Code http://www.cabinet-office.gov.uk/central/1999/cscode.htm, para. 5.

not to offer personal views or judgments on matters that may be of political controversy. To ask civil servants to do so would undermine their professional political impartiality."[32] Parliament is still not able to insist on a civil servant attending a select committee hearing. Parliament is unable to punish a civil servant; only a minister can do so. It therefore makes it difficult, if not impossible, to ascertain the true facts of a situation if one of the key players is unable to give evidence or gives evidence which is incomplete or misleading. However, the Public Service Committee noted in its report that the government has not generally refused to allow civil servants to give evidence except in a few cases where the civil servant was a member of the security services.[33] It notes however, that the Treasury is particularly reluctant to allow its officials to give evidence to other select committees.[34] In the Scott Inquiry, civil servants were able to given evidence on their own behalf, not on behalf of ministers and Scott recommended that this should be extended to appearances before select committees. The government however has resisted that idea.[35]

There will be occasions on which a civil servant feels that he is 12.12
being asked to do something, or not to do something, which is illegal, improper or unethical or in breach of a constitutional convention or is inconsistent with the Civil Service Code.[36] The Code gives the procedure for 'whistle-blowing' and reiterates that the civil servant must not disclose any information he is not authorised to disclose. The Code perpetuates the idea that civil servants have no constitutional duty to operate in the public interest but only in the interest of their minister. "Civil servants are servants of the Crown. Constitutionally all the Administrations form part of the Crown and, subject to the provisions of this Code, civil servants owe their loyalty to the Administrations in which they serve."[37]

However, the provisions of the Public Interest Disclosure Act 1998 apply to most civil servants. This Act gives protection from victimisation to most people in the workplace where they raise genuine concerns about malpractice. This can include breaches of civil, criminal, regulatory or administrative law, miscarriages of

---

32 Government Response to the Report of the Public Service Committee, above, p. ix.
33 Second Report, Ministerial Accountability and Responsibility, above, para. 75.
34 *ibid.* para. 81.
35 Government Response to the Report of the Public Service Committee, above.
36 Civil Service Code, para. 11.
37 *ibid.* para. 2. Note that the administrations referred to include the U.K. government, Scottish Executive and National Assembly for Wales.

justice, dangers to health safety or the environment, and the cover-up of any of these.[38] Employees of the Crown who are in the armed forces or involved in national security are not protected and if a civil servant is the subject of a ministerial certificate that his work safeguards national security, that civil servant is not protected either.[39] If a matter is covered by the Official Secrets Act 1989, then the civil servant will not be able to disclose that information and claim protection.

The fact that civil servants are unable to give any view other than the minister's to parliamentary select committees is problematic. It means that only one version of a matter will be heard publicly and that a civil servant will never be able to explain for instance that he tried to advise the minister to take a different course of action. Thus Parliament's ability to inquire into events is seriously curtailed. This could be seen in the Derek Lewis Affair, where any problems or disagreements between the Director of the Prison Service and the Home Secretary could not be disclosed by Mr Lewis. The weakness of the position of the civil servant in informing Parliament of his view is clearly demonstrated as is the powerfulness of the minister is being able to put forward his, possibly biased, viewpoint without fear of contradiction.[40]

12.13 The position of agency chief executives in giving evidence to select committees has been difficult in that, like Derek Lewis, they were only allowed to give the minister's view of how the agency was performing. The Public Service Committee, however, recommended that agency chief executives should be able to give evidence on matters falling within their responsibility under the framework documents without prior ministerial approval.[41] The government accepted this. However, civil servants who are not agency chief executives are still bound by the rules that prevent them from saying anything which has not been approved by the minister. They may report evidence of wrongdoing to a superior and ultimately to the Civil Service Commissioners but they may not disclose it to Parliament. An accounting officer, on the other hand, is required to report financial mismanagement to the Comptroller and Auditor-General.[42]

The government may refuse to allow a civil servant to give evidence to a select committee. This occurred in 1986 when the

---

[38] Employment Rights Act 1996, s. 43B as inserted by s. 1 of the 1998 Act.

[39] 1998 Act, s. 11(1).

[40] Tomkins, *op. cit.*, p. 88.

[41] Second Report, Ministerial Accountability and Responsibility, above, para. 114.

[42] Code of Conduct, para. 58.

Defence Select Committee wanted to interview the five civil servants involved in the Westland Affair. The Cabinet Secretary appeared instead along with Leon Brittan, the minister who had been forced to resign. Brittan's evidence was however limited, since he refused to comment on the circumstances leading to the leaking of the Law Officer's letter. In 1992, the Treasury and Civil Service Select Committee tried to investigate aspects of the Arms to Iraq affair but they were prevented from questioning two retired Ministry of Defence officials and obtaining evidence from the security and intelligence services. The refusal of the Ministry of Defence to allow the two civil servants to give evidence was made on the basis that it was inappropriate since civil servants gave evidence on behalf of their ministers and retired officers could not do so. The two retired officers gave evidence to the Scott Inquiry and Scott referred to the select committee incident in his report: "the refusal to facilitate the giving of evidence to the Treasury and Civil Service Committee by [the two retired officials] may be regarded as a failure to comply fully with the obligations of accountability owed to Parliament."[43]

The resolutions passed by Parliament in March 1997 have partly addressed the problem of civil servants giving evidence to select committees and the resolutions are, as has been previously mentioned, incorporated into the Ministerial Code. Thus paragraph 1(v) of the Code requires civil servants to be as helpful as possible in providing information to select committees, but the connection between minister and civil servant is not broken; the civil servant still gives evidence on behalf of the minister. The Code does not mention retired civil servants and the permission of the minister is still required before a retired civil servant may give evidence.

THE COURTS AND MINISTERIAL RESPONSIBILITY

Until relatively recently, the courts exercised a low level of regulation of the executive in respect of ministerial responsibility, taking the view that since it was exercised by virtue of the royal prerogative, it was not a matter they could review. The "low point" was the case of *Liversidge v. Anderson*[44] where a detention order 12.14

[43] Scott Inquiry Report, above, para. F4.66.

[44] [1942] A.C. 206.

was made in respect of a person whom the minister had 'reasonable cause' to believe to be hostile. The detainee argued that the order could only be made if the minister had objective reasonable cause for this belief. The order was, however, upheld by a majority of the House of Lords where it was found that some matters were so important they had to be determined personally by the minister, such as in this case the detention of an enemy alien in time of war. Lord Atkin dissented from this judgment, saying that the words "if a man has reasonable cause" did not mean, "if a man thinks he has reasonable cause". His dissenting judgment was later held to be the correct view of the common law position.[45]

The House of Lords had, however, previously stressed a minister's responsibility to Parliament in respect of his own and his officials' actions.[46] This was reiterated by the Master of the Rolls, Lord Greene, in *Johnston & Co. (Builders) Ltd v. Minister for Health*[47] where he commented: "In a nutshell, the decision of the minister is a thing for which he must be answerable in Parliament and his actions cannot be controlled by the courts." If Lord Greene's statement means that the courts cannot control a minister's decision because he is solely answerable to Parliament, then it has to be argued that this view is not sustainable. Bradley and Ewing have observed that judicial control and minister responsibility are not mutually exclusive; they coexist and are complementary to each other.[48] The general view now is that the judiciary will not become involved in political controversy but will act to review a decision if the executive act outwith their powers. In *R. v. Inland Revenue Commissioners, ex parte National Federation of Self-Employed and Small Businesses Ltd*[49] Lord Diplock said:

> "It is not, in my view, a sufficient answer to say that judicial review of the actions of officers or departments of central government is unnecessary because they are accountable to Parliament for the way in which they carry out their functions. They are accountable to Parliament for what they do in so far as regards efficiency and policy, and of that Parliament is the only judge; they are responsible to a court of justice for the lawfulness of what they do, and of that the court is the only judge."

---

[45] *R. v. Inland Revenue Commissioners, ex p. Rossminster Ltd* [1980] A.C. 952.

[46] *Local Government Board v. Arlidge* [1915] A.C. 120.

[47] [1947] 2 All E.R. 395 at 400.

[48] Bradley and Ewing, *Constitutional and Administrative Law* (11th ed. 1993), p. 125.

[49] [1982] A.C. 617.

There is a general presumption that statutes do not bind the Crown, although most statutes now do in fact expressly bind the Crown thus raising the question as to what will happen if the Crown disobeys a court order. Here the law differs between England and Scotland. The English courts have now decided that an officer of the Crown, acting in his official capacity, was amenable to final injunctions, interlocutory injunctions and contempt. Thus in *M v. Home Office*[50] the Home Secretary was held to be in contempt after he ignored an order of the court to procure the return of a political asylum-seeker who was the subject of judicial review proceedings. In Scotland, the Court of Session decided that section 21 of the Crown Proceedings Act 1947 applied to all forms of judicial proceedings, including judicial review, so that interdict (the Scottish equivalent of injunction) is still unavailable against the Crown.[51] 12.15

The courts will not interfere with the merits of a decision, only on the way in which it was made. There is still an assumption that ministerial responsibility is effective and more appropriate than judicial review. However, the House of Lords has said: "Many in government are answerable to Parliament and yet answerable also to the supervisory jurisdiction of this court."[52] The courts will now in certain circumstances have regard to parliamentary proceedings to interpret statutes which are ambiguous, obscure or absurd if the words are given their natural meaning.[53]

The major justification for the government being formed exclusively from members of the House of Commons and the House of Lords is that ministers can be held accountable to Parliament for their own conduct and that of their officials. In *Carltona Ltd v. Commissioner of Works*[54] the decision of the official was said to be the act of the minister since the minister was responsible to Parliament for its consequences. The Master of the Rolls, Lord Greene, remarked:

> "In the administration of government in this country the functions which are given to ministers (and constitutionally properly given to ministers because they are constitutionally responsible) are functions so multifarious that no minister

---

[50] [1993] 3 W.L.R. 433.

[51] See *McDonald v. Secretary of State for Scotland*, 1994 S.L.T. 692.

[52] *R. v. Parliamentary Commissioner for Administration, ex p. Dyer* [1994] 1 All E.R. 375.

[53] *Pepper v. Hart* [1992] 3 W.L.R. 1031.

[54] [1943] 2 All E.R. 560.

could ever personally attend to them . . . The duties imposed upon ministers and the powers given to ministers are normally exercised under the authority of the ministers by responsible officials of the department. Public business could not be carried on if that were not the case."[55]

12.16 The principle was reaffirmed in *R. v. Secretary of State for Home Department, ex parte Doody*[56] where it was held that the function of the Secretary of State in deciding the length of sentence for a life sentence could be delegated, in this case, to a junior minister. Although the courts have recognised that the minister's powers may be delegated to a junior minister or to an official, the courts have maintained that the minister remains responsible to Parliament. If an act is properly done by a civil servant on a minister's behalf, then the act is considered to have been done by the minister himself.[57]

In some instances, this general principle of delegation will not apply and the minister is required by statute to exercise the power personally, for instance with regard to exclusion or deportation orders.[58] If a certificate "purporting to be signed by the Secretary of State" is said to be conclusive of certain matters, then it is agreed that the certificate has to be signed by the Secretary of State personally.[59] The delegation to civil servants of some statutory Treasury functions was not possible until the Civil Service (Management Functions) Act 1992 which authorises the delegation and sub-delegation to any other Crown servant.

STANDARDS IN PUBLIC LIFE

12.17 During the premiership of John Major, 1990 to 1997, a number of vexed issues came to the fore and had to be dealt with. The problem of ministerial responsibility has been discussed above but there were other issues including the lobbying of ministers by M.P.s on behalf of outside interests and what constituted a registrable interest which should be included in the Register of Members'

---

55 [1943] 2 All E.R. 560 at 563.

56 [1993] 1 All E.R. 151.

57 *Re Golden Chemical Products Ltd* [1976] Ch. 300.

58 For instance the Immigration Act 1971, ss. 13(5), 14(3) and 15(4); and see *R. v. Secretary of State for the Home Department, ex p. Oladehinde* [1991] 1 A.C. 254.

59 *R. v. Clerkenwell Metropolitan Stipendiary Magistrates, ex p. Director of Public Prosecutions* [1984] Q.B. 821; [1984] 2 All E.R. 193.

Interests. In 1994 allegations were made that ministers and M.P.s had accepted money in return for putting down parliamentary questions. A political lobbyist, Ian Greer, had allegedly advised Mohamed Al-Fayed, the owner of Harrods, to bribe M.P.s to ask parliamentary questions and *The Guardian* newspaper subsequently reported that Al-Fayed had alleged that Neil Hamilton, a junior minister, had collected brown envelopes containing cash from his office. A libel action by Greer and Hamilton against *The Guardian* was dropped when the plaintiffs realised that the newspaper had evidence which would have led to the failure of their action. *The Guardian* had also named another junior minister, Tim Smith, who immediately resigned. Additional allegations of impropriety were made against the Chief Secretary to the Treasury, Jonathan Aitken, who resigned to pursue a libel action against the newspaper. He had to withdraw from the action in 1997 when evidence was presented to contradict his version of events. Aitken was later prosecuted for perjury and sent to prison in 1999 for 18 months.

Another newspaper, the *Sunday Times*, was also investigating the willingness, or otherwise, of M.P.s to accept money or benefits in kind in return for asking questions, and the newspaper offered money to two Private Parliamentary Secretaries, Graham Riddick and David Tredinnick, both of whom resigned.

These cases, coming as they did so closely together, led to suspicions of corruption, or 'sleaze' as the Opposition parties called it, within public life and the Prime Minister decided to set up a judicial inquiry into standards of conduct in public life. The committee was set up as a standing body under the chairmanship of Lord Nolan. Its terms of reference were:

> "To examine current concerns about standards of conduct of all holders of public office, including arrangements relating to financial and commercial activities, and to make recommendations as to any changes in present arrangements which might be required to ensure the highest standards of probity in public life.
>
> For these purposes, public life should include Ministers, civil servants and advisers, Members of Parliament and the United Kingdom Members of the European Parliament, members and senior officers of all non-departmental public bodies and of national health service bodies, non-ministerial office holders, members and other senior officers of other bodies discharging publicly funded functions and elected members and senior officers of local authorities."

12.18 In 1997, the Prime Minister, Tony Blair, announced additional terms of reference: "To review issues in relation to the funding of political parties, and to make recommendations as to any changes in present arrangements."

The committee's first report was published in May 1995 and it records a loss of public confidence in the probity of M.P.s. The committee suggested that there were seven principles of conduct applicable to public life: selflessness, integrity, objectivity, accountability, openness, honesty and leadership. The committee went on to make various recommendations on how M.P.s should conduct themselves. The Register of Members' Interests had not worked satisfactorily and there were areas of doubt and uncertainty as to the precise requirements of disclosure of interests. There was also poor enforcement of the requirements to register an interest. The House had already adopted a new register from January 1995 which required that M.P.s disclose their annual remuneration, estimated monetary benefits and any agreements or contracts which involved the M.P. acting in a parliamentary capacity for any outside interests.

The committee also proposed the appointment of an independent Parliamentary Commissioner for Standards who would be responsible for maintaining the Register and providing guidance on standards of conduct, propriety and ethics. The Commissioner was appointed in 1995 and is an officer of Parliament in the same way as the Comptroller and Auditor-General and the Parliamentary Commissioner for Administration. The Commissioner may receive and investigate complaints regarding the conduct of M.P.s; if he decides that further action is required, the matter is referred to the Committee of Standards and Privileges. The committee's first investigation was into allegations that David Willetts, the Paymaster General, had attempted to influence an investigation in 1994 into the 'cash for questions' row involving Neil Hamilton. Although Mr Willetts was cleared of the charge of improper influence, he was heavily criticised by the committee for 'dissembling', in other words the committee was not convinced that he had told the whole truth. Mr Willetts resigned. If the committee finds an allegation proved, it may recommend to the House that the M.P. concerned be reprimanded, suspended or expelled. The House of Commons alone will decide whether such action is warranted.

The Commissioner's decisions are not subject to judicial review. In *R. v. Commissioner for Standards and Privileges, ex parte Al-Fayed*[60] the Court of Appeal held that the Commissioner was

---

[60] [1998] 1 W.L.R. 669.

concerned with activities within Parliament and was accountable to the Special Standing Committee of the House of Commons and only the House of Commons could exercise a supervisory function over the Commissioner.

The first Commissioner had to investigate the 'Cash for Questions' Affair and his report was published in 1997. The Downey Report stated that five former ministers and M.P.s were guilty of breaking the parliamentary rules by not registering financial interests. All five had either resigned before the 1997 election or had lost their seats. Since the Downey Report, the House of Commons has tightened up its rules and procedure and passed a resolution to prevent any such recurrence of the affair. The resolution forbids any member accepting any remuneration, fee, payment, reward or benefit in kind, whether direct or indirect, in return for advocating or initiating any cause or urging any other Member to do so by means of a speech, question, motion, introduction of a Bill or amendment to a motion or Bill.

The House of Commons also approved a Code of Conduct for Members which sets out the general principles of standards and conduct expected of members. In addition, a Guide to the Rules relating to the Conduct of Members was approved and this gives detailed advice and examples of what the Code means.

SCOTTISH EXECUTIVE

The government was keen to ensure that the new Scottish Parliament did not have the same problems regarding members' interests as had occurred in the previous few years at Westminster. A Code of Conduct was drawn up by August 1999 setting out the expected standards of conduct for members of the Scottish Executive and junior ministers.[61] The Code follows very closely the Ministerial Code for U.K. ministers discussed above. Indeed there are only three significant differences. In paragraph (a) of the Scottish Code, the statement exhorting ministers to uphold the principle of collective responsibility ends by referring to a definition of the principle in section 2. The U.K. Ministerial Code does not have such a definition. It is submitted that the Scottish Code recognises that there is a different political reality in Scotland in that the Scottish Executive may well be a coalition government and the parameters of collective responsibility therefore have to be stated clearly. 12.19

---

[61] http://www.scotland.gov.uk/library2/doc03/smic-00.htm

In paragraph (b), the Scottish Code refers to a minister's duty to Parliament to account for the policies, decisions and actions taken "within their field of responsibility." The U.K. Ministerial Code refers to Departments and Next Steps Agencies. Again the reality for Scottish Ministers is that they do not have 'departments' in the same way as U.K. ministers; instead they are given certain areas of responsibility and civil servants are appointed to help them fulfil their responsibilities. It may well be that in the future, the groupings of civil servants will evolve into departments.

In paragraph (d) the Scottish Code requires "Ministers to be as open as possible with Parliament and the public, reflecting the aspirations set out in the Report of the C.S.G. on the Scottish Parliament." The U.K. ministers are required only to be as open as possible with Parliament and the public. The reason behind the Scottish Code is the feeling that the Scottish Parliament should be a different institution from Westminster and that ministers should conduct themselves in a more open and frank manner to avoid the unhappy incidents that were the subjects of the Scott Inquiry and the other investigations discussed above.

Collective responsibility

12.20 The principle of collective responsibility is defined in the Scottish Ministerial Code at paragraphs 2.2 and 2.3. These state:

> "2.2 The Executive operates on the basis of collective responsibility. The internal process through which a decision has been made should not be disclosed. Decisions reached by the Executive are binding on all its members. They are, however, normally announced and explained as the decision of the Minister concerned. On occasions it may be desirable to emphasise the importance of a decision by stating explicitly that it is the decision of the Scottish Executive; but this is very much the exception rather that the rule.
>
> 2.3 Collective responsibility requires that Ministers should be able to express their views frankly in the expectation that they can argue freely in private while maintaining a united front when decisions have been reached. This in turn requires that the privacy of opinions expressed and advice offered within the Executive should be maintained. It is therefore essential that, subject to the guidelines on the disclosure of information set out in the Code of Practice on Access to Scottish Executive Information, Ministers take the necessary steps to ensure that they and their staff preserve the privacy of Executive business and protect the security of Executive documents."

The principle applies to Deputy Scottish Ministers and to the Lord Advocate, except where he is acting in his capacity as head of the systems of criminal prosecutions and investigations of deaths in Scotland. "In that capacity, the Lord Advocate acts independently of other ministers."[62]

Ministerial Code

The Ministerial Code sets out the conduct expected of ministers 12.21 in the Scottish Executive and deputy ministers. There are separate sections dealing with the conduct of ministers *vis-à-vis* the executive, Parliament, their responsibilities and civil servants. As noted above, many of these follow the U.K. Ministerial Code closely.

Civil servants in the Scottish Administration are covered by the U.K. Civil Service Code since civil servants are still members of the Home Civil Service.[63] Thus, references within the Code to the government also refer to the Scottish Executive. The Code reiterates that civil servants are Crown servants and that "they owe their loyalty to the Administrations in which they serve."[64] Thus civil servants serving in the Scottish Administration owe their loyalty to the Scottish Administration, whilst civil servants serving in the Scotland Office will owe their loyalty to the U.K. government. It is easy to see that civil servants may be faced with conflicting interests should the government in Scotland and in the United Kingdom be drawn from different political parties.

Standards in the Scottish Parliament

The Scottish Parliament has set up a Standards Committee[65] to 12.22 consider whether a member's conduct is within the Standing Orders and Code of Conduct particularly regarding their interests. The committee is also responsible for advising the Scottish Parliament on the Code of Conduct, its adoption, amendment and application. If a member has transgressed, the committee may by motion recommend that a member's rights and privileges be withdrawn and may recommend the extent and period of withdrawal. There is no right given under Standing Orders for the committee to expel an MSP or indeed to fine him.[66] The Lord

---

[62] http://www.scotland.gov.uk/library2/doc03/smic-00.htm, para. 2.5.
[63] Scotland Act 1998, s. 51.
[64] Civil Service Code, para. 2.
[65] Scottish Parliament Standing Orders, r. 6.5.
[66] The committee faced its first challenge on Oct. 4, 1999 when *The Scotsman* newspaper sought judicial review of the committee's decision to hear evidence on the 'Lobbygate' Affair in private.

Advocate and the Solicitor General for Scotland are included in the provisions of section 39 since they are entitled to take part in the proceedings of Parliament.[67]

Section 30 of the Scotland Act provides for a Register of Members' Interests to be compiled, published and made available with public access. The section requires the Scottish Parliament to pass legislation, either primary or subordinate, to allow the various matters to have legal force. The requirement for a statutory scheme of regulation is in contrast to the system at Westminster, where regulation of members' interests and conduct is still controlled by the M.P.s themselves. The Nolan Committee Reports have made significant changes to the self-regulatory system at Westminster but it has yet to be established whether the changes will have restored public confidence in the House. The Scottish Parliament will not have such problems since the system of control will be statutory and thus less open to abuse and influence. Indeed, an MSP who fails to comply with the provisions of the section with regard to financial interests and paid advocacy will be guilty of a criminal offence, punishable on summary conviction by a fine up to Level 5 on the Standard Scale.[68] No such criminal sanction applies to the M.P.s at Westminster where the House has complete privilege to regulate its own affairs and matters such as accepting payment to ask questions fall within that privilege and outside the criminal law.

Section 39(2) requires that legislation should define what is meant by 'financial interests.' Members are required to declare any financial interest in the Register and again before the member participates in any proceedings in which that interest is discussed. Following the 'Cash for Questions' Affair and the House of Commons Resolution of 1995, the Act prohibits paid advocacy or the urging by means of payment of other MSPs to support a particular issue.

The Parliament is a public body for the purposes of the Prevention of Corruption Acts 1889 to 1916.[69] This includes members and staff of the Parliament but not members of the Scottish Administration. It prevents members and staff from accepting payments, of money or in kind, in respect of the activities of the Parliament. Thus MSPs are covered by sections 39 and 43 in regard to their activities.

---

[67] Scotland Act 1998, s. 27(1).

[68] Currently £5,000.

[69] Scotland Act 1998, s. 43.

CHAPTER 13

INDIVIDUAL RIGHTS AND FREEDOMS

INTRODUCTION

The constitutional law of the United Kingdom is now in a period of rapid change and development. The protection of individual rights and freedoms has been directly influenced by several major changes in the law in the last three decades. As well as the rights and freedoms which have traditionally existed under Scots law and United Kingdom law there is now additional protection provided by European law, by the Scotland Act and especially by the Human Rights Act which will incorporate the European Convention on Human Rights and Fundamental Freedoms into the domestic law of the United Kingdom. 13.01

The philosophy of the law regarding human rights within the United Kingdom has tended to be based more on the absence of prohibition than on assertions of freedom to act. Therefore a citizen of Scotland, or elsewhere in the United Kingdom, has had the freedom to do anything which is not prohibited by law. This has been a philosophy with which those in power have been very comfortable but it provides little protection for the citizen against any changes in the law which may be introduced by an oppressive government. Arguments against a Bill of Rights have tended to discount the possibility of an oppressive regime gaining governmental power within the United Kingdom. It cannot be denied, however, that there have been instances of limitations being placed on the freedom of individuals and the protection of international law provides an important safety net against future erosion of human rights and freedoms.

METHODS FOR PROTECTION OF RIGHTS

Traditional freedoms under Scots and U.K. law

It is usual for individual rights and freedoms to be guaranteed by a written constitution in a modern democracy. Written constitutions often create certain fundamental and unassailable rights for 13.02

the citizens of the state. Any attempt to erode such fundamental rights would be subject to legal challenge. In the absence of a written constitution there are no such unassailable fundamental rights and freedoms in the law of the United Kingdom. Historically the most important protection afforded to a citizen of the United Kingdom is the adherence to the doctrine of the rule of law. The rule of law means that the executive branch of the government, and those who serve it, should obey the law and should not exceed their lawful authority. Although the rule of law is held out as providing protection against infringement of individual rights and freedoms it does not actually fulfil such a role. The protection afforded by the rule of law is against the arbitrary use of power. It prevents a public official from infringing the rights of an individual unless he has legal authority for his actions. Where the official was acting within his powers the individual had no redress until the recent protection resulting from international treaties and European law. Individual rights and freedoms are therefore residual. This means that an individual is free to act in any way which is not prohibited by law.[1] There has been nothing to prevent individual rights and freedoms being gradually eroded by legislation.[2]

Rights protected by European law

13.03 The Treaty of Amsterdam[3] introduced three new elements for the protection of rights. First, the Treaty confirms that the ECJ has the power to review respect for fundamental rights by the Community institutions. In relation to the European Convention, to which all Member States of the Union, but not the Union itself, are signatories, the Treaty provides that Community law is subject to the European Convention as applied by the Court of Human Rights in Strasbourg. Limited judicial review is available in respect of justice and home affairs but not in relation to matters pertaining to foreign and security policy. No agreement could be reached with regard to making judicial review available in the fields of foreign and social policy at the Conference.

The Treaty of Amsterdam introduces a system of penalties for Member States that fail to respect rights. If the Heads of Government believe that there has been a breach of the principles of liberty, democracy and respect for human rights and fundamental

---

[1] See *Att.-Gen. v. Times Newspapers Ltd (No. 2)* [1988] 3 All E.R. 545 at 660.

[2] Examples include the Official Secrets Act 1989, Public Order Act 1986 and Prevention of Terrorism (Temporary Provisions) Act 1989.

[3] Treaty on European Union 1997.

freedoms a procedure to suspend some of the rights of the Member State may be brought into operation. Following a proposal by one-third of Member States or by the Commission, and after obtaining the assent of the European Parliament, the Council may decide, by a qualified majority, to suspend some of the rights of the Member State concerned. This may include suspension of voting rights in the Council.[4] New states intending to join the E.U. will have to demonstrate commitment to individual rights before their membership will be considered.

Rights protected by international treaties

International treaties are agreements between individual states. 13.04
The signing and ratifying of international treaties are prerogative acts of the Crown. Consequently treaties have no domestic legal force unless and until they are incorporated into the law of the United Kingdom by an Act of Parliament. They nevertheless have some impact on domestic law because, when the courts are interpreting a statute, they will presume that the intention of Parliament was not to infringe the international obligations that have been undertaken by the Crown. In cases where a statute is ambiguous or uncertain or open to different interpretations the courts will construe the legislation in the way which will achieve consistency with international treaty obligations. Where the meaning of an Act of Parliament is clear and the terms can only be interpreted one way, the courts must give effect to it even if it is inconsistent with a treaty obligation.

Where domestic law does not protect an individual from infringement of his rights, there may be remedies for the individual against the state under international law. If an individual is a victim of an infringement of the rights laid down in the European Convention on Human Rights he can petition the Court of Human Rights in Strasbourg. The United Kingdom granted the right of individual petition in 1966 and has since renewed it every five years. The first case from the United Kingdom which was deemed to be admissible and came before the court was *Golder v. United Kingdom*.[5] It was held in that case that the refusal by prison authorities to grant a convicted prisoner access to legal advice amounted to a breach of Article 8 (the right to respect for private life and correspondence) and Article 6(1) (the right to a fair trial).

---

[4] TEU, Art. 7.
[5] (1975) 1 E.H.R.R. 524.

CITIZENSHIP

13.05 The most important right is the right to reside in a state. The relationship between the state and the individual is historically based on mutual benefit. Any individual lawfully within the realm owed a duty of allegiance to the Crown, in return for which the Crown owed a duty of protection to the individual. This came to be regarded as a social contract under which citizens conceded power to a government to rule. The government holds its powers as a trustee of the individual's rights and freedoms.[6] British citizenship was formerly granted to all citizens of the United Kingdom and the colonies[7] but the need to restrict immigration to the United Kingdom gave rise to a series of measures to limit rights of immigration.[8]

Nationality

13.06 Nationality confers more than a simple right to reside in a country. Anyone who is a national of a state has the right to be protected by the state. When they travel abroad they are entitled to the protection of the diplomatic and consular services of that state. The British Nationality Act 1981 redefined U.K. citizenship to correspond with rights under immigration law. The former categories of citizenship of the United Kingdom and Colonies were replaced by three classes: British citizenship, British Dependent Territories citizenship and British Overseas citizenship. In addition to these categories there are Commonwealth citizens and citizens of the E.U. The status of Commonwealth citizenship confers few benefits except that Commonwealth citizens are not aliens. The Treaty on European Union 1992 (the Maastricht Treaty) introduced the concept of European citizenship. This has now been reaffirmed in the Treaty of Union 1997 (the Amsterdam Treaty),[9] which states that one of the objectives of the Union is to strengthen the protection of the rights and interests of nationals of its Member States through the introduction of a citizenship of the Union. Part Two of the revised E.C. Treaty provides that:

> "Citizenship of the Union is hereby established. Every person holding the nationality of a member State shall be a citizen of

---

[6] J. Locke, *Two Treatises on Government* (1690) (London 1977).

[7] British Nationality Act 1948.

[8] Commonwealth Immigration Act 1962, Commonwealth Immigration Act 1968, Immigration Act 1971.

[9] Art. 2.

> the Union. Citizenship of the Union shall complement and not replace national citizenship.
>
> Citizens of the Union shall enjoy the rights conferred by this Treaty and shall be subject to the duties imposed thereby."[10]

The consequences of this include a right for every citizen of the Union to stand as a candidate and to vote in municipal elections in the Member State in which he resides,[11] and a right to stand as a candidate and vote in elections to the European Parliament.[12] Union citizens are also entitled to protection from the diplomatic or consular services of any Member State.[13]

The rules relating to nationality may be changed to meet changing circumstances. By the Hong Kong Act 1985 a new status of British National (Overseas) citizens was created and a further change in favour of some people resident in Hong Kong was made by the British Nationality (Hong Kong) Act 1990. These changes gave more people the right to register as British nationals prior to the end of British Sovereignty in Hong Kong in 1997.

British citizenship may be acquired by birth, adoption, descent, registration or naturalisation.

Birth, adoption and descent

A child born legitimately in the United Kingdom becomes a British citizen if, at the time of the birth, one of its parents is either a British citizen or is settled in the United Kingdom. A person who is settled in the United Kingdom is a person ordinarily resident in the United Kingdom and not subject to any restriction on the time he or she may remain under immigration law.[14] A child born outside marriage acquires citizenship only through his or her mother. If the parents subsequently marry he or she becomes the legitimate child of both parents. A child who is adopted by a British citizen becomes a British citizen from the date of the adoption order. This is the case provided that either of the adoptive parents is a British citizen. A child born outside the United Kingdom becomes a citizen if one of his or her parents is a British citizen, provided that that parent has not also acquired citizenship by descent. An exception to this rule is where the parent is an employee of the Crown or other designated services in 13.07

---

[10] Art. 17.
[11] EC Treaty, Art. 19.
[12] *ibid.* Art. 19.
[13] *ibid.* Art. 20.
[14] Immigration Act 1971, s. 50(2).

which case the child of a person who became a citizen by descent may also acquire citizenship by descent.[15]

Registration

13.08 A person may acquire citizenship through residence in the United Kingdom. A child who is born in the United Kingdom, but who did not qualify as a citizen at birth, may register as a citizen at the age of 10 years unless he or she has been absent from the United Kingdom for more than 90 days in each of the first 10 years.[16] A child is also entitled to register if one of his or her parents acquires citizenship during the child's minority.[17] Certain classes of citizen who have been resident in the United Kingdom are entitled to register.[18] The Home Secretary has a general discretion to register any child as a British citizen.[19]

Naturalisation

13.09 Those who do not benefit from other provisions of the British Nationality Act 1981 may apply to acquire citizenship through naturalisation. They must first have been resident within the United Kingdom for five years. They may then apply to the Home Secretary who has a discretion as to whether or not to grant naturalisation. He must be satisfied that the applicant is of good character, has sufficient knowledge of English, Welsh or Gaelic and intends to have his or her principle residence in the United Kingdom. The latter condition may be waived where a person is employed in certain specified types of employment.[20] The spouse of a British citizen may acquire citizenship through naturalisation. The decision of the Home Secretary on an application for naturalisation is final. There is no right of appeal.[21]

Right of entry

13.10 Anyone who holds: (a) a valid British passport identifying them as a British citizen or as a citizen of the United Kingdom and Colonies having the right of abode in the United Kingdom;

---

[15] British Nationality Act 1981, ss. 2(1)(b) and 14.
[16] *ibid.* s.1(4).
[17] *ibid.* s.1(3).
[18] British Dependent Territories citizens, British Overseas citizens and British Protected Persons.
[19] British Nationality Act 1981, s. 3(1).
[20] *ibid.* s. 6(1).
[21] *ibid.* s. 44(2).

or (b) a travel document of a European Member State, is entitled to enter the United Kingdom. Passports are issued by the Passports Agency. They are usually issued for a period of 10 years but may be issued for a lesser period or a British visitor's passport of one year's duration may be issued. The holding of a passport is not conclusive proof of the right to enter. If an immigration officer suspects that a passport has been obtained as a result of fraud or theft he may require the passport holder to provide proof of his identity. Those who have a right of abode are entitled to live in and to come and go into and from the United Kingdom without let or hindrance, subject to restrictions enabling their status to be determined.[22]

Immigration

The law of immigration is extremely complex. The law is based 13.11 on the Immigration Act 1971, as amended, and on immigration rules which are laid down by the Home Secretary from time to time. Immigration is a matter which has been reserved as a responsibility of the Westminster Parliament and so responsibility for rules and policies with regard to immigration is not a responsibility of the Scottish Parliament. The immigration rules contain the details of the practice to be followed in the administration of the Act. The rules may be held to be *ultra vires* if they conflict with the provisions of a statute.

A person who is not a British citizen, or a Commonwealth citizen with a right of abode, shall not enter the United Kingdom unless he or she is given leave to enter.[23] Leave to enter may be given for an indefinite time or for a limited period. Where limited leave is given it may subject to conditions restricting an individual's right of employment or occupation, or requirements to register with the police or both. A person may for example be given leave to enter for a limited period to pursue a course of study or training. The leave to enter may be varied. The period of leave may be extended or curtailed and conditions may be added or revoked. Only those with a passport or a certificate giving entry clearance have a right of appeal against a refusal of entry into the United Kingdom.[24] Appeal can be made against any conditions attached to a leave to enter.

---

[22] Immigration Act 1971, s. 1(1).
[23] *ibid.* s. 3.
[24] *ibid.* s. 13(3).

It is a criminal offence to enter the country illegally, to fail to observe the conditions of leave to enter, to assist illegal immigrants or to obtain leave to remain by deception. Employees of organisations for the assistance of refugees do not incur criminal liability if they give assistance to asylum claimants.[25]

Deportation

13.12 A person who is not a British citizen is liable to be deported from the United Kingdom if he or she has a limited leave to enter and either fails to comply with the conditions or remains beyond the period of leave. A person who is not a British citizen may also be deported if the Home Secretary deems their deportation to be beneficial to society or if a member of his or her family is being deported.[26] Deportation may also be a result of a criminal conviction. If a person over the age of 17, who is not a British citizen, is convicted of an offence for which the punishment is imprisonment, the court may recommend that he or she be deported.[27]

Appeals may be made against deportation orders. The first appeal is from the decision of an immigration officer to an adjudicator appointed by the Lord Chancellor. Appeal then lies to the Immigration Appeal Tribunal. There is a right of appeal from a decision of the Immigration Appeal Tribunal, on a point of law, to the Court of Session.[28] The Home Secretary also has power to uphold or reverse a decision. A person will not be deported while an appeal is pending.

Extradition

13.13 Extradition is the means by which a fugitive from another country is returned to that country. The law of extradition applies to all persons regardless of citizenship. Extradition is a matter which has been reserved from devolution to the Scottish Parliament and so the rules relating to extradition apply on a United Kingdom wide basis. Extradition may be ordered to all foreign countries, Commonwealth states and colonies.[29] There are separate procedures for the Republic of Ireland. Extradition proceedings begin when another country submits a request to the Home

---

[25] Asylum and Immigration Act 1996.
[26] Immigration Act 1971, s. 5.
[27] *ibid.* s. 3(9).
[28] Asylum and Immigration Appeals Act 1993, s. 9.
[29] Extradition Act 1989.

Secretary for the return of the person.[30] Requests will only be considered from countries which have entered into a bilateral extradition agreement with the United Kingdom. If the Home Secretary is satisfied that the request is justified, the matter is referred to a sheriff who may issue an arrest warrant. Extradition will only be ordered for offences which would carry a sentence of at least 12 months' imprisonment both in the United Kingdom and in the country requesting extradition. Extradition will not be granted for a purely political offence, or where the request to return the person is based on race, religion, nationality or political opinions.[31]

The issue of extradition came before the House of Lords in March 1999 when an appeal was lodged against an extradition order against General Pinochet, the former President of Chile. There were two important issues to consider. First whether heads of state or former heads of state had immunity from extradition proceedings; and secondly whether extraterritorial acts of torture, murder and conspiracy to murder were acts which constituted extradition crimes.[32] An extradition order had been granted and then the order had been quashed on appeal. The Commissioner of the Metropolitan Police and the Government of Spain appealed against the ruling to quash the extradition warrants. The House of Lords had previously allowed the appeal by a majority,[33] but that decision was set aside and a rehearing ordered before a differently constituted committee.[34] Pinochet was alleged to have committed acts of torture, murder and conspiracy to murder. The Criminal Justice Act 1988, s. 134, which came into in force on September 29, 1988, made torture a crime under U.K. law and triable in the United Kingdom, regardless of where it was committed. This Act gave effect to the United Nations Convention against the Torture and other Cruel, Inhuman or Degrading Treatment or Punishment 1984, ratified by the United Kingdom with effect from December 8, 1988. Chile had ratified the Convention with effect from October 30, 1988.

---

30 Extradition Act 1989, s.7.

31 *ibid.* s.6(1).

32 *R. v. Bow Street Metropolitan Stipendiary Magistrate, ex p. Pinochet Ugarte (No. 3)* [1999] 2 W.L.R. 827; [1999] 2 All E.R. 97; (1999) 6 B.H.R.C. 24; (1999) 96(17) L.S.G. 24; (1999) 149 N.L.J. 497.

33 *R. v. Bow Street Metropolitan Stipendiary Magistrate, ex p. Pinochet Ugarte (No. 1)* [1998] 3 W.L.R. 1456.

34 *R. v. Bow Street Metropolitan Stipendiary Magistrate, ex p. Pinochet Ugarte (No. 2)* [1999] 1 W.L.R. 272.

It was held that to be an extradition crime Pinochet's conduct had to constitute a crime under both U.K. and Spanish law. Torture committed outside the United Kingdom was not a crime under U.K. law until September 1988. Under the Extradition Act 1989 an extradition crime had to have been criminal under U.K. law at the time it was committed. Extradition could only be allowed for the crimes committed after that date. It was also held that the former head of state had no immunity in relation to authorising or organising torture after December 8, 1988. However, Pinochet was entitled to immunity in respect of the charges of murder and conspiracy to murder. Pinochet could therefore be extradited to Spain but only in relation to some of the charges against him.

Freedom of Speech

13.14 Everyone is entitled to have their own opinions and beliefs and one measure of the extent to which individual liberty is valued in society is the extent to which citizens are able to express their opinions without fear of retribution. Freedom of speech is an essential element of democracy. The ability of citizens to exercise informed choice between political parties depends on members of each party being free to publicise their views. Without a reasonable degree of freedom of expression citizens are denied their role in the democratic process. Accountability of a government in power is diminished if criticism of the actions of the government can be suppressed.

Freedom of speech is important in wider spheres of life than those which affect the processes of democratic government directly. Freedom of speech allows informed discussion on religion, ideologies and ethics. Scientific developments can be impeded by rules which suppress the sharing of ideas. Nevertheless freedom of expression is never completely without restriction. The right of one individual to express his views has to be balanced against the rights of others. The rights which may need to be protected include national security, the right to a fair trial and the right not to be offended or shocked by obscene materials. Freedom of speech exists in the United Kingdom to the extent that anyone is free to express his views except where there is a law which prevents expression of a particular view or disclosure of certain types of information. Freedom of expression is protected under Article 10 of the European Convention of Human Rights and therefore any Acts of the Scottish Parliament and any actions by the Scottish Administration will need to be compatible with Article 10. The current restrictions on freedom of speech in the United Kingdom are broadly compatible with the permitted restrictions under Article 10. Although the protection of national security justifies restrictions on the freedom of speech the only restrictions which are justified are those which are absolutely necessary. If there is no risk of harm to national interests free speech should not be repressed.

Restrictions on freedom of speech

(1) Defamation

The purpose of the law of defamation is not to restrict freedom of speech but rather to protect individuals against false statements which may cause harm to their reputations and to provide a mechanism for compensation where such harm has occurred. Defamation is the communication of a false statement or idea which is defamatory. The law of defamation has been criticised as providing inadequate protection for the individual from unwarranted intrusion by the press into private lives. The process of gaining compensation for defamatory remarks is expensive and slow. People are often reluctant to undertake the expense of litigation. 13.15

The law of defamation could, however, be a serious threat to free and open debate in the course of debates in Parliament and to judicial proceedings. For this reason the protection of absolute privilege is given to: (a) words spoken in proceedings in the Westminster Parliament[35]; (b) statements in the course of judicial proceedings; (c) statements made by the Parliamentary Commissioner for Administration[36]; (d) statements made in the course of proceedings in the Scottish Parliament[37]; (e) publications made under the authority of the Westminster or Scottish Parliament, *e.g.* official reports of debates, committee papers and radio or television broadcasts of proceedings.

Absolute privilege means that whatever the accuracy of the statement or the intent with which it was made, no action for defamation can be based on it. Qualified privilege is given to reports of parliamentary or judicial proceedings. Qualified privilege applies where a statement is a fair and accurate report of the proceedings and it is made without malice.[38]

---

35 Bill of Rights 1689.

36 Parliamentary Commissioner Act 1967, s. 10(5).

37 Scotland Act 1998, s. 41.

38 Defamation Act 1996, s. 15.

(2) Obscenity

13.16 Restricting freedom of expression because of obscenity or indecency raises difficult constitutional questions. Can such restrictions be justified by the need to protect society as a whole or certain sectors of society from being shocked of offended? Arguments in favour of restrictions tend to emphasise the need to protect members of society from corrupting influences. Definitions of obscenity depend on contemporary standards of decency, taste and morality. It is difficult to apply an objective standard of acceptability for publications. Some publications which were regarded as obscene as little as 40 years ago are considered acceptable today.[39] Obscene publications are those which: "possess the liability to corrupt and deprave those to whom they are sold and exposed."[40]

The majority of cases involving obscene publications are heard before the courts in England and Wales because the majority of publishers are within the jurisdiction of the English courts. The control of obscene material is becoming increasingly difficult now that electronic communications and access to the internet make it possible for individuals to import material directly from outside the United Kingdom.

It is an offence under the Civic Government Scotland Act[41] to display any obscene material in any public place, or in any other place where it can be seen by the public. Material is defined as any book, magazine, bill, paper, print, film, tape, diskette or other kind of recording (whether of sound or visual images or both), photograph, drawing, painting, representation, model or figure. In a recent prosecution under this section a man was charged with operating computer bulletin board systems which contained visual images and text files of an obscene nature. The accused argued that "text files" did not fall within the definition of "material" provided by the 1982 Act. He was convicted and appealed unsuccessfully. It was held that text files could be considered to be a recording of a visual image and so are included in the definition of obscene material.[42]

Performances of plays or television and radio broadcasting are not restricted by the 1982 Act, although they are subject to controls through the licensing system. Performances of films and video recordings are subject to a classification system. It is also an offence under the Civic Government (Scotland) Act to publish, sell

[39] *e.g.* the novel, *Lady Chatterley's Lover* by D.H. Lawrence.
[40] *Ingram v. Macari*, 1983 S.L.T. 67.
[41] s. 51.
[42] *Ross (Crawford David) v. HMA*, 1998 S.L.T. 1313; 1998 S.C.C.R. 359.

or distribute any obscene material or to keep any obscene material with a view to its eventual sale or distribution. In the case of *Rees v. Lees*[43] the accused argued that he had not committed an offence if it could not be proved that he had sold any materials. A large quantity of sex articles had been seized from his shop during two police raids but he argued that there was no evidence that any actual sale had taken place and so he had not "sold" obscene material. He also argued that since the magazines were sealed in clear wrappers, they were not liable to corrupt or deprave. It was held that the word "sells" in section 51(2) included "offers for sale", and the sheriff had been entitled to infer that the articles were available for sale from evidence of sale on other occasions. Obscene magazines and videos visibly displayed with no warnings or age restrictions were liable to corrupt and deprave unsuspecting members of the public who found themselves exposed to the explicit and obscene covers visible through the wrappers. There is a defence of inadvertance. A person will escape conviction if he can prove that he used all due diligence to avoid committing an offence.[44]

(3) Contempt of court

The purpose of the law relating to contempt of court is to 13.17
protect the judiciary and judicial proceedings from actions or words which would impede or adversely affect the administration of justice.[45] Contempt of court is not strictly a crime but it is treated as a crime. Penalties may be imposed on a party in contempt. The law of contempt of court restricts freedom of expression, particularly on the part of newspaper journalists and radio and television broadcasters by preventing the reporting of anything which could be prejudicial to court proceedings. This type of contempt of court is regulated by statute.[46] The Contempt of Court Act applies to publications. A publication is defined as including any speech, writing, broadcast or other communication in whatever form, which is addressed to the public at large or to a section of the public.[47]

An example of the effect of the law of contempt on newspaper reporting was the case of *H.M. Advocate v. News Paper Group*

---

[43] 1997 S.L.T. 872; 1996 S.C.C.R. 601.

[44] Civic Government (Scotland) Act 1982, s. 51(4).

[45] *Report of the Phillimore Committee on Contempt of Court*, Cmnd. 5794 (1974), p. 2.

[46] Contempt of Court Act 1981.

[47] *ibid.* s. 2(1).

Newspapers.[48] Following the shooting of a Yugoslavian in Kirkcaldy two newspapers published articles of a fairly sensational nature relating to the incident. These articles were published the day after the shooting and subsequent arrest of a suspect. The Lord Advocate presented petitions against both newspaper companies on the ground that the articles were in breach of the Contempt of Court Act 1981, s. 2. Both newspapers were held to be in contempt of court. The article in one newspaper was fairly specific in its allegations, implying the suspect was guilty but not naming him. A heavier fine was imposed on that newspaper. The system of criminal justice in Scotland depended upon the proposition that jurors should arrive in the jury box without knowledge or impressions of facts, or alleged facts, relating to the crime charged. The articles in question had undermined this.

The newspapers companies were not able to plead in defence that they had no intention to interfere with the course of justice. Nor could it be a defence that they had procedures in place to vet articles to ensure that they did not create a risk of causing bias in court proceedings. The 1981 Act lays down a rule of strict liability and any publication which creates a substantial risk that the course of justice, in particular legal proceedings, will be seriously impeded or prejudiced will be in contempt of court regardless of the intent of the persons responsible for publication. The strict liability rule applies only when proceedings are active. Criminal proceedings are active from the time of arrest without warrant, or the time of granting of a warrant of citation, or the time when an indictment or other document specifying the charge is served on the accused. Civil proceedings become active in an ordinary action in the Court of Session or the sheriff court when the record is closed, or when a motion or application is made. In other proceedings the date when they become active is when the date of a hearing is fixed or a hearing is allowed.[49] A case remains active until it is disposed of or abandoned, discontinued or withdrawn.

An article which is published a considerable time before a trial is due to take place could still amount to contempt of court. The case of *H.M. Advocate v. Scotsman Publications Ltd*,[50] concerned a publication several months before a trial was expected to take place. Mohammed Sarwar, M.P. for a Glasgow constituency was charged with electoral fraud and attempting to pervert the course of justice. An article was published in *The Scotsman* newspaper

---

[48] 1989 S.C.C.R. 156.

[49] Contempt of Court Act 1981, Sched. 1.

[50] 1999 S.L.T 466; 1999 S.C.C.R. 163.

under the headline, "Sarwar charge witnesses ask for protection". The article alleged that two witnesses had sought police protection as a result of fears about intimidation. The Lord Advocate applied to the court to make findings of contempt in respect of the publisher, the editor and two journalists. It was held that there had been contempt of court. An ordinary reader was likely to conclude that it was intimidation by Sarwar which was to be feared. The likelihood of this was increased by the fact that Sarwar was well known. The suggestion that he would intimidate witnesses led people to suppose that he must be guilty. There would be a material risk of serious prejudice if any juror had read the article.

Actions for contempt of court are usually brought by the Lord 13.18
Advocate. They may also be brought by a party to a trial who considers that the course of justice will be impeded. An action for contempt of court may be brought, for example, by an accused person in a criminal trial. This happened in the case of *Robb v. Caledonian Newspapers Ltd.*[51] R had been arrested and charged in August 1993 with lewd, indecent and libidinous practices. He petitioned the court to make a finding of contempt against a newspaper company and its editor in respect of an allegedly prejudicial article published that month. It was held that the application was competent but should be dismissed on the ground of delay. It was argued that an accused person could not petition in this way without the consent of the Lord Advocate but it was held that his consent was not required. Contempt of court is not a crime and so bringing an action for contempt is not the same as trying to bring a private prosecution for a crime.

There are defences against an action for contempt of court. It is a defence to prove that, at the time of publication, or distribution of the publication, the writer or publisher does not know and has no reason to suspect that relevant proceedings are active.[52] Fair and accurate reports of legal proceedings, held in public, and published contemporaneously and in good faith do not attract the strict liability rule.[53] A publication which is a discussion in good faith of public affairs or matters of general public interest will not be held to be in contempt if the risk of impeding or prejudicing legal proceedings is merely incidental to the discussion.[54]

Section 10 of the Contempt of Court Act regulates the disclosure of sources. The court may not require disclosure, and a person will

---

[51] 1995 S.L.T. 631; 1994 S.C.C.R. 65.

[52] Contempt of Court Act 1981, s. 3(1), (2).

[53] *ibid.* s. 4.

[54] *ibid.* s. 5.

not be guilty of contempt as a result of failure to disclose a source of information, unless the court is satisfied that: "disclosure is necessary in the interests of justice or national security or for the prevention of disorder or crime".[55]

The behaviour of people present at court hearings may also be restricted by the law of contempt of court. Anything which amounts to disrespectful words or conduct may be held by a judge to be contempt of court. An example of this type of contempt arose in the case of *Young v. Lees*.[56] Young was present at the trial of his partner. When she was remanded in custody Young shouted "You guffy" at the sheriff. The sheriff found him in contempt of court. He was sentenced to 60 days' imprisonment.

(4) Incitement to racial hatred

13.19 A person may not speak or act in a public place in a manner which is likely to engender racial hatred.[57] An offence is committed by a person who, in a public place or at a public meeting, with the intention of stirring up hatred against a racial group in the United Kingdom, uses words or gestures which are threatening, abusive or insulting. It is also an offence to use threatening, abusive or insulting words or gestures in the knowledge that hatred against a racial group is likely to be stirred up. A racial group is defined as a group of persons defined by reference to colour, race, nationality or ethnic or national origins. Nationality in this context includes citizenship so a racial group could consist of the members of a state with a multi-racial community. The provisions of the Public Order Act apply to written material, videos, films and sound tapes as well as to the original words or gestures.

(5) Official secrecy

13.20 Certain categories of government information are protected from disclosure to the public by the Official Secrets Act 1989. This restricts the freedom of speech of Crown servants and government contractors in the interests of national security. Crown servants are Ministers of the Crown, members of the Scottish Executive or junior Scottish ministers, civil servants, office holders in the Scottish Administration, diplomats, police constables and members of the armed forces. The following categories of information are protected by the Act: (a) information relating to security and

---

[55] Contempt of Court Act 1981, s. 10.
[56] 1998 S.C.C.R. 558.
[57] Public Order Act 1986, s. 17.

intelligence[58]; (b) information relating to defence[59]; (c) information relating to international relations and any confidential information obtained from a state other than the United Kingdom or an international organisation[60]; (d) information the disclosure of which results in, or is likely to result in, the commission of an offence, to facilitate escape from lawful custody, or to impede the prevention or detection of offences or the apprehensions or prosecution of suspected offenders[61]; (e) any information obtained by reason of action taken under a warrant issued either under the Interception of Communications Act 1985, s. 2, or the Intelligence Services Act 1994, ss. 5 and 7, or relating to such a warrant.

Not every disclosure of information will automatically amount to a criminal offence. In some cases it is necessary to prove that the disclosure was damaging. A disclosure relating to defence, for example, will be regarded as damaging if it reduces the capabilities of the armed forces, endangers life or equipment or endangers the interests of the United Kingdom, or of British citizens abroad, or is likely to have any of these effects.[62] Some disclosures will be classed as criminal offences whether or not they are potentially damaging. Any disclosure by a member or former member of the security or intelligence services of information relating to security or intelligence is an offence, whether or not the disclosure is damaging.[63] The disclosure of information connected with warrants under the Interception of Communications Act and the Intelligence Services Act will also be an offence even if the disclosure is not damaging.

There are defences to a prosecution under the Official Secrets 13.21
Act. Where disclosure would only amount to an offence if it is damaging it will be a defence to prove that at the time of the alleged offence the accused did not know and had no reasonable cause to believe that disclosure would be damaging.[64] It will also be a defence to show that, at the time of the alleged offence, the accused did not know and had no reasonable cause to suspect that the information disclosed related to one of the protected categories. It will also be a defence for a person to prove that, at the time of the disclosure he believed that he had lawful authority to disclose the information and had no reason to believe otherwise.

---

[58] Official Secrets Act 1989, s. 1.
[59] *ibid.* s. 2.
[60] *ibid.* s. 3.
[61] *ibid.* s. 4(1).
[62] *ibid.* s. 1(1).
[63] *ibid.* s. 4.
[64] *ibid.* s. 1(1).

Where a third party such as a newspaper has received information which was disclosed in contravention of the Official Secrets Act it is not an offence merely to receive the information. It is an offence to fail to comply with an official direction for the return or disposal of written information.[65] Any subsequent disclosure by the third party will be an offence if it is made either knowing, or having reasonable cause to believe, that the information is protected under the Official Secrets Act. The maximum penalty for disclosing protected information is a period of imprisonment of up to two years, or a fine, or both. National security is a reserved matter under the Scotland Act 1998 and so responsibility for the regulation of official secrecy and the interception of communications remains with the Westminster Parliament.

Freedom of Association and Assembly

13.22 Freedom of assembly has always been regarded as an essential element in a society that claims to implement principles of civil and political freedom. Freedom of assembly is protected by Article 11 of the European Convention on Human Rights. The need for individuals to gather together in groups may be less important now that there are other means of communication such as television, telephones and the internet but two types of mass public meetings continue to be held:

(1) Public meetings are still important in industrial disputes where mass rallies and picketing of organisations are seen as a useful method of attracting publicity for a cause. During the miners' strike in the mid 1980s large numbers of pickets gathered at the steelworks at Ravenscraig and at Hunterston power station. The police diverted vehicles carrying pickets while they were some distance from either destination.

(2) Processions are still a popular way to attract the attention of the mass news media to a political or environmental cause. Certain traditional processions such as marches by members of Orange Orders still take place in parts of Scotland.

Scots law does not recognise a right of public protest. Freedom of assembly only exists to the extent that people can assemble

---

[65] Official Secrets Act 1989, s.8(4).

together in circumstances which are not subject to regulations or restrictions.[66] People may gather together in groups and may talk but the police could disperse them if they were obstructing the passage of others or if it was deemed likely that a breach of the peace may occur.[67]

Protection of assemblies

Where meetings are held on private property the regulation of the meeting is a matter for the owner of the property. Many meetings are held on premises belonging to local authorities and local authorities have statutory duties to make premises available for political meetings in the period prior to an election.[68] The law also takes steps to protect meetings from disruption by others. It is an offence for a person to attend a public meeting and to act in a disorderly manner for the purpose of impeding the business of the meeting.[69] There is a specific sanction in relation to political meetings in the period leading up to elections. The Representation of the People Act 1983 provides that a person who, at a political meeting held in any constituency between the date of issue of a writ for the return of a Member of Parliament and the date of the election, acts or incites others to act in a disorderly manner for the purpose of disrupting the meeting shall be guilty of an illegal practice.[70] 13.23

Restrictions on the freedom of assembly

Regulation of processions

Public processions are regulated by the Civic Government (Scotland) Act 1982 and the Public Order Act 1986 (as amended by the Criminal Justice and Public Order Act 1994). Local councils have the power to permit a procession to take place or to prohibit the holding of a procession.[71] The purpose of regulation is to prevent any violent confrontations which may take place between opposing groups and to ensure that provisions are in place for public safety. Seven days notice must be given prior to a procession taking place. Notice must be given to both the council 13.24

---

[66] *Aldred v. Miller*, 1925 J.C. 117.
[67] *Duncan v. Jones* [1936] 1 K.B. 218; *Aldred v. Miller*, above.
[68] Representation of the People Act 1983, ss. 95, 96.
[69] Public Meeting Act 1908.
[70] Representation of the People Act 1983, s. 97.
[71] Civic Government (Scotland) Act 1982, s. 63.

and the chief constable.[72] There are exceptions to this requirement. Advance notification is not required for processions which are customarily or commonly held. An example would be an annual children's gala and parade. The authority may decide to remove this exemption in the case of a particular procession or particular types of procession. A local authority may grant exemption from the requirement to give notice to certain types of procession or the processions of specific organisations. The local authority is also empowered to waive the full period of notice, but not the requirement for notification, in respect of processions which are spontaneous or organised urgently in response to a particular event where there is insufficient time to give the full seven days' notice.

When permission is given to hold a procession the council may impose conditions as to its date, time, duration and route. It may also prohibit the procession from entering into any public place specified in the order. A council may, for example, prohibit a march by an Orange Order from entering a predominantly Catholic street. Notice of the conditions must be given in writing at least two days before the procession is due to be held. Appeal against a prohibition of a procession or any conditions imposed may be made to a sheriff. Such an appeal must be lodged within 14 days of receipt of the order.[73] The grounds on which an appeal can be made are limited. The only ground is that the council has exceeded its powers. The sheriff may therefore only uphold an appeal if he considers that, in deciding to restrict or ban the procession, the council erred in law or based its decision on a material error of fact, or exercised its discretion unreasonably. The sheriff may not consider the merits of the decision, only whether the council was acting within its authority under the Civic Government (Scotland) Act.

It is an offence to hold a procession without permission or to contravene the conditions which have been laid down.[74] Any person who takes part in an unauthorised procession and who refuses to desist when required to do so by a policeman in uniform is also guilty of an offence. The powers of a council relate mainly to regulating the holding of processions in advance of them taking place. Regulation of processions at the time when they are taking place falls within the powers of the police.

---

72 Civic Government (Scotland) Act 1982, s. 62.

73 *ibid.* s. 64.

74 *ibid.* s. 65.

The Public Order Act gives power to a senior police officer who is present when a procession is taking place to impose conditions.[75] He may impose conditions before the procession has started once people are assembling with a view to taking part in the procession. The senior police officer may impose conditions if he reasonably believes that the procession may give rise to serious public disorder, serious damage to property or serious disruption to the life of the community, or that the purpose of the organisers is to intimidate others. Intimidation in this context means preventing people from doing what they have a right to do or compelling them to do something which they have no right to do. The senior police officer is the officer most senior in rank present at the scene. He need not be a high-ranking officer. Conditions may be imposed with regard to the time, place and manner of the procession. The conditions may be imposed only in so far as they are necessary to prevent serious disorder, disruption or intimidation. It is an offence to knowingly fail to comply with conditions imposed by the police on the day of a procession or to incite others to behave in a manner contrary to the conditions.[76] It is a defence for a person to prove that the failure to comply with the conditions arose from circumstances outwith his control.

Regulation of public assemblies

Similar powers to those by which the police regulate processions are conferred on the police in relation to other public assemblies.[77] These would include political protests, picketing in the course of an industrial dispute, and social occasions. Conditions may be imposed if the senior police officer present reasonably believes that there is a probability of serious public disorder, serious damage to property or serious disruption to the life of the community, or intimidation. The police officer may make conditions regarding the location of the assembly, the duration and the maximum number of people who may attend. As with processions the conditions imposed must not be more stringent than are required to prevent serious disorder, damage to property or disruption. The powers apply to a public assembly. A public assembly is where 20 or more persons assemble in a public place which is wholly or partly open to the air.[78] A public place means any road and any place to which at 13.25

---

[75] s. 12.
[76] Public Order Act 1986, s. 12(4), (5).
[77] *ibid.* s. 14.
[78] *ibid.* s. 16.

the material time the public or any section of the public has access, on payment or otherwise, as of right or by virtue of express or implied permission. A person who knowingly fails to comply with the directions of the police or who incites others to disregard the conditions is guilty of an offence.[79] Conditions may also be imposed in advance by the chief constable. Written notice of the conditions must be given to the organisers of the assembly.

Trespassory assemblies are prohibited. [80] A trespassory assembly is where 20 or more people assemble on land entirely in the open air, to which the public has no right of access or only limited right of access. If a chief constable reasonably believes that a trespassory assembly is about to take place and that it is likely to cause serious disruption to the life of the community, or significant damage to the land or a building or a monument on it, he may apply to the local authority for an order prohibiting all trespassory assemblies for a period of up to four days in an area not exceeding a radius of five miles from the intended location of the assembly. This power applies where the land, building or monument is of historical, architectural, archaeological or scientific importance. Examples include Stonehenge at the time of the summer solstice and areas around Faslane naval base. Any person who organises or takes part in an assembly which trespasses onto land in the area for which a prohibition order is in effect commits a criminal offence. A uniformed police officer is entitled to stop a person who he reasonably believes to be on his way to an assembly which has been prohibited.[81] People can only be stopped in this way if they are within the area covered by the prohibition order. The police officer can direct him not to proceed in the direction of the assembly. Failure to comply with the instructions of the police officer is an offence.

13.26 The Criminal Justice and Public Order Act also confers powers in relating to specific types of assembly such as raves and music festivals.[82] It also confers powers to remove groups of trespassers from land, which are aimed at controlling groups such as "new age travellers".[83] The offence of aggravated trespass is committed by a person who trespasses on land in the open air and does anything

---

[79] Public Order Act 1984, s. 14 (4), (5).

[80] *ibid.* ss. 14A, 14B (inserted by the Criminal Justice and Public Order Act 1994, s. 70).

[81] Public Order Act 1984, s. 14C (inserted by Criminal Justice and Public Order Act 1994, s. 71).

[82] Criminal Justice and Public Order Act 1994, ss. 63–67.

[83] *ibid.* ss. 61, 62.

intended to obstruct or disrupt any lawful activity or to intimidate persons with a view to deterring them from engaging in lawful activity.[84] This offence is likely to be committed by hunt saboteurs or anti-road protesters.

It may be an offence to wear uniforms at a public meeting. The wearing of uniforms which signify association with a political organisation or for the promotion of any political purpose at a public meeting or in a public place may be an offence under the Public Order Act 1936.[85] This act was passed to prevent uniformed fascists parading the streets in the 1930s. A uniform does not have to be a complete military outfit. The term uniform includes any article of clothing which is worn by each member of a group and which is intended to indicate his association with a political organisation or purpose. The article does not have to cover any major part of the body. The berets, dark glasses and dark pullovers worn by members of the IRA identify its members in the eyes of the public. Members of a political organisation may wear uniforms in private and even in meetings at which the only people present are members of the organisation. The wearing of uniforms in public may be permitted by a chief constable if he is satisfied that there is unlikely to be any risk of public disorder. Uniforms, such as badges or insignia, may be worn by the stewards who are engaged to assist in the preservation of order at a public meeting, provided that the number of stewards is not excessive.

The Public Order Act and the Criminal Justice and Public Order Act have, like many statutes, been drawn up to deal with a particular mischief which is perceived to be happening in society at the time. Sometimes, as in the case of the regulation of assemblies, the resulting statute has potential to be used in a wider range of circumstances. The powers which have been given to the police could be misused to prevent citizens gathering in groups to protest. The powers could be used against road protesters or anti-nuclear protesters.

Indirect restrictions on the right of assembly

Obstruction of the highway

The Civic Government (Scotland) Act provides that any person 13.27
who, "in a public place: (a) obstructs, along with another or others, the lawful passage of any other person and fails to desist on being

---

84 Criminal Justice and Public Order Act 1994, s. 61.

85 s. 1.

required to do so by a constable in uniform; or (b) wilfully obstructs the lawful passage of any other person" is guilty of an offence.[86] It is not necessary for a street or footpath to be completely blocked in order for the highway to be regarded as obstructed. It may be classed as obstruction if there is still room for people to pass by. People could, in theory be charged with the offence of obstruction if they gathered in a road for a few minutes and caused only a short delay to people wishing to use the road.

Obstruction of a police officer

13.28 It is an offence to obstruct a police officer in the execution of his duty.[87] Prosecutions for the obstruction of a police officer are not common. It is more usual for a person who has acted in a manner which impedes the work of a police officer to be charged with breach of the peace.

Breach of the peace

13.29 The all-encompassing common law offence of breach of the peace provides the grounds on which the police may prevent and control any public disorder.[88] It is not necessary for a breach of the peace to have occurred before a public assembly is dispersed or individual participants are apprehended. It is sufficient for there to be, in the opinion of the police, a reasonable probability that a breach of the peace may occur. In Scotland breach of the peace is a criminal offence in its own right. In *Alexander v. Smith* [89] a man was arrested and convicted of breach of the peace for selling newspapers. He had been selling National Front newspapers to football supporters. The police, who were concerned for his safety, asked him to move on. He refused to do so whereupon he was arrested.

An arrest for breach of the peace may take place even though there has been no rowdy conduct or loud noise. There have been instances where simply standing still and not speaking has been held to justify a conviction for breach of the peace. In *Montgomery v. McLeod* [90] a bystander was arrested in a hotel car park. There had been a disturbance in the car park earlier the same evening and the police returned to check that there had not been a reoccurrence. They found the accused standing in the car

---

[86] s. 53.
[87] Police (Scotland) Act 1967, s. 41.
[88] *ibid.* s. 17.
[89] 1984 S.L.T. 176.
[90] 1977 S.L.T (Notes) 77.

park waiting for a friend. The police asked him to move on. He refused and was then arrested. He was convicted of a breach of the peace and the conviction was upheld on appeal. It was said that an offence of breach of the peace could arise in two ways. First any conduct which creates "disturbance and alarm to the lieges" constitutes breach of the peace. A second set of circumstances which could be classed as breach of the peace is where there has been conduct "such as to excite the reasonable apprehension" that mischief might ensue. Even where there had only been passive conduct a police officer could be deemed to be justified in believing that a breach of the peace might occur. It was held that: "There is no limit to the kind of conduct which may give rise to a charge of breach of the peace."

It is not necessary to prove that an individual accused person was acting in breach of the peace. A person may be convicted of breach of the peace if he was part of a crowd of people acting in a disorderly manner and he did not disassociate himself from the crowd. In the case of *Winnick v. Allan* [91] the conviction was upheld of a man who had been part of a crowd of noisy and disorderly persons who shouted and swore and tore down a stone boundary wall and threw missiles at colliery buildings. His actions had not been singled out in the evidence at his trial but the evidence of the behaviour of the group was sufficient to give rise to the inference that he had supported, sympathised with and encouraged the actions of the crowd.

This power to intervene is not restricted to assemblies held in public places. The police are also entitled to attend where a public meeting is being held on private premises. They can do so if they have reasonable grounds for believing that an offence such as a breach of the peace is imminent or even that there is a strong probability that there may be a breach of the peace.[92]

It is not necessary for there to be members of the public present for a breach of the peace to occur. So even if there are no "lieges" to be alarmed or disturbed the police may arrest a person on the grounds of a real or apprehended breach of the peace. So in *Wyness v. Lockhart*[93] the appellant was charged with breach of the peace after approaching two police officers in a street, patting them on the shoulders and asking for money. Neither the police officers nor any other bystanders were alarmed or upset. The High

---

[91] 1986 S.C.C.R. 35. See also *MacNeill v. Robertson*, 1982 S.C.C.R. 468; *Tudhope v. Morrison*, 1983 S.C.C.R. 262.

[92] *Thomas v. Sawkins* [1935] 2 K.B. 249.

[93] 1992 S.C.C.R. 808.

Court held that, nevertheless the conduct of the accused was such as might reasonably be expected to cause alarm, upset or annoyance to members of the public.

Freedom from Discrimination

13.30 The laws which protect the citizen in the United Kingdom from discrimination on grounds of sex, marital status, race, colour, ethnic origin or disability all owe their existence to European directives which required Member States to establish a protective regime. Discrimination in relation to sex, racial or ethnic origin, religion or belief, disability, age or sexual orientation is contrary to Article 13 of the E.C. Treaty. Measures to combat discrimination under Article 13 are to be undertaken by the Council of Ministers, acting unanimously on a proposal from the Commission, following consultation with the European Parliament. Measures adopted under this Article will not have direct effect. This means that the potential for this Article is limited. Discrimination on grounds of religion or belief, age or sexual orientation remains permissible under U.K. law. One exception to this is Northern Ireland, where it is unlawful to discriminate on religious grounds. Article 12, which provides that discrimination on grounds of nationality is prohibited, has direct effect.

Discrimination on Grounds of Sex or Marital Status

13.31 The two major statutory provisions are the Equal Pay Act 1970 and the Sex Discrimination Act 1975. The Equal Pay Act 1970 makes it unlawful to discriminate between men and women in respect of pay and other contractual terms and conditions of employment. The Sex Discrimination Act 1975 ordains that it is unlawful to discriminate on grounds of sex or marital status in respect of employment, training, education, provision of goods and services, disposal and the management of premises. The laws to protect individuals from discrimination on grounds of sex have been passed in order to secure conformity with European Community law. Directive 76/207, for example, provides for equal treatment as regards access to employment and promotion, training, and working. The effects of the Sex Discrimination Act relate to many aspects of everyday life so, for example, it is unlawful for a bank or building society to discriminate in the terms on which a loan is offered. A public house cannot insist on women sitting at a table if it allows men to stand at the bar. The Act also outlaws discrimination on grounds of marriage in the context of employment.

Discrimination is unlawful if the reason for the discrimination is the sex of the person who is the victim of the discrimination. This was taken to mean either discrimination against a man because of his masculine gender or against a woman because of her female gender. It has also, however, been held to be unlawful discrimination to dismiss a transsexual who was undergoing gender reassignment since this was dismissal on the grounds of a person's sex and contrary to the Equal Treatment Directive.[94]

Unlawful discrimination may take one of three forms: direct discrimination, indirect discrimination or victimisation.

Direct discrimination

There is direct discrimination if a person is treated less favoura- 13.32 bly than a person of the opposite sex is or would be treated.[95] Therefore if a woman applied for a job selling cars and was told that it was not a woman's job that would amount to direct discrimination. However, if a feeble woman was rejected because the job needed a strong person to do it there would be no unlawful discrimination. She would have been rejected because she cannot do the job. However, if all women are rejected because an employer considers that all women are weak it would amount to unlawful discrimination. A balance has to be achieved between the rights of employers to hire employees who are suitably equipped to do the job required and the right of each individual not to suffer discrimination.

The purpose of the Sex Discrimination Act is to protect individuals from discriminatory acts. The motive of the person who discriminates against them is irrelevant. Whether or not he intended to discriminate is also irrelevant. Therefore it was held that, even where an employer acted on grounds which he thought were chivalrous, discrimination on grounds of sex would be unlawful. The employer had refused to allow women to earn extra payments by working in an area that was very dirty. The employer had discriminated against women by preventing them from earning additional payments and against his male employees by requiring them to work in different conditions from female employees.[96] Another successful claim was brought by a woman who had been preventing from starting her new job as a painter because she

---

94 76/207. See Case C–13/94 *P v. S and Cornwall County Council* [1996] E.C.R. 1–2143; [1996] I.R.L.R. 347.

95 Sex Discrimination Act 1975, s. 1(1)(a).

96 *Ministry of Defence v. Jeremiah* [1979] 3 All E.R. 833.

would have had to work with a team comprised entirely of men. The employer genuinely thought it would not be in her best interests to work with an all-male team. Nevertheless the tribunal held that she had been the victim of unlawful direct discrimination.[97] A long-established tradition will not justify discrimination. When women brought an action for a declarator that they had been unlawfully discriminated against by being denied an opportunity to participate in the Hawick common riding, it was held that the discrimination was unlawful. The fact that all of the roles had been traditionally taken by men did not justify the discrimination.[98]

It is also direct discrimination where assumptions are made on the basis of gender, for example to refuse to let a flat to men because they are untidy or to operate a policy of never employing young mothers because they are unreliable. In the case of *Hurley v. Mustoe*[99] it was held that there had been unlawful discrimination when the manager of a bistro refused to employ a mother who had young children. Ms Hurley had applied for a job as a waitress. She was given a one-night trial to see if she was satisfactory. The manager was happy with her work but the owner instructed him not to give her a job because she had four children and he thought women with children were unreliable. She had previously worked for 10 years as a waitress and had a good work record. The bistro owner made no attempt to check this. He based his decision on his assumptions about working mothers in general.[1]

13.33 Sexual harassment constitutes direct discrimination. Harassment is treatment which may include bullying or unwanted sexual advances. The most notable Scottish case involving sexual harassment is *Strathclyde Regional Council v. Porcelli*.[2] Mrs Porcelli was a laboratory technician in a school. She asked for a transfer to another school because of the behaviour of two male lab technicians. They sabotaged her work, let doors slam in her face as she was carrying equipment, and threw her personal possessions in the bin. They used obscene language, compared her body with nude pictures and one of them made suggestive remarks and brushed himself up against her. The employment tribunal held that if the two men had disliked a male colleague they would have treated him equally badly and dismissed her case. However, the Employment Appeal Tribunal and

---

[97] *Grieg v. Community Industry* [1979] I.R.L.R. 158.

[98] *Graham v. Hawick Common Riding Committee*, 1998 S.L.T. (Sh.Ct.) 42; 1997 S.C.L.R. 917.

[99] [1981] I.R.L.R. 208.

[1] See also *Coleman v. Skyrail Oceanic Ltd* [1981] I.R.L.R. 398.

[2] [1986] I.R.L.R. 134.

the Court of Session both found in Mrs Porcelli's favour. A man might have been treated badly, but the nature of the unpleasantness would have been different. The sexual element would not have been present. The council who employed her was held liable because no action had been taken by management when she had complained.

Actual physical contact is not necessary to establish that there has been sexual harassment. Nor is it necessary to prove that there has been a prolonged series of acts of harassment. A single serious incident will be sufficient.[3] In *Wileman v. Minilec Engineering Ltd*,[4] Popplewell J. stated: " 'Sexual harassment' is legal shorthand for activity which is easily recognisable as 'subjecting her to any other detriment'." Compensation for harassment relates to the degree of detriment and the courts have stated that evidence of the complainant's attitude to sexual matters is admissible in assessing injury to feelings. In *Wileman* a paltry sum of damages was awarded on the grounds that since the complainant had been scantily clad in posing for photographs, she had suffered little injury to her feelings.

The European Commission has issued a Recommendation and 13.34
Code of Practice on November 27, 1991 relating to the protection of dignity of men and women at work. Conduct of a sexual nature or conduct based on sex affecting the dignity of men and women at work is unacceptable if: (i) the conduct is unwanted, unreasonable and offensive to the recipient; (ii) the person's rejection of such conduct is used as a basis for employment decisions such as promotion, continued employment, or level of salary; or (iii) such conduct creates an intimidating, hostile or humiliating work environment.

Such conduct may be in breach of the Equal Treatment Directive 1976. The Recommendation asked Member States to implement the Code of Practice for employment within the public sector and to encourage its use in the private sector. In the United Kingdom it appears that the Recommendation has been taken into account by tribunals in sexual harassment cases.[5]

It may be possible for a woman (or man) to claim a delictual remedy in the civil courts for sexual or racial harassment.[6] In such actions it would not be necessary for the pursuer to base their action on the inequality of treatment on the basis of gender,

---

[3] *Bracebridge Engineering v. Darby* [1990] I.R.L.R. 3.

[4] [1988] I.R.L.R. 144 at 149.

[5] See *Insitu Cleaning v. Heads* [1995] I.R.L.R. 4.

[6] See S. Middlemiss "Civil remedies for Victims of Sexual Harassment: Delictual Actions", 1997 J.R. 241.

as would be required under the Sex Discrimination Act 1975. Harassment was recognised as a civil wrong in the case of *Khorasandjan v. Bush*.[7] The Criminal Justice and Public Order Act 1994 makes intentional harassment an offence. The Employment Rights Act 1996 ensures that there is a restriction on publicity in sexual harassment cases.

13.35 Unlawful discrimination may also occur where a woman is treated less favourably because she is pregnant. In the case of *Jennings v. Burton Group*[8] it was held that there had been unlawful discrimination by an employer against a pregnant employee. Mrs Jennings worked in a store in Edinburgh and was dismissed when she was absent for five weeks because of a threatened miscarriage. She had less than two years' service and so could not (at that time) bring an unfair dismissal claim. The tribunal compared the treatment of the pregnant employee with the treatment which the employer would have afforded to a male employee who was sick and had to go into hospital.[9]

Indirect discrimination

13.36 Indirect discrimination occurs when a condition or requirement is applied equally to both sexes but the application has a disproportionate adverse impact on the members of one sex.[10] If, for example, an employer hiring labourers for a building site stated that applicants must be over six feet tall the condition would be applied to both sexes and so would not amount to direct discrimination. However, since the vast majority of women are under six feet tall, it excludes a significantly larger proportion of women than men. It will therefore be classed as indirect discrimination and will be unlawful unless the employer can justify it.

A woman must show that it was to her detriment that she could not comply with the requirement. The condition or requirement must amount to an absolute bar to employment or promotion, etc. There is no indirect discrimination if the employer has produced a list of characteristics he would prefer applicants to have. The case of *Price v. Civil Service Commission*[11] was a challenge to a requirement

---

[7] [1993] Q.B. 727. See also J. Dine and B. Watt, "Sexual Harassment: Moving Away from Discrimination" [1995] 58(3) M.L.R. 362.

[8] 1988, Edinburgh I.T.

[9] See also *Dekker v. Stichting Vormingscentrum voor Jonge Volwassen Plus* [1991] I.R.L.R. 27; *Webb v. EMO Air Cargo (UK) Ltd (No. 2)* [1995] I.R.L.R. 645; *Gillespie v. Northern Health and Social Services Board* [1996] I.R.L.R. 214.

[10] Sex Discrimination Act 1975, s. 1(1)(b).

[11] [1977] I.R.L.R. 291.

by the civil service that applicants for a job as executive officer had to be no older than 28 years. Mrs Price was 35 years old and was therefore barred from joining the civil service as an executive officer. The age requirement applied equally to men and women, but Mrs Price argued that the proportion of women who could comply with the age requirement was considerably smaller than the proportion of men who could comply with it. Many women were out of the job market at that age because of childcare commitments. The employment tribunal dismissed her claim because they found that the numbers of men and women under 28 in the population were roughly the same. Therefore the same proportion of women as men could comply with the age requirement. The employment appeal tribunal disagreed with this reasoning. The proper test was to look at proportions of men and women who could comply in practice with the requirement. Fewer women could comply than men and Mrs Price's claim was upheld.[12]

In the case of *R. v. Secretary of State for Employment, ex parte Equal Opportunities Commission*[13] the House of Lords held that statutory provisions requiring part-time workers to complete five years' continuous service before they could claim unfair dismissal rights was unlawful on the grounds of indirect discrimination. The great majority of part-time workers were women while the great majority of full-time workers were men. Service thresholds had a disproportionate adverse effect on women. This case led to The Employment Protection (Part-time Employees) Regulations 1995 which came into force on February 6, 1995 and removed all hours of work thresholds and granted part-time workers the same statutory employment protection rights as full-time workers.[14]

Victimisation

It is important to provide protection from victimisation for individuals who bring complaints on grounds of discrimination. Victimisation occurs where a person is treated less favourably because: (i) he or she brought proceedings under the Sex Discrimination Act 1975 or the Equal Pay Act 1970, or (ii) he or she gave evidence in such proceedings, or (iii) he or she has alleged that a discriminator or other person has acted to contravene the 1975 Act or the 1970 Act.[15] 13.37

---

12 See also *Clarke and Powell v. Eley (IMI) Kynoch Ltd* [1982] I.R.L.R. 131; *Home Office v. Holmes* [1984] I.R.L.R. 299; *Greater Glasgow Health Board v. Carey* [1987] I.R.L.R. 484.

13 [1994] I.R.L.R. 176.

14 These regulations were revoked and re-enacted in the Employment Rights Act 1996.

15 1975 Act, s. 4.

This protection only applies where the allegations of discrimination are made in good faith. An example of a successful claim on grounds of victimisation was *Chadwick v. Lancashire County Council.*[16] Ms Chadwick was a deputy headteacher who alleged that appointing committees in Lancashire discriminated against women candidates when appointing headteachers. After making these allegations she applied for two headteacher posts but despite having suitable qualifications and experience, she was not short-listed. She alleged she had been discriminated against by way of victimisation. The tribunal held that she had been excluded from the short-list because of her allegations and so she had been victimised under section 4.

Discrimination against married persons

13.38 It is unlawful to discriminate against a person because he or she is married. Direct discrimination occurs where a married person is treated less favourably than an unmarried person of the same sex.[17] Indirect discrimination is also possible where a requirement or condition is such that a smaller proportion of married persons could comply compared with unmarried persons. In order to secure a remedy the married person must also show detriment. The discrimination may not be unlawful if it can be justified.

Protection against sex discrimination in relation to employment

13.39 In addition to the general protection against discrimination on grounds of sex, there are specific provisions which apply in relation to employment. It is unlawful for an employer to discriminate:

(a) In arrangements for seeking employees. This includes advertising, job descriptions, qualifications required and interviews.
(b) In terms of employment offered.
(c) By refusing or deliberately omitting to offer employment because of a person's sex or marital status.
(d) In respect of access to promotion, training, transfer or other benefits.
(e) By dismissing person because of their sex or marital status or subjecting them to detriment.[18]

---

[16] 1984, Liverpool I.T.

[17] Sex Discrimination Act 1975, s. 3. See, *e.g. Hurley v. Mustoe* [1981] I.R.L.R. 208.

[18] *ibid.* s. 6.

Originally the 1975 Act did not apply to provisions regarding death benefits or pensions. The Sex Discrimination Act 1986 was passed as a result of the milestone case of *Marshall v. South West Hampshire Area Health Authority*.[19] Ms Marshall had been forced to retire at the age of 62, although male colleagues could continue to work until they were 65 years old. Ms Marshall argued that her treatment was in breach of the Equal Treatment Directive.[20] The European Court of Justice held that different compulsory retiral ages for men and women were discriminatory. The Directive, having only vertical direct affect, only applied to public sector employees. The government therefore passed the 1986 Act to extend the same provisions to private sector workers.

Permissible discrimination

Not all acts of discrimination are unlawful. When sex is a 13.40
genuine occupational qualification, it is possible to discriminate lawfully.[21] A genuine occupational qualification may exist where:

(a) A man or woman is required for reasons of physiology or authenticity. An example would be a requirement for a female model for advertisement.
(b) The job needs to be held by one sex for reasons of decency or privacy. Examples include lavatory attendants and changing-room attendants.
(c) Where the job is residential, there is only single-sex sleeping and toilet accommodation and it would be unreasonable to expect the employer to provide additional facilities.
(d) The job is in a single-sex hospital, prison, or facility for persons requiring special care, attention and supervision, and it is reasonable for that job held by person of that sex.
(e) The job involves provision of personal services for welfare or education.
(f) The vacancy is for a post overseas and the laws or customs of that country are such that the duties could not be performed by a person of a particular sex.
(g) The job is one of two to be held by a married couple.

---

[19] [1986] I.R.L.R. 40.
[20] 76/207.
[21] Sex Discrimination Act 1975, s. 7.

An employer cannot plead that there is a genuine occupational qualification if he already has sufficient employees of that sex to perform the duties above.[22]

Exceptions to the 1975 Act

13.41 The protection of the Sex Discrimination Act does not extend to employment overseas.[23] There are also exceptions in relation to certain types of employment including: police, prison officers, and ministers of religion. Positive discrimination is permitted in order to redress imbalances.[24]

Remedies for sex discrimination

13.42 Actions under the 1975 Act are heard before an employment tribunal. There is no qualifying period or minimum number of hours. The claim must be made within three months of the prohibited act or omission unless the tribunal feels it is just and equitable to extend the limit.[25] If an applicant loses their case under U.K. law but then discovers that E.C. law is wider, they can bring their claim in the tribunal relying on E.C. law. Such a claim must be brought within a reasonable time of the clarification.[26] The remedies which may be granted include: an order declaring rights of parties, compensation and a recommendation that remedial action is taken within a certain period.[27]

Discrimination on Grounds of Race, Colour or Ethnic Origins

13.43 The Race Relations Act 1976 provides that it is unlawful to discriminate on grounds of race in employment, training, education, union membership, provision of goods and services and in disposal and management of housing and other premises. This Act is modelled closely on the Sex Discrimination Act 1975 and the concepts of direct and indirect discrimination, victimisation and genuine occupational qualifications are all included in the 1976

---

[22] See *Wylie v. Dee & Co. (Menswear) Ltd* [1978] I.R.L.R. 103; *Etam plc v. Rowan* [1989] I.R.L.R. 150.

[23] *Haughton v. Olau Lines (UK) Ltd* [1986] 1 W.L.R. 504; [1986] 2 All E.R. 47.

[24] Sex Discrimination Act 1975, s. 48. See *Kalanke v. Freie Hansestandt Bremen* [1995] I.R.L.R. 660.

[25] *ibid.* s. 76.

[26] *Methilhill Bowling Club v. Hunter* [1995] I.R.LR. 232.

[27] Sex Discrimination Act 1975, s. 65.

Act. The Act outlaws discrimination on the ground of colour, race, nationality or ethnic or national origins.[28] None of these is defined.

Direct discrimination

Direct discrimination occurs where persons are given less favourable treatment, or equal but segregated treatment, such as the provision of separate washing facilities. It will not amount to unlawful discrimination by an employer if workers segregate themselves and this is their choice, and has not been forced on them by the employer. An example of direct racial discrimination is the case of *King v. The Great Britain-China Centre.*[29] Ms King applied for job as deputy director at the China Centre but she was not interviewed. She had been born in China but brought up in the United Kingdom. She spoke Chinese and had spent three months travelling in China in the year prior to her application. There was no satisfactory explanation as to why she did not receive an interview, but evidence was shown which proved that no ethnic Chinese were interviewed although five had applied. Ms King's qualifications met the job requirements, and the centre had never employed an ethnic Chinese person. It was held there was direct discrimination.[30] 13.44

Indirect discrimination

Indirect discrimination on grounds of race, nationality or ethnic origin has four aspects: (i) there is a condition or requirement which is applied to all; (ii) the condition or requirement has a disproportionate effect on a racial group; (iii) the condition or requirement is not justifiable irrespective of race; and (iv) a member of the adversely affected racial group is unable to comply with the condition or requirement and this is to his detriment. 13.45

An example is the case of *J.H. Walker Ltd v. Hussain.*[31] Asian employees were disciplined for taking a day off work to mark the Muslim festival at the end of Ramadan. Muslim employees had previously been allowed to take time off for this festival but the employers had introduced a rule that no employees could have time off during the firm's busiest time, which fell around this

---

[28] Race Relations Act 1976, s. 3(1).

[29] [1991] I.R.L.R. 513.

[30] See also *Wilson v. T.B. Steelworks*, IDS Brief 150; *Showboat Entertainment Centre Ltd v. Owens* [1984] I.R.L.R. 7; *Burton v. De Vere Hotels* [1996] I.R.L.R. 596.

[31] [1996] I.R.L.R. 11.

festival. The employees asked the employers to reconsider but they refused even although the employees agreed to make up the lost working time. A large number of Asian workers took time off and all were issued with final written warnings. The court held that there was no direct discrimination against the workers as Muslims because Muslims do not constitute a racial group, but there was indirect discrimination against the Asian workers since they had suffered a detriment.

If the employer can prove justification then there will be no discrimination. Therefore in the case of *Panesar v. Nestle Co. Ltd*,[32] where a claim of indirect discrimination was brought against a rule prohibiting long hair, it was held that the rule was not unlawful because it was a condition justifiable in the interests of hygiene and safety. It had been argued that the rule against long hair indirectly discriminated against Sikhs in that a smaller proportion of Sikhs could comply with it compared to members of other racial groups.

Racial grounds

13.46 The Act defines racial grounds as: colour, race, nationality, ethnic or national origins.[33] National origin includes race and citizenship. Uncertainty has arisen from time to time with regard to the distinction between an ethnic group, who are protected from discrimination and a religious group who are afforded no protection under U.K. law. The case of *Mandla v. Dowell Lee*[34] hinged upon whether Sikhs were an ethnic or a religious group. It was held that an ethnic can be wider than a single race. Sikhs did constitute an ethnic group and were therefore a racial group for the purposes of the 1976 Act. This means that some, but not all religious groups will come within the protection of the Act. For a group to be protected it should have shared characteristics such as: common geographical origin; descent from common ancestors; common culture and social customs; long shared history distinguishable from other groups; common language, literature and religion; be a minority group within a larger community.

A common religion on its own is not enough to qualify as an ethnic group, the other factors must be present. So Sikhs and Jews may be protected, but Catholics and Muslims probably are not.

---

32 1980] I.R.L.R. 64.
33 Race Relations Act 1976, s. 3.
34 [1983] I.R.L.R. 209.

Racial discrimination in employment

The Race Relations Act makes it unlawful to discriminate against a person before he is in employment as regards matters such as the arrangements for interview.[35] It is also unlawful to offer less favourable terms to a person on the grounds of his race. A person must not be refused employment because of his race. Once a person is in employment discrimination on racial grounds is unlawful as regards opportunities for promotion, training and transfer. It is unlawful to dismiss someone on grounds of his race or subject him to detriment. An employer may insist on employing a person of a particular race where there is a genuine occupational qualification such as authenticity in an ethnic restaurant or where the holder of a job provides personal services to promote welfare of persons of the same racial group, such as a community relations officer.[36] The remedies are similar to those for sex discrimination. 13.47

Commission for Racial Equality

The Commission for Racial Equality was established by the Race Relations Act. It replaced the Race Relations Board, a statutory body which had no powers to investigate allegations of discrimination on racial grounds. The Commission for Racial Equality can assist claimants in the preparation of cases. It also has the power to intitiate investigations, provided that it has a reasonable suspicion that acts of discrimination have taken place.[37] There must be a strong reason to suspect that discrimination is occurring.[38] The Home Secretary may direct the Commission to carry out an investigation. If the Commission finds that discrimination has occurred, it has powers to issue a non-discrimination notice. For a period of five years from the issue of such a notice the Commission may seek an interdict to prevent any recurrence of discrimination. 13.48

Discrimination on Grounds of Disability

Disabled persons have not been protected against discrimination until relatively recently. The Disability Discrimination Act 1995 aims to end discrimination against disabled persons in employment, provision of goods, facilities and services, and in the disposal of premises. The Act allows individuals with a disability to seek 13.49

---

[35] s. 4.

[36] Race Relations Act 1976, s. 5.

[37] *R. v. Commission for Racial Equality, ex p. Hillingdon Council* [1982] A.C. 868.

[38] *Commission for Racial Equality v. Prestige Group plc* [1984] 1 W.L.R. 335.

unlimited compensation if they can establish unjustified discrimination on the part of an employer. The provisions relating to employment do not apply to employers with less than 20 employees.

Disability is defined as a physical or mental impairment which has substantial and long-term adverse effect on a person's ability to carry out normal day-to-day activities.[39] Physical impairment includes sensory impairment and severe disfigurement. Mental impairment is defined as mental illness which is 'clinically well recognised'. This includes mental disorders such as schizophrenia and manic depression. Protection against discrimination is not extended to people with anti-social disorders. Therefore it is not unlawful to discriminate against psychopaths, paedophiles and those addicted to tobacco, alcohol or drugs. Discrimination against a person whose disfigurement is self-inflicted by tattoos or body piercing is also not unlawful.

In order to qualify as a disability in terms of the Act an impairment must have long-term effects. It must be of a type which will last for 12 months or more. Persons with terminal illnesses who are expected to die within 12 months are, however, protected from discrimination. Conditions which recur, such as epilepsy or are progressive, such as cancer or multiple sclerosis are covered. The impairment must affect a person's normal daily activities. These include the ability to lift, mobility, manual dexterity, continence, speech, hearing, eyesight, memory or ability to concentrate, learn or understand.

Discrimination will occur if the person is treated less favourably than a non-disabled person and such treatment is unjustified. Consequently direct discrimination can be lawful if the person who acted in a discriminatory way can justify it. One example of this arose in the case of *Rose v. Bouchet*.[40] This case was an appeal against a sheriff court decision that there had been no unlawful discrimination. R contended that B had discriminated against him by refusing to let premises to him. B claimed that the refusal to let the premises was because the access was unsafe for a blind person. It was held that, although B had prima facie acted unlawfully by treating R less favourably on account of his disability, his treatment of R was justified if, in B's opinion, such treatment was necessary to avoid endangering R's safety. Evidence of the facts which gave

---

39 Disability Discrimination Act 1995, s. 1.

40 1999 G.W.D. 20–958.

rise to such an opinion could be considered in order to establish whether the belief that discriminatory treatment was justified was reasonable. This case is interesting because it does not set an objective standard for justifiable discrimination. Instead it establishes that discrimination will not be unlawful if the person who is discriminating believes, on reasonable grounds, that the discrimination is justified.

It is unlawful to discriminate against a disabled person in relation to recruitment, training, terms and conditions of employment or promotion.[41] The Act does not apply to persons working overseas, or to police, armed forces prison officers, fire-fighters. Employers are under a duty to take reasonable steps to make adjustments to any arrangements or physical features of premises which place disabled person at a substantial disadvantage. For instance an employer could install ramps for wheelchairs, and obtain special equipment or allow the work to be carried out on the ground floor. The Act only requires that reasonable steps be taken. This means that the courts will take account of the cost involved, the financial resources of employer and the amount of disruption in making the adjustment. The duty on employers is not a general one. It will apply only in individual cases. There is no express prohibition on indirect discrimination. The government argued that this was unnecessary because the terms of the prohibition on direct discrimination are so wide. Victimisation of a person who has made a complaint is unlawful. The remedies are similar to those available in cases of discrimination on grounds of race or sex. The tribunal can order a declaration of the parties' rights, compensation and a recommendation that the employer takes action.

Freedom of Movement

Article 61 of the E.C. Treaty provides that the Council, within five 13.50
years from the coming into force of the Treaty of Amsterdam, must adopt measures aimed at ensuring the free movement of persons, in accordance with Article 14. Article 14 provides that the internal market shall comprise an area without internal frontiers in which the free movement of goods, persons, services and capital is ensured. The Council will also adopt measures to deal with directly related matters such as external border controls, asylum and immigration and provisions to prevent and combat crime. Special provisions relate to Denmark, Ireland and the United Kingdom

---

[41] Disability Discrimination Act 1995, s. 4.

who have all formally derogated from Article 14 of the Treaty because of their special geographical boundaries. The Treaty of Amsterdam reaffirms the concept of European citizenship and states that every citizen of the Union shall have the right to move and reside freely within the territory of the Member States, subject to the limitations and conditions laid down in this Treaty and by the measures adopted to give it effect.[42] Residents of Member States do not have an unqualified right to enter and remain in the United Kingdom. Although there is free movement into the United Kingdom for the purposes of employment this does not confer unlimited freedom in relation to residence.[43] If a person has entered a Member State in order to seek work but has failed to find work after six months, the Member State is justified in requiring him to leave the country unless he can demonstrate that he is actively seeking work and has a real chance of finding a post.

---

[42] E.C. Treaty, Art. 18.
[43] *The Times*, Jan. 26, 1996.

CHAPTER 14

PROTECTION OF HUMAN RIGHTS

EUROPEAN CONVENTION ON HUMAN RIGHTS AND FUNDAMENTAL FREEDOMS

The U.K. government is a party to the European Convention on Human Rights which guarantees that certain rights freedoms and privileges will be enjoyed by individuals within States which adhere to the Convention. The European Convention on Human Rights was concluded under the auspices of the Council of Europe in November 1950. It was the first international human rights instrument to provide for individual remedies against States. The United Kingdom signed the Convention on November 4, 1950, and ratified it, on March 8, 1951. It came into force in 1953. 14.01

PRINCIPLES OF THE EUROPEAN CONVENTION ON HUMAN RIGHTS

The United Kingdom is obliged by Article 1 of the Convention to protect the rights therein. The Convention is to be interpreted: "in good faith in accordance with the ordinary meaning to be given to the terms of the treaty in their context and in the light of its object and purpose".[1] 14.02

PRINCIPLES OF INTERPRETATION

Purpose of the Convention

Any interpretation of the terms of the Convention must give consideration to the object and purpose of the Convention. As it is first and foremost an instrument for the protection of individual human beings its provisions should be interpreted so as to make its 14.03

---

[1] Vienna Convention on the Law of Treaties, Art. 31.

safeguards practical and effective.[2] This does not mean that there will be no restrictions whatsoever on individual rights or liberties since restrictions will often be justified. The legitimacy of each restriction on individual rights is considered on its own merits.

Uniform meaning for Convention terms

14.04 The Court of Human Rights interprets terms used in the Convention in a manner independent of their meaning under particular national laws. This is in order to secure consistent application regardless of the national legal systems from which a case originates. The terminology used under national law is taken it into account for clarification.

Convention as a dynamic and evolving instrument

The Court of Human Rights has repeatedly stressed that the Convention is a living instrument. It must be interpreted in the light of present-day conditions.[3] This means that the original negotiations for the development of the Convention and the original statements of intent are rarely taken into account. As the Convention is a living instrument the Court of Human Rights accepts that the effect of the Convention may change over time. The Court of Human Rights is aware of developing standards in human rights protection and its decisions take account of these changes in standards.

STATUS OF THE EUROPEAN CONVENTION OF HUMAN RIGHTS IN THE UNITED KINGDOM PRIOR TO THE HUMAN RIGHTS ACT 1998

14.05 The European Convention on Human Rights will not be incorporated into the domestic law of the United Kingdom until the Human Rights Act 1998 is in force. There has, however, been a gradual increase in the willingness of judges to regard it as a matter which should have been taken into account in the course of administrative decision-making. The English courts have led the way in this approach and the decisions of the Scottish courts in recent years have followed the same trend. In the absence of incorporation into U.K. law, the circumstances in which the

---

[2] *Loizidou v. Turkey* (A/310) (1995) 20 E.H.R.R. 99, para. 72.

[3] See *Loizidou v. Turkey*, above.

Convention should be taken into account are, however, limited to the following categories.

Where legislation is ambiguous or the law is uncertain

In *R. v. Secretary of State for the Home Department, ex parte* 14.06
Brind,[4] it was held that where a statute is clear and unambiguous international principles and standards, such as Convention rights may not be relevant. However, regard ought to be had to the Convention as an aid to interpretation. A presumption should be applied that Parliament must have intended to legislate in accordance with the Convention. This case was an unsuccessful challenge to the decision to ban broadcasts by IRA figureheads which featured their own voices.[5] A similar presumption was not accepted by the Scottish courts until 1996 when, in the case of *Re AMT (Known as AC)*,[6] Lord President Hope took the opportunity to clarify the extent to which regard should be given to the European Convention on Human Rights in Scots law. The case was an appeal against a decision by the Lord Ordinary refusing to allow an adoption of a child by a homosexual man. It was held that when legislation is found to be ambiguous, Parliament is to be presumed to have legislated in conformity with the convention and not in conflict with it. Lord Hope observed:

> "It is now an integral part of the general principles of European Community Law that fundamental human rights must be protected and that one of the sources to which regard may be made for an expression of rights is international treaties for the protection of rights on which member states have collaborated or of which they are signatories."

Where legislation has been passed to bring the domestic law into line with the Convention

In the case of *R. v. Secretary of State for the Home Department, ex* 14.07
parte Norney[7] it was held that, where legislation has been passed with the specific purpose of securing conformity with Convention standards in an aspect of domestic law, the court should have regard to the relevant provisions of the convention. The case

---

[4] [1991] A.C. 696.
[5] See also *Att.-Gen. v. Guardian Newspapers Ltd (No. 2)* [1990] 1 A.C. 109.
[6] 1996 S.C.L.R. 897.
[7] (1995) 7 Admin.L.R. 681.

involved referral of prisoners serving life sentences to the parole board. In considering the exercise of the discretion to refer prisoners by a government minister it would be perverse to ignore the relevant provisions of the convention.

Where administrative decisions affect fundamental rights

14.08 Where administrators are making decisions affecting fundamental rights and freedoms of individuals it has been held that the European Convention on Human Rights is a relevant consideration which the administrator should take into account before making a decision.[8] This did not mean that public authorities are bound to exercise their discretion consistently with the Convention only that the procedures followed should show that the Convention rights have been taken into consideration.[9]

SUBSTANTIVE RIGHTS

14.09 The rights guaranteed under the Convention are traditional individual rights. The language of the Convention fits in well with the British philosophy of freedom from unjustified interference rather than incontrovertible rights such as those which are found in some written constitutions. The term "Convention rights" means the rights and fundamental freedoms set out in: (a) Articles 2 to 12 and 14 of the Convention, (b) Articles 1 to 3 of the First Protocol, and (c) Articles 1 and 2 of the Sixth Protocol; as read with Articles 16 to 18 of the Convention.

The Articles

Article 1—Responsibility of the State

14.10 Article 1 simply states that the High Contracting Parties (*i.e.* the States) shall secure to everyone within jurisdiction the rights and freedoms defined in the Convention. The state is therefore not only responsible for actions taken by and on behalf of the government but has a duty to provide adequate protection for the citizens from any violations of the Convention. This includes an obligation to ensure that the substantive laws and legal procedures

---

[8] *R. v. Ministry of Defence, ex p. Smith* [1996] Q.B. 517, CA.

[9] *R. v. Horseferry Road Magistrates' Court, ex p. Bennet* [1994] A.C. 42; *Britton v. Secretary of State for the Environment*, Co/1348/96 and Co/1349/96, October 24, 1996.

are effective in preventing conduct harmful to others. After the stepfather of a nine-year-old boy had had been acquitted of assault, the child applied to the European Court of Human Rights, contending that his treatment constituted a violation of the European Convention on Human Rights 1950, Art. 3. It was held that there had been a breach of Article 3 because the child had suffered severe beatings. As to whether the U.K. Government should be held responsible for the ill-treatment the child received, Article 1 read with Article 3, demanded that contracting States adopt measures to ensure the protection of those within their jurisdiction and prevent them from suffering torture or inhuman or degrading treatment or punishment. Children and other vulnerable people deserve particular protection in the form of effective deterrence. The acquittal of the stepfather demonstrated that English law as it stood failed to provide adequate protection for children.[10]

Article 2—Right to life

> "1. Everyone's right to life shall be protected by law. No one shall be deprived of his life intentionally save in the execution of a sentence of a court following his conviction of a crime for which this penalty is provided by law. 14.11
>
> 2. Deprivation of life shall not be regarded as inflicted in contravention of this Article when it results from the use of force which is no more than absolutely necessary:
>
> (a) in defence of any person from unlawful violence;
> (b) in order to effect a lawful arrest or to prevent the escape of a person lawfully detained;
> (c) in action lawfully taken for the purpose of quelling a riot or insurrection."

This Article does not render all impositions of the death penalty unlawful. The death penalty for serious crimes may not be in violation of the Convention provided that the procedures for conviction are fair and there is no torture or degrading treatment in the manner of implementing the sentence. Whether euthenasia would be a violation of the Convention is not absolutely clear but it appears that it would be a breach of the Convention for a State to sanction mercy killing. There are arguments put forward to the effect that legalised abortion is in contravention of Article 2 but

---

[10] *A v. U.K.* [1998] 2 F.L.R. 959; [1998] 3 F.C.R. 597; (1999) 27 E.H.R.R. 611; [1998] Fam. Law 733; (1998) 5 B.H.C.C. 137; [1998] H.R.C.D. 870; [1998] Crim. L.R. 892.

the domestic law of the United Kingdom has consistently ruled that the legal protection of the person commences at birth.[11]

The exceptions to Article 2 excuse action in violent situations from which death unintentionally results. The use of plastic bullets, which are not designed to kill, has been held not to be a contravention of the convention.[12] In the case of *McGann, Farrell and Savage v. United Kingdom*,[13] the European Court of Human Rights ruled that the shooting of three Irish Republican Army members in Gibraltar did not violate Article 2. The action was justified, in the light of the information available to the security forces at the time, to prevent acts of terrorism. The action taken was, however, more than absolutely necessary. The operation should have been more tightly controlled so that the suspected terrorists were not killed. In order to be lawful the action must be proportionate to the circumstances in each case.

Article 3—Prohibition of torture

14.12 "No one shall be subject to torture or to inhuman or degrading treatment or punishment."

This Article protects people from two different types of treatment. Torture involves intense physical suffering and a probability of actual bodily injury. Inhuman or degrading treatment may involve mental or physical suffering and is the sort of treatment which arouses feelings of fear, anguish and inferiority. In the case of *Ireland v. United Kingdom*[14] it was held that the treatment of suspected terrorists in Northern Ireland amounted to inhuman and degrading treatment. Had the treatment resulted in more intense suffering it may have amounted to torture. An application to the European Court of Human Rights on the basis of a breach of Article 3 was made in the case of *Campbell and Cozens v. United Kingdom*.[15] Two mothers claimed that the use of the tawse in Scottish schools was a degrading punishment. The court rejected the argument that the use of the tawse was inhuman and degrading but held that there had been a violation of the Convention on other grounds.[16]

---

[11] See *Paton v. U.K.* (1980) 3 E.H.R.R. 408.

[12] *Stewart v. U.K.* (1985) 7 E.H.R.R. 453.

[13] (1995) 21 E.H.R.R. 97.

[14] (1976) 2 E.H.R.R. 25.

[15] (1982) 4 E.H.R.R. 165.

[16] See Protocol 1, Art. 2. See also *Costello-Roberts v. U.K.* (A/247-C) (1995) 19 E.H.R.R. 112; *Tyrer v. U.K.* (1980) 2 E.H.R.R. 1.

Article 4—Prohibition of slavery and forced labour

"1. No one shall be held in slavery or servitude. 14.13

2. No one shall be required to perform forced or compulsory labour.

3. For the purpose of this Article the term 'forced or compulsory labour' shall not include:

(a) any work required to be done in the ordinary course of detention imposed according to the provisions of Article 5 of this convention or during conditional release from such detention;

(b) any service of military character or, in case of conscientious objectors in countries where these are recognised, service exacted instead of compulsory military service;

(c) any service exacted in case of emergency or calamity threatening the life or well-being of the community;

(d) any work or service which forms part of normal civic obligations."

Contraventions of this provision are unlikely to arise in modern democratic states and so there is little case law. In the case of *Schmidt v. Germany*,[17] Schmidt challenged the rule that German men were required to serve as firemen or pay a fire service levy instead. The same obligation was not placed upon women. He claimed that he was the victim of discrimination on the ground of sex contrary to the European Convention on Human Rights 1950, Art. 14 in conjunction with Article 4(3)(d). It was held that compulsory fire service was one of the normal civic obligations within Article 4(3)(d). The obligation to pay a contribution in lieu of service also came within Article 4(3)(d). There had, however, been a breach of Article 14 as the difference in treatment between men and women was discriminatory.

Article 5—Right to liberty and security

"1. Everyone has the right to liberty and security of person. 14.14
No one shall be deprived of his liberty save in the following cases and in accordance with a procedure prescribed by law:

(a) the lawful detention of a person after conviction by a competent court;

---

[17] (1994) 18 E.H.R.R. 513.

(b) the lawful arrest or detention of a person for non-compliance with the lawful order of a court or in order to secure the fulfilment of any obligation prescribed by law;
(c) the lawful arrest or detention of a person effected for the purpose of bringing him before the competent legal authority on reasonable suspicion of having committed an offence or when it is reasonably considered necessary to prevent his committing an offence or fleeing after having done so;
(d) the detention of a minor by lawful order for the purpose of educational supervision or his lawful detention for the purpose of bringing him before the competent legal authority;
(e) the lawful detention of persons for the prevention of the spreading of infectious diseases, of persons of unsound mind, alcoholics, drug addicts or vagrants;
(f) the lawful arrest or detention of a person to prevent his effecting an unauthorised entry into the country or of a person against whom action is being taken with a view to deportation or extradition."

Everyone who is arrested shall be informed promptly, in a language which he understands, of the reasons for his arrest and any charges against him. Everyone arrested or detained on suspicion of having committed a crime shall be brought promptly before a judge or other officer authorised by law to exercise judicial power and shall be entitled to trial within a reasonable time or to release pending trial. Release may be conditioned by guarantees to appear for trial. Everyone who is deprived of liberty by arrest or detention shall be entitled to take proceedings by which the lawfulness of his detention shall be decided speedily by a court and his release ordered if the detention is not lawful. Everyone who has been the victim of arrest or detention in contravention of the provisions of this Article shall have an enforceable right to compensation.

This Article has given rise to a great number of cases, partly because the complexity of the Article itself has led to problems of interpretation. The difficulties have been caused by the need to draft an Article which will be applicable across a range of criminal jurisdictions. In *Murray v. United Kingdom*[18] it was held that there had not been a violation of Article 5 when a person had been detained in Northern Ireland by soldiers who suspected that they

---

[18] (1995) 19 E.H.R.R. 193.

had grounds of arrest. There was a delay of several hours between the time of the arrest and the time when the applicant was informed of the reason for the arrest but this was held to be too small a delay to amount to a breach of Article 5. In *Brogan v. United Kingdom*[19] detention of up to seven days, at the discretion of the Home Secretary, was held to be a violation of Article 5.

Article 5(e) permits the lawful detention of persons of unsound mind. Such detention must be strictly within the bounds of the relevant statute. In the case of *Winterwerp v. Netherlands*[20] the European Court of Human Rights stressed that Article 5 could not be taken as permitting the detention of a person simply because his views or behaviour deviated from the norms prevailing in a particular society. The detention must be lawful. No one may be confined as a person of "unsound mind" in the absence of medical evidence establishing that his mental state is such as to justify his compulsory hospitalisation. 14.15

Release from detention should only be refused if there is medical evidence establishing that continued compulsory hospitalisation is necessary or appropriate. In Scotland, until this year, under the Mental Health (Scotland) Act 1984 compulsory detention was only permitted where a person was suffering from a treatable mental illness and was receiving treatment. It has been held that patients must be released if they are not receiving treatment. Detention to protect the rest of society from a dangerous person is not lawful under that Act. In the case of *R. v. Secretary of State for Scotland*[21] a patient who had been convicted of culpable homicide, and who had a psychopathic personality, applied for discharge from hospital under section 64(1)(a) of the Mental Health (Scotland) Act 1984 on the ground that it was no longer appropriate for him to be detained for treatment as he suffered from a persistent mental disorder which was not treatable. The case eventually came before the House of Lords on appeal. The House of Lords held that a sheriff was bound to grant an application for discharge if treatment was not likely to "alleviate or prevent a deterioration of his condition". In this case, there was agreement among experts that medical treatment was not likely to lead to a cure but the treatability test was wide enough to include things other than medication and psychiatric treatment. The fact that the structured and controlled environment of the

---

19 (1989) 11 E.H.R.R. 117.

20 (1979–80) 2 E.H.R.R. 387, ECHR.

21 1999 S.C. (H.L.) 17; 1999 S.L.T. 279; 1999 S.C.L.R. 74; [1999] 2 W.L.R. 28; [1999] 1 All E.R. 481; (1999) 96(4) L.S.G. 37.

hospital resulted in an improvement in R's anger management could be considered as amounting to treatment. His continued detention was therefore lawful. This approach was not followed in the sheriff court case of *Ruddle v. Secretary of State for Scotland.*[22] The sheriff ordered the release of a potentially dangerous patient because his condition was not being alleviated by treatment in a secure institution.[23] The Scottish Parliament has now legislated to clarify the legal grounds on which persons of unsound mind may be detained.[24]

Article 6—Right to a fair trial

14.16 "1. In the determination of his civil rights and obligations and of any criminal charge against him, everyone is entitled to a fair and public hearing within a reasonable time by an independent and impartial tribunal established by law. Judgment shall be pronounced publicly but the press and public may be excluded from all or part of the trial in the interests of morals, public order or national security in a democratic society, where the interests of juveniles or the protection of the private life of the parties so require, or to the extent strictly necessary in the opinion of the court in special circumstances where publicity would prejudice the interests of justice.

2. Everyone charged with a criminal offence shall be presumed innocent until proved guilty according to law.

3. Everyone charged with a criminal offence has the following minimum rights:

(a) to be informed promptly, in a language which he understands and in detail, of the nature and cause of the accusation against him;
(b) to have adequate time and facilities for the preparation of his defence;
(c) to defend himself in person or through legal assistance of his own choosing or, if he has not sufficient means to pay for legal assistance, to be given it free when the interests of justice so require;
(d) to examine or have examined witnesses against him and to obtain the attendance and examination of

---

22 Lanark Sh. Ct, Aug. 2, 1999.

23 See also *Johnson v. U.K.* (1999) 27 E.H.R.R. 296; (1998) 40 B.M.L.R. 1; [1998] H.R.C.D. 41.

24 Mental Health (Public Safety and Appeals) (Scotland) Act 1999.

witnesses on his behalf under the same condition as witnesses against him;

(e) to have the free assistance of an interpreter if he cannot understand or speak the language used in court."

This Article applies to a wide range of judicial proceedings including cases before tribunals. It does not apply to decisions which are administrative rather than judicial. In *Lithgow v. United Kingdom*,[25] the court held that the shareholders in shipbuilding companies nationalised by the Aircraft and Shipbuilding Industries Act 1977 were entitled to rely on Article 6(1) in questioning the provision made by the Act for assessing compensation, since the right to compensation derived from owning shares was undoubtedly a civil right. However, the Court held that Article 6(1) did not guarantee shareholders an absolute right to a court for the determination of the right to compensation: The arbitration tribunal set up by the 1977 Act met the requirements of Article 6(1).

A failure to provide a forum for adjudication may amount to a breach of Article 6. In *W v. United Kingdom*,[26] it was held that there had been a breach of Article 6 as the procedures for parents to appeal against the decisions of local authorities were inadequate. The Court considered that this was a domain where, despite the difficult discretionary decisions to be made by the authorities, there was a great need for protection against arbitrary interference with parental rights. The decision-making process must ensure that the views and interests of parents were made known and taken into account by the local authorities. This was not a situation in which it was sufficient for an aggrieved parent to institute judicial review proceedings since the reviewing court would not be able to examine the merits of the local authority's decision on parental access. What was required by Article 6(1) in relation to the rights in question was that parents must be able to have the decision taken by a local authority with regard to access reviewed by a tribunal with jurisdiction to examine the merits of the matter. The powers of the courts in the United Kingdom did not extend to this and a breach of Article 6(1) had occurred.

In criminal cases it is important that trials are held within a 14.17
reasonable time after a person is charged because the accused may be being held in custody. However, even where the accused is at

---

[25] (1986) 8 E.H.R.R. 329.

[26] (1987) 10 E.H.R.R. 29.

liberty excessive delays may deny a person their right to a fair trial. The case of *Dougan v. United Kingdom*[27] related to a delay of more than 12 years. Dougan was arrested in May 1981 and charged with the attempted murder of his wife. He failed to appear at his trial diet in November 1981 and a warrant was issued for his arrest. In 1991 Dougan wrote to the procurator fiscal to ask whether there were still proceedings outstanding against him. He was told that there were no proceedings outstanding. The police were not informed of this inquiry and in 1992 Dougan was arrested. In the course of his trial a preliminary challenge was made to the proceedings on the ground of delay. This was rejected by the trial judge on the ground that there had been no oppression. No appeal was taken against that decision. Dougan pleaded guilty to assault and was sentenced to 240 hours community service and fined £1,000 for his failure to appear at the original trial. He brought an action before the European Commission on Human Rights claiming that there had been a breach of Article 6. The Crown invoked Article 26 of the Convention arguing that Dougan had failed to exhaust all domestic remedies as he had not appealed against the trial judge's decision. The Commission concluded that there had been a violation of Article 6(1) of the Convention. There had been several incidents of poor administration by the procurator fiscal's office. Dougan had been informed in 1991 that there were no outstanding proceedings against him. The reasonable time prescribed by Article 6(1) of the Convention had been exceeded. The application was admissible in terms of Article 26. The obligation to exhaust domestic remedies is limited to making normal use of those remedies which are likely to be effective. An individual is not obliged to pursue a remedy if it can be shown that it does not have a minimal prospect of success. Dougan was awarded damages of £2,000.

Article 6 also requires that those who need it are provided with legal assistance. In the cases of *Boner v. United Kingdom* and *Maxwell v. United Kingdom*,[28] it was held that there had been a violation of the right to a fair trial,[29] specifically the right to legal aid. Boner and Maxwell were both convicted in separate trials of offences of violence and given sentences of eight years and five years respectively. Despite the fact that both persons were having difficulty finding counsel who were willing to represent them it was held that the failure to award legal aid was a violation of the

---

27 1997 S.C.C.R. 56, ECHR.

28 (1995) 19 E.H.R.R. 246.

29 Art. 6(3).

Convention. The interests of justice required Boner and Maxwell to be granted legal aid bearing in mind: (i) the nature of the proceedings; (ii) the wide powers of the High Court; (iii) the limited capacity of an unrepresented appellant to put forward a legal argument; and particularly (iv) the importance of the issue at stake in view of the length of the sentences.

Article 7—Freedom from retroactive criminal convictions or penalties

> "1. No one shall be held guilty of an offence on account of any act or omission which did not constitute a criminal offence under national or international law at the time when it was committed. Nor shall a heavier penalty be imposed than the one that was applicable at the time the criminal offence was committed. 14.18
>
> 2. This Article shall not prejudice the trial and punishment of any person for any act or omission which, at the time when it was committed, was criminal according to the general principles of law recognised by civilised nations."

This Article is intended to protect individuals from arbitrary prosecution. It does not mean that the law cannot be developed by judicial interpretation. In the case of *SW v. United Kingdom*,[30] two men who had been convicted on charges of rape and attempted rape respectively upon their wives applied to the ECHR, arguing that the United Kingdom decisions violated Article 7 of the European Convention on Human Rights 1950, because at the date of their actions in 1989 and 1990 respectively, marital rape was not a criminal offence. It was held that the purpose of Article 7 was to ensure that no one should be subject to arbitrary prosecution, but that did not prevent the retrospective application of the criminal law provided that the development of criminal liability was clearly defined and foreseeable. At the time the two men committed the acts, the Government and Law Commission had provisionally recommended the immunity from prosecution for rape within marriage and the adaptation of the existing offence could be reasonably foreseen. The national courts' decisions did not violate Article 7 as they continued a perceptible evolution of case law which had reached the stage, at the dates of the applicants' actions, where they could have been found guilty of rape.

---

30 (A/355-B) [1996] 1 F.L.R. 434; (1996) 21 E.H.R.R. 363; [1996] Fam. Law 275.

Article 8—Right to respect for private and family life, one's home and correspondence

14.19 "1. Everyone has the right to respect for his private and family life, his home and his correspondence.

2. There shall be no interference by a public authority with the exercise of this right except which as is in accordance with the law and is necessary in a democratic society in the interests of national security, public safety or the economic well-being of the country, for the prevention of disorder or crime, for the protection of health or morals, or for the protection of the rights and freedoms of others."

This Article protects the rights of the individual in two distinct ways. They are entitled to respect for their private life and relationships. They are also entitled to privacy and non-intervention by the state. The right to privacy is subject to several exceptions and the interception of communications is permitted in a wide range of circumstances. There must, however, be clear, specific unambiguous legal authority for any invasion of privacy. In *Malone v. United Kingdom*[31] it was held that Article 8 had been violated by intercepting telephone conversations without specific legal authorisation. The law regarding interception of communications was unclear at the time. It has now been clarified by the Interception of Communications Act 1985. Whether the law should protect the interception of communications within private premises was considered in the case of *Halford v. United Kingdom*.[32] Telephone conversations of Alison Halford, Assistant Chief Constable in Merseyside, were intercepted by senior officers. She applied to the European Court of Human Rights, alleging a breach of her right to privacy, as guaranteed under Article 8. It was ruled that the convention had been violated and she was awarded compensation of £10,000. The Government argued unsuccessfully that interception of communications within government property was not a violation of the convention.

The concept of family life is not restricted to situations where there is a traditional family in which the parents are married to each other. It is the right to live as a family or to have personal relationships which the convention aims to protect. In a case before the European Court of Human Rights, the father and mother of a young child, who were not married at the time of his birth,

---

[31] (1984) 7 E.H.R.R. 14.

[32] [1997] I.R.L.R. 471, (1997) 24 E.H.R.R. 253; (1997) 3 B.H.R.C. 31; [1998] Crim. L.R. 753; (1997) 94(27) L.S.G. 24.

complained that their rights under the European Convention on Human Rights 1950, Arts. 6(1) and 8 had been violated when they had been denied access to social reports, during care proceedings in respect of the child, who had been taken into care. Children's hearings took a number of decisions concerning custody and access arrangements eventually freed the child for adoption. The parents had married by this time. The European Court of Human Rights held that the failure to give the mother access to the social reports was a breach of Article 6(1). Article 8 had been violated in respect of the right to respect for family life as there was evidence that the parents led a joint family life and acted together in their efforts to gain custody of the child.[33] In the case of *Dudgeon v. United Kingdom*[34] it was held that legislation in Northern Ireland which criminalised homosexual activities between consenting adult males was in breach of Article 8. The European Court of Human Rights has recently ruled that the ban on homosexuals serving in the British armed forces is in contravention of Article 8.

Article 9—Freedom of thought, conscience and religion

> "1. Everyone has the right to freedom of thought, conscience and religion; this right includes freedom to change his religion or belief and freedom, either alone or in community with others and in public or private, to manifest his religion and belief, in worship, teaching, practice and observance. 14.20
>
> 2. Freedom to manifest one's religion or beliefs shall be subject only to such limitations as are prescribed by law and are necessary in a democratic society in the interests of public safety, for the protection of public order, health or morals, or for the protection of the rights and freedoms of others."

There have been very few cases concerning breaches of Article 9. Laws prohibiting attempts to persuade others to join a religious group have been held to contravene Article 9. Jehovah's witnesses who have been fined for entering peoples' homes and attempting to recruit new members have applied successfully to the European Court of Human Rights. The court has held that freedom of religion includes the right to try and convince one's neighbour, provided that the means by which this is achieved are not improper.[35]

---

[33] *McMichael v. U.K.* [1995] 2 F.C.R. 718; (1995) 20 E.H.R.R. 205; [1995] Fam. Law 478.

[34] (1982) 4 E.H.R.R. 149.

[35] *Kokkinakis v. Greece* (1994) 17 E.H.R.R. 397.

Article 10—Freedom of expression

14.21 "1. Everyone has the right to freedom of expression. This right shall include freedom to hold opinions and to receive and impart information and ideas without interference by public authority and regardless of frontiers. This Article shall not prevent States from requiring the licensing of broadcasting, television or cinema enterprises.

2. The exercise of these freedoms, since it carries with it duties and responsibilities, may be subject to such formalities, conditions, restrictions, or penalties as are prescribed by law and are necessary in a democratic society, in the interests of national security, territorial integrity or public safety, for the prevention of disorder or crime, for the protection of health or morals, for the protection of the reputation or rights of others, for preventing the disclosure of information received in confidence, or for maintaining the authority and impartiality of the judiciary."

It was hoped by those in favour of freedom of information legislation in the United Kingdom, that the European Court on Human Rights would interpret Article 10 as requiring legislation to implement the rights. However, two cases decided by the Court, *Leander v. Sweden*[36]; and *Gaskin v. United Kingdom*,[37] found that Article 10 was limited to the right of a willing provider of information to communicate it, and did not imply a public right of access to government information.

In *Handyside v. United Kingdom*, the court said:

"Freedom of expression constitutes one of the essential foundations of a society, one of the basic conditions for its progress and for the development of every man. Subject to paragraph 2 of Article 10, it is applicable not only to 'information' or 'ideas' that are favourable received and regarded as inoffensive but also to those that offend, shock or disturb the state or any sector of the population. Such are the demands of that pluaralism, tolerance and broadmindedness without which there is no 'democratic society'".[38]

Freedom of expression has given rise to several cases under the Convention. In the case of *Sunday Times v. United Kingdom*,[39] it

---

[36] (1987) 9 E.H.H.R. 433.
[37] (1989) 11 E.H.H.R. 402.
[38] (1976) 1 E.H.R.R. 737, para. 49.
[39] (1979) 2 E.H.R.R. 245.

was held that the law of contempt of court in relation to publications as stated in the House of Lords in *Attorney-General v. Times Newspapers*[40] was in breach of Article 10. The United Kingdom was rather grudging in its approach to changing the law within the United Kingdom in order to secure compliance with Article 10. The Contempt of Court Act 1981 made only the minimum provision which was necessary to secure conformity with the Article. In *Goodwin v. United Kingdom*,[41] it was held that the United Kingdom had once again gone too far and had restrained proper news-gathering activities when a journalist was convicted for contempt of court when he refused to reveal his sources. The Court held in the case of *The Observer, The Guardian and the Sunday Times v. United Kingdom*[42] that the continuance in force of interim interdicts prohibiting press coverage of the allegations of malpractice within the British intelligence services made in the *Spycatcher* novel was in breach of Article 10. The interdicts could not be justified on grounds of protection of national security when the book had been published widely throughout the rest of the world.

Article 11—Freedom of assembly and association

> "1. Everyone has the right to freedom of peaceful assembly and to freedom of association with others, including the right to form and join trade unions for the protection of interests. 14.22
>
> 2. No restrictions shall be placed on the exercise of these rights other than such as are prescribed by law and are necessary in a democratic society, in the interests of national security, or public safety, for the prevention of disorder or crime, for the protection of health or morals, for the protection of the rights and freedoms of others.
>
> This Article shall not prevent the imposition of lawful restrictions on the exercise of these rights by members of the armed forces, of the police, or of the administration of the State."[43]

This Article only protects assemblies which are peaceful. There is no violation of the Article if the state regulates assemblies which are not peaceful or which are unlikely to be peaceful. The right to form and join trade unions includes the right to choose not to join

---

[40] [1974] A.C. 273.
[41] (1996) 22 E.H.R.R. 123.
[42] (1991) 14 E.H.R.R. 229.
[43] See *Artze fur das Leben v. Austria* (1991) 13 E.H.R.R. 204.

a trade union.[44] Deprivation of the right to join a trade union was considered in the case of *Council of Civil Service Unions v. United Kingdom*.[45] It was held that a ban on union membership at government communications headquarters was justified in the interests of national security.

Article 12—Right to marry and found a family

14.23 "Men and women of marriageable age have the right to marry and to found a family, according to the national laws governing the exercise of this right."

The right to marry and to found a family does not confer a right to end a marriage by divorce. In *Johnston v. Ireland*[46] an applicant claimed that his right to marry and found a family was violated by Irish law which prevented him divorcing his first wife and marrying the woman with whom he lived. Prisoners are entitled to marry but the right to marry does not extend to the right to conjugal visits whilst in prison.[47]

Article 13—Right to an effective remedy

14.24 "An effective remedy before a national authority must be secured to those whose rights and freedoms as set forth in the convention have been violated."

Article 13 is central to the co-operative relationship between the Convention and national legal system. More comprehensive and effective the national remedies mean that the number of applications to the European Court of Human Rights will decrease. The remedy need not be judicial. Remedies which consist of an appeal to a minister will suffice provided that they are effective. The obligations of the state to provide an effective remedy will depend upon the particular Article which has been contravened. It was held in *Halford v. United Kingdom*[48] that Article 13 had been violated in that the Interception of Communications Act 1985 did not apply to calls made through Merseyside Police's internal telephone system and H had no other means of redress under U.K. law.

---

[44] *Young, James and Webster v. U.K.* (1981) 4 E.H.R.R. 38.
[45] (1988) 10 E.H.R.R. 269.
[46] (1987) 9 E.H.R.R. 203.
[47] *X v. U.K.*, No. 6564/74, 2 DR 105 (1975).
[48] [1997] I.R.L.R. 471; (1997) 24 E.H.R.R. 253; (1997) 3 B.H.R.C. 31; [1998] Crim. L.R. 753; (1997) 94(27) L.S.G. 24.

Article 14—Prohibition of discrimination

"The enjoyment of rights and freedoms set forth in this convention shall be secured without discrimination on any ground such as sex, race, colour, language, religion, political or other opinion, national or social origin, association with a national minority, property, birth or status." 14.25

This Article does not give protection against discrimination *per se*. It gives a right not to be discriminated against in relation to any of the other rights and freedoms. In the case of *Abdulaziz, Cabales and Balkandali*,[49] it was held that the immigration rules for entry into the United Kingdom were in violation of Article 14 because it was easier for the wives of men residing in the United Kingdom to enter than it was for the husbands of women residing in the United Kingdom. The rules were amended as a result of the case.

Article 15—Restrictions on political activity of aliens

"Nothing in Articles 10, 11 and 14 shall be regarded as preventing the High Contracting Parties from imposing restrictions on the political activity of aliens." 14.26

Aliens enjoy all of the protection provided by the other Articles but the interests of national security may justify restrictions on political activities by aliens.

Article 17—Prohibition of abuse of rights

"Nothing in this Convention may be interpreted as implying for any State, group or person any right to engage or perform any act aimed at the destruction of any of the rights and freedoms set forth herein or at their limitation to a greater extent than is provided for in the Convention." 14.27

According to the Commission the purpose of this Article is to prevent exploitation of the Convention rights by totalitarian groups. Rights under Article 10, for example, cannot be used to protect those who possess literature promoting racial hatred.

Article 18—Limitation on use of restrictions on rights

"The restrictions permitted under this convention to the said rights and freedoms shall not be applied for any purpose than those for which they have been prescribed." 14.28

---

[49] (1985) 7 E.H.R.R. 471.

Since 1950 the Convention has been supplemented several times by the addition of Protocols. The first Protocol was signed in Paris in 1952.

Part II—The First Protocol

Article 1—Protection of property

14.29 "Every natural or legal person is entitled to the peaceful enjoyment of his possessions. No one shall be deprived of his possessions except in the public interest and subject to the conditions provided for by law and by the general principles of international law.

The preceding provisions shall not, however, in any way impair the right of a State to enforce such laws as it deems necessary to control the use of property in accordance with the general interest or to secure the payment of taxes or other contributions or penalties."

Even where the confiscation or destruction of property is justified there may be a breach of the Convention if adequate compensation is not provided. The case of *Booker Aquaculture Ltd v. Secretary of State for Scotland*[50] concerned the destruction of property which was justified in the national interest. In 1994 a notice was served on Booker requiring that it destroy some diseased fish stocks under the Fish Health Regulations 1992. In December 1994 Booker attempted to claim compensation but the Secretary of State informed Booker that there was no provision for compensation to be paid. Booker petitioned for judicial review. Booker contended that the Secretary of State's decision should be declared illegal on the basis of his failure to take account of the principles established by E.C. law and the European Convention on Human Rights 1950, which required the provision, by administrative or statutory measures, of compensation for those affected by regulation 7. It was held that the Secretary of State had acted illegally. Since the Regulations fell within the scope of E.C. law and were likely to interfere with a fundamental right, namely that of respect for freedom of property, the national court overseeing their application had to consider all the rules of E.C. law, including the right to compensation. The minimum E.C. provisions for the control of fish diseases allowed the enforcing authorities in each Member State discretion as to the extent to which of the measures would be applied in any particular case. It was important that national rules

---

[50] [1999] Eu.L.R. 54; 1998 G.W.D. 21–1089, *The Times*, Sept. 24, 1998.

designed to give effect to E.C. legislation did not remove that discretion, and with it the fundamental right to property which had to be observed by implication.

Article 2—Right to education

> "No person shall be denied the right to education. In the exercise of any functions which it assumes in relation to education and to teaching, the State shall respect the right of parents to ensure such education and teaching in conformity with their own religious and philosophical convictions." 14.30

In the case of *Campbell and Cozens v. United Kingdom*,[51] two mothers claimed that the use of corporal punishment in Scottish schools was a violation of Article 2. The court rejected the argument that the use of the tawse was inhuman and degrading but accepted that there was a violation of Article 2. 'Philosophical convictions' was interpreted by the Court as "such convictions as are worthy of respect in a democratic society" and which "are compatible with human dignity and which do not conflict with the right of the child to education". The United Kingdom pleaded in defence that the use of corporal punishment was necessary in order to provide efficient instruction and training and to avoid unreasonable expenditure on other forms of discipline. These arguments were not accepted. The Court held that a system of exemptions from corporal punishment would not conflict with efficient instruction. The use of corporal punishment in all state schools was abolished by the Education (No. 2) Act 1986.

Article 3—Right to free elections

> "The High Contracting Parties undertake to hold free elections at reasonable intervals by secret ballot, under conditions which will ensure the free expression of the opinion of the people in the choice of legislature." 14.31

None of the Convention Articles is absolute. Even the right to life may be infringed in circumstances where it is justified. Articles 8 to 11 may be subject to limitations which are prescribed by law and which are necessary in a democratic society. Restrictions may be deemed necessary in order to protect national security, to maintain public order, to prevent crime, to protect public health, safety or morals, to protect the rights and freedoms of others and to prevent the disclosure of confidential information.

---

[51] (1982) 4 E.H.R.R. 165.

Procedure under the Convention

14.32 After exhausting any effective and sufficient domestic remedies individuals may raise actions for compensation in the European Court of Human Rights in Strasbourg. The procedure until recently has been a two stage process with a filter stage to reduce the number of ill-founded petitions. Claims by both states and individuals went first to the European Commission on Human Rights, which was a body of independent experts. The Commission decided whether the application should be admitted for consideration on the merits. Only approximately 10 per cent of cases progressed beyond this filter stage. Petitions were rejected if they were out of time, or if the applicant had failed to exhaust all of the remedies available under domestic law, or because for one reason or another they were "manifestly ill-founded".[52] If the Commission found an application admissible it proceeded to the Committee of Ministers who attempted to negotiate a friendly settlement. If this failed it proceeded to a hearing before the European Court of Human Rights.

Protocol 11 to the Convention which came into force on November 1, 1998 introduced a new procedure. The Commission and the European Court of Human Rights have been replaced with a single court. The conciliation stage carried out by the Committee of Ministers has been removed. There is now one single permanent court considering the interpretation of the Convention. As well as simplifying, and possibly speeding up procedures, this will increase the consistency of decision-making. The Court is staffed by judges appointed by each of the States which is a party to the Convention. It carries out its work at four different levels. A committee of the Court, consisting of three judges considers applications and may by unanimous vote declare that an application is inadmissible.[53] This decision is final. If an application has not been declared inadmissible a Chamber consisting of seven judges decides on the admissibility and merits of inter-state applications. The judge representing the defendant State must be a member of the Chamber hearing the case against the State. Appeals may be made by either party from a decision of the Chamber to the Grand Chamber which consists of 17 judges.[54] A Chamber may choose to relinquish jurisdiction to a Grand Chamber where a case raises an important question affecting the interpretation of the Convention

---

[52] ECHR, Art. 27.
[53] ECHR, Art. 28.
[54] ECHR, Art. 43.

or where a decision is deemed to be likely to conflict with a previous judgment of the Court.[55] Finally, there is a plenary court which has the tasks of electing the President and Vice-President(s) of the Court, setting up Chambers and electing presidents of the Chambers, electing the Registrar and Deputy Registrar(s) and adopting rules of the Court.

Where an adverse judgment is given against it, the United Kingdom comes under an international legal obligation to change national law so as to comply with the Articles of the Convention. If the government does not wish to change the law it may enter a derogation from an aspect of the relevant Article.

Derogation and reservation

A few Convention rights are absolute and subject to no pos- 14.33
sibility of derogation. These are the prohibitions on torture, inhuman and degrading punishment,[56] of slavery,[57] and on retroactive criminal offences.[58] Some other provisions are subject to strictly limited derogation only. A State may, under Article 15, derogate from the right to life in time of war or grave public emergency but only in respect of deaths resulting from lawful acts of war. The only permitted restriction on the abolition of the death penalty is in respect of acts committed in time of war or imminent threat of war.[59] In general, however, the Convention follows a pattern of stating a right in general terms and then permitting restrictions on that right, to take account of other legitimate interests within a State. Following a decision that the United Kingdom had violated Article 5(3), which requires that persons arrested or detained shall be brought promptly before a judge, the United Kingdom entered a derogation from that Article.[60] The Court held that a delay of four days and six hours in bringing a person before a judge did not comply with Article 5(3). The four applicants had been arrested by the police in Northern Ireland as persons reasonably suspected of involvement in acts of terrorism. The detention had been authorised by section 12 of the Prevention of Terrorism (Temporary Provisions) Act 1984.

Convention cases are analysed in a standard way. The first stage is for the Court to consider whether there has been an interference

---

[55] ECHR, Art. 30.
[56] ECHR, Art. 3.
[57] ECHR, Art. 4(1).
[58] ECHR, Art. 7.
[59] ECHR, Protocol 6, Art. 2.
[60] *Brogan v. U.K.* (A/145-B) (1989) 11 E.H.R.R. 117.

with a right. If it is established that there has been interference with a right, it is then necessary to consider whether the interference is justified. In many cases some restriction on rights is justifiable. Restrictions are deemed to be justified if they meet the following four criteria: (i) they must be lawful; (ii) they must be intended to pursue a legitimate purpose; (iii) they must be "necessary in a democratic society"; and (iv) they must not be discriminatory.

Lawful restrictions

14.34 Interference with Convention rights is prima facie unlawful therefore any interference must be specifically authorised. In giving specific authorisation for an infringement of a right "the law must indicate the scope of any such discretion conferred on the competent authorities and the manner of its exercise with sufficient clarity, having regard to the legitimate aim of the measure in question, to give the individual adequate protection against arbitrary interference".[61] This concept is consistent with the rule that administrative discretion is never unfettered but must be exercised only within the confines of the power which has been delegated to the individual administrator.[62] It is also a restatement of Dicey's first principle of the rule of law as "the absolute supremacy or predominance of regular law as opposed to the influence of arbitrary power".[63] The Court of Session is experienced in judging whether administrative decisions are within the bounds of the powers which have been delegated by law. The Court will have have little difficulty in satisfying itself whether any restriction on Convention rights is lawful.

Restrictions intended to pursue a legitimate purpose

14.35 Any interference with individual rights must have a legitimate purpose. It has been very rare indeed for the Court of Human Rights to find that there has not been legitimate purpose for a restriction. The Court has been reluctant to find that a national government may have had an ulterior motive when imposing a restriction where there is a stated justification which meets the criteria. In the case of *Handyside v. United Kingdom*[64] the applicant was unable to prove that his books had been seized for political

---

[61] *Malone v. U.K.* (1985) 7 E.H.R.R. 14, para. 68.
[62] *Padfield v. Minister of Agriculture, Fisheries and Food* [1968] A.C. 997.
[63] A.V. Dicey, *The Law of the Constitution* (10th ed., Macmillan, 1959), p. 202.
[64] (1976) 1 E.H.R.R. 737.

reasons rather than for the "protection of morals" of a child audience.

Necessity for the restriction

The restriction must not exceed that which is necessary to meet the stated legitimate purpose. One important issue is the principle of proportionality: According to this principle, in order to be justified, a restriction must be proportionate to the legitimate aim pursued.[65] The extent of the restriction must be sufficient to achieve its aim without restricting individual freedoms any more than is strictly necessary. The law should aim for a fair balance between the rights of individuals, and the needs of the wider community. 14.36

The second important principle is the "margin of appreciation". The Court of Human Rights recognises that state authorities are in a better position than the Court to assess what the interest of the society requires in their particular country. In *Handyside v. United Kingdom*[65a] the Court recognised the ability of the U.K. government to assess the degree to which morality requires restrictions on obscene expressions. The margin of appreciation is a degree of deference accorded by the Court of Human Rights in recognition of the relative advantage of cultural awareness. This does not mean that states may take advantage to impose restrictions without limit. The restrictions have to be justified in each individual case before the Court. The attitude of the Court takes into account the context in which the restriction operates. A smaller margin of appreciation is allowed where the importance of the right at stake is greater. The Court also takes into account the particular purpose pursued by the state, and the degree to which practice varies among Convention States.

Restrictions must not be discriminatory

The Convention does not contain a general prohibition against discrimination *per se*. However, Article 14 prohibits discrimination in the enjoyment of the rights and freedoms set forth in this Convention. Under the Convention, discrimination is established where a distinction in treatment has no reasonable and objective justification.[66] The concept of a reasonable and objective justification for a difference in treatment may overlap with the consideration of whether a particular restriction is necessary in a democratic 14.37

---

[65] *Handyside v. U.K.* (1976) 1 E.H.R.R. 737.
[65a] (1976) 1 E.H.R.R. 737.
[66] *Belgian Linguistics Case*, Ser. A, No. 6; (1968) 1 E.H.R.R. 252, para. 10.

society. In both instances the principle question to be asked is whether a legitimate aim is sufficient to justify the distinction being made. The concept of discrimination relates specifically to circumstances where restrictions that are reasonable, when applied uniformly, may be unreasonable if applied in a different way to different groups of people.

INCORPORATION OF THE EUROPEAN CONVENTION ON HUMAN RIGHTS

14.38 The effect of incorporating the European Convention on Human Rights into U.K. law will be that, in addition to courts being required to construe statutes and common law as being consistent with the Convention, ministers, civil servants and other public authorities will be required to discharge the powers delegated to them by Parliament in a manner consistent with the Convention. Other international treaties protecting fundamental rights and freedoms are likely to be considered to be matters to which administrators should have regard when making decisions.

Human Rights Act 1998

14.39 Measures to incorporate the Convention into U.K. law have only recently been enacted.[67] The delay in incorporating the Convention into the law of the United Kingdom is attributable to the fact that successive governments have claimed that the required standards are already met by the existing laws of the jurisdictions within the United Kingdom. The United Nations Human Rights Committee was not convinced by these arguments. It noted that the legal system of the United Kingdom does not ensure that an effective remedy is provided for all victims of violations of the rights contained in the Convention. Concern has been expressed regarding the extent to which the implementation of the Covention in the United Kingdom is impeded by non-incorporation into U.K. law.[68] The Human Rights Act incorporates the European Convention on Human Rights into the domestic law of the United Kingdom. The incorporation of the Convention into domestic law is a significant constitutional innovation. The purpose of the Act is to see "rights brought home" by incorporating provisions for compliance with the

---

[67] Human Rights Act 1998; Scotland Act 1998.
[68] CCPR/C/79/Add. 55, July 27, 1995.

European Convention on Human Rights into the domestic law of the United Kingdom.[69] Where U.K. law appears to be in direct conflict with the Convention, cases will still need to be taken to the ECJ but the frequency with which resort to the ECJ is required should diminish.

The purpose of the Human Rights Act is to incorporate the European Convention on Human Rights into domestic law and to ensure that courts will consider and give effect to the Convention. In the course of interpreting and applying legislation there will be a presumption that the intention was to legislate in a manner compatible with the Convention. It will no longer be necessary to show that there is any ambiguity in the legislation before the presumption of compatibility is applied. The doctrine of parliamentary supremacy creates a barrier to the acceptance of externally protected human rights and the Human Rights Act has set out to reconcile the need for internationally protected human rights with the preservation of the doctrine of supremacy of Parliament. The Human Rights Act has therefore not provided that Parliament must legislate in conformity with the Convention. Parliament is, however, required to give consideration to the Convention when preparing legislation. A minister in charge of a Bill in the Westminster Parliament must make a written statement as to whether or not the provisions of the Bill are compatible with the Convention rights.[70]

A court or tribunal determining a question in connection with a Convention right must have regard to the relevant judgments, decisions, declarations and opinions of the European Commission and Court of Human Rights and the Committee of Ministers of the Council of Europe.[71] All courts and tribunals shall also, in construing primary and subordinate legislation passed, or to be passed, read and give effect to it, so far as possible consistently with the Convention rights. This will have no effect on the validity, continuing operation or enforcement of any legislation.[72]

Although Acts of Parliament will not be declared invalid on the ground of non-compliance with the Convention, if a judge is convinced that primary unambiguous legislation is inconsistent with the Convention, he can make a declaration of incompatibility. This

---

[69] See *Rights Brought Home: The Human Rights Bill*, Cm. 3782 (1997); Lord Irvine, "The Development of Human Rights in Britain under an Incorporated Convention on Human Rights" [1998] P.L. 221 at 225.

[70] Human Rights Act 1998, s. 19.

[71] *ibid.* s. 2.

[72] *ibid.* s. 3.

will draw the matter to the attention of ministers and Parliament. This does not give judges power to remedy inadequacies in human rights protection; but by making a declaration of incompatibility, they will publicise deficiencies in the law and pave the way for reform which may provide a satisfactory remedy. Declarations of incompatibility can only be made by certain specified courts. The courts which will have this power in relation to Scotland are: the House of Lords, the Judicial Committee of the Privy Council, the Courts Martial Appeal Court, the High Court of Justiciary sitting as a court of criminal appeal and the Court of Session.[73] It is expressly provided that a declaration of incompatibility has no effect on the validity, continuing operation or enforcement of the provision in respect of which it is given. It is not binding in any way on the parties to the proceedings.[74] The supremacy of Parliament will not be threatened by declarations of incompatibility since, theoretically at least, Parliament may ignore such declarations.

Power to take remedial action

14.40 If a provision of legislation has been declared to be incompatible with Convention rights, or if a Minister of the Crown is of the opinion that a provision of legislation is incompatible with the obligations of the United Kingdom arising from the Convention, the minister may, by a remedial order, make such amendments to the legislation as he considers appropriate.[75] This may involve the repeal of legislation. Where the incompatibility is in subordinate legislation he may, by remedial order, amend the enabling legislation where necessary.[76] A remedial order must be approved in draft by resolution of both Houses of Parliament. In exceptional circumstances where urgency requires an order to be implemented without delay, it may be laid before Parliament in final form. Each House must approve the order within 40 days or it will cease to have effect.

Administrative decisions of public authorities will be subject to a test of compatibility with the Convention. All public authorities, including courts, will be bound to act in a manner compatible with the Convention.[77] An administrative action which would otherwise be subject to challenge because it conflicts with the Convention will

---

[73] Human Rights Act 1998, s. 4(5).
[74] *ibid.* s. 4(6).
[75] *ibid.* s. 10.
[76] *ibid.* s. 10(3).
[77] *ibid.* s. 6(1).

not be susceptible to challenge if the course of action was required by statute and the public authority could not have acted differently. The same principle applies in the case of provisions in or under primary legislation which cannot be read as compatible with Convention rights where the authority was acting to give effect to or enforce those provisions. The term "public authority" includes all courts and tribunals and "any person certain of whose functions are functions of a public nature". It does not include either House of Parliament, except the House of Lords acting in a judicial capacity, or anyone exercising functions in connection with proceedings in Parliament.

An individual who claims that a public authority has acted or proposes to act in a way which is unlawful in terms of section 6 may bring proceedings against the public authority in the appropriate court or tribunal. Alternatively he may rely on the Convention right or rights in any legal proceedings against him.[78] The only person who may instigate a challenge or rely on a Convention right in proceedings against him is a person who qualifies as a "victim" of a violation of a Convention right. This means he has to show that he has been or is likely to be affected directly by the breach of the Convention. The court or tribunal may grant such relief or remedy, or make such order, within its jurisdiction as it considers just and appropriate. This may include an award of damages. Damages will only be awarded by a court which has the power to make an award of damages or to order the payment of compensation in civil proceedings. No award of damages may be made unless the court is satisfied, having regard to all the circumstances, that the award is necessary to afford just satisfaction to the person in whose favour it is made.[79]

SCOTLAND ACT 1998

The Scotland Act, which established the Scottish Parliament is now in force. It contains provisions which require compliance with the European Convention on Human Rights. Acts of the Scottish Parliament will be invalid if they are incompatible with the Convention. An important element of the legislation for the establishment of the Scottish Parliament was the establishment of the parameters within which the Scottish Parliament can legislate. 14.41

[78] Human Rights Act 1998, s. 7.

[79] *ibid.* s. 8.

The general principle is that the Scottish Parliament may legislate in relation to all matters other than those reserved for the Westminster Parliament. Legislation relating to human rights is within the legislative competence of the Scottish Parliament but, unlike legislation from the Westminster Parliament, the validity of Scottish Parliament legislation may be challenged. Section 29 ordains that an Act of the Scottish Parliament is not law so far as any provision of the Act is outside the legislative competence of the Parliament. One of the factors which would cause an Act of the Scottish Parliament to be outside the legislative competence is if it is incompatible with any of the Convention Rights or with Community law.[80] A condition for the introduction of a Bill into the Scottish Parliament is that a member of the Scottish Executive in charge of the Bill has to state that in his view the provisions of the Bill would be within the legislative competence of the Parliament.[81]

Executive actions taken by public officials are also subject to challenge if they are incompatible with the Convention.[82] A member of the Scottish Executive has no power to make any subordinate legislation, or to do any other act, so far as the legislation or act is incompatible with any of the Convention rights or with Community law.[83] There are some exceptions to this general rule. It is important that the exceptions which will be made under the Human Rights Act 1998 when it comes into force will apply now under the Scotland Act. Section 57(2) does not apply to an act of the Lord Advocate: (a) in prosecuting any offence, or (b) in his capacity as head of the systems of criminal prosecution and investigation of deaths in Scotland, which, because of the Human Rights Act 1998, is not unlawful.[84]

Section 6(1) of the Human Rights Act 1998 makes it unlawful for a public authority to "act in a way which is incompatible with a Convention Right". However, section 6(2) provides that there are the following exceptions: (a) as a result of provisions in primary legislation, the public authority could not have acted differently, or (b) in the case of provisions in or under primary legislation which cannot be read as compatible with Convention rights, the authority was acting to give effect to or enforce those provisions. This gives protection to any prosecution authority which seeks to prosecute a

---

[80] Scotland Act 1998, s. 29(2)(d).
[81] *ibid.* s. 31(1).
[82] *ibid.* ss. 57, 106. Challenges to executive actions are now coming before the courts: see Introduction.
[83] *ibid.* s. 57(3).
[84] *ibid.* s. 6(2)(1).

statutory offence which is itself contrary to Convention rights. It is important to ensure that, where such protection was afforded, it should remain fully available to all U.K. prosecution authorities. In circumstances where the Crown Prosecution Service is able to prosecute an offence in England, the Lord Advocate must be able to bring a prosecution under the same legislation in Scotland.

Challenges to the competence of an Act of the Scottish Parliament

Questions about the legislative competence of a Bill or Act of the Scottish Parliament may arise in a number of different circumstances. 14.42

Challenge by individuals

Ordinary citizens who have been adversely affected by an Act which is in force may raise actions in the Court of Session. The most likely ground of challenge is that an Act is incompatible with the standards of the European Convention on Human Rights. Members of the public may not instigate a challenge to a Bill before it has been enacted. Only a person who has been directly affected will be able to challenge an Act. The Act states that a person may not bring any proceedings in a court or tribunal on the ground that an act is incompatible with the Convention rights, or to rely on any of the Convention rights in any such proceedings, unless he would be a victim for the purposes of Article 34 of the Convention[85] if proceedings in respect of the Act were brought in the European Court of Human Rights.[86] Only those who are classed as "victims" have the right to challenge any other action or failure to act by a member of the Scottish Executive. The duty of public authorities to comply with the standards of the Convention will be a matter for the supervisory jurisdiction of the Court of Session. The procedure for challenge will be through judicial review procedure which provides a speedy and relatively simple process of consideration by a single judge. 14.43

The Scotland Act 1998 is already in force but there will be a period when the Human Rights Act is not in force. Provisions of the Scotland Act which are in force before the date of implementation of the Human Rights Act itself will continue to have the same effect after that date.[87] The consequence of the provisions in the

---

[85] Within the meaning of the Human Rights Act 1998.
[86] Scotland Act 1998, s. 100(1).
[87] *ibid.* s. 129(2).

Scotland Act is that citizens in Scotland currently have rights to challenge executive action on the ground of incompatibility with the European Convention on Human Rights which are not yet available in England.

Challenge by Law Officers

14.44 Action to prevent a Bill which is incompatible with the Convention becoming law is, however, possible. One of the three Law Officers may challenge a Bill which he deems to be outside the legislative competence. If no agreement on amendments can be reached the Bill would be referred to the Judicial Committee of the Privy Council prior to its receiving the royal assent.[88] The Lord Advocate is unlikely to challenge Bills unless there is a special purpose for doing so, such as to clarify any ambiguities with regard to the legislative competence but the Advocate General or the Attorney-General may do so. This may lead to conflict between the U.K. government and the Scottish Parliament.

---

[88] Scotland Act 1988, ss. 32, 33.

CHAPTER 15

ACCESS TO INFORMATION

"Freedom of information is a fundamental human right and is the touchstone for all the freedoms to which the United Nations is consecrated."[1] 15.01

"The public have a right to know what the government is doing in their name."[2]

The Labour Government came to power in 1997 on a mandate of constitutional change, and specifically on the promise that a Freedom of Information Bill would be introduced to Parliament. At the time of writing, half way through the Government's term of office, a Freedom of Information Bill has now been introduced to Parliament but has not yet become part of the law of the United Kingdom. In 1997, the then Chancellor of the Duchy of Lancaster, Dr David Clark, published a White Paper which went beyond the existing Code of Practice to give better access provisions. However, in mid-1998 the Freedom of Information Unit was moved from the Office of Public Service to the Home Office and the draft Bill published by the Home Office in May 1999 was in some ways more restrictive than the Code of Practice. It certainly contained major differences from the White Paper proposals. The suspicion was that the more liberal Dr Clark went too far in his proposals and frightened the very conservative and secretive senior civil servants. In any event the Prime Minister was persuaded that freedom of information was an issue that had to be dealt with by the department charged with the task of implementing the Human Rights Act, that is the Home Office. The Code of Practice, the White Paper and the Bill itself are discussed in turn below.

---

[1] UN General Assembly Resolution 59(2), Dec. 14, 1946.

[2] Bogdanor, "Freedom of Information: The Constitutional aspects" in McDonald and Terrill, *Open Government: Freedom of Information and Privacy* (1999), p. 8.

CODE OF PRACTICE ON OPEN GOVERNMENT

15.02 Freedom of information in the United Kingdom is currently regulated by a voluntary and non-statutory code of practice. The code was introduced in 1993 in a White Paper entitled *Open Government*.[3] The White Paper was introduced as a development of the Citizen's Charter programme which had been introduced by John Major in 1991 to set standards for public service organisations and to provide redress mechanisms for customers when the standards were not met.[4] There were a number of high-level releases of information during 1991 and 1992. These included the terms of reference and the membership of cabinet committees, the publication of questions of procedure for ministers (the forerunner of the Ministerial Code), the release of historical records and publication of the minutes of meetings between the Chancellor of the Exchequer and the Governor of the Bank of England. There were performance league tables for schools and hospitals as well as hundreds of charters all contributing to a greater public awareness of service provision and thus raising expectations as to future delivery. The Citizen's Charter was relaunched in June 1998 as the 'Service First' programme.

The *Open Government* White Paper recognised that the standards of the Citizen's Charter required that information on services was needed:

> "[T]he provision of full, accurate information in plain language about public services, what they cost, who is in charge and what standards they offer is a fundamental principle of the Citizen's Charter . . . public services appeared for too long to be shrouded in unnecessary secrecy. The government is now giving the public—often for the first time—the information they need."[5]

The Code of Practice was updated in 1997[6] and it sets out the circumstances in which government will volunteer information and where it will produce information on request. "The broad approach of the code is to balance the right to information against the public interest which may in certain circumstances, *e.g.* national security and commercial confidentiality, require non-disclosure."[7]

---

[3] Cm. 2290 (1993).
[4] *Citizen's Charter*, Cm. 1599 (1991).
[5] Cm. 2290 (1993), para. 23.
[6] http://www.open.gov.uk/m-of-g/code.htm
[7] Bogdanor, *op. cit.*, p. 3.

The code covers all bodies which are within the jurisdiction of the Parliamentary Ombudsman, including the Scottish Parliament and the Scottish Executive. The Parliamentary Ombudsman investigates complaints and issues special reports on the cases referred to him by members of the public.

The Code of Practice allows access to government information, not to government documents. Access is therefore dependent on the discretion of officials. Commentators have reflected that this is likely to prove to be unpopular with people seeking information. "Experience overseas suggests that many requesters will not be satisfied until they see the documents."[8] The White Paper said that the involvement of the Parliamentary Ombudsman would be a safeguard since he would have access to departmental working papers and could "check that the information is consistent with them and constitutes a proper response to the applicant."[9] The Ombudsman has recommended that documents be revealed since this may be the easiest way to deal with a request.

The reason for using a code instead of legislation was stated by 15.03
the Conservative government as making for greater flexibility than a statute could give. While this is certainly accurate, it is not the only reason for preferring a code of practice to legislation; legislation would be subject to judicial scrutiny, which the government wanted to avoid. The information allowed under the code does not include the process of decision-making, that is the advice tendered by officials and advisory committees to ministers. The basis of this exclusion is that the release of advice given by officials would undermine the convention of individual ministerial responsibility and the convention of civil service neutrality. Constitutionally a decision made by a civil servant will be regarded as the decision of a minister[10] and the minister is accountable to Parliament for the actions of civil servants. "The release of advice would allow a select committee to insert a wedge between the minister and the civil servant. It would enable a select committee to tell a minister—the advice your officials gave you was better than the decision which you took."[11] However, the Scott Inquiry Report took a different view of the convention of ministerial responsibility and the provision of information. Scott said: "The obligation of ministers to give information about the activities of their departments and to give information

[8] Hazell "Freedom of Information: Implications for the Ombudsman" (1995) Pub. Admin. 264.

[9] Cm. 2290 (1993).

[10] *Carltona Ltd v. Commissioner of Works* [1943] 2 All E.R. 560.

[11] Bogdanor, *op. cit.*, p. 5.

and explanations for the actions and omissions of their civil servants lies at the heart of ministerial accountability."[12] The government's need to keep policy advice secret was accepted by the Labour and Liberal Democratic Parties in their joint report on the constitution in 1997 when they declared themselves to be in favour of a Freedom of Information Act but insisted that there would need to be exemptions, one of which would be policy advice given by civil servants to ministers.

The code applies to applicants for information and a 'code request' will be an application which mentions the code specifically, or one where a charge is made for providing the information, or one where the request has been refused on the ground of a code exemption. If a request for information is refused, the code states that the applicant should first appeal through the department's internal resolution procedure. If the applicant is still dissatisfied, he may complain to the Parliamentary Ombudsman through his M.P. In normal complaints to the Ombudsman the applicant has to show that he has suffered injury or injustice because of maladministration by the department; in code appeals, however, it is enough that the applicant can show that he has not been given information he should have received.[13]

15.04 There are three main categories of exemption under the code. The first concerns documents which require a 'harm test' to justify their exemption. Examples include documents relating to defence and national security, international relations, proceedings of cabinet and cabinet committees. The Parliamentary Ombudsman indicated that he will expect a department to persuade him that harm or prejudice will result from the disclosure of the information; in other words, the onus of proof is on the department not the applicant.[14] The second category concerns documents which do not require the harm test such as information regarding immigration and nationality. The government indicated that these records are so sensitive that they should remain exempt. The exemptions apply only to individual cases not to information on government policy on immigration and nationality. The third category is more general and includes information relating to personal privacy, information

---

[12] Report of the Inquiry into the Export of Defence Equipment and Dual-Use Goods to Iraq and Related Prosecutions (Scott Inquiry) (1995–96 H.C. 115), para. K8.2.

[13] Second Report of the PCA, Access to Official Information: The First Eight Months (1994–95 H.C. 91), para. 3.

[14] Report of the Select Committee on PCA, Open Government: Minutes of Evidence (1994–95 H.C. 290).

given in confidence, unreasonable requests and information which should not be disclosed prematurely. As regards information given in confidence, the government argued that this should not be disclosed unless the party who originally gave the information has waived their right of confidentiality; otherwise there might be difficulty in obtaining such information in the future.

The code exempts internal discussions and advice, whether given by experts or by civil servants. This aspect of non-disclosure tries to protect civil servants in their role as neutral advisers to the government. However, departments are expected to publish or make available explanatory material on the department's dealings with the public except where publication will prejudice any matter which should be kept confidential. Thus material such as rules, procedures, internal guidance and administrative manuals may be made available.

Where the harm test is used to decide whether or not to release information, the code is clear that a balance should be struck between the harm or prejudice deemed to arise by disclosure and the public interest in making the information available.

The code does not allow access to public records held under the Public Records Acts 1958 and 1967 and the merits of decisions of the Lord Chancellor, the Secretary of State for Scotland and the Secretary of State for Northern Ireland are not reviewable by the Parliamentary Ombudsman if the decision not to disclose a public record is taken without maladministration.[15] The code does not apply to information held by the courts or contained in court documents.

Although the code has been criticised as maintaining a culture of secrecy in government, there is no doubt that it has had an impact. The Civil Service Code specifically exhorts civil servants to give as full information as possible about policies, decisions and actions. In 1997, the Cabinet Office published a guidance note, *Guidance to Officials on drafting answers to Parliamentary Questions,* setting out the principles for officials to follow in carrying out this activity. The creation of websites for all government departments, including the intelligence services, shows a greater willingness to give out more information, even if some of the information is of a trivial nature. Nonetheless, the trend has been towards more openness across the government as a whole.

---

[15] Parliamentary Commissioner for Administration Act 1967, s. 12(3).

Public Records Acts 1958 and 1967

15.05 These Acts ensure the selection of public records which should be preserved to safeguard them for posterity and to make them available for public inspection.[16] Most departmental records are reviewed after they have been inactive for five years and then destroyed because they are regarded as unimportant; only about one per cent of records are kept until the next review, which occurs after 25 years. At this time their historical content will be considered. Some records may be disclosed more quickly if they are part of a government inquiry. Documents relating to events leading to the Falklands conflict in 1982 were released very quickly because they were part of the Franks Inquiry Report.[17]

The Public Records Acts do not apply in Scotland but the procedures contained within them have been adopted as practice in Scotland. The relevant Scottish Act is the Public Records (Scotland) Act 1937.

The 1958 Act provided that the records of courts, government departments and some non-governmental public bodies are to be transferred to the Public Records Office before they are 30 years old and they then become available for public inspection when they are 50 years old. The 1967 Act reduced this latter period to 30 years. The closure times differ according to the type of document. Highly sensitive documents may be kept in departments for over 30 years if the Lord Chancellor approves. However, the documents must be reviewed after 30 years and periodically thereafter. Examples of the types of documents covered by this provision include Cabinet Office papers, records of the Ministry of Defence and of the U.K. Atomic Energy Authority. Other sensitive documents may be transferred to the Public Record Office but withheld from public inspection beyond the 30 years if the Lord Chancellor approves. Examples of these are: exceptionally sensitive papers, information received in confidence, and documents about individuals where disclosure would cause distress or might endanger them. These tend to be withheld for 50 years, although documents relating to individuals may be closed for up to 75 years and documents relating to the affairs of the Royal Family may be closed for 100 years.

There have been two reviews of the criteria for closure. In 1981 the Wilson Committee[18] recommended closure beyond 30 years

---

[16] Roper, "Access to Public Records" in Chapman and Hunt, *Open Government* (1987).

[17] Franks Inquiry on the Falklands War, Cmnd. 8787 (1983).

[18] Report of the Wilson Committee, *Modern Public Records*, Cmnd. 8204 (1981).

only if documents were exceptionally sensitive and disclosure was likely to harm the public interest, or they contained information supplied in confidence, or they contained information about individuals disclosure of which would cause distress or endanger their lives. In 1992, the then Lord Chancellor Lord Mackay of Clashfern ordered another review but the three criteria recommended by the Wilson Report were retained.

The White Paper made further recommendations on closure and disclosure. There should be one basic principle regarding the publication of information, that is, information should be released after 30 years unless first, it is possible to establish that actual damage will be caused by the release, and second, the damage would fall within the criteria in Annex C of the White Paper. The White Paper brought the time down to 40 years for most documents, but retains longer times for information given in confidence (75 years) and population census records (100 years). Many more documents are being released early as a result of the White Paper provisions.

The procedure for releasing documents is controlled by the Open Government Code of Practice. Once a document becomes an archive record, it is transferred to the department's archive for review. When the document becomes 30 years old, it becomes subject to the Public Records Acts and any restrictions on access are then determined by reference to these statutes. However, some documents are subject to access restrictions under other statutes and these were identified in the White Paper. The White Paper proposed to change the blanket restrictions in these statutes to a restriction controlled by the harm test but there has been little progress in changing them.

The current system of deciding whether or not a document is to be opened has three alternatives available: the document is open for inspection on its thirtieth birthday, or it is closed for a specified period (although limited access may be available if the material is not sensitive) or the document is retained in the government department. Applications for closing or retaining a document are scrutinised by four bodies. First, the department must set out its reasons for closing or retaining the document. Secondly, the Public Record Office checks the reason is one within the criteria set out by the Open Government Code of Practice. Thirdly, the application is sent to an independent body, the Lord Chancellor's Advisory Council on Public Records, which has the right to see the document and may refer the matter back to the department if it is not satisfied with the reasons given.[18a] The final 'arbiter' is the Lord Chancellor who has to approve closure or retention by authorising the inclusion of the document in a list published in a statutory instrument.

A researcher wanting access to a document which has been closed or retained as above may make representations to the Advisory Council, but this is not an appeal proper. It is not possible to appeal to the Parliamentary Ombudsman by making a code request since archives are not included in the remit of the code.

The Freedom of Information Bill discussed below contains some provisions with regard to historical records such as those held under the Public Records Acts. The Bill will allow access to documents exempted under the Bill when they are at least 30 years old. The types of documents are court records, relations within the United Kingdom, decision-making and policy formulation, commercial interests and legal professional privilege. Where the information relates to the granting of honours, the exemption is disapplied after 75 years while information on law enforcement will become available after 100 years.

Official Secrets Acts

15.06 The secrecy of the British government is well documented and is typified by the Official Secrets Act 1911, s. 2, which made it an offence for a Crown servant or agent to disclose, without authority, any information which had been acquired in the course of employment or contractual duties.[19] It was also an offence to willingly receive such information. Section 2 was essentially a 'catch-all' section which effectively meant that the unauthorised disclosure of all official information was prohibited regardless of its content. Thus a civil servant who disclosed information on the number of pencils used in the Ministry of Defence was as guilty under the Act as a civil servant who disclosed information on the location of a submarine. The section was heavily criticised over the years because of its lack of distinction between trivial matters and more serious issues. In 1972, the Franks Committee commented: "All information which a Crown servant learns in the course of his duty is 'official' for the purposes of section two, whatever its nature,

---

[18a] The Advisory Council also has the responsibility of advising on matters in the Freedom of Information Bill: see Sched. 5.

[19] Birkinshaw, *Freedom of Information: The Law, the Practice and the Ideal* (2nd ed., 1996).

whatever its importance, whatever its original source. A blanket is thrown over everything: nothing escapes."[20]

The 1911 Act had been passed by Parliament during a period of concern about German spies and it took just one hour's debate over one 24-hour period. Over a period of years, it became increasingly obvious that section 2 was not appropriate. In 1971, Jonathan Aitken, then a journalist,[21] obtained two documents which implied that inaccurate information had been given by the government concerning the war between Biafra and Nigeria. Aitken was prosecuted under section 2 along with the editor of the newspaper which published the article and the army officer who had given Aitken the papers. Their defence was that they had a moral duty to disclose the truth and this was accepted by the court. Aitken's acquittal led to the setting up of the Franks Committee to examine the workings of section 2.

In 1984, Sarah Tisdall, a junior civil servant, sent documents to *The Guardian* newspaper, giving details of when cruise missiles would arrive at the U.S. Airbase at Greenham Common. She was convicted under section 2 and given a six month prison sentence.[22] At the same time, a more senior civil servant was also leaking information, this time to an M.P. Clive Ponting sent information, relating to the sinking of the Argentinean ship *General Belgrano* in the Falklands conflict, to Tam Dalyell M.P. He gave the copy memorandum to the chair of the Foreign Affairs Select Committee who informed the minister. As a result, Ponting was charged under section 2 as having communicated information to someone who was not authorised to receive it. At his trial, Ponting argued that he had acted 'in the public interest' in disclosing the information. The trial judge disagreed and directed the jury to convict. However, the jury was persuaded by Ponting's argument and he was acquitted.[23] Why was Tisdall convicted but Ponting acquitted? The answer may lie in the fact that Tisdall had released information which was current; there were demonstrators at Greenham Common who had previously invaded the airbase and who might do so again, thus placing lives at risk. Ponting, however, had released information about past events and the only consequence of his act would be to embarrass the government.

---

[20] *Report and Evidence of the Committee on Section 2 of the Official Secrets Act 1911* (Franks Committee) Cmnd. 5104 (1972).

[21] The disgraced former cabinet minister imprisoned for perjury in 1999.

[22] *R. v. Tisdall*, *The Times*, Mar. 26, 1984.

[23] *R. v. Ponting* [1985] Crim. L.R. 318.

The House of Commons Treasury and Civil Service Committee reported[24] that section 2 was unenforceable after the Ponting fiasco. However, the government did not take action until another fiasco occurred, this time over the publication of the memoirs of a retired MI6 officer, Peter Wright. The government tried to prevent publication of the memoirs first in Australia where Wright lived and when this was unsuccessful, injunctions were sought against British newspapers to prevent them publishing extracts from the book *Spycatcher*. Interim injunctions were allowed[25] but final injunctions were refused because, as the court acknowledged, the material was already in the public domain and it was futile to attempt to restrain further publication.[26] A White Paper on reform of the 1911 Act was issued in 1988[27] and legislation followed shortly thereafter with the Official Secrets Act 1989.

In Scotland, another book had been published by a former member of the intelligence and security services and again the government tried to prevent its publication in a newspaper. In *Lord Advocate v. Scotsman Publications Ltd*[28] the Lord Advocate argued that the memoirs contained information which was covered by the Official Secrets Act 1989 and thus the author was prohibited from disclosing it. The Crown had already conceded that the information was harmless. The court held that the author was in breach of the Act but that when he circulated the memoirs to third parties, they did not commit an offence by disclosing harmless information. A third party could only be guilty of the offence if the information was damaging in the sense defined by the 1989 Act.

The civil courts have generally been more amenable to the government's requests for injunctions to prevent the disclosure of official information. In *Attorney-General v. Jonathan Cape Ltd*[29] the duty of confidentiality was effectively extended to 'public' secrets and the Lord Chief Justice stated that the courts had jurisdiction to restrain publication of official information if it could be shown that the public interest demanded it. The civil law is more attractive to the government than a criminal prosecution for a number of reasons: the standard of proof is lower, there is no jury to sympathise with a public interest defence and civil actions can be brought to

---

[24] Seventh Report (1985–86 H.C. 92–I).
[25] *Att.-Gen. v. Guardian Newspapers Ltd* [1987] 1 W.L.R. 1248.
[26] *Att.-Gen. v. Guardian Newspapers Ltd (No. 2)* [1990] 1 A.C. 109.
[27] *Reform of Section 2 of the Official Secrets Act 1911*, Cm. 408 (1988).
[28] [1989] 2 All E.R. 852, HL.
[29] [1976] Q.B. 752.

prevent the publication, whereas a criminal prosecution can only be brought after the offence has been committed and the harm done.[30]

The Official Secrets Act 1989 repealed section 2 of the 1911 Act and replaced it with a list of categories of information which are protected. The categories on the list are security and intelligence, defence, international relations and law enforcement. If information in the first three categories is released without lawful authority, no offence will be committed unless the information is 'damaging'. This defence does not apply with regard to information on law enforcement. A third party coming into possession of information obtained without authority will no longer commit an offence unless the information is used to make a further damaging disclosure and that party had reasonable cause to believe the disclosure would be damaging. It is not a defence that disclosure is made in the public interest; indeed it could be said that the Act is set up to make it easier to obtain a conviction rather than to allow access by the citizen to government information.[31] A member of the security or intelligence services, or a GCHQ officer, is prohibited for his whole life from disclosing information obtained by virtue of his position.[32] Criticism has been levelled at this provision since it would have prevented information being disclosed about several high profile cases, including the spying activities of Anthony Blunt.

The Act offers no protection to a civil servant who 'blows the whistle' in the public interest and a civil servant will not be able to claim protection under the Public Interest Disclosure Act 1998 for matters which are covered by the 1989 Act. The defence of 'prior publication' is not included in the 1989 Act although it may be that the Spycatcher cases have assisted in formulating such a defence. Civil servants who find themselves in a similar position to Clive Ponting could still be prosecuted under the 1989 Act. Alternative methods have been provided for a civil servant to pursue a grievance within their own department.[33]

Security and intelligence personnel have access to a staff counsellor; this officer has access to all documents and reports at least annually to the Prime Minister, the Home Secretary and the

---

[30] Oliver, *Government in the U.K.: The Search for Accountability, Efficiency and Citizenship* (1991), p. 173.

[31] Tant "The Campaign for Freedom of Information: A Participatory Challenge to Elitist British Government" (1990) 68(4) Pub. Admin. 477.

[32] 1989 Act s. 1(1), (2).

[33] See Chap. 11.

Foreign Secretary.[34] The Security Service Act 1989 established a tribunal to decide such matters of conflict.

The Freedom of Information Bill

15.07 The Labour Party promised in its 1997 manifesto to introduce a Freedom of Information Bill as soon as possible. In 1997, a White Paper, *Your Right to Know: The Government's Proposals for a Freedom of Information Act*[35] was published. The White Paper proposed that citizens would have a legal right to information and to the records in which that information is contained. The minister announced that this right was "central to a mature democracy". The proposals would apply to all public bodies such as government departments, nationalised industries, quangos, NHS bodies, armed forces, local government and police authorities. The public service broadcasters would be included as were schools and universities, any private bodies which carry out statutory functions and the privatised utilities.

As in all freedom of information legislation, the White Paper's proposals allowed for exempt categories to be included. The Open Government Code of Practice has 15 exempt categories and a simple 'harm' test. The White Paper suggested that there should be seven exempt categories but the test should be raised to 'substantial harm.' Partial disclosure will also be possible. The exempt categories were national security, defence and international relations; law enforcement; personal privacy; commercial confidentiality; safety of the individual, the public and the environment; information supplied in confidence; and integrity of decision-making and policy advice processes in government.

The White Paper proposed the appointment of an Information Commissioner to be independent of Parliament and answerable to the courts. The Commissioner would have the right to investigate complaints and to order disclosure of information. He would have the power to enter premises under warrant and to search for, examine and remove records suspected of being relevant to an investigation. If a body failed to comply with the Commissioner's direction to disclose information, an application could be made to the court to punish the body as being in contempt. It would be a criminal offence to tamper with or destroy documents.[36]

---

[34] Palmer, "Tightening Secrecy Law: Official Secrets Act 1989" (1990) P.L. Summer 243

[35] Cm. 3818 (1997).

[36] For discussion of the White Paper, see Birkinshaw and Parkin, "Freedom of Information" in Blackburn and Plant, *Constitutional Reform: The Labour Government's Constitutional Reform Agenda* (1999).

In May 1999, the long-awaited draft Bill was published by the Home Office, together with a consultation document.[37] The draft Bill was disappointing. It did not include many of the provisions of the White Paper and it strengthened the exemption categories. The draft Bill did not apply to the Scottish Parliament and Scottish Executive and other devolved bodies. The Scottish Executive stated that the existing Code of Practice would continue to be used but that a Freedom of Information Bill will be brought before the Parliament at the earliest opportunity. A consultation paper was published in late 1999.[37a]

The Freedom of Information Bill was introduced to Parliament on November 18, 1999. The White Paper had stated that all public authorities should have the duty to make information available as a matter of course and clause 17 of the Bill requires public authorities to adopt and maintain a scheme for the provision of information and to review this scheme. The scheme must be approved by the Information Commissioner, formerly the Data Protection Commissioner.

The Bill applies to all information, no matter how it is recorded.[38] The applicant has to describe the information requested so that the information can be identified. The applicant need not be a national or resident of the United Kingdom.

Clause 1 confers a general right of access to information held by public authorities and the public authority must confirm or deny that the information is held by the authority. The duty to confirm or deny that information is held may be disapplied by any provision in Part II of the Bill, which details the various exemptions. If the information falls within an exempt category, there is no duty on the public authority to disclose it, although the applicant may still be entitled to be told that the exempt information is held by the authority.

As in most freedom of information regimes, the applicant may have to pay a fee for the information and the public body need not disclose the information until the fee is paid. If the applicant does not pay within three months, the application for information will lapse. The Secretary of State is able to make regulations regarding the level of fees and how they are calculated. The government proposed that an upper limit of 10 per cent of "marginal costs of complying with the request" should be charged. If the cost of

---

[37] http://www.homeoffice.gov.uk/foi/dcon.1.htm

[37a] http://www.scotland.gov.uk/library2/doc07/opsc-00.htm

[38] http://www.scotland.gove.uk/library2/doc07/opsc-00.htm, cl. 1.

providing the information exceeds a threshold prescribed in the regulations by the Secretary of State, the public authority may refuse to disclose the information. Requests for information should be dealt with promptly and within 20 days of receipt of the request.

Where a public authority is not under a duty to disclose information under clause 1 because the information is exempt or it is too expensive to obtain, clause 13 requires the public authority to consider whether it may exercise its discretion and disclose the information. In doing so, the public authority must have regard to the public interest in freedom of information where the applicant does not have a right to the information. The authority may ask the applicant for further information regarding the motive for requesting the information and may impose reasonable conditions on the use of the information. Clause 13 does not apply to security services information covered by clause 21 or to court records (cl. 30).

If a request is refused, the public body must inform the applicant of this within the time-limit of 20 days and must also inform the applicant of the reason for the refusal.

Exemptions are covered by Part II of the Bill. Information reasonably accessible to the public by other means is exempted by clause 19. Examples would include certificates of birth, marriage and death which are available on payment of a fee, or books or pamphlets published by an authority. Information which will be published in the future may also be exempt if it is reasonable that the information should not be disclosed until the proposed publication date. This would include information relating to an incomplete research project or statistical information which is published to a specific timetable.

Clauses 21 and 22 exempt all information relating to the security services and information which, if disclosed, would damage national security. In both cases, a certificate may be signed by a Minister of the Crown that the information is exempt. Other examples of exemptions include defence, international relations, relations within the United Kingdom (for instance as between the Scottish Executive and the U.K. government), the economy, criminal investigations and proceedings and certain other investigations (such as investigations into accidents), law enforcement, court records, communications with the sovereign, health and safety, personal information, information provided in confidence. In total, there are 22 categories of exemption, seven more than the Code of Practice and 15 more than suggested in the 1997 White Paper. Some of the exemptions have 'class' exemptions, in that a document belonging to that class is automatically exempt regardless of its contents, although the authority may still be able to use its discretion under clause 13 to disclose it.

Information relating to decision-making and policy formulation is exempted as a class. It is also exempt if disclosure would prejudice the maintenance of the convention of collective responsibility or inhibit the free and frank provision of advice or exchange of views or prejudice the effective conduct of public affairs.[39] There is a proviso here that the disclosure must be prejudicial in the reasonable opinion of a qualified person, defined as a Minister of the Crown for his own department, or the person in charge of any other government department.

The White Paper envisaged a 'substantial harm' test; in other words the information should normally be disclosed unless there is the prospect of substantial harm being caused to the public interest. The Bill uses various tests according to the specific exemption. For national security matters, the test is whether the exemption is required for the purpose of safeguarding national security. For health and safety matters, the test is whether the disclosure would or would be likely to endanger the physical or mental health or safety of an individual. The government maintains that the test is one of probability, that is, "would or would be likely to prejudice". The prejudice will have to be real or actual or substantial and this standard will be tested, if necessary, by the Information Commissioner deciding whether there is prejudice of the kind alleged by the public authority.

The Secretary of State will be required to issue a code of practice giving details of the practices he considers should be adopted by public authorities. This should include a complaints procedure. An applicant who has been unsuccessful in obtaining information should appeal first to the authority's internal appeals mechanism and thereafter to the Information Commissioner. The Commissioner may not consider a case unless the internal procedure has first been used. The Commissioner may order the authority to disclose the information and a failure to comply with the Commissioner's order may be reported to the court and dealt with as contempt of court. There is a right of appeal against the decisions and regulatory action of the Commissioner to a new Information Tribunal with further appeal on a point of law to the courts.

---

[39] cl. 34.

Data Protection Act 1998

15.08 "English common law does not know a general right of privacy and Parliament has been reluctant to enact one. But there is some legislation to deal with particular aspects of the problem. The Data Protection Act . . . is one such statute."[40]

The Data Protection Act 1998 follows and extends the Data Protection Act 1984. This Act had originated from the U.K.'s treaty obligation after ratifying the Council of Europe Convention for the Protection of Individuals with regard to the Automatic Processing of Personal Data in 1981. The Convention, and the U.K.'s statute, applied to personal data held in electronic form and subject to automatic processing. They did not apply to manual records such as card indices or paper files. Since the information contained in manual records is as important to an individual as that held in electronic records, it was recognised that this was a major failing in the legislation. The E.C. adopted a Directive in 1995 to extend the Treaty's remit to manual records and Member States were given three years until October 24, 1998 to bring their domestic laws into line.[41] The Directive states that data protection is a human right: "In accordance with this Directive, Member States shall protect the fundamental rights and freedoms of natural persons, and in particular their right to privacy with respect to the processing of personal data."[42]

The 1998 Act gives individuals rights in relation to the processing by others of their personal data and these data controllers must not process personal data without complying with the eight data protection principles. These are set out in Schedule 1 of the Act and are very similar to those in the 1984 Act. However, there are two major changes: the first principle has important new provisions and the eighth principle is completely new. The principles are:

(1) Personal data should be processed fairly and lawfully, and should not be processed unless one of the conditions of Schedule 2 is met (for instance, the information has been fairly obtained). If the data relates to sensitive personal data, then in addition, one of the conditions in Schedule 3 must be met (such as the individual has given his explicit consent).

---

[40] *R. v. Brown* [1996] 1 All E.R. 545, *per* Hoffman L.
[41] E.C. Directive on Data Protection, Directive 95/46, adopted Oct. 24, 1995.
[42] *ibid.* Art. 1.

(2) The data must only be obtained for purposes that are specified and lawful, and must not be processed further in a manner incompatible with that purpose.
(3) The data must be adequate, relevant and not excessive in relation to the purposes for which they are held.
(4) The data must be accurate and up to date.
(5) The data must not be kept for longer than is necessary.
(6) The data must be processed in accordance with the rights of the data subjects. These rights include the provision of information regarding the processing and a copy of the data held.
(7) There must be security measures to prevent unauthorised or unlawful processing of personal data and against accidental loss or destruction to personal data.
(8) Personal data may not be transferred outside the European Economic Area unless the country concerned ensures an adequate level of protection for the rights and freedoms of data subjects in relation to the processing of personal data.

The 1998 Act repeals some provisions of the statutes which were passed piecemeal during the 1980s to give greater public access to information held by public bodies. Thus the Access to Personal Files Act 1987 is repealed in its entirety while the Access to Health Records Act 1990 has been partially repealed. The 1984 Act itself is repealed.

Section 1 of the 1998 Act defines the type of data covered by the Act. This includes data being processed by automatic equipment (*e.g.* computers and video surveillance equipment), data recorded as part of a filing system (including manual filing systems), and other data that form part of an accessible record (*e.g.* health records or educational records). Only personal data are caught by the Act so any data relating to a company or to a deceased person will not be covered. Personal data is interpreted widely to include mailing lists, photographs scanned on to a computer, DNA profiles and fingerprints. The definition of processing is very wide and will catch virtually every activity involving data. The 1984 Act excluded material held on a computer for the purpose of preparing text; such word-processing is not included in the 1998 Act. The definition of a manual filing system is again very wide, but three criteria must be met for the Act to apply. The information must be held in a structured form, the structure must be either by reference to individuals or criteria relating to individuals, and the specific information regarding individuals must be readily accessible. The set of information must have a common theme such as a set of customers or employees and the set must be structured so as to allow the ready extraction of information about individuals. If the filing system is very disorganised or arranged in a way that does not allow information to be easily extracted then it will not fall within the provisions of the Act. The Data Protection Commissioner issued guidelines in 1998 to assist in the interpretation of the Act.[43] The guidelines indicate that the decision as to whether or not a file is covered by the Act will depend on the decision of the courts. There are transitional arrangements for some manual records until October 23, 2001.

The Act continues to provide for the establishment of the office of Data Protection Commissioner (previously Registrar) and the Data Protection Tribunal.[44] The tribunal is chaired by a legally qualified person appointed by the Lord Chancellor after consultation with the Lord Advocate.

The Act gives individuals the right to access most personal data held about them.[45] A request for access has to be made in writing and contain sufficient detail to allow the information to be located; a fee may be payable but will be no more than a maximum amount set by the Commissioner. The request should be complied with within 40 days of receipt. The Act makes specific reference to credit reference agencies[46] where the individual must be given an opportunity to have inaccurate information rectified. The Act also assists individuals who have received, and no longer wish to receive, junk mail. Section 11 allows an individual to prevent their name being included on a mailing list and, even if they have previously given their consent to the inclusion, they may at any time withdraw their consent. A person's creditworthiness may be assessed by an automated process. Section 12 allows the individual to insist that this automated process is not the sole method of assessment.

The Freedom of Information Bill extends the rights of subject access and data accuracy under the 1998 Act to all personal information held by public authorities, including personal information held by either House of Parliament. However, the data controllers for each House are exempted from prosecution under the 1998 Act.[47]

---

[43] *The Data Protection Act 1998, An Introduction.*
[44] 1998 Act, s. 6.
[45] *ibid.* s. 7.
[46] *ibid.* s. 9.
[47] Freedom of Information Bill, Sched. 6.

CHAPTER 16

LEGAL REDRESS FOR THE INDIVIDUAL AGAINST THE STATE

INTRODUCTION

An important aspect of constitutional law is that there should be provision for remedies for individuals who have suffered losses or injuries because of action by the government or bodies acting under government authority. Where a person has suffered as a result of an act which has been authorised by statute there may be a provision for an appeal to a minister or to a tribunal. Where there has been maladministration there may be a right of redress through a complaint to an ombudsman. Where none of these apply there will usually be a right of recourse through judicial review procedure.[1] 16.01

NON-JUDICIAL PROCEDURES FOR LEGAL REDRESS

Ombudsmen

The word ombudsman is used to describe a public official who investigates the grievances of ordinary people. The term is also used in the private sector to describe an internal complaints adjudicator. An ombudsman exists to investigate the grievances of an individual but he also has a second important function, to raise the standards of service to the public within the department or industry concerned.[2] 16.02

In 1967 the Parliamentary Commissioner for Administration Act was passed. There then followed a flurry of Acts setting up other commissioners. Health Service Commissioners were established by

[1] V. Finch and C. Ashton, *Administrative Law in Scotland* (W. Green, 1997), pp. 223–245.

[2] See H. Wilkinson, "Complaining to the Ombudsman" (1992) 142 N.L.J. 1348.

the National Health Re-organisation Acts 1972 (for Scotland) and 1973 (for England and Wales). At present the office of Health Service Commissioner is held by the Parliamentary Commissioner for Administration but, following devolution, it is probable that a separate appointment will be made for Scotland. The Local Government Act 1974 established local commissioners for administration in England and Wales and a similar office was set up in Scotland by the Local Government (Scotland) Act 1975. The Maastricht Treaty made provision for the establishment of a European Parliament Ombudsman and an appointment to this position was eventually made in July 1995 after an 18-month search for a suitable candidate. The Scotland Act has not provided for the appointment of a parliamentary ombudsman to investigate complaints against the Scottish Parliament and the Scottish Administration but it has placed a duty on the Scottish Parliament to provide for the investigation of complaints of executive maladministration.[3] The role of the Parliamentary Commissioner for Administration is unchanged by the process of devolution. In Scotland however, the jurisdiction of the Ombudsman will be restricted to reserved areas of government. The reserved areas are those which have not been devolved to the Scottish Parliament, such as taxation. Most of the functions exercised by the Scottish ministers are no longer subject to the Ombudsman's supervision.

Parliamentary Commissioner for Administration

16.03 The Parliamentary Commissioner for Administration investigates complaints from members of the public who claim to have sustained "injustice in consequence of maladministration" from action taken by a government body or department "in exercise of the administrative functions of that department".[4] All complaints to the Parliamentary Commissioner for Administration should be made through an M.P. Complaints which have not been made through an M.P. are not automatically rejected. The Commissioner may refer a complaint to the M.P. if he believes that a case of maladministration is indicated. The M.P. will then refer the matter back to the Parliamentary Commissioner who can begin his inquiries. A complaint can only be made by a person claiming to have suffered injustice as a result of maladministration. The complaint must be made by the aggrieved person, or if he is

---

[3] Scotland Act 1998, s. 91.

[4] Parliamentary Commissioner for Administration Act 1967, s. 5(1)(a).

deceased, by his legal representative. Complaints can be made by individuals (including prisoners and immigrants) and corporate bodies but not by bodies such as local authorities or nationalised industries. There are no legal means to compel the Parliamentary Commissioner to investigate if he declines to do so.[5] The Parliamentary Commissioner may not investigate an issue unless there has been a written complaint from a member of the public. He has no direct legal powers to enforce his findings. He may only make recommendations. He may lay a special report before both Houses of Parliament and the select committee may then require the principal officer of the department to explain why the recommendations have been ignored.

Complaints against the Scottish Parliament

The Scotland Act requires the Scottish Parliament to make 16.04
provision for the investigation of relevant complaints made to its members in respect of any action taken by or on behalf of: (a) a member of the Scottish Executive in the exercise of functions conferred on the Scottish ministers, or (b) any other office-holder in the Scottish Administration. This means that complaints of a kind which could be investigated under the Parliamentary Commissioner Act 1967 if they were made to a member of the House of Commons will be investigated in a similar way in relation to the Scottish Parliament.

The Parliament may make provision for the investigation of complaints in respect of: (a) any action taken by or on behalf of an office-holder in the Scottish Administration, (b) any action taken by or on behalf of the parliamentary corporation, (c) any action taken by or on behalf of a Scottish public authority with mixed functions or no reserved functions, or (d) any action concerning Scotland and not relating to reserved matters which is taken by or on behalf of a cross-border public authority. The word "action" includes any failure to act.[6]

Local Government Ombudsman

The office of the Commissioner for Local Administration in 16.05
Scotland, was created by the Local Government (Scotland) Act 1975. The main role of the Local Government Ombudsman is to consider complaints of injustice arising from maladministration by

---

[5] *Re Fletcher's Application* [1970] 2 All E.R. 257.
[6] Scotland Act 1998, s. 91.

local authorities, water development boards, river purification boards, licensing boards and various joint committees. In addition, he may consider complaints on housing matters against New Town development corporations or against Scottish Homes in their capacity as landlords. The Local Government Ombudsman is appointed by the Crown on the recommendation of the Secretary of State for Scotland.[7] The Local Government Ombudsman has continued to operate following devolution. The accountability of the office has been affected by the establishment of the Scottish Parliament. The office falls into the devolved sector and therefore it will be subject to any legislative change made by the Scottish Parliament and it will be part of the Scottish Administration.

TRIBUNALS AND INQUIRIES

16.06 Tribunals and inquiries offer redress to individuals who have been aggrieved by government or administrative action. They are quite distinct from each other. Tribunals are concerned with ascertaining facts, applying legal rules to those facts and finally making a binding decision. Inquiries also ascertain facts but instead of making a decision, the inquiry makes recommendations to a minister regarding a matter of policy. The tribunal is judicial in nature whereas the inquiry is administrative. The inquiry exists to allow the citizen an opportunity to put forward their objections and give them a fair hearing before a decision is made. Tribunals are defined by statute and have a permanent existence, whereas inquiries are established or convened as needed or the law requires. Tribunals are sometimes referred to as 'administrative tribunals' but they deal with such a wide variety of disputes, not all of them administrative in nature, that now they are more properly and simply called 'tribunals'.

Tribunals are the primary mechanism provided by Parliament for the resolution of certain grievances between the citizen and the State but a few tribunals also cover disputes between citizen and citizen, for instance the industrial tribunal. There are around two thousand different tribunals in the United Kingdom today covering a wide range of topics such as social security appeals, VAT tribunals, immigration adjudicators, disability appeals, child support appeals, special education needs and one found only in

[7] Local Government (Scotland) Act 1975, s. 21.

Scotland, the children's hearing. Many of the tribunals come under the supervisory control of the Council on Tribunals.[8]

Most tribunals are set up by statute and their powers and duties are regulated either in the statute itself or in regulations made under the statute. The Tribunals and Inquiries Act 1992 gives the right of appeal to anyone who is dissatisfied in a point of law with the decision of a tribunal specified in the section, for instance tribunals dealing with schools, mines, nurses and so on.[9] The Court of Session, or High Court of Justice for England and Wales, is empowered to make a decision, or to order the tribunal to rehear the case or to give directions to the tribunal.[10] An appeal from a tribunal to an appellate tribunal or court of law is made according to the provisions of the statute which set up the tribunal. If no appeal to the court is provided by the parent Act or by section 11 of the Tribunals and Inquiries Act 1992, then challenge in the courts is by way of judicial review. In some tribunals, the appeal is to a minister rather than to a court or appellate tribunal.

Where there is a question of government policy affecting the rights of a citizen, such as the compulsory purchase of land for building a new road or the siting of a new power station, a statutory inquiry may be held before the final decision is taken. The rights of those affected are protected by the statute under which the work is required to be authorised, by the principles of natural justice and by the provisions of the 1992 Act. In *B. Johnston and Co. (Builders) Ltd v. Minister of Health*[11] Lord Greene M.R. described the inquiry as "merely a stage in the process of arriving at an administrative decision". The hearings often give a legal or judicial impression which can disappoint objectors when they realise that the inquiry does not make decisions, only recommendations, which may or may not be followed.

Classification of inquiries

Inquiries can be classified as appeals, objections, investigations 16.07
and post-mortems.

---

[8] For further reading, see Finch and Ashton, *op. cit.*, pp. 184–211; A. W. Bradley and K.D. Ewing, *Constitutional Law and Administrative Law*, pp. 737–746; P.P. Craig, *Administrative Law*, pp. 142–147.

[9] See *O'Brien v. Associated Fire Alarms Ltd* [1968] 1 W.L.R. 1916; [1969] 1 All E.R. 93; *L.A. v. Reliant Tool Co.* [1968] 1 W.L.R. 205; [1968] 1 All E.R. 162; *Woodhouse v. Peter Brotherhood Ltd* [1972] 2 Q.B. 520.

[10] Tribunals and Inquiries Act 1992, s. 11(4).

[11] [1947] 2 All E.R. 395.

Appeals

16.08 These inquiries cover such matters as appeals against refusal of planning permission. In Scotland, these are regulated by the Town and Country Planning (Scotland) Act 1972, s. 33. An applicant may appeal to the Secretary of State if a planning authority refuses planning permission, or if consent is granted subject to conditions, or if a planning authority has failed to come to a decision within two months of the application. The appeal will be decided either on the basis of written submissions or at a public local inquiry. Most appeals are now heard using the former method but it is open to the appellant or the planning authority to request an inquiry.

Objections

16.09 These are also mainly concerned with planning matters but, instead of an appeal against an adverse decision by a planning authority, objections are made by individuals or groups to proposals for planning permission by developers. The public inquiry thus generated is held on the same basis and on similar conditions to the appeal against planning permission. These inquiries may be held to inquire into major developments, such as the 'super-quarry' inquiry held on the Island of Harris in 1995.

Investigations and post-mortems

16.10 Inquiries may be set up either under statutory authority, for instance, fatal accident inquiries under the Fatal Accidents and Sudden Deaths Inquiry (Scotland) Act 1976, or in rare cases on a non-statutory basis to investigate issues of public interest and concern. Examples of this latter type include the Orkney Child Abuse Inquiry in 1991.[12] These inquiries will often lead to changes in legislation or administrative procedures. They are essentially retrospective in nature, examining why something occurred or did not occur. Formal versions of these inquiries may be held under the Tribunals of Inquiry (Evidence) Act 1921. These are held to investigate "a definite matter of urgent public importance" such as the events at Dunblane Primary School in March 1996 when a gunman killed 16 children and a teacher.[13]

---

[12] *Report by Lord Clyde of the Inquiry into the removal of children from Orkney in February 1991* (1991–92 H.C. 195).

[13] *The Public Inquiry into the Shootings at Dunblane Primary School on March 13, 1996* (Cullen Report), Cm. 3386 (1996).

JUDICIAL PROCESSES FOR THE REDRESS OF GRIEVANCES

There are several routes for obtaining legal redress through judicial process. The appropriate action will depend on the source of the authority for the decision which is being challenged. 16.11

Statutory appeal procedure

Where it is the exercise of a power derived from a statute which has caused an infringement of rights there may be a specific right of recourse provided by the statute. For example, the Social Security Act 1980, s. 14 gives a right of appeal on points of law from decisions of the Social Security Commissioners. The nature of a statutory right of appeal will depend on the provision in the relevant statute. It may allow a further inquiry into the factual basis of a decision, or it may be limited to reviewing the legality of the decision. The appeal may be to a court (often the sheriff court), or there may be a right of appeal to a government minister or, occasionally, to a tribunal. As a general rule, where there is a statutory right of appeal a litigant must make use of that right rather than seeking judicial review at common law. 16.12

Where a right of statutory appeal is being exercised the right to challenge a decision is normally granted to a "person aggrieved" by the decision. The Town and Country Planning (Scotland) Act 1997, s. 239(5) provides that where an authority has failed to follow the prescribed procedure in making a decision, the court should only intervene if the applicant has been "substantially prejudiced" by a failure to comply with any of the procedural requirements. In order to establish substantial prejudice it is not necessary to prove that the outcome would have been different if procedural requirements had been adhered to.

The fact that he has been deprived of the exercise of a right is sufficient alone to amount to substantial prejudice. In *Wordie Property v. Secretary of State for Scotland*,[14] Lord Cameron stated that: "where an applicant has been deprived of the exercise of a right conferred on him by Parliament, that fact alone would appear . . . to indicate that he has suffered substantial prejudice."

The grounds on which the courts can intervene through statutory appeal procedures will depend on the wording of the statute. For example, the statutory right of appeal in relation to planning decisions allow an appeal to be made on the grounds that the

---

[14] 1980 S.C. 210.

validity of a decision, notice or order can be questioned where: (1) the decision in question is not within the powers of the relevant statute or statutes, or (2) there has been a failure to comply with a relevant statutory requirement.

Action to enforce a statutory duty

16.13 Where there is a statutory duty on an official or body, such as a duty to provide a service, it may be possible for an individual to take action to enforce performance of that duty. A general power to enforce a statutory duty is provided by the Court of Session Act 1988, s. 45(b), which provides that the Court of Session may order the specific performance of any statutory duty. This section applies where a clear, definite duty is laid by statute upon some definite body or individual on whom the court can lay its hand and order the specific performance of the duty. It must be clear that the statute is imposing a duty, not merely conferring a power. In the case of *Docherty v. Burgh of Monifieth*,[15] the local authority was ordained to perform their statutory duty under the Burgh Police (Scotland) Act 1892 to construct sewers to the borders of land owned by Docherty.[16]

Nobile officium

16.14 An important 'safety net' in Scots law is the extraordinary jurisdiction of the Court of Session through the exercise of the *nobile officium*. The *nobile officium* provides a means to grant a remedy where justice requires it, but none is otherwise available. In the case of *Ferguson, Petitioners*,[17] an electoral registration officer wrongly removed the names of certain voters from the draft electoral register. There was no statutory procedure for revising the list of voters, however the court ordered the officer to reinstate the names on the register. The court makes sparing use of this power but there are still occasional cases.[18]

Judicial review

16.15 The Court of Session has a supervisory jurisdiction at common law to ensure that a decision-maker has acted within his powers. The procedure by which courts fulfil this function is known as

---

[15] 1970 S.C. 200.

[16] See also *Strathclyde Regional Council v. City of Glasgow District Council*, 1988 S.L.T. 144.

[17] 1965 S.C. 16.

[18] For further reading, see Finch and Ashton, *op. cit.*, pp. 218–223, 425–426.

judicial review. In Scotland the subject-matter of the supervisory jurisdiction extends not only to the actions of central government and of local authorities but also to some extent to voluntary associations and private bodies.[19] An application for judicial review is a remedy of last resort and, unless there are exceptional circumstances, judicial review is incompetent where there is an alternative remedy.[20]

Applications for judicial review are commenced by way of a petition to the Court of Session set out according to Form 58.6 of the Rules of Court. The court has a wide discretion as to the remedies which it can grant.

Petitions for judicial review may be sought for decisions made by a wide range of organisations including: inferior courts and tribunals, actions of the crown authorised by statute, public industries and services, nationalised industries and public boards, local authorities and certain decisions by the Parliamentary Commissioner for Administration.[21] The Court of Session may also review decisions made by various other statutory and non-statutory bodies such as: (a) disciplinary tribunals, *e.g.* Law Society of Scotland, Faculty of Advocates; (b) universities; (c) broadcasting authorities such as the BBC and IBA; (d) other bodies, *e.g.* parole board, Scottish Homes, Scottish Arts Council.

Judicial review of Scottish legislation

Although the courts have no power to declare a provision in an Act of the Westminster Parliament invalid, the same principle does not apply to Acts of the Scottish Parliament. Acts of the Scottish Parliament are only valid if they are within the legislative competence which has been devolved by the Scotland Act.[22] Acts of the Scottish Parliament and Scottish subordinate legislation are to be read as narrowly as is required for them to be within competence. A court or tribunal may remove or limit any retrospective effect of the decision, or to suspend its effect for a period to allow correction of the defect if it decides that provisions are *ultra vires*.[23] 16.16

---

[19] See Finch and Ashton, *op. cit.*, pp. 223–242.

[20] *Dante v. Assessor for Ayr,* 1922 S.C. 109; *Strathclyde Buses v. Strathclyde Regional Council*, 1994 S.L.T. 724; *West v. Secretary of State for Scotland*, 1992 S.L.T. 636; 1992 S.C.L.R. 385.

[21] *R. v. Parliamentary Commissioner for Administration, ex p. Dyer* [1994] 1 All E.R. 375; *R. v. Parliamentary Commissioner for Administration , ex p. Balchin* [1996] E.G.C.S. 166; [1996] N.P.C. 147.

[22] Scotland Act 1998, s. 54.

[23] *ibid*. s. 102.

This means that an individual may challenge the validity of an Act of the Scottish Parliament in any proceedings before a court or tribunal. This may include a court or tribunal elsewhere in the United Kingdom.[24] In order to avoid the possibility of inconsistency in judicial decisions the Judicial Committee of the Privy Council will act as a final court of appeal for all devolution issues. One possible ground of challenge is that a provision in an Act of the Scottish Parliament is incompatible with the European Convention on Human Rights.

Conditions for judicial review

16.17 The following conditions must normally be fulfilled before judicial review procedure can be used to challenge an administrative decision: (a) there are grounds for judicial review of acts complained of; (b) the person or body complained of is subject to judicial review; (c) the type of act complained of can be the subject of judicial review; (d) the person bringing action has both title and interest to sue; (e) the remedy sought is an appropriate remedy and is available against the person complained of; (f) there is no appeal procedure still open to the aggrieved person.

Title and interest

16.18 The courts can only exercise their supervisory jurisdiction over administrative decision-making when an action has been raised by an appropriate person. In order to qualify as an appropriate person to bring an action an individual or organisation must establish that he has *locus standi*, or standing.[25] Cases cannot be brought by persons whose rights and interests have not been affected by the decision which is being challenged.[26] An applicant who has interest but cannot establish that there is a relationship that gives him title has no standing to bring an action. In practice it is often difficult to separate title and interest and in some circumstances judges may simply state that a person has or has not 'title and interest' rather than deliberating separately on the qualifying title and interest.[27]

A definition of "title" was given in the judgment of Lord Dunedin in the case of *D. and J. Nicol v. Dundee Harbour*

---

[24] Scotland Act 1998, Sched. 6.

[25] See Finch and Ashton, *op. cit.*, pp. 387–407.

[26] *D. and J. Nicol v. Dundee Harbour Trs*, 1915 S.C. (H.L.) 7.

[27] *Cockenzie and Port Seton Community Council v. East Lothian District Council*, 1996 S.C.L.R. 209; *Lennox v. Scottish Branch of the British Show Jumping Association*, 1996 S.L.T. 105.

Trustees.[28] Lord Dunedin said that: "For a person to have title he must be a party (using the word in its widest sense) to some legal relation which gives him some right which the person against whom he raises the action either infringes or denies."

Even if a person qualifies as having title to raise an issue, the court must also be satisfied that he has an interest to do so. This requires that the particular issue is of real concern to the party and not an academic issue or merely something which is being raised as a matter of general public-spirited concern.[29] The case which is regarded as the current leading authority in relation to title and interest is that of *Scottish Old People's Welfare Council, Petitioners*.[30] The Scottish Old People's Welfare Council (commonly known as Age Concern Scotland) raised a petition for judicial review challenging the legality of a circular setting out the rules for extra social security payments in "severe weather conditions". The chief adjudication officer argued that the petitioners had no title and interest. In relation to the issue of title it was held that any member of the public had a title to sue, and accordingly there was no reason in principle why members of the public should be deprived of that title simply because they combined together into an association. It was held however, that the interest of the petitioners was too remote to give them a right to challenge the validity of the circular. An important factor was that Age Concern Scotland was an organisation whose purpose was to further the interests of elderly people. Its own membership did not necessarily include elderly people who would be in a position to benefit from a favourable decision. Age Concern Scotland was held therefore to have title but no interest to challenge the official guidance that limited the making of supplementary payment to old people during severe weather conditions. 16.19

In the case of *Wilson v. Independent Broadcasting Authority*,[31] three members of a group campaigning in the period leading up to the referendum on devolution of political power to Scotland were held to have title and interest to sue for an interdict to restrain the showing of certain political broadcasts by the Independent Broadcasting Authority. The broadcasts did not maintain a proper balance between opposing views. Lord Ross could see "no reason in principle why an individual should not sue in order to prevent a breach by a public body of a duty owed by that public body to the public."

---

[28] 1915 S.C. (H.L.) 7.
[29] *Docherty v. Burgh of Monifieth*, 1971 S.L.T. 13.
[30] 1987 S.L.T. 179.
[31] 1979 S.C. 351.

Grounds for challenging administrative decisions

16.20 The fundamental ground on which a decision may be challenged by judicial review proceedings is that there has been an excess of power on the part of the authority which made the decision. Every act or decision must be *intra vires*. The most widely recognised statement of the grounds for judicial review is that of Lord Diplock in the case of *Council for Civil Service Unions v. Minister for Civil Service*.[32] Lord Diplock stated that the grounds are: (i) illegality, (ii) irrationality, and (iii) procedural impropriety.

16.21 **Illegality** A decision may be quashed on grounds of illegality where a decision-maker has not understood correctly the law that regulates his decision-making power and has not given effect to that law.[33] Such a failure will render his decision unlawful. Illegality may arise where a public authority has: (i) acted in excess of its statutory powers, or (ii) where a decision has been made by taking into account irrelevant considerations, or (iii) where a decision has been taken after failing to take relevant considerations into account, or (iv) where a statutory power has been used for an improper purpose or where a policy has been adopted which amounts to a fettering of a future discretion.

16.22 **Irrationality** A decision may be quashed on the grounds of irrationality or unreasonableness. This applies to a decision which is so outrageous in its defiance of logic or of accepted moral standards that no sensible person who had applied his mind to the question to be decided could have arrived at it. In the case of *Associated Picture Houses v. Wednesbury Corporation*,[34] Associated Picture Houses challenged the validity of the decision by Wednesbury Corporation to grant permission for Sunday cinema performances only on condition that no children under 15 years of age should be admitted. The Sunday Entertainments Act 1932 gave a local authority power to permit cinemas to show films on Sundays "subject to such conditions as they see fit to impose." It was held that the local authority had not acted *ultra vires* as the decision was not so unreasonable that no reasonable authority could ever have come to it. The term "Wednesbury unreasonableness" is often applied to a decision which is so unreasonable that no reasonable authority could have come to it.

---

[32] [1984] 3 W.L.R. 1174.

[33] *Malloch v. Aberdeen Corp.*, 1973 S.C. 227; *Adams v. Secretary of State for Scotland*, 1958 S.C. 279.

[34] [1948] 1 K.B. 233.

Procedural impropriety A decision may be quashed on grounds of procedural impropriety: (i) where there has been a failure to observe the basic rules of natural justice, or (ii) where there has been a failure to act with procedural fairness towards the person who will be affected by the decision, or (iii) where there has been failure by an administrative tribunal to observe procedural rules. Many of the challenges which are made on the grounds of procedural impropriety arise because a failure to follow procedures has caused a breach of the principles of natural justice. The two main principles of natural justice are; *audi alteram partem* (both sides must be fairly heard) and *nemo judex in causa sua* (*potest*) (no one can be a judge in his own cause). The second of these is also known as the rule against bias. Underlying these there is a third principle that justice must not only be done but must be seen to be done. 16.23

An example of a breach of the principle that both sides must be fairly heard arose in the case of *Barrs v. British Wool Marketing Board*.[35] A wool producer, Barrs, appealed to a tribunal against a valuation of his wool by the appraisers under a wool marketing scheme. The tribunal examined the wool in the presence of a representative of the producer and the two appraisers who had originally valued it. The tribunal then retired for consideration. The representative of the producer was excluded at this stage but the two appraisers retired with the tribunal members although they took no part in the discussions. The tribunal dismissed the appeal and reduced the value of the wool by another penny per pound. Barrs successfully sought reduction of the tribunal's decision on the ground that it had reached its decision in circumstances which were contrary to natural justice.

This same principle applies where there has been a possibility that a person making a judicial decision has been biased. An example of possible judicial bias arose in the case of *Bradford v. McLeod*.[36] During a prolonged national strike by coal miners a conversation took place at a social function in Ayr in which the strike was discussed. A sheriff and a solicitor were both present. At one point the sheriff made remarks to the effect that he "would not grant legal aid to miners". Subsequently a miner represented by that solicitor appeared before that same sheriff accused of breach of the peace on a picket line. The solicitor moved that the sheriff should declare himself disqualified from hearing the case because

---

35 1957 S.C. 72.
36 1986 S.L.T. 244.

of the views which he had expressed. The sheriff declined to disqualify himself. The miner was convicted of the offence, as were 13 others in similar circumstances. They all sought to have their convictions and sentences suspended. It was held that there had been a miscarriage of justice. Although the sheriff himself might have been satisfied that he was not biased and would not act in a manner contrary to his judicial oath, circumstances existed which could create in the mind of a reasonable man a suspicion as to the impartiality of the sheriff.[37]

Remedies

16.24 Where an appeal against a decision is being made under a statutory appeal procedure the remedies which may be granted will be laid down in the relevant statute. Where a decision is challenged by way of the judicial review procedure in the Court of Session the court has a wide discretion as to the remedies which it can grant. The remedies sought must be listed in the petition but the court is not limiting to awarding only the remedies which have been listed. It can even make an order for a remedy which has not been sought in the application, although Lord Clyde, in *Mecca Leisure Ltd v. City of Glasgow District Council*,[38] observed that: "the court should not compel a petitioner to accept a remedy not sought and not desired by him or her."

The remedies which may be awarded include declarator. A declarator is simply a declaration as to the law. The remedy of reduction is usually sought in conjunction with declarator. Reduction is a legal decision that a decision is invalid and is therefore reduced. Petitioners are sometimes disappointed with this remedy because it does not prevent a similar decision being made in the future. For example, if a decision to permit a quarry to open has been reduced because the proper procedures were not followed, the authority could then follow all of the procedures to the letter and then make the same decision. All that would have been gained by the petition for judicial review was a delay. The court may make an award of financial compensation where a person has suffered a financial loss because of an *ultra vires* decision. The court may also make an order of specific implement. This requires a person to perform an act. For example a local authority may be required to

---

[37] See also *Lockhart v. Irving*, 1936 SLT 567; *London and Clydeside Estates v. Secretary of State for Scotland*, 1987 S.L.T. 459; *Wildridge v. Anderson* (1897) 25 R (J.) 27.

[38] 1987 S.L.T. 483 at 486.

give a place in a school to a child. The remedy of interdict can be awarded as an interim order and as a remedy following the disposition of a case. Interdict is an order prohibiting an action or a series of actions. Interim interdict is especially useful as it can be used to maintain the status quo until a petition comes before the court for a hearing. This could be useful if, for example, a petition was sought to challenge a decision to allow a change of land use which could result in damage to the environment. An interim interdict could be sought to ensure that nothing was done before the case was heard. The Court of Session can therefore award any of the remedies which it has the power to award in ordinary actions between individuals when it is exercising its supervisory jurisdiction over public authorities under judicial review procedure. There are some exceptions. The remedies of interdict and specific implement are not available against the Crown. The remedies which can be granted against the parliamentary corporation, the body set up to represent the Scottish Parliament in legal proceedings, are restricted. Orders for reduction, suspension, interdict, or specific performance including interim orders, may not be imposed against the parliamentary corporation. The remedy of declarator is available. The Scottish Parliament will decide what action to take when an order of declarator has been made.

CHAPTER 17

ENFORCEMENT POWERS OF PUBLIC AUTHORITIES

INTRODUCTION

17.01 Certain organisations within the United Kingdom have powers that have a direct impact on the rights and freedoms of individual citizens. The primary responsibility for enforcement of the law rests with the police forces throughout the United Kingdom but there are also other organisations whose activities have an impact on individual freedoms. The security services, for example, have powers to intercept communications, immigration officers control entry of persons into the United Kingdom, customs officers control the import and export of certain goods and local authorities exercise powers to permit or prohibit certain types of activity.

LIMITATIONS ON AND REGULATION OF POWERS

17.02 Powers can only be exercised within the limits of the authority that has been delegated. Where the power has derived from statute, whether or not an action is *intra vires* (*i.e.* within the powers) will depend on interpretation of the words of the statute. Challenges may be made if an action is illegal, irrational or if there has been a failure to follow procedures which have been laid down as mandatory by the statute. Any actions taken must be based on legal authority, carried out by the correct procedure and must not be unreasonable. An action will only be deemed to be unreasonable if it is one which is so outrageous in its defiance of logic or of accepted moral standards that no sensible person who had applied his mind to the question to be decided could have arrived at it.[1]

---

[1] *Associated Picture Houses v. Wednesbury Corp.* [1948] 1 K.B. 233.

THE POLICE

Organisation of the police

The United Kingdom has no national police force. Instead the police service is organised into forces on a local basis. This dispersed organisation has caused difficulties from time to time in the investigation of serious crimes which cross the boundaries of the various police forces and so there are a number of organisations which work on a national basis. The establishment of the Scottish Crime Squad in 1969 provided a means of tackling major crime affecting more than one police area. In 1986 a dedicated drugs wing was added to the squad with branches in Glasgow and Edinburgh and in 1988 a further unit was established in Stonehaven. A Technical Support Unit was set up in 1989 to provide equipment for the use of police forces in Scotland and to assist them in their technical operations. An office of the National Criminal Intelligence Service[2] is now based with the Scottish Crime Squad, H.M. Customs and Excise Investigation Division and the Scottish Criminal Intelligence Office. These law enforcement agencies are responsible for intelligence gathering, analysis and dissemination. The function of NCIS is to provide an intelligence service aimed at major criminals whose activities cross regional and national boundaries. The NCIS provides criminal intelligence to local forces. 17.03

Role of the Justice Minister and Justice Committee

Responsibility for the police has been devolved to the Scottish Parliament. The Justice Minister is responsible for civil and criminal justice, social work services, criminal policy in relation to drugs, police, fire and emergency planning, law reform, land reform policy and freedom of information. In relation to the police forces he will be responsible for developing police policy, providing resources and regulating the police forces. 17.04

He is supported in this function by the justice committee which may, from time to time, set up steering groups to consider future policy and operations of police forces. The remit of the justice committee is to consider and report on matters relating to the administration of civil and criminal justice, the reform of the civil and criminal law and such other matters as fall within the responsibility of the Minister for Justice.

---

[2] Police Act 1997.

Scottish police forces

17.05 There are eight police forces in Scotland. The boundaries of the police forces formerly corresponded with local authority boundaries. Since the reorganisation of local authorities in 1996, only two police force areas correspond to local authority areas: Fife, and Dumfries and Galloway. The other six: Strathclyde, Central, Lothian and Borders, Tayside, Grampian and Northern have a number of local authorities within their areas. In these cases the police authority for each force is a joint board. Each local authority appoints representatives to the joint police authority, which is not under the control of a single local authority. Joint boards can be a useful way of running a service where each council would be too small to run a police authority on its own. However, it can be problematic because the needs and priorities of one local authority may not coincide with those of another and conflict may then arise. Joint police authorities have operated for a longer period in England and Wales. Problems have arisen there from time to time when a local authority has refused to pay their agreed share of the costs on time or has persistently questioned the amounts being spent in other parts of the force area. In addition to the main police forces who have general responsibility for a geographical area there are a number of other forces whose responsibilities are for specific functions. For example, the British Transport Police is responsible for the maintenance of law and order on the railways,[3] and the Ministry of Defence Police force is responsible for the security of certain premises.[4] Reorganisation of the eight police forces is currently under consideration.

Every police officer in Scotland is a constable irrespective of the rank which he may attain. A police officer is neither a servant of the local authority, nor a servant of the Crown. A police officer is a public servant appointed to preserve law and order for and on behalf of the citizens. Although he has certain powers which the private citizen does not have, a police officer does not occupy any privileged position in the community. The legal responsibility for actions by a police constable does not differ from that of the private citizen. A police officer may be sued for damages if he acts in excess of the powers which have been conferred on him, for example, by wrongfully arresting a citizen. A police constable is also liable for punishment for any crime or offence which he may

---

[3] See Railways Act 1993, s. 10; Transport Police (Jurisdiction) Act 1994.

[4] Ministry of Defence Police Act 1987; Atomic Weapons Establishment Act 1991.

commit. A deliberate violation of the criminal law on the part of a police officer is more than likely to be regarded by the court as an aggravated offence, resulting in severe punishment.

Her Majesty's Inspectors of Constabulary, under the direction of the Scottish Ministers, visit and inquire into the state and efficiency of police forces and report to the Scottish Ministers. These reports are published. Her Majesty's Chief Inspector of Constabulary submits an annual report to the Scottish Ministers.

Police authorities

The police authority for most areas is a joint board whose 17.06 members come from the local councils covered by the force area. The authority contributes 49 per cent of the cost of the police and they have a statutory responsibility for the payment of the salaries of police officers and other employees and the provisions of buildings and equipment. The authority appoints the chief constable and assistant chief constables in consultation with and with the approval of the Scottish Executive. The authority is also the disciplinary body for the chief constable and assistant chief constables. The police authority may dismiss a chief constable or require him to resign his appointment. Disciplinary rules are made by the Justice Minister. The chief constable makes an annual report to the police authority and may be required to submit other reports concerned with policing in the force area.[5] Such requests for additional reports are not common. The Chief Constable for Strathclyde Police was asked to make a report on the events during the miners' strike in 1984–85. It is very important that the police should be free from political interference. The police must retain operational independence so that the police force cannot be used in favour of a particular cause or to further the wishes of a particular segment of society.

Functions of a chief constable

The performance of a police officer is subject to the direction of 17.07 the chief constable, who has operational control of his force and enjoys considerable autonomy. He cannot be instructed to do something unless that instruction comes from the sheriff principal or appropriate prosecutor. The Lord Advocate may issue instructions as to the reporting of offences for prosecution. Like any other public servant, a chief constable is constrained in what he can do by

---

[5] Police (Scotland) Act 1967, s. 15.

the level of financial resources which have been made available to the police force. Major incidents and inquiries will be resourced fully but other areas of concern may not be resourced all of the time. The Scottish Executive controls the finances for police forces and thus will have considerable influence over the manner in which each police force carries out its duties. Each force has a statutory relationship with both the Scottish Ministers and the local police authority. Issues of finance and policy arise as the funding of police forces comes partly direct from the executive and partly via local authorities.

The chief constable determines the priorities for his area in terms of resources and deployment of his officers. This is known as operational control over the police force. He may decide to have a campaign against burglary, or drug trafficking or speeding, or alcohol or drug related road traffic offences. Such campaigns have been seen regularly in Scotland over recent years. He may decide not to intervene in relation to certain minor offences such as prostitution or kerb crawling. The allocation of resources will also mean that he will have to make difficult choices regarding the geographic spread of his force. In the Northern Constabulary area, for example, many village police stations have been closed because of financial constraints. This discretion is recognised by the courts but a person who has suffered a loss or injury or an infringement of rights because of operational decisions made by the chief constable may challenge his decisions through judicial review procedure. In the case of *R. v. Metropolitan Police Commissioners, ex parte Blackburn*[6] it was held that the discretion of a chief constable does not extend to a right to refuse to enforce a particular law. He has a duty to enforce the law and could be compelled to do so. However, he has discretion as to the disposition of his force and can decide to give a low priority to the enforcement of a legal provision.[7]

The chief constable makes all appointments below the rank of assistant chief constable and is responsible for the maintenance of discipline in the force. He is vicariously liable for the wrongful actions of his police officers. The police are not liable for failing to prevent a crime or to catch a criminal before he commits another crime. In *Hill v. Chief Constable of West Yorkshire*,[8] Mrs Hill, the mother of one of the victims of the Yorkshire Ripper (Peter Sutcliffe), argued that the police had been negligent as they had

---

[6] [1968] 2 Q.B. 118.

[7] See also *R. v. Chief Constable of Devon and Cornwall, ex p. CEGB* [1981] 3 W.L.R. 967.

[8] [1988] 2 All E.R. 238.

interviewed Sutcliffe at an early stage of their investigations. They had failed to apprehend him and he had gone on to commit further crimes, including the murder of her daughter. Her claim failed. Opinion was expressed that there might have been liability if the police had identified and apprehended the killer and had then negligently allowed him to escape.

Disciplinary offences and complaints against the police

There is a Code of Discipline embodied in regulations made under statutory authority.[9] The code includes offences such as conduct prejudicial to discipline, breach of confidence, unlawful exercise of authority, conviction by a court of any criminal offence, and wilful or careless neglect of duty (including disobedience to lawful orders). Unlawful exercise of authority includes making an unlawful or unnecessary arrest and using unnecessary force against a prisoner or any other person. If an allegation of breach of the disciplinary regulations is made, a senior officer tries to mediate by speaking to the complainer and informing them of the duties of the police officer in the circumstances. If this mediation is unsuccessful, an investigating officer must be appointed to report on the matter. This must not be the same senior officer who mediated with the complainer. The report is considered by an assistant chief constable who can decide that no formal action should be taken, or deal with the officer under the police misconduct procedures, or report the matter to a procurator fiscal. The officer is entitled to a hearing before the assistant chief constable and any offence must be proved beyond reasonable doubt. The penalties which may be imposed include a reprimand, a fine, reduction in rank or dismissal from the force. Appeal against a request to resign, dismissal, or reduction in rank may be made to a police appeals tribunal.[10] The tribunal consists of a Queen's Counsel and an inspector of constabulary. The tribunal may allow or dismiss the appeal or may vary the punishment. When it is alleged that a criminal offence has been committed, the matter must be referred to the procurator fiscal. The procurator fiscal may decide not to prosecute if, for example, there is insufficient evidence to prove that a crime or offence has been committed beyond reasonable doubt. In such circumstances disciplinary proceedings may go ahead although, as the standard of proof for disciplinary hearings is the same as for criminal convictions, there may be little point. 17.08

[9] Police (Discipline) (Scotland) Regulations (S.I. 1967 No. 1021) (as amended).
[10] Police (Scotland) Act 1967, s. 30 (as amended).

If a complainant is not happy with the way in which their complaint has been handled, they may complain to the Inspector of Constabulary.[11] The inspector does not investigate the substance of the complaint, only the way in which proceedings were carried out. This process, which is in effect an ombudsman process, gives an element of independent supervision. This is augmented by the role of the procurator fiscal. In England and Wales a similar independent element is provided by the Police Complaints Authority which is required to supervise all serious complaints against police officers.

The Justice Minister has said that the Scottish Executive is considering what steps can and should be taken to ensure that serious complaints against police officers are independently investigated. Although the Scottish Ministers believe that the present system of investigating complaints is generally fair and impartial, with independence provided where appropriate by the procurator fiscal and the Inspectorate of Constabulary, they recognise that there is public concern about the police investigating themselves. A steering group is currently examining the feasibility of setting up an independent police complaints body.

Functions of Police

17.09 The general functions of constables in Scotland were laid down in section 17 of The Police (Scotland) Act 1967,[12] which states:

"It shall be the duty of the constables of a Police Force to:

1. Guard, patrol and watch so as to:
   (a) prevent the commission of offences;
   (b) preserve order; and
   (c) protect life and property.
2. Where an offence has been committed, to take all lawful measures and make such reports to the appropriate prosecutor as may be necessary for the purpose of bringing the offender, with all due speed, to justice.
3. Serve and execute, when required, any warrant, citation or deliverance issued or process endorsed by the courts, being a warrant, citation, deliverance or process relating to any criminal proceedings.

---

[11] Police and Magistrates' Act 1994, s. 61.

[12] Police Scotland Act 1967, s. 17, as amended by the Criminal Procedure (Scotland) Act 1975, s. 460.

4. Attend any Court of Law for the purpose of giving evidence."

In Scotland the responsibility for policing has been separated from the responsibility for the prosecution of crimes through proceedings in the criminal courts. Once a constable has made a report that a crime has been committed by an offender, the Scottish police have no part in the decision to prosecute, or any other part of the procedure other than to act as a witness should a prosecution take place.

POWERS OF THE POLICE

The wide range of actions which may be described as police powers 17.10 include: arrest, detention, search, seizure, power of entry to premises, inspection of premises, animals and vehicles, etc. These powers differ according to the law relating to them and the procedural rules which govern their execution can be complex. In some cases, the powers are not exclusive to police officers alone but may be exercised by the general public or even other authorised persons such as H.M. Customs and Excise Officers.

Detention

A power of detention does not necessarily mean the same as a 17.11 power to take someone into custody. There is no statutory definition of detention but it has been described as a form of limited or temporary arrest. There are different degrees of detention, ranging from simply stopping a person in the street for a few minutes to taking a suspect to a police station to be held in custody. The powers to detain suspects and to require the co-operation of witnesses are contained in the Criminal Procedure (Scotland) Act 1995.[13] Section 13(1) provides that where a constable has reasonable grounds for suspecting that an offence has been committed and he believes that a person has information regarding the offence he may require that person to give his name and address. A person commits an offence if he, without reasonable excuse, fails to comply with this requirement. He may then be arrested.

Where a constable has reasonable grounds for suspecting that a person has committed or is in the process of committing an offence

[13] ss. 13, 14.

he may ask him for an explanation of the circumstances which have caused the constable to be suspicious. These powers may only be exercised at the scene of the suspected crime, another public place or another place where the constable is entitled to be. The constable may require the suspect to remain with him while the details of the name and address are verified. A suspect can be physically constrained if he refuses to wait.

Whether the person is a witness or a suspect the constable must inform the person of the reason for the requirement and must warn him that failure to provide the information is an offence for which an arrest may be made without a warrant.

17.12 Section 14 of the Act differs from section 13 in that it gives the police the power to detain suspects rather than merely require their names and addresses. Where a constable has reasonable grounds to suspect that a person has committed an offence punishable by imprisonment, he may detain that person. He must take him as quickly as reasonably practicable to a police station or other premises in order to carry out an investigation into the offence and to decide whether criminal proceedings should be taken against that person. Reasonable force may be used. The question of what will amount to reasonable grounds to detain a suspect was considered in the case of *Wilson v. Robertson*.[14] Wilson and another were found guilty of theft from cigarette vending machines in a licensed club. They appealed against conviction on the basis that their conviction depended largely on their own alleged admissions, which had been made when they were detained. It was argued that they had been illegally detained as there were no reasonable grounds for suspecting that they had committed the offences. It was held that it was not necessary for there to be evidence as to guilt but only reasonable grounds for the relevant suspicion. The police were of opinion that a fire exit at the scene of the crime had been interfered with and there was evidence that the accused were in a position to have done so. The police therefore had reasonable grounds for suspicion, the detention was lawful and the admissions were admissible as evidence.[15]

A formal statement in the form of a statutory caution must be given to a suspect who has been detained. The statement informs him that he is being detained because he is suspected of committing an offence punishable by imprisonment. He must be told of the general nature of the offence and the reasons for the

---

[14] 1986 S.C.C.R. 701.

[15] See also *Keegan v. Gilchrist*, 1999 J.C. 185.

constable's suspicions. He must be told that is being detained to allow further investigation to be carried out. He must be told that he is being taken to a police station and that he will then be informed of his further rights. The statement then finishes with the following words: "You are not obliged to answer any further questions but anything you do say will be recorded and may be given in evidence." The police are permitted to use *aide memoire* cards to ensure that they convey the statutory caution accurately.

When a suspect is detained under section 14 of the Act the constable must record the following information:

(a) the time, date and place at which the detention commenced;
(b) the suspected offence or offences;
(c) the reason for the suspicions;
(d) the time at which the suspect has been read the cautionary statement and informed of his rights;
(e) name and address of the suspect;
(f) any reply made by the suspect;
(g) the police station to which he is being taken;
(h) the time of arrival at the police station;
(i) the time and place of any subsequent move during detention.

A person may not be detained indefinitely. Detention must cease 17.13
as soon as there are no longer grounds for reasonable suspicion that the person committed the offence. The period of detention is deemed to end if the suspect is arrested for the offence or detained under any other statutory provision. In any case the detention must be terminated after six hours. A person may be detained under more than one enactment provided that the cumulative period of detention remains less than six hours. For example, a person may be detained under the Criminal Procedure (Scotland) Act 1995 and under the Misuse of Drugs Act 1971.[16] Detention is not to be used as a means of delaying arrest and charge. Once there is sufficient evidence to justify an arrest the suspect must be arrested and charged. In the case of *Grant v. H.M. Advocate*[17] an objection was raised as to the admissibility of statements made during detention. In the course of a trial for firearms offences evidence was given by a police officer of an incriminating statement made by the accused while he was being detained. The accused had been detained at

---

[16] ss. 14, 23.
[17] 1990 J.C. 77; 1990 S.L.T. 402; 1989 S.C.C.R. 618.

9.20 a.m. but was not arrested until 3.40 p.m. The statement was made between 2.10 p.m. and 2.20 p.m. It was argued that the statement was not admissible because the detention was not terminated until after the six hour detention period had been exceeded. It was held, that processes carried out within the six hour period were not invalidated if that period happened to be exceeded. The incriminating statement was given within the six hour period and was therefore admissible as evidence.

The statutory caution must be repeated once the suspect arrives at the place of detention. A delay in delivering the caution at this stage may not invalidate the proceedings as long as there is no unfairness. In the case of *Scott v. Howie*,[18] the accused had been detained and taken to a police station but the statutory caution had not been read to him on arrival. When questioning of the suspect commenced he was read both the statutory caution and a full common law caution. The accused then made a statement which was used in evidence at his trial. The High Court held that the evidence was admissible. What had occurred was a procedural defect. There had been no unfairness to the accused person. Any statements which he had made between the time when he arrived at the police station and the time when he received the caution would have been inadmissible. The common law test of fairness is used to decide whether evidence is admissible. Giving a full common law caution ensures that a person has been treated fairly and knows that his words will be used in evidence.

17.14 Powers of detention may also be conferred from time to time by specific legislation and these powers may vary from the general powers under the Criminal Procedure (Scotland) Act 1995. One such example is the Prevention and Suppression of Terrorism (Supplemental Temporary Provisions) Order 1984.[19] The regulations provided for an initial period of detention of 12 hours which could be extended if the examining officer had reasonable grounds for suspecting that the person detained was or had been involved in terrorist acts. In such a case the Home Secretary had the power to extend the period for up to five days while consideration was given to the making of an exclusion order. In the case of *Breen v. Chief Constable of Dumfries and Galloway*,[20] a person who had been detained alleged that he had been wrongfully detained and sought damages from the police. While returning to Northern

---

[18] 1993 S.C.C.R. 81.

[19] Prevention and Suppression of Terrorism (Supplemental Temporary Provisions) Order 1984 (S.I. 1984 No. 418).

[20] 1996 S.L.T. 822.

Ireland from Scotland, Breen was detained at Stranraer and held for five nights by police. It was held that, in order for Breen to succeed in his claim he would have had to identify the factors necessary to make the detention lawful and plead that one or more of these was absent. He had not done so and in particular had not challenged the exercise of the statutory power under which the police had acted.[21]

Rights of detainees

All persons have the common law right not to be mistreated in custody and the right not to answer any questions, other than to give their name and address. Under section 15 of the Criminal Procedure (Scotland) Act 1995 a person over the age of 16 who is detained has the right to have intimation of his detention, and of the place where he is being detained, made to a solicitor and to one other person such as a friend or relative. The detained suspect should be informed of this right without delay, or with no more delay than is necessary in the interests of the investigation, the apprehension of offenders or the prevention of crime. A record must be kept of the time at which the suspect exercised his right to have information about his detention communicated. The time at which his request was complied with must also be noted. The suspect does not have a right to have direct access to a lawyer at this stage. The six hour period of detention has been challenged as being in contravention of Article 6 of the European Convention on Human Rights. Article 6 is concerned with the right to a fair trial, which includes the right of a person to legal representation and the right of an accused person to know the charges which are being made against him. 17.15

A person aged under 16 years does not have the same statutory right to have a solicitor or other reasonably named person informed of their detention. The police may inform such persons if they deem it appropriate. Instead the police have a duty to inform the parent or guardian of the suspect, without delay, even if the suspect does not wish them to be informed. If the parent or guardian cannot be found another relative or a social worker should be contacted. A parent or guardian must be given access to the suspect unless it is suspected that the parent was involved in the offence and the investigation requires the two suspects to be kept apart. Access may also be refused if it is in the interests of the

21 See also *Dahl v. Chief Constable of Central Scotland*, 1983 S.L.T. 420; *Shields v. Shearer*, 1914 S.C. 33.

child. A potentially violent parent, for example, may be refused access.

Whilst a person is detained, the police have certain powers to assist them with the investigation. They may question the suspect provided that the questions are fair. A common law caution must be administered prior to the commencement of questioning. They may search the suspect. They may take fingerprints, palm prints and such other prints and impressions as are deemed appropriate. The suspect may be removed to another location. The search of the suspect may include bags, such as handbags, which the suspect is carrying as well as a search of the suspect's clothing.[22]

Search

Search of persons

17.16 Unless a person has been arrested there is no power to search them under common law. Evidence obtained from a search where a person has voluntarily consented to be searched will, however, be admissible in a trial.[23] Apart from any statutory power, the police have no power to search a person prior to his arrest. There is no common law power to search a person in order to discover evidence for grounds of arrest. In situations of extreme urgency searches carried out before arrest may be excused and the evidence obtained may be used at trial. In *Bell v. Hogg*[24] it was held that searching or taking samples of substances from a person may be justified where the evidence was in danger of being destroyed. While investigating a suspected theft of copper in the early hours of the morning, the police stopped a van, told the four occupants the reason and cautioned them. The officer noticed marks which he suspected were made by copper on their hands, and took them to the police station. Before they were arrested or charged of any offence he asked them to give hand-rubbings on paper. They were not told that they need not do so. The substance from their hands matched the stolen wire and the four were prosecuted. Objection was taken to the evidence of the rubbings. It was held that in view of the urgency of preserving evidence, the officer was justified in taking the hand-rubbings. There had been no unfairness to the accused; and so the evidence was admissible.[25] When deciding

---

[22] *Skirving v. Russell*, 1999 G.W.D. 15–701.

[23] *Devlin v. Normand*, 1992 S.C.C.R. 875; *Davidson v. Brown*, 1991 S.L.T. 335; 1990 S.C.C.R. 304.

[24] 1967 J.C. 49; 1967 S.L.T. 290.

[25] See also *Miln v. Cullen*, 1967 J.C. 21.

whether or not evidence is admissible account is taken both of the public interest in the effective investigation of crime and the protection of the accused from arbitrariness, dishonesty or oppression. The court has a discretion in each case whether to allow the evidence and avoid an accused person being acquitted on a technicality or whether to disallow it and avoid condoning departures from procedures by the police.

Search before arrest may be authorised by a specific statutory provision such as the Civic Government (Scotland) Act 1982 which provides that a police constable has power to search a person suspected on reasonable grounds of being in possession of stolen property.[26] A constable may seize any suspected stolen property and any other evidence of the commission of theft. This power also enables police to stop and search vehicles and vessels in similar circumstances, although only uniformed officers are allowed to stop vehicles.[27] Before carrying out any power of search plain clothes officers must produce identification. The Criminal Law (Consolidation) (Scotland) Act 1995 provides the police with power to search a person reasonably suspected of being in possession of an offensive weapon. The person may be detained for that purpose and must be informed of the reason for the search and detention. Under the Misuse of Drugs Act 1971,[28] a person may be detained and searched if a constable has reasonable grounds to suspect that he is in possession of drugs. The police need not have seen a person acting in a suspicious manner in order to have reasonable grounds to suspect that he is in possession of drugs. Their suspicions may be based on evidence from other persons present or even from anonymous informants. In the case of *Weir v. Jessop*[29] it was held that there were reasonable grounds for suspicion based on information from an anonymous informant. The police had been told that a person was misusing drugs and had gone to the specified location. Weir was the only person there. When he was questioned he denied misusing drugs but did admit that, in the past, he had been involved with drugs. It was held that the police were justified in detaining him for the purposes of a search.

A person detained under this provision may be taken to a police 17.17
station for the purpose of being searched. Statutory powers of search must be exercised strictly in accordance with the procedures

---

[26] Civic Government (Scotland) Act 1982, s. 60.

[27] See *Chassar v. Macdonald*, 1996 S.L.T. 1331; 1996 S.C.C.R. 730.

[28] s. 23(2).

[29] 1991 S.C.C.R. 242.

laid down by the relevant statute.[30] Once they have been arrested the police have a power at common law to search a person. The power of search after arrest includes a power to photograph a person and to make a physical examination. This may include taking fingerprints, palm prints or other such prints and impressions of an external part of the body as the constable considers it appropriate to take, having regard to the circumstances of the suspected offence in respect of which the person has been arrested or detained.[31] On the authority of an officer of the rank of inspector or above, a constable may take samples of hair, fingernail or toenail clippings or scrapings, a sample of blood or other body fluids, a sample of saliva or body tissue obtained from an external part of the body by means of swabbing or rubbing.[32] Reasonable force may be used, if required, to obtain samples. Swabs may be taken from the mouth for the purpose of DNA fingerprinting where the circumstances of the offence justify this.[33]

Where a sample is sought before arrest or detention, or if samples are required which are not provided for in the statutory provisions, a warrant from a sheriff is required as authority. Such a warrant will only be granted where the circumstances are special and where the delicate balance that must be maintained between the public interest on the one hand and the interest of the accused on the other will not be disturbed. In the case of *Morris v. MacNeill*,[34] an accused person sought suspension of a warrant granted by a sheriff. A procurator fiscal had obtained from the sheriff a warrant to take a blood sample from a person suspected of having committed theft by housebreaking. There was blood found at the scene of the same blood group as blood found on the accused's clothing. The sheriff had regard to the facts that the crime was serious and that the blood analysis would greatly assist in clearing up the crime. The minimal invasion of the accused's body by a highly qualified doctor in obtaining a blood sample was outweighed by the public interest in solving crime. The sheriff accordingly granted the warrant and the accused thereafter sought suspension of it. It was held that the circumstances of the case were sufficiently special to justify taking a blood sample. Since the sheriff had considered balance of the public interest against the

---

30 *Normand v. McCutcheon*, 1994 S.L.T. 327.
31 Criminal Procedure (Scotland) Act 1995, s. 18(2).
32 *ibid.* s. 18(6).
33 *ibid.* s. 58; *Curley v. Fraser*, 1997 S.C.C.R. 705.
34 1991 S.L.T. 607.

accused's interest he was entitled to grant the warrant.[35] In a case where a warrant had been granted to take blood from a man charged with rape and assault of his wife it was held that the warrant could be modified in the interests of the accused. The accused had a phobia of needles. The warrant was amended to the taking of a sample of blood by means of finger pricks.[36]

Power of entry to premises

In order to enter private premises the police must have either the authority of the courts in the form of a warrant or be fully justified in their actions. At common law a constable is justified in entering premises only in certain limited circumstances. He can enter premises if he is in close pursuit of a person who has committed or attempted to commit a serious crime. Serious crimes include murder, rape, robbery, and theft by housebreaking. In *Cairns v. Keene*[37] the police followed a car because they suspected the driver of being under the influence of alcohol. After stopping his car the man ran into his house pursued by the police officers. He took a bottle from the fridge and drank from it. He claimed that there had been vodka in the bottle and that any breath test which he took would not be reliable. At his trial he argued that neither the breath test nor the subsequent blood test were admissible as evidence. The police were trespassers in his house and the breath test was not lawfully administered. He was convicted by the sheriff, appealed against the decision and the appeal was dismissed. The sheriff had not regarded the police as being justified in entering private premises because they were not in pursuit of a person suspected of being the perpetrator of a serious crime. He did, however, consider that the evidence was admissible despite this because vital evidence should not be excluded because of a technical flaw. The factors to be taken into account in deciding whether or not evidence is admissible are: (a) the urgency of the need to secure evidence; (b) the gravity of the crime; (c) the authority and good faith of those who obtained the evidence; (d) the general principle of fairness to the accused.[38] 17.18

---

35 See also *Brodie v. Normand*, 1995 S.L.T. 739; 1994 S.C.C.R. 924; *Walker v. Lees*, 1995 J.C. 125; 1995 S.L.T. 757; 1995 S.C.C.R. 445; *Hughes v. Normand (No. 1)*, 1993 S.L.T. 113.

36 *G v. Lees*, 1992 S.C.C.R. 252.

37 1983 S.C.C.R. 277.

38 *Lawrie v. Muir*, 1950 J.C. 19, *per* Lord Cooper.

A police officer may enter private premises to quell a disturbance which is actually proceeding,[39] if he hears cries of distress or if he is invited to enter by the occupant. In an emergency the police officer may force entry but only after first knocking loudly, stating that it is the police, indicating the nature of the business and demanding admission. Only then after the occupant fails to admit him, may he force entry. In *Campbell v. Vannet*[40] police officers saw a woman kneeling by the letter box of Campbell's front door receiving a package which they believed to contain heroin. One of the police officers shouted, "Police. Open the door." and saw Campbell run into the bathroom and lock the door. The police then forced open the front door and also the bathroom door where they found Campbell kneeling by the toilet with a brush in her hand. She was convicted of drug offences and appealed on the basis that the police had acted unlawfully. It was held that, as the police officers had just seen a serious crime being committed, they were entitled to enter the premises to detain the person suspected of that crime.

17.19 Several statutes authorise a police officer to enter premises without warrant. In each case the police may only take the specific actions which are authorised by the statute. Under the Licensing (Scotland) Act 1976 the police may enter licensed premises to investigate breaches of the licensing conditions. If premises are on fire the Fire Services Act 1947 gives authority to police officers to enter the premises, using force if necessary. Under the Betting, Gaming and Lotteries Act 1963 police may enter premises to investigate breaches of licensing conditions. The Crime and Disorder Act 1998, s. 24 amends the Civil Government (Scotland) Act 1982 to empower the police to enter premises without warrant where reasonable grounds exist for believing that an offence involving the use of noise-making equipment has occurred. This section authorises police to enter premises and to seize musical instruments, televisions and stereo equipment where there is reasonable ground for belief that their use is causing annoyance to others. This power can be exercised without the need for a warrant. The provision operates without prejudice to any other common law or statutory power of entry, search and seizure. Problems of noise caused by loud music might previously have been dealt with as a breach of the peace but difficulties could arise over retention of the property seized, pending any trial, particularly if the accused was

---

[39] *Moffat v. McFadyen*, 1999 G.W.D. 22–1038.

[40] 1997 S.C.C.R. 787.

not also the owner of the articles seized.[41] Where articles are seized a report must be submitted to the procurator fiscal. Once that is done the items can be retained until the prosecutor certifies that they are not needed as evidence, or until the conclusion of proceedings.

Search of premises

The police have no general power to search premises without a warrant. They may only search premises without a warrant if they have the full and free consent of the occupier of the premises. There must be corroborative evidence that consent has been given and the search must be conducted in the presence of the occupier. If, at any time, the consent is withdrawn the search must be terminated. Where a person has been arrested on a serious charge and a delay in carrying out a search may defeat the ends of justice a search without a warrant may be justified. Searches of premises may be carried out under specific statutory powers[42] or under the authority of a warrant. A general warrant to search premises or to remove articles is incompetent.[43] A warrant must be specific and its terms must be strictly adhered to.[44] If a search is carried out without a warrant any items seized may not be admissible in evidence. In *Graham v. Orr*[45] an accused person's car had been driven to a police station following his arrest on a drink-driving charge. It was held that a police constable, who opened the car door and looked inside the car, had carried out a search without having had the power to do so. Evidence of what he had found within the car was inadmissible. 17.20

An application for a warrant must specify the places to be searched, including outhouses and vehicles and the articles to be seized. The officers who are authorised to carry out the search must not actively search for any items other than those specified. In the case of *Leckie v. Miln*[46] officers who were searching a suspect's house removed a number of articles which were outside the terms of the warrant. The officers had not seen the warrant nor had they

---

41 Crime and Disorder Act 1998, s. 24 (3) and Sched. 1, enacted as Civic Government (Scotland) Act 1982, Sched. 2A.

42 *e.g.* Civic Government (Scotland) Act 1982, s. 60. See *Druce v. HMA*, 1992 S.L.T. 1110.

43 *Webster v. Behune* (1857) 2 Irv. 596; *Bell v. Black and Morrison* (1865) 5 Irv. 57.

44 *Leckie v. Miln*, 1982 S.L.T 177; *Drummond v. L.A.*, 1992 S.C.C.R. 290; *Thomson v. Barbour*, 1994 S.C.C.R. 485; *Bell v. McGlennan*, 1992 S.L.T. 237.

45 1995 S.C.C.R. 30.

46 1982 S.L.T 177.

been told what they were searching for. It was held that they had been unlawfully obtained and therefore could not be used in evidence. The conviction for theft was quashed. It often happens, however, that police, when conducting a search unexpectedly discover articles of an incriminating nature. In *Tierney v. Allan*,[47] the police found a typewriter, which matched the description of one which had been stolen, while they were searching for stolen gas cylinders. It was held that the police were justified in seizing the typewriter. In *H.M. Advocate v. Hepper*[48] the seizure of a briefcase was held to be justified. The initials on the briefcase did not match those of the occupier of the premises and so it was deemed to be plainly incriminating or of very suspicious character. In *Drummond v. H.M. Advocate*[49] it was held that the evidence of a police constable was not admissible when, operating under a warrant to search for the goods stolen from a furniture warehouse, he had admitted to searching also for and finding clothing stolen from another place. The evidence of another constable operating under the same warrant was admissible. He stated that he opened a wardrobe looking for small items such as pictures and table lamps stolen from the furniture warehouse and he happened to find woollen goods, which he suspected had been stolen from another place. A police officer was not prevented from taking possession of other articles of a plainly incriminatory character which he happened to come across in the course of a search. In the case of *Rollo v. H.M. Advocate*[50] it was held that a warrant to search for documents included data files held on computer. Rollo was convicted of being concerned in the supply of drugs. Information crucial to his conviction was seized by police acting on a warrant. The information was stored on a Memomaster electronic notepad and Rollo argued that such a device was not a "document" in terms of the section in terms of which the warrant was issued and that its contents were inadmissible in evidence and accordingly his conviction should be quashed. It was held that the essential essence of the term "document" was the information recorded on it and the seizure was within the terms of the warrant.

17.21 Only those authorised by the warrant may carry out a search and seize items as evidence. In *Hepburn v. Brown*[51] a warrant was obtained by Strathclyde police authorising a search of Hepburn's

[47] 1989 S.C.C.R. 334.
[48] 1958 J.C. 39.
[49] 1993 S.L.T. 476.
[50] 1997 J.C. 23; 1997 S.L.T. 958; 1996 S.C.C.R. 874.
[51] *sub nom. Hepburn v. Vannet*, 1998 J.C. 63; 1997 S.C.C.R. 698.

house. Information supplied by City of London police was used to obtain the warrant and a constable from London was involved in the search. During the search the English police officer found drugs. Hepburn objected to that evidence on the basis that the warrant authorised only the constables of the Strathclyde police force to carry out the search. Hepburn was convicted and appealed. It was held that the search was irregular because the English police officer had conducted part of the search himself. However, as the police officers had been acting in good faith and there had been no deceit on their part, the irregularity could be excused and the evidence could be ruled to be admissible.

Property seized under the authority of a warrant may only be retained by the police for the period authorised. Reasonable care must be taken of property and it must be returned to the owner at the end of the authorised period or at the end of the legal proceedings for which it is required as evidence.[52] Property which has been used in the commission of crimes may be seized under the authority of a warrant under the Proceeds of Crime (Scotland) Act 1995.[53] In *Shaw v. Colley*[54] it was held that neither the prosecutor nor the police had any power to seize a car prior to a trial as they had not applied for a warrant authorising the seizure. Shaws's car was seized by police officers. Shaw was alleged to have committed a number of road traffic offences over the previous two months and his solicitors were informed that the car was being kept pending an application for forfeiture if Shaw were convicted. It was held that the seizure without a warrant was unlawful.

Power to stop vehicles

The Road Traffic Act 1988[55] provides that a person driving a mechanically propelled vehicle on a road must stop the vehicle on being required to do so by a constable in uniform. In *Normand v. McKellar*[56] a person was charged with using or keeping on a public road a vehicle without a current tax disc. The police gave evidence that they were carrying out a routine road check when they stopped the accused person's vehicle and noticed that no vehicle excise disc was displayed on it. The accused claimed that this evidence was not admissible because the police had been carrying out an illegal road 17.22

---

52 *Bell v. McGlennan*, 1992 S.L.T. 237.
53 s. 23.
54 1998 S.L.T. 17; 1997 S.C.C.R. 597.
55 s. 163(1).
56 1995 S.L.T. 798.

stop at the time. The magistrate acquitted the accused. The procurator fiscal appealed by stated case and it was held that the power to stop vehicles under the Road Traffic Act was very general in its terms and the police officer was acting within the scope of that authority. Because the lack of a tax disc was obvious without any sort of search of the vehicle, there was nothing which could be described as an invasion of liberty or an excess of police powers.[57]

The Criminal Justice and Public Order Act 1994,[58] empowers a senior police officer to authorise the stopping of vehicles and persons if he reasonably believes that incidents of serious violence may take place in a particular location. He may order that vehicles are stopped and searched if he believes that this will prevent violence occurring. The Crime and Disorder Act 1998,[59] extends the power to stop vehicles. Having stopped a vehicle in anticipation of violence, a constable in uniform may require a person to remove an item, such as a mask, which he is wearing to conceal his identity and to seize the item.

A constable in uniform may require a person who is or has been driving, attempting to drive, or in charge of a motorvehicle on a road or public place, to supply a specimen of breath for a breath test. This power is limited to circumstances where the constable has reasonable cause to suspect hat the person has alcohol in their body or that the person has committed a moving traffic offence. Any police officer may require a person who has been driving and who has been involved in an accident to supply a breath test.[60] It is an offence for a person to fail, without reasonable excuse, to provide a breath specimen when required. In *Stewart v. Crowe*,[61] Stewart appealed against a conviction of driving with excess alcohol on the ground that the police had acted oppressively. He had been stopped as part of a police campaign against drunken driving in the period before Christmas. Officers had been instructed to stop all vehicles, inform the driver of the campaign and request them to take a breath test. If the driver refused, he was to be allowed on his way unless his breath smelt of alcohol. Stewart argued that in stopping vehicles in this way, the police were acting oppressively and outwith their powers. It was held that there was no unfair targeting of a particular

---

[57] See also *Beard v. Wood* [1980] R.T.R. 454; [1980] Crim. L.R. 384.
[58] s. 60.
[59] s. 25.
[60] Road Traffic Act 1988, s. 6.
[61] *sub nom. Stewart v. Brown*, 1999 S.L.T. 899; 1999 S.C.C.R. 327.

citizen because it was a general campaign. The imposition of random breath tests could have been unfair in other circumstances.

Arrest

Arrest, or apprehension, is the most fundamental invasion of the liberty of the individual. An arrest deprives a person of his liberty. Reasonable force may be used to effect an arrest if necessary. Arrests are almost always carried out by police officers. Police powers of arrest are derived from three sources of authority: arrest under the authority of a judicial warrant, arrest under authority of a specific statutory provision or arrest at common law. 17.23

It is possible in strictly limited circumstances for an ordinary person to carry out a citizen's arrest. A private citizen may arrest another person without a warrant where he has witnessed a crime. He may also arrest a person if he has been the victim of a crime and another witness points out the person who carried out the crime. A person who carries out a citizen's arrest in circumstances where it is not justified may be charged with assault. This happened in the case of *Bryans v. Guild*.[62] A person was convicted of assaulting a 15-year-old youth. A group of youths had been shouting and throwing objects at the accused's house. The accused chased the group of youths who ran away past the youth. The youth also ran away from the incident but was grabbed by the accused who twisted his arm up his back. The accused was convicted and appealed on the ground that he was justified in effecting a citizen's arrest of the youth. The appeal was refused because the accused had not witnessed an offence committed by the youth. A private citizen could only carry out an arrest if he was an eye-witness or he was a victim and had reliable evidence of identification from an eye-witness.

The meaning of arrest was considered in *Forbes v. H.M. Advocate*.[63] Forbes appealed against a conviction of conspiracy and various charges under the Explosive Substances Acts, Prevention of Terrorism Acts and Firearms Acts on the grounds that he had not been lawfully arrested. He claimed that statements he made to police were therefore not admissible as evidence. When police called at Forbes' he was told that the police had reasonable grounds to believe that Forbes had committed an offence under the Prevention of Terrorism Act 1984, s. 10. Forbes was informed

---

[62] 1990 S.L.T. 426.
[63] 1990 S.C.C.R. 69.

that he was being "detained". At the police station he signed a statement that he had been made aware of the reason for his "arrest". He argued that in terms of the statutory provision under which he was arrested detention had to be preceded by an arrest. He had been detained and not arrested. The court held that it was not strictly necessary to use the word "arrest" provided the suspect was sufficiently aware that he was under compulsion. Forbes was taken into custody in handcuffs and had signed the statement acknowledging that he was aware of the reason for his arrest. He must have understood that he had been arrested.[64] The general principle therefore is that a person is under arrest when he is no longer free to go about his business and he has been informed that he is under arrest.

Reasonable force may be used to effect an arrest.[65] It is an offence to resist a lawful arrest or to escape from police custody.[66] Every criminal prosecution is not preceded by an arrest. In many summary trials the accused is cited to appear in court by the service of a complaint. After he has been arrested and is in custody he has the right to have a third party informed that he is in custody and of the place where he is being held.[67] This intimation must be made with no more delay than is necessary in the interest of the investigation of the crime or the apprehension of offenders. The arrested person must be informed of this right as soon as he arrives at the police station. He must also be informed that he has the right to request the attendance of a solicitor at the place where he is being held.[68]

Powers of arrest under warrant

17.24 Where there is sufficient evidence to bring criminal charges a procurator fiscal will present a petition to the sheriff court seeking authority to arrest the suspect and bring him before the court. The petition for a warrant will set out the name and designation of the accused, specify the charge and seek warrants for a number of purposes, usually to arrest the accused and to search any premises occupied by him and the premises where he is located. The sheriff need not inquire into the grounds on which the warrant is sought provided that he has sworn information that there are reasonable

---

64 See also *Fox, Campbell and Hartley v. U.K.* (1990) 13 E.H.R.R. 157.
65 *Maclean v. Jessopp*, 1988 S.C.C.R. 13.
66 Police (Scotland) Act 1967, s. 41.
67 Criminal Procedure (Scotland) Act 1995, s. 15(1).
68 *ibid.* s. 17(1).

grounds for suspicion.[69] Warrants have been issued by justices of the peace until this year but the Lord Advocate has announced that they will now be issued only by sheriffs. The reason for this is that he believes that this will reduce the risk of arrest being challenged on the ground or irregularities in warrants. The European Convention on Human Rights is now incorporated into the domestic law of Scotland and there may be an increased number of challenges to the validity of criminal prosecutions. The validity of a warrant may be challenged by a bill of suspension in the High Court.[70] After a conviction challenge may be made by way of petition to the *nobile officium* of the High Court.[71] A warrant which is valid on its face cannot be challenged in the course of a trial in the sheriff court.[72]

Powers of arrest under specific statutory provisions

The police have the power to make arrests under a number of 17.25 statutes. The power usually arises where an offence under the particular statute has been committed. The powers of arrest vary greatly between statutes. A statute may confer an unconditional power of arrest for a particular offence in any circumstances. Examples of statutory provisions which place no conditions on the power of arrest are section 178 of the Road Traffic Act 1988, which makes it an offence to take and drive away a motorvehicle without the owner's consent and section 20 of the Firearms Act 1968, which makes it an offence to trespass on land with a firearm without reasonable excuse. Part I of the Sex Offenders Act 1997 requires those convicted of specified sexual offences to notify the police of their names and addresses and to keep the police informed of any changes. Once an order has been granted, a police constable is empowered to arrest an offender whom he has reasonable cause to suspect is in breach of any condition of a sex offender order.

It is more usual for a statute to give power of arrest for a specific offence, but only if specific conditions apply. An example of a conditional power of arrest occurs in section 47 of the Criminal Law (Consolidation) (Scotland) Act 1995. This section makes it an offence for a person to be in possession of an offensive weapon in public without an excuse. Police are given power to arrest persons committing this offence but only if the officer is not satisfied as to

---

[69] Renton & Brown, *Criminal Procedure According to the Laws of Scotland* (6th ed., W. Green); *HMA v. Rae*, 1992 S.C.C.R. 301.

[70] *Stewart v. Crowe, sub nom. Stewart v. Brown*, 1999 S.L.T. 899; 1999 S.C.C.R. 327.

[71] *HMA v. Rae*, above.

[72] *Allan v. Tant*, 1986 S.C.C.R. 175

the persons identity or address or the officer believes that arrest is necessary to prevent the offender committing some other offence using the offensive weapon.

The Civic Government (Scotland) Act 1982 gives the police power to arrest without warrant any person in or on a building with intent to commit theft.[73] In *Keegan v. Gilchrist*,[74] Keegan and others challenged the validity of their arrest under the Civic Government Scotland Act. They claimed that the police could only arrest them if they had seen them on or in the premises and suspected that they were about to commit theft. The police had been directed to the scene by a closed circuit television camera operator. It was held that the arrest was justified because the constable, having been directed to the scene, found the three accused persons running way. This behaviour was sufficient to give him reasonable ground to suspect that they intend to commit an offence.

17.26 The courts normally expect strict compliance with any conditions under which a statutory power of arrest is exercised. In *Wither v. Reid*[75] a woman who had been arrested under the Misuse of Drugs Act 1971, s. 24(1) resisted a clothing and body search for drugs. She was therefore charged with an offence under section 41 of the Police (Scotland) act 1967. The Misuse of Drugs Act gives only a conditional power of arrest. It states that a police officer may arrest a person if he reasonably suspects that they have committed an offence under the Act, but only if he believes with reasonable cause that the person will abscond if not arrested or if he has been unable to ascertain the name and address of the suspect or he believes that they have given a false name and address. It was held that the arrest was unlawful because none of those conditions was met. As the arrest was unlawful the woman was entitled to resist the search.

The usual ground on which an officer may arrest a person is that he has reasonable ground to suspect that the person has committed the offence. The test is rather subjective and the courts do not often seek evidence to ascertain whether the suspicion was objectively justified. Usually the court will be satisfied if the arresting officer honestly believed that the person arrested was committing or had committed the offence.[76] The arrest may be unlawful if there were no grounds whatsoever on which to base that belief. In

---

73 ss. 57, 59.

74 1999 J.C. 185, *sub nom. Keegan v. Friel*, 1999 S.C.C.R. 378.

75 1979 S.L.T. 192.

76 *McLeod v. Shaw*, 1981 S.C.C.R. 54.

Nicol v. Lowe,[77] Nicol and another had been seen by the police emerging from a driveway late at night, had been arrested and cautioned. They had then been searched and incriminating articles had been found. Nicol argued that his presence in the driveway was an insufficient basis for arrest and search. It was held that the police officers did not have reasonable grounds to suspect that an offence had been committed. The men had not acted suspiciously and the police had not asked the householder whether the men were there lawfully.

Arrest at common law

There is a general principle in Scots law that a person should not be arrested unless the arresting officer believes that it is necessary in the interests of justice so to do. Offenders may be arrested without a warrant but only if the circumstances justify apprehension and the ends of justice would not be equally served by a summons or arrest under warrant. A police officer has power to arrest without warrant where he sees a person committing an act which is a crime at common law. He may also arrest a person if he is informed, by an apparently credible witness that the person has just committed a crime at common law. A person who is seen running away from the scene of a crime pursued by others may also be arrested without warrant. The police may also arrest a person if he is threatening danger to members of the public or is behaving in a way offensive to public decency. 17.27

Where a person has committed a minor offence arrest is not usually necessary. A summons to appear in court for trial is usually sufficient. Arrests may be carried out in relation to minor offences where the ends of justice would be defeated if a person were not arrested. Arrest may be justified to avoid repetition of the offence or to stop the person offending. An example would be if a drunken man was throwing bricks at windows and refused to stop. If an offender refuses to give his name and address, or his name and address is not known and cannot be ascertained, he may be arrested. Arrest may be justified in the interests of the offender or in the interests of public safety. People who are excessively intoxicated may be arrested for their own safety. Arrest may also be justified to prevent an evident intention to run away in order to escape prosecution or to dispose of evidence.

---

[77] 1990 S.L.T. 543; 1989 S.C.C.R. 675.

Questioning

17.28 A person who has been detained by the police may be questioned so that the police may ascertain the truth of the matter which is being investigated.[78] Questioning may lead a suspect to provide information which will incriminate him by connecting him with the offence. A suspect may decide to make a confession when he is questioned. The general rule is that the courts will accept statements made by suspects during questioning as hearsay evidence provided that there has been no unfairness towards the suspect. In order to ensure that the suspect is aware of the fact that statements which he makes may be used in evidence he must be cautioned both at the time when he is detained and when he arrives at the police station where he is to be questioned. A full formal common law caution should be read to him before he is questioned.[79] There is no formal legal requirement for this caution to be read but it renders it more probable that the questioning will be deemed to be fair. There are circumstances where information given in response to a question without any caution being given will be admissible as evidence. In *Custerson v. Westwater*[80] the police asked Custerton if he had a knife in his possession. At this stage he had not been cautioned but the evidence that he had a knife was admissible in court. In *Young v. Friel*[81] it was held that it was not necessary to administer a second caution when a suspect volunteered information about another offence then unknown to the police, of which he was later convicted.[82]

Statements by a suspect to another ordinary person recorded without his knowledge are not admissible as evidence. In *H.M. Advocate v. Graham*[83] the police had interviewed a suspect on an assault charge and then released him. They still suspected him but did not have enough evidence to charge him. Prior to a business meeting they provided a colleague of Graham's with a radio transmitter. Graham made incriminating statements. It was held that the evidence was inadmissible. Although evidence should only be withheld from a jury in special circumstances, the unfair way in which the evidence had been obtained denied the accused his right not to incriminate himself. Evidence which has been obtained by

---

[78] Criminal Procedure (Scotland) Act 1995, s. 14.
[79] *Tonge v. HMA*, 1982 S.L.T. 506.
[80] 1987 S.C.C.R. 389.
[81] 1992 S.C.C.R. 567.
[82] *Pennycuick v. Lees*, 1992 S.L.T. 763.
[83] 1991 S.L.T. 416.

inducement, entrapment, deception, threats or oppression will not be admitted as evidence.

LOCAL AUTHORITIES

The powers of local authorities relate mainly to the power to permit certain activities to take place by means of licences. Under the Civic Government (Scotland) Act 1992, local authorities have the power to license certain types of business activity. Examples include scrap metal businesses, private car hire and taxi businesses, street trading, second-hand car dealing and public entertainment. Local authorities also regulate the sale of alcohol by the administration of a liquor licensing system under the Licensing (Scotland) Act 1976. Licences may be granted subject to conditions and may be revoked. 17.29

Under the Crime and Disorder Act 1998,[84] a local authority may make an application for an anti-social behaviour order if it appears to the authority that a person of, or over the age of 16, has acted in an anti-social manner or pursued a course of anti-social conduct likely to cause alarm or distress to one or more persons outside his household in the authority's area. The purpose of an anti-social behaviour order is to protect persons in the authority's area from further anti-social acts or conduct by them. The provision has been introduced to protect residents from 'neighbours from hell' whose behaviour infringes on the rights of those around them to enjoy a peaceful existence. An application is made to a sheriff who can make an order prohibiting the person from doing anything described in the order. An order can last for a specific period, or indefinitely, but either the local authority or the party named in the order can apply for its variation or revocation.[85]

Local authorities also have specific powers arising from their role as landlords. The Crime and Disorder Act 1998,[86] entitles a local authority to take account of a broad range of anti-social behaviour by a tenant, his companions or visitors at the house, or in its vicinity, as grounds for terminating a secure tenancy. Under the Housing (Scotland) Act 1987[87] the landlord of a secured tenant can apply to the sherifff or an eviction order to remove the tenant from the premises. The 1998 Act widens the categories of people

---

[84] s. 19.
[85] Crime and Disorder Act 1998, s. 21(7).
[86] s. 23.
[87] Sched. 3.

whose conduct at the tenanted house, or in its vicinity, can give rise to an eviction. A tenant may be evicted not only because of their own conduct or that of other people living in his house but also because of the actions of visitors. An eviction order may be granted if visitors to the premises have directed actions against the tenant's neighbours, or if they have committed criminal offences.

STATE SECURITY ORGANISATIONS

Security service (MI5)

Functions

17.30 The internal security service of the United Kingdom is known as MI5. The operations of MI5 and MI6 are co-ordinated by an Intelligence Co-ordinator, based in the Cabinet Office. MI5 was established in 1909 under royal prerogative powers as part of the defence of the realm. It was not regulated by statute until the Security Services Act 1989 was brought into force. The service is headed by the Director General who is responsible to the Secretary of State for the Home Office. The security service is not incorporated into the Home Office and so apart from the line of responsibility it stands alone. The Director General reports directly to the Prime Minister on matters of importance. The service is mainly concerned with gathering information in order to suppress terrorist activities. It holds about 440,000 files but many of these are historical as the service keeps files of all investigations over the last 90 years. About 13,000 files are active dossiers on British citizens.[88] The remit of MI5 has been extended to include investigations of serious crime, particularly the import and distribution of illegal drugs.[89] This role is intended to support, rather than replace the work of the conventional law enforcement agencies. The service is not, however, accountable to local police authorities and the actions of its members may not be the subject of complaints under the police complaints procedures.

The Security Services Act 1989 defines the functions of the security service and gives statutory authority for the issuing of warrants. The function of MI5 is defined as being:

> "The protection of national security and, in particular, its protection against threats from espionage, terrorism and

---

[88] *Hansard*, H.C. Vol. 317, col. 251.

[89] Security Services Act 1996.

sabotage, from the activities of agents of foreign powers and from actions intended to overthrow or undermine Parliamentary democracy by political, industrial or violent means.

It shall also be the function of the Service to safeguard the economic well being of the United Kingdom against threats posed by the actions or intentions of persons outside the British Islands."[90]

The duties of the Director General of the Service are defined in section 2. He is responsible for the efficiency of the Service.[91] He is also obliged to ensure that the Service only collects information which is necessary for the proper discharge of its functions.[92] He must also ensure that the Service does not take any action to further the interests of any political party.[93] The Intelligence Services Act 1994 established a Parliamentary Intelligence and Security Committee to scrutinise the work of the security services. This provides parliamentary scrutiny of the work of the security services for the first time but there is still provision for information to be withheld from Parliament. Information may be withheld if the Secretary of State has determined that it should not be disclosed.[94]

The security service has powers to interfere with property.[95] Interference with property includes forcing entry and bugging premises. Interference with property is lawful if it is authorised by the Secretary of State. The Secretary of State may issue a warrant to obtain information which he considers to be likely to assist the Service to carry out any of its functions. He may only do so if the information cannot be obtained by other means. Warrants are only effective for a period of six months. Warrants may be issued by an authorised senior civil servant where the matter is one of urgency.

The Commissioner

The Prime Minister is under a duty to appoint a Security 17.31
Services Commissioner.[96] He must be a person who holds or has held high judicial office. His function is to keep under review the exercise of the powers to interfere with property. All members of

---

[90] s. 1.
[91] Security Services Act 1989, s. 2(2).
[92] *ibid.* s. 2(2)(a).
[93] *ibid.* s. 2(2)(b).
[94] Intelligence Services Act 1994, Sched. 3, para. 3(1)(b)(ii).
[95] *ibid.*, ss. 5, 6.
[96] Security Services Act 1989, s. 4.

the Security Service and all departmental officials of the Home Office are under a duty to disclose information to him when requested. The Commissioner makes an annual report to the Prime Minister. This report is laid before Parliament but information may be excluded from the report if it appears to the Prime Minister, after he has consulted the Commissioner, that disclosure of the material would be "prejudicial to the continued discharge of the functions of the Service."[97] The Commissioner may instigate the investigation of complaints made by individuals.

The tribunal

17.32 The purpose of the tribunal is to investigate complaints about the service.[98] Any person may complain to the tribunal if he is aggrieved by anything which he believes the Service has done in relation to him or to any property of his.[99]

The tribunal is under a duty to investigate all complaints except those which are frivolous and vexatious. The scope of the investigations which the tribunal may make is very limited. It may investigate whether the Service had reasonable grounds to investigate the complainant. If the Service has disclosed information about the complainant to a third party, such as an employer, the tribunal may ascertain whether the information was true. Complaints about the issue of warrants are referred to the Commissioner who considers whether the Secretary of State was acting properly in issuing the warrant. There is no appeal from a decision of the tribunal and its decisions are not liable to be questioned in any court.

Secret intelligence service (MI6)

Functions

17.33 MI6 is the security service which deals with matters overseas. It gathers information for the defence of the realm and carries out espionage and covert operations outside the United Kingdom. The nature of its work requires a strict regime of secrecy. The existence of the Secret Intelligence Service was acknowledged officially for the first time in 1992. The Secret Intelligence Service is under the control of the Foreign and Commonwealth Office. The function of the Secret Intelligence Service is to obtain and provide information relating to the actions of persons outside the British Islands, and to

---

[97] Security Services Act 1989, s. 4(6), (7).
[98] *ibid.* s. 5.
[99] *ibid.* Sched. 1, para. 1.

perform other tasks relating to the actions or intentions of such persons. The actions which it carries out must be in the interests of national security, with particular reference to defence and foreign policies, or in the interests of the nation's economic well being and assisting in the prevention or detection of serious crime.[1]

Actions are carried out under the authority of warrants from the Secretary of State in the same way as actions by the Security Service. Complaints may be investigated by the Commissioner and tribunal. Where actions have been carried out under the authority of a warrant from the Secretary of State outside the British Islands, the authorised agent will be immune from any civil or criminal liability in the United Kingdom.[2]

---

1 Intelligence Services Act 1994, s. 2.

2 Security Services Act 1989, s. 7.

CHAPTER 18

LIABILITY OF THE CROWN AND PUBLIC AUTHORITIES

INTRODUCTION

18.01 Each year the Crown makes thousands of millions of pounds worth of contracts. It owns land, it employs staff, it purchases equipment and contracts for services. Other public authorities also enter into contracts with commercial and non-commercial organisations and with individuals. According to the doctrine of the rule of law, public authorities should be subject to the same rules of liability in contract and delict as private individuals and companies. In explaining this concept of equality before the law Dicey said: "With us every official, from the Prime Minister down to a constable or a collector of taxes, is under the same responsibility for every act done without legal justification as any other citizen."[1] It is unfair for a person who has entered into a contract with a government organisation to be denied the right to redress that he would have enjoyed had his contract been with a private individual. However, the extent to which the Crown will be liable for a breach of contract is not necessarily the same as in the case of a private individual and there are exceptions to the liability of public authorities and the Crown in delict.

LIABILITY OF THE CROWN IN CONTRACT

18.02 In Scotland, unlike England, it has always been possible to sue the Crown for breach of contract or in respect of contract. The common law principle that the Crown could sue and be sued in the courts was given statutory force by the Crown Suits (Scotland) Act 1857. Section 1 of the Act provides:

---

[1] *The Law of the Constitution* (10th ed., 1995), p. 193.

> "Every action, suit or proceeding to be instituted in Scotland on behalf of or against her Majesty or in the interest of the Crown, including the Scottish Administration, or on behalf of or against any public department, may be lawfully raised in the name of and at the instance of or directed against the appropriate Law Officer acting under this Act."[2]

It is not necessary for the individual office holder to be named in the action.[3] The "appropriate Law Officer" means: "(a) The Lord Advocate, where the action, suit or proceeding is on behalf of or against any part of the Scottish Administration, and (b) The Advocate General for Scotland in any other case."[4]

Petition of right

In England, prior to 1947, there was a presumption that the sovereign could do no wrong and so a direct action against the Crown in the courts was not possible. The courts were, after all, the sovereign's courts which he had provided for the settlement of disputes and it was considered he should not be called to account in his own courts. An action against the Crown for breach of contract was only possible by means of a petition of right. This was a device whereby the Crown consented to allow action to be taken against it. A person petitioned the Crown for his just rights and the Crown voluntarily referred the petition to the courts for a decision. The courts tried the case in the normal way except that the judgment took the form of a declaration of the rights of the individual. There was no way of enforcing this legally but, in practice, the Crown always respected such a decision. There was no remedy if the Crown refused to give consent. In practice however, consent was given whenever a subject had a possible claim. 18.03

CROWN PROCEEDINGS ACT 1947

The purpose of the Crown Proceedings Act 1947 was to provide for redress against the Crown through ordinary litigation. Section 1 of the Crown Proceedings Act 1947 (which does not apply to 18.04

---

2 The Crown Suits Act 1857 was amended by the Scotland Act 1998, Sched. 8, para. 2(1) to take account of the existence of the Scottish Parliament and the Advocate General.

3 *L.A. v. Black*, 1995 S.L.T. 540.

4 Scotland Act 1998, Sched. 8, para. 2(5).

Scotland) provides that any person having a claim against the Crown which previously might have been enforced by petition of right may now proceed directly against the Crown. This does not, however, render the Crown liable for breach of contract in the same way in which a private person would be liable. In the case of *Commissioners of Crown Lands v. Page*,[5] a tenant of land sought relief from the obligation to pay rent when the land was requisitioned by a government department. He was found liable to continue to make payments under the terms of the lease as the Crown is not contractually liable for actions taken by the government in the national interest. Devlin L.J. observed: "When the Crown, in dealing with one of its subjects, is dealing as if it too were a private person, and is granting leases or buying and selling as ordinary persons do, it is absurd to suppose that it is making any promise about the way in which it will conduct the affairs of the nation."

The Crown Proceedings Act did not alter the liability of the Crown under contract law in Scotland but it does have some relevance to contract law in Scotland. One example is section 50(2)(d), which provides that a government department cannot set debts owed to another government department against a claim made against the department without the consent of the court. In practice it appears that, if a person makes a claim against a government department, the court will usually consent to any debts owed to other government departments being taken into account. In the case of *Smith v. Lord Advocate*,[6] the liquidator of Upper Clyde Shipbuilders Ltd raised an action against the Lord Advocate, as representing the Ministry of Defence, for payment of £1,353,369. The Lord Advocate admitted that that sum was owed to Smith but sought leave under the Crown Proceedings Act 1947[7] to set off against that sum four debts owed by Upper Clyde Shipbuilders to other government departments. It was held on appeal that there were no circumstances which could properly justify a refusal to grant the leave sought by the Crown. It was observed that in common law and practice the Crown is regarded as an indivisible entity.

---

[5] [1960] 2 Q.B. 274.

[6] 1980 S.C. 227; 1981 S.L.T. 19.

[7] s. 50(2)(d).

LIABILITY IN DELICT

Liability of individual public servants

Every individual is liable for his own wrongful acts and omissions. Therefore, any person who is not protected by statutory duty can be sued for damages for negligence or breach of statutory duty. The most famous instance of this is the case of *Entick v. Carrington*.[8] King's messengers had broken into Entick's house and seized papers. They pleaded as a defence that they were acting under a warrant from the Secretary of State. It was held that this was no defence as the Secretary of State had no authority to issue the warrant. Superior orders will therefore not be a defence to an individual unless he is: (a) acting under the authority of a court acting within its jurisdiction, or (b) protected by statutory immunity whilst acting bona fide in the course of his duties. 18.05

A person who has suffered a loss because of the wrongful actions of a public official will usually prefer to sue the employing authority as being vicariously liable for the wrongful acts and omissions of their employee. However, there are some situations where a statute imposes a duty on an officer of central or local government as a designated officer rather than on the public authority which appoints him.[9] In the case of *Stanbury v. Exeter Corporation*[10] it was held that a local authority was not vicariously liable when their inspector of animals had seized sheep, which he had believed were diseased. The inspector was acting under a statutory duty, which was conferred on him personally by reason of his office and not on the authority which employed him. If the duty is one which is delegated to the employees of a local authority other than the designated official then the local authority may be vicariously liable. In the case of *Ministry of Housing and Local Government v. Sharp*,[11] it was held that an authority was liable where an employee had negligently certified that there were no local land charges registered against land which was being sold. The statutory duty of issuing certificates was imposed on the clerk to the local authority as registrar but, as this function was normally delegated to other employees, the local authority was vicariously liable.

---

8 (1765) 19 St.Tr. 1030.

9 Wade and Forsyth, *Administrative Law* (7th ed., Oxford University Press, Oxford, 1994), p. 764.

10 [1905] 2 K.B. 838

11 [1970] 2 Q.B. 223.

Acts and decisions giving rise to liability in delict

18.06 Liability will only arise if there has been an act which amounts to a legal wrong. In the case of *Malone v. Metropolitan Police Commissioner*,[12] it was held that no damages could be awarded at common law for the interception of telephone calls, which was held not to be a delict.[13]

Distinction between policy and operations

18.07 The formulation of a policy which may cause harm to others will not necessarily lead to a liability on the part of the Crown to pay compensation, unless the decision to formulate the policy is *ultra vires*. However, the negligent operation of activities authorised by that policy may give rise to liability in delict. In the case of *Dorset Yacht Company v. Home Office*,[14] it was held that borstal officers owed a duty to neighbouring property owners to carry out their activities with care. The Home Office was sued for the value of a yacht, which had been damaged when seven borstal boys absconded at night from a borstal summer camp on an island in Poole harbour. The plaintiffs claimed that the borstal officers had been negligent. It was held that the Home Secretary could not be held liable for the policy which set up the regime in operation at the borstal. The borstal officers, however, owed a duty of care to the plaintiff to exercise proper supervision of the borstal boys in their care. It was reasonably foreseeable that damage to the plaintiff's property (a yacht in Poole Harbour), would be likely to occur if the officers failed to exercise proper control or supervision. Lord Reid said that there would be no liability for the way in which a statutory power was exercised unless the person exercising the power had departed so far from its terms as to be outside it altogether. In other words it would need to be proved that they were not only acting negligently but also *ultra vires*. It was held that the Home Office was liable for the negligence of the officers. There was no ground in public policy for granting immunity to the Home Office or its officers and damages were awarded.

In accordance with this principle, in the case of *Bonthrone v. Secretary of State for Scotland*,[15] it was held that there was no liability for alleged official negligence in encouraging vaccination of

---

[12] [1980] Q.B. 49.

[13] Compensation for wrongful telephone tapping may now be payable under the Interception of Communications Act 1985.

[14] [1970] A.C. 1004.

[15] 1987 S.L.T. 34.

infants without adequate warning of risk. Lord Grieve said that the duty of care in exercising a statutory power "does not arise until the discretionary stage of its exercise has ceased and the executive stage has begun". This approach to Crown liability was also evident in *Shetland Line v. Secretary of State for Scotland*,[16] wherein it was held that damages could not be awarded in respect of the consequences of a decision of a Minister of the Crown in the absence of misfeasance or an abuse of power amounting to bad faith. A duty of care might arise, however, in respect of the manner in which a power was exercised. Lord Johnston said that:

> "There is to my mind a clear distinction between the manner in which a particular power may be exercised particularly when physical consequences may occur, *i.e.* personal injury and the way in which a minister sets about making a decision and informing himself of the basic facts that relate to that. The former may in itself create a situation which could be categorised as negligence and give rise to a duty of care, the latter as I understand the present law does not do so."

Effects of devolution on Crown liability

A new aspect of Crown liability has arisen following devolution of certain legislative and administrative functions to the Scottish Parliament and Scottish Administration. Provision has had to be made for contracts between the Scottish Administration and the Westminster Administration. Rights and liabilities may arise between the Crown in right of the sovereign's Government in the United Kingdom and the Crown in right of the Scottish Administration by virtue of a contract, by operation of law or by virtue of an enactment. In other words both administrations have contractual capacity and may incur liabilities towards each other. Property and liabilities may be transferred between the Westminster Administration and the Scottish Administration. The two administrations may bring actions against each other and they may act as joint defenders to an action.[17] For example, when a U.K. Minister of the Crown makes an order requiring some action to be taken by the Scottish ministers, it should be possible for the Scottish ministers to seek judicial review of the order. 18.08

The Scottish Parliament is an unincorporated association and so a body, known as the parliamentary corporation, has been

16 1996 S.L.T. 653.

17 Scotland Act 1998, s. 99.

established by the Scotland Act[18] to represent the Parliament in all legal proceedings by, or against, the Parliament. The purpose of this provision is to prevent the business of the Scottish Parliament being hindered by frivolous court proceedings against individuals. There is a limited number of remedies which can be granted against the parliamentary corporation. Orders for reduction, suspension, interdict, or specific performance (including interim orders), may not be imposed against the parliamentary corporation. The remedy of declarator is available. The Parliament will not be bound by a declarator to act or to refrain from acting. It is for Parliament itself to decide what action to take.

VICARIOUS LIABILITY OF PUBLIC AUTHORITIES

18.09 Unless they are acting within their powers public officials are liable in the same way as any other person for nuisance, negligence, defamation and so forth. Actions against individual officials serve little purpose because individuals usually do not have the financial resources to pay damages. An action against a vicariously liable employer gives a better prospect of adequate damages. A number of statutes provide that a public body is vicariously liable for the wrongful acts or omissions of those carrying out operations. One example is the Police (Scotland) Act 1967, s. 39, which provides that a chief constable is vicariously liable for the acts committed by police officers in the performance of their functions.

Liability for negligence

18.10 When actions are being carried out by or on behalf or a public authority, or by an official under statutory authority, there is a presumption that the actions are to be carried out lawfully. There can never be a presumption that Parliament intended to authorise activities to be carried out in a negligent manner. Persons working under statutory authority are under a duty to exercise the standard of care which would be expected of a reasonably competent member of their trade or profession. In the case of *Geddis v. Proprietors of Bann Reservoir*,[19] a reservoir company was held to be liable for a negligent failure to clean a stream. The stream had become blocked causing flooding to neighbouring property. Lord Blackburn said:

---

[18] Scotland Act 1998, s. 21.
[19] (1873) 3 A.C. 430.

> "[I]t is now thoroughly well established that no action will lie for doing that which the legislature has authorised, if it be done without negligence, although it does occasion damage to anyone; but an action does lie for doing what the legislature has authorised, if it be done negligently."[20]

In an action against the fire brigade, which failed because of lack of proof of negligence, it was held that the fire brigade is under a duty of care to owners of property. The claim for damages in the case of *Duff v. Highland and Islands Fire Board*[21] arose because a fire in a chimney was attended to by the fire brigade but restarted after they had left, causing the destruction of the house. It had been argued on behalf of the fire brigade that considerations of public policy prevented there being any duty of care owed by the brigade towards owners of property. They argued that, in any event the only loss which could be recovered would be loss beyond the loss which would have been sustained had the fire brigade never attended at all. It was held however, that fire fighters did owe a duty of care as there was a statutory duty imposed on fire authorities to make provision for fire fighting purposes. Damages for breach of the duty extended to all the loss resulting from the negligence.[22]

Where the activities which give rise to liability for negligence 18.11
comprise the provision of services such as roads, drains or sewers it is easy to establish the nature of the duty of care and the persons to whom that duty is owed. Matters are not so straightforward when the claim of negligence arises from the discretionary role of inspection or regulation carried out by a public authority. For some years there was an extension of the law in England which rendered a public authority liable for negligence in the performance of a regulatory function. It was held that, where local building inspectors failed to inspect, and then failed to inspect properly, the foundations of a new building, negligence by the council officials rendered the council liable for the cost of repairing the building. A block of flats developed cracks because it had been built on inadequate foundations. The council had a discretion whether or not to carry out inspections but once they exercised the discretion to carry out inspections, they were liable for any negligence in their operations.[23]

---

20 (1873) 3 A.C. 430 at 455.
21 1995 S.L.T. 1362.
22 See also *East Suffolk Rivers Catchment Board v. Kent* [1941] A.C. 74.
23 *Anns v. Merton London Borough Council* [1978] A.C. 728.

In Scotland although the decision in *Anns v. Merton London Borough Council* had some influence it was more cautiously accepted than in other parts of the United Kingdom. *Anns* was followed by a series of decisions which attempted to limit the wide duties of care which it established and this caused a degree of uncertainty as to the principles to be applied and a dependence on judicial discretion. Public authorities have been protected from liability, either by categorising actions of public authorities as 'policy' and so not giving rise to liability,[24] or by finding that a duty of care has not been established,[25] or by finding that liability will only arise if a statutory power has been exercised improperly. In the Scottish case of *Hallett v. Nicholson*,[26] it was held that where there is statutory authority there will be no liability on the part of the organisation for damages for acts or omissions committed in the proper exercise of its statutory duties or powers. Liability would arise, however, in respect of an act or omission committed in the course of an improper exercise of the authority's statutory powers. A statutory power or duty would be regarded as having been exercised improperly where it was not exercised in good faith in the interests of the public, or where it was not exercised in accordance with the statute. A failure to exercise a statutory power in accordance with the statute might include performing an authorised act in a negligent manner. The case arose following a fire in an Oban hotel in which a husband and wife had died. The hoteliers were sued on the grounds that they had failed to take reasonable care for the safety of the guests by providing adequate fire precautions. The hoteliers claimed that, under the terms of the Fire Precautions Act 1971, s. 5(3), the fire authority was bound to carry out an inspection of the hotel in order to award a fire certificate. They should have advised the hoteliers not to reopen. It was held that the fire authority was not under a duty to advise the hotel of risks of fire during inspections for fire certificates and was therefore not liable.

18.12 A statutory duty or power is exercised improperly where actions authorised by statute have been carried out in a biased way[27] or without taking reasonable precautions to avoid harm.[28] The case of *Rowling v. Takaro Properties Ltd*[29] was a decision of the Judicial

---

[24] *Ross v. Secretary of State for Scotland*, 1990 S.L.T. 13.
[25] *Gibson v. Strathclyde Regional Council*, 1992 S.C.L.R. 902.
[26] 1979 S.C. 1.
[27] *Wilson v. IBA*, 1979 S.L.T. 279.
[28] *Gillespie v. Lucas and Aird* (1893) 20 R. 1035.
[29] [1988] A.C. 473.

Committee of the Privy Council. The plaintiff owned a tourist lodge in New Zealand. After several years' unsuccessful trading he drew up a financial rescue package which included the sale of some shares to a Japanese company. This required the consent of the Minister of Finance who refused to give his consent. An action for judicial review had been allowed on the basis that the minister's refusal had been motivated by an irrelevant consideration of putting the land back into native New Zealand ownership. The Privy Council case was an appeal against an award of damages for breach of duty. The rescue package could no longer be implemented because of the delay. It was held that the distinction between policy and operations does not itself provide a touchstone of liability. The question is whether or not the case is suitable for judicial resolution, as in cases concerning the discretionary allocation of scarce resources or distribution of risks. Arguably the only private law action which should have been allowed to succeed in these circumstances was an action for malicious abuse of power.

In 1991 a case similar to *Anns v. Merton London Borough Council* arose; that of *Murphy v. Brentwood District Council*,[30] and the House of Lords held that *Anns* had been wrongly decided. The defendant council owed no duty of care to the plaintiff when it approved the plans for defective foundations for his house. The decision in *Murphy* was apparently influenced by a reluctance to award damages for pure economic loss. There was also concern that a local authority with a responsibility to ensure compliance with building regulations should not be held to owe a common law duty of care to avoid losses of the type suffered by the plaintiff. The court is not willing for councils to take on a role as insurers for those who suffer losses where the primary fault is with a third party (in this case the builder). Economic loss will not in general be recoverable unless it is the result of negligent misstatement or is consequential on injury or property damage. It was not decided whether negligence in administering building regulations might give rise to liability in the case of personal injury or damage to other property.

In the case of *Stovin v. Wise and Norfolk County Council*,[31] Lord 18.13
Hoffman said that the distinction between policy and operations is an inadequate tool with which to discover whether it is appropriate to impose a duty of care or not. Even if the distinction is clear cut, leaving no element of discretion in the sense that it would be

---

[30] [1991] 1 A.C. 398.

[31] [1996] A.C. 923; [1996] 3 All E.R. 801.

irrational for the public authority not to exercise its power it does not follow that the law should superimpose a common law duty of care. He stated:

> "This can be seen if one looks at cases in which a public authority has been under a statutory or common law duty to provide a service or other benefit for the public or a section of the public. In such cases there is no discretion but the courts have nevertheless been willing to hold that a member of the public who has suffered loss because the service was not provided to him should necessarily have a cause of action, either for breach of statutory duty or for negligence at common law."

Whether a statutory duty gives rise to a private cause of action depends on construction of the relevant statute. It requires an examination of the policy of the statute to decide whether it was intended to confer a right to compensation for breach. The case related to an alleged breach of a common law duty of care owed by a local authority by failing to take reasonable measures to reduce the dangers to road users at a road junction.

Duty of care

18.14 Liability for negligence will only arise where it can be proved that the person at fault owed a duty of care to the person who suffered the loss or injury. A duty of care is not owed to the world at large but only to those to whom it is reasonably foreseeable that harm could be caused by a breach of the duty of care. In the case of *Forbes v. City of Dundee District Council*,[32] damages were claimed from the local council for injuries sustained when Mrs Forbes fell down a flight of stairs. She claimed that the local authority was at fault for failing in its duty to take reasonable care to ensure that the stairs were built to comply with building regulations. It was held that Parliament did not intend any civil liability to arise from the Building (Scotland) Act 1959. The purpose of the Act was to enable a local authority to regulate building works. In order to establish that there is a duty of care one requirement is that there should be a sufficiently determinate class of persons to whom a duty of care could be said to be owed. This class must be smaller that the public at large. It was held that in this case there was no such class to whom a duty of care could arise.

---

32 1997 S.L.T. 1330; 1997 S.C.L.R. 682.

Need for a relationship of sufficient proximity

In order to claim compensation it is necessary to establish that there is some relationship between the person who has suffered the loss and the person who is under the duty. In the case of *Yuen Kun Yeu v. Attorney-General*,[33] Lord Keith said that, not only was there a test of reasonable foreseeability of harm, but also that it was necessary to show a relationship between the plaintiff and the public authority. The question to be considered was, taking into account the nature and extent of relevant statutory powers, did there exist between the public authority and the plaintiff such close and direct relationship as to place the authority under a duty of care to the plaintiff? The case of *Hill v. Chief Constable of West Yorkshire*[34] established that the police are not liable to members of the public for failure to apprehend an unknown criminal before he committed further crimes. There needed to be proximity of relationship in order for a duty of care to arise. The case was an action for damages raised by the parent of one of the later victims of the serial killer Peter Sutcliffe, known as the Yorkshire Ripper. It was alleged that the police had been negligent in not apprehending the killer earlier in the investigation. It was held, dismissing the plaintiff's appeal, that, in the absence of any special relationship between the police and a criminal arising out of the fact that the criminal was in police custody or had escaped from it, the general duty owed by the police to suppress crime did not give rise to a duty owed to individual members of the public. There was no special relationship between the police and Sutcliffe since he had neither been in police custody nor escaped from it. 18.15

Even where it has been established that a statute was intended to create a statutory duty which would give rise to a liability in damages, that liability extends only to those who fall within the class of persons which the Act was intended to protect or benefit. An individual who receives a benefit in consequence of the operation of a statute rather than as an intended recipient of a benefit or protection will not be entitled to damages. In the case of *X v. Bedfordshire County Council*,[35] a claim for damages was brought against a local authority for breach of its duties under child care legislation. Abused children claimed that the authority was in breach of its duty to protect them from harm. The court concluded that the child care legislation did not give rise to liability

33 [1988] A.C. 175.
34 [1988] 2 All E.R. 238.
35 [1994] 2 W.L.R. 554.

for breach of statutory duty. The purpose of the legislation was to establish an administrative system designed to promote the social welfare of the community. In such a context it would require exceptionally clear statutory language to show a parliamentary intention that there should be liability for breach of statutory duty.[36] In the case of *T v. Surrey County Council*,[37] damages were claimed from a local authority for injuries inflicted on a child by a childminder. The local authority had failed to maintain its register of childminders and was therefore in breach of the Nurseries and Childminders Regulation Act 1948. The name of the childminder should have been removed from the register as she had been implicated in a previous case involving injury to a child in her care. However, it was held that the local authority was not under a statutory duty to the child which would give rise to liability in damages.

Similarly in the case of *Armstrong v. Moore*[38] it was held that a building authority's statutory duty to ensure compliance with building regulations was not owed to owners of neighbouring properties. The purpose of the building standards regulations was to secure the health and safety of those inhabiting the new building, and there was nothing in the purposes of the Building (Scotland) Act 1959 giving rise to that proximity of relationship between the authority and the pursuers as proprietors of an adjacent building necessary to give rise to a duty of care on the part of the authority, even where defects in the new building were or ought to have been known to the authority and were such that damage to the pursuers' property or health was foreseeable.

Liability for breach of statutory duty

18.16 If a public authority fails to fulfil a statutory duty an action may be brought under section 45 of the Court of Session Act 1988 to enforce performance of the duty. A public authority may also incur liability for injury or loss caused by the non-performance of the statutory duty. This principle was stated by the House of Lords in the case of *Ferguson v. Earl of Kinnoul*,[39] in which it was held that a presbytery was liable in damages for refusal to accept a presentee to a church. Lord Lyndhurst said:

---

[36] *M v. Newham London Borough Council*; *X v. Bedfordshire County Council* [1994] 2 W.L.R. 554.

[37] [1994] 4 All E.R. 577.

[38] 1996 S.L.T. 690.

[39] (1842) 9 Cl. & F. 251.

> "When a person has an important duty to perform, he is bound to perform that duty; and if he neglects or refuses to do so, and an individual in consequence sustains injury, that lays the foundation for an action to recover damages by way of compensation for the injury that he has so sustained."[40]

Proof of negligence is not always necessary to establish a claim for breach of statutory duty. A statute may provide for stricter liability than common law. This will depend on the interpretation of the statutory provision which applies. In the case of *Mallon v. Monklands District Council*,[41] damages were awarded for psychiatric illness following a failure by a local authority to provide accommodation for a homeless person with a priority need and in *R. v. Lambeth London Borough Council, ex parte Barnes*,[42] it was held that the continued failure of a local authority to house an applicant for accommodation under Part III of the Housing Act 1985 was a breach of statutory duty which gave rise to liability in damages. Barnes had applied as homeless to her local authority who had accepted a duty to house her but failed to fulfil the duty. It was held that she was entitled to recover damages for the breach of statutory duty and also for the authority's negligence in failing to respond to correspondence for eight months.

Shortage of the resources necessary to fulfil statutory duties 18.17
imposed on local authorities creates difficult problems. Local authorities have many statutory duties and are often placed in a position where they have to ration the services which they provide and even reduce the level of provision which they make in performing statutory duties. If they fail to fulfil a duty they may incur liability in delict where those duties are owed to identifiable individuals. Specific provision for remedies may be made in a statute but, if this is not the case, then an action for damages at common law may be appropriate. In deciding whether there will be liability for a breach of statutory duty one approach is for the court to consider whether the legislation was passed primarily to protect a particular class of individuals as in the case of *R. v. Bexley London Borough Council, ex parte B*.[43] Bexley, a severely disabled boy with quadriplegic cerebral palsy and deafness, applied for judicial review of the council's decision to reduce the number of care-hours provided for him each week. The court held that authorities are under an obligation to

[40] (1842) 9 Cl. & F. 251 at 280.
[41] 1986 S.L.T. 347.
[42] (1992) 25 H.L.R. 140.
[43] July 31, 1995.

make provision under the Chronically Sick and Disabled Persons Act 1970 whenever they are satisfied that the relevant conditions have been met. The application failed for other reasons but the court observed that the duty laid upon authorities by section 2(1) of the 1970 Act was not merely a target duty, but was a duty owed to a specific individual, breach of which is capable of giving rise to a remedy in tort (delict). The very specific nature of the duties themselves means that they would readily be capable of evaluation in money terms. As Parliament provided no specific remedy, breaches of duty may give rise to a claim for damages in tort.

The House of Lords has considered the issue of the liability of a local authority for breach of statutory duty when there is a shortage of resources to maintain the level of service provided in the conjoined appeals of *R. v. Gloucestershire County Council and the Secretary of State for Health, ex parte Barry* and *R. v. Gloucestershire County Council, ex parte Barry*.[44] These cases were also related to the statutory duty to disabled persons under the Chronically Sick and Disabled Persons Act 1970. Section 2 of the Act provides that where a local authority is satisfied that a disabled person needs special arrangements, then the local authority is under a duty to make those arrangements. Mr Barry's needs were assessed and arrangements were made for home care, cleaning and laundry services and meals-on-wheels. In 1994 the council informed Mr Barry that they would no longer be able to provide him with his full needs as assessed as the money allocated to the council by central government had been reduced by £2.5 million. The House of Lords held that cost is now a relevant factor is assessing a person's needs for services. This does not mean that a local authority has a complete discretion over whether or not to allocate resources to fulfil a statutory duty. The local authority must carry out its functions in a reasonable fashion. In the event of a local authority acting with *Wednesbury* unreasonableness, a disabled person would have a remedy.

Breach of statutory duty under E.C. law

18.18 The Treaty of Rome and other Community legislation impose many duties on Member States and on the public authorities within Member States. Under the European Communities Act 1972, such duties are given legal effect in the United Kingdom and are enforced by courts within the United Kingdom. The extent to which duties under European Community law are enforceable will

---

[44] [1997] A.C. 584; [1997] 2 W.L.R. 459; [1997] 2 All E.R. 1.

depend on the nature of any particular duty and interpretation of the individual instrument by which that duty was imposed.

In the case of *Garden Cottage Foods Ltd v. Milk Marketing Board*,[45] the House of Lords held that the duty imposed by Article 86, not to abuse a dominant position, is to be regarded as a statutory duty. The majority of the judges expressed a view that damages would be awarded for breach of such a duty.[46] In the contrasting case of *Bourgoin SA v. Ministry of Agriculture, Fisheries and Foods*,[47] it was held that the implementation by a national government of measures which amount to a breach of Article 30 of the EEC Treaty does not of itself give a right to damages. Bourgoin was engaged in the business of importing turkeys from France. In 1981 the U.K. Government introduced a policy of preventing imports of turkeys from countries where disease was controlled by vaccination rather than slaughter. The ban prevented imports from France and caused Bourgoin to lose business. The European Court held that the new rules were in breach of Article 30 and Bourgoin was able to resume importing turkeys from France in November 1982. In an action before the U.K. courts he claimed damages for the loss of business in the intervening period, on the ground that the Ministry of Agriculture, Fisheries and Food was in breach of the statutory duty imposed by Article 30. It was held that a breach of Article 30 gave rise to a right to judicial review, by anyone with a sufficient interest, but there was no right to damages unless there had been an abuse of power. The purpose of Article 30 was not to protect individual traders but rather to protect the public at large. The measures implemented by the U.K. Government were a simple excess of power and not a breach of statutory duty and no damages were due.

The conflict between these two cases leaves some uncertainty as to the position in relation to breach of statutory duty under E.C. law. An underlying principle of E.C. law is that national courts should enforce rights under the E.C. Treaty by remedies which are not less favourable than those available for similar rights under domestic law. There is no overriding principle which establishes when liability for breach of statutory duty arises under national law. It is therefore logical to presume that a remedy which is not less favourable in relation to E.C. law is provided by following the same principle. The general principle is that liability will depend on the interpretation of the individual legislative instrument in each case.

---

45 [1984] A.C. 130.

46 See also *An Bord Bainne v. Milk Marketing Board* [1984] 2 C.M.L.R. 584.

47 [1986] Q.B. 716.

Liability for negligent mis-statement

18.19 The principle of liability for negligent misstatements was recognised by the House of Lords in the case of *Hedley Byrne & Co. v. Heller & Partners Ltd*,[48] in which it was established that liability may arise if a person is under a duty to take care that his statements are accurate and he fails to fulfil that duty.[49] The case of *T (A Minor) v. Surrey County Council*,[50] was brought on behalf of a child who had suffered a serious non-accidental injury while in the care of a registered childminder. The mother of the child, prior to engaging the childminder, had contacted the local authority's nursery and childminding adviser, who confirmed that the childminder was registered as a childminder under the 1948 Act and that there was no reason why a child could not safely be left in her care. In fact the adviser was aware that less than three months earlier another child in the care of the same childminder had been seriously injured. As a result of his injuries T claimed damages for personal injuries against the local authority. It was held that there was no liability to the child for breach of statutory duty. However, as the local authority knew or ought to have appreciated that there was a significant risk in placing a child in the care of a particular childminder, yet still informed a parent that there was no reason why a child should not be placed in that person's care, the local authority was liable for negligent misstatement and damages were awarded.

Vicarious liability for misfeasance in public office

18.20 Misfeasance in public office is fortunately a very rare occurrence. It is the wrongful use of a power by a public official with the intention of causing harm to an individual or organisation. The concept of a delict of misfeasance in public office is relatively new to Scots law but in the case of *Micosta v. Shetland Islands Council*,[51] Lord Ross expressed the opinion that Scots law is sufficiently flexible to accommodate a delict under such a description. The tort has a longer history under English law. In the early case of *Ashby v. White*,[52] the plaintiff was an elector who was wrongly prevented

---

[48] [1964] A.C. 465.

[49] See also *Ministry of Housing and Local Government v. Sharp* [1970] 2 Q.B. 223.

[50] [1994] 4 All E.R. 577.

[51] 1986 S.L.T. 193.

[52] (1703) 2 Ld Raym. 938, 3 Ld Raym. 320; 1 Smith's Leading Cases, 13th ed., 253. Wade and Forsyth, *Administrative Law*, (7th ed., Oxford University Press, Oxford, 1994), p. 790.

from voting in the Aylesbury election. He sued the borough constables in charge of the poll for damages of £200 on the grounds of fraud and malicious intent. The House of Lords held that damages were due to the plaintiff.[53] The most famous instance of misfeasance in public office occurred in the Canadian case, *Roncarelli v. Duplessis*,[54] in which damages were awarded against the Prime Minister of Quebec in person. He had directed the cancellation of a liquor licence for a restaurant because the owner of the restaurant had, on many occasions, provided bail for fellow members of the religious sect of Jehovah's Witnesses, which was then in conflict with the authorities. Damages of $33,123 were awarded. The cancellation of the liquor licence was an abuse of discretion based on irrelevant and illegal grounds. The Prime Minister had no legal authority to interfere with the jurisdiction of the liquor commission, which nevertheless followed his instruction to cancel the licence. Rand J. said: "Malice in the proper sense is simply acting for a reason and purpose knowingly foreign to the administration, to which was added here the element of intentional punishment by what was virtually outlawry."[55]

Oppressive action by a servant of the government is regarded as special circumstance in which exemplary or punitive damages could be awarded. Exemplary damages are calculated by reference to the outrageous conduct by the person at fault as well as the harm done to the victim. In the case of *Bradford Metropolitan City Council v. Arora*,[56] exemplary damages were awarded to a Sikh woman who had suffered sex and race discrimination in the course of applying for a post at a local authority college.[57] In the case of *AB v. South West Water Services*,[58] it was held that a claim for exemplary damages is not available where the cause of action is public nuisance or negligence. Aluminium sulphate was accidentally introduced into the drinking water system at a water treatment plant. A group action by injured parties in nuisance, negligence and breach of statutory duty claimed exemplary and aggravated damages in addition to the compensatory claim. On appeal it was held that exemplary damages were not available in those causes of action where they had not been awarded prior to 1964, which included public nuisance and negligence.

---

[53] See also *Racz v. Home Office* [1994] 2 W.L.R. 23, HL.
[54] [1952] 1 D.L.R. 680.
[55] *ibid.* at 706.
[56] [1991] 2 Q.B. 507.
[57] See also *Broome v. Cassell & Co. Ltd* [1972] A.C. 1027.
[58] [1993] 2 W.L.R. 507.

18.21 In the case of *Bennett v. Commissioner of Police of the Metropolis*,[59] it was held that intent to injure the plaintiff is an essential ingredient in the tort of misfeasance in public office and must be pleaded in a statement of claim. Bennett, a citizen of New Zealand, had been arrested in South Africa and was placed on a flight to New Zealand. The flight stopped off in London where Bennett was wanted on criminal charges. He was arrested and committed for trial. He applied for judicial review claiming that he had been detained in England as a result of an avoidance of the South African extradition procedure. Bennett had originally been refused access to documents but subsequently was held to be entitled to discovery of the documents as they were essential for his case. He then brought a claim for damages against, amongst others, the Secretary of State for the Home Department. He argued that, in not considering whether the public interest in non-disclosure was outweighed by the public interest in proper administration of justice, the Secretary of State had been negligent and committed an act of misfeasance. It was held that intent to injure was an essential ingredient of the tort of misfeasance in public office, and that, as no such intent had been pleaded, the statement of claim contained no cause of action.[60]

In *Bourgoin SA v. Ministry of Agriculture, Fisheries and Foods*,[61] in which Bourgoin failed to secure damages for the disruption of his business caused by an unlawful ban on the import of turkeys from France to the United Kingdom, it was held that, if it could be shown that in implementing the measures there had been an abuse of power then damages could be claimed for the commission of the tort of misfeasance in public office. The proof of malice upon the part of the officer concerned was not necessary but it must be proved that the officer knew that he had no power to act as he did and that he knew his act would injure the plaintiff.

18.22 In Scotland, although the term misfeasance in public office was not always used, there have been cases in which liability in damages for the wrongful use of a power has been held to exist. In the case of *B v. Forsey*,[62] a mental patient who had been unlawfully detained when the hospital authorities were aware that the detention was unlawful was awarded damages. In the case of *Micosta SA v. Shetland Islands Council*,[63] damages were claimed

---

[59] [1995] 1 W.L.R. 488.
[60] See also *Dunlop v. Woollahra Municipal Council* [1982] A.C. 158.
[61] [1985] 3 All E.R. 585.
[62] 1988 S.L.T. 572.
[63] 1986 S.L.T. 193.

against a harbour authority on the basis that the harbour master had used his powers in an improper way in the knowledge that he could not lawfully do so. It was held that there is a remedy in Scots law for a third-party loss which is a result of a deliberate misuse of statutory powers. There must be proof of malice, or proof that the statutory body knew that it did not have the power which it purported to exercise. In this case it was held that the harbour master's actions were in good faith and the action was dismissed.

The elements which have to be proved in order to establish misfeasance in public office are therefore: (1) the defender knows that he has no legal authority to act in a particular way; (2) the defender nevertheless does act in that manner either: (a) in order to injure the pursuer, or (b) in order to benefit a third party in the knowledge that by so doing, injury will inevitably accrue to the pursuer.[64] Malice, in the sense of a specific intention to cause harm to an individual as the primary purpose of the action or decision is not always required but there must be a conscious abuse of power in the knowledge that harm may occur.

LIABILITY OF THE CROWN FOR DELICT

Under the law of delict a person will be liable in damages for a 18.23
wrongful act or omission which causes harm to another person. Public authorities, including ministers of the Crown have no exemption from the ordinary law of delict unless the exemption has been provided by statute. In Scotland there was no legal barrier to an action against the Crown for a civil wrong until the case of *McGregor v. Lord Advocate*.[65] McGregor was knocked down by an army car, the driver being employed by the War Department and acting in the course of his employment. McGregor tried to sue the War Department but the action was held to be incompetent as the War Office represented the Crown. In England, before the Crown Proceedings Act 1947, the Crown was, in strict law, immune from proceedings. The monarch was subject to the law but there was no means of enforcing the law against a monarch as the sovereign could not be sued in their own courts. Since writs were issued in the name of the sovereign, they could not be issued against him.

---

[64] F. McManus, "Misfeasance in Public Office" in *Delict* (McManus, Bisacre, Russell *et al.* eds., Wylie, London, 1997).

[65] 1921 S.C. 847.

Nominated defenders

18.24 Action had, therefore, to be taken against the individual Crown servant. The Crown accepted its moral responsibility whenever a Crown servant was held to be liable and, in practice, the department concerned paid the compensation. This developed into the practice of using a nominated defender. The Crown would nominate an official to defend the action and would not use as a defence the fact that there was no evidence that he was personally liable. Where this was done the idea of an action against an individual servant of the Crown was mere fiction and in 1946 the House of Lords condemned this practice in the case of *Adams v. Naylor*.[66] A local commander of the Royal Engineers had been nominated to defend an action when two children were injured in a minefield. The House of Lords pointed out that whether or not the Crown stood behind the individual defendant, so as to make the trial really a matter of suit against the Crown, the reality was that judgment could only be given for the plaintiff if it could be shown that the individual defendant was himself liable.

The use of a nominated defender had not provided a universal solution for actions in delict against the Crown. It could not be used in cases where the only possible defender was the Crown itself, such as cases against the Crown as occupier of land or as an employer. It became obvious that a reform of the law to provide a right of action against the Crown was necessary and the Crown Proceedings Act was passed in 1947. Following the 1947 Act, petitions of right were abolished and the use of nominated defenders was no longer required. Section 17 of the Act requires the Treasury to publish a list of the authorised government departments and the names of the person against whom proceedings should be taken. If there is no appropriate department proceedings may be taken against: the Attorney-General in England; the Lord Advocate, where the action, suit or proceeding is on behalf of or against any part of the Scottish Administration; and the Advocate General for Scotland in any other case.[67]

Crown Proceedings Act 1947

18.25 Section 2 of the Crown Proceedings Act provides that, with exceptions, the Crown is subject to the same liabilities in tort/delict as if it were a private person of full age and capacity in respect of:

---

[66] [1946] A.C. 543.
[67] Scotland Act 1998, Sched. 8, para. 2(5).

"(1)(a) torts/delicts committed by its servants or agents.
(b) duties which an employer, at common law, owes to his servants or agents.
(c) breach of the common law duties attaching to the ownership, occupation, possession, or control of property.
. . .
(2)(d) breaches of statutory duty, provided that the statute is one which bonds the Crown as well as private persons."

By section 2(6) vicarious liability for torts/delicts of crown officers is restricted to an officer appointed directly or indirectly by the Crown and paid out of the Consolidated Fund, moneys provided by Parliament or a fund certified by the Treasury. And in order to protect the independence of the judiciary section 2(5) provides that there is no vicarious liability for acts done by officers acting in a judicial capacity or in execution of judicial process. Section 43(b) defines the meaning of tort in its application to Scotland as: "Any wrongful or negligent act or omission giving rise to liability in reparation."

In the case of *Hughes v. Lord Advocate*,[68] the Crown was held to be vicariously liable for injuries incurred by two boys as a result of Crown servants having left a manhole unguarded with a naked light inside. The Act does not authorise proceedings against the sovereign in their personal capacity.[69] There is also an exception where death or injury is caused by a member of the armed forces of the Crown to another serviceman in the execution of his duties where the minister certifies that the accident is attributable to the service for the purposes of a pension award (s. 10).[70] This exception is made on the grounds that compensation is already provided for in the pension award. The section would have been better expressed if it had made the exception only in cases where the pursuer stood to benefit from a pension, thus avoiding the effect that the section had in the case of *Adams v. War Office*.[71] It was held in that case that no action will lie whenever the minister issues a certificate that an accident is attributable to the service for the purposes of a pension award, even although no award is made.

---

68 1963 S.C. (H.L.) 31.
69 s. 40(1).
70 s. 10.
71 [1955] 1 W.L.R. 1116.

Adams was a reservist, serving in a territorial unit, who was killed by shell burst on a military exercise. His father alleged negligence on the part of the serviceman who allowed a live shell to be fired on an exercise. The War Office relied on section 10 of the Crown Proceedings Act 1947 as a defence as the Minister of Pensions had certified that the accident would give entitlement to pension. In fact, no pension was awarded as Adams was dead and his parents did not qualify as dependants. Section 10 was eventually put into suspension by the Crown Proceedings (Armed Forces) Act 1987. It may be revived if it appears to the Secretary of State necessary or expedient so to do. This may occur in the event of war. Until section 10 is revived, members of the armed forces (and, in the event of death, their dependants) may sue fellow members and the Crown for damages for death or injury arising from their service.

Statutory authority as a defence

18.26 Where Parliament expressly authorises something to be done, to do it in accordance with that authority cannot be wrongful. A public authority cannot therefore be held liable in delict where the loss or injury is the inevitable result of activities authorised by Parliament. The effectiveness of statutory authority as a defence will depend on interpretation of the specific legislation. There may be provision in the legislation for compensation for authorised infringement of private rights.

It is assumed that, when discretionary power is given to a public body, there is no intention to interfere with private rights, unless the power is expressed in such a way as to make such interference inevitable. In the case of *Metropolitan Asylum District v. Hill*,[72] hospital trustees were empowered by statute to build hospitals in London. A smallpox hospital was built at Hampstead in such a way as to create a nuisance at common law. It was held that the building of the hospital in such a place was unlawful because there were no express words or necessary implication in the statute authorising the commission of a nuisance. The Act gave no compulsory powers, it made no provision for compensation, and the inference was that it was not intended to permit interference with private rights. Lord Watson observed: "Where the terms of a statute are not imperative, but permissive . . . the fair inference is that the legislature intended that discretion be exercised in strict conformity with private rights and did not confer licence to commit

[72] (1881) 6 A.C. 193.

nuisance."[73] If the exercise of a statutory duty or power inevitably involves injury to private rights there is no remedy unless the statute itself makes provision for compensation. In the case of *Allen v. Gulf Refining Company Ltd*,[74] the House of Lords held that a local Act which envisaged the building of an oil refinery at Milford Haven, though it did not give express power to construct the refinery or define the site, did give authority by necessary implication, for its construction and use. Such authority protected the company against liability for nuisance caused to neighbouring owners which was the inevitable result of the building of the refinery. The Act made no provision for compensation and so neighbours who complained of excessive smell, vibration and noise had no remedy.

Liability for negligence in the operation of a function, however, may not be taken away by statutory authority where, as in the case of *Dorset Yacht Company v. Home Office*,[75] the negligent actings of officials rendered their actions *ultra vires* the statutory authority. In the case of *Bell v. McGlannan*,[76] it was held that whilst there would be no liability for actions taken in accordance with the statutory authority there may be liability for any actions which amounted to an excess of power. Acting under authority of a warrant from the sheriff under section 15(1) of the Wireless Telegraphy Act 1949 an officer of the radio investigation service of the Department of Trade and Industry searched premises and seized equipment. No criminal proceedings were raised within six months after which time proceedings were incompetent and in terms of section 83(1) of the Telecommunications Act 1984 the property should have been returned to the owner. After a further six weeks the property was returned but it was damaged. The owner of the property brought an action for damages against the procurator fiscal. He argued that the procurator fiscal was vicariously responsible for the actings of the investigation officer. The defender argued that, by virtue of section 456 of the Criminal Procedure (Scotland) Act 1975, he had immunity from damages in respect of acts done under Part II of the Act. As the warrant was lawful, statutory authority would preclude the award of damages for deprivation of the equipment seized during the authorised period of six months. Damages may be due for loss arising from detention of the 18.27

---

[73] See also *Manchester Corporation v. Farnworth* [1930] A.C. 171; *Tate and Lyle Ltd v. Greater London Council* [1983] 2 A.C. 509.

[74] [1981] A.C. 1001.

[75] [1970] A.C. 1004.

[76] 1992 S.L.T. 237.

property in respect of the period after the defender's statutory authority to hold it had expired.

Where a public authority can achieve an objective by exercising powers under more than one statute, each of which prescribes the procedures to be followed and the remedies which may be available to individuals affected, the authority may choose which statute to follow. The authority will not be called to account for failing to follow the course of action which is most advantageous to individuals who may be affected. An individual will not be able to claim compensation on the ground that the authority chose to follow procedures under one statute when alternative procedures would have provided for more generous compensation to individuals affected.[77] General powers under one Act may not, however, be used to achieve a regulatory goal which is authorised expressly in another Act.[78] In the case of *Westminster Bank Ltd v. Minister of Housing and Local Government*,[79] the House of Lords held that an authority's choice of action may be restricted by special circumstances.[80]

Statutes not applying to the Crown

18.28 It has long been established that the Crown is not bound or restricted by any statutory provision unless it is expressly stated or necessarily implied that it applies to the Crown. The application of statutes to the Crown was considered in the case of *Lord Advocate v. Strathclyde Regional Council*.[81] The Property Services Agency was carrying out work on the perimeter fence at Faslane. A temporary fence and works on part of the A814, a public road, caused an obstruction of the highway for which no permission had been sought from either the roads authority, Strathclyde Regional Council, or the planning authority, Dumbarton District Council. Both authorities took action to have the road cleared. The Lord Advocate on behalf of the Ministry sought judicial review of these acts. The Crown argued that it was not subject to the restrictions in the roads and planning legislation. There was no specific statutory

---

[77] *Montgomerie and Co. v. Haddington Corp.*, 1908 S.C. 127; 15 S.L.T. 474 (affirmed by the House of Lords 1908 S.C. (H.L.) 6; (1908) 15 S.L.T. 910); *Hawick Orange Lodge v. Roxburgh District Council*, 1980 S.C. 141; 1981 S.L.T. 33.

[78] *BAA v. Secretary of State for Scotland*, 1979 S.C. 200; 1979 S.L.T. 197.

[79] [1971] A.C. 508; [1970] 1 All E.R. 734.

[80] A. Bradley, "Administrative Law" in *Stair Memorial Encyclopaedia on the Laws of Scotland*, Vol. 1.

[81] 1990 S.L.T. 158.

exemption in this case, however, as the work was not on Crown land. In an appeal to the House of Lords, Strathclyde Regional Council and Dumbarton District Council argued that in modern circumstances the rule that statutes do not apply to the Crown, unless there was express provision to that effect, was limited to provisions which would affect prejudicially the property rights, interests and privileges of the Crown.[82] The House of Lords held that the Crown was not bound by any statutory provision unless there could be gathered from the relevant Act an intention to that effect. The Crown would be bound only by express words or necessary implication.

INTERDICT AGAINST THE CROWN

Interdicts were available against Ministers of the Crown in the Scottish courts until the Crown Proceedings Act 1947 came into force in 1948.[83] The Act transformed the procedure by which actions could be brought against the Crown in England but made no changes to the procedure in Scotland. In Scotland, accordingly, the procedure continues to be governed by common law, the Crown Suits (Scotland) Act 1857 and, in relation to the Secretary of State, the Reorganisation of Offices (Scotland) Act 1939. Prior to the Crown Proceedings Act 1947 it was competent in Scotland to seek the remedy of interdict against the Crown and when an officer of the Crown was sued in that capacity this was regarded as being an action against the Crown.[84] In *Somerville v. Lord Advocate*[85] Lord MacLaren stated: 18.29

> "I do not think that it ever was doubted in Scotland that the Crown might be called as a defender in a proper action, either through the Officers of State collectively, or through the King's Advocate or other officer representing the Crown in the matter of the action . . . His Highness, or His advocate as representing the King, may be convened in the Court of Session in actions and pleas at the instance of any private person."

---

82 See also *Somerville v. L.A.* (1893) 20 R. 1050; *Mags of Edinburgh v. L.A.*, 1912 2 S.L.T. 133.

83 *Russell v. Mags of Hamilton* (1897) 25 R. 350; *Bell v. Secretary of State for Scotland*, 1933 S.L.T. 519.

84 *Somerville v. L.A.*, above ; *Wilson v. 1st Edinburgh City Royal Garrison Artillery Volunteers* (1904) 7 F. 168; 12 S.L.T. 488.

85 (1893) 20 R. 105.

Section 21 of the Crown Proceedings Act 1947 provides that:

"(1) In any civil proceedings by or against the Crown the court shall, subject to the provisions of this Act, have power to make all such orders as it has power to make in proceedings between subjects, and otherwise to give such appropriate relief as the case may require: Provided that: — where in any proceedings against the Crown any such relief is sought as might in proceedings between subjects be granted by way of injunction or specific performance, the court shall not grant an injunction or make an order for specific performance, but may in lieu thereof make an order declaratory of the rights of the parties.

(2) The court shall not in any civil proceedings grant any injunction or make any order against an officer of the Crown if the effect of granting the injunction or making the order would be to give any relief against the Crown which could not have been obtained in proceedings against the Crown."

Section 38(2) provides *inter alia* that: "'Civil proceedings' includes proceedings in the High Court or the county court for the recovery of fines and penalties, but does not include proceedings on the Crown side of the King's Bench Division." Part V of the Act deals with the application of the Act to Scotland and provides that although Part II (which includes s. 21) does not apply to Scotland. There is an express exception in relation to section 21 with the result that section 21 does apply to Scotland. Section 43 of the Act of 1947 provides interpretation for the purposes of application to Scotland and states *inter alia* that for any reference to the High Court there shall be substituted a reference to the Court of Session, that the expression "plaintiff" means "pursuer", and that the expression "injunction" means "interdict".

Section 21 therefore has had the effect of changing the law of Scotland by exempting the Crown from interdict. The purpose of section 21(2) is to prevent avoidance of the Act by raising actions against officers of the Crown as individuals, and not against the Crown itself.[86] In circumstances where, but for the fact that the defender is the Crown, an interdict would have been granted, the court may instead make an order declaring the rights between the parties.[87]

---

[86] Mitchell, *Constitutional Law* (2nd ed., 1968), p. 309, *BMA v. Glasgow Health Board*, 1989 S.L.T. 493; 1988 S.L.T. 538.

[87] Crown Proceedings Act 1947, ss. 21(a), 23(a), as applied to Scotland by s. 43(a).

In the case of *Macdonald v. Secretary of State for Scotland*,[88] the Inner House confirmed that the effect of the Crown Proceedings Act 1947, s. 21 in Scotland, is that interdict cannot be obtained against the Crown or a Minister of the Crown. The *Macdonald* case was an action for reparation totalling £300,000 for, approximately, 3,000 searches which the pursuer claimed had been wrongfully carried out. Macdonald was a convicted prisoner serving his sentence in a Scottish prison. He sought interdict against the Secretary of State restraining him, or anyone acting on his behalf, from subjecting Macdonald to illegal searches. It was held that the effect of section 21 was that interdict was not available against the Crown in any civil proceeding. Lord Sutherland stated that: 18.30

> "[T]he construction of section 21 which prevents an individual from obtaining relief by way of interdict against the Crown is a restriction on the remedies available prior to 1947, which may seem strange in legislation designed to expand the remedies available against the Crown, but the wording of the section is such that there can be no doubt that this was the intention of Parliament."[89]

The current law in Scotland is therefore that, usually, an interdict will not be granted against the Crown.[90] An exception arises where the interdict relates to an area where European law impinges upon U.K. law. It was held in *Secretary of State for Transport, ex parte Factortame*[91] that, in such cases European law must prevail and the immunity of the Crown is removed.

---

88 1994 S.L.T. 692.
89 *ibid.* at 701.
90 Crown Proceedings Act 1947, s. 21. *Ayr Mags v. Secretary of State for Scotland*, 1950 S.C. 102.
91 [1991] 1 All E.R. 70.

BIBLIOGRAPHY

Allan, T.R.S. *Law, Liberty and Justice* (1993, Clarendon Press, Oxford)

Allen, M. and Thompson, B., *Cases and Materials in Constitutional and Administrative Law* (4th ed., Blackstone Press, London, 1996)

Alexander, A., "Wheatley To . . . What?" in *The Constitutional and Political Impact of Re-organisation* (1995, Black, S., ed., University of Edinburgh, Edinburgh)

Aristotle, *The Politics* (Sinclair T.A. (trans), Penguin, London, 1962)

Atkins, E. and Hogget, B, *Women and the Law* (1984, Blackwells, Oxford)

Bagehot, W., *The English Constitution* (1993, Fontana, London)

Bailey, S.H, Harris, D.J, and Jones, B.L, *Civil Liberties: Cases and Materials* (4th ed., Butterworths, London, 1995)

Barnett, H. *Constitutional and Administrative Law* (2nd ed., Cavendish, Newcastle-upon-Tyne, 1998)

Bates, St.J.T, *Devolution to Scotland: The Legal Aspects* (1997, T&T Clark, Edinburgh)

Birkenshaw, P, *Grievances, Remedies and the State* (2nd ed., Sweet & Maxwell, London, 1994)

Birkinshaw, P. and Parkin, A., "Freedom of Information" in Blackburn R. and Plant R., *Constitutional Reform: The Labour Government's Constitutional Reform Agenda* (1999, Longman, London)

Birkinshaw, P., *Freedom of Information: The Law, the Practice and the Ideal*, (2nd ed., Butterworths, London, 1996)

Black, S., "Constitutional and Political Issues in the Re-organisation of Scottish Local Government" in *The Constitutional and Political Impact of Re-organisation* (1995, Black, S., ed., University of Edinburgh, Edinburgh)

Black, S. (ed.), *The Constitutional and Political Impact of Re-organisation* (1995, University of Edinburgh, Edinburgh)

Blackburn, R. and Plant, R., *Constitutional Reform: The Labour Government's Constitutional Reform Agenda*, (1999, London, Longman)

Blackburn, R.W., *The Electoral System in Britain* (1995, Macmillan, London)

Bogdanor, V., and Butler, D., *Democracy and Elections* (1983, Cambridge University Press, London)

Bogdanor, V., *Power and the People* (1997, Gollancz)

Bogdanor, V., *The People and the Party System* (1981, Cambridge University Press, Cambridge)

Bogdanor, V., "Devolution: The Constitutional Aspects" in *Constitutional Reform in the U.K.* (1998, Hart, Oxford)

Bogdanor, V., "Freedom of Information: The Constitutional Aspects" in *Open Government: Freedom of Information and Privacy* (1999, McDonald, A., and Terrill, G., MacMillan, London)

Bradley, A., "Devolution of Government in Britain: Some Scottish Aspects" in *Devolution* (Calvert, H., ed., 1975)

Bradley, A., "The Sovereignty of Parliament: In Perpetuity?" in *The Changing Constitution* (3rd ed., Jowell, J. and Oliver, D., Clarendon Press, Oxford, 1994)

Bradley, A. and Ewing, K., *Constitutional and Administrative Law* (12th ed., Longman, London, 1997)

Brazier, R., *Constitutional Practice* (2nd ed., Clarendon Press, Oxford, 1994)

Butler, D., *Governing without a Majority: Dilemmas for Hung Parliaments in Britain* (1983, Collins, London)

Butler, D., and Ranney, A, (eds) *Referendums around the World* (1994, Macmillan, London)

Butler, D., *British General Elections since 1945* (1989, Blackwells, Oxford)

Calvert, H., *Constitutional Law in Northern Ireland* (1968, Stevens and Sons/Sweet & Maxwell, London)

Charlesworth, A., and Cullen, H., *European Community Law* (1994, Pitman)

Craig, P.P., *Administrative Law* (3rd ed., Sweet & Maxwell, 1994)

Craig, P.P., and de Burca, G., *European Community Law* (2nd ed., Oxford University Press, Oxford, 1998)

Deans, M., *Scots Public Law* (1995, T&T Clark, Edinburgh)

De Smith, S.A., *Judicial Review of Administrative Action* (4th ed., Penguin, London, 1980)

De Smith, S.A., and Brazier, R., *Constitutional and Administrative Law* (8th ed., Penguin, London, 1998)

Dicey, A.V., *Introduction to the Law of the Constitution* (19th ed., MacMillan, London, 1959)

Drewry G. (ed.) *The New Select Committees* (1989, Oxford University Press, Oxford)

Dummett, A., and Nichol, A., *Subjects, Citizens, Aliens and Others: Nationality and Immigration Law* (1990 Weidenfeld and Nicholson)

Dworkin, R., *A Matter of Principle* (1986, Clarendon Press, Oxford)

Edwards, O. (ed.), *A Claim of Right for Scotland* (1989, Polygon, Edinburgh)

Erskine May, *Parliamentary Practice* (21st ed., 1989)

Fawcett, J., *The Application of the European Convention on Human Rights* (1987, Clarendon Press, Oxford)

Fenwick, H., and Phillipson, G., *Sourcebook on Public Law* (1998, Cavendish, Newcastle-upon-Tyne)

Fenwick, H., *Civil Liberties* (2nd ed., Cavendish, Newcastle-upon-Tyne, 1998)

Finch, V., and Ashton, C., *Administrative Law in Scotland* (1997, W. Green, Edinburgh)

Finer, S., Bogdanor, V., and Rudden, B., *Comparing Constitutions* (1995, Clarendon Press, Oxford)

Finnie, W., Himsworth, C., and Walker, N. (eds), *Edinburgh Essays in Public Law* (1991, Edinburgh University Press, Edinburgh)

Fredman, S., *Women and the Law* (1997, Clarendon Press, Oxford)

Griffith, J.A.G., and Ryle, M., *Parliament, Functions, Practice and Procedures* (1989, Sweet & Maxwell, London)

Harlow, C., and Rawlings, R., *Law and Administration* (1984, Weidenfeld and Nicholson)

Harris, D.J., O'Boyle, M., and Warbrick, C., *Law of the Convention on Human Rights* (1995, Butterworths, London)

Hartley, T., *The Foundations of European Community Law* (4th ed., Clarendon Press, Oxford, 1998)

Himsworth, C., and Munro, C., *The Scotland Act 1998* (1999, W. Green, Edinburgh)

Himsworth C. *Local Government in Scotland* (1995, T&T Clark, Edinburgh)

Hood-Phillips, O., and Jackson, P., *Constitutional and Administrative Law*, (7th ed., Sweet & Maxwell, London, 1987)

Jennings, I., *The Law and the Constitution,* (5th ed., Hodder and Stoughton, London, 1959)

Jowell, J., "The Rule of Law Today" in *The Changing Constitution* (3rd ed., Jowell, J., and Oliver, D., Clarendon Press, Oxford, 1994)

Jowell, J., and Oliver, D., *The Changing Constitution* (3rd ed., Clarendon Press, Oxford, 1994)

Judge, D., *The Parliamentary State* (1993, Sage, London)

Le Sueur, A., and Sunkin, M., *Public Law* (1997, Longman, London)

Locke, J., *Two Treatises on Government* (1690 and 1977)

MacCormick, N., "Sovereignty or Subsidiarity? Some Comments on Scottish Devolution" in *Devolution and the British Constitution* (1998, Tomkins, A. ed., Key Haven, London)

McDonald, A., and Terrill, G., *Open Government: Freedom of Information and Privacy* (1999, MacMillan, London)

McEldowney, J., *Public Law* (2nd ed., Sweet and Maxwell, London, 1997)

McFadden, J., and Lazarowicz, M., *The Scottish Parliament: An Introduction* (1999, T&T Clark, Edinburgh)

McManus, F., "Misfeasance in Public Office" in *Delict* (1997, McManus, Bisacre, Russell *et al.*, Wylie, London)

Madgwick. P., and Woodhouse, D., *The Law and Politics of the Constitution of the U.K.* (1995) Harvester Wheatsheaf, Hemel Hempstead)

Marshall, G., and Moodie, G., *Some Problems of the Constitution* (5th ed., Hutchison, London, 1971)

Mathijsen, P.R.S.F., *A Guide to European Union Law* (1995, Sweet & Maxwell, London)

Mitchell, J.B., *Constitutional Law* (2nd ed., SULI/W. Green, Edinburgh, 1968)

Montesquieu, C., *L'Esprit des Lois*, (1989, Cambridge University Press, Cambridge)

Munro, C., *Studies in Constitutional Law* (1987, Butterworths, London)

O'Keefe,.D., and Twomey, P.M. (eds), *Legal Issues of the Maastricht Treaty* (1994, Chancery, London)

Oliver, D., and Drewry, G., *The Law and Parliament* (1998, Butterworths, London)

Oliver, D., *Government in the U.K.: The Search for Accountability, Efficiency and Citizenship* (1991, Open University Press, Milton Keynes)

Page, A., Reid, C., and Ross, A., *A Guide to the Scotland Act 1998* (1999, Butterworths, Edinburgh)

Paine, T., *The Rights of Man* (Collins, H, ed., Penguin, New York, 1998), Pt II

Palley, C., *The United Kingdom and Human Rights* (1991, Sweet & Maxwell, London)
Paterson, L., *The Autonomy of Modern Scotland* (1994, Edinburgh University Press, Edinburgh)
Payne, S., "The Royal Prerogative" in *The Nature of the Crown* (1999, Sunkin, M., and Payne, S., eds, Oxford University Press, Oxford)

Rawling, H., *Law and the Electoral Process* (1998, Sweet & Maxwell, London)
Renton, R.W., and Brown, H.H., *Criminal Procedure According to the Laws of Scotland,*(6th ed., W. Green, Edinburgh, 1996)
Roper, M., "Access to Public Records" in *Open Government* (1987, Chapman, R., and Hunt, M., Routledge, London)
Rush, M., "The Law Relating to Members' Conduct" in *The Law and Parliament* (1998, Oliver, D., and Drewry, G., eds., Butterworths, London)

Stair Memorial Encyclopaedia on The Laws of Scotland (1996, Law Society of Scotland/Butterworths), Vol. 15
Steiner, J., *Enforcing EC Law* (1995, Blackstone, London)
Steiner, J., *Textbook on EEC Law* (5th ed., Blackstone, London, 1996)
Sunkin, M., and Payne, S., *The Nature of the Crown* (1999, Oxford University Press, Oxford)

Tomkins, A. (ed.), *Devolution and the British Constitution* (1998, Key Haven, London)
Turpin, C., *British Government and the Constitution*, (3rd ed., Butterworths, London, 1995)
Tushnet, M., "The Politics of Constitutional Law" in *The Politics of Law* (1990, Kairys, D., ed., Pantheon Books, New York)

Wade, H.W.R., and Forsyth, C.F., *Administrative Law* (7th ed., Clarendon Press, Oxford, 1994)
Walker, N., "Constitutional Reform in a Cold Climate: Reflections on the White Paper and the Referendum on Scotland's Parliament' in *Devolution and the British Constitution* (1998, Tomkins, A., ed., Key Haven, London)
Walker, N., "The Antimonies of the Law Officers" in *The Nature of the Crown* (1999, Sunkin, M., and Payne, S., eds, Oxford University Press, Oxford)
Wheare, K., *Modern Constitutions* (2nd ed., Oxford University Press, Oxford, 1966)

Wheatley, S. (ed.), *Constitutionalism and Democracy* (1993, Oxford University Press, USA)
White, R., and Willock, I., *Scottish Legal System* (2nd ed., Butterworths, Edinburgh, 1999)
Woods, T. (ed.), *Administrative Law: Facing the Future* (1997, Blackstone, London)

Zander, M., *The Law-making Process* (5th ed., Butterworths, London, 1999)

ARTICLES

Austin, R., "Administrative Law's Reaction to the Changing Concepts of Public Service" (1988) C.M.L.Rev. 667

Bingham, T.H, "The European Convention on Human Rights: Time to Incorporate" (1993) 109 L.Q.R. 390
Bradley, A., "Parliamentary Privilege and the Common Law of Corruption: *R. v. Greenway and Others*" [1998] P.L. 356
Bradley, A., "Police Powers and the Prerogative" [1988] P.L. 298
Brazier, R., "The Scotland Bill as Constitutional Legislation" (1998) 19 Stat.L.R. 1-12
Brazier, R., 'Defending the Hereditaries: The Salisbury Convention' [1998] P.L. 371
Brazier, R., "The Constitution in the New Politics" [1978] P.L. 117
Brown, A., "Asymmetrical Devolution: the Scottish Case" (1998) 69 *Political Quarterly* 215
Brown, A., "Delimiting the Concept of Search" 1998 S.L.T. (News) 294
Brown, A., and McCrone, D., "A New Parliament and Scotland's Future" (1998) *University of Edinburgh*
Browne-Wilkinson (Lord), "The Infiltration of a Bill of Rights" [1992] P.L. 405

Churchill, R.R., and Young, J.R., "Compliance with judgments of the European Court of Human Rights" [1991] B.Y.I.L. 283
Coppel, J., "Horizontal Effect of Directives" [1997] I.L.J. 69
Cotterrell, R.B.M., "The Impact of Sex Discrimination Legislation" [1981] P.L. 469
Craig, P.P., "Dicey: Unitary, self-correcting democracy and public law" (1990) 106 L.Q.R. 105
Craig, P.P., "Directives: Direct effect, indirect effect and the construction of national legislation" (1997) 22 E.L.R. 519
Craig, P.P., "Sovereignty of the United Kingdom after Factortame" (1991) 11 Y.B.E.L. 221

de Burca, G., "Giving effect to European Community Directives" (1992) 55 M.L.R. 215

Dickinson, I.S., "Retrospective Legislation and the British Constitution", 1974 S.L.T. 25

Dickinson, I.S., "Still no interdicts against the Crown", 1994 S.L.T. (News) 217

Dine, J., and Watt, B., "Sexual Harassment: Moving Away from Discrimination" (1995) 58 M.L.R. 362

Eleftheriadis, P., "The Direct Effect of Community Law: Conceptual issues" (1996) 16 Y.B.E.L. 205

Ganz, G., "The Supreme Court (Offices) Act 1997: Loss of a constitutional safeguard" (1998) 6 *Amicus Curiae* 19

Gay, O., and Winetrobe, B., "Putting out the Writs" [1997] P.L. 385

Gearty, C.A., "The European Court of Human Rights and the Protection of Civil Liberties" [1993] C.L.J. 89

Griffith, J., "Crichel Down: The most famous farm in British constitutional history" (1987) 1 *Contemporary Record* 35

Hadfield, B., "The Nature of Devolution in Scotland and Northern Ireland" (1999) 3 Edin.L.R. 3

Hazell, R., "Freedom of Information: Implications for the Ombudsman" (1995) Pub.Admin. 264

Hazell, R., "Reinventing the Constitution: Can the state survive?", CIPFA/*Times* Lecture, Nov. 1998

Himsworth, C., "The Scottish Grand Committee as an Instrument of Government" (1996) 1 Edin.L.R. 79

Hopkins, J., "Devolution from a Comparative Perspective" (1998) 4 E.P.L. 323

Irvine (Lord), "The Development of Human Rights in Britain Under an Incorporated Convention on Human Rights" [1998] P.L.221

Jenkins, C., "Helping the Reader of Bills and Acts" (1999) 149 N.L.J. 798

Kerley, R., and Orr, K., "Joint Arrangements in Scotland" (1993) 19 L.G.S. 309

Lasok, P., "*Francovich* Overules *Bourgoin*: State liability for breach of Community law" [1992] I.C.C.L.R. 186

Laws, J. (Sir), "Is the High Court the Guardian of Fundamental Constitutional Rights?" [1993] P.L. 60

Lester (Lord), "Fundamental Rights" [1994] P.L. 70

Lester (Lord), "First Steps Towards a Constitutional Bill of Rights" (1997) 2 E.H.R.L.R. 124

Loveland, I., "Incorporating the ECHR into U.K. law" (1999) 52 Parl.Aff. 113

Marshall, G., "Parliamentary Sovereignty: The new horizons" [1997] P.L. 1

McFadden, J., "The Scottish Parliament: Provisions for Dispute Resolution", 1998 J.R. 221

Middlemiss, S, "Civil remedies for Victims of Sexual Harassment: Delictual Actions", 1997 J.R. 241

Midwinter, A., and McGarvey, N., "Local Government Reforms in Scotland: Managing the Transition" (1997) 23 L.G.S. 73

Mitchell, J., Denver, D., Pattie, C., and Bochel, H., "The 1997 Devolution Referendum in Scotland" (1998) 51 Parl.Aff. 166

Munro, C.R., "Power to the People," [1997] P.L. 579

O'Neill, A., "The Scotland Act and the Government of Judges", 1999 S.L.T. 61

O'Neill, A., "A Tale of Two Constitutions", 1997 S.L.T. 205

Olowofoyeku, A., "Decentralising the U.K.: The Federal argument" (1999) 3 Edin.L.R. 57

Palmer, "Tightening Secrecy Law: Official Secrets Act 1989" [1990] P.L. 243

Raz, J., "The Rule of law and its Virtue" (1977) 93 L.Q.R. 195

Ridley, F., "There is no British Constitution: A dangerous case of the Emperor's clothes" (1988) 41 Parl.Aff. 340

Ross, M., "Beyond *Francovich*," (1993) 56 M.L.R. 55

Sampford, C., "'Recognise and Declare': An Australian experiment in codifying constitutional conventions" (1987) 7 O.J.L.S. 369

Scott, R., "Ministerial Accountability" [1996] P.L. 410

Seaton, J., and Winetrobe, B., "The Passage of Constitutional Bills in Parliament" (1998) 4 J.L.S. 33

Steiner, J., "From Direct Effects to *Francovich*: Shifting means of enforcement of Community law" (1993) 18 E.L.R. 3

Tant, A., "The Campaign for Freedom of Information: A participatory challenge to elitist British government" (1990) 68 Pub.Admin. 477

Tracers, T., "More and More Go Hand in Hand" (1995) Local Government Chronicle, 9 June 1995

Wade, W., "Sovereignty: Revolution or evolution?" (1996) 112 L.Q.R. 568

Wilkinson, H., (1992) *Complaining to the Ombudsman* (1992) 142 N.L.J. 1348

Woodhouse, D., "Ministerial Responsibility in the 1990s: When do Ministers Resign?" (1993) 46 Parl.Aff. 277

Woodhouse, D., "The Attorney-General" (1997) 50 Parl.Aff. 98

Woolf, H., "Judicial Review: The Tensions between the Executive and the Judiciary' (1998) 114 L.Q.R. 579

Woolf (Rt. Hon. Lord), "Droit Public: English Style" [1995] P.L. 57

MISCELLANEOUS

Cabinet Office, *Your Right to Know: The Government's Proposals for a Freedom of Information Act*, Cm. 3818 (1997)

Civil Service Code http://www.cabinet-office.gov.uk/central/1999/cscode.htm (09.09.99)

Code of Conduct and Guidance of Procedures for Ministers (1997) http://www.cabinet-office.gov.uk/central/1997/mcode/index.htm (22.04.99)

Commission on Local Government and the Scottish Parliament, *Moving Forward: Local Government and the Scottish Parliament* (1999)

Constitution Unit, *Scotland's Parliament: The Fundamentals for a new Scotland Act* (1996)

Curtis, S., and Vidler, G., *Scottish Parliament Election Results*, Research Paper 99/1 (1999) Edinburgh: Scottish Parliament, http://www.scottish.parliament.uk/whats—happening/research/rp991-00.htm (05.08.99)

Government Response to the Report of the Public Service Committee on Ministerial Accountability and Responsibility (1996–97 H.C. 67)

Home Office, *Compensating Victims of Violent Crime: Changes to the Criminal Injuries Compensation Scheme*, Cm. 2434 (1993) London: HMSO

House of Commons, *The Code of Conduct together with the Guide to the Rules Relating to the Conduct of Members*, (1995–96 H.C. 688)

House of Lords Report, *Relations Between the United Kingdom Parliament and the European Parliament After Direct Elections*, (1977–78 H.L.)

Hughes, M., Clarke, M., Allen, H., and Hall, D., *The Constitutional Status of Local Government in Other Countries*, (1999, Scottish Office Central Research Unit)

Institute of Public Policy Research, *The Constitution of the U.K.* (1991)

Irvine (Lord) *Government's Programme of Constitutional Reform*, Constitution Unit, Dec. 8, 1998, http://www.open.gov.uk/lcd/speeches/1998/lc-const.htm (13.12.98)

Jenkins, Caines and Jackson, *Improving Management in Government–The Next Steps: Report to the Minister* (1988)

Mitchell, M., Standing Orders for the Scottish Parliament, Charter 88 (1998)

Public Service Committee, *Second Report on Ministerial Accountability and Responsibility* (1995–96 H.C. 313-I)

Report and Evidence of the Committee on Section 2 of the Official Secrets Act 1911(Franks Committee) Cmnd. 5104 (1972)

Report of the Committee on the Civil Service, Cmnd. 3638 (1968)

Report of the Committee, on Contempt of Court (Phillimore Committee), Cmnd. 5794 (1974)

Report of the Committee of Privy Councillors, Cmnd. 6386 (1976)

Report of the Committee on Scottish Administration (Gilmour Committee), Cmd. 5563 (1937)

Report of the Committee on Standards in Public Life (Nolan Committee), Cm. 2850-I (1995)

Report of the Inquiry into the Disposal of Land at Crichel Down, Cmd. 9176 (1954)

Report of the Inquiry into the Export of Defence Equipment and Dual-Use Goods to Iraq and Related Prosecutions (Scott Inquiry) (1995–96 H.C. 115)

Report of the Inquiry on the Falklands War (Franks Inquiry), Cmnd. 8787 (1983)

Report of the Inquiry into the Piper Alpha Disaster (Cullen Report), Cm. 130 (1990)

Report of the Inquiry into the Removal of Children from Orkney in February 1991 (Clyde Report) (1991–92 H.C. 195)

Report of the Inquiry into the Shootings at Dunblane Primary School on 13 March 1996 (Cullen Report), Cm. 3386 (1996)

Report of the Royal Commission on Local Government in Scotland, Cmnd. 4150 (1969)
Report of the Select Committee on PCA, *Open Government: Minutes of Evidence* (1994–95 H.C. 290)
Report of the Wilson Committee, *Modern Public Records*, Cmnd. 8204 (1981)
Report of the Working Party on Electoral Systems (1993)
Rights Brought Home: the Human Rights Bill, Cm. 3782 (1997)
Royal Commission on the Constitution (Kilbrandon Report), Cmnd. 5460 (1973)

Scottish Executive Consultation Paper on a Financial Framework for the Scottish Parliament (1999) http://www.scotland.gov.uk/library2/doc02/fdcon-00.htm (05.08.99)
Scottish Office, *The Scottish Parliament*, Factsheet 1 (1999)
Scottish Office *Scotland's Parliament*, Cm. 3658 (1997)
Scottish Office, *Scotland in the Union: A Partnership for Good*, Cm. 2225 (1997)
Scottish Office, *The Structure of Local Government in Scotland: Shaping the New Councils* (1992)
Scottish Office, *The Structure of Local Government in Scotland: The Case for Change*, (1991)
Scottish Office Consultative Steering Group, *Shaping Scotland's Parliament* (1999)
Second Report of the PCA, *Access to Official Information: The first eight months* (1994–95 H.C. 91)
Secretary of State for Scotland, *Shaping the Future: The New Councils*, Cm. 2267 (1993)
Select Committee on Modernisation of the House of Commons, *Third Report: Carry-over of Public Bills* (1997–98 H.C. 543)
Select Committee on Procedure, *Fourth Report: Procedural Consequences of Devolution* (1999) http://www.publications.parliament.uk/pa/cm199899/cmselect/cmproced/185/18503.htm (24.8.99)
Select Committee on Standards and Privileges, *Third Report: The Code of Conduct and the Guide to the Rules Relating to the Conduct of Members of Parliament* (1995–96 H.C. 604)
Select Committee on Standards in Public Life, First Report (1994–95 H.C. 637)

Taylor, M., and Douglas, A., *Local Authority Structures for Housing after Re-organisation* (1998)
Twigger, R., *The Barnett Formula*, H.C. Library Research Paper, House of Commons Library, Aug. 1998

White Paper, *Democracy and Devolution: proposals for Scotland and Wales*, Cmnd. 5732 (1974)

White Paper, *Modernising Parliament: Reform of the House of Lords* (1999)

Winetrobe, B., and Gay, O., *The House of Lords Bill: Options for Stage Two*, H.C. Library Research Paper, House of Commons Library, June 1999

INDEX